T0185554

Communications
in Computer and Information Science   1393

More information about this series at http://www.springer.com/series/7899

Ashish Kumar Luhach ·
Dharm Singh Jat · Kamarul Hawari Bin Ghazali ·
Xiao-Zhi Gao · Pawan Lingras (Eds.)

Advanced Informatics for Computing Research

4th International Conference, ICAICR 2020
Gurugram, India, December 26–27, 2020
Revised Selected Papers, Part I

 Springer

Editors
Ashish Kumar Luhach
Papua New Guinea University
of Technology
Lae, Papua New Guinea

Kamarul Hawari Bin Ghazali
Universiti Malaysia Pahang
Pekan, Pahang, Malaysia

Pawan Lingras
Saint Mary's University
Halifax, NS, Canada

Dharm Singh Jat
Namibia University of Science
and Technology
Windhoek, Namibia

Xiao-Zhi Gao
University of Eastern Finland
Kuopio, Finland

ISSN 1865-0929   ISSN 1865-0937   (electronic)
Communications in Computer and Information Science
ISBN 978-981-16-3659-2   ISBN 978-981-16-3660-8   (eBook)
https://doi.org/10.1007/978-981-16-3660-8

This Springer imprint is published by the registered company Springer Nature Singapore Pte Ltd.
The registered company address is: 152 Beach Road, #21-01/04 Gateway East, Singapore 189721, Singapore

Preface

This book "Advanced Informatics for Computing Research" contains selected and edited papers from the Fourth International Conference on Advanced Informatics for Computing Research (ICAICR 2020), targeting state-of-the-art as well as emerging topics pertaining to advanced informatics for computing research and its implementation for engineering applications. The objective of this international conference is to provide opportunities for researchers, academicians, industry professionals, and students to interact and exchange ideas, experience, and expertise in the current trends and strategies for information and communication technologies. Moreover, ICAICR aims to enlighten participants about the vast avenues, and current and emerging technological developments, in the field of advanced informatics and its applications, which are thoroughly explored and discussed.

The Fourth International Conference on Advanced Informatics for Computing Research (ICAICR 2020) was held during December 26–27, 2020, in Gurugram, India, in association with the Namibia University of Science and Technology, Namibia, and technically sponsored by the Mata Raj Kaur Institute of Engineering and Technology, Haryana, India, and Leafra Research Pvt. Ltd., Haryana, India.

We are extremely grateful to our valuable authors for their contributions and our Technical Program Committee for their immense support and motivation in making this edition of ICAICR a success. We are also grateful to our keynote speakers for sharing their precious work and enlightening the delegates of the conference.We express our sincere gratitude to our publication partner, Springer, for believing in us.

January 2021

Ashish Kumar Luhach
Dharm Singh Jat
Kamarul Hawari Bin Ghazali
Xiao-Zhi Gao
Pawan Lingras

Organization

Conference Chairs

Kamarul Hawari Bin Ghazali	Universiti Malaysia Pahang, Malaysia
Dharm Singh Jat	Namibia University of Science and Technology, Namibia
Ashish Kumar Luhach	The PNG University of Technology, Papua New Guinea

Publicity Chair

Aditya Khamparia	Lovely Professional University, Punjab, India

Technical Program Chairs

Pawan Lingras	Saint Mary's University, Canada
Xiao-Zhi Gao	University of Eastern Finland, Finland

Technical Program Committee

K. T. Arasu	Wright State University, USA
Rumyantsev Konstantin	Southern Federal University, Russia
Syed Akhat Hossain	Daffodil International University, Bangladesh
Sophia Rahaman	Manipal University, Dubai
Thippeswamy Mn	University of KwaZulu-Natal, South Africa
Lavneet Singh	University of Canberra, Australia
Pao-Ann Hsiung	National Chung Cheng University, Taiwan
Mohd Helmey Abd Wahab	Universiti Tun Hussein Onn, Malaysia
Shireen Panchoo	University of Technology, Mauritius
Sumathy Ayyausamy	Manipal University, Dubai
Kamarul Hawari Bin Ghazali	Universiti Malaysia Pahang, Malaysia
Dharm Singh Jat	Namibia University of Science and Technology, Namibia
Abbas Karimi	Islamic Azad University, Arak, Iran
Upasana G. Singh	University of KwaZulu-Natal, South Africa
Ritesh Chugh	Central Queensland University, Melbourne, Australia
Pawan Lingras	Saint Mary's University, Canada
Poonam Dhaka	University of Namibia, Namibia
Ashish Kumar Luhach	The PNG University of Technology, Papua New Guinea

Indra Seher	Central Queensland University, Sydney, Australia
Sugam Sharma	Iowa State University, USA
T. G. K. Vasista	King Saud University, Saudi Arabia
Akhtar Kalam	Victoria University, Australia
Ioan-Cosmin Mihai	Alexandru Ioan Cuza Police Academy, Romania
Abhijit Sen	Kwantlen Polytechnic University, Canada
R. B. Mishra	Indian Institute of Technology (BHU) Varanasi, India
Bhaskar Bisawas	Indian Institute of Technology (BHU) Varanasi, India

Contents – Part I

Computing Methodologies

Contents – Part II

Security and Privacy

Computing Methodologies

Analysis of Developers' Sentiments in Commit Comments

Rajdeep Kaur[✉] and Kuljit Kaur Chahal

Department of Computer Science, Guru Nanak Dev University, Amritsar, India
{rajdeep.rsh,kuljitchahal.cse}@gndu.ac.in

Abstract. Software development is a highly collaborative activity. Software is developed and maintained through cooperation among developers. In Open Source Software projects the development teams are distributed across the globe and collaborate through the Internet. They interact with each other through various communication artifacts and express their feelings therein. Nowadays, the study of the emotional aspects of software developers is essential for effective software engineering. In this paper, we used well known SentiStrength tool to analyze developers' sentiments in commit comments. We also investigated the association between developer sentiment and month of comment. Our findings revealed that the majority of sentiments expressed by developers in commit comments were neutral (46%). All observed months have a high count for neutral sentiments than positive and negative ones. July had the most negative sentiments.

Keywords: Sentiment analysis · Role of human factors in software engineering · Software developer · Developers' sentiment

1 Introduction

The process of software development is collaborative in nature. Software developers use many communication artifacts viz. forums, mailing lists, software code repositories, and issue tracking systems to collaborate with other team members and manage their work. They express their feelings regarding the project through these collaboration artifacts. For instance, they express their feeling related to satisfaction with the project or technical hitches associated with certain tasks [1, 2].

Sentiment analysis is extensively used in social media, economic events, and movie reviews [3]. It assigns a quantitative mood value (positive or negative) to a text snippet [4]. It is an opinion mining technique that is used in product reviews, movie reviews, microblogs, and tweets to analyze the polarity of small text [5]. In software engineering community research related to sentiments and emotional aspects of software development is becoming more popular. In recent time, Sentiment analysis is widely used in software engineering and applied to various software engineering tasks/artifacts for instance commit logs [4, 6–8] mailing lists messages [9], and issue comments [10, 11], code reviews [12], and bug reports [13].

© Springer Nature Singapore Pte Ltd. 2021
A. K. Luhach et al. (Eds.): ICAICR 2020, CCIS 1393, pp. 3–12, 2021.
https://doi.org/10.1007/978-981-16-3660-8_1

Many sentiment analysis tools are available that are used by software engineering researchers to identify the sentiment polarity of developers. Out of these tools Sentistrength is extensively used in software engineering and successfully applied on commit messages [6], commit comments [4], and mailing list messages [9]. It estimates the polarity and strength of sentiments. In this paper, we used Sentistrength tool to detect sentiment polarity of developers in the commit comments.

The work presented in this paper is influenced by study undertaken by Guzman et al. [4]. Guzman et al. study examined the association between sentiments projected in the commit comments and time and day of week, programming language, team distribution and project approval. But this study does not explore the relationship between sentiments expressed in the commit comments and month of comment that inspired us to conduct this study. To achieve our objective, we formulated the research questions that are mentioned below:

RQ1: What are the general developers' sentiments in commit comments?
RQ2: Do the developers convey more negative sentiment in commit comments than positive sentiment?
RQ3: Is there any relation between sentiment conveyed by the developer in commit comment and month of comment?

The rest of the paper is structured as follows. Related work is discussed in Sect. 2. The detail of the research methodology and sentiment analysis approach used in the study is presented in Sect. 3. The results with respect to research questions are described in Sect. 4. Limitations of study are reported in Sect. 5. Finally, conclusions and future work is presented in Sect. 6.

2   Related Literature

In software engineering, many researchers examined the sentiments of software developers in various software artifacts such as commit logs, commit comments, mailing list messages, and GitHub discussions concerned with security. In the year 2020, Romano et al. [14] examined the association between sentiments polarity of developers and bug introduction through conducting sentiment analysis on commit comments. In the year 2019, Paul et al. [12] examined the difference in the manifestation of sentiments based on the gender of developers throughout different software development tasks by using code review data of five open source projects. In the year, 2018 Bharti and Singh [15] analyzed the sentiments expressed by developers related to code cloning practices through surveying 20 software developers. In the year 2017, Singh and Singh [7] investigated the influence of 15 different code refactoring tasks on developers' sentiments. In the year 2016, Sinha et al. [6] analyzed the developer's sentiments in commit logs. In the year 2014, Guzman et al. [4] examined correlation among sentiments conveyed by developers in commit comments and programming language used in the project, time and day of the week when the comment was written, team distribution, and project approval. In the year 2014, Pletea et al. [16] investigated the sentiments associated with security-related discussions in commits and pull requests. In the year 2013, Garcia et al. [13] examined the connection between emotions and contributor activity.

In prior literature, several studies analyzed the sentiments of developers in various software artifacts. According to our knowledge, there is no single research that looks into the relation among developer emotions and month of the comment. Thus lack of research in the area encouraged us to perform this study.

In the current study, we used a lexical sentiment analysis approach to analyze the developers' sentiments associated with commit comments and examine the relation between developer sentiment and the month in which comment was made.

3   Research Methodology

This section provides the detail of data collection methodology as well as sentiment analysis approach used in our study.

3.1   Research Data

We extracted the data from SourceForge.net. It is a web-based archive of source code and provides a centralized place for control and management of OSS (Open Source Software) projects. We searched 50 OSS projects. In most of the projects commit comments was not available. We found only one project x64dbg that contains 58 comments that are written between 14 July 2015 to 2 October 2016. We extracted these comments using a manual approach. After manual analysis of comments, we included the comments of those participants who are either members or contributors and wrote one or more comments. Overall 37 comments were part of our dataset, after removing 21 comments of non-members.

Fig. 1. Description of the methodology

Figure 1 illustrated the detailed description of the methodology used for sentiment analysis. At the initial stage, we manually extract the comments. Then these comments were fed to the SentiStrength tool and then we analyzed the output of the tool. Finally, results are obtained.

3.2   Sentiment Analysis

Liu [17], first introduced Sentiment Analysis (SA). It is a method that assigns quantitative positive and negative sentiment value to a piece of text [4]. The plethora of tools are available in software engineering which deals with sentiment analysis viz. Alchemy, SentiStrength [18], Stanford NLP [19], NLTK [20] etc. Among these tools, SentiStrength is most frequently used tool in software engineering.

We utilized most popular SentiStrength tool to analyze sentiments conveyed by developers in commit comments. It is a lexical sentiment extraction tool that measures the polarity as well as strength of sentiments (positive, negative) in small, low quality text. We select this tool for our analysis because prior research shows that SentiStrength provides more precision to examine the polarity of the text of Twitter and movie review [3]. Manual investigation of comments reveals that comments were short and written in informal language. Therefore, SentiStrength is a suitable tool to analyze developers' sentiments projected in comments. It assigns sentiment value to each individual word and then calculates the overall sentence sentiment score by adding individual sentiment scores. The negative sentiment value of words ranges from -1 to -5 and score of words with positive value ranges from 1 to 5. The 1 and -1 indicate the neutral sentiment that is neither positive nor negative, while 5 and -5 are used to represent the extremely positive and highly negative emotion.

4 Results

This section presents the results obtained for each individual research question (RQ) that is formulated in the previous section.

RQ1: Developers general sentiments in commit comment?

The result of sentiment score of all comments that is obtained via SentiStrength tool is shown in Tables 1 and 2. We observed that 46% of sentiments projected by developers in commit comments were neutral. The positive and negative sentiments have an equal percentage (27%). The result proves that most of the sentiments expressed by developers in comments were neutral as compared to positive and negative sentiments. The major reason for this neutrality in sentiment is due to the presence of technical terms in commit comments. Developers use some technical terms and include URL when they write commit comments. Therefore, most of the sentiments in commit comments indicate neutral polarity.

RQ2: Do developers express more negative sentiments than positive sentiments in commit comments?

For this research question, we obtained contradictory results. The overall score of sentiments was neutral. We did not find any difference between positive and negative sentiments. The percentage of positive and negative sentiment was equal. In total 37 commit comments positive and negative sentiments have an equal percentage (27%).

RQ3: Is there any relation between developer sentiment in commit comment and month of comment?

In this research question, we examined the relationship between sentiments projected by developers in commit comments and month of comment. The numbers of positive, negative, and neutral sentiments with respect to month are presented in Table 3. Figure 2 shows the sentiments score across the month and Fig. 3 indicates the number of commits in each month. We classified sentiment (positive, negative, and neutral) according to month in which the comment was written. The 42.86% sentiments in July tend to be negative. November had most positive (40%) sentiment and the sentiment was more neutral (67%) in October. Moreover, developers did not express any negative sentiment in November.

Table 1. Commit Comments with Positive, Negative, and Neutral Score.

Sentiment	Commit comment	Final score
Positive	Yep, I have summer break :) and Nukem too I guess.	1
	I changed it around with commit 1e5c808 (It should be a better fix, along with the next one too)	1
	I noticed this right after I replied. 1eac42e#diff-a29958c5ad571425e6cec7f7f1896b9cR326 I guess it isn't very helpful to concentrate on multiple things at once: D	1
	Oh haha, totally forgot about that one	
	Yes, extended ASCII is supported. Apart from that everything is a UNICODE string so that is not supported.	1
	Like before, http://jenkins.x64dbg.com see workspace and then look in the 'release' directory	1
	Thanks, merged it!	1
	Haha yep, PWD doesn't work very well I discovered	1
	Haha yea...	1
	Visual studio is a far superior tool for development. I wanted to compile everything in visual studio, but that doesn't work very nicely so I decided to use qt creator. You can use qmake to generate visual studio project files if you want.	2
Negative	*Note for later: ntdll has no entry point and that's where this problem originated. On the flip side, malware has been known to replace the PE header in some places. I don't know if they can write at offset 0 and still be a Win32 valid PE.	-1
	The fix is wrong for executable. Entry of zero means it starts executing inside the header.	-1
	mrexodia trying to sabotage my code 👎	-1
	This brings back the problem with spaces in the path (FYI). -1	
	You must use quotes in the qt creator gui. Otherwise it will split the arguments anyway.	-1
	To be honest I kinda hate CMake. I think it's a waste of time to convert the everything.	-1
	The unicode string searching is not very straightforward unfortunately. Personally I don't know enough about unicode strings to determine if something is a viable string. I can make an option that attempts to detect Chinese and Japanese etc. string but it will most probably detect a lot of crap.	-3
	Oh never mind, I responded to the wrong issue.	-1
	Done. #392 The online editor added a new line at the end of the file sadly	-1
	I don't think using a memcmp is going to make this any clearer. We can add a comment that a path that starts with "virtual:\"	-1

(continued)

Table 1. (*continued*)

	denotes a virtual module.	
	Just curious, is there a reason for removing this? I tried to run init only once because it isn't foolproof with multiple threads - SectionLockerGlobal::Initialize () might cause issues if 1 thread calls it and another uses Acquire Lock ().	0
	I'm referencing this commit and be6dc8a. For line 55, why is this not set simply as a label instead of adding a custom if? Virtual modules use a label. (shamelessly taken from OllyDbg) I prefer these, but obviously it is your choice. I prefer these, but obviously it is your choice.	0
	Add on (@fileoffset): This will never work easily without quotes. A space in the directory path causes it to be interpreted as another parameter. Adding quotes in the .bat won't help.	0
	Topkek	0
	Sorry guys, I don't speak Chinese: D	0
	Should be return	0
Neutral	Page_execute bit mask isn't enough? I thought this was included in all of them. Page_execute|page_read should be the same as page_execute_read	0
	No, they are all individual bits. See:	0
	Right, then I'll push a fix later today or you can do a pull request	0
	Yea, I also noticed it. I think I'll change that indeed.	0
	I take this back; the CPU tab is completely screwed up somewhere in terms of rendering.	0
	My dreams are reuined.	0
	I'm going to assume you meant #429. https://xkcd.com/745/ 👍	0
	What does CommandLineEdit.cpp do? I don't know where it is used.	0
	I'm not sure actually...	0
	Oh, it's CommandHelpView	0
	Is this virtual:\\ or virtual:\? Let's use memcmp here?	0

As shown in Fig. 2 the neutral sentiments are higher than positive and negative sentiments in all months except July. This indicates that developers' sentiments are more neutral while writing commit comments. We conclude that July was the most negative month for the sentiment. The main reason is that July had maximum commits as compare to other months which turned the sentiment in a negative direction. Similarly, the number of commits made by developers in October was lowest. Hence, the sentiments were more neutral in this month.

Table 2. Sentiments across all comments

Sentiment	Sentiment Score	Number of comments	Percentage of Sentiment
Positive	1	9	27%
	2	1	
Negative	−1	9	27%
	−3	1	
Neutral	0	17	46%
	Total	37	

Table 3. Sentiments across all comments with respect to month.

Month of comment	Positive	Negative	Neutral
July	5	6	3
August	2	1	1
September	1	2	5
October	0	1	2
November	2	0	3

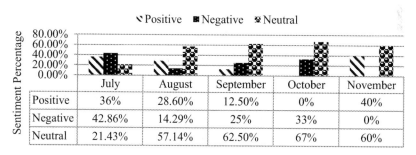

	July	August	September	October	November
Positive	36%	28.60%	12.50%	0%	40%
Negative	42.86%	14.29%	25%	33%	0%
Neutral	21.43%	57.14%	62.50%	67%	60%

Month of comment

Fig. 2. Percentage of sentiment (Positive, Negative, and Neutral) with respect to month.

We applied the Pearson correlation between positive, negative, and neutral sentiments and the number of commits in each month. We found a high correlation (>0.90) between positive sentiments and the number of commits. Negative sentiments and the number of commits were found to be moderately correlated (equal to 0.58).

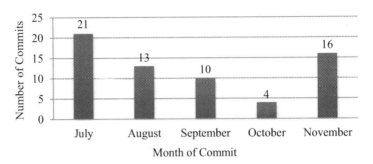

Fig. 3. Number of commits with respect to month

5 Threat to Validity

The first issue related to our study is that we used the SentiStrength tool to analyze developers' sentiments in commit comments. We observed that most of the commit comments contain technical terms and SentiStrength tool may have accuracy problems for the dataset that consists of technical terms. The second main problem is that comments for all months were not available. The dataset contains comments written from July to November.

6 Conclusions

In this work, we examined the developer sentiments in commit comments. To perform Sentiment analysis, we utilized SentiStrength, a well-known sentiment analysis tool used by researchers' in software engineering domain. To conduct our analysis, we manually extract 37 commit comments of x64dbg project available on SourceForge.Net website.

In this study, we identified that majority of comments had neutral (46%) sentiment and the percentage of neutral sentiment was higher than positive and negative ones. Out of 37 comments, 27% of comments represented positive sentiments and 27% denoted negative sentiments respectively. From these findings, we observed that most of the sentiments expressed by developers in commit comments were neutral. Moreover, commit comments having an equal percentage of positive and negative sentiments. We also look into the association between sentiments and month of the comment. All months have a high count for neutral sentiments than positive and negative ones. We see the opposite trend in July which have the most negative sentiments. November had more positive sentiments. The month of October had more neutral sentiments.

In the future, we will extend our work to cover more projects and use other sentiment analysis techniques such as deep learning to obtain better results. Our work detected the developers' sentiments in the commit comments. In the future, we will identify developers' sentiments in other software artifacts.

Acknowledgements. This research work is supported by UGC, Government of India. The authors are grateful to UGC for providing financial assistance under Rajiv Gandhi National Fellowship scheme to the first author. The authors are also thankful to Department of Computer Science,

Guru Nanak Dev University, Amritsar, and Punjab for providing infrastructure and pedagogic aid to accomplish this research work.

References

1. Storey, M., Deursen, A., Van Li-Te, C.: The impact of social media on software engineering practices and tools. In: Proceedings of the FSE/SDP Workshop on Future of Software Engineering, pp. 359–363 (2010)
2. Counts, S., De Choudhury, M.: Understanding affect in the workplace via social media. In: Proceedings of the 2013 Conference on Computer Supported Cooperative Work, pp. 303–316 (2013)
3. Ahmed, T.: Poster: measuring developers' sentiments in the android open source project. In: MobiSys 2016 Companion - Companion Publication 14th Annual International Conference on Mobile Systems, Applications, and Services, p. 7 (2016). https://doi.org/10.1145/2938559.2948838
4. Emitza, G., David, A., Yang, L.: Sentiment analysis of commit comments in GitHub.pdf. In: Proceedings of the 11th Working Conference on Mining Software Repositories, pp. 352–355 (2014)
5. Younis, E.M.G.: Sentiment analysis and text mining for social media microblogs using open source tools : an empirical study. Int. J. Comput. Appl. **112**(5), 44–48 (2015)
6. Sinha, V., Lazar, A., Sharif, B.: Analyzing developer sentiment in commit logs. In: Proceedings of the 13th International Conference on Mining Software Repositories. MSR 2016, pp. 520–523 (2016). https://doi.org/10.1145/2901739.2903501
7. Singh, N., Singh, P.: How do code refactoring activities impact software developers' sentiments? - an empirical investigation into GitHub commits. In: Proceedings - Asia-Pacific Software Engineering Conference. APSEC 2017-December, pp. 648–653 (2018). https://doi.org/10.1109/APSEC.2017.79
8. Islam, M.R., Zibran, M.F.: Sentiment analysis of software bug related commit messages. In: 27th International Conference on Software Engineering and Data Engineering SEDE 2018, pp. 3–8 (2018)
9. Tourani, P., Jiang, Y., Adams, B.: Monitoring sentiment in open source mailing lists: exploratory study on the apache ecosystem. In: CASCON '14 Proceedings of 24th Annual International Conference on Computer Science and Software Engineering, pp. 34–44 (2014)
10. Ding, J., Sun, H., Wang, X., Liu, X.: Entity-level sentiment analysis of issue comments. In: Proceedings - International Conference Software Engineering, pp. 7–13 (2018). https://doi.org/10.1145/3194932.3194935
11. Jurado, F., Rodriguez, P.: Sentiment analysis in monitoring software development processes: an exploratory case study on GitHub's project issues. J. Syst. Softw. **104**, 82–89 (2015). https://doi.org/10.1016/j.jss.2015.02.055
12. Paul, R., Bosu, A., Sultana, K.Z.: Expressions of sentiments during code reviews: male vs. female. In: SANER 2019 - Proceedings 2019 IEEE 26th International Conference Software Analysis Evolution Reengineering, pp. 26–37 (2019). https://doi.org/10.1109/SANER.2019.8667987
13. Garcia, D., Zanetti, M.S., Schweitzer, F.: The role of emotions in contributors activity: a case study of the GENTOO community. In: Proceedings - 2013 IEEE 3rd International Conference Cloud Green Computing, CGC 2013, 2013 IEEE 3rd International Conference Social Computing and Its Applications SCA 2013, pp. 410–417 (2013). https://doi.org/10.1109/CGC.2013.71

14. Romano, S., Caulo, M., Scanniello, G., Baldassarre, M.T., Caivano, D.: Sentiment polarity and bug introduction. In: Morisio, M., Torchiano, M., Jedlitschka, A. (eds.) PROFES 2020. LNCS, vol. 12562, pp. 347–363. Springer, Cham (2020). https://doi.org/10.1007/978-3-030-64148-1_22
15. Bharti, S., Singh, H.: Investigating developers' sentiments associated with software cloning practices. In: Luhach, A.K., Singh, D., Hsiung, P.-A., Hawari, K.B.G., Lingras, P., Singh, P.K. (eds.) ICAICR 2018. CCIS, vol. 955, pp. 397–406. Springer, Singapore (2019). https://doi.org/10.1007/978-981-13-3140-4_36
16. Pletea, D., Vasilescu, B., Serebrenik, A.: Security and emotion: sentiment analysis of security discussions on GitHub. In: 11th Workshop Conference Mining Software Repositories MSR 2014 – Proceedings, pp. 348–351 (2014). https://doi.org/10.1145/2597073.2597117
17. Liu, B.: Sentiment analysis and subjectivity. In: Handbook of Natural Language Processing (2010)
18. Thelwall, M., Buckley, K., Paltoglou, G., Cai, D., Kappas, A.: Sentiment strength detection in short informal text. J. Am. Soc. Inf. Sci. Technol. **61**(12), 2544–2558 (2013)
19. Jongeling, R., Datta, S., Serebrenik, A.: Choosing your weapons: on sentiment analysis tools for software engineering research. In: 2015 IEEE 31st International Conference Software Maintenance and Evolution ICSME 2015 – Proceedings, pp. 531–535 (2015). https://doi.org/10.1109/ICSM.2015.7332508
20. Thelwall, M., Buckley, K., Paltoglou, G.: Sentiment strength detection for the social web. J. Am. Soc. Inf. Sci. Technol. **63**, 163–173 (2012). https://doi.org/10.1002/asi.21662

Design of UML Diagrams for Intervention for Autism Children (IAC System)

S. Suriya[✉], R. Asmitha, V. G. Darshanaa, S. Priyadarshini, K. Priyanga, and J. R. Sanjeetha

Department of Computer Science and Engineering, PSG College of Technology, Coimbatore, India
ss.cse@psgtech.ac.in

Abstract. Autism Spectrum Disorder (ASD) or Autism is a complex developmental disability that typically appears during early childhood and can impact a person's social skills, communication, relationships, and self-regulation. Early recognition, as well as behavioural, educational and family therapies may reduce symptoms and support development and learning. Parent as well as the affected child faces severe challenges. IAC system enables the autistic child to overcome such challenges. The main functionalities of this system includes Training parent, Communicator, ABA, Schools nearby, Apprisal Provision, Financial Resources and Emotional Analyser. For this system, **StarUML** an open source software modelling tool is used to develop UML diagrams and provide users with ready-to-use, expressive modelling. The interesting quality of IAC is that it provides services both to the parent as well as the child affected by ADS.

Keywords: Autism · StarUML · UML diagrams

1 Introduction

Autism spectrum disorder (ASD) typically occurs in the first three years of life and continues throughout life. It is characterized by challenges with social skills, repetitive behaviours, speech and non-verbal communication. Though all people with autism show the same overall pattern of impairments, the severity of these issues will vary from case to case. Some people show mild impairments and others have severe issues. It also has direct and indirect cost implications on the nation that are incurred in providing health care, support for education, and rehabilitative services. Recent estimated prevalence of ASD in India ranges from 0.15% to 1.01% in various studies, depending on the screening method used, and the areas surveyed. In the INCLEN study, the prevalence of ASD was 1 in 125 in children 3–6 years and 1 in 85 in children 6–9 years of age. The prevalence in rural areas was 0.90%, 0.6% in hilly regions, 1.01% in urban areas, 0.1% in tribal areas and 0.61% in the coastal regions. No cure exists for autism spectrum disorder. The goal of treatment is to maximize the child's ability to function by reducing autism symptoms and supporting development and learning.

© Springer Nature Singapore Pte Ltd. 2021
A. K. Luhach et al. (Eds.): ICAICR 2020, CCIS 1393, pp. 13–28, 2021.
https://doi.org/10.1007/978-981-16-3660-8_2

2 Functionalities of the System

The main objective of Intervention for Autism Children (IAC system) is to avail children with autism spectrum disorder (ASD) to improve their social behaviour and to guide the children's parent. The services provided by IAC are Training Parent, Applied Behavioural Analysis (ABA), Apprisal Provision, Emotional Analyser, Financial Resources, Communicator and Schools Nearby. Training parent helps in guiding the parent to handle their disabled child. ABA is used to reinforce positive behaviour and teach new skills, self-management. Appraisal provision gives information about the technologies that help the disabled child. Emotional analyser is used to express their emotions through colours. Financial Resources gives information about the financial support available. Communicator helps the disabled child to convey their needs through pictures. Schools Nearby is used to find the nearby schools available for the autism child.

3 Proposed IAC System

3.1 System Architecture

System architecture is the conceptual model that defines the structure, behaviour and shows the relationship between different components. Usually they are created for systems which include hardware and software and these are represented in the diagram to show the interaction between them.

The architecture diagram shown in Fig. 1 includes all the functionalities of the system in an ordered manner based on the sequence of occurrence of these functionalities. It represents the work flow of the system starting from the registration till log out. This system is considered to have four phases namely register, login, features of intervention system and logout. To access the features of this system the person must register followed by login and then he/she will be permitted to access the features. Finally the person can logout of the system.

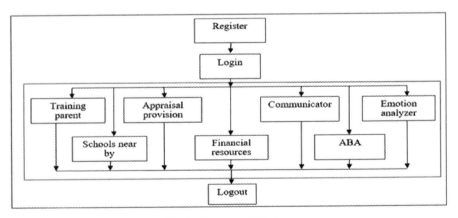

Fig. 1. System architecture

3.2 Data Flow Diagram

The Data Flow Diagram (DFD) depicts the logic models and expresses data transformation in a system. It depicts structured analysis and design method. It includes three levels namely level 0, level 1 and level 2 diagrams.

The Level 0 DFD is otherwise called as context diagram. It represents an overview of the system. Figure 2 represents level 0 DFD of the IAC system. The actors involved in the system are autistic children and their parents.

Fig. 2. Level 0 DFD diagram

Level 1 Data flow Diagram (Fig. 3) represents the main sub-process of the system. In this system the user is given various cases to visit and attain its benefits. The sub-process of the system are the functionalities available in the system namely Training Parent, Applied Behavioural Analysis (ABA), Apprisal Provision, Emotional Analyser, Financial Resources, Communicator, Schools Nearby (Table 1).

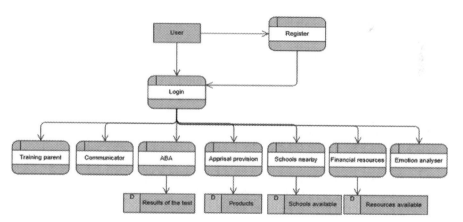

Fig. 3. Level 1 DFD diagram

Table 1. Comparison of proposed system and existing system

Existing system	Proposed system
Training parent	Training parent
ABA (Applied Behavioural Analysis)	ABA (Applied Behavioural Analysis)
Emotional analyser	Emotional analyser
Financial resources	Financial resources
Communicator	Communicator
-	Schools nearby - Introduction of a new feature which displays the nearby schools with the help of the details given by the user during registration
-	Apprisal provision – updates information about the technology available for the welfare of the autistic child
Existing systems provide anyone of the above mentioned functionality in a single system	Proposed system provides all the above mentioned services in a single system with some additional functionalities

4 UML Diagrams

4.1 UML Usecase Diagram

UML Usecase diagram is a simple representation of a user's interaction with the system that shows the relationship between the user and usecases. The usecase relationships are include, extend and generalization. UML Usecase diagram is illustrated in Fig. 4. Parent, Child and Admin are the actors. The functionalities of the system are Register, Login, Child options, Parent options, ABA, Emotion Analyser, Communicator, Schools Nearby, Training Parent, Appraisal Provision, Financial Resources, Post issues, Join committee, Place order, Update, End of child options, End of parent options and Logout. All the actors should initially register to the system. After login the system provides Child option and Parent option. The Child option is provided with three suboptions, ABA, Emotion Analyser and Communicator. All these three functionalities of Child option extends End of child option. The Parent option is provided with four suboptions, Schools Nearby, Training Parent, Appraisal Provision and Financial Resources. Training parent has options like post issue and join committee where parents can express their issues and give solutions for others issues. Appraisal provision includes Place order for placing order for the available technological equipment that helps the child. The information in the Training parent, Appraisal provision and financial resources are updated by Update functionality by the Admin. Finally the Logout extends End of child option, End of parent option and Update.

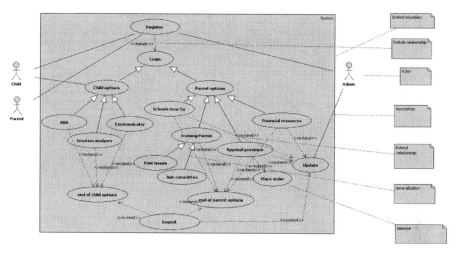

Fig. 4. UML usecase diagram for IAC system

4.2 UML Class Diagram

UML Class diagram provides the characteristic and behaviour of every entity in the system providing the logical view of the system. The major components are class, class name, attributes and operations. The class relationships include association, direct association, aggregation, composition, generalization, realization and dependency. Classes describes the structure of a system by showing the system's classes, their attributes, operations and their relationship among objects. In Fig. 5, all actors and usecases are considered classes, which represent the functional module of a system. User acts as an interface for Child and Parent which includes login and logout operations. Child and Parent class has username and password as attributes and login and logout as operations. ABA class has attributes namely mp3 and mp4 and operations namely view, listen and test. Emotion analyser class has an attribute named colour and analyse operation. Communicator class has the attribute picture and convey operation. Parent class includes Training parent class which has issue and name as attributes, and join and post issue as operations and Schools nearby class which has an attribute location and search operation. Appraisal provision class has an attribute tool and operations named view and place order. Financial resources class has an attribute amount and an operation request. The Resource Info class acts as the association class which contains the common functionalities like infotable and viewtable operations for parent and admin classes.

4.3 UML Activity Diagram

UML Activity diagram represented in the Fig. 6, portraits the control flow from a starting point to a finishing point including the various decision paths that exists by execution of any activity. The major components of this diagram are action, swimlanes such as horizontal and vertical, object, start state, final state, flow final, transition, subactivity and synchronizations such as fork, join, decision and merge. In Fig. 6, the vertical

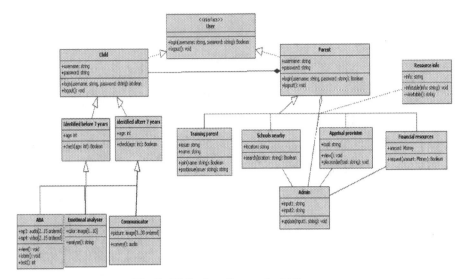

Fig. 5. UML class diagram for IAC system

swimlane contains three activities namely child, admin and parent. All these activities have separate subactivity, Register. Different register subactivities move to a common login using 'join'. Password validation is done using a decision component. Using fork component, it proceeds to either of the three activities namely child options of child, update of admin, parent option of parent. Again using a fork the child option is divided into three activities namely ABA, Communicator, Emotional Analyser from which the user can choose any one of them and can be continued. Similarly the parent option is split into four activities namely Schools nearby, Appraisal provision, Financial resources and Training parent using fork from which the user can choose any one of them. The update function is linked to schools nearby, Apprisal provision and financial resources for which frequent updates are required. If the user doesn't want to continue, then it can be logged out.

4.4 UML Sequence Diagram

UML Sequence diagram show how objects in a system or classes within code interact with each other. These diagrams show the sequence of events which is used by developers and business professionals to document processes. The main components are object, class, lifeline, focus of control, messages and fragments. The messages include synchronous, asynchronous, reply, self, lost, found, create and destroy messages. The types of fragments are ALT, OPT, PAR, NEG, LOOP, REF, SD. IAC system includes actors like Admin, Parent of the autism children and the autism child.

Figure 7 will explain the sequence of events between Admin and the Parent of the autistic child. PAR frame represents messages passed between entities in an environment which supports parallel execution. ALT frame represents if else scenario. The system checks whether the user is a registered user. If so, the user is allowed to login into the system. Synchronous message is used for login since response is needed. The login details

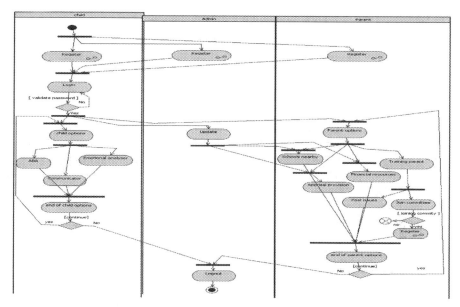

Fig. 6. UML activity diagram for IAC system

are validated for which self message is used. After login, the Parent is given access to parent options which is represented as a reply message. Parent's options include training parent, Appraisal Provision, Financial resources and schools nearby. An OPT frame represents simple if scenario. Training Parent option will have two more OPT frames such as Post Issues and Join Committee. Parent can send a synchronous message to post issues for which a reply message is sent regarding the information to guide. Parent sends a synchronous message to join a committee, which undergoes validation followed by a reply message that he/she has joined the committee. In the Appraisal Provision option, the Admin will provide info about the new technology. The Admin will update the system which is represented as a self message. The Parent places order to the admin for which delivery details are sent as reply message. If Parent is in need of financial resources, synchronous message is sent by the parent, resource availability is checked by admin followed by availability status is sent to Parent as reply. Admin provides info about the schools nearby to the parent. Parent searches for schools, Admin will check the availability and then school information is sent as reply message. If the user is not a registered user, user will register, the details get validated by the admin and the reply message of registration is sent to the Parent.

Figure 8 will explain the sequence of events between Admin and the Autistic child. Login validation is similar to every user as described above. Child options include ABA, Emotion analyser and communicator. OPT frame is used to enable if scenarios. Admin teaches skills with audio and video. The child is supposed to complete and submit the test which is analysed by the admin and test result is sent using reply message. If emotion analyser is chosen, the child is provided with different colours, it is analysed by the Admin and emotions of the child are returned. Synchronous and self messages are used

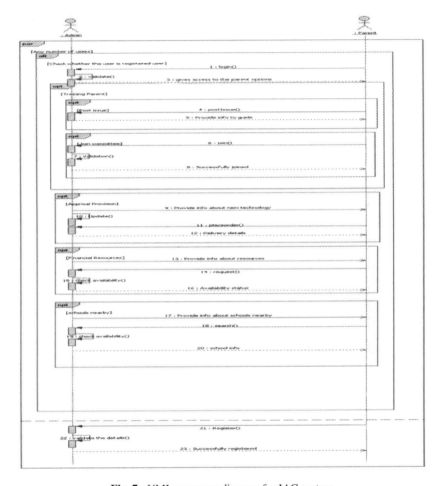

Fig. 7. UML sequence diagram for IAC system

in these types of scenarios. If communicator is chosen, the child is supposed to chose an image which is analysed and an audio is sent as reply message. This feature is for children who finds have in conveying information. If the user is not a registered user, user will register, the details get validated by the admin and the reply message of registration is sent to the Child.

4.5 UML Collaboration Diagram

UML Collaboration diagram represents a set of messages passed during an interaction between the objects in order to portray the flow of events in a usecase. The components of collaboration diagram are object, class, link and the messages which includes synchronous, reply, asynchronous, self, create, destroy, iterative, iterative conditional, conditional and mutually exclusive messages. Figure 9 deals with the communication between the parent and the admin system. Initially, the user who is a parent, sends the

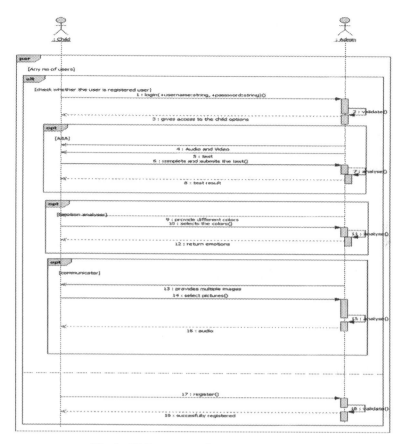

Fig. 8. UML sequence diagram for IAC system

synchronous message to login into the system and these details are validated by the admin's self-message and the parent gets the reply message describing about the status of the login. If the parent is not a registered one, then user sends the synchronous message to get registered into the system and details are checked by the admin's self-message and gets the reply message confirming about the registration. Among the available services for parent, if the parent chooses the parent training, the parent sends the synchronous message to post issue and can get responses. Otherwise, the parent can send the synchronous message to join the committee and gets the response confirming about the registration in the committee. If the parent chooses Apprisal Provision option, the system gives the information through the asynchronous message. If the parent wishes to place order, it can be done through the synchronous message and the delivery details are given by the system as reply message. In Financial Resources option, the details about the resources are as asynchronous message. The parent can request for the financial help through the synchronous message and it's availability is checked through the admin's self-message and the status is returned as response. The admin updates the information in Apprisal Provision through the self-message. The Schools nearby option provides information about the schools available in different locations through asynchronous message, through which parents can select school and its availability is checked through the admin's self-message and the status is returned as a reply message.

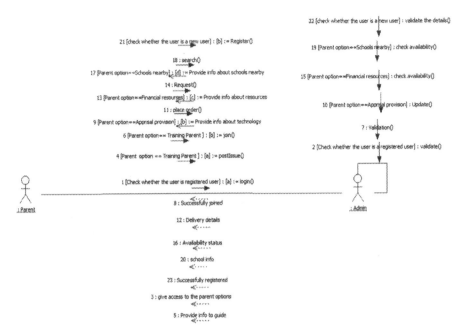

Fig. 9. UML collaboration diagram for IAC system

Figure 10 deals with the communication between the child and the admin system. Login validation is similar for every user. Among the available services for child, if the child chooses the ABA, it provides audio and video as asynchronous message to teach the child. The child attends and submits the test as a synchronous message and it is analysed by admin's self-message and the results are given as reply message. In Emotional Analyser, it provides the details of the colours as asynchronous message. The child uses the colour to express his/her expressions through synchronous message and it is analysed through admin's self-message and emotion is returned as reply message. In Communicator, pictures are provided by the system through asynchronous message. The child can express his/her needs by selecting messages and the audio is returned as the reply message.

4.6   UML State Machine Diagram

UML State Machine diagram shows the different states of every entity and its response to various events while changing from one state to another and focuses on dynamic view of a system. The components include simple state, composite state, initial state, final state, junction point, choice point, flow final, shallow history, deep history and transition. UML State Machine diagram is depicted in Fig. 11. If the registration is not successful,

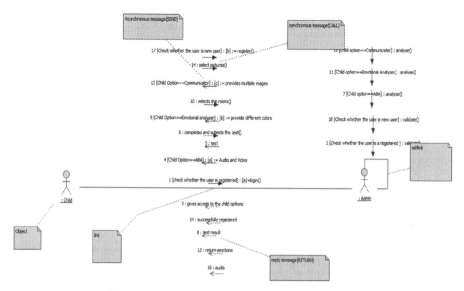

Fig. 10. UML collaboration diagram for IAC system

the Register state will be terminated using flow final. In Login state, user can go to either parent option or child option for which a choice point is used. If 'Parent Option state is chosen, using a choice point, the user is allowed to choose any of the different sub states namely training parent or financial resources or schools nearby or apprisal provision. The parents are given training in Training Parent state. Post Issues and Join Committee are the substates of training parent where issues faced can be posted and can join committee who come up with solution respectively. If the user wants to find a school for their autistic child, the user can choose schools through Schools Nearby state. If the user requires financial assistance, the user can send request and gets the availability status through Financial Resources state. If the user wants to know the new technologies available, the user can search for the technologies through Apprisal Provision state and the user can place order for that device online through 'Place Order' state. If Child Option is chosen, using a choice point, the user is allowed to choose any of the different sub states namely ABA, emotional analyser, communicator. If the user wants to learn new skills, the skills can be learned through ABA state. If the user wants to express emotions, the user can choose colour which returns an emotion through Emotion Analyser state. If the user wants to communicate with others, through pictures the user can communicate which returns audio through Communicator state.

4.7 UML Component Diagram

UML Component diagram, Fig. 12 shows the dependencies and interactions between software components. It focuses on how components of a system actively interact with each other to execute a specific task. The major components are component that represents every individual module, subcomponents, stereotypes that includes component, subsystem, service and process, port, part, interfaces such as required, provider and

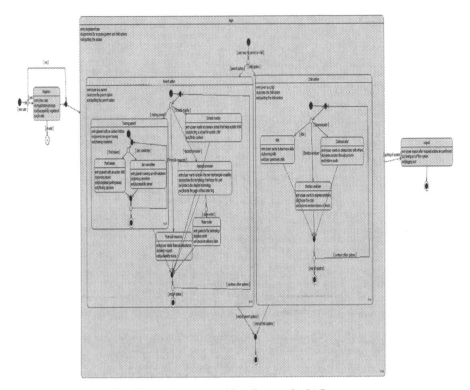

Fig. 11. UML state machine diagram for IAC system

assembly, artifacts, relations such as dependency, realization and association. Parent, Child, Database, Admin, Training Parent, Schools Nearby, Apprisal Provision, Financial Resources, Emotional Analyser, Communicator, ABA are the components in the diagram which represents the modules of the IAC system. Database is considered as subsystem because it contains the artifacts like Parent Details, Child Details, Medical Device Details, School Details. Training Parent, Schools Nearby, Apprisal Provision and Financial Resources are the services provided by the Parent component. Join committee and Post issues are the operations of the Training Parent component. Likewise, Schools Nearby contains search, Apprisal Provision contains Place order and view as parts. Emotional Analyser, Communicator and ABA are the services provided by the Child component. Emotional Analyser performs analyse as part, Communicator performs convey as part and ABA contains view, listen and test as parts. Admin interacts with Child and Parent for performing the update operations.

4.8 UML Deployment Diagram

UML Deployment diagram describes the integration of run time processing elements and software components that live on it. The major components are node such as device node and execution environment node, port, part, interfaces and interface relations. UML Deployment diagram is represented in the Fig. 13. The client includes the Child and

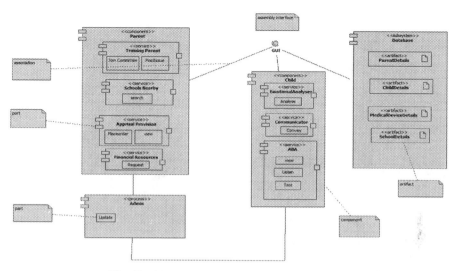

Fig. 12. UML component diagram for IAC system

Parent and the server includes Admin and Database. Client uses the Window 10 OS and the Chrome browser. Server uses Window 7 OS and Tomcat web server. Training Parent, Schools Nearby, Appraisal Provision and Financial Resources are the nodes of the parent. Emotional Analyser, ABA, Communicator are the nodes of the Child. Training Parent contains Join Committee and post issues parts. Schools Nearby includes search as a part. Appraisal Provision contains view and Place Order as parts. Financial Resources contains request part. Emotional Analyser contains analyse as its part. Communicator contains convey as its part. ABA contains view, listen, test as its parts. Admin contains update as its part. Database contains the artifacts like Parent Details, Child Details, Medical Device Details, School Details.

5   Experimental Results

See Fig. 13.

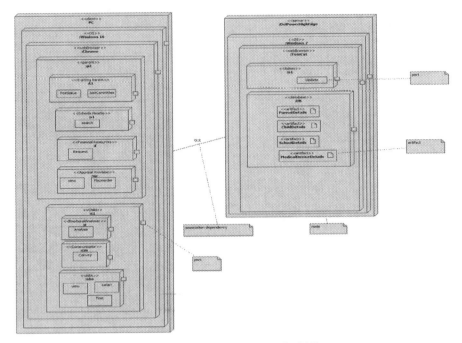

Fig. 13. UML deployment diagram for IAC system

6   Conclusion and Future Enhancement

The UML diagrams used for the development of this system permits us to specify the structure or behaviour of a system, helps visualizing the system, provides template that guides in constructing the system, helps to understand complex system part by part. With the help of UML diagrams, executable code can be generated with which the application can be developed and implemented. The future enhancement of this system can focus on the communicator which could be developed to convey complete sentences.

References

1. Milovancevic, M., et al.: UML diagrams for dynamical monitoring of rail vehicles. Phys. A: Stat. Mech. Appl. **531**, 121169 (2019)
2. Cvetković, J., Cvetković, M.: Evaluation of UML diagrams for test cases generation: case study on depression of internet addiction. Phys. A: Stat. Mech. Appl. **525**, 1351–1359 (2019)
3. Hashmani, M.A., Zaffar, M., Ejaz, R.: Scenario based test case generation using activity diagram and action semantics. In: Human Factors in Global Software Engineering, pp. 297–321. IGI Global (2019)
4. Mala, D.J.: IoT functional testing using UML use case diagrams: IoT in testing. In: Integrating the Internet of Things into Software Engineering Practices, pp. 125–145. IGI Global (2019)
5. Voit, N., Kanev, D., Kirillov, S., Ukhanova, M.: The method of translation of the diagram with one type directed links into the inhibitor petri net. In: Misra, S., et al. (eds.) ICCSA 2019. LNCS, vol. 11623, pp. 562–572. Springer, Cham (2019). https://doi.org/10.1007/978-3-030-24308-1_45

6. Planas, E., Cabot, J.: How are UML class diagrams built in practice? A usability study of two UML tools: Magicdraw and Papyrus. Comput. Stand. Interfaces **67**, 103363 (2020)
7. Anwar, M.W., Azam, F., Khan, M.A., Butt, W.H.: The applications of Model Driven Architecture (MDA) in Wireless Sensor Networks (WSN): techniques and tools. In: Arai, K., Bhatia, R. (eds.) FICC 2019. LNNS, vol. 69, pp. 14–27. Springer, Cham (2020). https://doi.org/10.1007/978-3-030-12388-8_2
8. Nanthaamornphong, A., Leatongkam, A.: Extended For UML for automatic generation of UML sequence diagrams from object-oriented Fortran. Sci. Program. (2019)
9. Assunção, W.K., Vergilio, S.R., Lopez-Herrejon, R.E.: Automatic extraction of product line architecture and feature models from UML class diagram variants. Inf. Softw. Technol. **117**, 106198 (2020)
10. Zahoor, M., Azam, F., Anwar, M.W., Yousaf, N., Kashif, M.: A UML profile for the service discovery in the Enterprise Cloud Bus (ECB) framework. In: Barolli, L., Hussain, F.K., Ikeda, M. (eds.) CISIS 2019. AISC, vol. 993, pp. 269–279. Springer, Cham (2020). https://doi.org/10.1007/978-3-030-22354-0_25
11. Yildiz, O.: Object-based modeling of restrictions on the sale of agricultural land. Land Use Policy **82**, 538–549 (2019)
12. Lozynska, O., Savchuk, V., Pasichnyk, V.: Individual sign translator component of tourist information system. In: Shakhovska, N., Medykovskyy, M.O. (eds.) CSIT 2019. AISC, vol. 1080, pp. 593–601. Springer, Cham (2020). https://doi.org/10.1007/978-3-030-33695-0_40
13. Ruiz, P., Dorronsoro, B.: A novel CAD tool for electric educational diagrams. Appl. Sci. **9**(4), 810 (2019)
14. Störrle, H.: Structuring large models with MONO: notations, templates, and case studies. In: Model Management and Analytics for Large Scale Systems, pp. 141–166. Academic Press (2020)
15. Júnior, A.A.C., Misra, S., Soares, M.S.: A systematic mapping study on software architectures description based on ISO/IEC/IEEE 42010:2011. In: Misra, S., et al. (eds.) ICCSA 2019. LNCS, vol. 11623, pp. 17–30. Springer, Cham (2019). https://doi.org/10.1007/978-3-030-24308-1_2
16. Pathak, N., Sharma, G., Singh, B.M.: Trusted operating system-based model-driven development of secure web applications. In: Hoda, M.N., Chauhan, N., Quadri, S.M.K., Srivastava, P.R. (eds.) Software Engineering. AISC, vol. 731, pp. 421–432. Springer, Singapore (2019). https://doi.org/10.1007/978-981-10-8848-3_40
17. Abdelhadi, F., Ait Brahim, A., Zurfluh, G.: Applying a model-driven approach for UML/OCL constraints: application to NoSQL databases. In: Panetto, H., Debruyne, C., Hepp, M., Lewis, D., Ardagna, C.A., Meersman, R. (eds.) OTM 2019. LNCS, vol. 11877, pp. 646–660. Springer, Cham (2019). https://doi.org/10.1007/978-3-030-33246-4_40
18. Fitzgerald, K., Browne, L.M., Butler, R.F.: Using the Agile software development lifecycle to develop a standalone application for generating colour magnitude diagrams. Astron. Comput. **28**, 100283 (2019)
19. Mohanan, M., Bajwa, I.S.: Requirements to class model via SBVR: RECM via SBVR tool. Int. J. Open Sour. Softw. Process. (IJOSSP) **10**(2), 70–87 (2019)
20. Chien, C.F., Chen, G.Y.H., Liao, C.J.: Designing a connectivist flipped classroom platform using unified modeling language. Int. J. Online Pedagogy Course Des. (IJOPCD) **9**(1), 1–18 (2019)
21. Bluemke, I., Malanowska, A.: Tool for assessment of testing effort. In: Zamojski, W., Mazurkiewicz, J., Sugier, J., Walkowiak, T., Kacprzyk, J. (eds.) DepCoS-RELCOMEX 2019. AISC, vol. 987, pp. 69–79. Springer, Cham (2020). https://doi.org/10.1007/978-3-030-19501-4_7
22. Traoré, M.K.: Unified approaches to modeling. In: Model Engineering for Simulation, pp. 43–56. Academic Press (2019)

23. Wang, Y., Bai, L.: Fuzzy spatiotemporal data modeling based on UML. IEEE Access **7**, 45405–45416 (2019)
24. Mumtaz, H., Alshayeb, M., Mahmood, S., Niazi, M.: A survey on UML model smells detection techniques for software refactoring. J. Softw.: Evol. Process **31**(3), e2154 (2019)
25. Korableva, O.N., Kalimullina, O.V., Mityakova, V.N.: Designing a system for integration of macroeconomic and statistical data based on ontology. In: Arai, K., Bhatia, R., Kapoor, S. (eds.) CompCom 2019. AISC, vol. 998, pp. 157–165. Springer, Cham (2019). https://doi.org/10.1007/978-3-030-22868-2_12
26. Jovic, S., Cukaric, A., Raicevic, A., Tomov, P.: Assessment of electronic system for e-patent application and economic growth prediction. Phys. A: Stat. Mech. Appl. **520**, 93–105 (2019)
27. Bocciarelli, P., D'Ambrogio, A., Falcone, A., Garro, A., Giglio, A.: A model-driven approach to enable the simulation of complex systems on distributed architectures. Simulation. https://doi.org/10.1177/0037549719829828. (2019)
28. Tekinerdogan, B., Babur, Ö., Cleophas, L., van den Brand, M., Akşit, M.: Introduction to model management and analytics. In: Model Management and Analytics for Large Scale Systems, pp. 3–11 (2020). Academic Press
29. Baklouti, A., Nguyen, N., Mhenni, F., Choley, J.Y., Mlika, A.: Improved safety analysis integration in a systems engineering approach. Appl. Sci. **9**(6), 1246 (2019)
30. Mehryar, S., Sliuzas, R., Schwarz, N., Sharifi, A., van Maarseveen, M.: From individual fuzzy cognitive maps to agent based models: modeling multi-factorial and multi-stakeholder decision-making for water scarcity. J. Environ. Manag. **250**, 109482 (2019)

Data Analysis and Forecasting of COVID-19 Outbreak in India Using ARIMA Model

Binal Kaka[1]($\boxtimes$), Dweepna Garg[1], Parth Goel[2], and Amit Ganatra[1]

[1] Department of Computer Engineering, Devang Patel Institute of Advance Technology and Research, Charotar University of Science and Technology (CHARUSAT), Nadiad, India
{binalkaka.dce,amitganatra.ce}@charusat.ac.in
[2] Department of Computer Science and Engineering, Devang Patel Institute of Advance Technology and Research, Charotar University of Science and Technology (CHARUSAT), Nadiad, India

Abstract. Nowadays COVID-19 has created a pandemic for the whole world. This is also known as Novel Coronavirus-2019. In this paper, time series analysis using the ARIMA model is brought forward for COVID-19 prediction on the confirmed cases in India. ARIMA model can significantly give precise forecast results based on AIC (Akaike Information Criteria) value. ARIMA model can considerable reduce the errors of the prediction results with 24418 AIC value for predicting confirmed cases in India. The work is implemented gathering the data of confirmed cases from different states of the country. The duration from 30th January 2020 to 28th April 2020 has been taken into consideration for verifying the positive cases of corona in India. Moving average and auto regressive models are used for accurate prediction and maintaining seasonal differencing and second order differencing. The graphical representation is demonstrated applying the technique named Data Visualization in python programming. It shows the increasing amount of confirmed cases as well as the number of cured cases and death cases in India. It is examined that the p, d, q parameter in ARIMA can locate the best AIC value. According to the analysis in this context rolling mean and standard deviation test Statistic value is -1.186895. ADF Statistic value is 1.186895. Data sets are divided in training and testing module respectively for approximate judgement of positive cases.

Keywords: Data visualization applying python · Time series analysis · ARIMA model · AR model · MA model

1 Introduction

On 31st december 2019, the united nations agency was investigating on unusual cases of reposistary disorder of unknown causes in urban area town, China. One of the unique Coronavirus was detected because it was triggered by the authority of China on 7th of January, 2020, and the disease was given the name as "2019-nCoV". Coronavirus (CoV) is a local unit of an external family of viruses that causes abnormalities from respiratory infections to many serious infections. A unique Coronavirus may be called new shear

© Springer Nature Singapore Pte Ltd. 2021
A. K. Luhach et al. (Eds.): ICAICR 2020, CCIS 1393, pp. 29–38, 2021.
https://doi.org/10.1007/978-981-16-3660-8_3

that has not been previously known to human beings. Countries around the globe have heightened their police investigation to quickly identify possible new cases of 2019-nCoV. Hundreds of infected people have been known in China, similarity in european countries are also expand new cases WHO has issued guidelines in various countries guiding all how to examine sick people, how to test samples, treat patients, reign infection in health facilities, maintain and manage the right goods, and communicate with people based on present market information. WHO doesn't advocate any restriction of travel to common place. Recommendations are there to forestall infection and restrictions for travelers in or from affected areas incorporate regular hand laundry, covering mouth and nose once coughing and symptom, and avoiding shut contact with anyone showing symptoms of disease are precaution to be taken [1]. The loss of life meets 50 on first April, 100 on fifth April, 500 on nineteen April, and 1,000 on twenty-nine April. One minister who came back from moving to Italy and Germany, conveying the infection, transformed into "very fast-spreading" by going to a Sikh celebration in Anandpur Sahib from tenth–twelveth March. 27 COVID-19 cases were followed back to it [2]. Approximately 40,000 individuals in twenty towns of Punjab was required to be isolated on Twenty Seventh of March to restrict the spread. A Tablighi Jamaat strict gathering occasion that occurred on 31st of March in Delhi toward the beginning of March rose as another infection hotspot which gave a high rise to the spread of virus throughout the country. On an average 9,000 teachers possibly had attended the assembly, maximum from different parts of the country, and 960 participants which were belonging to 40 Regions outside the country. As per the Government, 4,291 out of 14,378 patients are connected to this occasion in Twenty-three Indian states and association domains till Eighteen April [3]. On Six April 2020, in Mumbai, 26 attendants and 3 specialists were found to have been tainted with the infection. The medical clinic was incidentally closed down and proclaimed a control zone. The carelessness of the emergency clinic organization has been accused of the contaminations [4]. Starting at Twenty Seventh of April, the conditions of the state named Goa, the state named Sikkim, as well as Nagaland, Arunachal Pradesh, Manipur, & Tripura was announced as "Covid-19 Free" with no single dynamic cases by the Indian Officials [4, 5]. Numerous research studies have been conducted to solve the problem of predicting the relations by individually keeping into consideration about different aspects of similarity [6, 7]. Several fields in which AI, ML, and DL act as From Automated Coronavirus Disease Detection, Deep Transfer Learning for Medical Image Processing, Data Processing, Analytics, Methodologies of Data Science, Text mining and analysis of natural languages, Validation Methodology for COVID-19 Events, Computational biology, and medicine, Internet of things for patient management and various diagnostic decision-making, Therapy, risk reduction and administration [8, 9].

Health Security
All printed material, including text, illustrations, and charts, must be kept as per the global health panel. It can be said that there are some standard for how humanity can take a safe keeping from the coronavirus. The important cause of this project is it shows the total danger from septicemia of the disease epidemic that would cause world wild outbreak and infestation together with work out response potentiality for each state. There are some important aspects which are specified by GHS index [10]. The first one is prevention. It represents how to take prevention from the coronavirus. It is the

Anticipation of the disclosure or let out of pathogens. There is mainly the observation to be done for extensive of budding international concern. Seconadly, immediate reaction to and relocation of the increase of an outbreak satisfactorily. Lastly the surity of the wellbeing of the laborers is important. Duties to enhance public limit, capitalize intends to mark holes, and sticking to worldwide standards. Generally speaking, dangerous condition and nation powerlessness leads to dangers. The major GHS Index discoveries were:

- Although America scored 83 out of one hundred focuses, properly-being protection around the globe is feeble and no country is enough arranged for plagues or outbreaks. The ordinary rating turned into simply 42 out of 100. Preparedness may be very vulnerable, and capacities have now not been examined properly.
- Capitalization and spending plans are deficient [11].
- Synchronization is missing between state governments and central government in teaching about precautions from the diseases like plague and pandemic like covid-19. Now it is standing them in India Government was choose to make some vital move for the individuals wellbeing through the lockdown [12]. On 4 March 2020 India's government declared obligatory screening of every single worldwide traveler showing up. Total number of 589,000 individuals have been screened at air terminals, more than 1,000,000 screened at fringes with Nepal and round 27,000 had been as of now beneath community reconnaissance [13]. On fifth of March the government of Delhi reported that every single fundamental faculty throughout Delhi will remain closed till thirty-first of March as a security cause [13]. On seventh March, grade faculties in Jammu vicinity as well as Samba location have been shut down till thirty-first March [3]. On ninth of March, gatherer as well as region justice of Pathanamthitta locale of Kerala introduced 3 days of prolonged holidays for every single instructive foundation in the region. On 10 March, Kerala declared a conclusion everything being equal and schools over the country until thirty-first March, w.e.f (with effect from) eleventh March. The government declared on twelveth March, that each schools, universities, and movie corridors in New Delhi could be shut until the finish of March. On thirteenth March, the Punjab and Chhattisgarh governments reported closing in all schools and universities until 31 March. Manipur authorities declared that each one of schools within the state, wherein assessment is not being held could stay close till 31 March. The Himachal Pradesh boss priest announced on 14 March, that every instructive establishment along with auditorium would stay shut up to thirty-one March as a prudent step taking into account the risk of Covid_19. Likewise, in the West Bengal government reported that every single instructive foundation will be closed up-to 31st March, and the board exam assessments will be managed. The government of Maharashtra asked shopping-malls, cinemas, recenters and all academy and universities in the state's urban zones to stay lockdown up to thirty-one March 2020. Administration of Rajasthan reported closing all instructive institutions, rec centers, as well as film corridors till thirty March, but progressing school and school tests will proceed [4]. On fifteenth March, in Goa government proclaimed that every single instructive employer might stay close until thirty-first of March. At the same time, the assessments of the tenth and twelveth students of Goa state could be conducted in accordance with plot. Brihanmumbai Municipal enterprise closed down Jamaat

Udaan until further requests. The government of Gujarat mentioned that each one of schools, as well as universities, movie corridors may be shut till Thirty-one March, besides the board checks may be led. Shrine Board of Vaishno Devi gave a caution urging non-occupant Indians as well as outsiders to restrict the visit the sanctuary for the Twenty-eight days their post-arrival in the country. The Tamil Nadu & Telangana governments announced the college-break, purchasing centers including theatres till Thirty-first of March. All the landmarks and exhibition halls under Archaeological Survey of India were closed down until thirty first March by Ministry of culture. On 24 March, the government of India asked a shutdown across country for twenty-one days, affecting the survival of 1.3 billion populace of the country as a safety measure opposing the 2020 coronavirus pandemic in India. There was a reopen of few markets following a 14-h wellful open time limitation on 22 March, trailed by the requirement of a progression of guidelines in the nation's COVID-19 affected areas. The lockdown was set when number of positive coronavirus cases in India was around 500. Likewise, the Indian Government Continuously propeled the individuals that they will be remaining at home. Government advised to use cover and sanitizer for your their own security. There are numerous individuals in india who required nourishment parcel for their wellbeing from the government during lockdown, all the specialists, Police, government employees made a solid effort to help the Indian Government's choice.

2 Related Work

In the recent year, Covid-19 problem is targeted as the relevant problem for conducting research. For the prediction of the exact number of novel coronavirus (COVID-19) confirmed recorded cases for 32 Indian states as well as union territories, deep learning-based models are used. It is noted that for short-term prediction, the proposed approach yields high precision with errors of less than 3% for daily predictions and less than 8% for weekly predictions. Long term memory (LSTM) cells based on recurrent neural networks (RNN) are used as prediction models. In 32 states/union territories, LSTM variants such as deep LSTM, coevolutionary LSTM, and bi-directional LSTM models are tested and the model with maximum accuracy is chosen based on absolute error. Bi-directional LSTM provides the best outcomes based on prediction errors, and convolutional LSTM gives the worst [11]. To calibrate, a newly developed Trust-region-reflective algorithm, which is one of the robust least-squares numerical optimization techniques, has been deployed. The publicly accessible COVID-19 data has been carefully analyzed to assess the possible peak dates and sizes for the developing COVID 19 hotspots called Russia, Brazil, India, and Bangladesh. Russia may be based on the forecast results as of May 11, 2020, In terms of regular cases of infections and deaths, Russia could hit a peak around the end of May. In terms of daily and symptomatic infectious cases and deaths, Brazil, Bangladesh and India could hit a peak around the middle of June [10].

3 Methodology

The Dataset of Total Confirmed, recovered and death cases of COVID-19 infection are collected for the globe wiled also as India as per World Health Organization region classification from the official website of Kaggle from 22nd January 2020 to 1st May 2020. Using this data build a predictive model [15].

3.1 Proposed Methodology

ARIMA displaying is one of the least complex demonstrating methods. ARIMA models are constantly spoken to with the help of certain framework and furthermore, the design is communicated as Auto regressive integrated moving Average (p, d, q) [17]. Well, p represents the request for auto-relapse, d means the level of pattern contrast while q is that the request for moving normally. We have applied an ARIMA model to the measurement information of confirmed COVID-19 cases in India. Autocorrelation work (ACF) chart and incomplete autocorrelation (PACF) diagram are utilized to look out the underlying number of ARIMA models [18]. These ARIMA models are then tried for fluctuation in ordinariness and fixed. Next, they're checked for exactness by watching their MAPE, MAD, and MSD qualities to work out the best model to conjecture. also, the most straightforward fit ARIMA model is contrasted and Linear Trend, Quadratic Trend, S-Curve Trend, Moving Average, Single Exponential also as Double Exponential models utilizing a yield of the proportion of precision, viz. MAPE, MAD, MSD, so on select the best model to calculate. The best model is the one which has an exceptionally modest incentive for all the measures. In the wake of fitting the model, its parameters are evaluated followed by verification of the model. Using the ARIMA model in this paper we are going the evaluate expected data and predicted data. P, d, q parameters are decided using 5 the AIC (Akaike Information Criteria) value. The Akaike Information Criteria (AIC) is a generally utilized proportion of a factual model [19, 20]. It essentially measures (1) the integrity of fit, and (2) the effortlessness/miserliness, of the model into a solitary measurement. When looking at two models, the one with the lower AIC is by and large "better". Presently, let us apply this incredible asset in looking at different ARIMA models, regularly used to show time arrangement.

4 Result Analysis

Covid_19 Effect on India

The current work envelops the advancement of a model to estimate Coronavirus frequencies in the advancing days. The outcomes for the proportion of model exactness for ARIMA, Autocorrelation, Quadratic Linear, S-Curve Trend, Moving Average, Single Exponential just as Double Exponential model, moving mean, and moving abandoned. A gander at the MAPE, MAD, and MSD values proposes what p, d, q ARIMA model worth is the most precise of just for anticipating future frequencies as it has a minimal incentive for all the measures. P-cost of the test is much less than the importance stage (0.05) then you reject the null speculation and infer that the time collection is indeed stationary (Fig. 1).

Figure 2 shows the total count of cured cases in India. Here different state wise analysis on cured cases shown in Fig. 2.

Figure 3 shows the total count of Deaths cases in India. Here different state wise analysis on Death cases shown in Fig. 2.

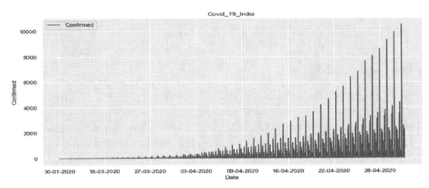

Fig. 1. Analysis of total confirmed cases in India

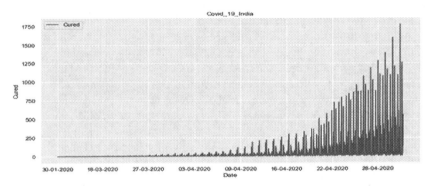

Fig. 2. Analysis on total cured cases in India

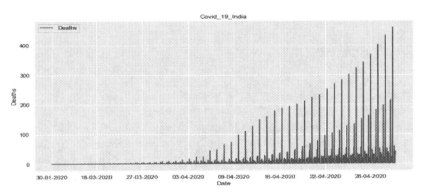

Fig. 3. Analysis of total deaths cases in India

Figure 4 shows the original data with the calculated mean and standard division line. According to the analysis in this case Test Statistic value is −1.186895. ADF Statistic: −1.186895 p-value: 0. 679208. The invalid speculation of the augmented dickey-fuller test is that the time arrangement is non-fixed. In this way, if the p-estimation of the

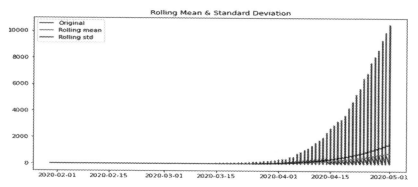

Fig. 4. Analysis of rolling mean and standard deviation

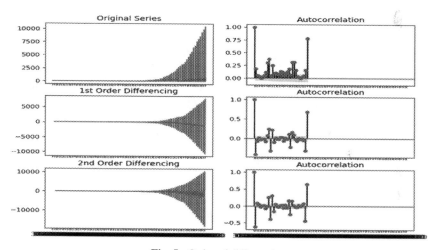

Fig. 5. Order of differencing

experiment is not exactly the essentialness level (0.05) at that point you dismiss the invalid theory and surmise that the time arrangement is without a doubt fixed. In this way, for our situation, if P cost less than 0.05 we proceed with uncovering the request for differencing. Since the p esteem is more noteworthy than the necessity, we move towards the distinction the arrangement and perceive how the autocorrelation plot resembles.

Figure 5 Shows For the above diagrams, the time arrangement arrives at stationarity with two sets of differences. In any case, on taking a gander at the autocorrelation plot for the second differencing the slack goes into the far negative zone genuinely snappy, which shows, the arrangement may have been over difference. Along these lines, we are going to likely fix the request for differencing as 1 despite the fact that the arrangement isn't consummately fixed. So next we are going to discovering AR expression for the arrangement.

Figure 6 shows just like what we looked like at the PACF plot for the quantity of AR terms, we can take a gander at the ACF plot for the quantity of MA terms. A MA expression is in fact, the blunder of the slacked estimate. The ACF tells what number of MA terms are required to evacuate any autocorrelation in the stationary arrangement. The above figure it shows the autocorrelation plot of the differenced arrangement. A couple of slacks are well over the centrality line.

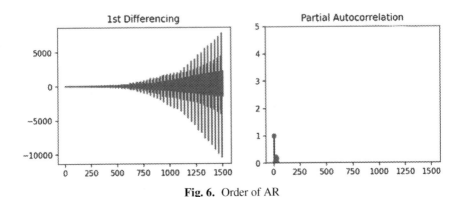

Fig. 6. Order of AR

In this way, it allows likely fix q as 1. If all else fails, go with the more straightforward model that adequately clarifies the Y.

Figure 7 shows the Just like what we looked like at the PACF plot for the quantity of AR terms, we can take a gander at the ACF plot for the quantity of MA terms. A MA expression is in fact, the blunder of the slacked estimate. The ACF tells what number of MA terms are required to evacuate any autocorrelation in the stationary's arrangement. In the above fig it shows the autocorrelation plot of the differenced arrangement. Couple of slacks are well over the centrality line. In this way, allows likely fix q as 1. If all else fails, go with the more straightforward model that adequately clarifies the Y.

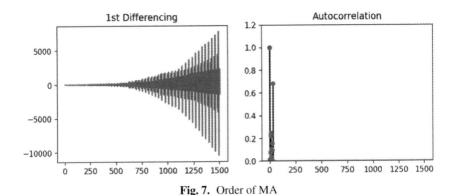

Fig. 7. Order of MA

Figure 8 Shows the result of ARIMA model on Data set of India. Here using the (2, 0, 2) p, d, q parameter we found best AIC value for the Prediction.

Figure 9 Shows the Expected and Predicted value of the Covid_19 Confirmed cases in India. The blue line represents the Expected value and red Line Represent the Predicted value.

```
                              ARMA Model Results
==============================================================================
Dep. Variable:              Confirmed   No. Observations:              1510
Model:                      ARMA(2, 2)  Log Likelihood            -12203.222
Method:                       css-mle   S.D. of innovations          781.692
Date:              Sat, 09 May 2020     AIC                        24418.444
Time:                        13:31:23   BIC                        24450.363
Sample:                             0   HQIC                       24430.331

==============================================================================
                    coef     std err          z      P>|z|     [0.025      0.975]
------------------------------------------------------------------------------
const             477.5841   430.179      1.110      0.267   -365.551    1320.719
ar.L1.Confirmed     0.1365     0.015      8.902      0.000      0.106       0.167
ar.L2.Confirmed     0.8629     0.015     56.267      0.000      0.833       0.893
ma.L1.Confirmed    -0.0016     0.005     -0.330      0.742     -0.011       0.008
ma.L2.Confirmed    -0.9726     0.005   -208.853      0.000     -0.982      -0.963
                                   Roots
==============================================================================
                 Real          Imaginary           Modulus         Frequency
------------------------------------------------------------------------------
AR.1           1.0003          +0.0000j            1.0003            0.0000
AR.2          -1.1585          +0.0000j            1.1585            0.5000
MA.1           1.0132          +0.0000j            1.0132            0.0000
MA.2          -1.0148          +0.0000j            1.0148            0.5000
------------------------------------------------------------------------------
```

Fig. 8. ARIMA model results

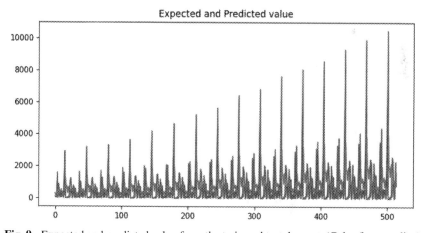

Fig. 9. Expected and predicted value from the train and test data set. (Color figure online)

5 Conclusion

In this paper, ARIMA Model is used for forecasting increasing confirmed cases of Covid-19 in India in different states. In case of rolling mean and standard deviation analysis p value is 0.067, which is not up to the mark p value should be 0.05. So, auto correlation plots are used to achieve the precise estimated value it is observed that the auto correlation plot divides the analysis according to original series, first order differencing and second order differencing. ARIMA Model is used for detailed analysis for confirmed cases in future. The p, d, q values in ARIMA Model is set to (2, 0, 2) respectively. The values helped to achieve the best AIC value which will in-turn help to predict the number of confirmed COVID-19 cases in future. Expected and predicted values are achieved using training and testing datasets. In future the same model can be used for predicting the cured cases as well as the death cases in the country as well as the whole world.

References

1. Coronavirus disease (COVID-19) pandemic. http://www.euro.who.int/en/health-topics/hea lthemergencies/coronaviruscovidcoronavirus-2019-ncov
2. A history of Corona virus. https://www.labmanager.com/lab-health-and-safety/covid-19-a-history-ofcoronavirus-20-2021
3. Global Health Security Index. https://www.ghsindex.org/about/
4. All Delhi malls to be closed, grocery and pharmacy stores exempted: CM Arvind Kejriwal. Deccan Herald. Press Trust of India. 20 March 2020 (2020). Accessed 20 Mar 2020
5. Sharma, S.: How conference hall at health ministry emerged as coronavirus-control war-room. Hindustan Times. Archived from the Original on 7 March 2020 (2020). Accessed 7 Mar 2020
6. Chen, N., et al.: Epidemiological and clinical characteristics of 99 cases of 2019 novel coronavirus pneumonia in Wuhan, China: a descriptive study. Lancet **395**(10223), 507–513 (2020)
7. Arora, P., Kumar, H., Panigrahi, B.K.: Prediction and analysis of COVID-19 positive cases using deep learning models: a descriptive case study of India (2020)
8. Kumari, A., et al.: Supervised link prediction using structured-based feature extraction in social network (2020)
9. Nabi, K.N.: Forecasting COVID-19 pandemic: a data-driven analysis (2020)
10. Shen, M., Peng, Z., Xiao, Y., Zhang, L.: Modelling the epidemic trend of the 2019 novel coronavirus outbreak in China. BioRxiv (2020)
11. Read, J.M., Bridgen, J.R., Cummings, D.A., Ho, A., Jewell, C.P.: Novel coronavirus 2019-nCoV: early estimation of epidemiological parameters and epidemic predictions. MedRxiv (2020)
12. Ruiz Estrada, M.A., Koutronas, E.: The networks infection contagious diseases positioning system (NICDP-System): the case of Wuhan-COVID-19. SSRN 3548413 (2020)
13. Ramoliya, D., Patel, A., Pawar, C., Ganatra, A.: Application of artificial intelligence, machine learning and deep learning in fight against Coronavirus (COVID-19): a detailed analysis. JASC: J. Appl. Sci. Comput.
14. Wilder, B., et al.: The role of age distribution and family structure on Covid-19 dynamics: a preliminary modeling assessment for Hubei and Lombardy. SSRN 3564800 (2020)
15. Novel Coronavirus 2019 Dataset. https://www.kaggle.com/sudalairajkumar/novel-corona-virus-2019-dataset
16. Chang, S.L., Harding, N., Zachreson, C., Cliff, O.M., Prokopenko, M.: Modelling transmission and control of the COVID-19 pandemic in australia. arXiv preprint arXiv:2003.10218 (2020)
17. Johns Hopkins Coronavirus Resource Center (2020). https://coronavirus.jhu.edu/. Accessed 16 May 2020
18. Moriarty, L.F., Plucinski, M., Marston, B.J.: Public health responses to COVID-19 outbreaks on cruise ships-worldwide. Morb. Mortal. Wkly. Rep. **69**, 347–352 (2020)
19. Grenfell, R., Drew, T.: Here's why it's taking so long to develop a vaccine for the new coronavirus. Science Alert Archived from the original on 28 2020 (2020)
20. Wang, L., Li, J., Guo, S., Xie, N., Yao, L., Cao, Y., et al.: Real-time estimation and Real-time estimation and prediction of mortality caused by COVID-19 with patient information based algorithm. Sci. Total Environ. **727**, 138394 (2020)

Analysis Paper on Different Algorithm, Dataset and Devices Used for Fundus Images

Priyanka Arora$^{(\boxtimes)}$ and Babanpreet Singh$^{(\boxtimes)}$

CSE Department, Guru Nanak Dev Engineering College, Ludhiana, India

Abstract. Analysis of images with deep learning and machine learning has recently show more accuracy in medical image processing. The paper review the major machine learning methods is used for the extraction of retinal fundus image. It describes how hardware has been modified according to time for retinal eye segmentation that device is helpful for the environment and also useful for humans The algorithms used for image extraction, clear and noise-free Images of different color scales are used to improve image quality. The paper gives a review of how researchers and scientists have been trying different methods to improve vessel segmentation in the future.

Key words: Artificial intelligence · Deep learning · Local phase (LP) · ROI (Region of Interest) · Area under ROC Curve (AUC) · Point of care (POC) · Visual Geometry Group (VGG) · Rectified Linear Unit (ReLU) · Digital fundus images (DFIs) · Multiview Test (MVT) · Computer-aided diagnosis (CAD)

1 Introduction

Retina Blood Veins visitation is required mostly in the medical group to diagnose complicated disease hypertension, heart vessel disease, eye glaucoma, blood stroke, arteriosclerosis to identify diseases in the early stage. Retina vessel images (Ananthamoorthy 2019) are very helpful within the center of the retina as they are more hidden, rough place, the macula remains, whose middle is well known because of the fovea, this is effective for clear vision. In blind spot as well as eyecup may be a deep oval patch (Besenczi et al. 2016). Glaucoma leads to a different group of disorders that damage the nerves optics and field of vision (VF) (Jonas et al. 2017). There were many difficulties faced by peoples of United Kingdom. First and principal, the numbers of people with diabetes and un-diagnosed diabetes are significantly above within the UK (Federation 2015). This vessel segmentation formation plays a critical role in normal visual, developmental, and metabolic function. The choroid may be a vascular film layer filling the posterior eye found inside the retina and hence, the controller of ocular temperature and refractive error improvement is a sign of the essential duties of the choroid (Nickla and Wallman 2010) this eye disease is detected by useful devices (Fig. 1).

The Latest tabletop fundus cameras are used for quality improvement of the image that uses a light LED camera with a machine on a table that gives different angle images of the retina that is visible on a computer screen with autofocus device lens that makes

© Springer Nature Singapore Pte Ltd. 2021
A. K. Luhach et al. (Eds.): ICAICR 2020, CCIS 1393, pp. 39–52, 2021.
https://doi.org/10.1007/978-981-16-3660-8_4

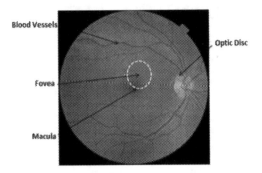

Fig. 1. Retina eye image (Michael Goldbaum et al.)

Table 1. Machine learning methods used by different researchers

Reference	Methods	Application remark
Ananthamoorthy and balasubramanian (Ananthamoorthy 2019)	CNN and SVM	Image visitation using CNN and SVM
Soares et al. (Soares et al. 2006)	Supervised classification and 2-D Gabor wavelet	Retinal vessel analysis using the supervised classification and 2-D Gabor wavelet
Wang et al. (Wang et al. 2015)	CNN and random forest	Level wise retinal blood vessel segmentation based on feature and group learning
J. Zhao et al. (Zhao et al. 2018)	Multi-scale superpixel chain tracking	Self-workable retinal vessel analysis using multi-scale super pixel chain tuacking
E. Sutanty et al. (Sutanty et al. 2017)	Combined filters	Blur selection Using combined filters and blood vessel Segmentation
J. Zilly et al. (Zilly et al. 2017)	Selective sampling and ensemble learning	Glaucoma finding using selective sampling and group learning for automatic optic cup and disc analysis
P. Smith et al. (Smith et al. 1979)	Gray-level histograms	Inception selection technique from gray-level histograms(Paul M. Muchinsky 2012)
Roychowdhurys. et al. (Roychowdhury et al. 2015)	Iterative algorithm	Iterative vessel visitation of fundus images (Paul M. Muchinsky 2012)
Sun Song and Maninis.K.K et al. (Maninis et al. 2016)(Mateen et al. 2020)	DCNN "Deep convolutional Neural Network" (Paul M. Muchinsky 2012)	DRIU "Deep Retinal Image Understanding" (Paul M. Muchinsky 2012)

(*continued*)

Table 1. (*continued*)

Reference	Methods	Application remark
Xu ziyue et al. (Wu et al. 2016)	Probabilistic approach via deep learning	Deep vessel tracking
Chen Xiangyu et al. (Zilly et al. 2017)	Deep convolutional neural network	Glaucoma finding based on DCNN
Greinvan jj and Hoyng et al. (Van Grinsven et al. 2016)	FCNN "Fast Convolutional Neural Network"	The methods to hemorrhage "an escape of blood from ruptured blood veins" finder in color fundus images
Worral D.E et al. (Hutchison et al. 2016)	Convolutional Neural Networks	Automated retinopathy of leister case detection with CNN
Chain Singh et al. (Singh et al. 2013)	Genetic Algorithms used focused crawling improving	Latest crawling method to build domain specific collection for search engines
Luhach KA et al. (Kumar et al. 2019)	Perspective modeling with deep learning	Malignancy in mammograms early detection

vessel and lesion detection easy. Evolution in technology shrinks devices to human hands as shown in Fig. 2, this new device known as combined adaptor-detector-based hand-held ophthalmic cameras. Each ocular device is united with a display screen forming an easy hand-held LED, LCD tool (Panwar et al. 2016) (Table 1).

The financial value of known damages and sicknesses is another issue of workplace accidents and infection. In extension to limitless human suffering, certain accidents and sick fitness purpose significant financial losses for companies and communities as a whole, including lost productivity and decreased job ability. Some research has selected that an approximated that around 4% of the world's gross domestic product (GDP) is suffered due to many direct and indirect losses, including damages, therapeutic expenses, assets damage, missed earnings and replacement practice (Table 2).

2 Analysis Color Fundus Images

Fundus picture-taking is a low-cost and common technique for average filters, Applied by origin equalizing and sharpens image quality qualified remedial experts. There is an improvement that a picture can be The back frame picture was then reduced from the first one to be tried at another section or time by authorities and gives a selection of the satisfactory image pre-processing systems and photos documentation for future reference (Panwar et al. 2016). Lately obtained the state-of-the-art technic proposed to pick an optimal hybrid of early select early operation methodologies for fundus picture-taking. Currently, possible fundus cameras wound and tumor aspirant extractors by modern research that gives another viewpoint to predict and create a surgical environment.

Table 2. Accuracy achieved on different datasets

Reference	Accuracy	Dataset used
Balasubramanian and Anathamoorthy (Ananthamoorthy 2019)	98.12%	DRIVE
	98.67%	STARE
Soares et al. (Soares et al. 2006)	96.14%	DRIVE
	96.71%	STARE
J. Zhao et al. (Zhao et al. 2018)	95.92%	DRIVE
	96.53%	HRF
S. Wang et al. (Wang et al. 2015)	98.83%	DRIVE
J. Zilly et al. (Zilly et al. 2017)	90.00%	DRISHTI-GS
S. Roychowdhury et al. (Roychowdhury et al. 2015)	96.23%	CHASE_DB1
K. Maninis et al.(Maninis et al. 2016)	97.10%	DRIONS-DB
	95.90%	RIM-ONE
A. Wu et al. (Wu et al. 2016)	97.01%	DRIVE
D. Wong et al. (Wong et al. 2008)	96%	SiMES
Van Grinsven et al. (Van Grinsven et al. 2016)	89.40%	Ses
	97.20%	NSeS
D.E. Worrall et al. (Hutchison et al. 2016)	93.60%	Canadian dataset
X. Xu et al. (Xu et al. 2016)	93.3%	DRIVE
	92%	STARE
Y. Lu et al. (Lu et al. 2019)	83.10%	ORIGA
	88.70%	SCES

Fig. 2. Smartphone attached with retinal photo camera (Source:Besenczi et al. 2016) (Besenczi et al. 2016)

These are often classified into three principal groups:

- The old purpose of pre-processing programs through this group-based rule is that the fundus camera is very simple to use by a skilled person also that device is cost-efficient but on the other hand special clinical stays are needed by the sufferers. Surgeries held by devices require highly qualified medical staff.

- Small tabletop fundus cameras are analyzed, but for all that, individually client has to visit the clinic. These devices are costly so that's why those expensive devices are not widely used. These devices are not easily available in any general clinic.
- Aim and ignite cameras are light, handheld devices. They need the best image quality at a low cost. Supervised classification uses preliminary results with multi-scale transformation using wavelet transform
- that improves by a Gaussian mixture. Bayesian classifier model as test held with ROC analysis is used for segmentation methods. Pixel is given by feature vector measure on many scales get from 2D Gabor wavelet transform. The result made by this transformation classifies every pixel of a vessel or non-vein area. That classification is rapidly complete by Gaussian mixture on a model of the complex decision surface (Soares et al. 2006).

2.1 Image Pre-processing

- Pre-analysis is that the ultimate task for fundus photo-shoot the finding of (Scanlon et al.) and (Philip et al. (2005)). Finds that 20.8% and 11.9%, each were pictures from a point of one eye that can't be examined clinically due to unfinished image property. The foremost reasons for the poor shape of irregular lighting, decreased contrast, media darkness (e.g., cataract), and change of the recognition. earlier selection and modification is a moderate process that shall reduce these problems tone (Philip et al. 2005)
- Green channel Fragment with the highest vascular response. The green channel is held the perceptive focus of main retinal images it improves the big vessel intensity differentiating on a different region. The solution is in two phases:

  - Gaussian blur algorithm is used to eliminate vessel surfaces and capture local light scattering
  - The Gaussian filter shall be big enough to fade a large vessel update from this equation.
  - Image pre-processing decreases the workload of doctors. That is also used for accurate analysis of medical pictures so useless paperwork is easily detected by Digital images.

$$v'_p = v_p . \frac{v_m}{\frac{b}{v_p}} \qquad (1)$$

Enhance the contrast in the vascular area and backdrop a quadrature filter called local phase (LP) is applied. It wants to improve the formation of the image. That filter is selected because filter measurement in terms of the first scale N parameter is got to fit huge vessels eliminating undesired edge effects is operated to expand the tracking region along the sting of ROI (Zhao et al. 2018). A general-purpose representation of the ROI of a medical image could be declared as a subset of a medical picture, known for a special intention. Researcher introduces here an easy way of thresholding method to partition (Na'am at al. 2018) the preference of non-uniform environment brilliance, an active methodology called median filtering is applied. (Ananthamoorthy 2019) median filtering may be a simple filter that is used for edge improvement smoothing filter sets. it includes the fine details about the softened image (Sutanty et al. 2017) center esteem are ideal "central state" than the traditional esteem that time is calculated by

$$\text{"}Median[A(x)+B(x)] \neq median[A(x)]+median[B(x)]\text{"(Vijikala \& Dhas, 2016)}$$
(2)

A center base filter to assume every pixel value of surrounding or not. rather than changing that alter the pixel matrix with a center value (Vijikala and Dhas 2016).

Bifurcation is used for the following method of segmentation combined filtering-:

o Extraction fundus photo green channel.
o Making a balance to fundus photo green methods.
o Executing Adaptive Histogram (Sutanty et al. 2017).

A pixel features Red Green Blue (RGB) elements of colored pictures are reflected individually, green channel is most suited for vein/background variance. On another side blue and red channels show fewer colors and very blur images. the green channel is chosen feature applied by method wavelet to scale back false detection border of the camera gap wavelet transformation use the iterative method in developing ROI neighbors using four-block pixel internally each pixel point change with mean value pixel. This equivalent Fourier meaning of the wavelet transform (Soares et al. 2006).

$$T_\varnothing(b, \theta, a) = C_\varnothing^{-1/2} a \exp \int (jkb)\psi^*(ar_{\theta k})\hat{f}(k)d^2k$$
(3)

the optic disc is improved by applying a two-stage method segmented supported by the smaller eyecup then uses domain-independent pre-processing this improves the information of images. The blind spot first applies round Hough transformation on the green channel icon each image front cropped image and take away any quantity of background but around blind spot held then training scheme to take crucial feature of images which concentrate also on the receiver operation characteristics (ROC). Cropping also trims the calculative load. Take retinal fundus Picture are in Red Green Blue color season change into L * a * b color season applying unconditional change that copies the rational answer of the study on express image concentration is decreased from every pixel violence followed by the group with the quality deviation (Zilly et al. 2017).

2.2 Dataset

The experiment in retinal fundus images is performed on an easily available dataset on the internet. The dataset is a combination of images holding valuable knowledge. In this review, a dataset that is commonly used by different researchers is by applying various techniques on the image processing algorithm's in the operations, some of the images are used to train the system and some are used for testing purpose *K. B. N. P. Ananthamoorthy* (2019). Also, the STARE dataset includes many retinal images, which is taken using

Topcon TRV 50 fundus camera including spatial resolution of 700 × 605 pixels and greyscale resolution of 24 bit. The review evaluation is approved for a different sample of retinal images with approx. 240 images of training and approx. 260 of testing images are used STARE and DRIVE dataset which has includes 400 images of STARE dataset and Approximately. 400 images of Drive dataset test on different accuracy methods like kappa index, Sensitivity, Specificity, Accuracy, Kappa index (Mateen et al. 2020).

2.2.1 STARE Dataset

The Dataset holding a total number of 400 Approximately. STARE dataset is an open-source accessible dataset presented by the University of California, San Diego holding 400 Approx images. Retinal fundus images. All the retinal fundus images. STARE dataset is implemented by *K. B. N. P. Ananthamoorthy* (2019). (Ananthamoorthy 2019) using CNN and SVM methods (Michael Goldbaum 1996).

2.2.2 DRIVE Dataset

This dataset holds 40 retinal fundus photographs taken by Canon CR5 camera. DRIVE dataset is also an open-source accessible dataset provided by Netherlands research and education purposes. In this dataset, used by (Zhao et al. 2018) standard segmentations of personal witnesses where the events of the first author are recognized as the spot fact anatomy is in this paper (Ginneken, 2012).

2.2.3 HRF Dataset

The dataset contains 3 types of images database healthy eyes, glaucomatous eyes, diabetic retinopathy. Which is available on Field of view (FOV)mask, Vessel Segmentation Gold standard, Optic Disk Gold standard. This HRF dataset is Used by the researcher (Zhao et al. 2018). Every collection includes 15 RGB retinal photographs, and each picture is associated with a mask image or a manually segmented area fact image (Budai et al. 2013).

2.3 DRISHTI-GS

This dataset is provided by IIIT, Hyderabad. This dataset must stay gathered and explained by Aravind Eye Hospital, Madurai, India. The dataset meant for validation of segmenting OpticDisc, cup, and identifying notching. This dataset is of a particular group as all cases whose eye images are part of this dataset are Indian people (Zilly et al. 2017) uses.

DeepCNN on 50 images to gives trained a network (Sivaswamy 2011) (Table 3).

2.3.1 CHASE_DB1

That dataset is provided by IDIAP Research Institute. The dataset includes 28 eye fundus images with a pixel range of 1280 × 960. Two assortments of ground-truth vessel explanations are accessible. The first set is commonly used for training and testing. The second set acts as a "human" baseline. That dataset is used by (Roychowdhury et al. 2015) every image is observed by two researchers (M.M Fraz et al. 2012).

Table 3. Devices used of fundus images.

Category name	Design principle	Pupil	Field of view	Focusing range	Fixation targets	Photo sensor display	Extra features
Miniature table –Top design							
EasyScan	Confocal SLO, with green, NIR	Nonmydriatic	60° H 45° V Topcon	Autofocus	Not Specified	Photo detector-based computer interface; network connectivity	Enhanced view of periphery, better resolution, auto- mated iris detection, pseudo-color
Topcon TRC-NW8Fplus19	Reflective imaging using white light	Nonmydriatic	45°	Autofocus, -13D to 12D (without lens correction)	Internal/external fixation target (can be selected)	8 MP digital SRL camera	Stereo photography, color, red-free images. fluorescein angiography
Canon CR-2	Reflective imaging using white ligh	Nonmydriatic	45o	Autofocus	Internal and external	18 MP EOS digital camera	Cobalt- and red-free imaging

(continued)

Table 3. (*continued*)

Category name	Design principle	Pupil	Field of view	Focusing range	Fixation targets	Photo sensor display	Extra features
Point-and-shoot off-the-shelf digital camera-based	Conventional optics + camera lens	Mydriatic	50o	Manual	NO	Camera CMOS senso	-
Smartphone-based (hand-held)							
Ocular Cellscope	iPhone + conventional optics	Not specified	55o	Autofocus	No	iPhone	-
PEEK	iPhone + external lens	Not specified	Not specified	Filmic Pro application	No	iPhone	-
Harvard Medical School prototype	iPhone + external lens	Mydriatic	Not specified	Filmic Pro application	No	iPhone	-

2.3.2 DRIONS-DB

This dataset provides by Akande Noah Oluwatobi et al. Landmark University, kwara state, Nigeria. Dataset used by (Maninis et al. 2016) he applies optic disc segmentation on DRIONS-DB used 110 images split by 60 for training and 50 images for Testing (Baidaa Al-Bander 2018).

3 Partitioning

Partitioning is that the way of separating images into separate sections Thresholding for every Pixel. This OD (optical disk) Thresholding is necessary for grouping it from the backdrop for more OD (optical disk) classification (Ullaha et al. 2018) the research paper feature extraction of the things described by various parameter shapes, texture, and color, etc. Otsu's partitioning value does not allow such a lot of images than what's preferred so that that algorithm is modified by different technique's (Smith et al. 1979) an unsupervised technique like Iterative vessel segmentation by adaptive Thresholding by process subdued image create by hiding out the current segmented artery view from the vein improved picture. (Roychowdhury et al. 2015) Segmentation width of a vessel using pixels that paper developed saliency-based vessel extraction methods and vessel width measurement graph-theoretic methods that convert saliency image to ROI that algorithm builds 2D graph-based vessel model. That system requirement on-site diagnostic tool. Which is used to convert all types of images and RGB images.

A user-friendly form was created to facilitate on-site image recovery, review or supervision (Xu et al. 2016) make two different system map volumes both perform different task eye vessel analysis volume has 4 finer processes of optic disc finding and other for coarser stage (Maninis et al. 2016) the following devices with a different feature used.

4 Fundus Photography Sustainability with the Latest Devices in Current Health-Care Also

Image-processing with Technical equipment is very useful for eye retinal to examine as latest hardware are developed according to time that gives accurate and signified result in low cost as compared to earlier days fundus photography was done with heavy and costly equipment. The field of view (FOV) was first developed in 1927 Metzger developed fundus photography invention of flashlight enables to see the pupil of the eye with retina images at different angles used to detect clearer images and newly, moveable. Popular devices in the market nowadays are Canon, CenterVue and Topcon.

In any hospital, cases need a complete physique check than a precise and particular physical examination. Modernistic physicians are experts at communicating with complex devices that encouraged by skilled technical person. so the conclusion is that as much as the device is easy to handle and less complex to operate that much charges of the medical test are decreased (Picano 2004).

5 Limitations in the Earlier Fundus Camera

- The heavy system's devices a host of a mechanical or optical part are connected with other components to get good quality images.
- Requirement of a skilled person. Heavy mechanical equipment is difficult to handle and accessible in remote rural settings (Panwar et al. 2016).

6 Machine Learning Methods for Vessel Extraction

The State-of-Art method is used in a deep convolutional neural network (DCNN) to acquire the characteristics of the look of the point. A imaging techniques, optic imaging, computed tomography and local structure pattern.

Two major challenges (i) manual identification of vascular tree, (ii) biological vasculatures which is very time consuming and tedious.

Challenges to get a common description model of vein model design for a particular task

- State of art methods - problems in numerical modeling the form over a selection regarding individual practice data, in most samples is also resolvable.
- Probabilistic tracking - multiple studies of robustness and efficiency.
- Continuous Gaussian method - that is used for the evaluation.
- Monte Carlo Random Sampling - Anywhere weight is defined following Bayesian rule. justify the vessel tracking route (Wu et al. 2016).

Moreover, it gave minimum detached veins. This system will also use in that place where some pixels are segmented in the tracking system as related to the full CNN method and this CNN used with DRIU deep retinal image understand which improves the result of impressive progress to solve the problem with base network architecture. That start from seminal Alex Net. more complex and more accurate VGGNet. single forward pass of CNN segments vessel network and optic disc CNN coupled with rectified Linear Unit (ReLU) 4 max-pooling layer architecture separates the network 5 stage which uses Loss function formula that implements a particular set of the parameter of CNN with back-propagation (Maninis et al. 2016); (Wu et al. 2016).

Digital fundus image is the latest method for diagnosing glaucoma. DFIs are a noninvasive manner that is used for mega-scale screening. DFIs not involving the introduction of an instrument into the body (noninvasive) makes the identification of disease pattern complex and hidden. Because all decisions are taken only on behalf of DFIs this study improve by Deep learning architecture which creates the combination of various direct and in-direct transformations. Further improved by ROI (Region of interest) is a recommended deep convolutional neural network in a pre-processing level reduction or reduces the shiny border which includes getting the core of the trimming finished and the trim space. mean value of round picture pixel is deducted from per pixel to eliminate the impact of color change for images in this system will suffer from much overfitting that is removed. Data development consists of making image translations and flat reflection. This rule also identifies the glaucoma of low-quality images (Lu et al. 2019).

7 Conclusion

Artificial neural network renewing the design of deep learning has developed the correctness of various design verification task, so as a group of gadgets, pictures, and several other items in digital images in retinal fundus base image encouraging results should be performed in image-based Treatment. Machine learning and artificial intelligence are easy to implement on hardware devices that also give accurate predictions on a testing dataset. This compresses the hardware of the device. In the future researchers focus on digital images processing retinal fundus image as 3-D developed Algorithm.

In the literature, many of the researcher's trail had been done that worked on developing many layer structure identification of severe disease with help of image photo detection radio genomic approach are very effective in lung cancer detection with help of textual feature extraction and classification (Shallu et al. 2019).

Eventually, researcher' views has described in review focusing on important methods and orientation to research questions for a scientific researcher in the field of eye retina fundus images Besides, the purpose of evaluation metrics has improved with computer-aided diagnosis (CAD) systems.

Deep neural network improved with an increment of size to add several unit in each layer. Generally increases or decreases the accuracy. Combining specialties for the success of highly simple prototype. Neural networks and fuzzy logics advance technics that can be used in non-blind watermark methods this is used for watermark message in normal image (Kumar et al. 2013).

A genuine innovation in medical image. We have to implement the law into clinical tradition Donors or experts: My views are based on 35 research papers are many imaging technique have developed to improve achieve target of accurate diagnosis without any risk or at lesser possible cost.

References

Balasubramanian, K., Ananthamoorthy, N.P.: Robust retinal blood vessel segmentation using convolutional neural network and support vector machine. J. Ambient. Intell. Humaniz. Comput. **12**(3), 3559–3569 (2019). https://doi.org/10.1007/s12652-019-01559-w

Al-Bander, B., et al.: Dense fully convolutional segmentation of the optic disc and cup in colour fundus for glaucoma diagnosis. Adv. Med. Image Seg. **10**, 87 (2018). https://doi.org/10.3390/sym10040087

Besenczi, R., Tóth, J., Hajdu, A.: A review on automatic analysis techniques for color fundus photographs. Comput. Struct. Biotechnol. J. **14**, 371–384 (2016). https://doi.org/10.1016/j.csbj.2016.10.001

Budai, A., Bock, R., Maier, A.: High-Resolution Fundus (HRF) Image Database (2013). https://www5.cs.fau.de/research/data/fundus-images/

Federation, I.D.: Grading model on referrals to ophthalmology services (2015). Group.Bmj.Com. https://doi.org/10.1136

van Ginneken, B.: DRIVE dataset (2012)

Carneiro, G., et al. (eds.): LABELS/DLMIA -2016. LNCS, vol. 10008. Springer, Cham (2016). https://doi.org/10.1007/978-3-319-46976-8

Jonas, J.B., Aung, T., Bourne, R.R., Bron, A.M., Ritch, R., Panda-Jonas, S.: Glaucoma. Lancet **390**(10108), 2183–2193 (2017). https://doi.org/10.1016/S0140-6736(17)31469-1

Kumar, A., Luhach, A.K., Pal, D.: Robust Digital Image Watermarking Technique using Image Normalization and Discrete Cosine Transformation. Int. J. Comput. App. **65**(18), 5–13 (2013)

Kumar, A., Mukherjee, S., Luhach, A.K.: Deep Learning With Perspective Modeling for early detection of malignancy in mammograms. J. Disc. Math. Sci. Cryptogr. **22**, 627–643 (2019). https://doi.org/10.1080/0920529.2019.1642624

Lu, Y., Sun, J., Ma, S.: Moving objectdetection based on deep convolutional neural network. Xitong Fangzhen Xuebao J. Syst. Simul. **31**(11), 2275–2280 (2019). https://doi.org/10.16182/j.issn1004731x.joss.19-FZ0368

Fraz, M.M., et al.: CHASE_DB1. IEEE Trans. Biomed. Eng. (2012). https://doi.org/10.1109/TBME.2012.2205687

Maninis, K.-K., Pont-Tuset, J., Arbeláez, P., Van Gool, L.: Deep Retinal Image Understanding. In: Ourselin, S., Joskowicz, L., Sabuncu, M.R., Unal, G., Wells, W. (eds.) MICCAI 2016. LNCS, vol. 9901, pp. 140–148. Springer, Cham (2016). https://doi.org/10.1007/978-3-319-46723-8_17

Mateen, M., Wen, J., Hassan, M., Nasrullah, N., Sun, S., Hayat, S.: Automatic detection of diabetic retinopathy: a review on datasets, methods and evaluation metrics. IEEE Access **8**, 48784–48811 (2020). https://doi.org/10.1109/ACCESS.2020.2980055

Michael Goldbaum, M.: STARE DATASET (1996). https://cecas.clemson.edu/~ahoover/stare/

Na'am, J., Harlan, J., Putra, I., Hardianto, R., Pratiwi, M.: An automatic ROI of the fundus photography. Int. J. Elect. Comput. Eng. **8**(6), 4545–4553 (2018). https://doi.org/10.11591/ijece.v8i6.pp4545-4553

Nickla, D.L., Wallman, J.: The multifunctional choroid. Prog. Retin. Eye Res. **29**(2), 144–168 (2010). https://doi.org/10.1016/j.preteyeres.2009.12.002

Panwar, N., et al.: Fundus photography in the 21st century -a review of recent technological advances and their implications for worldwide healthcare. Telemed. E-Health **22**(3), 198–208 (2016). https://doi.org/10.1089/tmj.2015.0068

Muchinsky, P.M.: Conference program. Psychol. Appl. Introduct. Industr. Organ. Psychol. Tenth Edn. Paul **53**(9), 1689–1699 (2012). https://doi.org/10.1017/CBO9781107415324.004

Philip, S., Cowie, L.M., Olson, J.A.: The impact of the Health Technology Board for Scotland's grading model on referrals to ophthalmology services. Br. J. Ophthalmol. **89**(7), 891–896 (2005). https://doi.org/10.1136/bjo.2004.051334

Picano, E.: Sustainability of medical imaging. BMJ **328**(7439), 578–580 (2004). https://doi.org/10.1136/bmj.328.7439.578

Roychowdhury, S., Koozekanani, D.D., Parhi, K.K.: Iterative vessel segmentation of fundus images. IEEE Trans. Biomed. Eng. **62**(7), 1738–1749 (2015). https://doi.org/10.1109/TBME.2015.2403295

Shallu, N.P., Kumar, S., Luhach, A.K.: Detection and analysis of lung cancer using radiomic approach. In: Luhach, A.K., Hawari, K.B.G., Mihai, I.C., Hsiung, P.A., Mishra, R.B. (eds) Smart Computational Strategies: Theoretical and Practical Aspects, pp.13–24. Springer, Singapore (2019). https://doi.org/10.1007/978-981-13-6295-8_2

Singh, C., Luhach, A., Kumar, A.: Improving focused crawling with genetic algorithms. Int. J. Comput. Appl. **66**(4), 40–43 (2013)

Sivaswamy, J.: DRISHTI-GS1 (2011). https://cvit.iiit.ac.in/projects/mip/drishti-gs/mip-dataset2/Home.php

Smith, P., Reid, D.B., Environment, C., Palo, L., Alto, P., Smith, P.L.: A tlreshold selection method from gray-level histograms. IEEE Trans. Syst. Man Cybern. **9**(1), 62–66 (1979)

Soares, J.V.B., Leandro, J.J.G., Cesar, R.M., Jelinek, H.F., Cree, M.J.: Retinal vessel segmentation using the 2-D Gabor wavelet and supervised classification. IEEE Trans. Med. Imaging **25**(9), 1214–1222 (2006). https://doi.org/10.1109/TMI.2006.879967

Sutanty, E., Rahayu, D.A., Rodiah, Susetianingtias, D.T., Madenda, S.: Retinal blood vessel segmentation and bifurcation detection using combined filters. In: Proceeding - 2017 3rd International Conference on Science in Information Technology: Theory and Application of IT for Education, Industry and Society in Big Data Era, ICSITech 2017, 2018-January, pp. 563–567 (2017). https://doi.org/10.1109/ICSITech.2017.8257176

Ullaha, H., et al.: Optic disc segmentation and classification in color fundus images: a resource-aware healthcare service in smart cities. J. Ambient. Intell. Humaniz. Comput. 1–13 (2018). https://doi.org/10.1007/s12652-018-0988-8

Van Grinsven, M.J.J.P., Van Ginneken, B., Hoyng, C.B., Theelen, T., Sánchez, C.I.: Fast convolutional neural network training using selective data sampling: application to hemorrhage detection in color fundus images. IEEE Trans. Med. Imaging 35(5), 1273–1284 (2016). https://doi.org/10.1109/TMI.2016.2526689

Vijikala, V., Dhas, D.A.S.: Identification of most preferential denoising method for mammogram images, pp. 173–179 (2016). https://doi.org/10.1109/icedss.2016.7587786

Wang, S., Yin, Y., Cao, G., Wei, B., Zheng, Y., Yang, G.: Hierarchical retinal blood vessel segmentation based on feature and ensemble learning. Neurocomputing 149(PB), 708–717 (2015). https://doi.org/10.1016/j.neucom.2014.07.059

Wong, D.W.K., et al.: Level-set based automatic cup-to-disc ratio determination using retinal fundus images in argali. In: Proceedings of the 30th Annual International Conference of the IEEE Engineering in Medicine and Biology Society, EMBS 2008 - 'Personalized Healthcare through Technology, vol. 2, pp. 2266–2269 (2008). https://doi.org/10.1109/iembs.2008.4649648

Wu, A., Xu, Z., Gao, M., Buty, M., Mollura, D.J.: Deep vessel tracking: a generalized probabilistic approach via deep learning. In: Proceedings - International Symposium on Biomedical Imaging, 2016-June(April), pp. 1363–1367 (2016). https://doi.org/10.1109/ISBI.2016.7493520

Xu, X., et al.: Smartphone-based accurate analysis of retinal vasculature towards point-of-care diagnostics. Sci. Rep. 6(April), 1–9 (2016). https://doi.org/10.1038/srep34603

Zhao, J., et al.: Automatic retinal vessel segmentation using multi-scale super pixel chain tracking. Digital Signal Process. Rev. J. 81, 26–42 (2018). https://doi.org/10.1016/j.dsp.2018.06.006

Zilly, J., Buhmann, J.M., Mahapatra, D.: Glaucoma detection using entropy sampling and ensemble learning for automatic optic cup and disc segmentation. Comput. Med. Imaging Graph. 55, 28–41 (2017). https://doi.org/10.1016/j.compmedimag.2016.07.012

Fuzzy Controller for Indoor Air Quality Control: A Sport Complex Case Study

Bakhytzhan Omarov[1]([✉]), Aigerim Altayeva[2], Akhan Demeuov[3], Adilbay Tastanov[1], Zhakipbek Kassymbekov[4], and Arman Koishybayev[4]

[1] International University of Tourism and Hospitality, Turkistan, Kazakhstan
[2] International Information Technology University, Almaty, Kazakhstan
[3] Auezov South Kazakhstan University, Shymkent, Kazakhstan
[4] Khoja Akhmet Yassawi International Kazakh-Turkish University, Turkistan, Kazakhstan

Abstract. Currently used automatic control systems for electric drives of ventilation systems do not fully meet the requirements for the quality of performance of heat engineering production processes. It is necessary to develop new management systems through the use of intelligent technologies. The mathematical description of the control object is obtained by the methods of the classical theory of automatic control. Optimization of control loops is performed using fuzzy algorithm synthesis methods. A model of a ventilation system using a fuzzy controller is considered. Methods for developing intelligent control systems for electric drives of ventilation and air conditioning systems are proposed. It is established that the developed intelligent methods of control of electric drives of ventilation systems can be used under strict requirements to the microclimate in the room to ensure comfortable conditions. The developed fuzzy model was applied in a university sport complex, and the results showed the effectiveness of the proposed model when comparing traditional systems.

Keywords: Fuzzy controller · Air quality · Indoor air · Building · Sport complex

1 Introduction

At the present stage of development of the classical theory of automatic control, there is a pronounced tendency to increase the complexity of mathematical and formal models of real control systems and processes [1–3]. This is due to the desire to improve their adequacy and take into account an increasing number of different factors that affect the operation of the system [4, 5].

As a rule, ventilation systems operate in modes characterized by non-stationary parameters of the object of regulation [6], so the quality of these systems depends not only on the correct choice of the fan and coordination of its aerodynamic characteristics and the ventilation network of the mine, but also on the method and efficiency of regulating its operation modes [7].

It is possible to ensure high quality of heat engineering processes by applying intelligent control technologies that allow achieving high control parameters with significant

© Springer Nature Singapore Pte Ltd. 2021
A. K. Luhach et al. (Eds.): ICAICR 2020, CCIS 1393, pp. 53–61, 2021.
https://doi.org/10.1007/978-981-16-3660-8_5

non-linearity of the object and the presence of many disturbing factors [8]. Let us consider the implementation of an intelligent control system that ensures the maintenance of a comfortable indoor air temperature and the necessary level of air exchange.

In such cases, it is most appropriate to use such methods that are specifically focused on building models that take into account the incompleteness and inaccuracy of the source data [9–12]. It is in these situations that fuzzy modeling technology is most constructive.

As an example of a fuzzy inference system in control problems, the model of fuzzy control of air conditioning in a building is considered. Adjusting the speed of rotation of the supply and exhaust fans allows you to change the intensity of air exchange and, consequently, the concentration of harmful impurities in the air environment of the room.

2 Background

A distributed system of different sensors has been installed to analyze the chemical composition of indoor air [13]. The measured values are concentrations of carbon dioxide (CO_2), carbon monoxide (CO), humidity (H_2O) and other harmful impurities (OD) [14–17]. The number of fans may vary and depends on the functional purpose and size of the room. Thus, in potato storage facilities, one or several fans can be used [18]. In this case, building a control system based on a PID controller is very difficult, since the object has a nonlinear mathematical description, and you also need to process several input signals at once [19]. The best way to represent the behavior of various gases and impurities in the air is to use a linguistic description [17]. This can be done by using fuzzy modeling of the corresponding process.

3 Model

The building has a household air conditioner that cools or heats the air in the building. The most comfortable conditions in the building are created at a certain stable air temperature. Since the ambient temperature outside the building changes during the day and largely depends on external weather conditions, all this destabilizes the air temperature in the building and leads to the need for manual adjustment of the operating mode of the household air conditioner. The task is to make the air conditioner adjustment automatic, ensuring a constant temperature of the air in the building. The model of fuzzy control of air conditioning in a building is shown in Fig. 1. The Mamdani algorithm is used as a fuzzy inference algorithm [20].

The practice of using household air conditioners shows that the process of cooling or heating the air in a building has some inertia. Namely, after switching on the "cold" mode, cold air is pumped, and therefore the air temperature in the room gradually drops [25]. However, when this mode is disabled, the temperature continues to drop for a short but finite period of time. A similar pattern is observed when switching on and off the "heat" mode [26]. Suppose that in the considered model the inclusion of a mode "cold" is done by turning the slider to the left, the inclusion of "heat" by turning the knob toward the right relative to a point in which the air conditioner is off.

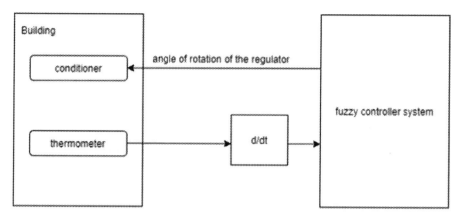

Fig. 1. A model of fuzzy control of indoor air conditioning

The output parameter is considered not only the indoor air temperature, but also the rate of its change [27, 28]. With this in mind, heuristic rules are drawn up, which are applied in the case of manual control of the air temperature in a room with air conditioning:

– if the air temperature in the room is very warm and the rate of temperature change is positive, then turn on the "cold" mode by turning the air conditioner controller at a very large angle to the left;
– if the air temperature in the room is very warm and the rate of temperature change is negative, then turn on the "cold" mode by turning the air conditioner controller at a small angle to the left;
– if the air temperature in the room is warm and the rate of temperature change is positive, then turn on the "cold" mode by turning the air conditioner controller at a large angle to the left;
– if the room temperature is warm and the rate of temperature change is negative, turn off the air conditioner;
– if the room temperature is very cold and the rate of temperature change is negative, then turn on the "heat" mode by turning the air conditioner controller at a very large angle to the right;
– if the air temperature in the room is very cold and the rate of temperature change is positive, then turn on the "heat" mode by turning the air conditioner controller at a small angle to the right;
– if the room temperature is cold and the rate of temperature change is negative, turn on the "heat" mode by turning the air conditioner controller at a large angle to the right;
– if the room temperature is cold and the rate of temperature change is positive, turn off the air conditioner;
– if the air temperature in the room is very warm, and the rate of temperature change is zero, then turn on the "cold" mode by turning the air conditioner controller at a large angle to the left;

- if the room temperature is warm and the rate of temperature change is zero, then turn on the "cold" mode by turning the air conditioner controller at a small angle to the left;
- if the room temperature is very cold and the rate of temperature change is zero, then turn on the "heat" mode by turning the air conditioner controller at a large angle to the right;
- if the room temperature is cold and the rate of temperature change is zero, turn on the "heat" mode by turning the air conditioner controller at a small angle to the right;
- if the air temperature in the room is within the normal range, and the rate of temperature change is positive, then turn on the "cold" mode by turning the air conditioner controller at a small angle to the left;
- if the air temperature in the room is within the normal range, and the rate of temperature change is negative, then turn on the "heat" mode by turning the air conditioner controller at a small angle to the right;
- if the room temperature is within the normal range and the rate of temperature change is zero, the air conditioner should be turned off.

This information is used in the construction of the fuzzy inference system rule base, which allows implementing the considered fuzzy control model.

4 Fuzzy Controller

In the course of the study, a number of ways of using fuzzy control to control certain parameters in various technological modes were analyzed [6, 22–24]. Fuzzy controllers based on rule bases. On the basis of "rule bases", we can simplify programming of technological processes, in our case, indoor microclimate control.

The experience of using household air conditioners shows that the process of cooling or heating the air in the room has some inertia. Namely, after switching on the "cold" mode, cold air is pumped, and therefore the air temperature in the room gradually drops. However, when this mode is disabled, the temperature continues to drop for a short but finite period of time. A similar pattern is observed when switching on and off the "heat" mode. Suppose that in the considered model the inclusion of a mode "cold" is done by turning the slider to the left, the inclusion of "heat" by turning the knob toward the right relative to a point in which the air conditioner is off.

To take into account this feature of the air conditioner control process and eliminate the additional costs associated with frequent switching on and off of these modes, it is necessary to consider as an output parameter not only the temperature of the air in the room, but also the speed of its change. In this case, empirical knowledge about the problem area under consideration can be presented in the form of heuristic rules that are applied in the case of manual control of the air temperature in an air-conditioned room. Based on a number of heuristic rules, we will build a rule base for the fuzzy inference system, which allows us to implement this model of fuzzy regulation [25].

5 Results

To conduct the experiments, we used a sport hall of our university when students were played different games. Figure 2 shows the plan of the sport facility that experiments have conducted.

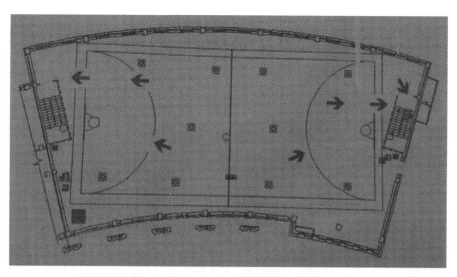

Fig. 2. Indoor CO_2 concentration level monitored in January

Fig. 3. Indoor CO_2 concentration level monitored in January

Figure 3 illustrates the sport facility and the experiment process. During the experiment, we measured the level of air quality and how our fuzzy model copes with this task. In addition, we asked from students, how they feels about air quality in the facility.

Figure 4 illustrates CO_2 level changes during one working day in January 2020. It can be see that, when the working day started, the CO_2 concentration level was low, and around 9.00 it increased sharply because of employers coming to work, and then, due to the controller's work, it fell to less than 1000 ppm. After the lunchtime, CO_2 concentrations increased immediately, followed by a comparatively steady state level. After the working day, the CO_2 concentration level decreased.

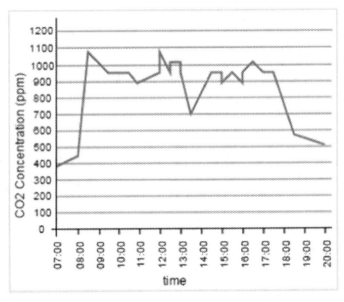

Fig. 4. Indoor CO_2 concentration level monitored in January

Figure 5 shows the average monthly value of internal CO_2 during the experiment, from December 2019 to May 2020. The average monthly level of CO_2 in the room during working hours from 9:00 to 18:00, and they vary between 875–944 ppm. In normal conditions, the average monthly CO_2 level in the room is between 939–994 ppm. Therefore, the CO_2 concentration in the room is maintained at an acceptable level, and a small, steady error means that during the working day, when the controller is operating, there is no excessive ventilation.

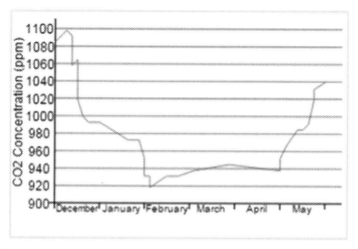

Fig. 5. The average monthly level of CO_2 taken during the scheduled occupied period.

6 Conclusion

The proposed method of fuzzy control for regulating the operating modes of heating, ventilation and air conditioning systems in a building has the following advantages:

1. Easy data entry into the control system.
2. Classic PI and PID controllers are able to eliminate established errors, but require configuration for each type of device, and reconfiguration if the choice of equipment changes. A comparative analysis of the results revealed certain advantages of using fuzzy control in a sports complex designed to maintain a given air quality.
3. Automatic air quality control systems based on fuzzy logic are able to work effectively at any volume of premises, which is an important technical feature of this development. In our case, the fuzzy controller was applied to the sport hall and shown good results and efficiency compared to the conventional system.
4. The use of fuzzy control is more justified in complex control system.

References

1. Földváry, V., Bukovianska, H.P., Petráš, D.: Analysis of energy performance and indoor climate conditions of the slovak housing stock before and after its renovation. Energy Procedia **78**, 2184–2189 (2015). https://doi.org/10.1016/j.egypro.2015.11.314
2. Omarov, B., Altayeva, A.: Design of a multiagent-based smart microgrid system for building energy and comfort management. Turk. J. Electr. Eng. Comput. Sci. **26**(5), 2714–2725 (2018)
3. Omarov, B., et al.: Agent based modelling of smart grids in smart cities. In: Chugunov, A., Misnikov, Y., Roshchin, E., Trutnev, D. (eds.) Electronic Governance and Open Society: Challenges in Eurasia: 5th International Conference, EGOSE 2018, St. Petersburg, Russia, November 14-16, 2018, Revised Selected Papers, pp. 3–13. Springer International Publishing, Cham (2019). https://doi.org/10.1007/978-3-030-13283-5_1

4. Yu, T., Lin, C.: An intelligent wireless sensing and control system to improve indoor air quality: monitoring, prediction, and preaction. Int. J. Distrib. Sensor Netw. 2015(8), 1–9 (2015).https://doi.org/10.1155/2015/140978

5. Abraham, S., Li, X.: A cost-effective wireless sensor network system for IAQ monitoring applications. Procedia Comput. Sci. **34**, 165–171 (2014)

6. Altayeva, A., Omarov, B., Im Cho, Y.: Towards smart city platform intelligence: PI decoupling math model for temperature and humidity control. In 2018 IEEE International Conference on Big Data and Smart Computing (BigComp), pp. 693–696. IEEE, January 2018

7. Taleghani, M., Tenpierik, M., Kurvers, S.: A review into thermal comfort in buildings. Renew. Sustain. Energy Rev. **26**, 201–215 (2013)

8. Minnesota Department of Health: Carbon Dioxide (CO_2) (2014). http://www.health.state.mn.us/divs/eh/indoorair/co2/index.html

9. Altayeva, A., Omarov, B., Im Cho, Y.: Multi-objective optimization for smart building energy and comfort management as a case study of smart city platform. In: 2017 IEEE 19th International Conference on High Performance Computing and Communications, IEEE 15th International Conference on Smart City, IEEE 3rd International Conference on Data Science and Systems (HPCC/SmartCity/DSS), pp. 627–628. IEEE, December 2017

10. Song, Y., Wu, S., Yan, Y.: Development of self-tuning intelligent PID controller based on 115 for indoor air quality control. Int. J. Emer. Technol. Adv. Eng. **3**(11), 283–290 (2013)

11. Seppänen, O.A., Fisk, W.J., Mendell, M.J.: Association of ventilation rates and CO2 concentrations with health and other responses in commercial and institutional buildings. Indoor Air **9**, 226–252 (1999)

12. Apte, M.G., Fisk, W.J., Daisey, J.M.: Associations between indoor CO2 concentrations and sick building syndrome symptoms in US office buildings: an analysis of the 1994-1996" (LBNL 44385). Indoor Air **10**(4), 246–257 (2000). https://doi.org/10.1034/j.1600-0668.2000.010004246.x

13. Brennan, T., Clarkin, M., Turner, W., Fisher, G., Thompson, R.: School buildings with air exchange rates that do not meet minimum professional guidelines or codes and implications for radon control. In: Proceedings of ASHRAE IAQ 1991 Healthy Buildings, Atlanta, GA, ASHRAE, pp. 228–229 (1991)

14. Weschler, C.: Changes in indoor pollutants since the 1950s. Atmosp. Environ. **43**(1), 153–169 (2009). https://doi.org/10.1016/j.atmosenv.2008.09.044

15. Levy, R.J.: Carbon monoxide pollution and neurodevelopment: a public health concern. Neurotoxicol. Teratol. **49**, 31–40 (2015)

16. Omarov, B.: Exploring uncertainty of delays of the cloud-based web services. In: 2017 17th International Conference on Control, Automation and Systems (ICCAS), pp. 336–340. IEEE, October 2017

17. Omarov, B., et al.: Ensuring comfort microclimate for sportsmen in sport halls: comfort temperature case study. In: Hernes, M., Wojtkiewicz, K., Szczerbicki, E. (eds.) Advances in Computational Collective Intelligence: 12th International Conference, ICCCI 2020, Da Nang, Vietnam, November 30 – December 3, 2020, Proceedings, pp. 626–637. Springer International Publishing, Cham (2020). https://doi.org/10.1007/978-3-030-63119-2_51

18. Omarov, B., et al.: Indoor microclimate comfort level control in residential buildings. Far East J. Electron. Commun. **17**(6), 1345–1352 (2017)

19. Omarov, B., et al.: Fuzzy-PID based self-adjusted indoor temperature control for ensuring thermal comfort in sport complexes. J. Theor. Appl. Inf. Technol **98**(11), 1–12 (2020)

20. Pradityo, F., Surantha, N.: Indoor air quality monitoring and controlling system based on IoT and fuzzy logic. In: 2019 7th International Conference on Information and Communication Technology (ICoICT), pp. 1–6. IEEE, July 2019

21. Yan, H., Xia, Y., Xu, X., Deng, S.: Inherent operational characteristics aided fuzzy logic controller for a variable speed direct expansion air conditioning system for simultaneous indoor air temperature and humidity control. Energy Build. **158**, 558–568 (2018)
22. Setayesh, H., Moradi, H., Alasty, A.: Nonlinear robust control of air handling units to improve the indoor air quality & CO_2 concentration: a comparison between H∞ & decoupled sliding mode controls. Appl. Thermal Eng. **160**, 113958 (2019)
23. Sarkheil, H., Rahbari, S.: Development of case historical logical air quality indices via fuzzy mathematics (Mamdani and Takagi-Sugeno systems), a case study for Shahre Rey Town. Environ. Earth Sci. **75**(19), 1319 (2016)
24. Giosuè, C., Pierpaoli, M., Mobili, A., Ruello, M.L., Tittarelli, F.: Influence of binders and lightweight aggregates on the properties of cementitious mortars: from traditional requirements to indoor air quality improvement. Materials **10**(8), 978 (2017)
25. Alhasa, K.M., et al.: Calibration model of a low-cost air quality sensor using an adaptive neuro-fuzzy inference system. Sensors **18**(12), 4380 (2018)
26. Faouzi, D., Benmoussa, N., Bibi-Triki, N., Abene, A.: Modeling and simulation of heating cooling and ventilation systems to optimize the microclimate management of the greenhouse by fuzzy logic controller. SDRP J. Comput. Sci. **1**, 1–12 (2017)
27. Jiménez-Bravo, D.M., Lozano Murciego, Á.H., De la Iglesia, D., De Paz, J.F., Villarrubia González, G.: Central Heating Cost Optimization for Smart-Homes with Fuzzy Logic and a Multi-Agent Architecture. Applied Sciences **10**(12), 4057 (2020). https://doi.org/10.3390/app10124057
28. Mohd, T.A.T., Hassan, M.K., Aris, I., Azura, C.S., Ibrahim, B.S.K.K.: Application of fuzzy logic in multi-mode driving for a battery electric vehicle energy management. Int. J. Adv. Sci. Eng. Inf. Technol. **7**(1), 284–290 (2017)

Cancer Prediction Using Novel Ranking Algorithms and Machine Learning

A. Lakshmanarao[1(✉)], A. Srisaila[2], and T. Srinivasa Ravi Kiran[3]

[1] Department of IT, Aditya Engineering College, Surampalem, A.P, India
[2] Department of Information Technology, V.R Siddhartha Engineering College,
Vijayawada, Andhra Pradesh, India
[3] Department of Computer Science, P.B.Siddhartha College of Arts and Science,
Vijayawada, Andhra Pradesh, India

Abstract. Cancer is the second leading cause of death globally. Especially, breast cancer is the most problematic cancer with more death rates. In this paper, we proposed a novel fusion classifier model based on a combination of various machine learning algorithms to improve accuracy. First, the base level models are trained and then we applied a ranking based algorithms for predicting final accuracy. The proposed model is tested on two different cancer datasets from UCI, Kaggle repository. The experimental results on two different datasets shown the effectiveness of the proposed framework. We used Python for implementing all our experiments.

Keywords: Cancer · Ranking based algorithms · Machine learning

1 Introduction

Cancer disease is the second leading reason for death rates globally. The total number of deaths in 2018 are estimated as 9.6 million. In global health environment, one of the six deaths happening duo to cancer only [1]. In very low, middle income countries,70% of deaths occurring due to cancer. 10% of the women are affected by breast cancer. 25% of the women are affected by all types of cancer disease [2]. Late-stage presentation and inaccessible diagnosis and treatment are common. WHO, through its malignant growth research organization, International Agency for Research on Cancer (IARC), keeps up an arrangement of disease-causing specialists. Over the previous decades, a nonstop advancement identified with disease research has been performed. Researchers applied various techniques, for example, screening in be-ginning period, so as to discover sorts of malignant growth previously they cause side effects. Besides, they have grown new techniques for the early expectation of malignant growth treatment result. With the approach of new advances in the field of medication, a lot of disease information have been gathered and are ac-cessible to the clinical exploration network. Be that as it may, the exact expecta-tion of a malady result is one of the most intriguing and testing errands for doc-tors. Therefore, ML techniques have become a famous device for clinical special-ists. These procedures can find and distinguish examples and connections between them, from complex datasets, while they can successfully anticipate future results of a malignancy type.

A. K. Luhach et al. (Eds.): ICAICR 2020, CCIS 1393, pp. 62–70, 2021.
https://doi.org/10.1007/978-981-16-3660-8_6

2   Literature Survey

Several researchers applied machine learning models to cancer detection. J. Sivapriya et al. [3] applied various classification algorithms for cancer classification. They applied Support Vector classifier, Logistic Regression, Naïve Bayes classification, Random Forest model and achieved best results with random forest classification. Rasool Fakoor [4] et al. applied deep learning tech-niques for cancer diagnosis and classification. Konstantina Kourou et al. [5] proposed various classifier models Bayesian classifier, Support Vector classification algorithms, Artificial Neural Networks (ANNs), Decision Tree classification (DTs) for cancer prediction and classification. Joseph A. Cruz et al. [6] compared the performance of various machine learning models that are being applied to cancer prediction and prognosis. Gigi F. Stark et al. [7] applied different machine learning techniques for predicting breast cancer risk using personal health data. They applied logistic regression, linear discriminant analysis, and neural network models. Youness Khourdifi et al. [8] applied Random Forest,Naïve Bayes, Support Vector Machines, K-Nearest Neighbors (K-NN) for Breast Cancer Predic-tion and Classification and achieved better results. Wen WU1 et al. [8] applied Support Vector Machines on cervical cancer dataset and achieved an accuracy of 93%. Priyanka K Malli et al. [9] applied various machine learning techniques for detection of cancer and achieved an accuracy of 84% with K-Nearest Neighbor algorithm. Devi R.D.H et al. [12] applied neural network model on cancer dataset and achieved an accuracy of 93%. Nanglia et al. [13] applied radiomic technique for detection and analysis of lung cancer and achieved good results. Kumar, A. et al. [14] proposed deep learning techniques for cancer detecton and achieved good results.

3   Research Methodology

First, we applied data preprocessing techniques on two different cancer da-tasets collected from UCI repository [10], Kaggle [11]. Later, we applied base clas-sifiers (single classifier) on two datasets. Later we used our proposed ranking based algorithms to decide the performance of base classifiers. Based on pro-posed ranking based algorithms, we find the best combination of final algorithms. The fusion classifiers are then applied to predict cancer. The proposed frame-work for cancer detection is depicted in Fig. 1.

3.1   Ranking Based Algorithms

We proposed three ranking based algorithms MAR (Mean Accuracy Ranking), CDR (Class Differential Ranking), PCR (Per Class Ranking). First, we applied these three ranking based algorithms on the datasets. Later we identified the best combination of algorithms for final evaluation.

3.2   MAR (Mean Accuracy Ranking)

MAR considers both True positive rate and True Negative rate. The rank was assigned by averaging the true positive rate and true negative rate. If the average is more, then the rank is good.

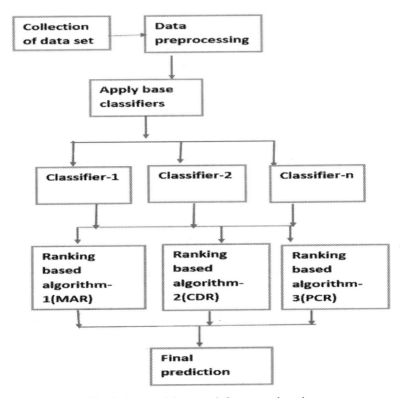

Fig. 1. Proposed framework for cancer detection

3.3 CDR (Class Differential Ranking)

In CDR, Class Differential Value (CDV) is used for assigning the ranks. With this approach, the classifier that performed good in both classes will get good rank.

CDV = (Average of TPR & TNR)/(|TPR-TNR|).

3.4 PCR (Per Class Ranking)

In PCR algorithm, more importance is given to a base classifier that performs good in both classes.

4 Experimentation and Results

4.1 Dataset

Two different cancer datasets are downloaded from Kaggle, UCI machine learning repository. Dataset-1 contains 36 features with 858 samples. Dataset2 contains 32 features with 569 samples. For each dataset, we applied three-fold cross validation technique. Table 1 shows the number of total samples, number of training samples and number of testing samples used in the experiments.

Table 1. Datasets details

	Number of training samples	Number of testing samples	Total
Dataset-1	572	286	858
Dataset-2	380	189	569

4.2 Evaluation Metrics

The following metrics are used for evaluating the model performance. Three measures namely True Positive Rate, True Negative Rate and Accuracy are used for evaluation.

True Positive Rate (TPR)
The ratio of correctly classified cancer samples to the total number of cancer samples.
TPR = True Positives/(True Positives + False Negatives).

True Negative Rate (TNR)
The ratio of correctly classified non-cancer samples to the total number of non-cancer samples.
TNR = True Negatives/(True Negatives + False Positives).

Accuracy
The ratio of total correctly classified samples (positive samples as positive and negative samples as negative) to the total number of all samples in the dataset.
Accuracy = (True Positives + True Negatives)/(True Positives + True Negatives + False Positives + False Negatives).

4.3 Applying Base Classifiers

For dataset-1 four different base classifiers are applied. Various base classifiers are tried and Logistic Regression, Adaboost, Random Forest, K-NN are the best among them.

For dataset-2, we tried with different algorithms and final best classifier algorithms are Logistic-Regression, Adaboost, Random Forest classifier, Decision Tree classifier.

For the two datasets, we find True Positive Rate(TPR), True Negative Rate(TNR). Results of the experiments are shown in Table 2.

4.4 Applying Ranking Based Algorithms

Three ranking algorithms MAR, are applied on two different datasets.

4.4.1 Applying MAR (Mean Accuracy Ranking) Algorithm

In MAR, the ranking is directly proportional to mean accuracy of True Positive Rate (TPR) and True Negative Rate (TNR). If the average is more, then higher rank is assigned. If the average is low, lower rank is assigned. Average = (TPR + TNR)/2 (Table 3).

Table 2. Base classifiers results

	Algorithm	True negative rate (%)	True positive rate (%)
Dataset-1	Logistic regression	98.1	71.4
	Adaboost	97.3	61.9
	Random forest	99.2	42.8
	Decision tree	97.7	61.9
Dataset-2	Logistic regression	93.8	95.3
	Adaboost	95.2	93
	Random Forest	96.5	97.6
	Decision Tree	91.7	93

Table 3. Results of MAR

		TNR	TPR	Average	MAR ranking
Dataset-1	Logistic regression	98.1	71.4	84.75	4
	Adaboost	97.3	61.9	79.6	2
	Random forest	99.2	42.8	71	1
	K-NN	97.7	61.9	79.8	3
Dataset-2	Logistic regression	93.8	95.3	94.5	3
	Adaboost	95.2	93	94.1	2
	Random forest	96.5	97.6	97	4
	Decision tree	91.7	93	92.3	1

4.4.2 Applying CDR (Class Differential Ranking) Algorithm

In CDR, the ranking is directly proportional to the mean accuracy of TPR and TNR and inversely proportional to the absolute difference between the TPR and TNR.

CDV (Class Differential Value) = Average accuracy/|TPR-TNR|

If CDV is more, then higher rank is assigned. If CDV is low, lower rank is assigned (Table 4).

4.4.3 Applying PCR (Per Class Ranking) Algorithm

In PCR,CDR, the ranking is directly proportional to the sum of TPR and TNR rankings.

Sum = TPR rank + TNR rank.

Table 4. Results of CDR

		TNR	TPR	Average	Difference	CDV	CDR ranking
Dataset-1	LG	98.1	71.4	84.75	26.7	3.17	4
	ADB	97.3	61.9	79.6	35.4	2.24	3
	RF	99.2	42.8	71	56.4	1.25	1
	K-NN	97.7	61.9	79.8	35.8	2.22	2
Dataset-2	LG	93.8	95.3	94.5	1.5	1.5	3
	ADB	95.2	93	94.1	2.2	2.2	4
	RF	96.5	97.6	97	1.1	1.1	1
	DT	91.7	93	92.3	1.3	1.3	2

If sum is more, then higher rank is assigned. If sum is low, lower rank is assigned (Table 5).

Table 5. Results of PCR

		TNR	TPR	TNR rank	TPR rank	Sum	PCR ranking
Dataset-1	LG	98.1	71.4	3	4	7	4
	ADB	97.3	61.9	1	2	3	1
	RF	99.2	42.8	4	1	5	3
	K-NN	97.7	61.9	2	2	4	2
Dataset-2	LG	93.8	95.3	2	3	5	3
	ADB	95.2	93	3	1	4	2
	RF	96.5	97.6	4	4	8	4
	DT	91.7	93	1	1	2	1

4.5 Final Model

The final fusion of models is decided by results of above three algorithms.The algorithms which performed good in teo of the three ranking algorithms are considered for fusion.In some cases only one classifier became final model and sometimes final model can be formed with ensemble of more than one classfier.

4.6 Comparison of Results with Previous Work

The accuracy comparison of the proposed work with previous work is depicted in Table 6. In [8], Support Vector Machine classification technique applied and achieved an accuracy

Table 6. Results of final model

		TNR	TPR	Accuracy
Dataset-1	LG	98.1	71.4	94.7
Dataset-2	LG + RF	95.8	97.6	96.2

of 93%. In [9], K-Nearest Neighbor classification technique applied and achieved an accuracy of 84%. In [12], Neural Networks technique applied and achieved an accuracy of 91%. In this paper, the authors applied novel fusion model on two different datasets and achieved an accuracy of 94.7%, 96.2% respectively (Fig. 2).

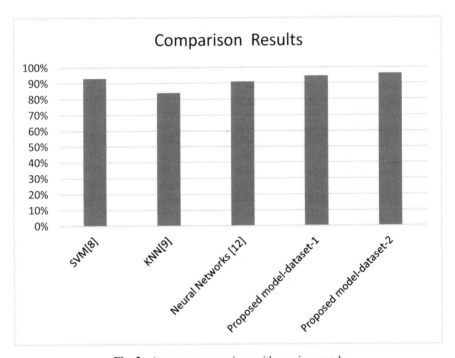

Fig. 2. Accuracy comparison with previous work

From Table 7, it was shown that the novel ranking algorithms outperforms other classifiers for two different datasets and achieved an accuracy greater than 94% in two cases.

Table 7. Accuracy comparison with previous work

Method	Accuracy
SVM [8]	93%
KNN [9]	84%
Neural networks [12]	91%
Proposed model-dataset-1	94.7%
Proposed model-dataset-2	96.2%

5 Conclusion

In this paper, the authors proposed a novel Fusion classifier model based on three different ranking algorithms MAR (Mean Accuracy Ranking), CDR (Class Differential Ranking), PCR (Per Class Ranking). First, base classifiers are applied on two different datasets (one from UCI repository, one from Kaggle) and later, three ranking algorithms are applied to find the final model. Experimental results on two datasets shown a good accuracy when compared to previous work.

References

1. Scott, C.D., Smalley, R.E.: Diagnostic ultrasound: P.M.I. Jordan and T.M. Mitchell, "Machine learning: trends, perspectives, and prospects. Science **349**(6245), 255–260 (2015)
2. Shkolnikov, V.M., Andreev, E.M., Tursun-zade, R., Leon, D.A.: Patterns in the relationship between life expectancy and gross domestic product in Russia in 2005–15: a cross-sectional analysis. Lancet Public Health **4**(4), e181–e188 (2019). https://doi.org/10.1016/S2468-2667(19)30036-2
3. Agarwal, P., Shetty, N., Jhajharia, K., Aggarwal, G., Sharma, N.V.: Machine learning for prognosis of life expectancy and diseases. Int. J. Innov. Technol. Explor. Eng. (IJITEE) **8**(10), 1–7 (2019)
4. Schultz, M.B., Kane1, A.E., Mitchell, S.J.: Age and life expectancy clocks based on machine learning analysis of mouse frailty. Nat. Commun. **11**, 1–12 (2020). https://doi.org/10.1101/2019.12.20.884452
5. Barardo, D.G., Newby, D., Thornton, D., Ghafourian, T., Magalhães, J.P., Freitas, A.A.: Machine learning for predicting lifespan-extending chemical compounds. Aging **9**(7), 1721–1737 (2017). https://doi.org/10.18632/aging.101264
6. Kang, J.J., Adibi, S.: Systematic predictive analysis of personalized life expectancy using smart devices. Technologies **6**, 74 (2018). https://doi.org/10.3390/technologies6030074
7. Leng, C.H., Chou, M.H., Lin, S.-H., Yang, Y.K., Wang, J.-D.: Estimation of life expectancy, loss-of-life expectancy, and lifetime healthcare expendi-tures for schizophrenia in Taiwan. Schizophr. Res. **171**, 97–102 (2016)
8. Wen, W., Zhou, H.: Data-driven diagnosis of cervical cancer with support vector machine-based approaches. IEEE Access **5**, 25189–25195 (2017). https://doi.org/10.1109/ACCESS.2017.2763984
9. Malli, P.K., Nandyal, S.: Machine learning technique for detection of cervical cancer using kNN and artificial neural network. Int. J. Emerg. Trends Technol. Comput. Sci. (IJETTCS). **6**(4), 1–10 (2017)

10. https://archive.ics.uci.edu/ml/datasets/Cervical+cancer+%28Risk+Factors%29
11. https://www.kaggle.com/imdevskp/cancer-classification-using-knn#Data
12. Devi, R.D.H., Devi, M.I.: Outlier detection algorithm combined with decision tree classifier for early diagnosis of breast cancer. Int. J. Adv. Eng. Tech. **7**(2), 98 (2016)
13. Nanglia, P., Kumar, S., Luhach, A.K.: Detection and analysis of lung cancer using radiomic approach. In: Luhach, A.K., Hawari, K.B.G., Mihai, I.C., Hsiung, P.A., Mishra, R.B. (eds) Smart Computational Strategies: Theoretical and Practical Aspects, pp. 13–24. Springer, Singapore (2019). doi: https://doi.org/10.1007/978-981-13-6295-8_2
14. Kumar, A., Mukherjee, S., Luhach, A.K.: Deep learning with perspective modeling for early detection of malignancy in mammograms. J. Disc. Math. Sci. Cryptogr. **22**(4), 627–643 (2019). https://doi.org/10.1080/09720529.2019.1642624

Supervised Learning Algorithm: A Survey

Kanksha[1]([✉]), Harjit Singh[1], and Vijay Laxmi[2]

[1] Lovely Professional University, Jalandhar, India
[2] Guru Kashi University, Talwandi Sabo, India

Abstract. The supervised learning algorithm is exactly what in which we've input as well as output variable which is able to be A or maybe B which uses an algorithm to find out the mapping feature from the feedback to the output. supervised algorithms like SVM, decision tree, naive Bayes distinction, etc. The primary motive of this particular paper is actually discussing the supervised learning methods that can help to the distinction of information on real-life information sets. It also details the charts of references within the last second area in which we compared which algorithm is perfect in which situation and exactly why based on particular parameters. The potential range of this paper is to survey on supervised learning algorithms and the comparison between them so that a brand new individual who's wanting to master machine learning could comprehend in layman language.

Keywords: SVM · Logistic regression · Random forest

1 Introduction

This specific paper centers around gathering the key prons of various, normally utilized, and in a few notices in AI calculations that are used for the characterization technique. Breaking down which calculation is immaculate in which state as examined in the diagram of the reference's table, one may perceive which calculation is really used when and dependent on which parameter [1]. Characterization techniques could be put on an unstructured or organized dataset. Individuals from datasets are really answered as per a mark which is really used in administered learning in which we did on name information. Right now the directed acing class mark is as of now characterized that implies we can figure esteems dependent on the datasets. A differentiation calculation is actually a methodology that will assist with finding from the guidance set and next use fresh out of the box new data in a specific way.

Additionally, this calculation assists with making sense of a no of sorts of unmistakable techniques. An extra system Binary classification in which we're assessed 2 last results that are conceivable. For example, climate forest (it is going to rain or possibly maybe not). This is really Binary classification in which data could be grouped relying upon the double methodology. Each other model is really of Email spam recognition whether a particular email is really spam or even average mail(placed in inbox). Multi-name order is actually a fresh out of the plastic new system with 2 or over feasible results. for example, Classify the scholastic abilities of understudies as brilliant or extraordinary or maybe average [1]. Inside or maybe exceptionally terrible order, an example might be mapped to significantly more in correlation with one-time label item names [1].

A. K. Luhach et al. (Eds.): ICAICR 2020, CCIS 1393, pp. 71–78, 2021.
https://doi.org/10.1007/978-981-16-3660-8_7

2 Methodologies Analysis in Supervised Learning

2.1 Logistic Regression

Logistic regression is a numerical analysis used to perform classification and to demonstrate the Connection between one dependent variable or one or even more independent, integer, period or proportion independent variables [2] (Fig. 1).

$$= \log\left(\frac{p(y=1)}{1-(p=1)}\right) = \beta_0 + \beta_1 x_{l2} + \beta_2 \cdot x_{l2} + \dots + \beta_j \cdot x_{ln}$$

Fig. 1. Logistic regression mathematically equation (12, p.2).

There can be no outlier in the data that can be measured by transforming constant predictors to uniform scores and eliminating values below-3.29 or below-3.29. No high correlations among the predictors.Mathematically equations of logistic regression are shown above.

2.2 Support Vector Classifier

It handles dataset objects, potentially logging each except 'n' variety of components mapped as n-dimensional space regions divided into groups by a distinct gap as wide as possible defined as a hyper – plane [1]. Within the same n-dimensional space, data objects are mapped to calculate the class to which they belong, based on the edge of the hyperplane they land.

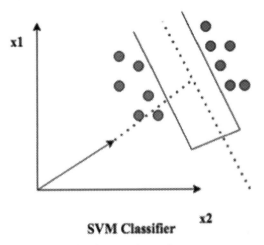

SVM Classifier

Fig. 2. SVM hyperplane.

A very good example of this particular technique as seen above on the basis of the differentiation form of color circle and the red color of circle shapes are actually classified as mentioned above in Fig. 2. The segregating line consists of all the circular objects on the right side as well as the circle items on the left side In case it is located on the proper section of the dividing boundary or the hyperplane (Fig. 3). With this in mind, the bulk of classification responsibilities are not straightforward and typically contribute to complex positions that need to be completed in order to be able to obtain an optimal distinction of the condition of those intricate approaches. SVM can conveniently be separated into two categories: Nu Svm and C Svm.

2.3 Decision Tree

This algorithm uses the prediction model to transfer from the item's assumptions (values that present in branches) to the target value projections of the item (described at leaf node). This is one of the computational mathematics techniques used for programming, data analysis and artificial intelligence.

The decision tree can be used to clearly and specifically reflect judgments and decision-making in the study of decisions. Data mining is defined in the decision tree (but the resulting classification tree can be an input for decision making).

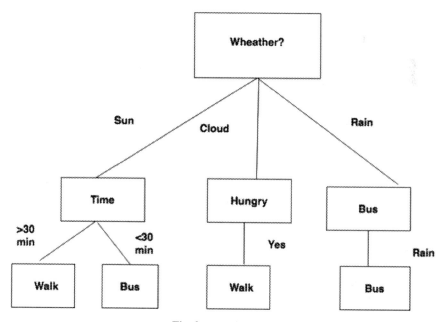

Fig. 3. Decision tree.

2.4   Random Forest Classifiers

Random forests or randomised decision-making forests are a collective testing algorithm for categorization, regression and other tasks performed by creating a mixture of state forests at the time of training and producing a type that would be class mode (classification) or average tree prediction [2].

The extension of the algorithm was developed by Leo Breiman and Adele Cutler, and their signature is "Random Forests". This extension combines the Breiman idea of "bagging" with a random set of functions, first suggested by Ho and then independently [2] (Fig. 4).

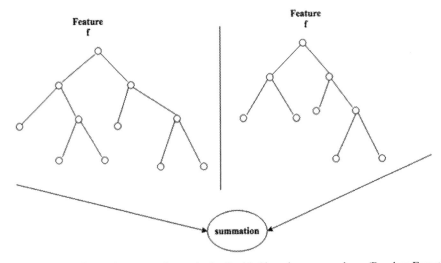

Fig. 4.   Random forest. A comparative analysis of guided learning as seen above (Random Forest).

3   Related Work

See Table 1.

4   Chart of References

Below there are comparisons of various algorithms with respect to various parameters such as learning speed,classification speed (Table 2).

Table 1. Comprehensive explanation of each papers like title, of author etc.

Citations	Year	Journal/conference	Title of the journal	Author	Technology used	Description
[1]	17 July 2019	Springer	Supervised classification algorithms in machine learning: a survey and review	Pratap Chandra Sen et al.	Describes the various techniques of active learning and their specifications	Compare various forms of classification algorithms that are very common on the basis of certain basic principles
[3]	23 Jan 2020	Computer Science	Machine learning and value generation in software development: a survey	Barakat et al.	Support Vector Machine is frequently mentioned in respect to predicting schedule as well as budget risks	Used for programming energy estimation, predicting risks and detecting and determining defects
[4]	March 2008	Journal of Artificial Intelligence Research (JAIR)	A Literature Survey on domain adaptation of statistical classifiers	Jing Jiang	There is a need for domain adaptation is common in several true classification problems	AdaBoost algorithm to address the domain adaptation problem
[5]	2020	Interactive Learning Environments	Facebook messages in predicting learning achievement within the personal learning environment	Jiun-Yu Wu et al.	Developed 3 distinction styles with instruction information of 76,936 posts	Used for text recognition
[6]	June 2015	IEEE Transactions	Object detection in optical remote sensing images Based on weakly supervised learning and High-Level feature learning	Junwei Han et al.	The innovative programme to address the subject of accurate RSI optical detections	Combination of weakly controlled learning (high-level dimension along with wsl) research

(continued)

Table 1. (*continued*)

Citations	Year	Journal/conference	Title of the journal	Author	Technology used	Description
[7]	Dec. 2014	IEEE transaction on Cybernetics	Semi supervised and Unsupervised Extreme learning machine	G.Huang et al.	The issue of object detection in optical RSIs	Semi-supervised ELM (SS ELM) as well as the unsupervised ELM (US ELM) exhibit mastering capability as well as computational effectiveness of ELMs;
[8]	June 2016	IEEE transaction on Geoscience and remote	Semantic annotation of high-resolution satellite images via weakly supervised learning	X. Yao et al.	Developed as an ultimate optimization issue, which may be fixed effectively with our recommended alternative iterative SEO programs	The vague and complicated quality of the satellite pictures, as well as the high man's labour price, induced by the processing of an immense volume of instructio
[9]	April 2013	IEEE Transactions	A survey of discretization techniques: taxonomy and empirical analysis in supervised learning,	S. García et al.	Outcomes of their performances assessed in phrases of accuracy, selection of intervals, and inconsistency	A survey of discretization strategies suggested in the literature from an empirical and theoretical perspective
[10]	17 July 2019	Springer	Supervised classification algorithms in machine learning: a survey and review	Pratap Chandra Sen et al.	Distinct schemes of supervised learning as well as the parameters of theirs which impact to attain accuracy	Compare various kinds of classification algorithms exactly popular ones on the foundation of some fundamental conceptions

Table 2. Chart of references (12, p.1).

	Decision Tree	Neural Network	Naive Bayes	K-nearest neighbour	SVM
Proposed by	Quilan	Rosenblatt	Duba and Hurt	Cover and Hart	Vapnik
Accuracy in General	Good	V.Good	Average	Good	Excellent
Speed of Learning	V.Good	Average	Excellent	Excellent	Average
Speed of Classification	Excellent	Excellent	Excellent	Average	Excellent
Tolerance to missing value	V.Good	Average	Excellent	Average	Good
Tolerance to irrelevant attribute	V. Good	Average	Good	Good	Excellent
Tolerance to redundant	Good	Good	Average	Good	V. Good
Tolerance to Highly independent attribute	Good	V.Good	Average	Average	V. Good
Dealing with Continuous/Discrete attribute	All	Not Discrete	Not Continous	All	Not Discrete
Tolerance to Noise	Good	Good	V.Good	Average	Good
Dealing with Danger of Overfitting	Good	Average	V.Good	V.Good	Good
Attempt for Incremental Learning	Good	V.Good	Excellent	Excellent	Good
Explanation Ability	Excellent	Average	Excellent	Good	Average
Support multiclassification	Excellent	Naturally Extended	Naturally Extended	Excellent	Binary Classfier

5 Conclusion and Future Scope

This article will focus on summarising the core advantages of a number of widely-reputed publications and completing comparative analysis on them to decide which algorithm is most successful based on a variety of specifics. The forthcoming range of this paper would extend datasets to all of those computer mastering algorithms that are better optimised for.

References

1. Sen, P.C., Hajra, M., Ghosh, M.: Supervised classification algorithms in machine learning: a survey and review. In: Mandal, J.K., Bhattacharya, D. (eds.) Emerging Technology in Modelling and Graphics. AISC, vol. 937, pp. 99–111. Springer, Singapore (2020). https://doi.org/10.1007/978-981-13-7403-6_11

2. Ray, S.: A Comparative Analysis and Testing of Supervised Machine Learning Algorithms. https://doi.org/10.13140/RG.2.2.16803.60967 (2018)

3. Akinsanya, B.J., et al.: Machine learning and value generation in software development: a survey. In: Kalenkova, A., Lozano, J.A., Yavorskiy, R. (eds.) TMPA 2019. CCIS, vol. 1288, pp. 44–55. Springer, Cham (2021). https://doi.org/10.1007/978-3-030-71472-7_3

4. Jiang, J.: A Literature Survey on Domain Adaptation of Statistical Classifiers (2008)

5. Jiun-Yu, W., Hsiao, Y.-C., Nian, M.-W.: Using supervised machine learning on large-scale online forums to classify course-related Facebook messages in predicting learning achievement within the personal learning environment. Interact. Learn. Environ. 28(1), 65–80 (2018). https://doi.org/10.1080/10494820.2018.1515085

6. Han, J., Zhang, D., Cheng, G., Guo, L., Ren, J.: Object detection in optical remote sensing images based on weakly supervised learning and high-level feature learning. IEEE Trans. Geosci. Remote Sens. 53(6), 3325–3337 (2015)

7. Huang, G., Song, S., Gupta, J.N.D., Wu, C.: Semi-supervised and unsupervised extreme learning machines. IEEE Trans. Cybern. 44(12), 2405–2417 (2014)

8. Yao, X., Han, J., Cheng, G., Qian, X., Guo, L.: Semantic annotation of high-resolution satellite images via weakly supervised learning. IEEE Trans. Geosci. Remote Sens. 54(6), 3660–3671 (2016)

9. García, S., Luengo, J., Sáez, J.A., López, V., Herrera, F.: A survey of discretization techniques: taxonomy and empirical analysis in supervised learning. IEEE Trans. Knowl. Data Eng. 25(4), 734–750 (2013)

10. Sen, P.C., Hajra, M., Ghosh, M.: Supervised classification algorithms in machine learning: a survey and review. In: Mandal, J.K., Bhattacharya, D. (eds.) Emerging Technology in Modelling and Graphics. AISC, vol. 937, p. 99. Springer, Singapore (2020)

11. Mane, D.T., Kulkarni, U.V.: A survey on supervised convolutional neural network and its major applications. In: Deep Learning And Neural Networks: Concepts, Methodologies, Tools, and Applications (2020)

12. Zhang, J.M., Harman, M., Ma, L., Liu, Y .: Machine learning testing: survey, landscapes and horizons. IEEE Trans. Softw. Eng.

13. Abdallah, A., Maarof, M.A., Zainal, A.: Fraud detection system: a survey. J. Netw. Comput. Appl. (2016)

14. Sharma, P., Sufi, J.: Supervised classification algorithms in machine learning: a survey and review (2016)

Searching Sub-classes Within Type Ia Supernova Using DBSCAN

Neha Malik[1(⊠)], Shashikant Gupta[2], Vivek Jaglan[3], and Meenu Vijarania[1]

[1] Amity University, Gurgaon, Haryana, India
[2] G D Goenka University, Gurgaon, Haryana, India
[3] Graphic Era Hill University, Dehradun, Uttarakhand, India

Abstract. Type Ia Supernovae (SNe Ia) represents a distinct class of stellar objects which is crucial for cosmological applications such as estimating expansion rate of the universe and measuring the matter density at large scales. Spectroscopic and photometric observations (Light Curves) are used to identify these objects. Recent studies indicate heterogeneity among SNe Ia which is a vital issue for cosmological studies. We investigate the existence of subgroups within SNe Ia class using the photometric properties such as decline rate of light curve and the position of SN in the host galaxy. For this study, a sample of 40 SNe Ia from Asiago Supernova Catalogue and Calan/Tololo survey is taken. Density Based Spatial Clustering of Applications with Noise (DBSCAN) algorithm is implemented on the data sample. Our results show the presence of sub-groups in the SNe Ia sample. Strong correlation among various parameters of SNe Ia is found in each sub-group.

Keywords: Supernova · Clustering · Silhouette score · Spatial

1 Introduction

Supernovae (SNe) explosions occur at the last stage of the stars and are among the biggest explosions known so far. All the heavy elements required for the origin of life are produced and expelled in the space during the Supernova (SN) explosion. Thus, SNe explosions play major role in origin of life in the universe. Based on the spectrum, SNe are divided into Type Ia, Ib, Ic and Type II classes. However, based on the explosion mechanism, SNe can be divided into two categories as thermonuclear and core-collapse. Type Ia Supernovae fall in the category of thermonuclear explosions and rest i.e. Type II, Type Ib and Type Ic SNe belong to the category of core-collapse explosions.

During the main sequence stage, a star burns Hydrogen into Helium via nuclear fusion. The pressure of the radiation produced in this reaction holds the star against its own gravity. The successive fusion can lead to production of heavy elements in the massive stars. However, in the low mass stars the fusion halts at early stage and the star ends up creating a White Dwarf (WD) of Carbon and Oxygen. During this stage the degeneracy pressure of the electrons holds the star against its gravity. WD often exists in a binary system and it steals matter from its companion star. This process is known as accretion. If the mass of WD reaches the Chandrasekhar limit (M_{Ch}) due to accretion of

© Springer Nature Singapore Pte Ltd. 2021
A. K. Luhach et al. (Eds.): ICAICR 2020, CCIS 1393, pp. 79–88, 2021.
https://doi.org/10.1007/978-981-16-3660-8_8

matter, the degeneracy pressure is no longer sufficient to hold the WD. Thus, collapse of WD takes place and the star now explodes completely due to thermonuclear reactions and high-speed shock waves. This explosion is termed as Type Ia Supernova. Light Curve (LC) of Supernova are used to represent the brightness of SN Ia that changes with time. Shape of Light Curve (LC) is found similar in all Type Ia Supernovae. Due to this feature of light curve, SN Ia are considered as standard candle and hence are used to measure distance to distant galaxies [4, 8].

Like Supernovae explosions, galaxies are also classified into four main types as elliptical, spiral, barred spiral, and irregular in the Universe [15]. Almost 77% of the galaxies observed so far are spiral shape galaxies (SDSS). Almost two-thirds of all spiral galaxies have a bar-shaped structure, that is why they are classified as barred spiral galaxies. Elliptical galaxies are generally made from old stars or low-mass stars.

However, recent studies have shown diversity among SNe Ia [7, 9, 10, 13, 14] and indicate the possibility of sub-classes within the SNe Ia class. This may lead to serious conflicts among cosmological studies and is a matter of concern. In this paper we have tried to investigate the possibility of sub-classes within the SNe Ia class based on location of Supernovae within their host galaxy using DBSCAN algorithm [12].

2   Data Set

A sample of 40 Supernovae is collected from various sources [1–3]. Table 1 contain 40 supernovae along with their tag in column 1. Column 2 and 3 contains information of Supernova offset from the galaxy nucleus, in the E/W and N/S direction, respectively. So offset is calculated using equation given below as:

$$offset = \sqrt{(x^2 + y^2)}. \tag{1}$$

where 'x' is supernova offset from the galaxy nucleus in the E/W direction and 'y' is supernova offset from the galaxy nucleus, in the N/S direction.

Information regarding decline rate (Δm_{15}) and b-band absolute magnitude (M_B) of the supernova parent galaxy is given in Column 4 and 5. Column 6 and 7 contains information regarding host galaxy and morphological type. Column 8 contains information about Morphology type code.

3   Methodology

Density based spatial clustering of applications with noise (DBSCAN) is one of the famous clustering algorithms [6] in the field of data science, machine learning and data mining. It is applied on data points that are generally categorised based on Euclidean distance. Other distance calculating techniques like Manhattan distance can also be used as per need. The algorithm also identifies noise as outliers during clustering. Working of DBSCAN is based on two main parameters:

Epsilon (ε): It is the minimum distance between two points. Two points are considered as neighbours if the distance between them is less or equal to ε.

Table 1. Table of 40 Supernovae

SN name	x	y	Δm_{15}	M_B	Galaxy	Morphology type	T
SN1992A	3	62	1.47	−18.81	NGC1380	S0	−1.9
SN1989B	15	50	1.34	−18.87	NGC3627	SBb	3
SN2003kf	9.2	14.3	1.01	−19.37	M-02-16-02	Sb?	3
SN1996X	52	31	1.25	−19.24	NGC5061	E0	−5
SN1999ee	13	3.5	0.94	−19.46	IC5179	Sbc	4
SN1990N	63.2	1.8	1.08	−19.23	NGC4639	SBbc	3.8
SN1994D	9	7	1.32	−19.06	NGC4526	S0	−2
SN2003du	8.8	13.5	1.06	−18.93	UGC 9391	SBdm	8
SN2001el	22	19	1.15	−18.71	NGC1448	Sc	5.9
SN1997br	20.6	51.6	1.04	−19.62	E576-G40	SBd:pec	7
SN1999cw	21.1	1.5	0.94	−19.24	M-01-02-01	SBab pec:	1.5
SN1991T	26	45	0.95	−19.62	NGC4527	SBbc	3.8
SN1998bu	4.3	55.3	1.04	−19.12	NGC3368	Sab	2
SN1983G	17	14	1.37	−18.62	NGC4753	S0	−2.2
SN2002bo	11.6	14.2	1.17	−19.42	NGC3190	Sa pec	1
SN2002er	12.3	4.7	1.33	−19.45	UGC10743	Sa?	1
SN1984A	15	30	1.21	−19.46	NGC4419	SBa	1
SN1989A	21	18	1.06	−19.21	NGC3687	SBbc	4.1
SN2002dj	8.9	2.8	1.12	−19.05	NGC5018	E3:	−5
SN1981B	41	41	1.11	−19.21	NGC4536	SBbc	4.5
SN1999by	100	91	1.87	−16.64	NGC2841	Sb	3
SN1991bg	2	57	1.93	−16.81	NGC4374	E	−4.7
SN1997cn	6.8	11.7	1.86	−16.95	NGC5490	E	−5
SN1993H	1	12.3	1.7	−18.2	E445-G66	SBab	1.9
SN1986G	120	60	1.78	−17.48	NGC5128	S0	−2.2
SN1990O	21.8	3.9	0.96	−19.4	M + 03-44-03	SBa	1
SN1990T	24.8	1.9	1.15	−19.17	PGC0063925	S0	−2
SN1991S	4.4	17.3	1.04	−19.24	UGC 5691	Sab	1.8
SN1991U	2.2	5.8	1.06	−19.49	IC4232	Sbc	3.8
SN1991ag	4.4	22.1	0.87	−19.4	IC4919	SBd	7.9
SN1992K	1.9	15.4	1.93	−17.72	E269-G57	SBab	1.9
SN1992P	4.3	9.8	0.87	−19.34	IC3690	Sbc	4

(*continued*)

Table 1. (*continued*)

SN name	x	y	Δm_{15}	M_B	Galaxy	Morphology type	T
SN1992al	19	12	1.11	−19.47	E234-G69	SBc:	5.1
SN1992bc	16	5	0.87	−19.64	E300-G09	Sc	5
SN1992bk	12	21	1.57	−19.03	E156-G08	E	-5
SN1992bl	15	22	1.51	−19.13	E291-G11	SBa	1
SN1992bo	47.3	54.7	1.69	−18.76	E352-G57	S0/a	−1.5
SN1993ah	1	8	1.3	−19.28	E471-G27	S0	−2
SN1937C	30	40	0.87	−19.56	IC4182	Sm	8.9
SN1972E	38	100	0.87	−19.69	NGC5253	Sd	8

Minimum Points (*minPoints*): It is minimum number of points each cluster must contain i.e. if we choose minpoints as 4 then each cluster will contain at least 4 data points. Epsilon value should be selected carefully, if ε value is too small then most of data points will be left to become part of any cluster and taken as outliers. If ε value is too large, then most of data points will fall in same cluster. Minimum points can be selected from the dimension of data set as *minPoints* ≥ *Dimension* + 1. This algorithm has got 3 types of data points.

Core Points: Core points are the points that have at-least *minPoints* with in its ε neighbourhood. A point that is not a core point is either a boundary point or a noise point.

Boundary Point: Boundary point neighbourhood has points less than *minPoints* but it has core points within its neighbourhood.

Outliers: Outliers are the noise points of data sets that are neither core point nor boundary points.

A point is Directly Density Reachable (DDR) to core point if that point is in neighbourhood of core point i.e. within ε radius of core point. Steps of DBSCAN algorithm are:

- Find all core points, boundary points in the data set.
- For every core point if it is not assigned to any cluster, a new cluster is created.
- Recursively find all its density connected core and boundary points and assign them to the same cluster.
- Iterate through all remaining unvisited points in the data set.
- Points that were not assigned to any cluster are marked as outliers.

DBSCAN algorithm is applied to determine clusters within dataset of 40 supernovae listed in Table 1. Euclidean distance formula has been used to calculate distance between core points and its neighbours. To determine best value of ε, a technique referred as silhouette score coefficient has been used.

3.1 Validity of DBSCAN

Silhouette Score Coefficient technique has been used to prove the validity of DBSCAN Algorithm [5]. Silhouette Score Coefficient determines, how well the data points, belongs to their respective cluster as compare to other clusters.

Silhouette coefficient is calculated for each sample and its value lies between $+1$ and -1. The best value is $+1$ and the worst value is -1. Value 0 shows overlapping clusters. The Silhouette Coefficient is calculated as:

$$S = \frac{y - x}{max(x, y)} \tag{2}$$

where 'x' is the mean intra-cluster distance and 'y' is the mean nearest-cluster distance. Silhouette coefficient values for each data-point can be obtained separately also using Silhouette samples technique.

Figure 1 shows graph between Silhouette-Score and epsilon. Graph clearly shows the value of epsilon with highest silhouette score. DBSCAN algorithm is implemented on offset and Δm_{15} using best epsilon value obtained from Silhouette Score Coefficient technique.

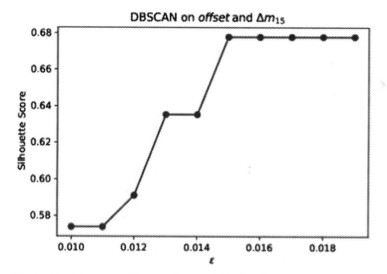

Fig. 1. Graph between Silhouette-Score and Epsilon for DBSCAN algorithm.

4 Results

DBSCAN is implemented on data sample presented in Table 1. The parameters for our analysis are the offset and Δm_{15}. The decline rate Δm_{15} has been plotted against the SNe absolute brightness in Fig. 2. It displays a strong correlation between the two as expected [4]. Contrary, Fig. 3 shows a poor correlation between M_B and offset. Table 2

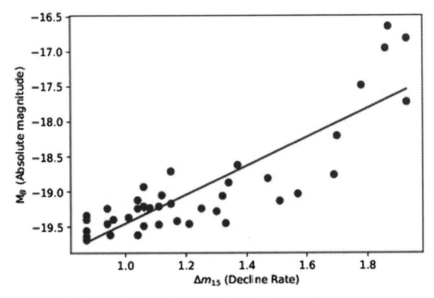

Fig. 2. Correlation graph between M_B and Δm_{15} for 40 Supernovae.

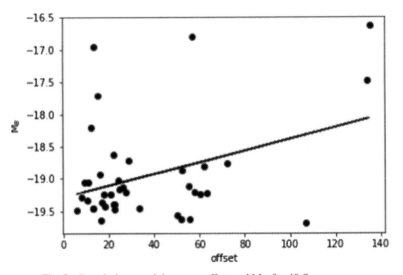

Fig. 3. Correlation graph between offset and M_B for 40 Supernovae.

contains the values of Pearson correlation coefficient among various parameters. The correlation between offset and decline rate is quite poor.

Table 3 contains results of DBSCAN algorithm when implemented on offset and Δm15. Two clusters are obtained within the data which contain 32 and 6 SNe respectively and the result is validated using silhouette score technique. Two SNe do not belong to any of these clusters and are shown as noise by DBSCAN. It is found that correlation

Table 2. Correlation among various parameters of 40 SNe

Parameter	Correlation
$\Delta m15 - MB$	0.86
Offset - MB	0.37
offset - Δm_{15}	0.28

between Δm_{15} and M_B in each cluster is as strong as it was for the full data set. However, correlation between offset and decline rate is quite strong within the clusters as compared to the overall data and same is the case with offset and absolute magnitude. The average value of each parameter is presented in Table 4. The bigger cluster (32 SNe) due to low value of M_B, contains brighter SNe on average while due to high value of M_B, the smaller cluster contains relatively dimmer SNe. Also, the average value of T corresponding to the bigger cluster is larger indicating that these SNe belong to Spiral galaxies. Figure 4 displays two clusters within dataset as explained in Table 3 and Table 4

Table 3. Correlations within clusters when DBSCAN is implemented on offset and Δm_{15}

Cluster no.	No. of data points	Δm_{15}-M_B	offset-M_B	offset-Δm_{15}
1	32	0.844	0.572	0.523
2	6	0.884	0.561	0.840

Table 4. Mean values within clusters when DBSCAN is implemented on offset and Δm_{15}.

Cluster no.	No. of data points	$\overline{M_B}$	offset	$\overline{T}$
1	32	−19.028	43.789	2.307
2	6	−18.405	12.548	−1.2

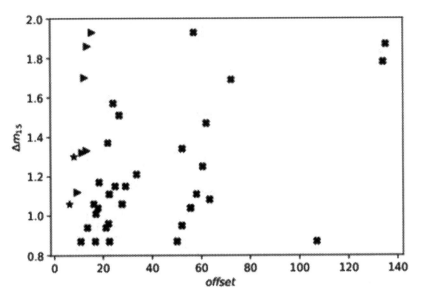

Fig. 4. Graph between offset and Δm_{15} with two clusters.

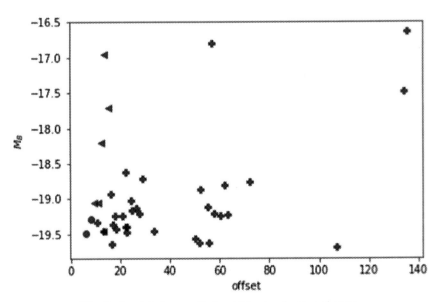

Fig. 5. Graph between offset and M_B showing two clusters.

5 Conclusions

To study the dependence of SNe Ia brightness on the location inside the host galaxy, DBSCAN algorithm is implemented on two parameters i.e. offset and Δm_{15} in the set of 40 Type Ia SNe. The analysis indicates the presence of clusters within the SNe data. Two prominent clusters can be seen clearly with good correlation within parameters. Figure 5 shows the graph between offset and M_B when DBSCAN is implemented on offset and Δm_{15} and it clearly displays that almost all the brighter SNe are found closer to the nucleus of galaxy. Table 4 further established that supernovae with higher brightness exist in early type galaxies and supernovae with low brightness are found in late type galaxies. These results can be linked to the distribution of heavy elements, in different type of the host galaxies and at different locations within the host galaxy.

6   Scope of Study

This study contributes to understand the matter and energy density of the universe. The presence of sub-groups with in SNe Ia is studied based on dependence on location within the host galaxy which is related to variation of metallicity within host galaxy. Also, all the heavy elements required for the origin of life are produced and expelled in the space during the Supernova (SN) explosion. Thus, the study can help to understand the origin of the universe along with heavy elements distribution.

With all these contributions related to matter density of the universe, the study can help to understand the nature of dark matter and dark energy that is believed to be responsible for the accelerated expansion of the universe [11].

References

1. Hamuy, M., et al.: The absolute luminosities of the calan/tololo Type Ia Supernovae. Astrophys. J. **112**(6), 2391–2396 (1996)
2. Benetti, S., et al.: The diversity of Type Ia Supernovae: evidence for systematics? Astrophys. J. **623**(2), 1011–1016 (2005)
3. Barbon, R., et al.: Asiago Supernova Catalogue. Astronomy and Astrophysics Supplement 81, no. 3/DEC, pp. 421 (1989)
4. Phillips, M.M., et al.: The absolute magnitudes of Type Ia Supernovae. Astrophys. J. **413**(2), L105–L108 (1993)
5. Peter, J.: Rousseeuw: silhouettes: a graphical aid to the interpretation and validation of cluster analysis. J. Comput. Appl. Math. **20**, 53–65 (1987)
6. Ester, M., Kriegel, H., Sander, J., Xu, X.: A density-based algorithm for discovering clusters in large spatial databases with noise. In: Proceedings of the 2nd International Conference Knowledge Discovery and Data Mining (KDD 1996), pp. 226–231. Montreal, Canada (1996)
7. Foley, R.J., et al.: Type Iax supernovae: a new class of stellar explosion. Astrophys. J. **767**(1), 1–28 (2013)
8. Perlmutter, S., et al.: Measurements of Ω and Λ from 42 high-Redshift Supernovae. Astrophys. J. **517.2**, 565 (1995)
9. Malik, N, et al.: A search of diversity in type Ia supernova using self organizing maps (SOM). In: Algorithm for Intelligent Systems, pp. 737–744. Springer, (2020)
10. Parrent, J.: A review of Type Ia Supernova spectra. Astrophys. Space Sci. **351**, 1–52 (2014)
11. Nugent, P.E., et al.: Supernova 2011fe from an exploding carbon-oxygen white dwarf star. Nature **480**, 344 (2011)
12. Malik, N., et al.: Supernova Type Ia diversity: a study using DBSCAN algorithm. Int. J. Adv. Trends Comput. Sci. Eng. **9**(3), 3398–3402 (2020)

13. Malik, N., et al.: Search for sub-classes within Type-Ia Supernovae using Hierarchical Agglomerative Clustering (HAC). Int. J. Emerg. Trends Eng. Res. **8**(9), 5248–5254 (2020)
14. Kobayashi, C., et al.: Subclasses of Type Ia Supernovae as the Origin Of [α/Fe] Ratios in Dwarf Spheroidal Galaxies. Astrophys. J. Lett. **804**(1), L24 (2015)
15. Jarrett, T.H., et al.: Near-Infrared Galaxy Morphology Atlas. Astronomical Society of the Pacific (2007)

Abnormality Detection Based on ECG Segmentation

Mayur M. Sevak[(✉)], Dhruv Patel, Parikshit Mishra, and Vatsal Shah

Birla Vishvakarma Mahavidyalaya, Anand, Gujarat, India
mayur.sevak@bvmengineering.ac.in

Abstract. In present scenario, the cause of death due to the heart related disease has been observed at a rapid growth. In order to diagnose the heart associated diseases the study of ECG is very much important. ECG stands for electrocardiogram. It is the technique that is used to measure heart rate. Basically ECG segmentation is a process of locating waves, segments and intervals and carry out comparison of this with the known patterns through its time and characteristics. So by applying segmentation technique on ECG one can predict the normality and abnormality present in the waveform of ECG. This paper deals with the design of ECG segmentation which detects the QRS complex and based on detection system computes bpm, breathing rate and statistical feature of ECG as after that based on the input BPM detail classification of normality and abnormality of ECG takes place. The purpose of the article is to provide an effective solution on the present system so that life efficiency of any patient suffering from the heart disease increases. We have utilized noisy ECG dataset of MIT-BIH for testing purpose.

Keywords: ECG · ECG segmentation · Python · Hypokalemia · Hyperkalemia · Junctional Tachycardia · Hypocalcemia · Ventricular Tachycardia · SDNN · SD1 · SD2

1 Introduction

SCA (Sudden Cardiac Attack) is the emerging disease in the twenty-first century irrespective of a person's age. Heart failure is one of the essential reasons that cause many people to lead to death. ECG is a technique used to measure the electrical activity of the human heart that offers cardiologists information about the functioning of the human heart. It is useful in determining heart rate, breathing Rate, abnormality, heart sound, proper heart functioning, blockage in the veins. The whole ECG signal is decomposed in P-wave, QRS complex and T-wave. P-wave is a positive and first wave in ECG also known as atrial complex. It is produced due to the depolarization of atrial musculature. Small negative wave is a Q wave that is followed by tall positive R wave that is further followed by a small negative s wave. The QRS complex is also called the initial ventricular complex. It is due to the depolarization of ventricular musculature. Q wave is due to the depolarization of the basal portion of the interventricular septum. R wave is due to depolarization of the apical portion of ventricular septum and muscle. S wave is due

A. K. Luhach et al. (Eds.): ICAICR 2020, CCIS 1393, pp. 89–99, 2021.
https://doi.org/10.1007/978-981-16-3660-8_9

to depolarization of the basal portion of the ventricular muscle near the atrioventricular ring. The positive T wave due to the repolarization of ventricular musculature is the final ventricular complex The wave form of ECG is shown in Fig. 1 [1].

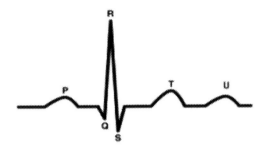

Fig. 1. ECG waves

Analysis and processing of the ECG signal help to find the length of ECG segments (PR interval, ST interval, QT interval) and BPM of the signal to detect different types of heart activity or diseases. The length and BPM of the signal are used to indicate normal and abnormal behavior. The presence of noise may cause a change in amplitude and frequency of the signal that may cause an interruption in detecting the actual abnormality and may lead to error. A Digital filter can be used for the filtering of the ECG signal. The eminent analysis technique to determine the characteristic of ECG is by doing Segmentation of this wave. The main purpose of this analysis is to locate P, Q, R, S, T indices and to find out length of ECG Segment. A short detailed analysis of ECG can be achieved by using these techniques. In the Segmentation process, the whole signal is divided into characteristics like amplitude and frequency. Since ECG is a non-stationary signal, it is essential to preprocess the ECG signal before segmentation. For segmentation of ECG various algorithms like Wavelet Transform, Pan-Tompkins algorithm, METEOR algorithm etc. are available. From the ECG segmentation, we can calculate the wave indices and length of P, Q, R, S, T waves and from that one can predict normality and abnormality in the ECG signal. The ECG segmentation is shown in the figure below (Fig. 2):

Python is a general purpose programming language that uses simple easy to use syntax. Due to this Characteristics Python is an excellent language for the beginners. The python libraries that we have utilized are Heartpy, Matplotlib and Pandas and environment that we have used is Jupyter notebook. HeartPy is a Python Heart Rate Analysis Toolkit used to handle the noisy data that are collected through the sensors. Matplotlib library describes the plotting of the mathematical operations and using the collected data for making 2D plots. Abnormality of the ECG is classify into 5 main categories they are: Hyperkalemia, Hypokalemia, Hypocalcemia, Ventricular Tachycardia and Junctional Tachycardia. Hyperkalemia is the phenomenon in the abnormality in which the body potassium level increases compare to normal. This can cause cardiac arrest and death. Other symptoms include kidney failure and rhabdomyolysis. Hypocalcemia is that state of the abnormality in which body concentration of the calcium decreases compare to normal. Calcium is an important element in the nervous system so the patient with such abnormal ECG has impaired growth. Hypokalemia is the condition in the abnormality in

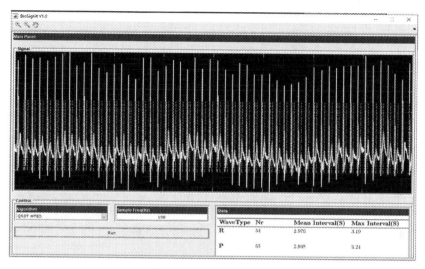

Fig. 2. ECG segmentation

which the body potassium level decreases. So as potassium decreases in the body which leads to the weakness in the muscle of the heart which leads to abnormal ECG. Ventricular Tachycardia is the abnormality condition of heart which occurs due to abnormal signal in the lower chambers of the heart. Junctional Tachycardia is the heart disorder in which the abnormality occurs in junction better the Upper and Lower chamber of the Heart. This place is known as Atrioventricular Node. Figures below indicate the different abnormality waveforms (Fig. 3).

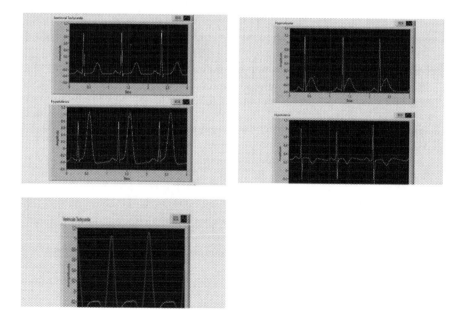

Fig. 3. Abnormal ECG

2 Literature Review

In article "Classification of Arrhythmia from ECG signal using MATLAB", the author Priyanka Mayapur et al. [2] has described the various arrhythmia associated with ECG and classify it based on length of the segments of the ECG as well as to detect the P, Q, R, S, T wave in ECG. The author has taken MIT-BIH, ECG recording then the software will remove the noise with Digital filters like IIR and FIR filters and detect the P, Q, R, S, T waves and states whether the ECG is normal or abnormal. The AHA and ESC database for analysis. The author has used inbuilt algorithms of MATLAB. In article "Abnormalities State Detection from P-Wave, QRS Complex, and T-Wave in Noisy ECG", The authors Chandra Wijaya, Andrian, Mawaddah Harahap, Christnatalis, Mardi Turnip, ArjonTurnip [4] have utilized Bitalino and connect the ECG sensor with it after ECG recording Bitalino transfers the ECG recording through the cloud to the software. If the noise is present in the ECG recording then the software will remove the noise. In the software Digital filters like FIR and Butterworth filters are used to remove the noise. After filtering segmentation is done which computes the QRS complex and R-R interval. Finally feature extraction is done which detects P, Q, R, S, T wave indices. In article "Optimizing the Detection of Characteristic Waves in ECG Based" on Processing Methods Combinations. The author KresimirFriganovic, DavorKukolja, Alan Jovic, Mario Cifrek, and Goran Krstacic [3] has described the various algorithm like Pan Tompkins, Elgendi's algorithm based on two moving average filters, Sun Yan's algorithms based on Mathematical Morphology operations, Martinez's algorithms based on Wavelet Transform, Martinez's algorithm based on Phasor Transform withmodifications on MIT-BIH arrhythmia, Q-T database and detect the P, Q, R, S, T waves and compare the computation complexity as well as accuracy. In article " Analysis of ECG Signal and Classification of Heart Abnormalities Using Artificial Neural Network". The authors TanoyDebnath and Md. Mehedi Hasan [6] describes the Preprocessing of the ECG signal and then feature extraction is done using the Pan Tompkins algorithm and Artificial Neural Network. Pan Tompkins algorithm is used for the detection of QRS complex and Artificial Neural Network used to detect P and T wave. On testing, they calculate the R-R interval and Heart rate interval of these ECG samples and they have classified... If it is abnormal they have classified it as Bradycardia, Tachycardia, and based on it they have determine the possibility of having heart attack.

3 Proposed Model

3.1 Software Requirements

- Jupyter Notebook Python 3
- Python Library:

  1. HeartPy: HeartPy is used for ECG Segmentation and Statistical Analysis of ECG
  2. Pandas: It is used to load ECG Signal.
  3. Matplotlib: For Plotting ECG Signal.

3.2 Our Methodology

Abnormality in ECG occurs due to change in the concentration of the important constituent in the body. So in order to detect abnormality we have done segmentation of the ECG and detect QRS complex using Pan-Tompkins algorithm and base on QRS detection we have calculated BPM, Breathing Rate, SDNN, SDSD, SD1, SD2. And first of all we have done the preprocessing of the ECG using band pass filter having cut-off frequencies 0.8–2.5 Hz and order of 3 and sample rate is 100. The equation of the Band pass filter is given by: After band pass filtering unwanted noise is removed and one can now apply the Pan-Tompkins algorithm.

$$H(\omega) = \frac{1}{\sqrt{1 + \epsilon^2 \left(\frac{\omega_s}{\omega_p}\right)^{2n}}} \tag{1}$$

where H (ω) = frequency response

ϵ is the all pass gain

ω_s is the stop band cut-off frequency

ω_p is the pass band cut-off frequency

Basically SDNN stands standard deviation of NN intervals (R-R intervals) is the measurement of change in heart rate per cycle measured in milliseconds calculated over a period of 24 h. The Equation of SDNN is shown below: SD1 is the standard deviation for instantaneous variation of BPM and SD2 is standard deviation for a continuous variation of BPM.

$$SDNN = \sqrt{\frac{1}{N-1} \sum_{n=2}^{N} [I(n) - I]^2} \tag{2}$$

The various types of noise that are present in ECG signal will degrade the quality of ECG data. The Pan Tompkins algorithm gives an accurate result for detection of abnormality of the ECG. These algorithm was experimented on an annotated arrhythmia. In Pan Tompkins algorithm the preprocessed ECG signal is integrated then threshold is set which is adaptive in nature then QRS complex is detected. The figure below describes the Pan-Tompkins algorithm [5] (Fig. 4).

4 Flowchart of the Proposed Model

(Figure 5)

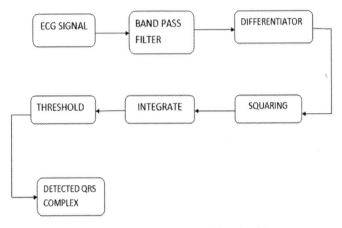

Fig. 4. Flowchart of Pan-Tompkins algorithm

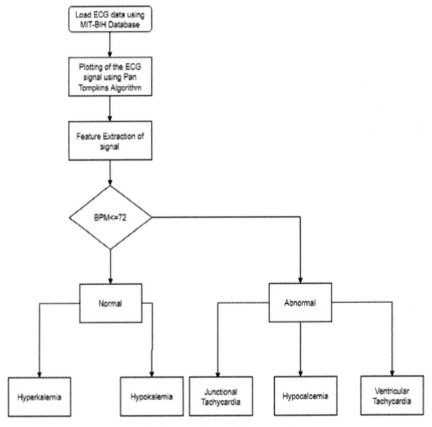

Fig. 5. Flow chart of the research

5 Experiments and Results

In order to detect abnormality of the ECG Data we have load the Noisy MIT-BIH database utilizing pandas library in python then we have plot it using Matplotlib library then we have applied band pass filtering in ECG in order to remove unwanted noise then using heartpy library we have initialized Pan-Tompkins Algorithm detected QRS complex and statistical parameters that we have listed and based on the value of BPM we detected abnormality and normality. If value of bpm is less or equal to 72 then it is normal and in normal ECG If BPM value between 50–60 then Hypokalemia or else BPM value less than 50 then Hyperkalemia. In abnormal case If value of BPM is between 100–150

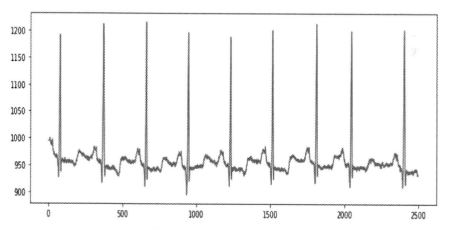

Fig. 6. Loaded ECG waveform

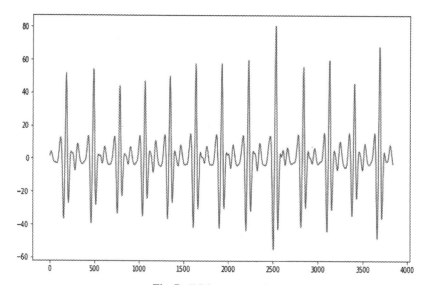

Fig. 7. ECG preprocessing

then Junctional Tachycardia. If value of BPM is between 80–100 then Hypocalcemia or else BPM between 150–250 then ventricular Tachycardia. The results are shown in the figures below (Figs. 6, 7, 8 and 9):

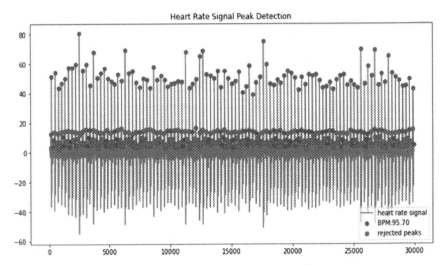

Fig. 8. QRS complex detection using Pan-Tompkins algorithm

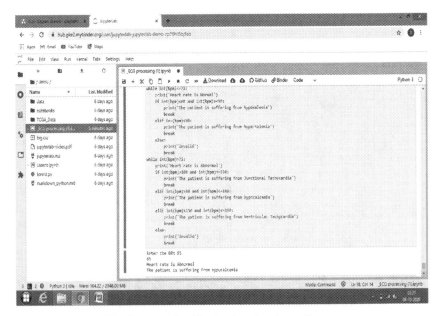

Fig. 9. BPM classification based on heart diseases

5.1   Observation Table

(Table 1)

Table 1. Observation table

ECG sample	Breathing rate	Beats per minute	SDNN	SD1	SD2	Type of ECG
1	1.87	58.89	65.76	45.75	82.92	Hypokalemia
2	0.203	116.30	47.18	59.69	63.20	Junctional Tachycardia
3	0.78	119.63	90.14	115.12	78.75	Junctional Tachycardia
4	0.39	95.19	126.67	128.52	120.11	Hypocalcemia
5	0.23	89.10	185.47	168.48	175.94	Hypocalcemia
6	0.42	71.74	89.48	96.90	105.32	Normal
7	0.63	92.85	299.48	225.11	76.19	Hypocalcemia
8	0.51	87.91	129.67	139.92	115.40	Hypocalcemia
9	0.12	67.77	89.82	168.12	194.83	Normal
10	0.30	75.73	118.42	36.48	34.61	Abnormal
11	1.00	121.99	69.37	19.00	27.48	Junctional Tachycardia
12	0.41	95.22	105.83	74.64	84.43	Hypocalcemia
13	0.55	92.08	188.03	190.13	178.17	Hypocalcemia
14	0.56	103.26	57.60	65.72	35.22	Junctional Tachycardia
15	0.45	72.43	195.64	245.06	143.69	Abnormal
16	0.47	66.04	167.92	141.30	202.90	Normal
17	0.04	84.85	183.52	196.75	182.97	Hypocalcemia
18	0.30	63.57	30.73	10.17	13.65	Normal
19	0.57	115.85	9.05	1.00	1.00	Junctional Tachycardia
20	0.27	76.67	151.44	160.99	167.37	Abnormal

6   Conclusion

To detect the abnormality of ECG, segmentation of ECG is done and for QRS complex detection, Pan Tompkins algorithm have been utilized and based on that calculation of BPM and SDNN is done. From the 20 samples taken, one was the hypokalemia with 58.89 BPM and 65.76 SDNN value, there were 5 samples of Junctional Tachycardia having 116.30 BPM and 47.18 SDNN near value, 7 samples of hypocalcemia with 95.19 BPM and 126.67 SDNN near value and there were 4 normal samples with 71.74 BPM and 89.48SDNN value. Finally, 3 abnormal samples with 75.73 BPM and 118.42 SDNN value are detected. Based on the results, various types of abnormality have been detected. One could easily use this algorithm for the detection of various abnormality types.

References

1. Haibing, Q., Xiongfei, L., Chao, P.: A method of continuous wavelet transform for QRS wave detection in ECG signal. In: 2010 International Conference on Intelligent Computation Technology and Automation, pp. 22–25. Changsha (2010). https://doi.org/10.1109/icicta.201 0.402
2. Mayapur, P.: Classification of Arrhythmia from ECG Signals using MATLAB. Int. J. Eng. Manage. Res. **8**, 15 (2019). https://doi.org/10.31033/ijemr.8.6.11
3. Friganovic, K., Jovic, A., Kukolja, D., Cifrek, M., Krstacic, G.: Optimizing the detection of characteristic waves in ECG based on exploration of processing steps combinations. In: Eskola H., Väisänen O., Viik J., Hyttinen J. (eds.) EMBEC & NBC 2017. EMBEC 2017, NBC 2017. IFMBE Proceedings, vol. 65. Springer, Singapore (2018). https://doi.org/10.1007/978-981-10-5122-7_232
4. www.semanticscholar.org
5. Sevak, M.M., Pawar, T.D.: Wearable ECG recorder using MATLAB (2019). https://www.ijeat.org/wp-content/uploads/papers/v9i1/A9473109119.pdf
6. Debnath, T., Hasan, M.M., Biswas, T.: Analysis of ECG signal and classification of heart abnormalities using Artificial Neural Network, pp. 353–356 (2016). https://doi.org/10.1109/icece.2016.7853929
7. Roonizi, E.K., Fatemi, M.: A modified Bayesian filtering framework for ECG beat segmentation. In: 2014 22nd Iranian Conference on Electrical Engineering (ICEE), pp. 1868–1872. Tehran (2014). https://doi.org/10.1109/iraniancee.2014.6999844
8. Kumar, A., Mukherjee, S., Luhach, A.K.: Deep learning with perspective modeling for early detection of malignancy in mammograms. J. Disc. Math. Sci. Cryptograp. **22:4**, 627–643 (2019). https://doi.org/10.1080/09720529.2019.1642624
9. Shallu, N.P., Kumar, S., Luhach, A.K.: Detection and analysis of lung cancer using radiomic approach. In: Luhach, A.K., Hawari, K.B.G., Mihai, I.C., Hsiung, P.A., Mishra, R.B. (eds.) Smart Computational Strategies: Theoretical and Practical Aspects. Springer, Singapore (2019). https://doi.org/10.1007/978-981-13-6295-8_2
10. Pradeepa, S., Manjula, K.R., Vimal, S., et al.: DRFS: detecting risk factor of stroke disease from social media using machine learning techniques. Neural Process. Lett. (2020). https://doi.org/10.1007/s11063-020-10279-8
11. Ouni, K., Ktata, S., Ellouze, N.: Automatic ECG segmentation based on Wavelet Transform Modulus Maxima. In: The Proceedings of the Multiconference on "Computational Engineering in Systems Applications, pp. 140–144. Beijing (2006). https://doi.org/10.1109/cesa.2006.4281639
12. Clifford, G.D., Zapanta, L.F., Janz, B.A., Mietus, J.E., Younand, C.Y., Mark, R.G.: Segmentation of 24-hour cardiovascular activity using ECG-based sleep/sedation and noise metrics. Computers in Cardiology, pp. 595–598. Lyon (2005). https://doi.org/10.1109/cic.2005.158 8171

13. Kaminski, M., Chlapinski, J., Sakowicz, B., Balcerak, S.: ECG signal preprocessing for T-wave alternans detection. In: 2009 10th International Conference - The Experience of Designing and Application of CAD Systems in Microelectronics, pp. 103–106. Lviv-Polyana (2009)

14. Zhang, Q., Frick, K.: All-ECG: A least-number of leads ECG monitor for standard 12-lead ECG tracking during motion*. In: 2019 IEEE Healthcare Innovations and Point of Care Technologies, (HI-POCT), pp. 103–106. Bethesda, MD, USA (2019). https://doi.org/10.1109/hi-poct45284.2019.8962742

15. Francisco, A., Gari, C., Patrick, M.: Advanced Methods and Tools for ECG Data Analysis. In: Advanced Methods and Tools for ECG Data Analysis, Artech (2006)

16. Kurniawan, A., Yuniarno, E.M., Setijadi, E., Yusuf, M., Purnama, I.K.E.: QVAT: QRS complex detection based on variance analysis and adaptive threshold for electrocardiogram signal. In: 2020 International Seminar on Intelligent Technology and Its Applications (ISITIA), pp. 175–179. Surabaya, Indonesia (2020). https://doi.org/10.1109/isitia49792.2020.9163784.k

17. Tan, F., Chan, K.L., Choi, K.: Detection of the QRS complex, P wave and T wave in electrocardiogram. In: 2000 First International Conference Advances in Medical Signal and Information Processing (IEE Conf. Publ. No. 476), pp. 41–47. Bristol, UK (2000). https://doi.org/10.1049/cp:20000315

Detection and Classification of Toxic Comments by Using LSTM and Bi-LSTM Approach

Akash Gupta[1](✉), Anand Nayyar[2], Simrann Arora[1,3], and Rachna Jain[1]

[1] Department of Computer Science and Engineering, Bharati Vidyapeeth's
College of Engineering, New Delhi, India
rachna.jain@bharatividyapeeth.edu
[2] Graduate School, Duy Tan University, Da Nang 550000, Viet Nam
anandnayyar@duytan.edu.vn
[3] Faculty of Information Technology, Duy Tan University, Da Nang 550000, Viet Nam

Abstract. With the advancement in the technology, a lot of comments has been produced on a regular basis through the various online communication platforms like Wikipedia, twitter, Glassdoor etc. Although, many of these comments really benefit the people, but the various high toxic comments are also responsible for the increasing online harassment, mental depression and even personal attacks. Toxic Comment Classification is one of the active research topics at present. In the following study, a multi-label classification model is presented to classify the various toxic comments into six classes namely toxic, severe toxic, obscene, threat, insult and identity hate. The proposed classification model has been built using deep learning algorithms explicitly Long Short-Term Memory (LSTM) and Bi-Directional Long Short-Term Memory (Bi-LSTM) along with the word embeddings by adapting insights from previous proposed works. The dataset for this research is obtained from the Kaggle and is provided by the Conversation AI team (a research ingenuity co-founded by Google as well as Jigsaw). The accuracy score of both the proposed techniques is evaluated and compared. Finally, the empirical results show that Bi-LSTM algorithm achieved better in comparison to LSTM with an increased accuracy of 98.07%.

Keywords: Toxic comments classification · LSTM · Bi-LSTM · Word embeddings · Multi-label classification · Online harassment · Personal attack

1 Introduction

As the world is progressing with an ever-increasing rate, the surge in technological advancements is also at an all-time high [1]. This has caused more and more people around the globe to have access to several platforms on the internet and express their views and opinions on almost every other thing [2]. The social media sites are becoming easily accessible each passing day, thereby increasing the number of users and intensifying their vulnerability. On one side, this has helped many people to interact with each other, discuss over various eclectic issues around the globe while sitting at the comfort of their homes and provide information on certain topics in the form of comments, but

© Springer Nature Singapore Pte Ltd. 2021
A. K. Luhach et al. (Eds.): ICAICR 2020, CCIS 1393, pp. 100–112, 2021.
https://doi.org/10.1007/978-981-16-3660-8_10

on the other hand it has increased the cases of online harassment and misconduct among people [3]. The social media sites especially, do have photographs of people and may provide a glimpse of their personal life as well. Inappropriate comments on such sensitive content can also harm mental or physical well-being of people and force them to take some inappropriate actions. Such comments are identified as being toxic in nature and they contain abusive words, foul language, aggression, hate, insulting remarks and threats of various types [4]. There is a need to help identifying these comments and stop them from causing any harm or loss of life further. Thus, this topic becomes an extensive and challenging area of research and might help in earlier and faster detection of typical comments in future.

Some of the key objectives of this research are:

- Detection and classification of toxic comments to prevent online harassment and misconduct to a large extent
- Development of a multi-label classification model using deep learning models, namely, LSTM and Bi-LSTM LSTM along with the word embeddings by adapting insights from previous proposed works into 6 different categories of abusive words, foul language, aggression, hate, insulting remarks and threats of various types.
- Achieved a high accuracy of 98.07% by using the Bi-LSTM which performed better than LSTM approach and facilitate research in this field.

The rest of the paper is organized in the following manner. Section 2 provides a detailed review of the various researches takes place in the world for the classification and detection of toxic comments. Section 3 discusses the algorithms and techniques used in this research work. Section 4 deliberates the proposed methodology steps along with the proposed model of the entire research work in detail. Later, Sect. 5 discusses about the experimental results and simulations along with the various evaluation plots used in this research. Finally, Sect. 6 concludes the paper with future scope.

2 Literature Review

The advent in technology has brought people closer by interacting through comments on various platforms. These comments mostly are neutral, but some comments include hate, aggression, abusive words which can seriously cause harm to the other person. Thus, toxic comment classification has been a major concern these days to prevent people from online harassment and mental breakdown. Many types of researches are being done on this issue. Here, are some of the researches listed below from all over the world.

van Aken et al. [7] worked on the comparison of various deep learning models along with the shallow approaches on a novel, huge dataset of comments and proposed an ensemble method that outshined all the other individual models. Subsequently, the findings were validated on another dataset. The results obtained by the ensemble method facilitated the authors for performing an all-embracing error scrutiny, which consequently revealed the encounters for the advanced approaches along with guidelines for the scope of future research. The challenges contained the inconsistency in dataset labels along with the missing paradigmatic context.

Srivastava et al. [8] proposed a solitary model capsule network which had a focal forfeiture to accomplish the chore of identifying the aggression as well as toxic comments. This approach is well suited for the production environment. The proposed model achieved an outstanding result as compared to other baselines models, showing its efficacy and depicting that the focal loss displays crucial improvement in the cases where the imbalance of classes is a major concern. Along with this the concerns regarding extensive data augmentation and processing are dealt with the proposed network. The model also tackles the transliteration problem in an effective manner, which had comments in both English and Hindi languages.

Saeed et al. [9] worked on several Deep Neural Network (DNN) techniques for classification of the overlapping sentiments with a high accuracy. Furthermore, the proposed framework used for classification did not necessitate a large volume of text pre-processing and is able to handle this concern implicitly. The pragmatic validation performed on a practical dataset supported the authors' claim by giving superior results.

Vaidya et al. [10] evaluated various advanced models with particular focus on the reduction of model prejudice towards the most vulnerable and attacked identity groups. The authors proposed a multi-task erudition framework with a consideration layer that with a joint focus, predicts the identities in the comment as well as its toxicity to reduce the bias. Then they compared the model to an arrangement of deep learning and shallow learning models by leveraging the metrics that have been devised for testing the bias within these groups of identity.

Deshmukh et al. [11] presented a novel approach which used RNNs as well as Capsule networks as the backbone and captured the information (contextual) to a greater extent while learning the representations of word in the text. Experiments were steered on Wikipedia's talk leaf controls. The results showed that the proposed model outperformed the conventional advanced models and displayed the efficacy of capsule networks. After discussing the various researches, this study is focused on the recognition and cataloguing of toxic comments by means of the Bi-LSTM and LSTM approaches.

3 Algorithms and Techniques Used

In this section, the algorithms and techniques used in this research are discussed in detail.

3.1 Long Short-Term Memory (LSTM)

Long Short-Term Memory (LSTM) network is a specialized sort of Recurrent Neural Network (RNN) which is able to learn the dependencies that are long-term [11]. They perform exceptionally well on the sequence modelling problems and are devised to circumvent the problem of long-term dependency [12]. Their behavior is to retain the information for long periods of time. Figure 1 below displays the LSTM architecture.

With slight linear interactions across this path, cell state C allows information to be passed unchanged across the complete LSTM which allows LSTM to recognize multiple times steps, the context in the past [14]. There are many inputs and outputs throughout this line which enable us to add or remove the cell state information. Gates control the insertion or deletion of the information [15].

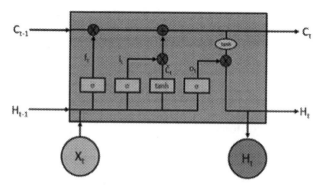

Fig. 1. LSTM architecture [13]

The Sigmoid layer outputs zero-to-one numbers, specifying how much of every part should be allowed through. A zero value suggests letting nothing at all in, whereas a one means getting everything into it [16]. The architecture of LSTM includes 3 gates, namely, the forget gate, the input gate as well as the output gate.

Some applications of LSTMs are in:

- Generation of Handwriting
- Image Captioning
- Language Modelling
- Chatbots for Question/Answering

3.2 Bi-directional Long Short-Term Memory (Bi-LSTM)

Bi-directional RNN basically means a combination of two individual RNNs [17]. This structure enables the network to contain forward and backward, both information regarding the sequence at each and every time step [18]. Utilizing the bidirectional approach, the input can be run in 2 behaviors that are from past to future as well as future to past [19]. It is different from the unidirectional LSTM in a way that backward run in this saves the future information and utilizing the latent states collated together, the information can be saved from both the future as well as the past [20]. Figure 2 below shows its architecture.

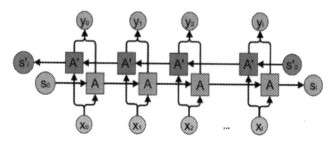

Fig. 2. Bi-LSTM architecture [21]

In this, the activation values are also used, not only the candidate values. Along with this, two outputs are obtained from the cell, a novel activation as well as a novel candidate value [22]. Its architecture also has 3 gates, that are, update gate, forget gate and the output gate. Bi-LSTMs have a major application in text related problems where the previous and future response generation comes into picture [23].

4   Proposed Methodology

In the following section, the research methodology is discussed in depth. The proposed prototype of this research is represented in Fig. 3. Initially, the toxic comments dataset obtained from the Kaggle is provided as the input to the model. After the analysis of the data, the dataset is pre-processed for further analysis. The pre-processing steps includes removal of punctuations, stopwords and null values followed by the stemming techniques. After the pre-processing, the dataset is converted to a suitable input matrix by employing tokenization, padding and the word embedding techniques. After this, the dataset is fragmented into the training and the validation set. 75% of the data is utilized for the training resolution while 25% of the data is used for the validation resolution. The proposed model is then trained by using LSTM and Bi-LSTM algorithms. Finally, the model is validated upon validation set and the presentation of both the algorithms is gauged and compared with each other.

4.1   Dataset Description

The dataset for the research is attained from Kaggle and is made available by the Conversation AI team, which is an examination initiative co-founded by Jigsaw and Google [5]. The dataset consists of a huge number of toxic Wikipedia remarks which had been categorised into the six classes explicitly toxic, sever toxic, obscene, threat, insult and identity hate. These are categorised by the professional ratters. The dataset consists of around 1,60,000 comments taken from the Wikipedia talk pages. Since, it is multi-label classification problem, hence, the comments can belong to more than one classes i.e., a particular remark can be toxic, threat or an insult at the same time. The dataset consists of Comment ID, Comment Text, and the Boolean entries against the corresponding toxic comment category.

4.2   Data Analysis

There are around 1,60,000 comments are present in the dataset. Figure 4 shows the distribution of these comments according to its length. After the analysis of Fig. 4, we conclude that, most of the comments (around 1,20,000) are generally short and having words in the range of 0–100. Also, the average length of the comments is calculated to be around 80 words.

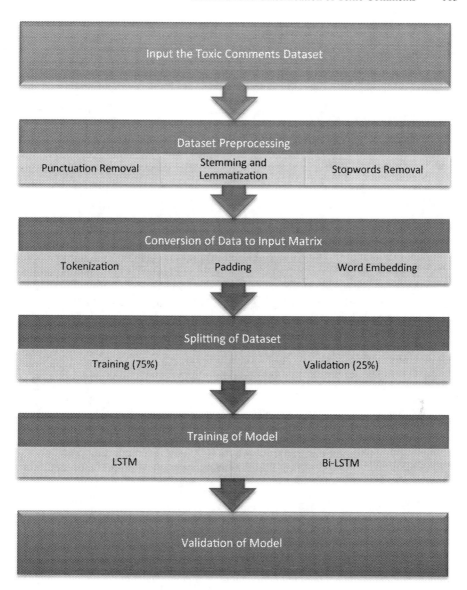

Fig. 3. Flow of proposed methodology

Figure 5 shows the further distribution of these comments into six labels according to its length. After the analysis of Fig. 5, we can conclude that large number of remarks fits to the toxic, obscene in addition to insult classes.

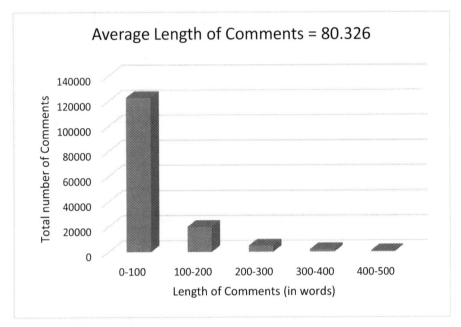

Fig. 4. Distribution of comments according to length

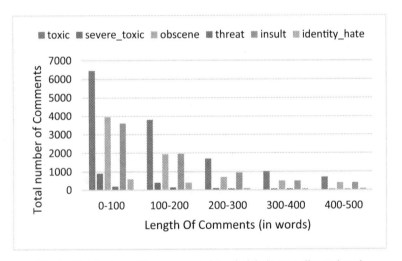

Fig. 5. Distribution of the comments into six labels according to length

4.3 Data Pre-processing

The following steps are employed in this research for the pre-processing of the dataset:

1. Initially, all the null values are removed from the dataset.
2. Then, all the punctuation signs and the numerical digits are removed from the dataset.
3. After that, all the Stopwords like for, this, in, the etc. are removed from the dataset.
4. Finally, stemming and lemmatization is performed which converts the various forms of verbs present in the comments to its base word.

4.4 Data Conversion to Input Matrix

The following steps are employed in this research for the conversion of the data to suitable input matrix.

1. **Tokenization:** It is employed to convert the comments into a series of tokens.
2. **Padding:** Since the average length of the comments is determined as 80, hence, the standard length is taken to be of 80 words.
3. **Word Embedding:** It is performed to get insights from the previous research works. In this research, Glove.6B.300D is used which contain 6 billion tokens and each token is represented by 300D vector representation. This glove dataset is obtained from the web [6].

4.5 Build LSTM and Bi-LSTM Model

After conversion of tokens data into a suitable input matrix, the data is fragmented into the training along with the validation set. 75% of the data is used for the training resolution, while the 25% of the data is utilized for the validation resolution. After splitting, the model is then trained by using Long Short-Term Memory (LSTM) and Bi-Directional Long Short-Term Memory (Bi-LSTM) algorithms.

5   Experimental Results and Analysis

In this section, experimental results are discussed and analysed in detail. The elementary approach of both the algorithms is same and is discussed here.

1. The LSTM or Bi-LSTM network is initialised with 100 neurons.
2. Four dense layers are used in these models in which, three of them having ReLu as its activation function with 100, 70 and 30 neurons respectively. The last layer has sigmoid as its activation function with 6 neurons, as comments are belonging to the 6 classes in total.
3. The dual cross-entropy is chosen as the loss function here.
4. The model is further optimized using Adam optimization technique with learning rate equals to 0.01.
5. Number of epochs is selected to be 2. Because more than 2 epochs overfits the model as shown in Fig. 6 and 7.

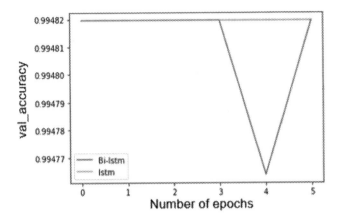

Fig. 6. Validation accuracy with increase in figure of epochs

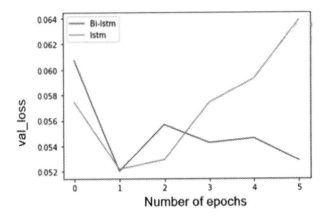

Fig. 7. Validation loss with surge in figure of epochs

Then, after selecting the epoch size as 2 and batch size as 128, the training and validation accuracy and the loss curves for the LSTM and the Bi-LSTM models are plotted then compared. Figure 8 and 9 represents the training accuracy and the training loss for the LSTM and Bi-LSTM neural networks.

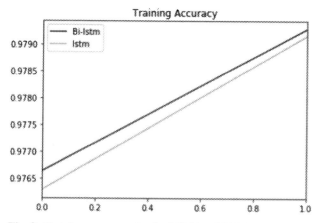

Fig. 8. Training accuracy plot for LSTM and Bi-LSTM networks

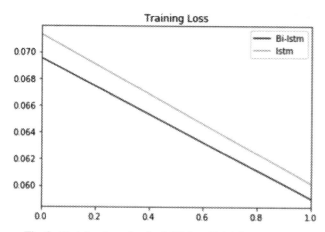

Fig. 9. Training loss plot for LSTM and Bi-LSTM networks

Figure 10 and 11 represents the validation accuracy and validation loss for the LSTM and Bi-LSTM neural networks.

After analysing the training and validation accuracy and loss curves, it is concluded that Bi-LSTM neural network shows improved recital as compared to LSTM network for both the training and the validation set. The validation accuracy score of Bi-LSTM is nearly equals to 0.9807 which is considerably higher than the LSTM network.

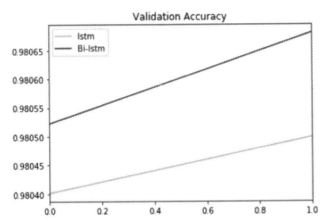

Fig. 10. Validation accuracy plot for LSTM and Bi-LSTM networks

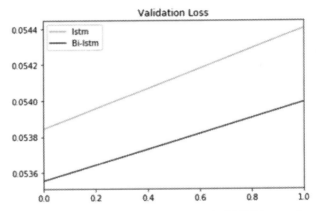

Fig. 11. Validation loss plot for LSTM and Bi-LSTM networks

6 Conclusion and Future Scope

This research work is carried out to offer a multi-label classification model for the classification of various toxic comments collected from the Wikipedia talk pages dataset. The dataset for the following research is obtained from Kaggle. Here, the comments are categorised into six classes namely toxic, severe toxic, threat, insult, obscene, and identity hate. The proposed classification model is build using deep learning algorithms namely Long Short-Term Memory (LSTM) and Bi-Directional Long Short-Term Memory (Bi-LSTM) along with the word embeddings by adapting insights from previous proposed works. In this research, both the proposed models are gaged and equated using the accuracy and the loss curves for the training and the validation datasets. Finally, the pragmatic results display that the Bi-LSTM network shows improved performance with an increased accuracy of 98.07%. The model can be enhanced in future either by developing a denser neural network by increasing the number of dense layers or by employing other RNN techniques.

References

1. Georgakopoulos, S.V., Tasoulis, S.K., Vrahatis, A.G., Plagianakos, V.P.: Convolutional neural networks for toxic comment classification. In: Proceedings of the 10th Hellenic Conference on Artificial Intelligence, pp. 1–6 (2018)
2. Mohammad, F.: Is preprocessing of text really worth your time for toxic comment classification?. In: Proceedings on the International Conference on Artificial Intelligence (ICAI), pp. 447–453. The Steering Committee of The World Congress in Computer Science, Computer Engineering and Applied Computing (WorldComp) (2018)
3. Carta, S., Corriga, A., Mulas, R., Recupero, D.R., Saia, R.: A supervised multi-class multi-label word embeddings approach for toxic comment classification. In: KDIR, pp. 105–112 (2019)
4. D'sa, A.G., Illina, I., Fohr, D.: Towards non-toxic landscapes: automatic toxic comment detection using DNN. arXiv:1911.08395 (2019)
5. Toxic Comment Classification Challenge: Identify and classify toxic online comments (2018). Accessed from https://www.kaggle.com/datamunge/sign-language-mnist
6. Pennington, J., Socher, R., Manning, C.D.: GloVe: Global Vectors for Word Representation (2014). Accessed from https://nlp.stanford.edu/projects/glove/
7. van Aken, B., Risch, J., Krestel, R., Löser, A.: Challenges for toxic comment classification: an in-depth error analysis. arXiv:1809.07572 (2018)
8. Srivastava, S., Khurana, P., Tewari, V.: Identifying aggression and toxicity in comments using capsule network. In: Proceedings of the First Workshop on Trolling, Aggression and Cyberbullying (TRAC-2018), pp. 98–105 (2018)
9. Saeed, H.H., Shahzad, K., Kamiran, F.: Overlapping toxic sentiment classification using deep neural architectures. In: 2018 IEEE International Conference on Data Mining Workshops (ICDMW), pp. 1361–1366. IEEE (2018)
10. Vaidya, A., Mai, F., Ning, Y.: Empirical analysis of multi-task learning for reducing model bias in toxic comment detection. arXiv:1909.09758 (2019)
11. Deshmukh, S., Rade, R.: Tackling toxic online communication with recurrent capsule networks. In: 2018 Conference on Information and Communication Technology (CICT), pp. 1–7. IEEE (2018)
12. Sherstinsky, A.: Fundamentals of recurrent neural network (RNN) and long short-term memory (LSTM) network. Physica D **404**, (2020)
13. Liu, J., Wang, G., Hu, P., Duan, L.Y., Kot, A.C.: Global context-aware attention LSTM networks for 3d action recognition. In: Proceedings of the IEEE Conference on Computer Vision and Pattern Recognition, pp. 1647–1656 (2017)
14. Kim, H.Y., Won, C.H.: Forecasting the volatility of stock price index: a hybrid model integrating LSTM with multiple GARCH-type models. Expert Syst. Appl. **103**, 25–37 (2018)
15. Ma, Y., Peng, H., Cambria, E.: Targeted aspect-based sentiment analysis via embedding commonsense knowledge into an attentive LSTM. In: Thirty-Second AAAI Conference on Artificial Intelligence (2018)
16. Zhao, Z., Chen, W., Wu, X., Chen, P.C., Liu, J.: LSTM network: a deep learning approach for short-term traffic forecast. IET Intell. Transp. Syst. **11**(2), 68–75 (2017)
17. Alzaidy, R., Caragea, C., Giles, C.L.: Bi-LSTM-CRF sequence labeling for keyphrase extraction from scholarly documents. In: The World Wide Web Conference, pp. 2551–2557 (2019)
18. Tourille, J., Ferret, O., Neveol, A., Tannier, X.: Neural architecture for temporal relation extraction: A Bi-LSTM approach for detecting narrative containers. In: Proceedings of the 55th Annual Meeting of the Association for Computational Linguistics, Volume 2: Short Papers, pp. 224–230 (2017)

19. Minaee, S., Azimi, E., Abdolrashidi, A.: Deep-sentiment: Sentiment analysis using ensemble of cnn and Bi-LSTM models. arXiv:1904.04206 (2019)
20. Lin, J.C.W., Shao, Y., Zhou, Y., Pirouz, M., Chen, H.C.: A Bi-LSTM mention hypergraph model with encoding schema for mention extraction. Eng. Appl. Artif. Intell. **85**, 175–181 (2019)
21. Li, C., Zhan, G., Li, Z.: News text classification based on improved Bi-LSTM-CNN. In: 2018 9th International Conference on Information Technology in Medicine and Education (ITME), pp. 890–893. IEEE (2018)
22. Hua, Q., Qundong, S., Dingchao, J., Lei, G., Yanpeng, Z., Pengkang, L.: A character-level method for text classification. In: 2018 2nd IEEE Advanced Information Management, Communicates, Electronic and Automation Control Conference (IMCEC), pp. 402–406. IEEE (2018)
23. Zhang, Y., Liu, Q., Song, L.: Sentence-state lstm for text representation. arXiv:1805.02474 (2018)

On the Effects of Substitution Matrix Choices for Pairwise Gapped Global Sequence Alignment of DNA Nucleotides

Rajashree Chaurasia[1,2(✉)] and Udayan Ghose[2]

[1] Guru Nanak Dev Institute of Technology, Directorate of Training and Technical Education (Govt. NCT of Delhi), Delhi, India
rajashree.14416490019@ipu.ac.in
[2] University School of Information Communication and Technology, Guru Gobind Singh Indraprastha University, Delhi, India
udayan@ipu.ac.in

Abstract. Substitution matrices for nucleotides and amino acids are one of the critical parameters of sequence alignment algorithms. In the case of amino acids, standard substitution matrices like PAM and BLOSUM were derived from evolutionary models. Modern amino acid scoring models based on maximum likelihood like VTML have also been recently developed. However, for nucleotides, there exist no standard scoring matrices. The case of nucleotide substitution matrix choices for global gapped pairwise alignments has been explored little, whereas much literature exists on amino acid substitution matrices pertaining to multiple local alignments. This manuscript aims to offer insights into how different substitution scores may affect the optimal global alignment scores and the statistical significance of nucleotide sequences. The manuscript is organized as follows: Sect. 1 gives a succinct background of the work done in this direction, Sect. 2 specifies the data analysis methodology, Sect. 3 discusses the results obtained, and Sect. 4 concludes the paper with some comments on laying the foundation for potential research that may be done to strengthen this empirical analysis.

Keywords: Global pairwise alignment · Nucleotide substitution matrix · Scoring matrix · Statistical significance · Gapped alignments

1 Background

Homology between nucleotide sequences can be gauged from their global alignments. Many improvements to the standard global pairwise alignment, which is the Needleman-Wunsch [13] algorithm, exist [2, 7, 9, 12, 15]. One of these improvisations, the Myers-Miller algorithm [12], uses the dynamic programming paradigm in conjunction with graph theory to represent the global alignment in linear space. Several online tools employ basic Needleman-Wunsch and other faster linear space extensions [18]. Two of the most notable from EMBL-EBI's (European Bioinformatics Institute) EMBOSS package are the EMBOSS 'needle' and the EMBOSS 'stretcher' programs (see https://

© Springer Nature Singapore Pte Ltd. 2021
A. K. Luhach et al. (Eds.): ICAICR 2020, CCIS 1393, pp. 113–125, 2021.
https://doi.org/10.1007/978-981-16-3660-8_11

www.ebi.ac.uk/Tools/psa/), which implement the Needleman-Wunsch and the Myers-Miller algorithms, respectively. NCBI's (National Centre for Biotechnology Information) BLAST (Basic Local Alignment Search Tool) suite of programs implements the Needleman-Wunsch algorithm as well [1]. These tools give an optimal alignment of the two sequences along with an optimal alignment score and a percentage identity/similarity. Percent similarity or percent identity is a measure of the evolutionary distance between two nucleotide sequences aligned globally, i.e., across their entire lengths. For amino acids, percent similarity and percent identity are different quantities, whereas they mean the same thing for nucleotides. Percent identity is given by the ratio of exactly matching bases (for nucleotides) or residues (for amino acids) to the alignment's total length. On the contrary, percent similarity measures the number of similar residues (of amino acids) over and above the exact matches to the alignment's total length.

Several parameters govern the optimal alignment scores obtained using these alignment algorithms, viz. the match and mismatch scores and the gap penalties. The scoring matrices consist of match scores and mismatch penalties among the four bases, A, T, G, and C, for nucleotides. Therefore, the scoring or substitution matrices are 4×4 matrices wherein the main diagonal gives the uniform match scores (positive quantities) for the nucleotides, and the non-diagonal elements contain the uniform mismatch penalties (negative quantities) for the misaligned bases. Several standard scoring models exist for protein sequences, viz., PAM (Point Accepted Mutation), BLOSUM (BLOcks Substitution Matrix), VTML (Variable Time Maximum Likelihood), JTT (Jones-Taylor-Thornton), etc. [4, 6, 8, 10, 11]. However, there are no standard models for nucleotide sequences. The default values for match and mismatch scores used by the EMBOSS package for the global pairwise alignment programs are $+5$ and -4, respectively. NCBI's BLASTN (Nucleotide BLAST) uses $+2$ and -3 as the match and mismatch scores for global pairwise alignment. Like amino acid PAM scores, States et al. [16] point out that nucleotide scoring matrices can also be modeled as log-odds ratios of the alignment frequency in homologs versus the frequency of random alignment. Their study of the PAM scoring efficiency at varying evolutionary distances provides a table of match and mismatch scores targeted at sequences of a particular percent identity. In their study, States et al. conclude that scoring matrices should be chosen such that database similarity searches for the query sequence are optimized for a small range of percentage identity. According to States et al., as the percentage identity diverges from the optimum, the scoring matrices' efficacy decreases, and so does the amount of information carried by the alignment. They also compared the static scoring scheme of uniform match and mismatch scores for transitions (A↔G) and transversions (C↔T) with the more complex mutational model, wherein the transitions are scored higher than the transversions. However, the research they have conducted is primarily targeted at BLASTP (Protein BLAST) multiple local sequence alignments or protein database similarity searches. According to this study, the EMBOSS score defaults are optimized for approximately 66% identity, whereas the BLASTN Needleman-Wunsch program scoring defaults are optimized for approximately 98% identity. Either of these online tools do not use complex mutation-biased scoring matrices. An online tool for evaluating the optimum target percent identity for DNA scoring matrices, based on the work of States et al., is available at [17]. This tool takes the uniform match and mismatch scores as input and calculates the percentage identity for which this particular scoring model is best suited. It also provides an expected entropy for the scoring model selected. Pearson [14], in his study on scoring matrix choices for amino acids, also finds that different matrices are best suited to be applied at different levels of homology. He further distinguishes between 'shallow' and 'deep' scoring matrices and concludes that these two types of matrices result in different sensitivities and affect the length of the alignments produced. According to Pearson, 'shallow' substitution matrices have higher scores for both matched and mismatched residues than 'deep' matrices. Therefore, 'shallow' matrices result in shorter alignments with higher percent similarity and carry more residue pair entropy. These studies target amino acid multiple local alignment searches and do not directly apply to global pairwise alignment for nucleotides. The alphabet for nucleotides is very much smaller, consisting of only four bases against 22 amino acid residues. Furthermore, global nucleotide alignment lengths are more massive than protein local alignments. Therefore, the principle of choosing between 'shallow' or 'deep' matrices does not apply to them. However, the relationship between percent identity and scoring matrices may be explored for nucleotide global pairwise alignment.

Alignment scores are also heavily dependent on the gap score model. Gap penalties are of many types viz., constant, linear, affine, convex, and profile-based. Of these, affine gap penalties are the most popular in alignment problems. Affine gap penalties are of the form:

$$gap_{penalty} = gap_{open} + (n - 1) * gap_{extend} \tag{1}$$

$$where\ gap_{open} > gap_{extend}$$

In Eq. 1, 'n' is the gap length, 'gap_{open}' is the penalty of beginning a new gap in the alignment, and 'gap_{extend}' is the penalty for extending the newly opened gap beyond one gap length. The gap opening score is generally set higher than the extension penalty because we do not want a large number of very short gaps in the alignment, which would render the alignment practically meaningless. Gap costs are directly related to alignment quality. Gap penalties are set appropriately high so that the resultant alignment is not overextended with unnecessary gaps. Overextension makes the alignment lose its reliability. Both the EMBOSS package programs 'needle' and 'stretcher,' as well as the BLASTN global alignment program, use affine gap penalties. The EMBOSS default 'gap_{open}' cost is set at 16, and 'gap_{extend}' cost is set at 4 for nucleotide sequences. However, the BLASTN global pairwise module sets the 'gap_{open}' penalty to 5 and 'gap_{extend}' cost to 2 by default.

The statistical significance of global nucleotide alignments may be calculated by determining the p-value of the optimal scores compared to a random model. For a static scoring matrix and a predetermined gap cost model, it has been found that the alignment scores tend towards the Gumbel distribution [3]. Therefore, the p-values obtained from such a distribution help assess the significance of a global pairwise alignment.

2 Methods

The EMBOSS 'stretcher' module that implements the linear space Myers-Miller global pairwise alignment is used to generate the alignments in this study. The EMBOSS 6.5.0.0 package can be downloaded for Windows (see ftp://emboss.open-bio.org/pub/EMBOSS/windows/, free and open-source), and its documentation can be found at [5]. We have used the following two sets of affine gap equations:

$$EMBOSS \ \ Default : gap_{penalty} = 16 + (n - 1) * 4 \tag{2}$$

and

$$BLASTN \ \ Default : gap_{penalty} = 5 + (n - 1) * 2 \tag{3}$$

Sixteen pairs of real nucleotide sequences have been selected from the NCBI nucleotide database, with varying lengths (~1000 base pairs to ~10,000 base pairs) and varying percentage identities (see Table 1). As is evident from the table, pairs 1 and 6 contain sequences that vary considerably in length, while in all others, the target and query sequences are of similar length. Further, pair 10 is a non-gapped global alignment; i.e., it contains zero gaps for the EMBOSS default gap model. Sequence pairs 2–15 have been used in [3] to study the nature of the statistical significance of such alignments. A set of 25 uniform scoring matrices with equal match and mismatch scores among the four nucleotide bases have been studied (see Table 2). The target percent identity is evaluated using the online tool available at [17].

Table 1. Sequence pairs selected from the NCBI database for analysis along with the accession numbers. The target sequence is the first sequence input to the 'stretcher' program. The query sequence is the second sequence, which is also used to generate the random model.

Pair no.	Target sequence	Query sequence	Target sequence length (in base pairs)	Query sequence length (in base pairs)
1	AF531299.1	NC_030679.2: c135757942 - 135758641	1620	700
2	NC_000079.6: 23763668 -23764412	NC_030679.2: c135757942 - 135758641	745	700
3	NM_000523	NM_008275	1008	1020
4	KC978991.1	NC_038958.1	1001	1021
5	NM_000522	NM_008264	1167	1151
6	AF531299.1	NC_000079.6: 23763668 -23764412	1620	745

(*continued*)

Table 1. (*continued*)

Pair no.	Target sequence	Query sequence	Target sequence length (in base pairs)	Query sequence length (in base pairs)
7	NC_038298.1	KX066124.1	1958	1996
8	NC_000006.12: 31575565 - 31578336	M64087.1	2772	2610
9	NC_026662.1	NC_014480.2	3907	3322
10	NC_026662.1	MH649256.1	3907	3904
11	NC_004764.2	AB453162.1	4981	4981
12	NC_048296.1	KY985463.1	5736	5729
13	U31789.1	U31790.1	7100	7184
14	NC_001362.1	AB187565.1	8323	8319
15	M10060.1	Y14570.1	8952	8855
16	NC_001802.1	KT284376.1	9181	9579

Table 2. Scoring matrix choices considered for analysis. EDNAS23 and EDNAS54 are the NCBI BLASTN default and EMBOSS default, respectively.

S.no.	Datafile name	Match score	Mismatch score	Target % identity
1	EDNAS11	1	-1	75
2	EDNAS12	1	-2	95
3	EDNAS13	1	-3	99
4	EDNAS14	1	-4	100
5	EDNAS15	1	-5	100
6	EDNAS21	2	-1	42
7	EDNAS22	2	-2	75
8	EDNAS23	2	-3	89
9	EDNAS24	2	-4	95
10	EDNAS25	2	-5	98
11	EDNAS31	3	-1	Not defined
12	EDNAS32	3	-2	56
13	EDNAS33	3	-3	75
14	EDNAS34	3	-4	85

(*continued*)

Table 2. (*continued*)

S.no.	Datafile name	Match score	Mismatch score	Target % identity
15	EDNAS35	3	−5	91
16	EDNAS41	4	−1	Not defined
17	EDNAS42	4	−2	42
18	EDNAS43	4	−3	62
19	EDNAS44	4	−4	75
20	EDNAS45	4	−5	83
21	EDNAS51	5	−1	Not defined
22	EDNAS52	5	−2	32
23	EDNAS53	5	−3	51
24	EDNAS54	5	−4	65
25	EDNAS55	5	−5	75

The query sequences are used to construct a null model of 200 random sequences that preserve the query's composition. The random model for each sequence pair is generated using the EMBOSS package 'shuffleseq' module (see http://emboss.bioinf ormatics.nl/cgi-bin/emboss/shuffleseq). Each of the 200 sequences is globally aligned to the target for every scoring matrix and gap model employed. Thus, there are a total of 25 * 16 * 2 = 800 result sets (25 scoring matrix models, 16 sequence pairs, and 2 gap models), each containing 201 alignments (200 random global alignments + 1 target to query alignment). A p-value is then calculated from the Gumbel distribution's cumulative distribution function to measure the statistical significance of the alignment scores obtained. The alignment scores are then compared among the 25 scoring matrices for both gap models. All analysis has been done using the Python programming language.

3 Results and Discussion

Figures 1, 2, 3 and 4 show the relationship between the 25 scoring matrices and the corresponding alignment scores for all pairs of sequences. Figures 1 and 2 employ the EMBOSS default gap model, and Figs. 3 and 4 use the BLASTN default gap model. The red lines indicate the linear relationship between mismatch scores when the match score is constant. As the mismatch scores become more negative, the alignment scores decrease accordingly. The blue lines indicate the linear relationship between the match scores when mismatch scores are constant. As the match scores increase, the alignment scores also increase linearly. This is evident from Eq. 4–6. The alignment score also depends on the gap model employed. However, the total score accounting for gaps is independent of each gap block's length in the optimal alignment (see Eq. 6).

All the alignment scores are statistically significant, having p-values near to zero. The linear equation intercept parameter has no meaning in our analysis since the x-axis displays labels of scoring matrix data file names. However, the slope of the line equations

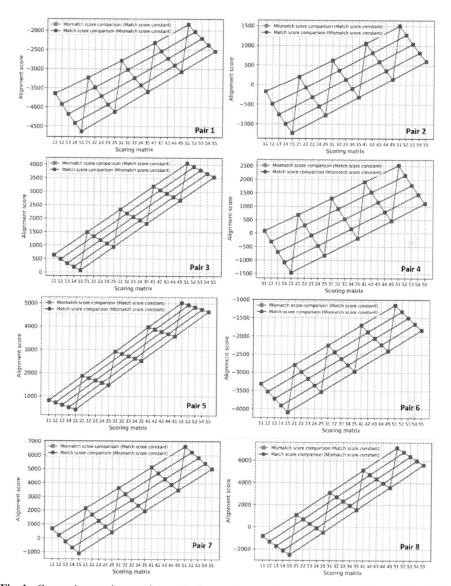

Fig. 1. Comparing scoring matrices and alignment scores for sequence pairs 1–8 and EMBOSS default gap model. The x-axis labels correspond to the data file names (shortened) from Table 2, where the prefix 'EDNAS' has been dropped for brevity. E.g., 21 refers to datafile 'EDNAS21', where the match score is +2, and the mismatch score is −1.

obtained are of interest here. The slopes of the red and blue lines are very close to the mean of their corresponding set of values. This means that the slope parameter of the linear equation segments of mismatch scores (when match scores are constant) and match scores (when mismatch scores are constant) can be represented by the mean of the number of mismatches and matches for that set of values, respectively.

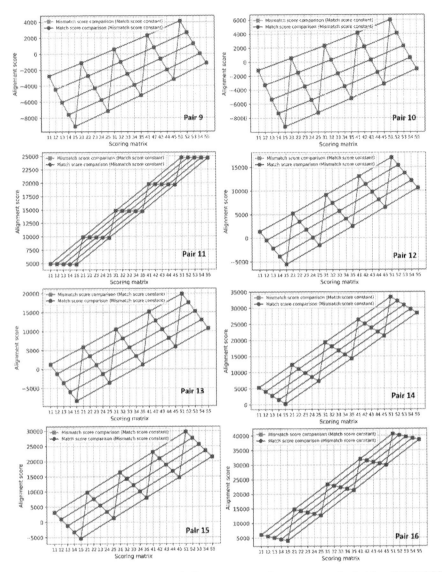

Fig. 2. Comparing scoring matrices and alignment scores for sequence pairs 9–16 and EMBOSS default gap model.

For the un-gapped model (pair 10 in this study), the following equation holds for alignment score calculation:

$$Score = n_{matches} * score_{match} - n_{mismatches} * score_{mismatch} \qquad (4)$$

where

$n_{matches}$ = number of matched bases, $score_{match}$ = the match score of the scoring matrix, $n_{mismatch}$ = number of mismatched bases, and $score_{mismatch}$ = mismatch score

Table 3. Scoring matrix for which the percent identity or opt$_{align}$ ratio is maximum as against the matrix recommended for the target percent identity of the corresponding sequence pair (according to States et al. [16]).

Pair no.	Scoring matrix (shorthand) for BLAST default gap model for which opt$_{align}$ is maximum	Scoring matrix (shorthand) for EMBOSS default gap model for which opt$_{align}$ is maximum	Scoring matrix (shorthand) for the target optimum percent identity
1	54	45, 55	52
2	43	53, 54	43, 54
3	43	42, 43, 44, 45, 51, 52, 53, 54, 55, 33, 34, 35, 24, 25, 14, 15	45
4	53	55	43, 54
5	54, 54, 44, 34	52, 53, 54, 55, 43, 44, 45, 34, 35, 25	35
6	55	54, 55	52
7	53	45, 53, 54, 44, 35	44, 55, 33, 22, 11
8	43, 53	55, 45	54
9	43, 53	55	53, 21, 42
10	43, 53	55	53, 21, 42
11	53, 54, 55, 43, 44, 45, 34, 35, 24, 25, 15	all	13, 14, 15, 25
12	43	55	43, 54
13	43, 53	55	54
14	43, 53	55, 45	45, 34
15	43, 53	55, 45	44, 55, 33, 22, 11
16	43, 53	55, 54	23, 35

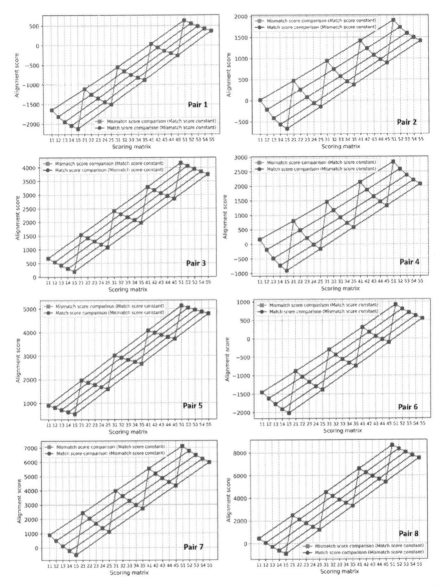

Fig. 3. Comparing scoring matrices and alignment scores for sequence pairs 1–8 and BLASTN default gap model.

of the scoring matrix. For the gapped model, the following equation can be used to calculate the global optimum alignment score:

$$Score = n_{matches} * score_{match} - n_{mismatches} * score_{mismatch} - (gap_{score}) \qquad (5)$$

and,

$$gap_{score} = gap_{open} * n_{gapblocks} + gap_{extend} * \left(n_{gaps} - n_{gapblocks}\right) \qquad (6)$$

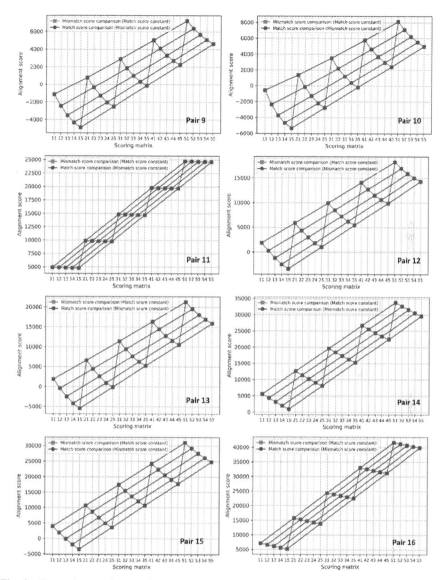

Fig. 4. Comparing scoring matrices and alignment scores for sequence pairs 9–16 and BLASTN default gap model.

where $n_{gapblocks}$ = the number of gap chunks of length one or more, n_{gaps} = the total number of gaps in the alignment. The percent identity can also be represented by the ratio, $opt_{align} = \frac{n_{matches}}{n_{mismatches}+n_{gaps}}$, and this ratio can be used to calculate the maximal optimal alignment among the 25 scoring matrices to compare which of them is most effective for a particular sequence pair and gap model. In some cases, the alignment length and the number of gaps are the same across all scoring matrices. For these pairs, the ratio $opt_{align} = \frac{n_{matches}}{n_{mismatches}}$ can be used instead. Table 3 gives the summarized results for scoring matrix choice comparison across all pairs and gap models.

As can be seen from Table 3, no specific scoring matrix is optimum for all sequence pairs. However, the scoring matrix with match score +4 and mismatch score −3 as well as the one with match score +5 and mismatch score −3 appear in 11 out of 16 pairs for the BLASTN default gap model. The scoring matrix with match score +5 and mismatch score −5 appears in 14 out of 16 cases for the EMBOSS default gap model. Scoring matrices targeted for the optimum percent identity do not appear in many cases for either gap model.

Since all the alignment scores are highly statistically significant, this suggests that the application-specific scoring scheme [16] may not apply to the case of the global pairwise alignment of nucleotides. The scoring matrices targeted at 50–75% identities (like EDNAS43, EDNAS53, and EDNAS55) are producing maximal optimal alignments for sequence pairs containing 30–99% identities as well. Therefore, these scoring matrices may be suitable for any pairwise global alignment.

4   Conclusion and Future Work

In this research, we have attempted to present an analysis of the effects of applying different uniform scoring matrices to nucleotide sequence pairs with varying percentage identities. For the two gap models and twenty-five substitution matrices, sixteen pairs of sequences were studied. The scoring matrix versus alignment score plots signified a positive linear relationship between increasing match scores and a negative linear relationship between negatively increasing mismatch scores. However, the overall effect of increasing match scores is a positive linear increase in alignment scores. The statistical significance of each global alignment was ascertained using p-values, and it was found that all the alignments were highly statistically significant. However, on comparing the percentage identity equivalent ratios, it was found that the application-specific scoring schemes may not apply to the global alignments of pairs of nucleotide sequences. Further, it was observed for the sixteen pairs that scoring matrices that were targeted at an optimal percent identity of 50–75% were equally suitable for sequence pairs having 30–99% similarity. Therefore, it is reasonable to conclude that, for the sequences studied, such scoring schemes are suitable for any global alignment of two nucleotide sequences.

Regardless, more research is necessary to strengthen this empirical study. Scaling up to larger sequences with varying percentage identities and employing numerous gap models may be the way forward to support this work. Uniform scoring matrices may be compared to mutation-based schemes. Exploration of the effects of different mutational scoring matrices is also further warranted.

References

1. BLAST Global Alignment. https://blast.ncbi.nlm.nih.gov/Blast.cgi?PAGE_TYPE=BlastS earch&PROG_DEF=blastn&BLAST_PROG_DEF=blastn&BLAST_SPEC=GlobalAln& LINK_LOC=BlastHomeLink

2. Chakraborty, A., Bandyopadhyay, S.: FOGSAA: fast optimal global sequence alignment algorithm. Sci. Rep. **3**, 1746 (2013). https://doi.org/10.1038/srep01746

3. Chaurasia, R., Ghose, U.: Assessing the statistical significance of pairwise gapped global sequence alignment of DNA nucleotides using Monte-Carlo techniques. In: Smys, S., Tavares, J.M.R.S., Bestak, R., Shi, F. (eds.) Proceedings of the 4th International Conference on Computational Vision and Bio-Inspired Computing (ICCVBIC 2020), Coimbatore, India, Advances in Intelligent Systems and Computing Series, vol. 1318, Ch. 5, pp. 57–70 (2021), Springer Nature Singapore Pte Ltd. Volume https://doi.org/10.1007/978-981-33-6862-0, Chapter https://doi.org/10.1007/978-981-33-6862-0_5

4. Dayhoff, M.O., Schwartz, R., Orcutt, B.C.: A model of evolutionary change in proteins. In Atlas of protein sequence and structure. Nat. Biomed. Res. **5**(3), pp. 345–358 (1978). ISBN 978-0-912466-07-1

5. EMBOSS Stretcher Help and Documentation. https://www.ebi.ac.uk/seqdb/confluence/display/JDSAT/EMBOSS+Stretcher+Help+and+Documentation

6. Henikoff, S., Henikoff, J.G.: Amino acid substitution matrices from protein blocks. In: Proceedings of the National Academy of Sciences of the United States of America, vol. 89, Issue 22, pp. 10915–10919 (1992). https://doi.org/10.1073/pnas.89.22.10915

7. Hirschberg, D.S.: A linear space algorithm for computing maximal common subsequences. Commun. ACM **18**, 341–343 (1975). https://doi.org/10.1145/360825.360861

8. Jones, D.T., Taylor, W.R., Thornton, J.M.: The rapid generation of mutation data matrices from protein sequences. Comput. Appl. Biosci.: CABIOS **8**(3), 275–282 (1992). https://doi.org/10.1093/bioinformatics/8.3.275

9. Kahveci, T., Ramaswamy, V., Tao, H., Li, T.: Approximate global alignment of sequences. In: Fifth IEEE Symposium on Bioinformatics and Bioengineering (BIBE'05), pp. 81–88. Minneapolis, MN, USA (2005). https://doi.org/10.1109/bibe.2005.13

10. Müller, T., Vingron, M.: Modeling amino acid replacement. J. Comput. Biol.: J. Comput. Mol. Cell Biol. **7**(6), 761–776 (2000). https://doi.org/10.1089/10665270050514918

11. Müller, T., Spang, R., Vingron, M.: Estimating amino acid substitution models: a comparison of Dayhoff's estimator, the resolvent approach, and a maximum likelihood method. Mol. Biol. Evol. **19**(1), 8–13 (2002). https://doi.org/10.1093/oxfordjournals.molbev.a003985

12. Myers, E.W., Miller, W.: Optimal alignments in linear space. Bioinformatics **4**, 11–17 (1988)

13. Needleman, S.B., Wunsch, C.D.: A general method applicable to the search for similarities in the amino acid sequence of two proteins. J. Mol. Biol. **48**, 443–453 (1970). https://doi.org/10.1016/0022-2836(70)90057-4

14. Pearson, W.R.: Selecting the right similarity-scoring matrix. Current Protoc. Bioinf. **43**, 3.5.1–3.5.9 (2013). https://doi.org/10.1002/0471250953.bi0305s43

15. Powell, D.R., Allison, L., Dix, T.I.: A versatile divide and conquer technique for optimal string alignment. Inf. Process. Lett. **70**, 127–139 (1999). https://doi.org/10.1016/s0020-0190(99)00053-8

16. States, D.J., Gish, W., Altschul, S.F.: Improved sensitivity of nucleic acid database searches using application-specific scoring matrices. METHODS: A companion to Methods in Enzymology, vol. 3, pp. 66–70 (1991)

17. Tammi, M.T.: Evaluate DNA scoring matrix values - find out what is the DNA scoring target frequency (2018). https://bioinformaticshome.com/online_software/evaluateDNAscoring/evaluateDNAscoring.html

18. Wikipedia contributors.: List of sequence alignment software, Wikipedia, The Free Encyclopedia. Retrieved from 15 Oct 2020. https://en.wikipedia.org/w/index.php?title=List_of_sequence_alignment_software&oldid=979369078

Case Based Reasoning Approaches for Reuse and Adaptation in Community Question Answering System

Lushaank Kancherla[✉] and Rajendra Prasath

Indian Institute of Information Technology, Sricity, Andhra Pradesh, India
{lushaank.k17,rajendra.prasath}@iiits.in

Abstract. A study was undertaken to fetch a set of similar questions asked through Community Question Answering system. Our aim is to propose a better generic and effective similarity method to question answering structure. We used a Case Based Reasoning system in Knowledge Reprocess as it explains fresh problems with elucidation of related challenges or cases solved in the past. The key idea in this approach is recovery of like cases. Data was gathered from Stackoverflow as well as GeeksforGeeks databases. Four computer languages *i.e.,* C, C++, Java and Python were used for the study. Generation of graphical tree of similar keywords was done with the help of Bayesian and Semantic similarities. Multiple questions were generated based on keywords using the above computer languages. The reuse and adaptation methods are involved in this model to improve the retrieval of queries.

Keywords: Case Based Reasoning · Community Question Answering · Bayesian similarity · Semantic similarity

1 Introduction

Development of a large number of Question Answering systems has taken place since 1960's [1, 2]. Traditionally, information retrieval was done through web exploring engines leading to beginning of query-response in Community Question Answering approaches (CQA). In the present system of social networking, CQA methods in the form of Stack Overflow and Yahoo! Answers, where general public ask questions and get their doubts clarified by others and at the same time provide information by answering the queries raised by clients [3]. Answering the queries raised by clients in existing QA systems is usually done after mining information through semantic resources [1, 4]. A change in answers structure would effect from text to multimedia text structure [5]. The existing QA systems are of various types *i.e.,* information (answers) may be provided in the form of paragraphs about a specific content or it may provide as precise statements giving details of persons, places, dates, etc.

Semantic related responses were studied through "word matching" methods and "bag-of-words" characteristics along with natural language processing challenges arising

R. Prasath—This work is supported by the seed grant fund provided by IIIT Sri City, Chittoor.

© Springer Nature Singapore Pte Ltd. 2021
A. K. Luhach et al. (Eds.): ICAICR 2020, CCIS 1393, pp. 126–140, 2021.
https://doi.org/10.1007/978-981-16-3660-8_12

in CQA scenario [3]. The CQA systems are able to make use of both implicit and explicit information to answer huge fresh queries in comparison to that of traditional knowledge mining methods. There exist several modes in performing the question answering, which could be done in the form of either Query–Response or Query-Query similarities [1, 6, 7]. Common query – query similarity method was proposed in favour of CQA methods through semantic graphs consisting of domain explicit keywords [8–10].

The online Community of Practice (CoP) situation was designed and developed in the form of CQA method allowing clients supporting one another mutually. The important functionalities of CoP supporting environment are to reprocess and transfer information along with assisting societal interactions [11]. The previous trials with virtual CoPs indicate that distribution of information increases vCoP with the application of social networking functionalities [12]. Hence, community information is utilized to the maximum extent based on community interactions.

In this context, the present study was undertaken to recommend an efficient and common similarity method for query - response system using Bayesian and Semantic similarities.

2 Research Perspective

2.1 CQA Approach

The approach offers appropriate answers for fresh questions in a short span of time. In contrast to that of conventional knowledge retrieval systems, they also bind explicit information, which are entrenched in varied populations in solving numerous novel queries added daily [3]. The researchers in open domain working in Yahoo! reply annals are involved in covering a broad range of themes [6, 13]. Some researchers involved in Stack overflow are enhancing the client knowledge by suggesting fresh themes as per client's fascination and knowledge [14]. Few researchers are involved in insurance sector through a constrained QA system [8]. The experience of CQA can be enhanced by adding superior queries, so that its environment can create more interest to its community [15].

A retrieval version was developed for identifying same queries through kernels and syntactic trees [16, 17]. Similarity evaluation could be determined through QA and Question-Question (QQ) resemblances. Some researchers respond to new queries by compiling the remarks of queries made by clients and ranking them, while few obtain responses for a query through matching a large number of query-response pairs [7, 8]. Few researchers [18–20] have done resemblances of query-responses through neural network types.

2.2 Case Based Analysis for Reuse of Information

The main purpose of CQA method is to benefit the information to community in general and existing clients in specific. Case based analysis is generally used for adjusting earlier solutions to acquaint to fresh challenge, employing earlier instances to describe novel circumstances, utilizing earlier cases to review new answers and initiating an unbiased elucidation to a fresh challenge [21]. While investigating for earlier similar queries, fresh queries sought by the client may not be akin to earlier queries, nevertheless pertinent subject matter could be seen within the associated conversation sequence. A case can be described as a query characterized with a text depiction along with supplementary keywords and elucidation of responses [6].

A case is illustrated in a structured CBR method by means of a restricted and organized collection of attribute data pair, which exemplifies the question and explanation (Fig. 1). In conversational CBR, clients are generally involved in a query–response discussion to augment a question which explains the conundrum [6]. Cases in textual CBR are free text and difficult to describe fuzzy logic, which are vague in nature. Hence, appropriate answers are difficult to get for precise questions. In order to overcome such circumstances, it is required to obtain semantic core of query texts ahead of lexical stage.

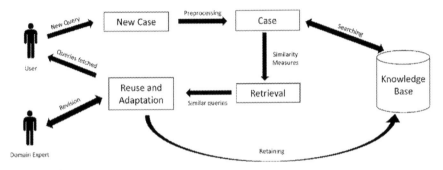

Fig. 1. Flow diagram of CBR for information reuse and adaptation

2.3 Textual Comparison Systems

Text similarity can be categorized into semantic and lexical similarity. Semantic similarities approaches are either graph or corpus build. Graph based similarity measures semantic association of words by utilizing details from knowledge or semantic graphs [22, 23]. Textual similarity process generally utilizes the methods of machine learning along with statistics to manage problems in research *viz.*, information mining, text depiction, categorization, etc. [24]. Generally, the queries in context of research are brief textual explanations along with supplementary keywords. Lexical similarity approach works on character structure and string categorization by manipulating distance measurement between text threads for estimated string comparison without involving the connotation of nearer words and whole phrase.

Text similarity approaches are utilized for applications like document grouping, categorization of texts, retrieval of information, finding of topics, generation of queries, tracing of topics, etc. Knowledge based similarity can be defined as one of semantic resemblance which recognizes extent of semblance among words with the help of knowledge gained from Semantic system. Corpus based similarity can be described as a semantic resemblance that establishes comparison involving words as per knowledge benefited from the big text corpus [22].

Vocabulary disparity problem have been reported, if document and question does not contain any common terms. In such cases, they tend to get less similarity marks irrespective of their semantically relationship. Context is another problem, which occur during the measurement of resemblance between two small text segments. While small texts give a partial context, larger texts and documents offer a realistic text to deduce an appropriate connotation of word or phrase [25]. Lexical matching and probabilistic approaches were found to be satisfactory for identifying semantically similar and topically interested matches respectively. A combined method of lexical, probabilistic and stemmed matches' results in better performance compared to that of a single approach [26, 27].

2.4 Graphical Textual Likeliness Approach

Semantic graphs from texts is generally done by expressing texts and term series as nodes and edges respectively. The resemblance of texts is measured by calculating distance relating to their characteristic graphs. Text similarity could be truncated as two components namely edge and note similarity. The individual component is measured and aggregate of two components is text similarity [27, 28]. Some researchers could prepare graphs from documents along with incorporation of supplementary details mined from freebase knowledge base. Similar studies have been undertaken, wherein measurement of graph nodes was done based on DBpedia knowledge base [29, 30].

A customised WordNet supported semantic similarity approach was proposed for disambiguated words and use of lexical sequence for mining primary semantic characters conveying subject of texts. Associating text to information graph and relating the resemblance between texts are generally done by evaluation and calculating paths in phases in reference graph [31]. A general semantic resemblance approach was suggested for undertaking knowledge graphs, which merges path length and statistical knowledge so as to describe precision and commonness of model [32].

2.5 Bayesian System for Query-Responses

Bayesian network is a plausible graphical version which denotes arbitrary set of variables along with its restrictive dependencies through directed acyclic graph. Researchers have studied the utility of a Bayesian network connecting every node term to nodes of document, which denotes documents catalogued with its term and suggested a comprehensive Bayesian network to understand the degree of association among documents, which is done by measuring its conditional probability of a given document whether it is relevant or not. SBN constituted document and term nodes in tiers are connected by every term to that of document nodes, which are catalogued [33].

Bayesian networks are done from lexical knowledge base WordNet through constructing synsets of WordNet along of query words and these synsets have been connected through lexical and semantic associations [34]. Machine learning was adopted in twin stages for making Bayesian framework, which could foresee creating precise response to queries. Various heuristics have been recreated for every client query into varying questions for redrafting a query and BN is utilized to test the validity of responses connected with that of a redrafted question [35].

3 Experimentation and Methodology

The authors have planned an overview of Semantic Bayesian approach for answering queries, which would be used for retrieval of queries and responses. The planned skeleton is depicted in Fig. 2.

Fig. 2. Skeleton for query retrieval based on Semantic Bayesian approach

This part explains studies performed for assessing the functioning of planned Semantic – Bayesian similarity models in CBR supported CQA approach. Datasets were collected from Stackoverflow and GeeksforGeeks database and created our own knowledge base. Semantic graphs were generated on various programming languages - "C", "C++", "Java", and "Python", which modelled domain specific semantics and was automatically developed. Dataset also consisted of queries as discussion strings by means of preliminary query along with responses.

Attempts were made to pre-process and adaption for the needs of this investigation. In this context, dataset queries were gathered manually from different online archives along with domain professional's queries – responses. The following characteristics were ascertained – values of A1 and A2 for semantic similarities, Bayesian limit, Semantic limit and Adaptation limits for similarity. The illustration of a case from knowledge base is portrayed in Fig. 3.

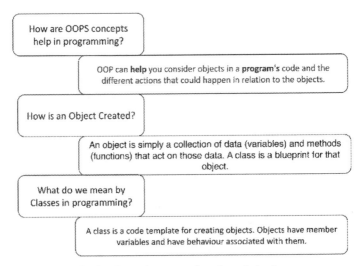

Fig. 3. Illustrating a case from knowledge base

3.1 Graphical Configuration

The keywords were made as a semantic graph in a hierarchical mode so that root node symbolises a broad model and nodes correspond to broad subject idea [9]. Once a fresh query is included in a case base, it would be held by combining with its matching keywords within semantic graph (Fig. 4).

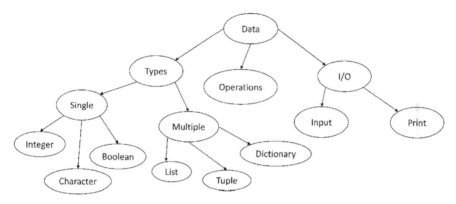

Fig. 4. Section of semantic graph based on Python language

3.2 Initial Processing

Before advancing to similarity evaluation, the initial phase was to alter query-context to keywords set. The questions might miss some important keywords, which might only be found in its context, but not in its keywords. There might also be some synonyms and we tried to find those terms from query-context and tried to add these in the keywords part. The keywords were then ranked according to semantic graph and keywords with better ranks are searched first.

Keywords given by clients are considered and seem to be insufficient to signify the queries gist. Later, the entire keywords are searched in graph and matching node. The node of keyword {nwi} would be saved, if present. Also, every node consisting of keyword along with their synonyms possessed a benefit, as various words are employed by clients in explaining a similar model. Every fresh query (FQ) consisted of a keywords set {nwi}. The measurement of similarity was done later by partitioning into Bayesian and Semantic assumptions.

3.3 Similarity Methods

3.3.1 Semantic Similarity

The influence of main identical queries in case base was done in keywords belonging to a fresh query. The associated keywords are characterized with the help of models semantically connected through graph. Fresh keywords are mined for similarity on the basis of their keywords re-appearance in queries and graphical nomenclature.

Postulation # 1 - Every keyword is clearly associated semantically with nodes, which are nearer to its nomenclature compared to that of distant nodes. In support of this hypothesis, distance metric can be described as semantic nearness amidst 2 keywords.

Distance_metric (w1, w2) = number of traversed arcs between w1 and w2

The algorithm of Dijkstra's is utilized for measuring distance metric for arriving at smallest distance amidst 2 keywords.

Postulation # 2- Keywords of several common parents are better associated with that of lesser common parents. The semantic nearness is described as depth *i.e.,* keywords farther from root node tend to be more precise and explanatory of its problem originated in query.

Postulation # 3- Keywords which are frequently found collectively in queries seem to be semantically associated. This means possessing same used contexts even though not alike with regard to that of Proximity and Distance.

Proximity (w1, w2) = number of common parents between w1 and w2

Postulation # 3 - Keywords which are frequently found collectively in queries seem to be semantically associated. This means possessing same used contexts even though not alike with regard to that of Proximity and Distance.

Cooccurrence (w1, w2) = number of shared questions between w1 and w2

The following evaluations were done in the investigation:

Path evaluation: This is done on the basis of proximity and distance. Similarity between 2 models is the function of location of model in nomenclature and distance of path associated with model [36], which is originated in Wu & Palmer's scaled model [37] that does not consider lso (w1, w2) measuring its depth but replaced with proximity.

Similar1(w1, w2) = (2 *Proximity (w1, w2))/(Distance_metric(w1, w2)+2 *Proximity(w1, w2))

Corpora evaluation: The rate of co-occurrence of queries in situation base is equal to belief of knowledge in a document [36, 38] as supplementary knowledge available in nodes of keywords is sum total of queries appeared.

Similar2(w1, w2) = (Cooccurence(w1, w2))/(nb_qry(w1) + nb_qry(w2))

The concluding similarity procedure is done by uniting the two measures (similarity 1 and similarity 2) along with allocation of a1 and a2 coefficients to each measure so as to maintain their involvement in equation that allows this stage in reaching queries, which don't consist of precise keywords to a fresh query but may include semantically alike keywords.

Sem_SIM(w1, w2) = a1(Similar1(w1, w2)) + a2(Similar2(w1, w2))

```
Algorithm: Semantic similarity
Input: {nwi} new query keywords
Output: {skj}keywords similar to nwi
For i in nw:
sk.append(nw[i])
        for j in key:
                s = Sem_sim(nw[i], key[j])
                if (nw[i] != key[j]) & (s > μ):
sk.append(key[j])
return sk
```

3.3.2 Bayesian Similarity

During queries retrieval method, the authors possessed keyword list {fkj}, which consisted of preliminary keywords to fresh query sought by client along with majority of like keywords used in the graph. Keyword query associations in graph were studied in sub graph of Bayesian, which allowed conducting the uncertainty limit in query similarity. A fresh query is regarded as an occurrence due to presence or absence of keywords. Later, the procedure of inference is operated with the help of equation consisting of query Qi, P(Qi|FQ) as probability significance of keywords {fwj} (denoting FQ).

$$Bay\_SIM = P(Qi|FQ) = \Sigma Nj = 1 P(fwj|Qi) * P(Qi)/P(fwj)$$

Queries are classified in descending probability and each query possessing probability higher than a given upper limit is mined and shown to clients. When semantic assumption step is omitted and continued retrieving similar queries on the basis of FQ keywords, there is a chance of preventing queries semantically linked to fresh queries as precise words are not utilized, which is the huge advantage. The similar questions were then fetched from the following results - Questions with more similarity are chosen first and Questions with more matched keywords are chosen.

```
Algorithm: Bayesian similarity
Input: {ski} keywords from semantic similarity
Output: {FQ} semantic similar queries from knowledge base for a
fresh query
For i in sk:
        for j in q:
                if sk[i] in q [j][key]:
                        b = P(q[j][ques] | sk[i])
                        if (b >α):
FQ.append(q[j])
return FQ
```

3.4   Reuse and Adaptation

The probability from Bayesian similarity measure is used for reuse and adaptation of new questions. Each question asked would be stored as logs with an answer and flag, representing a fully answered or partially answered or couldn't find the answer for the question asked. This could be achieved from keeping barriers in probability range of question, we get.

This part can be explained from probabilities and three main categories were explained:

1. No Change – If probability in a fresh query and old reached a certain threshold (namely, second threshold), then the new question isn't added directly to case base, but new keywords in a new question are added to questions that are in case base.
2. Some Change – When no question similarity could reach the second barrier, but some questions could be in between the two barriers. This is a special case in which questions in case base might provide just a part of solution but not the whole. This could either give parts of answer in case base or some parts might be missing. So, this will be added to case base after confirming with domain expert for the model.
3. Changes – When the threshold couldn't reach the first barrier. That means related question and answers aren't found in case base and domain expert needs to take the case and manually update it to case base manually.

Algorithm: Reuse and Adaptation

Input: {fq} new query with keywords

Output: whether added to knowledge base or not

```
For i in oq:
s = sim(fq, oq[i])
      c = 0
      if s > β1:
            for j in fq[keywords]:
                  if fq[keywords][j] not in oq[i][keywords] :
                        oq[i][keywords].append(fq[keywords][j])
                        c = 2
      elif s < β2:
            continue
      else:
pfq.append(oq[i])
            c = 1
if len(pfq) != 0:
      FQ = adap_sem(pfq)
if c == 0:return("No new questions found")
elif c == 1: return("Answer found")
else: return("Answer found, but repeated")
```

4 Assessment

4.1 Characteristics and Threshold Limits

The characteristics of similarity were performed and similarity was measured between w1 and w2 keywords with the help of using a1 and a2 for combining corpora and taxonomy measures. The following activities were performed - few arbitrary queries were selected from information base comprising semantic graph and keywords. Both the similarities were measured with previous keywords for each query. The five important keywords were taken for matching using similarity measures. Lastly it was decided to ask the human in evaluating the model.

4.1.1 Acceptance Rates for a1 and a2

While conducting similarity approach for variables a1 and a2 with lot of queries in case base, we might come up with this type of conclusion, that for less queries, acceptance rate would be higher due to the fact that there aren't a lot of queries in getting an accurate result (Table 1). But in later cases, we might say that it could be better, when both variables are equal to 0.5, while 'a1' being just slightly larger than 'a2'.

Table 1. Acceptance rates (AR) for a1 and a2 with variable number of queries.

No. of queries	a1	a2	AR %	No. of queries	a1	a2	AR %	No. of queries	a1	a2	AR %
10	0	1	15	100	0	1	32	1000	0	1	40
	0.25	0.75	17		0.25	0.75	45		0.25	0.75	58
	0.50	0.50	22		**0.50**	**0.50**	**66**		**0.50**	**0.50**	**65**
	0.75	**0.25**	**30**		0.75	0.25	56		0.75	0.25	48
	1	0	26		1	0	33		1	0	30

4.1.2 Semantic Limit

Generally, Sem_SIM model is utilized in semantic conclusion stage on every fresh keyword (nwi) for ascertaining the precise word from semantic graph. When keywords possessing value Sem_SIM (nwi, wi) was found lesser than a threshold, it is not used in the study. The following activities were performed – similar related test was conducted as given above. The similarity performance was utilized for measuring keywords in queries along with others in semantic graph. The results indicated that uppermost 32 percent of classified keywords are nearly similar semantically. In general, we use this value in place of a predetermined limit.

4.1.3 Bayesian Limit

When a fresh query is sought by client, a group of similar queries are got from earlier queries associated with preliminary keywords corresponding to the fresh query along with keywords mined during the earlier stages. During Bayesian conclusion stage, probability for every client query is evaluated along with its importance to fresh query with the help of Bayesian conclusion. Each query possessing probability of $P(Qi|FQ)$ higher than the limit is regarded same and sent back to client. The authors have taken into account thirty per cent random selections for regarding a fresh query for which algorithm similarity was done to recover related queries. Semantic likeliness was done initially to every fresh query for deciding semantically like keywords. A record of similar queries was later recovered from complete dataset originated from keywords. Bayesian conclusions were used on every query and arranged based on decreased probability limits. Lastly human evaluation was done by domain professional in selecting lowest probability limit beyond which the entire queries are pertinent for a particular query. The mean Bayesian conclusion limit was found to be 0.22.

4.1.4 Adaptation Limits

Given a new query, similarity approaches are initially checked and later retrieve like queries from case base. Appropriate evaluations were done for measuring similarity along with bifurcating similarity of queries into different classes. Initially, an array of queries as fresh queries are taken and algorithm similarities were run for retrieving. Semantic likeliness was operated followed by Bayesian similarity towards a fresh query. Similarity approaches were verified for various tasks and limits were worked out. Lastly, human evaluation was done for every task and limits were again worked out. The adaptation limit was established and $\beta 1$ was found to be 0.31, while $\beta 2$ was found to be same as that of Bayesian conclusion limit.

4.2 Association with Human Assessment

The precision and efficiency of used Bayesian and Semantic similarities was verified with mandatory retrieved queries to that of results given by domain professional. This was intended to investigate whether this approach could identify similar queries akin to human professional. The series set contained thirty per cent of arbitrary sample of dataset taken and human professional would manually appraise (1–5 scale) for every 2 queries taken from dataset. Later, algorithm of similarity approach was employed for allocating a routine rate of similarity between every two queries taken in same dataset (Fig. 5).

4.3 Recall and Precision

A better precision approach for query response method and search engines is its capacity to give back a related result along with entire related results. Precision is a component of related occurrences among retrieved occurrences, while recall is a component of related occurrences over retrieved occurrences. The best possible balance has to be found

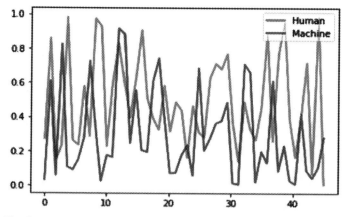

Fig. 5. Association of our proposed approach to that of human evaluation

between recall and precision for getting more likely similar queries that are semantically pertinent. There is also a chance of getting less related findings, which are fairly similar and could be handy to client. With the help of this test, Bayesian conclusion coefficient could be evaluated and human evaluation have judged that the approach obtained elevated precision (P is equal to 0.82) along with high recall (R = 0.70).

5 Discussion

The query-context likeliness method in this study is supported through semantic graphical system, which consists of query, context and keywords. The use of context in text could be useful for identifying keywords missed from the query, while mentioning keywords would help semantically as both query and context seems to be short texts. The user asks a query in a textual format and query is broken down into keywords. Similar queries for every keyword could be arrived by using Semantic and Bayesian similarities. Reuse and adaptation method can then be used for checking, if the new question could be revised or retained. Besides, association graph has been made by evaluating the method with a human, which showed the efficiency of our method. This investigation proves that we could efficiently perform reuse and adaptation in Community Question Answering model.

6 Conclusions

Knowledge reuse and adaptation has been recommended in our research paper that would efficiently be used for retrieval of queries from the model. Bayesian conclusion model was used for semantic improbability from texts in ordinary dialects. Using a Community Question Answering model, a case base was created. The model was checked by asking a new query and tested it with existing query in the case base. The model works better for shorter natural language texts, which require textual similarity. Instead of simply having query-query similarity approach, a query-context similarity approach was also included for better results. This approach along with reuse and adaptation method gave a better retrieval process. Such models might be also used in question duplicate detection models and question recommendation.

References

1. Mishra, A., Jain, S.K.: A survey on question answering systems with classification. J. King Saud Univ. Comput. Inf. Sci. **28**, 345–361 (2016)
2. Kolomiyets, O., Moens, M.F.: A survey on question answering technology from an information retrieval perspective. Inf. Sci. **181**, 5412–5434 (2011)
3. Bielikova Srba, M.: A comprehensive survey and classification of approaches for community question answering. ACM Trans. Web **10**(3), 1–63 (2016)
4. Suresh Kumar, G., Zayaraz, G.: Concept relation extraction using Naive Bayes classifier for ontology-based question answering systems. J. King Saud Univ. Comput. Inf. Sci. **27**, 13–24 (2014)
5. Burger, J., et al.: Issues, Tasks and Program Structures to Roadmap Research in Question and Answering, NIST (2002)
6. Oumayma, C., Ahlame, B., Groux-Leclet, D.: Integrating a Bayesian semantic similarity approach into CBR for knowledge reuse in community question answering. Knowl. Based Syst. **185**, 104919 (2019)
7. Joty, S., et al.: Global thread-level inference for comment classification in community question answering. In: Proceedings of the Conference on Empirical Methods in Natural Language Processing, Lisbon, Portugal, pp. 573–578 (2015)
8. Feng, M., Xiang, B., Glass, M.R., Wang, L.: Applying deep learning to answer selection: a study and an open task. In: IEEE Workshop on Automatic Speech Recognition and Understanding, Scottsdale, USA, pp. 813–820 (2015)
9. Chergui, O., Begdouri, A., Groux-leclet, D.: A knowledge-based approach for keywords modeling into a semantic graph. Int. J. Inf. Sci. Technol. **2**(1), 12–14 (2018)
10. Wheeler, S.: Creating social presence in digital learning environments: a presence of mind? In: Proceedings of TAFE Conference, Queensland, Australia, p. 6 (2005)
11. Chergui, O., Begdouri, A., Groux-Leclet, D.: CBR approach for knowledge reuse in a community of practice for university students. In: Colloquium on Information Science and Technology Cist, pp. 553–558 (2017)
12. Jadidinejad, A.H., Mahmoudi, F., Meybodi, M.R.: Conceptual feature generation for textual information using a conceptual network constructed from Wikipedia. Expert Syst. **33**(1), 92–106 (2016)
13. Zhang, W.N., Liu, T., Yang, Y., Cao, L., Zhang, Y., Ji, R.: A topic clustering approach to finding similar questions from large question and answer archives. PLoS ONE **9**(3), e71511 (2014)
14. Tumenbayar, G., Kao, H.Y.: Topic suggestion by Bayesian network enhanced tag inference in community question answering. In: Conference on Technologies and Applications of Artificial Intelligence, Hsinchu, Taiwan, pp. 178–185 (2016)
15. Baltadzhieva, A.: Question quality in community question answering forums: a survey. SIGKDD Explor. **17**(1), 8–13 (2015)
16. Wang, K., Ming, Z., Chua, T.S.: A syntactic tree matching approach to finding similar questions in community-based QA services. In: Proceedings of the 32nd International ACM SIGIR Conference on Research and Development in Information Retrieval, Boston, USA, pp. 187–194 (2009)

17. San Martino, G.D., Cedeno, A.B., Romeo, S., Uva, A., Moschitti, A.: Learning to re-rank questions in community question answering using advanced features. In: Proceedings of the 25th ACM International on Conference on Information and Knowledge Management, Indianapolis, Indiana, USA, pp. 1997–2000 (2016)
18. Severyn, A., Moschitti, A.: Learning to rank short text pairs with convolutional deep neural networks. In: Proceedings of the 38th International ACM SIGIR Conference on Research and Development in Information Retrieval, Santiago, Chile, pp. 373–382 (2015)
19. Cedeno, A.B., et al.: ConvKN at SemEval-2016 Task 3: answer and question selection for question answering on Arabic and English fora. In: Proceedings of the 10th International Workshop on Semantic Evaluation, San Diego, USA, pp. 896–903 (2016)
20. Mohtarami, M., et al.: SLS at SemEval-2016 Task 3: neural based approaches for ranking in community question answering. In: Proceedings of the International Workshop on Semantic Evaluation, San Diego, USA, pp. 828–835 (2016)
21. Kolodner, J.L.: An introduction to case-based reasoning. Artif. Intell. Rev. **6**, 3–34 (1992)
22. Gomaa, W.H., Fahmy, A.A.: A survey of text similarity approaches. Int. J. Comput. Appl. **68**(13), 975–8887 (2013)
23. Atif, M.: Utilising Wikipedia for text mining applications. Ph.D. dissertation, College of Engineering and Informatics, National University of Ireland, Galway (2015)
24. John, S.F.: Semantic networks. In: Encyclopedia of Artificial Intelligence, 2nd edn. Wiley, New York (1992)
25. Gabrilovich, E., Markovitch, S.: Wikipedia-based semantic interpretation for natural language processing. J. Artif. Intell. Res. **34**, 443–498 (2009)
26. Metzler, D., Dumais, S., Meek, C.: Similarity measures for short segments of text. In: Amati, G., Carpineto, C., Romano, G. (eds.) ECIR 2007. LNCS, vol. 4425, pp. 16–27. Springer, Heidelberg (2007). https://doi.org/10.1007/978-3-540-71496-5_5
27. Paul, C., Rettinger, A., Mogadala, A., Knoblock, C.A., Szekely, P.: Efficient graph-based document similarity. In: Sack, H., Blomqvist, E., d'Aquin, M., Ghidini, C., Ponzetto, S.P., Lange, C. (eds.) ESWC 2016. LNCS, vol. 9678, pp. 334–349. Springer, Cham (2016). https://doi.org/10.1007/978-3-319-34129-3_21
28. Liu, Z., Chen, A.: A graph-based text similarity algorithm. In: National Conference on Information Technology and Computer Science, pp. 614–617 (2012)
29. Wang, C., Song, Y., Li, H., Zhang, M., Han, J.: KnowSim: a document similarity measure on structured heterogeneous information networks. In: Proceeding of IEEE International Conference of Data Mining, Atlanta city, USA, pp. 1015–1020 (2015)
30. Schuhmacher, M., Ponzetto, S.P.: Knowledge-based graph document modeling. In: ACM International Conference on Web Search and Data Mining, pp. 543–552 (2014)
31. Wei, T., Lu, Y., Chang, H., Zhou, Q., Bao, X.: A semantic approach for text clustering using WordNet and lexical chains. Expert Syst. Appl. **42**, 2264–2275 (2015)
32. Zhu, G., Iglesias, C.A.: Computing semantic similarity of concepts in knowledge graphs. IEEE Trans. Knowl. Data Eng. **29**(1), 72–85 (2017)
33. Acid, S., De. Campos, L.M., Fernández-Luna, J.M., Huete, J.F.: An information retrieval model based on simple Bayesian networks. Int. J. Intell. Syst. **18**(2), 251–265 (2003)
34. Wordnet: A lexical database for English. https://wordnet.princeton.edu/
35. Azari, D., Horvitz, E., Dumais, S., Brill, E.: Actions, answers, and uncertainty: a decision-making perspective on web-based question answering. Inf. Process. Manage. **40**, 849–868 (2004)
36. Meng, L., Huang, R., Gu, J.: A review of semantic similarity measures in WordNet. Int. J. Hybrid Inf. Technol. **6**(1), 1–12 (2013)

37. Wu, Z., Palmer, M.: Verb semantics and lexical selection. In: Proceedings of 32nd Annual Meeting of the Association for Computational Linguistics, Las Cruces, New Mexico, pp. 133–138 (1994)
38. Zhou, Z., Wang, Y., Gu, J.: New model of semantic similarity measuring in Wordnet. In: 3rd International Conference on Intelligent System and Knowledge Engineering, Xiamen, China, pp. 85–89 (2008)

Depression Detection During the Covid 19 Pandemic by Machine Learning Techniques

Sofia Arora$^{(\boxtimes)}$, Arun Malik$^{(\boxtimes)}$, Parul Khurana, and Isha Batra

Lovely Professional University, Jalandhar, Punjab, India
{arun.17442,parul.khurana,isha.17451}@lpu.co.in

Abstract. Coronavirus disease 2019 is a global pandemic caused by the (SARS-CoV-2) Severe Acute Respiratory Syndrome. During the outbreak of an infectious disease, the population's psychological reactions play a crucial role in affecting both the spread of the disease and the occurrence of emotional distress. It is recognized that there are number of techniques and tools which are used to detect the depression. To assess whether the individual is depressed or not, machine learning techniques are used. The course of action is based on texts, images, videos and emoticons etc. Among different techniques, it is analyzed that none of the technique is using the probability method to detect the depression. In probability method, one can create a database, which is a collection of words related to emotions like happiness, sadness and anger etc., The probability would be set for all such words in the database and then it will be calculated by various techniques which shows the level of depression of a person. This paper summarized the findings on the identification of depressive mood disorders, using emotion analysis methods and techniques. The author focused on research that identifies irregular activity patterns on social networks automatically. The studies selected used the classic off-the-shelf classifiers to evaluate the knowledge available for lexicon use. To resolve this problem, the web application will be developed which will perform sentiment analysis with the help of classification function which recognizes the ratio of depressive and non-depressive thoughts.

Keywords: COVID-19 · Depression · Machine-learning · Probability

1 Introduction

Psychological reactions to pandemics include maladaptive behaviors and emotional distress. Particularly vulnerable are those who are susceptible to psychological problems. COVID-19 is taking its toll, leaving many with profound emotional wounds. On the positive side, through numerous acts of encouragement, compassion and kindness, this pan-demic shows the strength of humanity; people assist each other in a number of imaginative ways. Yet other negative characteristics, including greed and what we call pathological racism, a form of modern-day tribalism, are still being exposed. Furthermore, the vulnerabilities of some subpopulations are revealed: the elderly, the imprisoned, the disabled and people living in poverty. Concern related to COVID-19 (e.g., main-training

© Springer Nature Singapore Pte Ltd. 2021
A. K. Luhach et al. (Eds.): ICAICR 2020, CCIS 1393, pp. 141–151, 2021.
https://doi.org/10.1007/978-981-16-3660-8_13

employment, coronavirus testing) may be associated with symptoms of mental health. The early weeks of the pandemic saw dramatic changes in daily life, with students moving remotely during university closures and attending classes, transitioning to remote work for other young adults, or losing jobs. Such disturbances can present a greater risk to mental health problems for an already vulnerable group. A depressed person regularly feels sad, hopeless and loses interest in physical symptoms such as activities and experiences Chronic or digestive ailments. Depression is one of the biggest societal issues, and is rising millions of people suffered from depression every day and just a small proportion fractions of these are handled appropriately. Depression is one of the leading causes of mental illness and has been shown to raise early death risk. This is also a significant cause of suicidal ideation and leads to serious disability in daily life. According to WHO, depression has 2nd rank in all over the world. Social networking sites are nowadays the most common way for people to exchange information, from work problems to personal issues. People with health issues prefer to share their thoughts about counselling, helping or actually relieving pain. It offers a tremendous incentive for all users to be proactively identified and directed to medical assistance as soon as possible. On social networking sites people share their thoughts, beliefs, emotions and feelings. Analysis of sentiment and opinion mining help to understand the beliefs, thoughts, behaviors, emotions and feelings of the people.

2 Related Work

Social networking is another type of medical assistance to recognize mental illness signs, such as depression. This paper summarized the findings on the identification of depressive mood disorders, using emotion analysis methods and techniques. The author focused on research that identifies irregular activity patterns on social networks automatically.

I.   In order to assess the information available for lexicon use, the selected studies used classic off-the-shelf classifiers. The author also identified the complexity of processing temporal information and the mixture of various types of information [1]. A person who is depressed will always feel sad, hopeless and often loses his interest in regular basis activities and also faces physical symptoms. In the past decades, the doctors analyzed depression through face to face interaction and provide the treatment to the patients. However, past research shows that most patients in their early stages of depression did not take the aid of doctors which gives the results of declination in their mental health condition [2].

II. On the other hand, many individuals in this world use social networking sites like Twitter, Facebook, Instagram, etc. to share their emotions and opinions. According to the author, there is a lack of work in this application which is used to identify depression on social media like twitter etc. To resolve this problem, the web application is developed that perform sentiment analysis with the help of classification function which recognizes the ratio of depressive and non-depressive thoughts [3, 4]. Due to the number of electronic documents accessible from various resources, the study of supervised learning is growing in importance today. Text classification is defined because the work characterizes a group document into predefined groups according to its subjects. The main purpose of classifying text is to extract textual resource information. It deals with the process of retrieving the information, classification and machine learning techniques to identify various patterns [5].

III. One ground breaking area of research that deserves attention is Persian opinion mining. The Persian language is classified into approaches based on machine learning and lexicons. Such techniques are used to overcome polarity. In this paper, a systematic approach to machine learning and lexicon-based techniques is carried out, and then the issue of rating prediction in Persian is suggested by the Hybrid approach.. At last the part of machine learning, feature selection process, methods of normalization are investigated. The experimental results indicate this approach is efficient in detecting polarity [6]. In today's world, health is an important aspect of society. A quick burst of any disease becomes a fright among people. So, it is very important to identify a disease at early stage so that it is not increasing in a region. With the rapid development of social media, public can easily precise its opinion, which can be helpful to observe the spread of disease in different regions. Twitter is one of the famous social media on which people post their feelings and opinions. Author offered twitter analysis of health care which deals with tweets related to health through sentiment analysis. The author also reveals the contrast of current work with the proposed method as regards accuracy [7].

IV. The proposed method is a novel approach to classifying depression health tweets which helps identify health status in a living environment [8, 9]. Internet these days, is a sea of raw data, only after processing, establishing and arranging of raw data, it can be observed as information. According to the author, sentiment analysis tools were slow, huge and computationally weighty to observe such data [10, 12]. To solve this problem of effectively analyzing feelings, a novel process, called partial textual entailment, was implemented. It was used to measure semantic similarity between the posted tweets so that grouping of related tweets could be easier. This approach was first used in this paper to decrease the computational overhead according to the author [13]. The World Health Organization (WHO) recognises that depression is increasingly growing in today's world. More than 300 million persons suffered from depression in these days. There are many types of methodologies which are helpful to come out from this problem but still there are controversies and criticisms between clinicians among the accuracy of the results [14, 15].

V. In terms of patient medical information, the structure of this analysis was considered in the context of data mining, data analytics, and data visualization. The main goal was to construct a self-serving psychometric analyzer capable of conducting rapid computational linguistics, delivering a mental well-being summary based on previous patient records, medications and treatments [16, 17]. Depression can be considered as a common disabling mental disorder which has a high impact on society. The Opinion Research covers the use of methodologies for the production of natural languages and text mining. The aim of an examination of sentiments is to recognize opinions or feelings [18]. Methodologies for sensitivity analysis may provide useful methods and frameworks for tracking mental illness and depression [19, 20].

VI.   The applications of sentiment analysis and appropriate methodologies for assessing detection of depression were explored in this paper. An initial design of a hybrid multimodal system for tracking depression conditions based on SA and AC methodologies has been suggested [21, 22]. While mental illness has improved in recent eras, many instances remain unnoticed. On Twitter, Facebook, on which depression is easy to find, the symptoms of mental illness are observed. The depressed users are identified using screening surveys and their posts on twitter. To identify the depressed users, automated detection methods are used [23, 24]. The researchers indicated that in various online settings, depression and other mental illnesses became observable. Technological advances in the processing of natural languages and machine learning techniques are helpful because of the enormous amount of data available on social media [25]. Amount of work to diagnose depression through Twitter using natural language processing and machine learning techniques [26].

VII. In today's age, social networking has the highest rank in the society to communicate. Due to the immense use of social networking, it can be seen that one to one interaction is mostly avoided by most of the people [27]. The prime reason for preference of social networking over personal interaction is that it has its own culture, which scatters the personal communication of individual or communities or society to all over the world. Twitter is one of the social media sites most widely used these days [28]. To perform opinion mining of customer reviews on twitter, author has collected 600 million public tweets. These tweets were collected using security tool and feature generation. Further, Hybridization technique was used for classification accuracy in sentiment analysis [29]. Used technique with machine learning classification gives 90% accuracy for classifying sentiment tweets into positive, negative and neutral. Mood analyzer that is a revolutionary approach to emotion analysis, it describes the changes in the user's mood by adopting an unsupervised learning technique. This novel approach uses an internal model to define and classify the polarity of feelings into classes [30, 31]. In this paper the internal model identifies the polarization of the messages which decreases the need of normalization. With this internal model the efficiency of algorithm is increasing. The algorithmic approach alongside with the results also show the functioning of the application in an well-organized manner and this approach is also useful to hold the suicide attempts which is due to cyber-depression [32]. Social Network Sites (SNS) offers a forum for people to express their thoughts, emotions and beliefs, enabling study groups to explore a variety of facets of human behavior and psychological distress. It also indicates mental illness and can be categorized into depression, nervousness, bipolar disorder, and so on. Depression is the most common psychiatric illness with symptoms such as depression, depressed mood, and tiredness, insufficient concentration, feeling bad and attempted suicide.

VIII. In this article, the author suggested a method for categorizing individuals into depression of the displayer and non-displayer. The advanced method is used for individual treatment of a major depressive disorder (MDD). This built method used Facebook as a responsible source for detecting individual depression trends

[33]. Depression is the most common psychiatric illness, and the most severe. Owing to flawed methods of study, it is not easily identified and provides significant consequences for public and individual safety. Recent studies show the detection of the depression by use of social media because amount of people share their feelings, thoughts and views on social media. In order to provide new perspectives for public health research, the author has analyzed spatial trends to apply GIS methods to social media data. The tool is designed to classify distressed Twitter users and use GIS technology to analyze the spatial designs. This technique can improve the depression treatment techniques [34, 35]. There are many datasets creating from social networks which are appreciated in several arenas such as sociology and psychology. In this paper the author relates psychology field data mining to find dissatisfied consumers of social network services. Firstly, emotion analysis is provided for the application of vocabulary and man-made guidelines for measuring depression, the author says [36]. A model of depression detection is then developed which is based on expected process, although this model of depression was based on Chinese vocabulary. It was also found that homophilia is evident in the depression user community, indicating the depressed individual's friends are more likely to be suicidal and different types of experiences provide different results [37]. Naive Bayes classifier, it is a common algorithm in classification field. This classifier is easy to recognize and implementation of classifiers are particularly fast. A model of depression detection is then developed which is based on expected process, although this model of depression was based on Chinese vocabulary. It was also found that homophilia is evident in the depression user community, indicating the depressed individual's friends are more likely to be suicidal and different types of experiences provide different results. The experimental findings have proved the efficiency of this algorithm as opposed to other algorithms such as CART, DT, and MLP's [38, 39] (Fig. 1).

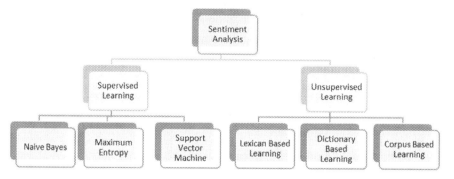

Fig. 1. Sentiment analysis

3 Proposed Methodology

This proposed methodology is novel, prediction based and it would be helpful for the society to identify the depression level of the person at early stages of this disease. Proposed Methodology provides the flow of activities to be performed for the completion of each of the objective for the research work. For the tracking of work progress flow (Fig. 2):

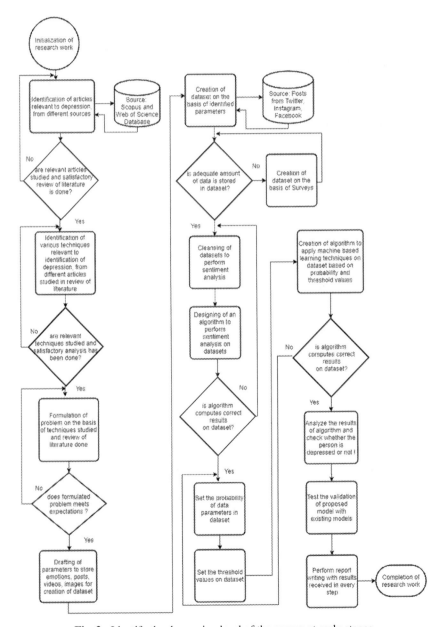

Fig. 2. Identify the depression level of the person at early stages

In this figure, firstly formulate the problem with the help of literature survey and identifying various techniques which is used to detect the depression. In the next step, parameters will be identified and dataset will be created. After creating the dataset, the data will be cleaning and design an algorithm to perform sentiment analysis. Furthermore, if the algorithm computes correct result, the probability will be set of data with threshold value. After this the algorithm will be introduced for machine leaning techniques which will apply on datasets. At the end analyze the results and testing will be done.

4   Result Analysis from Literature Survey

In this section, analysis was performed using different parameters such as survey-id, gender, age, married, N-of-children, educational level, total-member, gained-asset, durable-asset, save-asset, living-expenses, depressed. The various outcomes of these parameters are given by a literature survey.

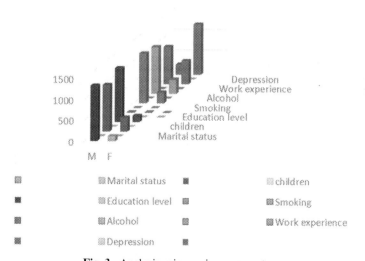

Fig. 3. Analysis using various parameters

These figures show the analysis of different methods 3 and 4 on the basis of certain factors, i.e., sex, age, married, N-of-children, level of education, total-member, gained-asset, durable-asset, save-asset, living-expenses, depressed, (Fig. 3 and 4).

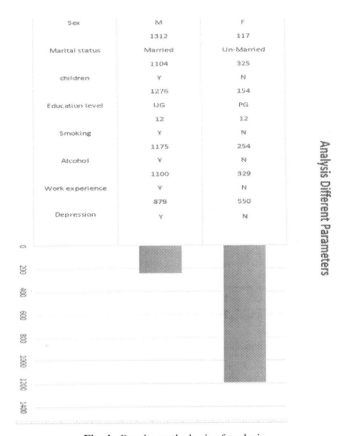

Fig. 4. Results on the basis of analysis

5 Limitation

In this proposed methodology, the dataset will be collected from the surveys also. But the survey will not give more samples. Because everyone is not interested to take part in survey. So, to resolve this problem we will also fetch the data from the social networking sites.

6 Conclusion and Future Work

The various techniques used for data collection are compared in this paper. On the basis of their research aims, suggested methods, input and output, this comparison was carried out. Later, it demonstrates an overview of the outcomes of some of the current techniques. These techniques assess performance on the basis of survey-id, gender, age, married, n-of-children, education-level, total-member, gained-asset, durable-asset, save-asset, living-expenses, depressed. It illustrates that better tools have been used for some systems and others degrade the functionality of the corresponding process. It shows the outcomes that can be further strengthened and can be used as potential directions for study.

Acknowledgements. The writers are grateful to Mr. Baljinder Singh.

References

1. Giuntini, F.T., Cazzolato, M.T., de Jesus Dutra dos Reis, M., Campbell, A.T., Traina, A.J.M., Ueyama, J.: A review on recognizing depression in social networks: challenges and opportunities. J. Ambient Intell. Hum. Comput. **11**, 4713–4729 (2019)
2. Wisnu, H., Afif, M., Ruldevyani, Y.: Sentiment analysis on customer satisfaction of digital payment in Indonesia: a comparative study using KNN and Naïve Baye (2020)
3. Ziwei, B.Y., Chua, H.N.: An application for classifying depression in tweets. In: Proceedings of the 2nd International Conference on Computing and Big Data, pp. 37–41 (2019)
4. Kadhim, A.I.: Survey on supervised machine learning techniques for automatic text classification. Artif. Intell. Rev. **52**(1), 273–292 (2019). https://doi.org/10.1007/s10462-018-096 77-1
5. Padhanarath, P., Aunhathaweesup, Y., Kiattisin, S.: Sentiment analysis and relationship between social media and stock market: pantip. com and SET. In: IOP Conference Series: Materials Science and Engineering, vol. 620, no. 1, p. 012094. IOP Publishing (2019)
6. Basiri, M.E., Kabiri, A.: HOMPer: a new hybrid system for opinion mining in the Persian language. J. Inf. Sci. **46**, 101–117 (2019)
7. Alamsyah, A., Bernatapi, E.A.: Evolving customer experience management in internet service provider company using text analytics. In: 2019 International Conference on ICT for Smart Society (ICISS), vol. 7, pp. 1–6. IEEE (2019)
8. Arora, P., Arora, P.: Mining Twitter data for depression detection. In: 2019 International Conference on Signal Processing and Communication (ICSC), pp. 186–189. IEEE (2019)
9. Aragón, M.E., López-Monroy, A.P., González-Gurrola, L.C., Montes, M.: Detecting depression in social media using fine-grained emotions. In: Proceedings of the 2019 Conference of the North American Chapter of the Association for Computational Linguistics: Human Language Technologies, vol. 1 (Long and Short Papers), pp. 1481–1486 (2019)
10. Nagarajan, S.M., Gandhi, U.D.: Classifying streaming of Twitter data based on sentiment analysis using hybridization. Neural Comput. Appl. **31**(5), 1425–1433 (2018). https://doi. org/10.1007/s00521-018-3476-3
11. Wongkoblap, A., Vadillo, M.A., Curcin, V.: Researching mental health disorders in the era of social media: systematic review. J. Med. Internet Res. **19**(6), e228 (2017)
12. Priya, B.G.: Emoji based sentiment analysis using KNN. Int. J. Sci. Res. Rev. **7**(4), 859–865 (2019)
13. Wu, L., Qi, M., Jian, M., Zhang, H.: Visual sentiment analysis by combining global and local information. Neural Process. Lett. **51**(3), 2063–2075 (2019). https://doi.org/10.1007/s11063-019-10027-7
14. Gupta, S., Lakra, S., Kaur, M.: Analysis using partial textual entailment sentiment. In: 2019 International Conference on Machine Learning, Big Data, Cloud and Parallel Computing (COMITCon), pp. 51–55. IEEE (2019)
15. Hee, V., et al.: Automatic detection of cyberbullying in social media text. PloS one **13**(10), e0203794 (2018)

16. Malik, M., Naaz, S., Ansari, I.R.: Sentiment analysis of Twitter Data using Big Data Tools and Hadoop ecosystem. In: Pandian, D., Fernando, X., Baig, Z., Shi, F. (eds.) ISMAC. LNCVB, vol. 30, pp. 857–863. Springer, Cham (2019). https://doi.org/10.1007/978-3-030-00665-5_83

17. Samareh, A., Jin, Y., Wang, Z., Chang, X., Huang, S.: Detect depression from communication: how computer vision, signal processing, and sentiment analysis join forces. IISE Trans. Healthcare Syst. Eng. **8**(3), 196–208 (2018)

18. Vij, A., Pruthi, J.: An automated psychometric analyzer based on sentiment analysis and emotion recognition for healthcare. Procedia Comput. Sci. **132**, 1184–1191 (2018)

19. Zhang, W., Xu, M., Jiang, Q.: Opinion mining and sentiment analysis in social media: challenges and applications. In: Nah, F.F.H., Xiao, B.S. (eds.) HCIBGO. LNCS, vol. 10923, pp. 536–548. Springer, Cham (2018). https://doi.org/10.1007/978-3-319-91716-0_43

20. Biradar, A., Totad, S.G.: Detecting depression in social media posts using machine learning. In: Santosh, K.C., Hegadi, R.S. (eds.) RTIP2R. CCIS, vol. 1037, pp. 716–725. Springer, Singapore (2019). https://doi.org/10.1007/978-981-13-9187-3_64

21. Fatima, I., Mukhtar, H., Ahmad, H.F., Rajpoot, K.: Analysis of user-generated content from online social communities to characterise and predict depression degree. J. Inf. Sci. **44**(5), 683–695 (2018)

22. Deshpande, M., Rao, V.: Depression detection using emotion artificial intelligence. In: 2017 International Conference on Intelligent Sustainable Systems (ICISS), pp. 858–862. IEEE (2017)

23. Aldarwish, M.M., Ahmad, H.F.: Predicting depression levels using social media posts. In: 2017 IEEE 13th International Symposium on Autonomous decentralized System (ISADS), pp. 277–280. IEEE (2017)

24. Zucco, C., Calabrese, B., Cannataro, M.: Sentiment analysis and affective computing for depression monitoring. In: 2017 IEEE International Conference on Bioinformatics and Biomedicine (BIBM), pp. 1988–1995 IEEE (2017)

25. Hassan, A.U., Hussain, J., Hussain, M., Sadiq, M., Lee, S.: Sentiment analysis of social networking sites (SNS) data using machine learning approach for the measurement of depression. In: 2017 International Conference on Information and Communication Technology Convergence (ICTC), pp. 138–140. IEEE (2017)

26. Guntuku, S.C., Yaden, D.B., Kern, M.L., Ungar, L.H., Eichstaedt, J.C.: Detecting depression and mental illness on social media: an integrative review. Curr. Opinion Behav. Sci. **18**, 43–49 (2017)

27. Singh, J., Singh, G., Singh, R.: Optimization of sentiment analysis using machine learning classifiers. Hum.-Centric Inf. Sci. **7**(1), 1–12 (2017). https://doi.org/10.1186/s13673-017-0116-3

28. Tao, X., Zhou, X., Zhang, J., Yong, J.: Sentiment analysis for depression detection on social networks. In: Li, J., Li, X., Wang, S., Li, J., Sheng, Q.Z. (eds.) ADMA. LNCS, vol. 10086, pp. 807–810. Springer, Cham (2016). https://doi.org/10.1007/978-3-319-49586-6_59

29. Alessia, D., Ferri, F., Grifoni, P., Guzzo, T.: Approaches, tools and applications for sentiment analysis implementation. Int. J. Comput. Appl. **125**(3) (2015)

30. Kaushik, A., Naithani, S.: A study on sentiment analysis: methods and tools. Int. J. Sci. Res. (IJSR), 2319–7064 (2015)

31. Dinakar, S., Andhale, P., Rege, M.: Sentiment analysis of social network content. In: 2015 IEEE International Conference on Information Reuse and Integration, pp. 189–192. IEEE (2015)

32. Gupta, E., Rathee, G., Kumar, P., Chauhan, D.S.: Mood swing analyser: a dynamic sentiment detection approach. Proc. Natl. Acad. Sci. India Sect. A: Phys. Sci. **85**(1), 149–157 (2015)

33. Hussain, J., et al.: SNS based predictive model for depression. In: Geissbühler, A., Demongeot, J., Mokhtari, M., Abdulrazak, B., Aloulou, H. (eds.) ICOST. LNCS, vol. 9102, pp. 349–354. Springer, Cham (2015). https://doi.org/10.1007/978-3-319-19312-0_34

34. Yang, W., Lan, M.: GIS analysis of depression among Twitter users. Appl. Geogr. **60**, 217–223 (2015)
35. Nunzio, D., Maria, G.: A new decision to take for cost-sensitive Naïve Bayes classifiers. Inf. Process. Manage. **50**(5), 653–674 (2014)
36. Wang, X., Zhang, C., Ji, Y., Sun, L., Wu, L., Bao, Z.: A depression detection model based on sentiment analysis in micro-blog social network. In: Li, J. (ed.) PAKDD. LNCS, vol. 7867, pp. 201–213. Springer, Heidelberg (2013). https://doi.org/10.1007/978-3-642-40319-4_18
37. Hsu, C.-C., Huang, Y.-P., Chang, K.-W.: Extended Naive Bayes classifier for mixed data. Expert Syst. Appl. **35**(3), 1080–1083 (2008)
38. Kumari, A., Behera, R.K., Sahoo, K.S., Nayyar, A., Kumar Luhach, A., Prakash Sahoo, S.: Supervised link prediction using structured-based feature extraction in social network. Concurr. Comput.: Pract. Exp., e5839 (2020)
39. Dash, S., Luhach, A.K., Chilamkurti, N., Baek, S., Nam, Y.: A Neuro-fuzzy approach for user behaviour classification and prediction. J. Cloud Comput. **8**(1), 17 (2019)

Mucus Plug Blockage Detection in COVID-19 Patient's Chest X-Ray Using Instance Segmentation

Piyush Juyal and Sachin Sharma[✉]

Department of Computer Science and Engineering, Graphic Era Deemed To Be University, Dehradun, Uttarakhand, India
sachin.cse@geu.ac.in

Abstract. COVID-19 has fundamentally changed our lives and is rapidly impacting the world's population, and it has become a total human tragedy. Figures are rising fast in both diseases and mortality. It is crucial that patients who are infected are quickly recognized and supported in these challenging times following this plague. We also created a deep analysis method for detecting the blockage of mucus with X-ray images in the lungs. Not only is the system observed for COVID-19 patients, but also stresses the enhanced strength and credibility of the system due to the mucus in the lung.

Keywords: CNN · Mask-RCNN · COVID-19 · Mucus plugs

1 Introduction

COVID-19 is a newly discovered infectious disease, with a community of coronaviruses that cause breathing problems. It is quick to spread and the world is terrifying high infectious rate. The COVID-19 pandemic stopped the world, not only impacting the economy, but also socially distancing us. Even if the locks used to slow down its growth curve, people lose their livelihoods at an infection rate. Covid19 is a virus that actually has no vaccine due to disorder and death. It is primarily transmitted through goutlets of saliva or release from the person's nose. It is fatal for elders or individuals with past illnesses in particular. Everyone is concerned about the increasing mortality rate. No doubt the world and the way we live are deadly in this pandemic. Humans are classified into four separate subgroups such as beta, alpha, gamma and delta. The main indicators for the tracking of all viruses are symptoms; currently discovered symptoms are shortness of breath, toxins becoming severe over time, fever gradually increasing in temperatures, fatigue, chills, sore throat and much otto are common types that affect persons NL63 (alpha), 229E (alpha), HKU1 (beta) and three less common ones are SARS CoV, SARS CoV-2, MERS CoV. But pneumonic symptoms are particularly highly detectable.

Pneumonia is a condition which causes inflation in the lungs. The virus or bacteria are usually caused and not usually the fungi and parasites. The inhale of pathogen happens as a bacterial pneumonia. Viral pneumonia mainly results from inhalation into

© Springer Nature Singapore Pte Ltd. 2021
A. K. Luhach et al. (Eds.): ICAICR 2020, CCIS 1393, pp. 152–160, 2021.
https://doi.org/10.1007/978-981-16-3660-8_14

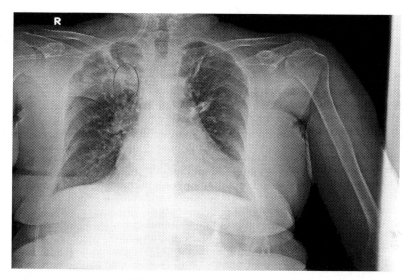

Fig. 1. Annotated X-ray image.

the lungs of ill-defined droplets. The alveoli affecting our lungs are small sacks. Mucus generation, which causes mucus plugs in pneumonia, is typically increased, and leaky capillaries can hint blood to the mouth. An accumulation of mucus in the airways is a mucus plug. These clumps can look like pus or blood streaked. In extreme pneumonia, mucus plugs and fluid accumulation limit gas exchange capacity in the lung together. Pneumonia leads to lung mucus plugs that can be seen in the chest x-ray as in Fig. 1. A patient with COVID-19 has similar symptoms of chest blockage from mucus plugs. Such mucosal plugs appear in the x-rays as nebulous or translucent regions. Using the lung X-ray has been effective in screening patients. Chest X-ray has been one of the most effective tool of screening. It is important that its high rate of infection recognizes its patients as soon as possible. The Artificial intelligent community has come forward and brought innovative approaches to speed up this process of detection of COVID-19 in chest x-rays. But just classifying an x-ray image whether it is COVID-19 or not is not very credible for doctors. We can make these predictions more understandable for doctors by highlighting mucus plugs in x-ray images and makes the approach more credible.

2 Literature Survey

Since COVID-19 is recently identified in the human body, various research is continuously proposed by multiple researchers. Due to the power of AI, it can be introduced in numerous fields. Therefore, we can suggest using the power of AI and giving a brain to computers. We have looked into some published works:

In [1], authors used chest X-ray images of various pneumonia and COVID-19 patients with other diseases, and healthy individual chest X-rays to create the dataset for training intent in Microsoft's Custom Vision. Microsoft's Custom Vision is an automated object detection and image classification service. With this research, high training, testing, and validation accuracy are achieved. The developed model makes a sensitivity accuracy of 100. In [2] authors suggested the SODA model name for the semi-supervised Open set domain opponent network. This model supports the distribution of line-up data in a general domain and in a common source and target data sub-space across different domains. It is effective in separating COVID-19 from standard pneumonia compared to recent state-of-the-art versions. In [3], authors proposed an effective mechanism, which is also known as transfer learning, his approach is powered by utilizing the knowledge acquired from generic object recognition tasks and use it on domain-specific tasks. The previously developed CNN may adapt and validate by the domain specific tasks which is also called Transfer, Decompose and Compose (DeTraC). It is also used for the classification of COVID-19 CXRs.

3   Proposed Methodology and Result Analysis

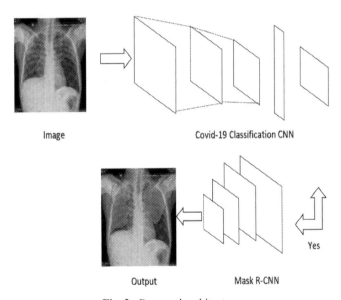

Fig. 2. Proposed architecture.

In the proposed methodology, the dataset consists of 211 positive pictures of COVID-19 and 199 normal radiographic images. These pictures are for binary COVID-19 classification; after that if we find it ideal for COVID-19, then we send the image to the R-CNN mask for further processing [6]. King George's Medical University has collected the annotated information about mask RCNN training. The machine efficiency is improved by CNN deployment before R-CNN mask. The R-CNN mask [9] addresses the problem of instance segmentation following classification as it can achieve a complete pixel-level identification of an object border. The method is binary classifying the image as

COVID-19 or normal. If found positive for COVID-19, then pass it to mask R-CNN which will apply a mask to that image. The proposed method is depicted in Fig. 2. Data for training and testing of mask R-CNN needs to be prepared separately. To prepare it, we have utilized the guideline annotated pictures shown in Fig. 2 and have annotated about 108 images for this task. The images have been annotated through an image annotating software that prepares a JSON file containing the image's coordinates. This JSON file, along with the images, is supplied to the network for training.

Convolutional Neural Networks [7, 8] in short CNN, is a made up of convolution operation connected with an artificial neural network (ANN). It is commonly used in the area of computer vision. As the name suggests, the convolution part of the neural network typically comprises of normalization layers, convolutional layers, fully connected layers and pooling layers [10]. It picks up Temporal and spatial dependencies in an image through the application of appropriate filters. The main element of CNN is the convolutional layer. It consists of filters, also known as the kernel. Kernels vary in size example, 5×5 or 3×3. These kernels slide across the image performing element-wise matrix multiplication and add the result, which is then stored in a matrix known as a feature map. The results are added to the feature map as the filter slides over the image. These filters work like edge detectors detecting various edges and finding unique features [11]. The next operation is the pooling operation. It is used to reduce the dimensionality of our matrix. It facilitates in depreciating the number of parameters, combating overfitting and cutting the training time. Pooling layers down sample e feature maps individually. Pooling layers reduces height and width of the feature maps while keeping its depth intact. A primary type of pooling is max pooling. This operation also has kernels but does not compute elementwise multiplication; instead, it grabs the maximum value from the filter and then adds it to a feature map. After a desired number of pooling and convolution operations, resulting feature matrices are then flattened and are routed to a neural network. Convolution operation extracts the appropriate feature from an image and helps a neural network to classify class-specific features. The picture size is changed to 224×224. There are four operations combined with the max operation of the pool. The role maps will then be flattened and transported to a completely connected neural network. Figure 3 illustrates the plot of testing accuracy versus training accuracy of CNN. Figure 4 illustrates the plot of overall loss of the training and validation of mask R-CNN.

Region-based CNN is the full form of mask R-CNN [3, 4]. It helps to resolve the enigma of instance segmentation. Instance segmentation is detecting and delineating various distinct objects of interest appearing together in an image. This network splits the objects in an image. It supplies bounding boxes, classes, and masks to bind the object in the image. The structure of the Mask R-CNN architecture network is illustrated in Fig. 5. This is an update to the R-CNN architecture more exponentially. The object branch produces a binary mask when an object is bound to a given pixel. The overhead for faster R-CNN is insignificant, and it's computationally cheap [5]. It is made up of two stages. First it allows suggestions for places where an object may be in the picture. The second is the object type. The bounding box is improved and based on the previous proposals a binary mask is generated. We have a backbone that is an FPN to connect these stages. The FP Network for Recognition Systems is a deep neural network. FPN has a side-linked up and down route. In the identification of objects at different levels it

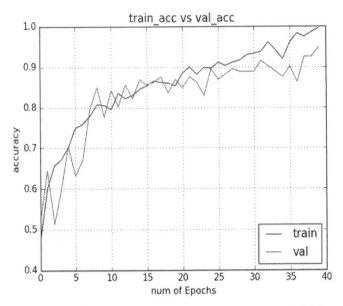

Fig. 3. Plot of testing accuracy versus training accuracy of CNN.

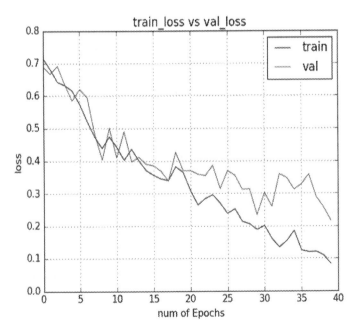

Fig. 4. Plot of testing loss versus training loss of CNN.

plays an important role. This model reads all feature maps and recommends only those feature maps which are likely to contain the object. Anchors are used to link features to the object located in the images. Grouping by ground reality is done because boundary boxes are separated by the intersection of each anchor. There is a binary classification between the object and the context at this point. Anchor has several dimensions and is connected to various levels of characteristic maps. Region proposal network utilizes anchors computes the location of the object for the feature maps. It also decides the size of the bounding box. Proposed regions are also used by another neural network which assigns them to different areas of the map level. These areas are scanned by the network which supplies masks, classes and boundary boxes for the object in the image. Alternatively, anchors are not utilized at this stage to discern the correct sections of the feature map. Figure 6 illustrates plot of training loss vs validation loss of mask R-CNN and Fig. 7 illustrates plot of training mask R-CNN class loss vs validation mask R-CNN Class loss. Figure 8 illustrates the plot of training mask R-CNN mask loss vs validation mask R-CNN mask loss. Figure 9 illustrates the result of proposed methodology using mask R-CNN, first image is the one which supplied to the network and the next image is its result. The red patch highlights the area where mucus plug is located.

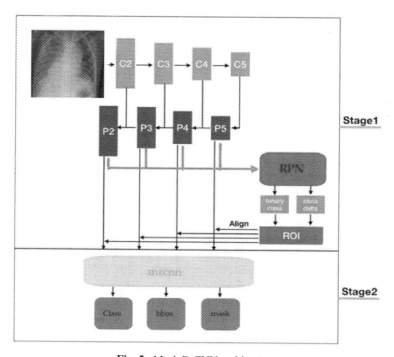

Fig. 5. Mask R-CNN architecture.

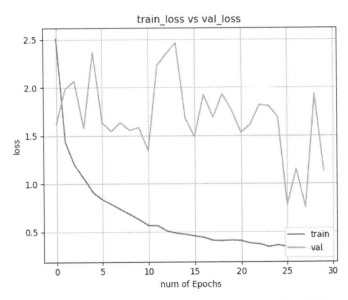

Fig. 6. Plot of training loss versus validation loss of mask R-CNN.

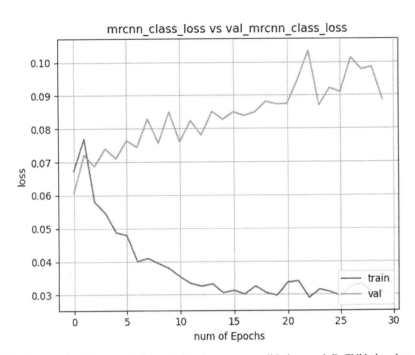

Fig. 7. Plot of training mask R-CNN class loss versus validation mask R-CNN class loss.

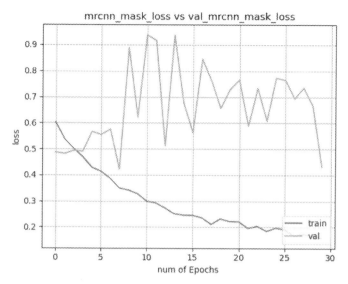

Fig. 8. Plot of training mask R-CNN mask loss versus validation mask R-CNN mask loss.

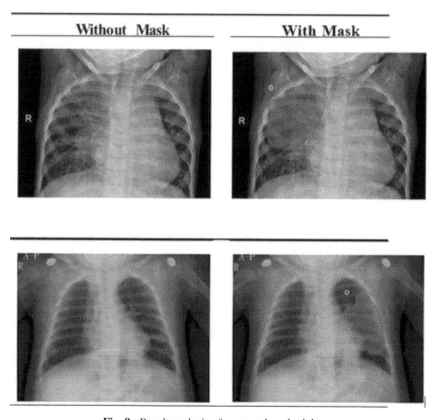

Fig. 9. Result analysis of proposed methodology.

One of the popular metrics for gauging the accuracy of the object detection is the mean average precision (mAP) score. It is the average of average precision and It is calculated by taking the mean average precision over all classes and overall IoU thresholds. For our model the mAP is 0.84.

4   Conclusion

This proposed technique provides a new perspective for medical personnel. Analyses of literature show that different methods of research have been used to tackle this question, but this approach provides a constructive, systematic approach to the problem. Deep learning will assist physicians and other medical employees in this crisis. If adopted, the methods will certainly aid in the COVID-19 classification, and with the help of real-time data availability the R-CNN masks may become much more precise, reliable and accurate.

References

1. Borkowski, A.A., et al.: Using artificial intelligence for COVID-19 chest X-ray diagnosis. medRxiv (2020)
2. Zhou, J., Jing, B., Wang, Z.: SODA: detecting Covid-19 in chest X-rays with semi-supervised open set domain adaptation. arXiv preprint arXiv:2005.11003 (2020)
3. Juyal, P., Sharma, S.: Estimation of tree volume using mask R-CNN based deep learning. In: 2020 11th International Conference on Computing, Communication and Networking Technologies (ICCCNT), pp. 1–6. IEEE (2020)
4. He, K., Gkioxari, G., Dollar, P., Girshick, R.: Mask R-CNN arXiv:1703.06870v3 [cs.CV] 24 Jan 2018
5. Abbas, A., Abdelsamea, M.M., Gaber, M.M.: Classification of COVID-19 in chest X-ray images using DeTraC deep convolutional neural network. arXiv preprint arXiv:2003.13815 (2020)
6. Liu, B., Yan, B., Zhou, Y., Yang, Y., Zhang, Y.: Experiments of federated learning for covid-19 chest x-ray images. arXiv preprint arXiv:2007.05592 (2020)
7. Juyal, P., Kulshrestha, C., Sharma, S., Ghanshala, T.: Common bamboo species identification using Machine Learning and Deep Learning algorithms. Int. J. Innov. Technol. Explor. Eng. (IJITEE) 9(4) (2020)
8. Bhadula, S., Sharma, S., Juyal, P., Kulshrestha, C.: Machine Learning algorithms based skin disease detection. Int. J. Innov. Technol. Explor. Eng. (IJITEE) 9(2) (2019)
9. Yin, S., Li, H., Teng, L.: Airport detection based on improved faster RCNN in large scale remote sensing images. Sens. Imaging 21(1), 1–13 (2020). https://doi.org/10.1007/s11220-020-00314-2
10. Singh, K., Rajput, A., Sharma, S.: Vision based patient fall detection using deep learning in smart hospitals. Int. J. Innov. Technol. Explor. Eng. (IJITEE) 9(2) (2019)
11. Sharma, S., Mishra, R.R., Joshi, V., Kour, K.: Analysis and interpretation of global air quality. In: 2020 11th International Conference on Computing, Communication and Networking Technologies (ICCCNT), pp. 1–5. IEEE (2020)

Applying Machine Learning to Detect Depression-Related Texts on Social Networks

Shirinkyz Shekerbekova[1], Meruyert Yerekesheva[2], Lyailya Tukenova[3],
Kuralay Turganbay[4], Zhazira Kozhamkulova[5], and Batyrkhan Omarov[6,7(✉)]

[1] Abai Kazakh National Pedagogical University, Almaty, Kazakhstan
[2] K. Zhubanov Aktobe Regional University, Aktobe, Kazakhstan
[3] Narxoz University, Almaty, Kazakhstan
[4] Kazakh National Womens Teacher Training University, Almaty, Kazakhstan
[5] Almaty University of Power Engineering and Telecommunication, Almaty, Kazakhstan
[6] Al-Farabi Kazakh National University, Almaty, Kazakhstan
[7] Khoja Akhmet Yassawi International Kazakh-Turkish University, Turkistan, Kazakhstan

Abstract. This interdisciplinary study is aimed at determining the informative signs of behavior of users of the social network Vkontakte of the Kazakh segment in connection with the level of severity of signs of depression in them. We applied six machine learning algorithms with different features to depression related post detection problem. Our experimental results show that the problem can be successfully solved and applied to detect depressive or suicidal behavior or texts in online user contents. Experiment results with depressive and suicide related texts detection show that we can achieve high accuracy in depression related text classification using the collected dataset.

Keywords: Depression · Suicide · Classification · Detection · Machine learning · NLP

1 Introduction

According to a 2016 report by the who European office, the current health system is not entirely successful in dealing with depression, and evidence-based approaches to its treatment should be developed using a public health support and prevention strategy [1]. The effectiveness and accessibility of preventive measures to the population should also be significantly improved [2]. Existing problems encourage the search for ways to automate mental health projects and develop new forms of diagnosis and information [3].

Research shows that the analysis of users' personal pages in social networks can be a source of information not only about the user's socio-demographic characteristics, but also about their current psychological state [4]. Thus, a whole field of research has emerged that is related to the study of the ability to predict the psychological states of individuals and the level of subjective well-being by analyzing profiles in social networks [5].

© Springer Nature Singapore Pte Ltd. 2021
A. K. Luhach et al. (Eds.): ICAICR 2020, CCIS 1393, pp. 161–169, 2021.
https://doi.org/10.1007/978-981-16-3660-8_15

This diagnostic methodology allows you to solve several problems at once:

1 early detection of signs of psychological distress for its timely diagnosis and prevention;
2 the transition from subjective methods of diagnosis to objective ones based on real behavioral signs;
3 reduce the cost of psychological diagnostics through passive data collection mode;
4 gaining access to groups of the population who do not seek psychological help for various reasons (socio-economic status, subjective barriers and stigmatization, etc.).

Special attention of researchers is directed to the study of signs of depression based on informative parameters of Internet users' behavior. Depression is the leading disease in terms of prevalence, affecting 9% of men and 17% of women in Europe, which are about 33.4 million people. This condition is characterized by a depressed mood, cognitive and motor inhibition, loss of interest, and motivation to important areas of life for a person, so it is one of the main causes of disability in the world [6–8].

The purpose of this interdisciplinary study was to identify the most informative signs of behavior of users in Kazakh social segment of the Vkontakte social network in order to identify their belonging to groups of respondents with high and low levels of depression.

We tested the assumption that machine learning models are able to classify people with and without signs of depression by various activity parameters and psycholinguistic markers of their texts in the social network Vkontakte.

2 Related Works

Recently, artificial neural networks have proven to be effective for many tasks. For example, neural networks can recognize numbers, images, classify objects, and so on. One of these networks is a recursive neural network. Recursive neural networks have achieved significant success in solving natural language processing problems [9–11].

In [12], it was found that people with pronounced neuroticism use the Internet as a resource where they can Express their "true Self", while avoiding doing so in real life. The study [13] shows that the more often a person uses "Facebook", the more pronounced their neuroticism, loneliness, shyness, and narcissism are. In [14], it was confirmed that neuroticism positively correlates with the number of "likes" and the groups that the user belongs to. Building predictive models that include personality traits, depression symptoms, and various parameters of user behavior in social networks revealed the moderating role of neuroticism in the relationship between depression indicators and Facebook use. Until the level of neuroticism reaches a certain point, depression is positively associated with a variety of activity on Facebook—broadcasting, the number of "likes", comments, hashtags. When the level of neuroticism exceeds this point, the correlation between depression and social network activity becomes negative [15].

The study [16] found that people with signs of depression change the pattern of behavior, which can also be manifested in social networks. For example, respondents suffering from mild to moderate depression are more likely to listen to music, especially classical music, while people with severe depression stop listening to it altogether. The intensity of social interactions is changing, despite the General trend of reducing the number and duration of offline contacts with family and colleagues, respondents with severe depression talk more on the phone than people with mild to moderate depression.

The study [17] found that the instability of the use of words expressing negative emotions can be a simple but sensitive measure for diagnosing depression in social media users, but its usefulness may depend on the platform for Facebook users, this indicator is a predictor of greater severity of depression, and in Twitter, on the contrary, it is lower.

The paper [18] shows the high accuracy of artificial neural networks (ins) in assessing the risks of depression. The authors argue that (ins) can be used for large-scale research on mental health and, in particular, depression.

The study [19] suggests an approach to creating statistical models that can predict depression. The models rely on a metric called the Social Media Depression Index (SMDI), which is used to determine depressive-indicative messages on Twitter and identify levels of depression in the population. Twitter messages are represented as feature vectors (for example, emotions, time, n-grams, style, signs of participation). To reduce the feature space, the principal Component Analysis (PCA) method was used. The test sample obtained classification completeness of more than 70%, accuracy 82%.

In [20], the "CES-D" questionnaire, which is a score scale of 20 indicators, was used as the main tool for determining the level of depression. Four features of the emotional state that appears in messages were considered as positive affect (PA), negative affect (NA), activation, and dominance. Some descriptive analyses of differences in two classes of messages were presented as "depressive" and "standard" messages. It is noted that authors who are prone to depression publish fewer messages, which indicates a possible loss of social connectedness. In addition, a decrease in the number of subscribers and subscribed pages indicates that these authors show a decrease in the desire to communicate or tend to consume external information and remain connected to others. The high NA rate that characterizes these authors may reflect their mental instability and helplessness. Moreover, low activation and dominance can indicate loneliness, anxiety, exhaustion, lack of energy and sleep, which are clear signs and symptoms of depression.

In social networks, there is a high risk of spreading prohibited information or leaking confidential data, such as photos, files from user correspondence histories, which can later become prohibited content in the hands of hackers [21]. The network distributes information that encourages any undesirable actions, such as suicidal content, instructions for suicide, and others [22]. Once in social networks, such content can spread very quickly between groups of users.

In addition to distributing prohibited content, you can find resources on the network that distribute prohibited products. Many of these sites selling various narcotic substances, and the methods of payment using cryptocurrency. It is because of the use of cryptocurrencies that special services can practically not track the activities of such sites in hidden networks [23].

Opening obfuscated texts of messages, as we noted in [24], is a non-trivial task, since there are a huge number of options for obfuscating even a single word, and today there is no single technique used for opening obfuscated messages in social networks. The hidden Markov model (SMM) and the N-gram model are among the most frequently used models for solving the problem of opening obfuscation of texts. There are other methods, however, as our experiments have shown, they are not able to solve the problem of opening obfuscated texts for all methods of their creation, and the best results were obtained using SMM-86% of successfully opened texts.

To identify stable communities of participants in virtual social networks, a software package for clustering these networks is used, which provides the following functions: input of source data; determination of the membership function; determination of clustering parameters; clustering; visualization of graphs of distributions of parameter values across clusters; scaling of source data; and report generation.

3   Methodology

3.1   Data Collection and Analysis

Since data about people who have committed suicide is confidential, we collected depressing messages from social media users. A lot of work has been done to create a parser that collects posts from public groups with depressive or suicidal content. We collected about 32 000 depressing messages and 32 000 regular messages, such as news, blogs, add-ons, and so on.

Before you start working with messages, you need to pre-process them. In our case, preprocessing will include tokenization, lemmatization, stemming, removing stop words, and removing punctuation marks.

First, tokenization is performed – this is the process of splitting the text into smaller parts, tokens. The tokens in the General case are the words, numbers and punctuation. You need to separate words into separate elements so that you can perform operations on each of them.

Next, you need to bring the words to the normal form, that is, to conduct lemmatization – this is the process of bringing the word form to the Lemma. In Russian, normal forms are: for nouns-nominative case, singular; for adjectives-nominative case, singular, masculine; for verbs, participles, and adverbs-a verb in the infinitive of an imperfect form.

You also need to get rid of words that do not carry any meaning in the text themselves, i.e. stop words after deleting them, the meaning will not change. Stop words include prepositions, particles, conjunctions, adverbs, pronouns, introductory words, and so on. Dropping them has almost no effect on the size of the dictionary, but it can significantly reduce the length of some texts. It should be noted that such stop words as "not", "no" and others that have an emotional connotation will not be deleted.

Along with stop words, it makes sense to remove symbolic values from texts, i.e. words consisting only of numbers, punctuation marks, and other symbols, although this step may depend on the specific goals that the model should meet.

3.2 Tools

Python 3 was chosen as the programming language. This language is one of the most popular in machine learning tasks, as it provides various built-in libraries for neural networks. The TensorFlow library is an open source software library for machine learning developed by Google. It allows you to create and train neural networks of various architectures. TensorFlow calculations are expressed as data flows through a state graph. In these graphs, vertices have 0 or more inputs and 0 or more outputs and represent mathematical operations, while edges are data that is usually represented as multidimensional arrays or tensors that are communicated between these edges. PyCharm is an integrated development environment for the Python programming language.

4 Data Exploration

This section describes the collected data and its main characteristics. Figure 1 demonstrates the distribution of posts by text length.

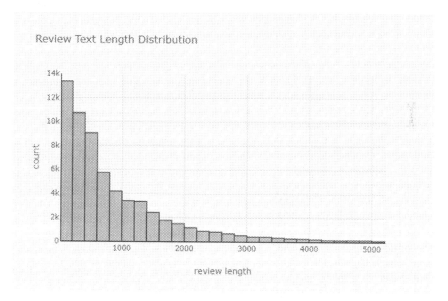

Fig. 1. Text length distribution of depression-related posts.

Figure 2 shows the distribution of depressive and neutral posts in the collected corpus. Figure 3 shows the age distribution of authors of depressive posts.

Distribution of posts Lengths Based on labeled posts

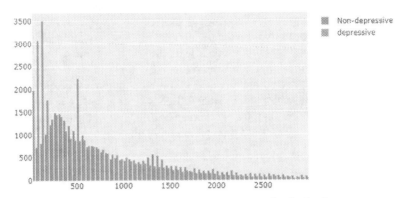

Fig. 2. Depression-related and neutral posts distribution law.

Reviewers Age Distribution

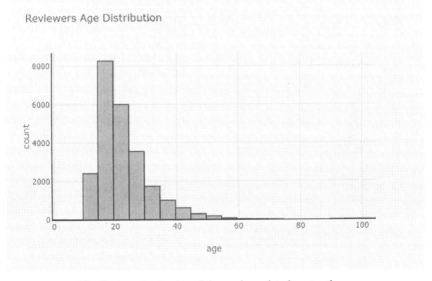

Fig. 3. Age distribution of depression-related post authors.

5   Experiment Results

In this section we apply different machine learning methods to our dataset. In the experiment, we applied six machine learning algorithms for text classification problem to classify depression-related and neutral posts. The applied algorithms are Support Vector Machine, Decision Tree, Random Forest, K nearest neighbor, Random Forest, and Logistic Regression (Table 1). Figure 4 illustrates AUC performance of the results.

Table 1. Experiment results. Applying machine learning to depressive-related post detection/classification.

Methods	Acc.	Prec.	Rec	F1	AUC
SVM	0.8115	0.6502	0.7253	0.6778	0.8676
Decision Tree	0.7957	0.6467	0.7142	0.6181	0.8254
Random Forest	0.7898	0.6795	0.7361	0.7071	0.8402
K Nearest Neighbours	0.8236	0.6336	0.7434	0.6362	0.8043
Naïve Bayes	0.8041	0.6183	0.7527	0.6816	0.8198
Logistic Regression	0.8247	0.6571	0.7758	0.6184	0.8289
SVM	0.8125	0.6223	0.7296	0.6773	0.8334

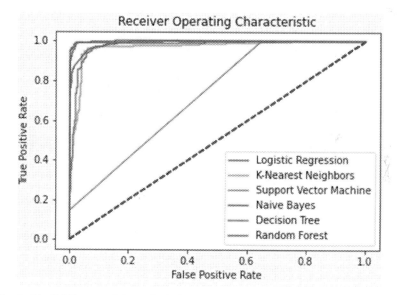

Fig. 4. The ROC curve of six methods for depression related text classification problem.

6 Conclusion and Future Work

In this paper, we applied machine learning to text classification problem for detection of depressive or suicidal behavior. To solve the given problem, we applied various classification algorithms.

Our experimental results show that the problem can be successfully solved and applied to detect depressive or suicidal behavior or texts in online user contents. Experiment results with depressive and suicide related texts detection show that we can achieve high accuracy in depression related text classification using the collected dataset.

Analyzing the above, it can be noted that the analysis of posts in social networks can be one of the methods that can improve the prevention of suicide among patients, when it is implemented in practice. At the same time, preventive measures can be extended to a larger number of people, which will significantly improve the situation with suicide prevention and, as a result, reduce the negative consequences of suicide.

References

1. Pande, N., Karyakarte, M.: A review for semantic analysis and text document annotation using natural language processing techniques (2019). Available at SSRN 3418747
2. Alshemali, B., Kalita, J.: Improving the reliability of deep neural networks in NLP: a review. Knowl.-Based Syst. **105210** (2019)
3. Yankah, S., Adams, K.S., Grimes, L., Price, A.: Age and online social media behavior in prediction of social activism orientation. J. Soc. Media Soc. **6**(2), 56–89 (2017)
4. Costello, M., Hawdon, J.: Who are the online extremists among us? Sociodemographic characteristics, social networking, and online experiences of those who produce online hate materials. Violence Gend. **5**(1), 55–60 (2018)
5. Ferrara, E.: Contagion dynamics of extremist propaganda in social networks. Inf. Sci. **418**, 1–12 (2017)
6. Awan, I.: Cyber-extremism: Isis and the power of social media. Society **54**(2), 138–149 (2017)
7. Chetty, N., Alathur, S.: Hate speech review in the context of online social networks. Aggress. Violent. Beh. **40**, 108–118 (2018)
8. Kruglanski, A., Jasko, K., Webber, D., Chernikova, M., Molinario, E.: The making of violent extremists. Rev. Gen. Psychol. **22**(1), 107–120 (2018)
9. Chen, H.: Exploring extremism and terrorism on the web: the dark web project // Pacific-Asia Workshop on Intelligence and Security Informatics. Springer, Berlin Heidelberg (2007), pp. 1–20
10. Finlayson, M.A., Halverson, J.R., Corman, S.R.: The N2 corpus: a semantically annotated collection of Islamist extremist stories // LREC (2014), 896–902
11. Chepovskiy, A., Devyatkin, D., Smirnov, I., Ananyeva, M., Kobozeva, M., Solovyev, F.: Exploring linguistic features for extremist texts detection (on the material of Russian-speaking illegal texts), in: 2017 IEEE International Conference on Intelligence and Security Informatics: Security and Big Data, ISI 2017 Institute of Electrical and Electronics Engineers Inc., pp. 188–190 (2017)
12. Tosun, L.P., Lajunen, T.: Why do young adults develop a passion for Internet activities? The associations among personality, revealing "true self" on the Internet, and passion for the Internet. Cyberpsychol. Behav. **12**(4), 401–406 (2009)
13. Li, C., Shi, X., Dang, J.: Online communication and subjective well-being in Chinese college students: the mediating role of shyness and social self-efficacy. Comput. Hum. Behav. **34**(5), 89–95 (2014). https://doi.org/10.1016/j.chb.2014.01.032

14. Bachrach, Y., Kosinski, M., Graepel, T., Kohli, P., Stillwell, D.: Personality and patterns of Facebook usage", WebSci'12 Proceedings of the 4th Annual ACM Web Science Conference (June 22–24, 2012, Evanston, Illinois, USA), pp. 24–32 (2012), ISBN 978-1-4503-1228-8

15. Wee, J., Jang, S., Lee, J., Jang, W.: The influence of depression and personality on social networking. Comput. Hum. Behav. **74**, 45–52 (2017)

16. Tasnim, M., Shahriyar, R., Nahar, N., Mahmud, H.: Intelligent depression detection and support system: statistical analysis, psychological review and design implication. Proceedings of IEEE 18th International Conference on e-Health Networking, Applications and Services (Healthcom) (September 14–16, 2016), p. 6. Munich, Germany (2016)

17. Seabrook, E.M., Kern, M.L., Fulcher, B.D., Rickard, N.S.: Predicting depression from language-based emotion dynamics: longitudinal analysis of Facebook and Twitter status updates. J. Med. Internet Res. **20**, 5 (2018)

18. Yates, A., Cohan, A., Goharian, N.: Depression and self-harm risk assessment in online forums. Proceedings of the 2017 Conference on Empirical Methods in Natural Language Processing (September 7–11, 2017, Copenhagen, Denmark), pp. 2968–2978 (2017)

19. Choudhury, M.D., Counts, S., Horviz, E.: Social media as a measurement tool of depression in populations. WebSci'13 Proceedings of the 5th Annual ACM Web Science Conference (May 02–04, 2013, Paris, France), 2013, ISBN 978-1-4503-1889-1, pp. 47–56

20. Radloff, L.S.: The CES-D scale: A self-report depression scale for research in the general population. Appl. Psychol. Meas. **1**(3), 385–401 (1977)

21. Purohit, G.N., Priti, S., Praveen, D.: Content filtering on social networking sites with fuzzy logic. Int. J. Adv. Res. Comput. Sci. Softw. Eng. **7**(6), 175–179 (2017)

22. Morch, C.-M., Cote, L.-P., Corthesy-Blondin, L.: The darknet and suicide. J. Affect. Disord. **241**, 127–132 (2018)

23. Yannikos, Y., Schäfer, A., Steinebach, M.: Monitoring product sales in darknet shops. Int. Conf. Avail. Reliab. Security (2018)

24. Coley, C.W., Green, W.H., Jensen, K.F.: Machine learning in computer-aided synthesis planning. Acc. Chem. Res. **51**(5), 1281–1289 (2018)

Usability Improvements in E-Governance Applications with Simple and Usable Interface (Design Stage)

Rajul Betala[✉] and Sushopti Gawade

Pillai College of Engineering, Panvel 410206, Maharashtra, India
sgawade@mes.ac.in

Abstract. To improve the usability of e-governance applications and to remove the issues of corruption, unaccountability, and irresponsibility of government departments, Citizen-Centric-Model of Performance-Related-Pay is proposed. In this proposed model, a link to the portal will be given to the citizen who received the service. Portal will consist of 5 Usability Related Questions (Q1–Q5) and Rating using Dichotomous Rating Scale (Yes/No) will be stored in the database (Yes = 1, No = 0). The proposed formula for Rating of Department (RD), Incentive Rate (IR) and Incentive Amount (IA) will be applied. For model validation, a manual survey of 10 citizens is conducted by considering the Postal and Telecommunications Department and Basic Salary is 15000 units. Results are RD as 2, IR as 4 and IA as 600 units. Accordingly, the departments of government will evolve themselves constantly to improve RD, IR and IA to get satisfactory incentives thereby giving proper and fully usable online services.

Keywords: E-governance application · E-government application · Usability analysis · Dichotomous rating scale · Citizen-Centric-Model · Performance-Related-Pay

1 Introduction

According to ISO 9241–11:1998, Usability is the extent to which a product can be used by specified users to achieve specific goals with effectiveness, efficiency, and satisfaction in a specified context of use [1]. Higher usability is needed to provide a good user experience.

In the context of governance, citizens are the end-users. And still in the current scenario, according to many pieces of research like the one of B. Mahalingam and Akash Raj DP in 2016, citizens are facing many issues due to long-queues to complete tasks, irresponsibility and un-accountability of government employees, corruption in the system, etc. [2]. So, to tackle these issues, Improvement in the current system is needed and this can be achieved by improving the usability of e-governance applications for users (citizens).

© Springer Nature Singapore Pte Ltd. 2021
A. K. Luhach et al. (Eds.): ICAICR 2020, CCIS 1393, pp. 170–180, 2021.
https://doi.org/10.1007/978-981-16-3660-8_16

As per the studies of Aksel Sundstrom in 2019, to improve the user experience, Performance Related Pay (PRP) was proposed which has been said to reduce government employee's wish for bribes, making them more accountable and responsible towards service delivery and have therefore been promoted. But in highly corrupt settings, its effect cannot be seen because of the presence of corrupt senior managers and so PRP isolates honest employees and they receive no addition to their salary. So this scheme is adversely affecting user experience by promoting more corruption, irresponsibility, and un-accountability [3].

As there is no process in which the end-users i.e. citizens participate in the analysis of the performance of employees and so the result of the existing system is that the user experience is still not improved. So, the Citizen-Centric-Model of Performance-Related-Pay (CCMPRP) is proposed where the performance of the department will be judged and analyzed by their end-users i.e. Citizens and relevant ratings will be used to provide the hike to the employee or department thereby minimizing the effects of un-accountability, irresponsibility, corruption and so on.

The remaining paper is structured as follows. In the second section, the Literature Survey is given. The third section shows the Methodology which is used to describe the tools, techniques, and data to be used in the proposed model. Forth section provides the Results and Discussion of the manual survey conducted on 10 citizens to validate the proposed model. The fifth section gives the Conclusion and Future Scope of the work.

2   Literature Survey

The literature survey shows many researchers conducted their research on Performance Related Pay as shown in Table 1 and on Citizen-Centric-Model as shown in Table 2. But very less research is done in the area of the combination of Citizen-Centric-Model with Performance-Related-Pay as shown in Table 3. So to bridge the missing gap, the design of Citizen-Centric-Model of Performance Related Pay is proposed in this paper where Citizen will be the main stakeholder to decide the Performance of Government and the incentive pay will be accordingly given to the departments.

3   Proposed Methodology

E-governance was assumed to provide many benefits such as Single-point access, increased accountability, reduction in corruption, reducing the cost of delivery, etc. The Citizen-Centric-Model of Performance-Related-Pay System (CCMPRP) will try to solve the problem of corruption and increase accountability by creating e-governance applications with a simple and usable interface. This proposed system uses Performance-Related-Pay as an anti-corruption tool.

Table 1. Literature review on Performance Related Pay

Year	Area of research	Key points
2020	Performance-related pay in South Korean public enterprise	Research shows that increasing pay in the performance-related-pay model is worthwhile, and also describes the issues present in it [4]
2020	Improve Performance of public sector of Korea	Research shows that to improve the quality of services, it is essential to improve the working conditions, advance the personnel management, and upgrade the organizational culture [7]
2020	Relation between Performance-related pay (PRP), Public Service Motivation (PSM), State-Owned Enterprises (SOEs)	Research shows links in the fields of accounting, leadership, corporate governance, public policy research, organizational sciences, and psychology [5]
2020	Relation between Corruption, Public Administration, Accountability, Transparency and Virtual Social Networks (VSNs)	Research shows that e-government improvement can remove corruption by improving the effectiveness of its government administration [6]
2020	PRP in Public and Private Sector of Southern Italy	Research shows that Performance-related Incentives motivate employees [8]
2019	Rank Order Tournament in Italian Public Institution	Research shows that employees have to compete with themselves and others and the result will be known at the end [9]
2018	Performance Measurement system in the Italian case	Research shows that the technical, operational, Theoretical and Methodological level affects the Performance Measurement System [10]
2018	Public Sector Employees of Northern Greece	Research shows that the performance is significantly and positively related to job satisfaction [11]
2018	Performance Related Pay (PRP) of Iranian government	Research shows that Performance Related Pay is just behaving as a means to distribute money to the employees and not as a means to improve performance [12]

Table 2. Literature review on Citizen-Centric Model

Year	Area of research	Key Points
2020	Citizen centric model and e-democracy	Research shows that the perceived ease of use determines the attitudes of citizens toward e-democracy [13]
2019	Citizen-Centric Model status in the Rwanda government	Research shows that lack of change management strategy, cooperation among organizations, incomplete automation of processes, and intermediary management mechanisms are major challenges [14]
2019	Citizen centric model	Research tries to illustrate the process, stages, and factors of e-government adoption in a proposed citizen-centric e-government model [19]
2018	Citizen survey for Usability of e-government portal in the federal state of Rhineland Palatinate, Germany	Research shows that the citizen's preferences of the future use, the importance of online public service delivery are high and also shows the aspects indicating performance and quality fulfillment [17]
2006	Citizen-centric E-Governance System Approach	Research provides a framework using citizen-centric-model for e-governance system [18]

Table 3. Literature review relation of Citizen with Performance of employees

Year	Area of research	Key Points
2019	Citizen feedback and performance of government officials	Research shows that a huge effect can be achieved if citizen feedback were included as performance indicators for government employees [20]
2018	Israeli Local Government	Research shows that the Performance of department employee is strongly related to the trust and satisfaction of citizen (performance management → satisfaction → trust) [21]
2018	Performance management	Research shows that the Citizen's Report Card (CRC) can be used as a tool in the performance management system. Also, research suggests that time demands to do a paradigm shift in ensuring accountability by service agreements and involving the citizen in appraising the performance [22]

In this system, citizens will give the ratings to the Unit which performs the tasks or gives the service to the citizen. This will be used to design the salary structure of the unit working for citizens, thereby holding more accountability to give that service to the public.

If a citizen accesses the postal service, he will be asked to give a rating for that department. The rating of the whole month of all the users will be accumulated. Then, the average rating will be calculated by dividing the sum of ratings given by users by the total number of users. This Average rating will be multiplied with Basic Salary and its percentage will be calculated. The higher the rating, the higher will be the incentives (other than basic salary) for the employee involved and or unit involved. If the rating is lower for a consecutive 1 year, Public Administrator can ask the unit to improve the usability of the application.

3.1 Proposed Tools and Technique

In this system, the web application portal is proposed to be created on which the citizen will be able to provide the rating and Government Department's Employee will be able to view their rating along with their Pay Slip document containing calculated incentive amount with other salary components.

The portal will be named as Rating Portal. The homepage will contain the List of Department showing the current ratings. Initially, when the portal will be launched, the rating will be 0 for all departments.

The Citizen has to use this portal to give the rating for the department with which they have dealt. Considering an example that if a citizen had paid an online electricity bill, then the citizen will get a link for this Rating Portal for providing feedback. The citizen has to click on the feedback link and visit the Rating Portal. The citizen has to click on the Postal and telecommunications services Department. Then the citizen has to provide the Rating for all the 5 Questions (Q1, Q2, Q3, Q4, Q5) in which the user has to provide the rating on Dichotomous scales of Yes and No, where internally in the backend it will be stored as Yes $= 1$ and No $= 0$ in database. The sum of the rating of all 5 questions will be calculated for that citizen. This sum will be abbreviated in this paper as SM and can be depicted as in (1).

$$SM = sum\left[Rating(Q1, Q2, Q3, Q4, Q5)\right] \tag{1}$$

For every citizen, this SM will be calculated and stored in the database of the department.

Considering NC $=$ Number of Citizens who have given ratings, then the SC $=$ Sum of SM of each citizen will be calculated. After this, the AM $=$ Arithmetic Mean will be calculated by using SC and NC. This can be depicted as in (2).

$$AM = SC/NC \tag{2}$$

This AM will be rounded-off to a Natural number having no decimal. Consider this Rounded AM as Rating of the Department $=$ RD.

This RD will be linked to the Incentive calculation of the department. For this Incentive Rate IR, the RD will be multiplied by 2 as depicted in (3).

$$IR = RD * 2 \tag{3}$$

This IR is the Incentive Rate Percent. This IR will be used to calculate the Incentive Amount IA. For this, IR% will be multiplied by Basic Salary = BS as depicted in (4).

$$IA = IR\% * BS = (IR/100) * BS \tag{4}$$

This IA will be shown to the Department's Employee in their Pay Slip in the Incentive Amount field.

For this complete architecture, the infrastructure proposed is:

1. Database server
2. Application server
3. Webserver
4. Load balancer servers
5. Internet access
6. Website Application

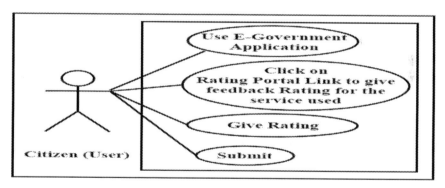

Fig. 1. Use-case diagram depicting Citizen as main entity and its actions

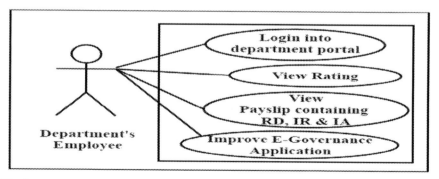

Fig. 2. Use-case diagram depicting Department's Employee as the main entity and its actions

Figure 1 and Fig. 2 diagrams of the proposed application. Figure 3 shows the Architecture diagram which can be used to model the Architecture of the application. Figure 4 shows the Flowchart diagram which depicts the flow of the application proposed [16].

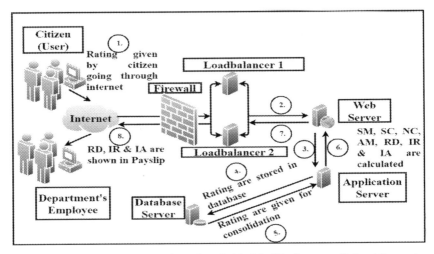

Fig. 3. Architecture diagram of Citizen-Centric-Model of Performance-Related-Pay system

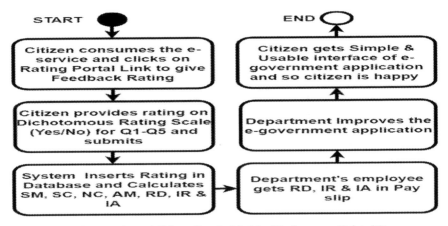

Fig. 4. Flowchart of Citizen-Centric-Model of Performance-Related-Pay

3.2 Proposed Data

The data will consist of a Questionnaire to be asked on Portal from Citizen.

The e-governance application can be assessed on seven Parameters of Accessibility, Content Availability, Ease of Use, Integrated Service Delivery, Status, and Request Tracking, Information Security and Privacy, and End Service Delivery [15].

The following 5 questions Q1, Q2, Q3, Q4, and Q5 are formulated after studying these parameters. The citizen shall provide the rating on Dichotomous scales of Yes and No, where internally in the backend it will be stored as Yes $= 1$ and No $= 0$.

Q1. Are the government services made available without personally visiting the office?
Q2. Are the facilities to upload the documents provided?
Q3. Did the verification of all documents required to get the service was done online by Government officers without personally visiting the office?
Q4. Are you able to get the proper status of your application?
Q5. Is the application timely processed without personally visiting the office? [15]

4 Result and Discussion

To validate the proposed Citizen-Centric-Model of Performance-Related-Pay, a manual survey of 10 citizens is conducted. These citizens were asked to give Yes or No for the above listed 5 Questions (Q1–Q5) for the Postal and Telecommunications Department.

The response of the citizen taken in the survey along with the sum of responses SM for each citizen is given in Table 4 where $1 =$ Yes and $0 =$ No response of Citizen and C1–C10 column headings are depicting the Citizens.

Table 4. Result of the manual survey done to validate proposed Rating Portal. (C1–C10 = Citizens, Q1–Q5 = Questions, SM = Sum of response of each question given by Citizen, 1 = Yes, 0 = No)

		Citizen									
		C1	C2	C3	C4	C5	C6	C7	C8	C9	C10
Questionnaire	Q1	1	1	0	1	1	0	1	1	1	0
	Q2	0	0	0	0	0	0	0	0	0	0
	Q3	0	0	0	0	0	0	0	0	0	0
	Q4	1	1	1	0	1	1	0	1	0	1
	Q5	1	1	0	1	1	1	1	1	1	0
	SM	3	3	1	2	3	2	2	3	2	1

Then the remaining parts SC, NC, AM, RD, IR are calculated as shown below and consolidated and shown in Table 5:
SC = Sum of each SM = 22.
NC = Total Number of Citizens participated in survey = 10.
AM = NC/SC = 22/10 = 2.2
RD = Round-off(AM) = 2.
IR = RD * 2 = 2 * 2 = 4.
Here, for this study, BS is considered as 15000 Rupees. So the IA is calculated as
IA = (RD/100) * IR = (4/100) * 15000 = 600.

As this is manual validation, so considering that these feedbacks are given by citizens for the month of March 2020 in the proposed Rating Portal. Then this RD = 2 will be shown on the portal in that month to both citizen and employee and this IA = 600 will be given in March Pay Slip of Postal and Telecommunications Department's Employee in the Incentive Amount field.

Table 5. Results of the remaining components calculated using the responses of 10 citizens.

Components	Results
SC	22
NC	10
AM	2.2
RD	2
IR	4
BS	15000
IA	600

It is assumed that this RD and IA will be taken by the department as the scope of improvement as the maximum of 10% incentive hike can be achieved by it each month. Also, it is assumed that the Public Administrator can easily track the RD of each department and so it can analyze the issues by studying the response of citizens for each question from Q1 to Q5 and can instruct the departments to improve. Once the department starts scoring RD = 5, the public administrator can look into other minor usability issues of citizens and get the questions changed on the portal to further improve the usability of e-governance applications.

5   Conclusion and Future Scope

As citizens are the end-users of the government and still in the current scenario, citizens are facing many issues due to long-queues to complete tasks, irresponsibility and un-accountability of government employees, corruption in the system, etc. So, to tackle these issues, Improvement in the current system is needed and this can be achieved by improving the usability of e-governance applications for users (citizens). For this, the Citizen-Centric-Model of Performance-Related-Pay is proposed in this paper. To implement this, the design of the Rating Portal is proposed in this paper. It is assumed that the government will link this portal to each department's service portal. Once service is received by the citizen, the citizen will get a link for this Rating Portal where the rating has to be given on the dichotomous rating scale (Yes/No) for Questions (Q1–Q5). This rating will be stored in the database and based on these ratings, SM, SC, NC, AM, RD, IR will be calculated. This IR will be applied on BS and the final IA will be given in the Pay-slip of the department's employee and the RD will be shown to the user as the current rating of the department.

The future scope are described as follows:

5.1 Future Scope for Researchers

First, as the design of the proposed model is given in this paper, the researchers can implement it and provide the actual response for all departments with as many citizen's responses as possible. Second, in this paper, only the dichotomous rating scale is considered, so the Likert scale rating can also be considered for taking the response of Q1–Q5, and accordingly, the model can be customized and research can be conducted. Third, in this paper, the maximum incentive that can be given is considered as 10%, but the researcher can customize it and perform the research.

5.2 Future Scope for Public Administrator

The design of Citizen-Centric-Model of Performance-Related-Pay is proposed in this paper. This model can be implemented and linked to each service providing portal of each department. At the places where the citizen finally receives the service, a link can be provided which will redirect the citizen to this Rating Portal. This model will also help Public Administrator to track the level of e-governance achieved and will help to reach the final stage of e-governance where everything will be completed online and on-time. Thus this model is assumed to remove the major issues faced by citizens like long-queues to complete tasks, irresponsibility and un-accountability of government employees, and corruption in the system by compelling the active participation of each stakeholder of the governance. This model is assumed to help to link the citizen's e-participation with the Performance of Government Departments, thereby achieving citizen satisfaction by continuously tracking and improving the usability.

References

1. ISO 9241–210: Ergonomics of human-system interaction (2010)
2. Mahalingam, B., Akash, D.P.: Major drawbacks of public distribution system in india-a review. Int. J. Sci. Res. Dev. **4**, 602–605 (2016)
3. Sundström, A.: Exploring performance-related pay as an anticorruption tool. Stud. Comp. Int. Dev. **54**, 1–18 (2019). https://doi.org/10.1007/s12116-017-9251-0
4. Lee, H.-W.: The pros and cons of increasing the proportion of performance pay: an evidence from South Korean Public Enterprise. Public Perform. Manag. Rev. **43**, 1150–1173 (2020)
5. Ulf, P., Florian, K.: Does performance-related pay and public service motivation research treat state-owned enterprises like a neglected Cinderella? A systematic literature review and agenda for future research on performance effects. Public Manag. Rev. **22**, 1119–1145 (2020)
6. Arayankalam, J., Khan, A., Krishnan, S.: How to deal with corruption? Examining the roles of e-government maturity, government administrative effectiveness, and virtual social networks diffusion. Int. J. Inf. Manage. **58**, 1–22 (2020)
7. KIM, Y.S.: Analyzing factors that affect job attitude, job satisfaction and job performance in public sector. Thesis. KDI School of Public Policy and Management, pp. 1–54 (2020)
8. Renato, R., Giuseppe, M., Roberta, S., Matteo, T., Marco, B.: Is merit pay changing ethos in public administration? Cogent Bus. Manage. **7**, 1–15 (2020)

9. Cainarca, G.C., Delfino, F., Ponta, L.: The effect of monetary incentives on individual and organizational performance in an italian public institution. Adm. Sci. **9**, 1–19 (2019)
10. Barbato, G., Salvadori, A., Turri, M.: There's a Lid for every Pot! The relationship between performance measurement and administrative activities in Italian Ministries. Cogent Bus. Manage. **5**, 1–20 (2018)
11. Evangelia, M., Dimitrios, M.: Enhancing employees' work performance through organizational justice in the context of financial crisis. A study of the greek public sector. Int. J. Public Adm. **42**, 509–519 (2019)
12. Alessandro, S., Patrizio, M.: Performance-Related payments in local governments: do they improve performance or only increase salary? Int. J. Public Adm. **41**, 321–334 (2017)
13. Hujran, O., Abu-Shanab, E., Aljaafreh, A.: Predictors for the adoption of e-democracy: an empirical evaluation based on a citizen-centric approach. Trans. Gov. People Process Policy **14**, 523–544 (2020)
14. Mukamurenzi, S., Grönlund, Å., Islam, M.S.: Challenges in implementing citizen-centric e-government services in Rwanda. Electron. Gov. **15**, 283–302 (2019)
15. Department of Administrative Reforms & Public Grievances. National e-Governance Service Delivery Assessment 2019, Ministry of Personnel, Public Grievances & Pensions, Government of India.https://nesda.gov.in/publicsite/NeSDA_2019_Final_Report
16. UML diagrams creation website. https://app.diagrams.net/
17. Wirtz, B.W., Kurtz, O.T.: Local e-government services: quality aspects and citizen usage preferences. Electron. Gov. Int. J. **14**, 160–176 (2018)
18. Gupta, D.N.: Citizen-centric approach for e-governance. In foundations of e-government. In: 5th International Conference on E-Government, International Congress of E-government (ICEG) (2007)
19. Ghareeb, A.M., Ramadan, N., Hefny, H.A.: E-government adoption: a literature review and a proposed citizen-centric model. Electron. Gov. Int. J. **15**, 392–416 (2019)
20. Iqbal, H.: Improving public service delivery in Pakistan through citizen feedback. Glob. Delivery Initiative, 1–5 (2019)
21. Beeri, I., Uster, A., Gadot, E.V.: Does performance management relate to good governance? a study of its relationship with citizens' satisfaction with and trust in Israeli local government. Public Perform. Manage. Rev. **42**, 241–279 (2018)
22. Trivedi, P.: Performance management in government: a primer for leaders. The Commonwealth, pp. 1–135 (2018)

PGF Cyberpolicing to Defuse Fake Government of Telangana (FGoT), Fake Government of India (FGoI) and Cybercriminal Legacy

B. Malathi[1]($\boxtimes$), P. Munesh[2], and K. Chandra Sekharaiah[3]

[1] Jawaharlal Nehru Technological University, Hyderabad, Telangana, India
[2] Jagan College of Engineering, Nellore, Andhra Pradesh, India
[3] Jawaharlal Nehru Technological University, Manthani, Telangana, India

Abstract. FGoT/FGoI are known as the Twin Big Data Cybercriminally Seditious Fake Governments that are first of the kind in Indian history (TBDCS-FGsIIH). FGoI and FGoT are the obverse and the reverse of the same coin of the JNTUHJAC's cybercriminal website, http://www.jntuhjac.com. The mitigation and defusion of cybercrimes in the case study are challenging tasks for cyberpolicing. Consequently, the case study of FGoT and FGoI has a very good potential for a cyberpolicing legacy of the remedial forum, PGF's counterintelligence alternatives for the mitigation and defusion of cybercrimes. We conclude that PGF's cyberpolicing legacy is significant in the development of the Smart City, Hyderabad as well as Telangana/India. PGF successfully endeavored ICT usage based on cybersafe, cybersmart academics in Telangana. The empirical results indicate that PGF successfully imparted national education to the higher education students by cyberpolicing for positive quality of national digital life on the bedrock of good national character. We reiterate, however, that it is important that GoI/GoT/Cyberabad Police/JNTUH take initiatives by prohibition orders and white paper release to remedy and recover from the national losses due to the FGoI/FGoT cybercrimes and to mitigate the cybercriminal legacy in academics due to the TBDCSFGsIIH.

Keywords: Semantic Web and Social Networks (SWSN) · Cyberpolicing cognitive engineering · Fractional cognitive engineering · Cybercriminally Seditious Twin Fake Governments in Indian History (CSTFGsInIH) · Fake Government of Telangana (FGoT) · Fake Government of India (FGoI) · Cybercriminally Seditious Twin Fake Governments in India (CSTFGsII) · NFGoT = Not Fake GoT = GoT2Jun2014 · National cognition impairment

1 Introduction

At the outset, we assert that this paper presents some new perspectives of IT and governance in the present day world. The authors have great respect for the GoI and the GoT as responsible citizens of Mother India. However, for reliable, sustainable democracy, we highlight the cybercrimes that have GoI-abusive and GoT-abusive impact and legacy

© Springer Nature Singapore Pte Ltd. 2021
A. K. Luhach et al. (Eds.): ICAICR 2020, CCIS 1393, pp. 181–191, 2021.
https://doi.org/10.1007/978-981-16-3660-8_17

and assert that correct remedies and recovery from these cybercrimes are required as ICT initiatives from the GoI, GoT, JNTUH, Cyberabad and the general masses such that we have truly real-time, smart governance which strengthens the roots of democracy in India. We are in a time wherein NISG (https://www.nisg.org/), CGG (https://www.cgg.gov.in/) and RTGS (https://www.rtgs.ap.gov.in/) are some governance models in India. In [28], "Countering Negative Models that Surround Disruptive ICT Usage: Ensuring a Successfully Sustainable Society, Nation and Culture" contains an abstract and a lecture for its elaboration. The FGoT/FGoI are considered negative models of web applications because they are India-abusive.

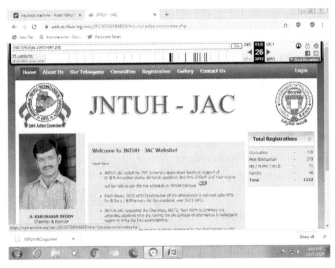

Fig. 1. JNTUHJAC website homepage dt.26Feb2012 snapshot crawled from Wayback Machine

AI Agent software, wayback machine, was used as a tool for cyberforensic diagnostics. The many snapshots of the traces of the TBDCOs were captured as screenshots and presented in [2, 17]. The crux of the matter in our earlier works was cyberpolicing to defuse the TBDCOs. But, now, new perspectives of the cyberpolicing case study have come up. One such perspective is that the case study involves, apart from the TBDCOs, the Fake Government of India, the First Fake Government of India in Indian history. Figure 1 shows the Indian national emblem in the logo used in the cybercriminal website http://www.jntujac.com. The usage of the Indian national emblem is simply indicative of the forgery of the National Seal of India. In earlier works, we highlighted that the usage was violative of the State Emblem of India (Prevention of Improper Use) Act 2005. But, the point that this amounted to the prevalence of a Fake Government of India was overlooked. So, we, now, emphasize this dimension of the case study. The first FIR registered in Jan2014 for this case study of India-abusive crimes in JNTUH academic environment was against the violation of the State Emblem of India (Prevention of Improper Use) Act 2005. In the course of judicial examination, the mention of the sedition crime was impressively recorded by the Magistrate. In [22], the second FIR registered in Jan 2018 in the Cybercrimes P.S., Cyberabad was against Identity Theft (ITAct 2008), Section 66-C violation as the FGoT/FGoI cybercrimes.

The seditious cybercrimes are evaluated to have 80,000 as the degree of cybercrime owing to which they are considered big data crimes. Of late, the cybercriminally seditious dimension of FGoT/FGoI generated considerable pabulum in the frontranks of cybersecurity world of R&D in IT as well as in the cyberpolicing organizations such as Cyberabad Metropolitan Police and Peoples' Governance Forum (PGF). This is clear from it that there were best research paper awards for the R&D work by FGoT/FGoI-remedial PGF's cyberpolicing thinktank for the defusion of the FGoI/FGoT. In this paper, we highlight that the case study involves Fake Government of India (FGoI) as another organization apart from the Twin Big Data Cybercriminal Organizations (TBDCOs) which were highlighted in our earlier works. We conclude that PGF's cyberpolicing legacy is significant in the development of the Smart City, Hyderabad as well as Telangana/India as long as the prevalence and existence of FGoT/FGoI and their variegated forms such as online and offline dimensions are not ruled out by a white paper release by the Cyberabad police/JNTUH/Not FGoT (GoT2Jun2014-?)/GoI together with prohibition orders against the TBDCSFGsIIH.

The rest of the paper is organized as follows: Sects. 2 and 3 detail about FGoI/FGoT cybercrimes and PGF's solution approach. Section 4 presents the degree of crime details and comparison of the Cybercrimes with Corona. Section 5 presents the visuals of the social media campaign using Google+. Section 6 concludes the paper.

2   What Is Fake Government of India - The First FGIIH?

It is already well proven by the many publications of PGF that the case study involves CSFGoT. Nevertheless, the mention of the national seal of India opens new vistas of the cybercrimes spectrum for the case study. The mention of the national seal may be considered as forging the signature of GoI. This means that a Fake Government of India was prevalent by means of the cybercriminal website. Now, important questions arise. Who was the Prime Minister of the FGoI? Who was the home minister of the FGoI? Who was the foreign affairs minister of the FGoT? The issue should not be seen as just merely a misdeed of a miscreants group in Telangana. It is rather a thoroughly contemplated act of violation of the sedition law, the constitution of India, the IT Act 2008 Section 66-C. Because JNTUH has many foreign students with a well-established directorate for foreign students, it is to be looked into as to whether the foreign students partnered through the cybercriminal website knowingly or unknowingly, covertly or overtly by such means as online registrations for constituting the population under FGoI. Interestingly, JNTUH did not issue prohibition orders against the CSTFGsII and the cybercrimes.

3   PGF's AI Solution Approach to CSFGoT

PGF is a cyberpolicing organization. It consists of cyberpolicing professionals whose R&D presentations/publications span such institutions as IIT Madras, IIT Guwahati, IIT

Roorkee, IIT Kanpur, IIT Kharagpur, IIT Delhi, IRMA Anand, JNU Delhi. PGF's cyber-policing by online guidance and counselling is an example of cybercognitive approach for cyberpolicing solution, the defusion of the CSFGoT/FGoI.

Each and every student is made to develop one's own website with innovative features for PGF awareness drive for its Cyberpolicing Solutions. A remedy for the Cyber-criminally Seditious Fake GoT (CSFGoT = GoT2011-?) is to make public the PGF's cyberforensic findings through awareness drive by the PGF members. Each and every student considered oneself a PGF member and generate public awareness within one's own circle of friends, relatives, neighbors, pupils and organizational citizens as well as by social media means. One should imbibe the spirit of the PGF for social, national and academic good and follow creative approaches for inculcating the cyberpolicing attitude and for volunteering for the PGF's solutions and for the realization of the goals of PGF's cyberpolicing. Mother India Consciousness has been generated and regenerated such that the engineering solutions give rise to transforming the "Make in India" campaign as "Make in India Successfully" campaign. A foreign solution or foreign involvement for the cyberpolicing solutions should be rather dispensed with. In a higher education institution like JNTUH, there are foreign students and the prevalence of CSFGoT due to their presence in the JNTUH academic environment should be considered sensitively such that national exploits by the foreign students do not become a possibility. The Cyberabad Police should reveal the details of the data of the online registrations in the cybercriminal website in our case study for cyberpolicing and issue a public declaration about whether any foreign students in JNTUH academic environment partnered with the CSFGoT. The pupils who are PGF members study the PGF publications and its unche-quered R&D services and tread on the similar pathway to excel in academic performance and development.

4   Disaster Management of Big Data Crimes

The CSFGoT-cybercrimes phenomenon involved a national hazard. The CSFGoT-cybercrimes have imperilled the voyage of the national ship hazardously and the realization of the national goals for Telangana became challenged. Telangana engineering academics became infested with cybercrimes of big data degree. As per the latest statistical analytics, the degree of cybercrimes in the case study is 1,20,000 i.e. 2500 registrations * 4 cybercrimes * min. 4 years of incidence (2011–2014) * 3 cybercriminal organizations (JNTUHJAC, FGoT and FGoI). This is considered a big data crime because of the many varieties of factors involved in the DoC. The DoC value of 1,20,000 is considered so high that we designate it as a big data crime. Digital India in the context of ICT development has been the catchphrase nowadays. Now, every Indian has digital life. But, what is the quality of digital life (QoDL)? The QoL parameters may be extended to the QoDL in the ICT usage context. QoDNL refers to Quality of Digital National Life. It refers to the national character of the citizen in the ICT context. The encompassing parameters span national amity, national solidarity, national integrity, national unity etc. Nation means its people. Nation-building means developing the national character of the citizens of the nation. The big data crimes of FGoI/FGoT indicate that the Positive Quality of Digital National Life (QoDNL) parameters such as national amity, national solidarity, national integrity, national unity, national consciousness of Indian netizens are at stake.

So we have to reverse engineer the national digital lifecycle and management. This is possible by the issue of the prohibition orders against the CSTFGsII and by the government's initiatives by releasing a white paper w.r.t. the CSTFGsII. Basically, FGoI/FGoT crimes led to national cognition impairment. The national cognitive engine has to be repaired by the prohibition orders and the white paper release by the governments in authority.

Foreign students are many in Hyderabad in Osmania Univ. and JNTUH. The prevalence of India-abusive cybercrimes gives cues to foreigners for a degraded outlook w.r.t. the academics and the nation itself. In the age of cyberwarfare, the resultant poses a national menace as the foreigners can easily partner with the cybercriminals for disruptive academics which imperils the nation. So, the PGF has undertaken the task of cyberpolicing the maladaptive management in Telangana academics.

4.1   The Corona Menace vis-a-vis the FGoT/FGoI Menace

Corona has the potential of the kind of a national disaster. Hence, the GoI applied the Disaster management Act 2005 in dealing with Corona. Corona has the potential to lead one to death. Corona spread can imperil the nation. Some experts including a Japanese Nobel Laureate termed Corona as artificial which meant 'fake biological entity'. Some considered Corona as having the potential as a biological warfare weapon (Fig. 2).

Some considered FGoT/FGoI as having the potential as a cyberwarfare weapon. The national breakdown due to FGoT is imperceptible. The national lockdown due to Corona is perceptible.

Corona is a pandemic and is incident through out the length and breadth of India. All sates and UTs are affected. But, FGoT/FGoI are cybercriminal organizations. Only Telangana is affected by these cybercrimes. The higher education environment is badly affected due to FGoT/FGoI. FGoT/FGoI are not health hazards. In the backdrop of cybercriminal setting, the Telangana polity turned detrimental to national ethos. Both Corona and FGoT/FGoI have had viral spread. But, Corona is a biological entity. The viral spread of FGoT/FGoI in the sense that nearly 2500 registrations were online for citizenship/membership under FGoT/FGoI meant that the Telangana higher education environment turned foul to assume cybercriminal dimensions. National response is a necessity for FGoT/FGoI cybercrimes too such that they are not seen as a precedence for recurrence of similar India-abusive cybercrimes. Prohibition orders against the FGoI/FGoT are to be issued by the GoI/NFGoT.

PGF STRESSES NEED TO CREATE AWARENESS ON CYBERCRIMES

Hyderabad: People's Governance Forum (PGF) said there is an urgent need for creating awareness about cybercrimes to keep a vigil on the misuse of the virtual world by vested interests. Addressing media here on Sunday the PGF founder Prof Dr K Chandra Sekhariah after conducting an awareness camp cited how a group of cybersecurity specialists has figured out a group of people hosting a fake website in the name of Government of Telangana and tried to organise people both online and offline.

He said a police complaint was registered in January 2018 in the Cybercrimes wing of the city police on the issue He said people hosting such fake websites in the name of elected governments of various States and even the Government of India, to lure and organise people should be treated seriously, as such cyber activities might pose a problem for the government as well the society.

"He said such illegal activities could also be used to encourage people to disturb the peace in the society and creat a security threat for the safet and security of the people an the country," he added.

It was against this backdro that the PGF has taken up th awareness activities to prevent adverse impact on those taken for a raid and misuse their talents by joining hands with such activities, he said.

The contents of the R.K. Math publications book, "Vivekananda His call to the Nation" gave us inpiration to be patriotic with a strong sense of national values. The national values are in variegated forms such as national consciousness, national solidarity, national amity, national integrity, national solidarity, national character, national life, digital national life, quality of national life, quality of digital national life, national sovereignty, national integration and national fervor, national spirit, national education, national heritage, national motto, national development, ...

PGF is a Cyberpolicing Thinktank. PGF is an R&D organization in JNTUH. It is for developing a Swachch, Secure Digital India. It strives for better QoDNL(Quality of Digital National Life) and for cybercrime-free Netizens with a sense of the aforementioned national values and for improvement in cyberethics standards among the JNTUH university academics stakeholders in Telangana Higher Education. Swachch Telangana should not mean just merely open defecation free(ODF) Telangana. It should mean cybercrime-free Telangana as well wherein the cybercriminal legacy of the TBDCOs(Twin Big Data Cybercriminal Organizations, viz. FGoT(2011-) & JNTUHJAC) is extirpated. Swachch Bharat should not mean just merely ODF-Bharat. It should mean also Bharat that is free from the clutches of the GoI-abusive, India-abusive(involving the TBDCOs) cybercrimes in its higher education academics. Prohibition order against the TBDCOs is an impending necessity to extirpate the cybercriminal legacy due to the TBDCOs and the underlying deleterious effects. JNTUH should not be considered a university of good standard or accreditation as long as it does not issue the prohibition orders against the TBDCOs and their cybercriminal legacy that prevails in its academic environment causing academic and national losses compoundingly? Hyderabad should not be considered a real Smart City as long as the smart crimes affecting the netizens of Hyderabad and the academics of the universities in Hyderabad, Telangana, A.P. and India are left sparingly without prohibition orders.

PGF has more than 1000 members consisting of Ph.D. students, senior faculty in JNTUH colleges, Ph.D./M.Tech/B.Tech/M.C.A. /M.Sc./ B.A./ B.Sc. students. It is a remedial forum for solutions to the FGoT cybercrimes of sedition. It is http://sites.google.com/site/pgovernanceforum. Many members have their own PGF websites which contain the hyperlinks to their respective YouTube channels. These YouTube channels contain the video presentations of the respective Ph.D. students for the R&D publications under PGF. The Google drive contents of its members contain the R&D publications which are also freely downloadable. The social media associated with PGF include sound cloud, twitter, facebook, youtube, ...

Fig. 2. Hans India News about PGF in 2018

5   Cognitive Visuals of Cyberpolicing R&D Chief's PGF Organizational Efforts for Adaptive Academic Management: Google Plus Social Network Account, Kcraiah's Snapshots

The Google plus data is captured and archived in 3 parts-Part one consists of the contents in https://drive.google.com/file/d/1rixynGS1qVYgspwkB16V18xu6z17pvX-/view?usp=sharing;

Part 2 consists of the contents in https://drive.google.com/file/d/1yX_3xvy6wamKxDr3x71bHsz2cFixdloZ/view?usp=sharing.

Part 3 consists of the cognitive visuals which are depicted as 5 snapshots in the Figs. 3, 4 and 5 below. The data in the contents of these three parts are put together for holistic analytics (Figs. 6 and 7).

Fig. 3.   Google Plus Account kcraiah and its Profile Picture

Fig. 4. The Teacher (kcraiah)'s 'profchandswsnsubjectclass' student group for teaching 'Semantic Web and Social Networks' students for 2 semesters consisted of 74 members of MCA and M.Tech. courses in School of IT, JNTUH

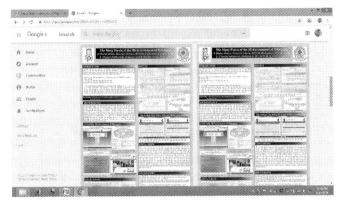

Fig. 5. Cracking the Conundrum: "The Many Facets of the 3D-Government of Telangana" Poster presentation in NAoP2018 New Delhi

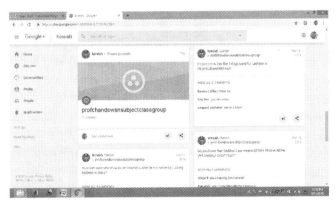

Fig. 6. Evaluating the Awareness of the School of IT students w.r.t. Sedition Law and Implications of its Violation by the TBDCOs

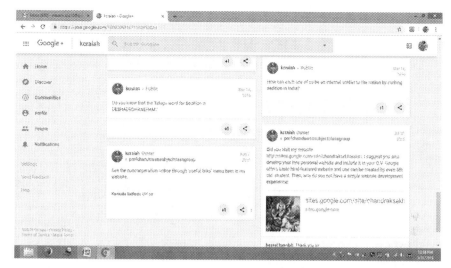

Fig. 7. Training the Students to partner with kcraiah's PGF for Cyberpolicing

6 Conclusions

PGF has evolved as a cyberpolicing forum owing to the intense R&D work w.r.t. the case study for the defusion of the TBDCOs. We conclude that the PGF's cyberpolicing legacy is significant in the development of the key Smart City, Hyderabad in India as long as the prevalence and existence of FGoT and the FGoI and their variegated forms such as online and offline dimensions are not ruled out by a white paper release by the Cyberabad police/JNTUH/Not FGoT (GoT2Jun2014-?) together with prohibition orders against the TBDCSFGsIIH. As long as PGF's work and conclusions are not honored by the GoT, GoI, Cyberabad Police and JNTUH in the form of prohibition orders for the defusion of the TBDCSFGsIIH, so long Hyderabad cannot be considered a Smart City. This is so because we opine that Smart Policing is essential for a city to be termed a Smart City. A city where cybercrimes are left without conviction and cybercriminal organizations are left without prohibition orders, by the police, against them, cannot be truly a Smart City. PGF's findings are crucial for the development of a Smart City such as Hyderabad. A city wherein PGF's counterintelligence alternatives are neglected cannot be considered a Smart City. PGF's cyberpolicing legacy is as relevant as or much more relevant than the cybercriminal legacy of the TBDCSFGsIIH. PGF generated significant impact in Telangana Engineering academics by cyberpolicing in the presence of TBDCSFGsIIH.

References

1. Usha Gayatri, P., Chandra Sekharaiah, K.: Encasing the baneful side of Internet. In: National Conference on Computer Science & Security (COCSS 2013), 5–6 April 2013. Sardar Vallabhbhai Patel Institute of Technology, Vasad, Gujarat, India (2013)
2. Tirupathi Kumar, B., Chandra Sekharaiah, K., Mounitha, P.: A case study of web content mining in handling cybercrime. Int. J. Adv. Res. Sci. Eng. **04**(01) (2015). ISSN 2319-8354, www.ijarse.com

3. Usha Gayatri, P., et al.: Exploring cyber intelligence alternatives for countering cyber crime: a continuing case study for the nation. In: Proceedings of the International Conference@Bharati Vidyapeeth's Institute of Computer Applications and Management (BVICAM), New Delhi (India)

4. Usha Gayatri, P., Chandra Sekharaiah, K.: A case study of multiple cybercrimes against the union of India. In: Presented in NCIST 2017@Manipur Institute of Technology, Manipur University & Published in Int. J. Comput. Math. Sci. IJCMS **6**(3), 71–79 (2017). ISSN 2347-8527

5. Aparna, G., Usha Gayatri, P., Mounika, S., Radhika, D., Chandra Sekharaiah, K.: Reviewing a judicial case study of multiple cybercrimes. In: IndiaCOM2016 International Conference, BVICAM, New Delhi (2016)

6. Usha Gayatri, P., Chandra Sekharaiah, K., Premchand, P.: Analytics of judicial case study of multiple cyber crimes against the union of India. School of Law, Pondicherry University, Pondicherry, 2–3 March 2018 (2018)

7. Ravi Kumar, S., Chandra Sekharaiah, K., Sundara Krishna, Y.K., Gouri Shenkar, M.: Cybercrimes-trends and challenges in achieving Swachh Digital India: a case study. In: MRITCISTCSE-2018, pp. 6–8 (2018). ISBN 97893 83038 596

8. Ravi Kumar, S., Chandra Sekharaiah, K., Sundara Krishna, Y.K.: Cybercrimes-trends and challenges in achieving Swachh Digital India using a public cloud: a case study. School of Law, Pondicherry University, Pondicherry, 2–3 March 2018 (2018)

9. Madan Mohan, K., Chandra Sekharaiah, K.: A case study of ICT solutions against ICT abuse: an RTI Act 2005 success story. In: National Seminar on S&T for National Development, Manipur Univ., Imphal (2017)

10. Srihari Rao, N., Chandra Sekharaiah, K., Ananda Rao, A.: An approach to distinguish the conditions of flash crowd versus DDoS attacks and to remedy a cyber crime. School of Law, Pondicherry University, Pondicherry, 2–3 March 2018 (2018)

11. Srihari Rao, N., Chandra Sekharaiah, K., Ananda Rao, A.: An approach to distinguish the conditions of flash crowd versus DDoS attacks and to remedy a cyber crime. Int. J. Comput. Eng. Technol. **9**(2), 110–123 (2018)

12. Srihari Rao, N., Chandra Sekharaiah, K., Ananda Rao, A.: A survey of Distributed Denial of Service (DDoS) defense techniques in ISP domains. In: 5th International Conference on Innovations in Computer Science and Engineering (ICICSE 2017) (2017)

13. https://sites.google.com/site/sekharaiahk/apeoples-governanceforumwebpage

14. Chandra Sekharaiah, K.: Impact of the RTI act within a public authority organization towards employee-employer engagement: a case study. In: Proceedings of the International Conference on "Enriching Employee Engagement in Organization-Role of Psychology", 30 January–1 February 2015 (2015)

15. Madan Mohan, K., Chandra Sekharaiah, K., Premchand, P.: Impact of RTI act with in public authority organization toward employee employer engagement: a case study. School of Law, Pondicherry University, Pondicherry, 2–3 March 2018 (2018)

16. Ramesh Babu, J., Chandra Sekharaiah, K.: Adaptive management of cybercriminal, mal-adaptive organizations, in the offing, that imperil the nation. In: IIT Kharagpur, March 2018, ICDMAI, Pune, January 2018 (2018)

17. Tirupathi Kumar, B., Chandra Sekharaiah, K., Suresh Babu, D.: Towards national integration by analyzing the web mining results of a case of cybercrime. In: 2nd International Conference on Information and Communication Technology for Competitive Strategies (ICTCS 2016), Udaipur, Rajasthan, India, 4–5 March 2016 (2016)

18. Gouri Shankar, M., Usha Gayatri, P., Niraja, S., Chandra Sekharaiah, K.: Dealing with Indian Jurisprudence by analyzing the web mining results of a case of cybercrimes. In: Modi, N., Verma, P., Trivedi, B. (eds.) Proceedings of International Conference on Communication and Networks. AISC, vol. 508, pp. 655–665. Springer, Singapore (2017). https://doi.org/10.1007/978-981-10-2750-5_67
19. Srihari Rao, N., Chandra Sekharaiah, K., Ananda Rao, A.: Janani Janmabhoomischa Swargaadapi Gareeyasi. In: BVRIT, International Conference on Research Advancements in Applied Engineering Sciences, Computer and Communication Technologies, (ICRAAESCCT 2018), 12–13 July 2018. Conference Proceeding of 3rd International Conference on Research Trends in Engineering, Applied Science and Management (ICRTESM 2018) Osmania University Centre for International Programmes, Osmania University Campus, Hyderabad, Telangana State, India, 4 November 2018 (2018). ISBN 978-93-87433-44-1 330
20. Srihari Rao, N., Chandra Sekharaiah, K., Ananda Rao, A.: Janani Janmabhoomischa Swargaadapi Gareeyasi. Int. J. Eng. Technol. (IJET) 7(3.29), 225–231 (2018)
21. Santhoshi, K., Chandra Sekharaiah, K., Lakshmi Kumari, N.: ICT based social policing for Swatch Digital India. School of Law, Pondicherry University, Pondicherry, 2–3 March 2018 (2018)
22. Santhoshi, N., Chandra Sekharaiah, K., Madan Mohan, K., Ravi Kumar, S., Malathi, B.: Cyber intelligence alternatives to offset online sedition by in-website image analysis through WebCrawler cyberforensics. In: Wang, J., Reddy, G.R.M., Prasad, V.K., Reddy, V.S. (eds.) Soft Computing and Signal Processing. AISC, vol. 900, pp. 187–199. Springer, Singapore (2019). https://doi.org/10.1007/978-981-13-3600-3_18
23. Madan Mohan, K., Chandra Sekharaiah, K., Santhoshi, N.: ICT Approach to defuse the cyber-criminal sedition dimension of Telangana movement. In: BVRIT, International Conference on Research Advancements in Applied Engineering Sciences, Computer and Communication Technologies (ICRAAESCCT 2018), 12–13 July 2018 (2018)
24. Madan Mohan, K., Chandra Sekharaiah, K., Santhoshi, N.: ICT approach to defuse the cyber-criminal sedition dimension of Telangana movement. Int. J. Eng. Technol. (IJET) 7(3.29), 360–363 (2018)
25. Pavana Johar, K., Malathi, B., Ravi Kumar, S., Srihari Rao, N., Madan Mohan, K., Chandra Sekharaiah, K.: India-abusive Government-of-Telangana (GoT2011): a constitutional IT (an SMI) solution. In: Proceedings of International Conference on Science, Technology & Management (ICSTM 2018), Punjab University Campus, Chandigarh, India, 12 August 2018 (2018). ISBN 978-93-87433-34-2
26. Pavana Johar, K., Malathi, B., Ravi Kumar, S., Srihari Rao, N., Madan Mohan, K., Chandra Sekharaiah, K.: India-abusive Government-of-Telangana (GoT2011): a constitutional IT (an SMI) solution. Int. J. Res. Electron. Comput. Eng. (IJRECE) 6(3), 1118–1124 (2018). ISSN 2393-9028 (Print), ISSN 2348-2281
27. Singh, K.P.: Hostile witness: legal and judicial contours in Indian laws. Haryana Police J. 1(1), 26–36 (2017)
28. https://sites.google.com/site/chandrasekharaiahk/hyderbadbulbulcharminarchalchal

Energy Consumption Analysis of R-Based Machine Learning Algorithms for Pandemic Predictions

Shajulin Benedict[1]([⊠]), Prateek Agrawal[2,3], and Radu Prodan[3]

[1] Indian Institute of Information Technology Kottayam, Kottayam 686635, Kerala, India
shajulin@iiitkottayam.ac.in
[2] Lovely Professional University, Phagwara, Punjab, India
prateek@itec.aau.at
[3] University of Klagenfurt, Klagenfurt, Austria
radu@itec.aau.at
http://www.sbenedictglobal.com

Abstract. The push for agile pandemic analytic solutions has attained development-stage software modules of applications instead of functioning as full-fledged production-stage applications – i.e., performance, scalability, and energy-related concerns are not optimized for the underlying computing domains. And while the research continues to support the idea that reducing the energy consumption of algorithms improves the lifetime of battery-operated machines, advisable tools in almost any developer setting, an energy analysis report for R-based analytic programs is indeed a valuable suggestion. This article proposes an energy analysis framework for R-programs that enables data analytic developers, including pandemic-related application developers, to analyze the programs. It reveals an energy analysis report for R programs written to predict the new cases of 215 countries using random forest variants. Experiments were carried out at the IoT cloud research lab and the energy efficiency aspects were discussed in the article. In the experiments, `ranger`-based prediction program consumed 95.8 J.

Keywords: Analysis · Energy consumption · Machine learning · R-program · Tools

1 Introduction

Since the very earliest days of the rise of COVID-19 deaths, the havoc due to social distancing practices, researchers, and practitioners have put forth novelty in societal/health-care products, creating a haze of mystery owing to hasty developments. The declaration of COVID-19 as a global pandemic by WHO on 11 March 2020 has motivated several startups and research labs to seriously work on developing solutions, including ICT-enabled intelligent solutions.

There exist solutions to predict the gene characteristics of COVID-19 patients; to visualize the arrival of patients nearer to the vicinity – i.e., mobile

© Springer Nature Singapore Pte Ltd. 2021
A. K. Luhach et al. (Eds.): ICAICR 2020, CCIS 1393, pp. 192–204, 2021.
https://doi.org/10.1007/978-981-16-3660-8_18

applications; to visualize the statistical data relating to COVID-19 and forecast the next few days of the pandemic in various geographical locations – i.e., COVID-19 dashboards; to warn or alert the disease and side effects; to track the pathway of patients and predict the spread of diseases, and so forth. Most of these solutions apply machine learning (ML) algorithms, mostly written in R or python, combined with a few other sophisticated technologies such as IoT, visualization, cloud services, or modern ICT technologies to reach the objectives.

Several research questions need to be addressed in the present real-world prediction scenario:

- Are the existing prediction approaches performance-efficient and energy-efficient?
- Are these software/hardware developments remaining as a prototype-stage of development which needs to be optimized?
- Are the developers capable to investigate into the performance/energy efficiency of ML algorithms?

This paper delves into the energy efficiency aspects of R-based ML algorithms. The energy monitoring mechanism of R-based ML algorithms was discussed and the energy efficiency procedures were highlighted in the work.

Although the proposed energy analysis framework could be adapted to any data science applications, in this paper, the energy analysis of the COVID-19 prediction problem was studied. Towards this end, programs were written in R to predict the new cases of COVID-19 in 215 countries across the globe. The experiments were carried out at the IoT cloud research laboratory and the findings were reported. The energy analysis outcome and the other associated performance issues relating to the developed COVID-19 prediction applications were studied in this paper.

The rest of the paper is organized as follows: Sect. 2 dictates state-of-the art research work in the energy efficiency aspects of COVID-19 products; Sect. 3 showcases the proposed energy monitoring approach for R-based ML algorithms; Sect. 4 illustrates the most commonly applied ML algorithms with more emphasis to `RandomForest` algorithm and its variants in the recent pandemic-related applications; Sect. 5 manifests the observations due to energy improvement aspects; and Sect. 6 concludes the article with a few suggestions.

2   Related Work

Pandemic-causal diseases such as Asian Flu, HIV/AIDS, SARS, Swine Flu, MERS, Ebola, Zika, and COVID-19 have been emerging in the world to create losses and distract humanity. The recent surge of COVID-19 has spread across the globe COVID-19 related research works have abruptly increased in recent months due to a combined effort of the large volume of researchers and practitioners belonging to various domains. A keyword search results on COVID-19 topics at the google scholar site throws light on the increasing research works

Table 1. Literature on COVID-19-related search keywords

Keywords	2019		2020	
	Title	Body	Title	Body
COVID	226	40000	130000	173000
+predict	X	11900	208	52300
+learning	X	3750	13	23400
+Algorithm	X	1840	X	10400
+Performance	X	1360	X	7830
+Energy	X	1070	X	5630

(see Table 1). The keyword "COVID" in the title of the articles increased from 226 to 1,30,000 articles within a few months of the pandemic.

The available COVID-19 solutions are broadly classified into detection, prediction, tracking, and services aspects. These categories are described as follows:

1. detection-based solutions ensure the early detection of COVID-19 patients and perform pattern analysis for the spread of the disease;
2. prediction-assisted solutions model the infection scenario for a given location considering various parameters, including the visits of patients;
3. tracking-enabled solutions identify the source of the pandemic and the rise for the community-spread of the virus; and
4. services-based solutions include the online services that promote the well being of humans in a society – for instance, distribution of food to quarantined patients/visitors.

Researchers, recently, have adopted prediction algorithms to solve COVID-19 problems in varied fashion: i) the author of [2] have applied deep neural network learning algorithm to predict the gene classification leading to COVID-19; ii) Nita et al. [9] have applied prediction algorithms to anticipate the virus transmission pattern among humans in a city; iii) Qian et al. [10] have studied the pattern of human behavior with respect to the spread of the virus over air; iv) Mohamed et al. [8] have proposed a hybrid model combining a marine predator algorithm and a ranking-based diversity prediction strategy to predict the COVID-19 cases using x-ray images; v) Furkan et al. [3] have studied the impact of various ML algorithms such as support vector machine, Linear Regression, Lasso Regression, and so forth, while predicting the COVID-19 cases on tenth day in terms of RSE; and, so forth. Obviously, a large volume of research works have been involved in the past few months that apply prediction algorithms to analyze, classify, or predict the COVID-19 cases.

Apart from predictions, a few researchers have proposed innovative ideas for quantifying data on the web as wrong data could lead to wrong predictions [12]. Similarly, the application of novel security features to address the COVID-19 issues [15] and engaging citizens through social media [11] have been enlightening researchers. In addition, a few researchers have applied ML algorithms to classify COVID cases from pneumonia [1].

As it could be observed, a lot many research works have been carried out to apply prediction algorithms for COVID-19 problems. However, there are not many research works that highlight the energy consumption aspect of these algorithms, more preferably the R-programs. Analyzing the energy consumption of prediction or ML algorithms foregrounds the importance of the present scenario of adopting COVID-19-related applications on battery-operated devices or power-scarce datacenters.

This article proposes an energy analysis framework for R-based prediction programs by extending the EnergyAnalyzer tool. The article highlights the energy consumption of the most commonly applied prediction algorithms by revealing the prediction of COVID-19 new cases in 215 countries.

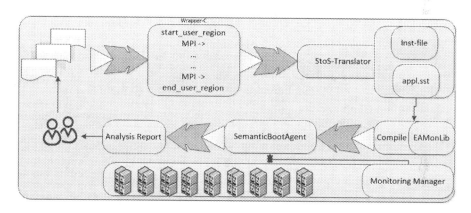

Fig. 1. Energy analysis framework – an extension of EnergyAnalyzer for analyzing R-programs

3   Energy Analysis – An Extended Version

One of the primordial objectives of application developers for decades has been to decipher the behavior of complex algorithms when executed on different architectures. This section explains the performance and energy monitoring approach of R-based ML algorithms which could be applied in predicting the COVID-19-related societal products.

Energy consumption of ML algorithms needs to be analyzed when executed on computing machines so that diligent actions could be performed either manually or by automated machines. The important entities and their primordial functionalities involved in monitoring and analyzing the energy consumption of ML algorithms are extended from the EnergyAnalyzer tool [13] – i.e., in this work, the tool is extended to measure R-based programs; the major extension that is carried out in this work is to analyze R-based ML algorithms – i.e., a wrapper C-module is inserted for measuring the energy consumption of R-programs. A brief outline of the EnergyAnalyzer tool and the extension levied in the work are given below:

1. *SSTranslator: SSTranslator* translates the C/C++ HPC applications or programs with sufficient additional monitoring functions so that the *Semantic-Boot Agent* could monitor the performance/energy measurements of them. Besides, it highlights the measurement outcome in various formats, including HTML and XML.
   In this work, the *SSTranslator* parses the R-programs and inserts the functions into a customized wrapper-C module of the tool.
2. *SemanticBoot Agent:* The *SemanticBoot Agent* is responsible to execute the ML algorithms for the appropriate datasets; it invokes *Monitoring Manager* module to pursue performance/energy measurements.
3. *Monitoring Manager:* The *Monitoring Manager* entity measures the energy consumption and performance metrics such as Execution Time, L1 cache misses, and so forth. The energy measurement of R-based programs is based on the RAPL energy monitoring hardware unit of modern processors – i.e., sandybridge and above in Intel architectures. The measurement values are uploaded into `mongodb`-based *EAPerfDB* database of the tool. Accordingly, the energy analysis report or the performance analysis report is formulated in various formats such as CSV, HTML, and graphs.

Figure 1 illustrates the functional components of the proposed energy analysis framework that was extended from the previous EnergyAnalyzer tool.

4   COVID-19 and ML Algorithms

The emphasis of this work is to reveal the findings of the performance/energy impacts of ML algorithms that are applied in predicting the COVID-19 cases of various countries. Towards this end, a few programs for predicting the COVID-19 cases from various countries were developed based on the `RandomForest` algorithm.

This section explores the R-programs that were developed for predicting COVID-19 new cases based on available datasets. In fact, there exists several dataset for COVID-19. However, the most commonly utilized dataset for developing prediction services is from WHO [17]. This dataset is applied in this article to analyze newer COVID-19 cases and to enable energy-efficient innovative predictive services.

4.1   RandomForest – A Brief

In short, `RandomForest` algorithm is a supervised machine learning algorithm that is widely applied in several research problems. The algorithm is an ensemble learning algorithm based on the bagging technique; it creates decision trees, i.e., objective answers, that are formulated depending on the input labels/parameters. The algorithm is initially designed by Leo Breimen [5] and it is quite popular due to the wide applicability in various domains such as medicine, IoT, finance, and so forth.

4.2   COVID-19 Predictions

In this work, programs were written in R to predict the new cases of COVID-19 from various countries. In order to predict the number of new COVID-19 cases/patients in the vicinity, the following steps are adopted:

1. *Data Collection:* Initially, COVID-19 pandemic data are collected from WHO site [17].
2. *Process Data:* Next, the data are processed to ensure a complete availability of information – i.e., NULL values need to be removed and numeric representation of columns has to be enabled for pursuing mathematical modeling during the training process of the algorithm.
3. *Split Data:* Next, the data are split into training, validation, and testing dataset. This step enables the creation of models and predictions accordingly.
4. *Modeling:* During the training phase of the algorithm, decision trees are created based on a bootstrapping technique for a given set of samples. The training model attempts to reduce the variance while avoiding bias to the learning processes.
5. *Validation:* Once after the creation of the training model, validation and testing of data are carried out. The validation of the model is based on mean squared error which is represented as *RSE*. The *RSE* value is represented as a percentage – i.e., higher the percentage, higher is the quality of the model; and, vice-versa.
6. *Prediction:* The testing phase of the algorithm attempts to identify the best possible tree based on the given dataset while considering the decision variables.

4.3   Popular Packages

There exist a few popular R packages that represents `RandomForest` algorithm. These algorithm variants could be applied for predicting COVID-19 cases by writing specific codes. A few notable R packages that are adapted in the work to predict the new COVID-19 cases and their highlights are given below:

1. *randomForest:* The `randomForest` package of R [6] suggests the utilization of `mtry` and `ntree` features. `mtry` defines the number of variables to be sampled at each split in trees; `ntree` defines the number of trees that needs to frame a forest. Typically, the `ntree` parameter of `randomForest` package should be higher in number for manifesting a better prediction result.

2. *ranger:* The *ranger* package of R [7] is a fast implementation of the `RandomForest` algorithm. Compared to the other implementations, `ranger` returns a probability estimate for each tree of random forests during the modeling phase of the algorithm.

3. *rPart:* The *rPart* package of R [14] is named after the recursive partitioning concept of the basic `RandomForest` algorithm. This package emphasis on the way how the splitting or partitioning should occur while creating the training models. For instance, the parameters such as `minsplit` and `minbucket` of *rPart* package urges the partitioning to occur in a pre-defined fashion – i.e., `minsplit` defines the minimum number of observations of a node.

4. *RandomForestSRC:* The *randomForestSRC* package of R [4] is a fast parallel version of RandomForest algorithm. The package is implemented using the OpenMP parallel programming model where hardware threads are utilized to execute the algorithm. As similar to *randomForest* package, it has `mtry` and `ntree` parameters to define the number of split in each trees of a randomForest. However, additionally, the package includes the OpenMP style of implementation to speedup the training or testing processes.

5. *party:* The *party* package of R [16] is similar to the *rPart* package which recursively partition the data while framing the trees in a randomForest. However, in *party*, the partitioning is emphasised on the formation of conditional inference trees (ctrees) while modeling data.

Are these variants of `RandomForest` algorithm providing an energy-efficient solution while executing them on computing machines, especially when the prediction of COVID-19 cases are considered? This question could be addressed by analyzing the R implementations of ML algorithms using the proposed energy analysis mechanism (discussed in Sect. 3).

5   Experimental Results

In this section, the energy analysis report while predicting the increase of COVID-19 cases in a country is disclosed. Throughout the experiments, the dataset available at WHO is considered – i.e., "WHO-COVID-19-global-data.csv" [17]. The dataset has 35762 entries from 215 countries across the globe; it has information relating to new COVID-19 patients/cases, cumulative cases, new deaths, and cumulative number of deaths starting from 24 February 2020 to 18 August 2020.

All the experiments were carried out at the DELL Precision Tower 7810 machine of the IoT Cloud Research laboratory of the Institute. The machine consists of 48 CPUs belonging to Intel(R) Xeon(R) CPU E5-2650 v4; it has ubuntu-18.04 kernel 5.4.0-42-generic for executing the energy analysis framework while monitoring R programs which were written in R version 4.0.0.

5.1   Validation Analysis

Although any R-programs or prediction algorithms could be analyzed, in this work, a few most popularly utilized random forest packages, such as, `rpart`, party, randomForest, randomForestSRC, and ranger, are utilized in the context of predicting and analyzing COVID-19 newly arising cases in different countries.

The programs were manifested, at first, to validate the prediction models due to the inclusion of appropriate packages. To do so, the dataset was subdivided into two parts: training and testing – 50% data were utilized for establishing a training model and the other 50% were utilized for predicting data. In the experiments, the rise of new COVID-19 patients/cases of a country was considered as a prediction variable, and the other parameters such as the number of new deaths, and the cumulative number of deaths, were considered as dependent variables. The validation results, while utilizing the packages, are depicted in Fig. 2.

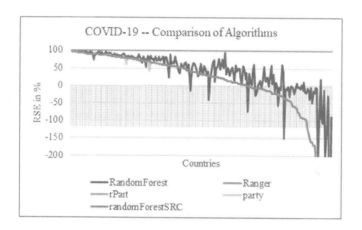

Fig. 2. RSE observed from 215 countries – validation of packages

It could be observed from the Fig. 2 that the packages have suffered from noise or overfitting problems for the dataset available with over 75 countries. The negatively predicted values of the Fig. 2 manifest the poor adoption of prediction algorithms to the given dataset. Obviously, there is a requirement for tuning the dataset and validating the appropriate fit to the algorithms/packages in an iterative manner. This aspect of handling the prediction algorithms in an iterative manner could reduce the battery life of certain COVID-19 aware applications or increase the electricity costs of dataservers in real-world associated applications.

The top 10 countries that were benefited by the prediction algorithms are showcased in Table 2.

5.2 Prediction Analysis

Similarly, the prediction of the number of new cases reported in these countries was analyzed. To restrict the prediction results to higher qualities, the

Table 2. Countries showing top 10 prediction results – RSE in percent

Sl.No	Country	RandomForest	Ranger	rPart	Party	randomForestSRC
60	SV	98.15	99.87	96.39	96.39	96.39
94	IN	98.64	100	95.42	95.42	95.423
210	UZ	95.27	100	94.60	94.60	94.60
97	IQ	97.56	99.99	94.47	94.47	94.47
130	MX	95.99	100	94.44	94.48	94.44
43	CO	97.17	99.99	93.34	93.34	93.34
164	RO	95.21	98.99	93.21	93.21	93.21
8	AR	96.88	100	93.20	93.20	93.20
28	BR	95.10	99.99	92.22	92.22	92.22
165	RU	94.42	100	92.18	92.18	92.18

dataset resembling the highly accurate top 6 countries during the validation stage of the prediction analysis was considered. The possibility of new COVID-19 cases/patients that would be reported for the tenth day was analyzed.

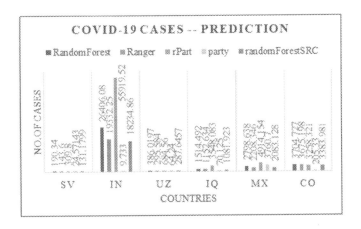

Fig. 3. COVID-19 prediction results for tenth day

The following points could be observed from the prediction results of Fig. 3:

- The prediction algorithms revealed the arise of the probable new cases for the tenth day of the future incidents. Notably, *rPart* package was able to nearly predict the future COVID-19 cases when compared to the other packages. For instance, the COVID-19 entry on 18/8/2020 of countries such as India and Uzbekistan was 550709 and 587. These numbers have increased in the prediction results to 55919 and 684 when predicted using *ranger* assisted R-program.

– India showed a higher number of cases when compared to the other countries such as SV, UZ, IQ, MX, and CO.

5.3   Energy Consumption Analysis

The energy consumption analysis and the performance analysis of the R programs which were written to predict to COVID-19 cases of 215 countries were analyzed.

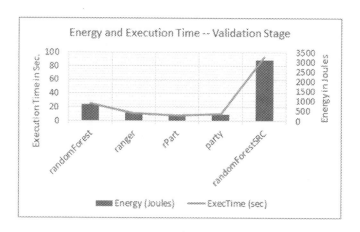

Fig. 4. COVID-19 validation stage – energy and execution time

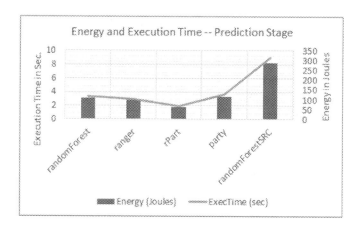

Fig. 5. COVID-19 prediction stage – energy and execution time

Figure 4 highlights the energy consumption in Joules and the execution time in seconds when the prediction algorithms were executed on the machine. It could be observed that rPart package has the minimal energy consumption and execution time – i.e., 279.288 J and 8.03 s. However, the prediction results were not as accurate as the ranger package. Notably, the ranger package was able to provide better prediction results with minimal energy consumption and execution time values – i.e., 412.65 J and 11.42 s.

Figure 5 was obtained when the programs were executed to showcase the energy consumption and execution time value of predictions. During the predictions for COVID-19 new cases in countries (i.e., the tenth day from the date of inception), the execution time was comparatively very low. This reveals the fact that the execution time would be higher for establishing a training model than testing the model. In Fig. 4, it is noticed that the execution time was less than 8 s for most of the prediction programs. Consequently, the energy consumption of the programs was lesser than the previous case for establishing training models. This shows that there is a strong relationship between the execution time and the energy consumption of R programs.

Besides the energy and execution time analysis, the proposed energy analysis framework is able to measure the performance bottleneck of prediction algorithms. Table 3 illustrates the performance metrics that were measured while executing the COVID-19 prediction algorithms on the machine. The performance metric values such as Total Number of Instructions (Total INS), Level 1 Data Cache Misses (L1 DCM), Unconditional Branch Instructions (BR UCN), and Level 3 Total Cache Misses (L3 TCM) were recorded by the measurement framework for the COVID-19 prediction programs.

Table 3. Performance analysis for COVID-19 predictions

Packages	Total INS	L1 DCM	BR UCN	L3 TCM
randomForest	44759	1035	2868	1594
ranger	45093	1013	2871	1539
rPart	43831	1038	2820	1585
Party	44123	1039	2827	1539
randomForestSRC	45326	999	2886	1688

The following performance-related points were inferred:

- the total number of instructions for the programs was in the range of 44000;
- the party package based prediction program showed the highest L1 cache misses – i.e., the L1 cache miss for the program was 1039;
- the BR UCN, L1 DCM, and L3 TCM were almost similar for the different prediction programs of consideration.

6 Conclusion

The era of the post-eruption of the COVID-19 pandemic has marked the composite culture of innovations in varied departments, including machine learning associated research/product developments. Tens of thousands of solutions have been tested and practiced with the application of ML algorithms, often written in R/python languages, without much satisfactory notes owing to several performance/energy bottlenecks, especially when battery-operated IoT-enabled solutions were considered.

This article proposed an energy analysis framework for R-based ML algorithms by extending the previous EnergyAnalyzer tool. The framework was experimented after a set of prediction programs based on random forest algorithm for predicting the new COVID-19 cases were written in R. Experiments were carried out at the IoT Cloud Research laboratory and the energy consumption analysis of the prediction programs were manifested. Besides, the capability of the framework to pinpoint the performance bottleneck of the prediction programs was illustrated in the work.

Acknowledgement. This work is supported by IIIT-Kottayam faculty research fund and OEAD-DST fund.

References

1. Hasan, A.M., Al-Jawad, M.M., Jalab, H.A., Shaiba, H., Ibrahim, R.W., AL-Shamasneh, A.A.: Classification of COVID-19 coronavirus. Pneumonia and healthy lungs in CT scans using Q-deformed entropy and deep learning features. Entropy J. **22**(517), 1–15 (2020). https://doi.org/10.3390/e22050517

2. Heni, B.: COVID-19, Bacille Calmette-Guerin (BCG) and tuberculosis: cases and recovery previsions with deep learning sequence prediction. Ingenierie des Systemes dInformation **25**(2), 165–172 (2020)

3. Rustam, F., et al.: COVID-19 future forecasting using supervised machine learning model. IEEE Access **8**, 101489–101499 (2020). https://doi.org/10.1109/ACCESS.2020.2997311

4. Ishwaran, H., Kogalur, U.B.: Fast Unified Random Forests for Survival, Regression, and Classification (RF-SRC) (2020). https://cran.r-project.org/web/packages/randomForestSRC/randomForestSRC.pdf. Accessed Aug 2020

5. Breimen, L.: Random Forests (2020). https://www.stat.berkeley.edu/~breiman/randomforest2001.pdf. Accessed Aug 2020

6. Breiman, L., Cutler, A.: Breiman and Cutler's Random Forests for Classification and Regression (2020). https://cran.r-project.org/web/packages/randomForest/randomForest.pdf. Accessed Aug 2020

7. Wright, M.N., Wager, S., Probst, P.: A Fast Implementation of Random Forests (2020). https://cran.r-project.org/web/packages/ranger/ranger.pdf. Accessed Aug 2020

8. Abdel-Basset, M., Mohamed, R., Elhoseny, M., Chakrabortty, R.K., Ryan, M.: A hybrid COVID-19 detection model using an improved marine predators algorithm and a ranking-based diversity reduction strategy. IEEE Access **8**, 79521–79540 (2020). https://doi.org/10.1109/ACCESS.2020.2990893

9. Shah, N.H., Suthar, A.H., Jayswal, E.N.: Control strategies to curtail transmission of COVID-19. Int. J. Math. Math. Sci. **2020**(2649514), 1–12 (2020). https://doi.org/10.1155/2020/2649514

10. Liu, Q., et al.: Spatiotemporal Patterns of COVID-19 Impact on Human Activities and Environment in Mainland China Using Nighttime Light and Air Quality Data. Remote Sens. **12**(1576), 1–14 (2020). https://doi.org/10.3390/rs12101576

11. Chen, Q., Min, C., Zhang, W., Wang, G., Ma, X., Evans, R.: Unpacking the black box: how to promote citizen engagement through government social media during the COVID-19 crisis. Comput. Hum. Behav. **110**, 106380 (2020). https://doi.org/10.1016/j.chb.2020.106380

12. Sear, R.F., et al.: Quantifying COVID-19 content in the online health opinion war using machine learning. IEEE Access **8**, 91886–91893 (2020). https://doi.org/10.1109/ACCESS.2020.2993967

13. Benedict, S., Rejitha, R.S., Preethi, B., Bright, C., Judyfer, W.S.: Energy analysis of code regions of HPC applications using energy analyzer tool. Int. J. Comput. Sci. Eng. **14**(3), 267–278 (2017). Inder Science Publishers

14. Therneau, T., Atkinson, B., Ripley, B.: Recursive Partitioning and Regression Trees (2020). https://cran.r-project.org/web/packages/rpart/rpart.pdf, Accessed Aug 2020

15. Weil, T., Murugesan, S.: IT risk and resilience cyber security response to COVID-19. IT Prof. **22**, 4–10 (2020). https://doi.org/10.1109/MITP.2020.2988330

16. Hothorn, T., Hornik, K., Strobl, C., Zeileis, A.: A Laboratory for Recursive Partytioning (2020). https://cran.r-project.org/web/packages/party/party.pdf. Accessed Aug 2020

17. WHO COVID-19 Global Dataset (2020). https://covid19.who.int/. Accessed in Aug 2020

Performance Analysis of Deep Learning Classification for Agriculture Applications Using Sentinel-2 Data

Gurwinder Singh[1]([✉]) [ID], Ganesh Kumar Sethi[2] [ID], and Sartajvir Singh[3] [ID]

[1] Punjabi University, Patiala 147 002, Punjab, India
[2] Multani Mal Modi College, Patiala 147 001, Punjab, India
[3] Chitkara University School of Engineering and Technology, Chitkara University, Solan 174 103, Himachal Pradesh, India
sartajvir.singh@chitkarauniversity.edu.in

Abstract. North Indian states are largely covered with agricultural land which plays an important role in nation's economy development. Remote sensing offers a cost-effective and efficient solution for sustainable monitoring and mapping of agricultural land. In past, various classification algorithms were developed and implemented for agriculture applications. But the conventional techniques are generally based on machine learning algorithms which are easy to implement but at the same time require human intervention on decision making. Nowadays, deep learning algorithms are becoming more popular due to the presence of trained models and one-time processing. However, the deep learning model required a large amount of computation time and needs to be tested in different regions for different applications. In the present work, the deep learning algorithm has been tested over agricultural land (over a part of Punjab state, India) using Sentinel-2 imagery. The major classes considered in the present analysis are vegetation area, water, and buildup area. For validation purposes, output classified maps are compared with reference datasets which were acquired from field observations for some points. The statistical results have shown that more than 80% of accuracy has been obtained using a deep learning algorithm. This study has many applications in the monitoring and mapping of land use land cover regions using a deep learning algorithm.

Keywords: Sentinel-2 · Deep learning · Agriculture mapping · Classification · Remote sensing

1 Introduction

Agriculture land is the backbone of the Indian economy and the major source of national income via agriculture and allied activities. Agriculture is acting as a supply chain of food products and raw material for industrial development, commercial activities, and international trade [1]. It has also been observed that in India, agriculture activities have been continuously decreased due to urbanization or the growth of other sectors [2].

© Springer Nature Singapore Pte Ltd. 2021
A. K. Luhach et al. (Eds.): ICAICR 2020, CCIS 1393, pp. 205–213, 2021.
https://doi.org/10.1007/978-981-16-3660-8_19

But still as compared to other countries the rate is high [3]. It is more important to perform a comprehensive assessment of agriculture concerning crop production which is essential to meet the demands of the food supply chain [4]. For mapping and validating the agricultural land, field observation methods are generally followed which are time-consuming, expensive, and tedious tasks and also sometimes not feasible for inaccessible areas [5].

For large land-use and land-cover mapping and monitoring, remote sensing plays an important role at a lower cost. Remote Sensing (RS) dataset can be broadly categorized into two types first is optical sensor and another is microwave [6]. The optical remote sensing dataset is further classified such as Landsat-8 [7], Sentinel-2 [8], MODIS (Moderate Resolution Imaging Spectroradiometer) [9], AVIS (Avian Information System) the classification requires the training data to classify the input data such as DL (Deep Learning), ANN (Artificial Neural Network), CNN (Convolutional Neural Network). The microwave remote sensing dataset is also classified such as SAR (Synthetic Aperture Radar), SCATSAT-1 (Scatterometer Satellite-1) [10] represents the classified dataset obtained from two different classifier LMM (Linear Mixer Model) and ANN (Artificial Neural Network), respectably. In past, various techniques have been developed and modified to improve the utilization of remotely sensed data [11]. However, most of the traditional techniques or models are generally based on machine learning algorithms and proven as significant in large area mapping [12]. But such methods are generally based on either supervised or unsupervised models [13]. From the literature [14], it has been seen that unsupervised methods are not able to extract the actual information satellite imagery due to dependency on untrained data [15]. On the other hand, supervised methods provide better results but are limited by the requirement of training data which varies from person to person [16].

In literature, various datasets have been explored such as Sentinel 1 dataset for agriculture land mapping [17], a high-resolution satellite dataset to classify the cloud, shadow, and land cover [18] as shown in Table 1. Moreover, [19] investigated the suitability and potential of DCNN in the supervised classification of POLSAR (Polarimetric Synthetic Aperture Radar) dataset. Spatial information was naturally employed in terrain classification due to the properties of convolutional networks. The deep learning algorithms take the advantage of the trained model to reduce the intervention of the user's skill. However, the deep learning model requires more computation power and time and needs to be tested in different regions for different applications [20].

The main aim of this research paper is to estimate and validate agriculture using a deep learning algorithm over a part of Punjab state, India using the Sentinel-2 dataset. In the study area, the major classes are vegetation area, water, and buildup area [23]. Previously the classification of the agriculture land is done to the door-to-door survey. Here in the proposed work remote sensing dataset is being used for automatic classification of agriculture land. The introduction is followed by the study site and the associated dataset in Sect. 2; Sect. 3 describes the methodology of the deep learning algorithm with the Tensor Flow model for agriculture land cover classification using the sentinel-2 dataset. The experimental results are discussed in Sect. 4. At last, the conclusion has been drawn in Sect. 5.

Table 1. Some papers on agricultural land, the number of classes, and classification accuracy.

Author	Species	Accuracy	Dataset	Approach
[18]	11	96%	Sentinel-1	RNN[a], K-NN[b], RF[c] and VSM[d]
[21]	22	86.2%	Colour Plant Images	DCNN[f]
[22]	10	77%	WV-2[e]	ANN[g]
[23]	5	87.3%	Landsat-8 OLI/Sentinel-2 MSI	ML[h]
[24]	11	85%	Sentinel-1	CNN[i]
[25]	14	92%	Sentinel-2	ML[h] and DL[j]
[26]	8	94.94%	Sentinel-1/Sentinel-2	TWINNS[k]
[27]	4	94.85%	Landsat-8/Sentinel-2	FCNs[l]
[28]	15	96.5%	Sentinel-2	R-CNN[m]
[29]	10	98.7%	Sentinel-2	CNN[i] and R-CNN[m]
[30]	3	97.53%	Digital images	R-CNN[m]
[31]	2	91%	Landsat-8/Sentinel-2	DL[j]
[32]	55	85%	NS-55	DLCD[n]

[a]RNN: Recurrent Neural Network, [b]K-NN: K-Nearest Neighbors, [c]RF: Random Forest, [d]VSM: Vector Support Machines, [e]DCNN: Deep Convolutional Neural Networks, [f]WV-2: World View-2, [g]ANN: Artificial Neural Network, [h]ML: Machine Learning, [i]CNN: Convolutional Neural Network, [j]DL: Deep Learning, [k]TWINS: TWIn Neural Network for Sentinel Dataset, [l]FCNs: Fully Convolutional Networks, [m]R-CNN: Recurrent-Convolutional Neural Network, [n]DLCD: Deep Learning Change Detection

2   Study Area and Satellite Dataset

The study site lies in district Fatehgarh Sahib and Patiala, Punjab, having geographic coordinates between $30^{\circ}26'N-30^{\circ}33'N$ in latitude and $76^{\circ}21'E-76^{\circ}29'E$ in longitude as shown in Fig. 1. The class categories existing over the study area are agriculture, buildup, and water. The data is acquired on 19 February 2018 using the European Space Agency (ESA) based on Sentinel-2. It offers the information in twelve different spectral bands such as (a) 4 VIS and NIR bands at 10 m of spatial resolution, (b) 6 Red and SWIR bands at 20 m of spatial resolution, and (c) 3 atmospheric correction bands at 60 m of spatial resolution. The sentinel dataset offers a range of applications in various scientific domains.

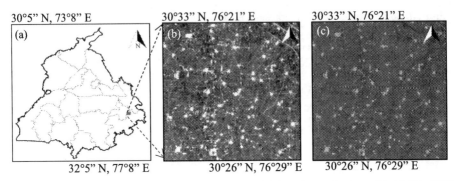

Fig. 1. Study area: (a) Punjab state (India) map highlights the study area, (b) 19-Feb-2018 Sentinel-2 imagery at RGB 432 (Natural color), and (c) 19-Feb-2018 Sentinel-2 imagery at RGB 843 (color infrared that highlights the healthy and unhealthy vegetation). (Color figure online)

3 Methodology

The flowchart of the proposed methodology is shown in Fig. 2 which involves the three basic steps: (a) Pre-processing that involves the area of interest (AOI) acquisition from atmospherically and radiometrically correction sentinel-2 data, (b) implementation of deep learning module to train the model, (c) classification. This framework is designed specifically to work with remotely sensed imagery to solve geographic problems through deep learning technologies [33]. The model must be trained to look for specific features using a set of input label raster that indicates know samples of the features [34].

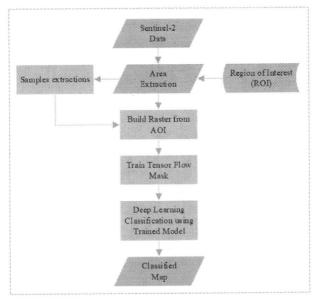

Fig. 2. The flowchart is shown the proposed methodology of the deep learning algorithm.

3.1 Preprocessing

In the present work, we are dealing with the agricultural land and therefore, the data has been pre-processed using the "Sen2cor" software tool for performing atmospheric and radiometric corrections [25]. Afterward, the AOI is extracted from the Sentinel-2 tile and fed to the deep learning model.

3.2 Deep Learning Process

Initially, the sample was extracted from the input dataset with the knowledge of field data and then, builds the raster with the help of training samples. Afterward, the Tensor Flow model is used to train the models using specific parameters. Once the model is trained, then it is used as the input to the classification procedure. It is noted that while implementing the deep learning process, the computer specification includes the Intel Xeon 3.2 2400 MHz 8.25 4C CPU, 16 GB of RAM, 512 GB of SSD, and NVIDIA Quadro P620 2 GB (4) MDP GFX.

3.3 Classification

Once the activation output is obtained, the classified maps have been generated using the automatic Otsu threshold method for each class category i.e. build-up area, agricultural, water, and rest all the categories have been assigned to mixed categories.

4 Experimental Analysis

The methodology shown in Fig. 3 was applied to process the dataset sentinel-2. There after the processed dataset was further analyzed to map in the form of classified dataset. To get the desired classified dataset such as vegetation, water and build-up area the classification scheme has been performed. The land cover regions were generated for each of the deep learning-based classification approaches for each category separately i.e. (a) vegetation area, (b) buildup area, and (c) water area, respectively [35].

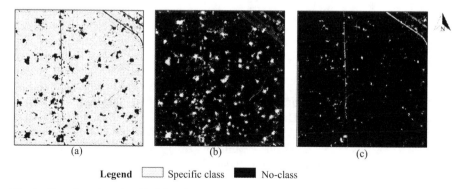

Fig. 3. Deep learning classified fractional maps (a) Vegetation area; (b) Build-up area; and (c) water area.

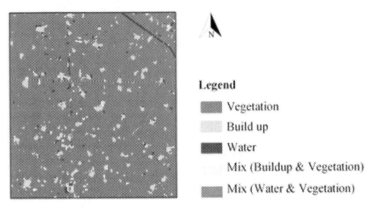

Fig. 4. Deep learning algorithm classified output after Otsu threes holding function.

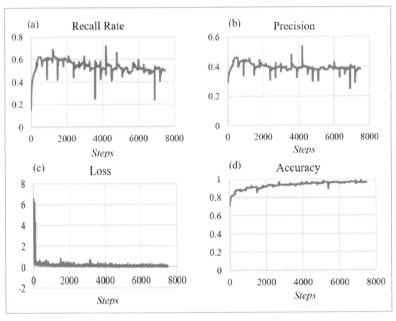

Fig. 5. The average training model recall-rate, precision, loss, and accuracy of 100 epochs for the 10 k folds.

From Fig. 4, the thematic map derived from sentinel-2 and additional data using deep learning classification algorithm show the variation in vegetation, buildup, water, mix (buildup & vegetation), and mix (water & vegetation) [36]. The main reason behind the existence of mixed categories due to limited spatial resolution. District Fatehgarh Sahib and Patiala had the samples to be collected of total number and were the effective category within the study area [37].

Moreover, the statistical analysis has also been computed for deep learning algorithms such as recalls rate, precision, loss, and accuracy. Figure 5 represents the statistical analysis to highlight the performance of the deep learning model. From the statistical analysis, the validated precision (88% accuracy) and average (98% accuracy) at the 100th epoch for 10 k folds and while the loss and recall rate started to raise. To hand was no significant raise or reduction after the 100th epoch, and the training was completed at that epoch to attain the highest accuracy possible without any over-fitting the network [21].

5 Conclusion

This study highlights the performance of a deep learning algorithm for agricultural land using the Sentinel-2 satellite dataset. The deep learning algorithm confirmed that all classes contributed in the classification process. Also, all the mixed categories have been separated to improve the accuracy of classification [38]. From the present study, it has been concluded that deep learning plays a significant role in the extraction of accurate class categories from satellite images. However, the results may be affected due to the limited spatial resolution of the satellite dataset. It is expected that different vegetation types could be explored using high spatial resolution and hyperspectral dataset. This research has a wide contribution in agriculture field to decide the area suitable for crop field. This research will prove to be more useful in finding areas that burn straw. Future recommendations also involved the exploration of deep learning algorithms for different land-use and land-cover types using different sensors at the global level.

Acknowledgment. The authors would like to thank the U.S. Geological Survey (USGS), NASA for providing the ESA's Sentinel-2 dataset via an online platform (https://earthexplorer.usgs.gov/). They also like to thank Chitkara University, HP for providing infrastructural and laboratory facilities for the smooth conduct of the experiment.

References

1. Sicre, C.M., Fieuzal, R., Baup, F.: Contribution of multispectral (optical and radar) satellite images to the classification of agricultural surfaces. Int. J. Appl. Earth Obs. Geoinf. **84**, 1–13 (2020)
2. Lu, D., Mausel, P., Brondízio, E., Moran, E.: Change detection techniques. Int. J. Remote Sens. **25**, 2365–2401 (2004). https://doi.org/10.1080/0143116031000139863
3. Adepoju, K.A., Adelabu, S.A.: Improving accuracy evaluation of Landsat-8 OLI using image composite and multisource data with Google Earth Engine. Remote Sens. Lett. **11**, 107–116 (2020). https://doi.org/10.1080/2150704X.2019.1690792
4. Singh, G., Sethi, G.K.: Automatic land cover classification using learning techniques with dynamic features. Int. J. Innov. Technol. Explor. Eng. **8**, 499–503 (2019)
5. Khamparia, A., Singh, A., Luhach, A.K., Pandey, B., Pandey, D.K.: Classification and identification of primitive Kharif crops using supervised deep convolutional networks. Sustain. Comput. Inform. Syst. (2019). https://doi.org/10.1016/j.suscom.2019.07.003

6. Sood, V., Gusain, H.S., Gupta, S., Taloor, A.K., Singh, S.: Detection of snow/ice cover changes using subpixel-based change detection approach over Chhota-Shigri glacier, Western Himalaya, India. Quat. Int. (2020). https://doi.org/10.1016/j.quaint.2020.05.016

7. Zhong, L., Hu, L., Zhou, H.: Deep learning based multi-temporal crop classification. Remote Sens. Environ. **221**, 430–443 (2019). https://doi.org/10.1016/j.rse.2018.11.032

8. Virnodkar, S.S., Pachghare, V.K., Patil, V.C., Kumar, S.: CaneSat dataset to leverage convolutional neural networks for sugarcane classification from Sentinel-2. J. King Saud Univ. - Comput. Inf. Sci. (2020). https://doi.org/10.1016/j.jksuci.2020.09.005

9. Singh, S., Sood, V., Prashar, S., Kaur, R.: Response of topographic control on nearest-neighbor diffusion-based pan-sharpening using multispectral MODIS and AWiFS satellite dataset. Arab. J. Geosci. **13**, 1–9 (2020). https://doi.org/10.1007/s12517-020-05686-z

10. Sood, V., Gusain, H.S., Gupta, S., Singh, S., Kaur, S.: Evaluation of SCATSAT-1 data for snow cover area mapping over a part of Western Himalayas. Adv. Sp. Res. **66**, 2556–2567 (2020). https://doi.org/10.1016/j.asr.2020.08.017

11. Singh, S., Tiwari, R.K., Sood, V., Gusain, H.S.: Detection and validation of spatiotemporal snow cover variability in the Himalayas using Ku-band (13.5 GHz) SCATSAT-1 data. Int. J. Remote Sens. **42**, 805–815 (2021). https://doi.org/10.1080/2150704X.2020.1825866

12. Aznar-sánchez, J.A., Piquer-rodríguez, M., Velasco-muñoz, J.F., Manzano-agugliaro, F.: Worldwide research trends on sustainable land use in agriculture. Land Use Policy **87**, 1–15 (2019)

13. Singh, S., Tiwari, R.K., Gusain, H.S., Sood, V.: Potential applications of SCATSAT-1 satellite sensor: a systematic review. IEEE Sens. J. **1748**, 1 (2020). https://doi.org/10.1109/jsen.2020.3002720

14. Sood, V., Gupta, S., Gusain, Sh.S., Singh, S.: Spatial and quantitative comparison of topographically derived different classification algorithms using AWiFS data over Himalayas. J. Indian Soc. Remote Sens. **4**, 1–12 (2018). https://doi.org/10.1007/s12524-018-0861-4

15. Singh, S., Tiwari, R.K., Gusain, H.S., Sood, V.: Potential applications of SCATSAT-1 satellite sensor: a systematic review. IEEE Sens. J. **20**, 12459–12471 (2020). https://doi.org/10.1109/JSEN.2020.3002720

16. Sankar, S., Srinivasan, P., Luhach, A.K., Somula, R., Chilamkurti, N.: Energy-aware grid-based data aggregation scheme in routing protocol for agricultural internet of things. Sustain. Comput. Inform. Syst. **28**, 100422 (2020). https://doi.org/10.1016/j.suscom.2020.100422

17. Shendryk, Y., Rist, Y., Ticehurst, C., Thorburn, P.: Deep learning for multi-modal classification of cloud, shadow and land cover scenes in PlanetScope and Sentinel-2 imagery. ISPRS J. Photogramm. Remote Sens. **157**, 124–136 (2019)

18. Ndikumana, E., Ho, D., Minh, T., Baghdadi, N., Courault, D., Hossard, L.: Deep recurrent neural network for agricultural classification using multitemporal SAR Sentinel-1 for Camargue, France. Remote Sens. **10**, 1–16 (2018). https://doi.org/10.3390/rs10081217

19. Zhou, Z., Li, S., Shao, Y.: Crops classification from Sentinel-2A multi-spectral remote sensing images based on convolutional neural networks. In: IGARSS, pp. 5300–5303 (2018)

20. Viana-Soto, A., Aguado, I., Martínez, S.: Assessment of post-fire vegetation recovery using fire severity and geographical data in the mediterranean region (Spain). Environ. - MDPI **4**, 1–17 (2017). https://doi.org/10.3390/environments4040090

21. Dyrmann, M., Karstoft, H., Midtiby, H.S.: Plant species classification using deep convolutional neural network. Biosyst. Eng. **151**, 72–80 (2016). https://doi.org/10.1016/j.biosystemseng.2016.08.024

22. Omer, G., Mutanga, O., Abdel-Rahman, E.M., Adam, E.: Performance of support vector machines and artificial neural network for mapping endangered tree species using WorldView-2 data in Dukuduku Forest, South Africa. IEEE J. Sel. Top. Appl. Earth Obs. Remote Sens. **8**, 4825–4840 (2015). https://doi.org/10.1109/JSTARS.2015.2461136

23. Ka, A., Sa, A.: Improved Landsat-8 Oli and Sentinel-2 Msi classification in mountainous terrain using machine learning on Google earth engine, pp. 632–645 (2018)
24. Kussul, N., Lavreniuk, M., Skakun, S., Shelestov, A.: Deep learning classification of land cover and crop types using remote sensing data. IEEE Geosci. Remote Sens. Lett. **14**, 778–782 (2017). https://doi.org/10.1109/LGRS.2017.2681128
25. Adagbasa, E.G., Adelabu, S.A., Okello, T.W.: Application of deep learning with stratified K-fold for vegetation species discrimation in a protected mountainous region using Sentinel-2 image. Geocarto Int. 1–21 (2019). https://doi.org/10.1080/10106049.2019.1704070
26. Ienco, D., Interdonato, R., Gaetano, R., Ho, D., Minh, T.: Combining Sentinel-1 and Sentinel-2 Satellite Image Time Series for land cover mapping via a multi-source deep learning architecture. ISPRS J. Photogramm. Remote Sens. **158**, 11–22 (2019). https://doi.org/10.1016/j.isprsjprs.2019.09.016
27. El Mendili, L., Puissant, A., Chougrad, M., Sebari, I.: Towards a multi-temporal deep learning approach for mapping urban fabric using Sentinel 2 images. Remote Sens. **12**, 423 (2020). https://doi.org/10.3390/rs12030423
28. Mazzia, V., Khaliq, A., Chiaberge, M.: Improvement in land cover and crop classification based on temporal features learning from Sentinel-2 data using recurrent-Convolutional Neural Network (R-CNN). Appl. Sci. **10**, 1–23 (2020). https://doi.org/10.3390/app10010238
29. Campos-Taberner, M., et al.: Understanding deep learning in land use classification based on Sentinel-2 time series. Sci. Rep. **10**, 1–12 (2020). https://doi.org/10.1038/s41598-020-742 15-5
30. Ganesh, P., Volle, K., Burks, T.F., Mehta, S.S.: Orange: mask R-CNN based orange detection and segmentation. IFAC Pap. **52**, 70–75 (2019). https://doi.org/10.1016/j.ifacol.2019.12.499
31. Peterson, K.T., Sagan, V., Sloan, J.J., Sloan, J.J.: Deep learning-based water quality estimation and anomaly detection using Landsat-8/ Sentinel-2 virtual constellation and cloud computing. GIScience Remote Sens. **57**, 1–16 (2020). https://doi.org/10.1080/15481603.2020.1738061
32. Wang, M., Zhang, H., Sun, W., Li, S., Wang, F., Yang, G.: A coarse-to-fine deep learning based land use change detection method for high-resolution remote sensing images. Remote Sens. **12** (1933)
33. Vreugdenhil, M., et al.: Sensitivity of Sentinel-1 backscatter to vegetation dynamics: an Austrian case study. Remote Sens. **10**, 1–19 (2018). https://doi.org/10.3390/rs10091396
34. Grosso, M.M.: Optical and SAR remote sensing synergism for mapping vegetation types in the endangered Cerrado/Amazon Ecotone of Nova. Remote Sens. **11**, 01–25 (2019)
35. Stendardi, L., et al.: Exploiting time series of Sentinel-1 and Sentinel-2 imagery to detect meadow phenology in mountain regions. Remote Sens. **11**, 1–24 (2019). https://doi.org/10.3390/rs11050542
36. Jozdani, S.E., Johnson, B.A., Chen, D.: Comparing deep neural networks, ensemble classifiers, and support vector machine algorithms for object-based urban land use/land cover classification. Remote Sens. **11**, 1–24 (2019). https://doi.org/10.3390/rs11141713
37. Otunga, C., Odindi, J., Mutanga, O., Adjorlolo, C.: Evaluating the potential of the red edge channel for C3 (Festuca spp.) grass discrimination using Sentinel-2 and Rapid Eye satellite image data. Geocarto Int. **34**, 1123–1143 (2019). https://doi.org/10.1080/10106049.2018.1474274
38. Sood, V., Gusain, H.S., Gupta, S., Taloor, A.K., Singh, S.: Detection of snow/ice cover changes using subpixel-based change detection approach over Chhota-Shigri glacier, Western Himalaya, India. Quat. Int. **575**, 204–212 (2020). https://doi.org/10.1016/j.quaint.2020.05.016

Smart Approach for Identification of Pneumonia Using Real-Time Convolutional Neural Networks

Darshankumar C. Dalwadi[✉], Yagnik Mehta, Nisarg Patel, Neel Macwan, and Deep Sakhiya

Birla Vishvakarma Mahavidyalaya Engineering College, V.V. Nagar 388120, Gujarat, India
darshan.dalwadi@bvmengineering.ac.in

Abstract. Pneumonia is one of symptom cause for one of the most widespread Contagious diseases emerged as Coronavirus 2019 known as CoVID-19. This diseases is sharply spreading in most of part of the world effecting small aged and elderly aged people which is causing more than Nine Thousand deaths from all parts of the world. Identification of Pneumonia in Covid cases is happened by analysis of Posteroanterior views (P.A.) X-Rays. Thus, developing a smart and efficient system for detecting Pneumonia must-have utilities even in the future. In Recent Researches, Convolutional neural networks were found to be more accurate and efficient. Nowadays, Features are pre-trained in CNN models on a vast scale of datasets that make medical image identification more efficient. However, analyzing the medical image for Pneumonia's detection is hard to assess because professional expertise is needed to label them. This Paper shows how a convolutional neural network can be used to detect Pneumonia using any generic python notebook with computer vision support.

Keywords: Convolutional neural networks · Radiology · Artificial intelligence · Computer vision · Feature extraction

1 Introduction

There is a serious danger of Pneumonia in developing countries where there are unhygienic living conditions and dirtying types of assets. One out of three passing in India was because of Pneumonia, as revealed by WHO. Investigation of Chest X-rays has been a significant part of Doctors or radiologists for checking how serious the pneumonia disease has happened. The Centers for Disease Control and Prevention (CDC, Atlanta, GA, USA) reveals that 1.7 million grown-ups in the United States Are confronting issues concerning Pneumonia each year, and around 50,000 individuals have been confronted passing in the United States from Pneumonia in 2015 [1]. In 2019–2020 almost 200000 instances of Covid had been accounted for, and almost 8000 have confronted demise till walk 2020, which has side effects of Cold Pneumonia. The World Health Organization (WHO, Geneva, CH) announced that Pneumonia is one of the driving reasons for Child mortality of over 1.4 million, which is about 18% of all youngsters passing younger than

© Springer Nature Singapore Pte Ltd. 2021
A. K. Luhach et al. (Eds.): ICAICR 2020, CCIS 1393, pp. 214–225, 2021.
https://doi.org/10.1007/978-981-16-3660-8_20

5 years overall [2]. The quickly rising danger of respiratory ailments like Pneumonia, CoVid-19 have made this subject increasingly lively for research right now.

Chest X-Rays are an essential thing to analyze Pneumonia, and it needs master doctors and radiologists for evaluation. Conventional profound inclining was utilized, which was additional tedious, and it depended on try completed on people, who make it much increasingly entangled because of an assortment of previous cases. To Overcome these issues in regards to clinical picture characterization, a straightforward way to deal with investigation x-ray and give grouping dependent on reports has been presented right now model consequently plays out the undertaking of isolating Pneumonia non-pneumonia cases. A Deep Convoluted Neural Network Which runs ongoing makes the whole procedure progressively necessary yet cost proficient and with the least computational costings.

In This Decade, CNN-based deep learning algorithms have emerged as a prominent alternative for medical image classifications. However, the last Generation of CNN-based image classifications had similar rigid network architectures relying on the traditional trial-and-error method. U-Net, SegNet, ResNet50, ResNet100, and CardiacNet are prominent architectures for medical imaging. We have used ResNet50 and ResNet100 architectures due to its fast computation and low power requirements. Existing Models like evolutionary-based algorithms and reinforcement learning (R.L.) have been introduced to locate optimum network parameters. However, these methods were more complex yet more power-consuming, making it less efficient than what it can be.

2 Literature Review

The medical risk of Pneumonia in developing countries like India, Bangladesh, Africa, Bhutan, etc., is immense. The treatment of such a disease is time-consuming and requires high expertise, which results in inexpensive treatment. To cure any disease, it is necessary to study it and get verified reports on whether the person under treatment is a patient of Pneumonia or not. It may happen that due to lack of knowledge as well as standardized resources, the doctors may not find the sign of Pneumonia. This case is even worse in 54 countries of Africa, where there is a massive gap of 2.3 million doctors in the number who can be a vital asset in detecting and curing the disease So. To tackle this problem, scientists and researchers have developed, using Machine Learning cases, various models on different architectures.

For example, researchers of Yokohama in January 2018 [3], developed a classifier using RNA sequencing data for the identification of usual interstitial pneumonia pattern. They were successful in defining a decision boundary that specified $\geq 85\%$ accuracy. Another example states that The Deep Radiology Team at San Francisco [4] proposed advances in the detection techniques that used CoupleNet architecture that analyzed the input image and merged them after passing them through spontaneous convolutional networks to generate predictions based on both local and global information. The result generated metrics that segregated the analyzed data into 4 different stages of conclusion. Thus, it was, in turn, difficult to precisely predict and display results. Further research by the radiologists of the Department of Computer Technology of Firat University [5] extracted and combined the features from equivalent layers of CNN architectures like

AlexNet, VGG-16, and VGG-19 and classified the results from all three architectures, which decided analysts over operationalized and confusing [6].

In 2010 a breakthrough research was done by scientists gathered from all over the globe, where they used various image classification like You Only Look Once (YOLO3), U-Net, and Mask R-CNN, producing distributed prediction results [7]. In our model, our approach relies on Mask-RCNN that aims to identify lung opacity that is likely to predict and judge the case of Pneumonia. The CNN technique is being used to improvise and increase the confidence level of accurately detecting the symptoms. This technique is also in utilization for Hemorrhage classification and identification [8].

3 System Blueprint

3.1 Processing System

In Our Case, we have used Our system processor, an i5 generation intel core processor containing AMD graphics processor, which was sufficient to run our python algorithms for Haar Cascade to run the algorithms we have used the anaconda ide for running the whole project.

3.2 Setting up System for Use

Making a system capable of working, we have used the Anaconda Ide. Anaconda is a scientific Python distribution. It has no IDE of its own. The default IDE bundled with Anaconda is Spyder, just another Python package installed even without Anaconda. Additionally, it provides its package manager (conda) and package repository. Nevertheless, it allows installing packages from PyPI using pip if the package is not in Anaconda repositories. It is especially good if you are installing on Microsoft Windows to easily install packages that would otherwise require you to install C/C++ compilers and libraries if you were using pip. It is undoubtedly an added advantage that condo, besides being a package manager, is also a virtual environment manager allowing you

Fig. 1. Anaconda welcome screen

to install independent development environments and switch from one to the other (like victualing). Below is a Screenshot of Anaconda IDE: Fig. 1.

3.3 Anaconda IDE and Jupyter Notebook

The Jupyter notebook is Web Application Integrated along inside the anaconda. Ideas they can use to create Data-Visualizations live code performance and text the python scripts it supports Julia, Python, and R programming languages [9]. It contains the command cell the menus here is List of Features in current menus: Here is a list of the current menus:

- File
- Edit
- View
- Insert
- Cell
- Kernel
- Widgets and Help

Here is a figure for the general layout of Jupyter ide where we have written our algorithms: Fig. 2.

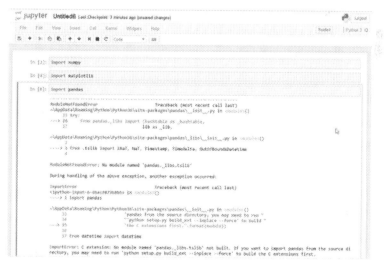

Fig. 2. Jupyter workbook layout

3.4 Project Environment

We have done a setup consisting of binary segregation of Posteroanterior views (P.A.) of X-rays on various classifications of lung opacities as with opacity, without opacity and abnormal and normal cases Main Challenge in analyzing X-Rays is brightness, Resolution settings, and quality of medical images obtained at the end for analyses. In such cases, we have to make our model a way to interpret the received information from X-Ray or medical images. It can give support logic that whether a person is suffering from Pneumonia more precisely is about giving positive or negative report for Pneumonia case-patient.

3.5 Proposed Model

We have described our modeling approach based on fast R-CNN to predict Pneumonia's intensity level based on opacity levels obtained from different X-rays of Chest Samples [10]. A Mask layer of the CNN network is developed to solve the instance segregation of available samples. We have implemented fast R-CNN-based dot pixel-wise segmentation for the classification of samples. We have first implemented the Region of Interest-based Align Classifier that bound the image and only do the process on Region of interest rather than segmenting the entire area following ROIAlign [11]. We have Applied individual pixel segmentation for available medical images. This process is shown in Fig. 3 below [12].

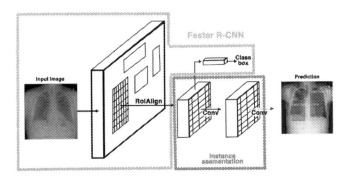

Fig. 3. Model segmentation for opacity distribution using Fast R-CNN [6].

3.6 Modeling

We have applied fast R-CNN as our working algorithm, which we found to be more accurate and efficient for low-cost systems. There were preexisting algorithms like SEGNET, UNET, RESNET, and CARDIACNET architectures, but some have failed to be most efficient while using the least optimum resources. A Mask is applied to R-CNN with optimum weights, and Residual network layers like RESNET50 and RESNET100 are used in our model to analyze the Posteroanterior view of chest X-Rays. Individual Pixel wise segmentation of Chest X-Ray image is done to obtain opacity in provided samples for training the model. We have applied segmentation of the data with an initial learning rate of 0.0015 times. The overall time for training was around 12 h for the training of 20 epochs with batches of 20 and a resolution of 540 × 540. The model's post-processing is done in separate phases to get the maximum sustainable confidence for the model. We achieved a confidence score of 0.95 for each bounding box of Region of Interest by the following equation.

$$\alpha = \frac{1}{F} \sum \alpha i \tag{1}$$

Where α is the confidence score of each with a bounding box for any set. The bounding box for the group is calculated by

$$\hat{\beta} = median\{\beta\} + \mathcal{X}\sigma \tag{2}$$

Where β denoted the group pixel location of corners (Top-right, Top-Left, bottom-right, bottom-left). There is a standard deviation of 0.1 in β and $\hat{\beta}$ For those who have a value, the model has discarded less than 0.4.

3.7 Training

Our model has used a dataset of Chest X-Ray given by the Radiological Society of North America (RSNA) [16]. We have used several examples provided we have used a fewer number of samples in stage 2 than used in stage 1 we have used 7211 datasets, which is less than 8283 in stage two. Where ground truth for lung opacity is 6365 in stage one and 7028 in stage two. We have found over 11832 abnormal cases in stage 1 dataset and over 12221 in stage two dataset [17] (Table 1).

Table 1. Properties of RSNA data [18]

# Features	Phase 1	Phase 2
Normal	7211	8283
Lung opacity	6365/9565	7028/10015
Abnormal	11,832	12221

Below is the brief information of the dataset used combinedly in this model in both stages. In Figs. 2 and 3, there is information about the dataset taken from different age groups looking at the occurrence of symptoms. It occurs mostly in ages of childhood and elderly aged people [18] (Table 2).

Table 2. Training and testing of image data [19]

# Features	Phase 1	Phase 2
Training set	25684	26684
Testing set	1000	3000

4   Experimental Results and Outcomes

4.1   Data Enrichment

We initialized augmentation on lungs relative opacity and pictures information with arbitrary enlargement, remembering moving for arranging space just as expanding/diminishing brilliance and balance incorporating obscuring with Gaussian haze under clumps. Following this picture growth, we discovered pictures after the increase was revealed. Thinking about the result in Fig. 2 means the condition of patient and marks from the X-Ray pictures, we come across an exceptionally imbalanced dataset; similar aspects can be observed from Fig. 3. We test in the case of adjusting the class conveyance would yield any improvement right now. In our usage, we have prepared our model on two informational collections, either adjusted. At that point, we make a fair dataset by increasing more pictures to the negative (0) class. We already talked about the expansion steps that incorporate flipping, pivoting, scaling, trimming, interpreting, and clamor. Presenting the pictures in a non-positive class can make a fundamentally new element that does not exist in a different class [20] (Fig. 4).

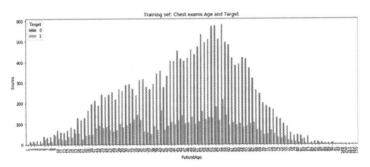

Fig. 4. Positive and negative features among patients of different age groups.

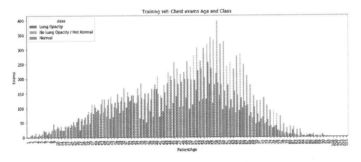

Fig. 5. Feature class of patients among the different age groups.

We similarly aggregate the circulation of location view highlights, a radio-realistic view, which corresponds to the patients' condition given in preparing and testing information such as Table 5: Data Cleansing: Data Cleaning: We played extensive data cleaning the front of the Audience 2 dataset. Moreover, investigated class likelihood positions among boys and girls. This is calculated in Fig. 5. It shows more chest x-ray images of boys, with both sexes having too many grades "No Lung Opacity/Not Normal. "However, in contrast to this reality, men have "Lung Opacity," but the ladies are somewhat uncertain.

4.2 Performance Measures

We apply IoU coordinating mechanisms for truth boxes and ties in various directions. The IoU is calculated from the circumferential peak region of bound binding boxes and the necessary binding boxes as basic metrics in diagnosing Pneumonia (Table 3).

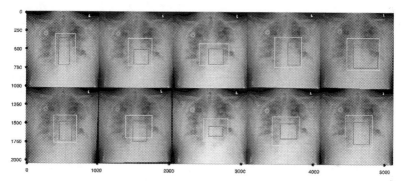

Fig. 6. Augmentation on chest X-ray images.

Table 3. Distribution based on coordinate classification in RSNA dataset

Coordinate feature	Phase 1		Phase 2	
	Train set	Test set	Train set	Test set
Anterior/Posterior	19645	470	13145	1458
Posterior/Anterior	14561	465	15487	1700

$$IoU_{region}\left(B_{predicted}, B_{ground-truth}\right) = \frac{B_{predicted} \cap B_{ground-truth}}{B_{predicted} \cup B_{ground-truth}} \qquad (3)$$

The E.U. decides a genuine positive while matching the anticipated article with the correct object over the edge, ranging between 0.4 to 0.75 at a stage size of 0.05 to arrange "misses" and "hits." Pairing among anticipated bouncing boxes and ground-truth jumping encloses surveyed sliding requests of the expectations and carefully injective which depends on their certainty levels. Given any limit esteem, the mean edge esteem over the results for a specific edge can be processed after the True Positives (T.P.), negatives (T.N.), and false positives (F.P.).

$$MTV(t) = \frac{C_{TP(t)}}{C_{TP(t)} + C_{FP(t)} + C_{FN(t)}} \tag{4}$$

Mean scores for all threshold values and Dataset values are determined by the following:

$$MS_i = \frac{1}{|Image|} \sum_i MTV(t) \quad MS_{dataset} = \frac{1}{|Image|} \sum_i^{image} MS_i \tag{5}$$

5 Experimental Results

5.1 Results

We report that our assessment brings results from the Group Model about this area. Due to the identified dataset, we maintain the collection in Phase 2, although the dataset in Phase 1 is exceptionally mismatched. The change in the dataset is that radiologists ignore every move without examining the large volume of images. We talked about this in the previous section of this article. In Fig. 6, we overlap the probabilities of ground truth marks to see if it is rotated. It likewise shows compelling predictions that describe manipulated-between-truth and reference jumping boxes.

We prepared the Nvidia 1050Ti GPU in Phase 2 and the Nvidia 1050Ti in Phase 1 and illustrated the need for a productive figure resource to perform such tasks on an exceptionally unbalanced dataset. Our model's findings at a given edge are calculated in Table 4, which gives the best waiting set of jumping boxes and ground-truth results. The model is calculated in Fig. 7.

Table 4. Result: prediction at the given threshold

Model	Threshold	Phase 1	Phase 2
RCNN (ResNet50)	0.32	0.097689	0.193730
RCNN (ResNet100)	0.978	0.102155	0.201352

5.2 Accuracy and Loss of Proposed Model

As represented toward the start of this segment, our proposed approach infers a regular gathering and post-preparing step that is then utilized to get a forecast set of Pneumonia patients. We Grouped our R-CNN to put together a model and created it concerning ResNet50 and ResNet100, and the outcome is reported in Table 5.

Accuracy and loss of model which is trained by us areas described in Figs. 8 and 9.

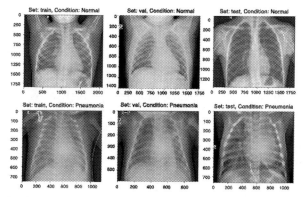

Fig. 7. The results from the stage 2 dataset. The probability overlaid on a few images which include all patient classes and labels

Table 5. Results of the aggregated model

Model	Phase 2
RCNN (ResNet50 + ResNet100)	0.197541

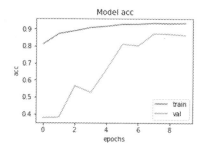

Fig. 8. Accuracy of model

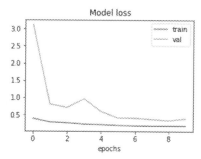

Fig. 9. Loss of model

6 Conclusion and Future Scopes

We introduced our classifying Pneumonia method and to see how lung image size plays a vital role in modeling. We have found that the stems are less prone to images between the proximity or malfunction of the forearms, the larger the image can be by using the most critical data. In any case, the cost of computation is similarly problematic when managing a large image. Our proposed spatial engineering, for example, Mask-RCNN, has provided an additional provision for direct effects. Similarly, using the edges at the base while adjusting our system to perform better in this case. With the use of the image in the crease, space outage and L2 is excessive traffic.

Even though this promise is still a long way from being perfect, it is impressive to see the reach of comprehensive learning on such evolving issues. Later, this work can be achieved by identifying and arranging X-Ray images containing malignant growth of the lungs and Pneumonia. Viewing X-Ray images containing lung malignant and Pneumonia has been a significant problem since late, and our next approach should be to address this issue.

References

1. National Center for Health Statistics (NCHS); Centers for Disease Control and Prevention (CDC) FastStats: Pneumonia. http://www.cdc.gov/nchs/fastats/pneumonia.htm. Accessed Feb 2017
2. Nanglia, P., Kumar, S., Luhach, A.K.: Detection and analysis of lung cancer using radiomic approach. In: Luhach, A.K., Hawari, K.B.G., Mihai, I.C., Hsiung, P.A., Mishra, R.B. (eds.) Smart Computational Strategies, pp. 13–24. Springer, Singapore (2019). https://doi.org/10.1007/978-981-13-6295-8_2
3. Choi, Y., et al.: Identification of usual interstitial pneumonia pattern using RNA-Seq and machine learning: challenges and solutions. BMC Genom. **19**, 147–159 (2018). https://doi.org/10.1186/s12864-018-4467-6
4. Yadav, S.S., Jadhav, S.M.: Deep convolutional neural network based medical image classification for disease diagnosis. J. Big Data **6**, 113 (2019)
5. Jaiswal, A.K., Tiwari, P., Kumar, S., Gupta, D., Khanna, A., Rodriguese, J.J.P.C.: Identifying Pneumonia in chest X-rays: a deep learning approach
6. Jamaludin, A., Kadir, T., Zisserman, A.: SpineNet: automatically pinpointing classification evidence in spinal MRIs. In: Ourselin, S., Joskowicz, L., Sabuncu, M.R., Unal, G., Wells, W. (eds.) MICCAI 2016. LNCS, vol. 9901, pp. 166–175. Springer, Cham (2016). https://doi.org/10.1007/978-3-319-46723-8_20
7. Heron, M.: Deaths: leading causes for 2010. Natl. Vital. Stat. Rep. **62**, 1–96 (2013)
8. Wang, X., Peng, Y., Lu, L., Lu, Z., Bagheri, M., Summers, R.M.: Chestx-ray8: hospital-scale chest x-ray database and benchmarks on weakly-supervised classification and localization of common thorax diseases. In: Proceedings of the IEEE Conference on Computer Vision and Pattern Recognition, pp. 2097–2106 (2017)
9. Stein, A.: Pneumonia Dataset Annotation Methods. RSNA Pneumonia Detection Challenge Discussion (2018). https://www.kaggle.com/c/rsna-pneumonia-detection-challenge/discussion/64723
10. Dalwadi, D., Mehta, Y., Macwan, N.: Face recognition-based attendance system using real-time computer vision algorithms. In: Hassanien, A.E., Bhatnagar, R., Darwish, A. (eds.) AMLTA 2020. AISC, vol. 1141, pp. 39–49. Springer, Singapore (2021). https://doi.org/10.1007/978-981-15-3383-9_4

11. Ren, S., He, K., Girshick, R., Sun, J.: Faster R-CNN: towards real-time object detection with region proposal networks. Adv. Neural Inf. Process. Syst. **39**, 91–99 (2015)
12. He, K., Zhang, X., Ren, S., Sun, J.: Deep residual learning for image recognition. In: Proceedings of the IEEE Conference on Computer Vision and Pattern Recognition, pp. 770–778 (2016)
13. Dalwadi, D.C., Shah, V., Navadiya, H., Mehta, Y.: AIDS detection using genomics signal processing techniques on DNA. In: Favorskaya, M.N., Mekhilef, S., Pandey, R.K., Singh, N. (eds.) Innovations in Electrical and Electronic Engineering. LNEE, vol. 661, pp. 651–663. Springer, Singapore (2021). https://doi.org/10.1007/978-981-15-4692-1_50
14. Kumar, A., Mukherjee, S., Luhach, A.K.: Deep learning with perspective modeling for early detection of malignancy in mammograms. J. Discrete Math. Sci. Cryptogr. **22**(4), 627–643 (2019)
15. Avni, U., Greenspan, H., Konen, E., Sharon, M., Goldberger, J.: X-ray categorization and retrieval on the organ and pathology level, using patch-based visual words. IEEE Trans. Med. Imaging **30**(3), 733–746 (2011)
16. Ronneberger, O., Fischer, P., Brox, T.: U-Net: convolutional networks for biomedical image segmentation. In: Navab, N., Hornegger, J., Wells, W.M., Frangi, A.F. (eds.) MICCAI 2015. LNCS, vol. 9351, pp. 234–241. Springer, Cham (2015). https://doi.org/10.1007/978-3-319-24574-4_28
17. Arnab, A., Torr, P.H.: Pixelwise instance segmentation with a dynamically instantiated network. In: Proceedings of the IEEE Conference on Computer Vision and Pattern Recognition, pp. 441–450 (2017)
18. Pradeepa, S., Manjula, K.R., Vimal, S., et al.: DRFS: detecting risk factor of stroke disease from social media using machine learning techniques. Neural Process. Lett. (2020). https://doi.org/10.1007/s11063-020-10279-8
19. Rajpurkar, P., et al.: CheXNet: radiologist-level pneumonia detection on chest x-rays with deep learning. arXiv:1711.05225
20. Khobragade, S., Tiwari, A., Patil, C., Narke, V.: Automatic detection of major lung diseases using chest radiographs and classification by feed-forward artificial neural network. In: 2016 IEEE 1st International Conference on Power Electronics, Intelligent Control and Energy Systems (ICPEICES), pp. 1–5. IEEE (2016)

A Comparative Study of Deep Learning Techniques for Emotion Estimation Based on E-Learning Through Cognitive State Analysis

Maragoni Mahendar[✉], Arun Malik, and Isha Batra

Lovely Professional University, Jalandhar, Punjab, India
{arun.17442,isha.17451}@lpu.co.in

Abstract. Due to dynamic changes in education filed, e-learning plays a crucial role in the success of students. Unlike in classroom sessions it is hard to estimate learning efficiency in e-learning. In order to assert this situation, we need a technology that can understand, analyze and calculate the efficiency of learners in the class. Emotion estimation using deep learning is one such technique that can determine the competence of the learner based on facial expression using cognitive state analysis. In a typical e-learning environment, we extract emotions of learner from facial images using deep learning technique to analyze cognitive state. In the present day approaches for cognitive state analysis, emotions are not considered to a significant extent. However, emotion estimation has significant role in cognitive state analysis. Image, audio and video sequences contribute in estimating the emotional quotient of the learner in the class. Moreover, studies show numerous solutions proposed facial expressions as source to estimate emotional quotient. The primary focus of this paper is to research multiple techniques used in existing methodologies for emotion estimation and attempt to compare across each other to unveil the merits and demerits. At the end, the focal point of this paper is to research and analyze the emotion estimation and make it available to the e-learning ecosystem.

Keywords: Emotion estimation · Cognitive state analysis · Facial expressions · Deep learning

1 Introduction

In present days there is a need of e learning to improve young people's academic outcomes, but these outcomes depends on each individual interest. The experience and perception of student shows academic successes or failures, which leads to academic achievement. To this end, cognitive emotions gained to learn or develop new skill can play a crucial role when faced with challenging tasks, as they reflect a student's flow of emotions. In innovative teaching models, evaluation of learning was focused mainly on self reports and tests that neglected the real time detection of emotions, e.g. by recording or accessing facial expressions. Recognition of facial expressions is complex task for machine learning methods [1] as people can vary significantly in the way they express themselves.

© Springer Nature Singapore Pte Ltd. 2021
A. K. Luhach et al. (Eds.): ICAICR 2020, CCIS 1393, pp. 226–235, 2021.
https://doi.org/10.1007/978-981-16-3660-8_21

1.1   Emotion Identification with Facial Expressions

Facial expressions have a primary role to play in the identification of emotions and are helpful for fulfilling the non-verbal communication procedure, and individual's recognition. It is regarded as quite significant factor for emotional communication in day to day life, just after the tone of voice. Also, they act as indicators of feelings, helping a person in expressing his/her emotional state of mind. The individual emotional state can be related instantly and consequentially, the recurrent utilization of facial expressions helps in the emotion identification in automatic manner. The objective of this work is recognition of seven fundamental emotional states: neutral, happiness, surprise, anger, sadness, fear and disgust depending on facial expressions [2] and Fig. 1 shows the illustration images of actors pertaining to facial expressions deliberating seven emotional states.

Fig. 1. Seven fundamental emotions in facial expression identification [2].

Lastly, in facial expression recognition, several attempts have been done for the classification of these fundamental facial expressions. It has been endeavoured to measure the facial geometric, definition of facial look and its movement, inclusive of the categorization of facial expressions. The general architecture for facial expression identification resembles the shown Fig. 2.

Generally, the system comprises of facial acquisition, facial expression extraction and representation, and classification of facial expression. In particular, the face acquisition phase tries for face region extraction from the input pictures or videos and at times, organization of all the faces into a reference model is done with the help of facial marks, next the process of facial expression extraction and representation attempts for extraction of the features for the proper representation of facial expressions, and at last, the classification step helps in designation of input pattern to a particular groups. Facial expression representation has a predominant part to play in facial expression recognition. Very particularly, facial expression features tries efficiently defining the facial muscle or facial movement for stationary or active facial pictures pertaining to basic features like shape, colour and texture. Fisher criterion can be greatly exploited for mitigating the within-class changes of facial expressions when increasing the between-class changes are calculated based on smart computational strategies [3].

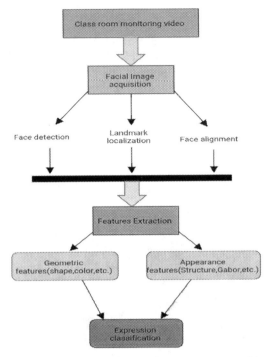

Fig. 2. Classical pipeline of facial expression recognition

Presently, the Emotion Recognition in the wild challenge and workshop [4] primarily examined the emotion recognition techniques performance for the wilderness. Also, facial expression analysis system reveals that the capability of automatically identifying the facial expressions may results in poorer resolution and deals with the complete head motion. Emotion recognition is applied in different domains like medicine (therapy rehabilitation, counselling, etc.), e-learning, emotion monitoring, entertainment, marketing, and law. Among these applications, E-Learning has paved the way for a greater revolution in delivering the learning process with the help of fast progress made in Internet technology.

1.2 Facial Expression Analysis in E-Learning Systems

E-learning has achieved much popularity among universities and colleges, considering its benefits over conventional methods where the students are capable of studying and learning at their own comfort anywhere and anytime. But, human educators are still considered best in few places as they can monitor the progress by the student and render sufficient guidance and assistance. Also, teachers with ample experience are capable of introspecting the changes in the student's emotions so that the necessary actions can be taken. At present, the shift is towards a new path, where the behaviours of students are revealed by their heartbeat, pose, gesture, mouse pressure and movement, eye gaze, voice pitch,facial expressions, and given as proper system inputs for further improvement headed for the learners.

Facial expression is considered as the primary modality since researches reveals its contribution is about 55% as far as communicating messages is concerned [5]. Since the earlies of 1970, Ekman (1973) has carried out elaborate analysis of human facial expression and has got proof to emphasis on facial expressions through facial movements [6]. The designed algorithms encompassed face detection, facial features extraction ranging till the facial expression classification. Even though the attempts towards the automated machine recognition of human FER are fascinating besides the advancement are acceptable, it is quite the same circumstance that people are eager for learning about how to solve the problems through the development of ever more complex algorithms, rather than understanding for what they would use the information for.

In addition, as it can be observed, many of the so known automated recognition machines are being run under particular limitations. Comparatively, very less work has been carried out in the education field. Generally, FEA comprises of 3 important steps, which include face detection, facial features extraction and expression classification [7].

Academic e-efficacy encourages academic engagement [5] and accomplishment [8] pertaining to performance. Moreover, it is observed that academic self-efficacy [5] has a positive correlation with the experience achieved due to positive emotions during e-learning practice, and has a negative association with negative emotions. The higher positive emotions that the students experienced during e-learning activities, reflects in their increased perception of themselves being capable of interacting usefully with further learners besides teachers by means of learning platform. Conversely, wteamviewerith more students experiencing negative emotions in the course of e-learning practice, the fewer would be the students perceiving themselves to be capable of using the learning tools besides managing their learning process.

Several studies above mentioned have employed self-report measures and in fact, the real emotions of the students 'in the moment' are not taken into account as soon as participating in learning processes. eLearning settings has grabbed the attention of researchers for elementary emotions, or contrast amid positive and negative emotions. The cognitive emotions in e-learning environments associated with individual beliefs, academic welfare and performance are not explored properly. Still, research is being carried out to focus on the facial expressions, which are significant and generic for e-learning. Hence, Cognitive state learning is regarded a crucial aspect, which decides learning efficiency in class, and analyzing the cognitive state of the learners has emerged a hot topic in the research field and a huge issue in education domain [9].

1.3 Introduction to Cognitive State Analysis in Education

Big Data plays a major role in the learner's cognitive state recognition of educators quantitatively using a massive amount of time series data and this facilitates individual attention to improve the outputs of learning. A high-throughput multiple social signal analysis, e.g., emotion and attention is terms as learning cognition state [9]. But, many of the available cognitive state analysis techniques highlight on neglecting the roles played by human learning emotion. Hence, an emotion-sensitive learning cognitive state analysis model is presented here, which provides an estimate on the students' attention depending on head pose and emotion depending on facial expression in a non-intrusive manner.

The expression intensity estimation and facial expression classification analysis at the same time is done for the knowledge of emotions learning through CNN [10]. But, it is hard to use these techniques in the practical classroom as they need complex wearable gadgets for measuring these physiological signals. As an alternative, since facial expression is regarded as extremely strong social signals for human beings for their emotion and intension, which is utilized for emotion exploration.

The face detection, landmark location, and head pose estimation is acquired through multi-task learning system with deep learning based technique [11]. The face detection and positioning removes the head pose variations effect on facial expression analysis. The head pose estimation and landmarks are accomplished for analyzing the learner's attention. After this, the facial expression is studied for estimating of the learners' emotion while the focus of the learner is on the whiteboard. The facial expression classification and expression intensity estimation is shown in Fig. 4 (Fig. 3).

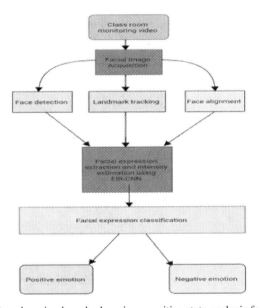

Fig. 3. Deep learning based e-learning cognitive state analysis framework.

The nonverbal communication is acquired by one of the strongest mediums namely face. The emotion, motive, alertness, pain, personality, controls interpersonal behaviour, and transmits psychiatric and biomedical status among the other functions is stated by facial expression. The automated facial expression analysis has grabbed the attention of researchers in the computer vision and machine learning approaches. The next section provides a review on the basic techniques for facial assessment by behavioural researchers and present endeavours in automated FER. The issues pertaining to feature detection, tracking, and representation, and in cooperation with supervised and unsupervised learning highlighted also on deep learning are considered.

2 Related Work

This section presented review of different articles on emotion estimation:

i.   Presented an innovative approach on the basis of Two-Part Convolutional Neural Network (CNN), namely Facial Emotion Recognition Using Convolutional Neural Networks [12]. Nevertheless, the face fragmentation granularity into local regions and there exist great demand due to its consequence on the performance, predominantly for random occlusion deprived of a static location, size, and shape.

ii. The Directed acyclic graph SVM for facial emotion classification employing the combined feature is used [13]. But, owing to the deficit of appropriate standard databases, direct contrasts amid statistical model based techniques and additional mechanisms quiet remain non-examined in the available researches. Consequently, their performance benefits over other mechanisms have to be verified deeper.

iii. A new reliable feature extraction process is called as local directional position pattern (LDPP) is suggested [2]. A new FER mechanism is introduced in this research work employing LDPP, PCA, GDA, and Deep Belief Network (DBN) depending on a depth sensor-based video camera images. First, the LDPP features extraction are performed on the facial expression depth images followed by Principal Component Analysis (PCA) deployed for dimensionality reduction. In addition, the categorization of face features is accomplished using Generalized Discriminant Analysis (GDA) for robustness improvement. But, facial expression evaluation or analysis from video information is a huge challenge besides its accuracy.

iv. Designed a new U-Net Conditional Generative Adversarial Network for FES in which retaining of input face property, comprising the identity information besides facial specifics is achieved [14]. Practically, there require personalized outcomes which is not achieved.

v.   An advanced algorithm combined with linear discriminant analysis (LDA) to improve the feature selection in a still image-based facial expressions system [15], however they do not exhibit resistance towards changes in illumination.

vi. Deployed a Deep Convolutional Neural Network (DCNN) features for facial expressions recognition in automatic manner [16]. The single image is the key element for identification of facial expressions of a distinct person, but the illumination variation is not handled properly.

vii. Obtained a multi view and view invariant classification of facial expressions by utilizing a discriminative shared Gaussian process latent variable model (DS-GPLVM) from various views [17]. But, the primary drawback of these techniques is that they do not succeed in explicit modelling the correlations between multiple views.

viii. Introduced Markov random fields for designing an ensemble system for emotion detection [18]. This research article, has considered the fact that the primary indicators of emotions are the eye and mouth expressions. The validation pertaining to other classifiers like ANN, BN, HMM, and CRF is to done besides improving identification of seven fundamental expressions.

3 Comparison Among Various Methods

This Section, Table 1: showing the complete comparison among various emotion estimation methods given below. This analogy made from litrecture review, from the year 2016–20. The Following table of Comparison is done on proposed techniques,merits and demerits.

Table 1. Comparison between different methods

Author	Proposed technique	Merits	Demerits
Mehendale et al. (2020)	Convolutional neural networks	When there are wide training data sets and computing tools, such as several CPU cores and or GPUs, it showed impressive results	The ability of the feature recognition will reduce because the information varies between the two dada sets, however needs a large number of labelled samples
Dagher et al. (2019), Ramos et al. (2020)	SVM	Over fitting is less observed compared to other models	It experienced some problems detecting occluded faces and displaying the surprise expression
Li et al. (2018)	ACNN	It can perceive the facial features of occlusion and rely on the most discriminatory unoccluded regions	How to establish bits of focus in faces without landmarks is a difficult challenge
Uddin et al. (2017)	Local Directional Position Pattern (LDPP)	extract a large number of facial features representing various facial deformation patterns and speed up the computation speed	It had significant difficulties with natural materials illuminated with different directions and images degraded by an additive noise
Wang et al. (2019)	Conditional Generative Adversarial Network	Only requires standard pre processing, does not include extraction of complicated features matching	However, as there are significantly more background items than faces, the training can be extremely unbalanced

(continued)

Table 1. (*continued*)

Author	Proposed technique	Merits	Demerits
Zhang et al. (2017)	Part-based Hierarchical Bidirectional-RNN	A fully connected structure with higher speed and lower cost of computation	Optimizing deep auto encoders using back propagation turned out to be very complex
Mayya et al. (2016)	DCCN	High recognition score, and uses the knowledge during preparation of dataset	It is not tried to manage the illumination variation

4   Result Analysis from Literature Review

This section comprehensively scrutinizes the various methods and strategies performed for detecting human facial expressions, aiming to identify the emotions. Besides, summarizes the associated steps of machine-learning and deep learning-based approaches that assist during the process of face detection, and explains the emotion recognition accompanying classification as well as a few significant concerns of recognition. In order to conquer/evade the struggles (facial expression, pose variations, illumination changes, etc.) existed in FR, the deep-learning methods have utilized to the core, as they perform well during the processes of heterogeneous face matching, video, and RGB-D. Also, provided an analysis made on associated face databases (video footages, various facial images data for cross-modal Face Recognition, and static images). The accuracies on faces recognition significantly enhanced over face matching on the basis of the static image, yet there are a few practical difficulties remain, Occlusion problem with non-frontal head pose, class imbalance problem, Low quality images, High quality and balanced distributions of input dataset and More focus need on multimodal information based FER.

Here are two vital factors that affect the automatic Facial Expression Recognition, namely Occlusion, and semi-frontal head pose. With this, the actual facial expressions visual aspect might vary. The class imbalance has considered being a further challenge in facial expression that generally occurred while at attaining the data. Even though the annotation and elicitation may easy for a smile, yet the real difficulty is with information capture of infrequent expressions, like anger, disgust, etc. Though the networks have presented with the enormous number of face images with various qualities in the training phases, yet the deep-learning approaches struggle to process with the quality variations of the face image. To overcome this problem, designing more efficient deep-learning has necessitated.

Associated processes of the face that relies on deep-learning methods comprise the possibility to get heavily influenced by the training set factors, such as the size and quality. Nevertheless, the accumulation and tagging of sufficiently high-quality samples with enough quantity, as well as the stable allocation, are not an easy task yet, as they require great endeavour and cost. Therefore, the training dataset has prominently enhanced through several data enhancement methods. The employment of multimodal information through hybrid intelligent approaches is unable to help the system to recognize the sentimental statuses of the learner,for example, recognition of facial expression, tracking of eye gaze, head pose, etc.

5 Conclusion

This paper presented the analogy of various methods used for emotion estimation. On the basis of their research objectives, suggested methods, merits and demerits, this comparison was carried out. Later, it demonstrates an overview of the outcomes of some of the current strategies. These techniques assess outcomes on high quality images, video and audio sequences. it shows that some methods provided good results and some reduce efficiency of the relevent method. It shows the outcomes that can be more optimised and can be used as future research directions.

References

1. Pradeepa, S., Manjula, K.R., Vimal, S., Khan, M.S., Chilamkurti, N., Luhach, A.K.: DRFS: detecting risk factor of stroke disease from social media using machine learning techniques. Neural Process. Lett. 1–19 (2020). https://doi.org/10.1007/s11063-020-10279-8
2. Uddin, M.Z., Hassan, M.M., Almogren, A., Alamri, A., Alrubaian, M., Fortino, G.: Facial expression recognition utilizing local direction-based robust features and deep belief network. IEEE Access **5**, 4525–4536 (2017)
3. Nanglia, P., Kumar, S., Luhach, A.K.: Detection and analysis of lung cancer using radiomic approach. In: Luhach, A.K., Hawari, K.B.G., Mihai, I.C., Hsiung, P.A., Mishra, R.B. (eds.) Smart Computational Strategies: Theoretical and Practical Aspects, pp. 13–24. Springer, Singapore (2019). https://doi.org/10.1007/978-981-13-6295-8_2
4. Dhall, A., Goecke, R., Joshi, J., Wagner, M., Gedeon, T.: Emotion recognition in the wild challenge 2013. In: Proceedings of the 15th ACM on International Conference on Multimodal Interaction, pp. 509–516, December 2013
5. D'Errico, F., Paciello, M., Cerniglia, L.: When emotions enhance students' engagement in e-learning processes. J. e-Learning Knowl. Soc. **12**(4) (2016)
6. Ekman, P.: Cross-cultural studies of facial expression. In: Darwin and Facial Expression: A Century of Research in Review, vol. 169222, no. 1 (1973)
7. Loh, M.P., Wong, Y.P., Wong, C.O.: Facial expression analysis in e-learning systems-the problems and feasibility. In: Fifth IEEE International Conference on Advanced Learning Technologies (ICALT 2005), pp. 442–446. IEEE, July 2005
8. Di. Mele, L., D'Errico, F., Cerniglia, L., Cersosimo, M., Paciello, M.: Convinzioni di efficacia personale nella regolazione dell'apprendimento universitario mediato dalle tecnologie. Qwerty-Open Interdiscip. J. Technol. Cult. Educ. **10**(2), 63–77 (2015)
9. Xu, R., Chen, J., Han, J., Tan, L., Xu, L.: Towards emotion-sensitive learning cognitive state analysis of big data in education: deep learning-based facial expression analysis using ordinal information. Computing **102**(3), 765–780 (2019). https://doi.org/10.1007/s00607-019-00722-7
10. Sekaran, K., Chandana, P., Krishna, N.M., Kadry, S.: Deep learning convolutional neural network (CNN) with Gaussian mixture model for predicting pancreatic cancer. Multimedia Tools Appl. **79**(15–16), 10233–10247 (2019). https://doi.org/10.1007/s11042-019-7419-5

11. Kumar, A., Mukherjee, S., Luhach, A.K.: Deep learning with perspective modeling for early detection of malignancy in mammograms. J. Discrete Math. Sci. Cryptogr. **22**(4), 627–643 (2019)
12. Mehendale, N.: Facial emotion recognition using convolutional neural networks (FERC). SN Appl. Sci. **2**(3), 1–8 (2020). https://doi.org/10.1007/s42452-020-2234-1
13. Sen, D., Datta, S., Balasubramanian, R.: Facial emotion classification using concatenated geometric and textural features. Multimedia Tools Appl. **78**(8), 10287–10323 (2018). https://doi.org/10.1007/s11042-018-6537-9
14. Wang, Y., Li, Y., Song, Y., Rong, X.: The application of a hybrid transfer algorithm based on a convolutional neural network model and an improved convolution restricted Boltzmann machine model in facial expression recognition. IEEE Access **7**, 184599–184610 (2019)
15. Boubenna, H., Lee, D.: Image-based emotion recognition using evolutionary algorithms. Biol. Inspired Cogn. Archit. **24**, 70–76 (2018)
16. Mayya, V., Pai, R.M., Pai, M.M.: Automatic facial expression recognition using DCNN. Procedia Comput. Sci. **93**, 453–461 (2016)
17. Eleftheriadis, S., Rudovic, O., Pantic, M.: Discriminative shared Gaussian processes for multiview and view-invariant facial expression recognition. IEEE Trans. Image Process. **24**(1), 189–204 (2014)
18. Maglogiannis, I., Vouyioukas, D., Aggelopoulos, C.: Face detection and recognition of natural human emotion using Markov random fields. Pers. Ubiquit. Comput. **13**(1), 95–101 (2009)

Detection of Epileptic Seizures in Long-Term Human EEG by Improved Linear Discriminant Analysis (ILDA)

V. Nageshwar[1(✉)], Y. Padmasai[1], and K. Subba Rao[2]

[1] VNR Vignana Jyothi Institute of Engineering and Technology, Hyderabad, India
{nageshwar_v,padmasai_y}@vnrvjiet.in
[2] CBIT, Hyderabad, India

Abstract. In a recent survey conducted by WHO, it is stated that 70 million people across the globe are said to have epileptic seizures. In India, as per the data from recent studies mentioned that 12 million out of 70 million people who are suffering from various epileptic conditions are from India. Although each epileptic condition may have different medication, the detection process is almost the same. Many algorithms have been developed to detect the epileptic seizures. In this paper, epileptic seizures detection is done through Convolutional Neural Networks (CNN) based feature extraction and Linear Discriminant Analysis (LDA) based classification. This attempt of combining a basic old LDA algorithm with recent developed deep learning algorithm i.e. CNN gave satisfactory results with 96% accuracy of detection.

Keywords: Feature extraction · Convolutional Neural Networks (CNN) · Linear Discriminant Analysis (LDA)

1 Introduction

Every year around 2.4 million new cases of Epilepsy are registered across the globe. When compared to a normal person, the probability that the epileptic person may die prematurely is two or three times. Epileptic Seizure is a chronic disorder, which arises due to abnormal neural activity of the brain. It is likely to affect the people of any age. More often, due to abnormal neural activity, a person may have an attack of fits. During this attack, normal activity of neurons is spiked to extremely hyperactivity. A Person during this state, lose consciousness and may also have physical damage while collapsing. Hence, epilepsy is the most important topic to carry out the study on.

First and Foremost, step in the study is to know about EEG waveforms and their nature. Based on the frequency of waves, EEG waveforms are broadly classified into Delta (0.5 Hz–4 Hz), Theta (4 Hz–7 Hz), Alpha (7 Hz–13 Hz), Beta (13 Hz–39 Hz) and Gamma (>40 Hz). These waves give information about state of mind. In order to acquire the EEG signals, electrodes are placed on the patient's scalp according to 10–20 system. All the lobes are covered with electrodes and readings are recorded on paper.

© Springer Nature Singapore Pte Ltd. 2021
A. K. Luhach et al. (Eds.): ICAICR 2020, CCIS 1393, pp. 236–245, 2021.
https://doi.org/10.1007/978-981-16-3660-8_22

Long term Human EEG is continuous monitoring of neural activity of the patient. This monitoring duration may be several hundreds or thousands of hours. All the recordings are cut short into several files, for further processing.

In work carried out in this paper in brief is to analyze the EEG waveforms that are available in the form of datasets. After preprocessing the input signal, features are extracted based on Convolutional Neural Networks (CNN) and then according to the features signal is classified as normal/severe epileptic condition by Linear Discriminant Analysis (LDA). Details in particular are:

- Usage of Bonn Dataset
- A 6th order Butterworth low pass filter with cut-off frequency of 300 Hz.
- Convolutional Neural Networks with 5 layers - 1 Input, 2 Convolutional, 2-Pooling layers for feature extraction.
- Linear Discriminant Analysis Algorithm as Classifier.

2 Literature Survey

According to U.R. Acharya et al. (2013)'s work on "Automated EEG analysis of epilepsy", discussed the need of a diagnostic system aided by computer to detect the conditions of epileptic seizures. It details about the various feature extraction methods and their results. Paper also reveals about the work done by several other publishers to detect the seizures in a computerized way.

Graupe and Nigam (2004) found the usage of Artificial Neural Networks (ANN) in detection of epilepsy in their paper "A neural-network-based detection of epilepsy". They used a multistage filter as a part of preprocessing along with ANN. It fetched 97.20% accuracy. In addition to this, they worked on Adaptive Neuro-Fuzzy Interference Systems (ANFIS) and accuracy is found to be 92.22%.

Srinivasan (2007)'s work on the Elman network fetched the accuracy of 100%, which is mentioned in the paper entitled "Approximate entropy-based epileptic EEG detection using artificial neural networks". He used entropy approximation as a feature to detect the epileptic condition. It is the work on two class detection i.e. either normal or EEG epileptic condition.

Guo et al. (2009) worked on different theories and went through all the possible combinations, in order to improve the accuracy of automated detection. As part of this, classification based on ANN gave 95.2% accuracy. It involved feature extraction based on relative wavelet energy. Additional combinations include Wavelet Transform with ApEn feature extraction, Wavelet Transform with line length feature extraction and Genetic programming-based feature extraction with KNN classifier gave 99.85%, 99.60%, 99% of accuracy respectively. The paper "Classification of EEG signals using relative wavelet energy and artificial neural networks" discloses these details.

Fast Fourier Transform based welch method is mentioned in "Classification of epileptiform EEG using a hybrid systems based on decision tree classifier and fast Fourier transform" and is used by Polat and Gunes et al. (2009) which gave the maximum value of accuracy i.e. 98.72% when used along with decision tree classifier. They also worked on the FFT-welch method for the purpose of feature extraction.

The famous Discrete Wavelet Transform (DWT) is used by subasi et al. (2007) in their work. DWT is used to decompose the EEG signal into frequency sub-bands. They extracted four statistical features based on DWT coefficients. This combination is referred to as modular neural networks, which is often called "Mixture of Experts (MEs)". The entire work progressed by providing 94.5% accuracy.

Tzallas et al. proposed two class differentiation models of automated detection using time-frequency methods. Accuracy kept varying between 97.72% and 100%. This method is supported by the latest technology - Artificial Neural Networks.

A three-class classification technique is mentioned by chua et al. (2009) in "Automatic identification of epileptic EEG signals using higher order spectra", which is based on HOS feature extraction. With the HOS feature extraction method, accuracy is found to be 88.18%. Power spectrum extraction is also carried out inorder to improve the accuracy. When the power spectrum method is used as a feature extraction technique, accuracy is found to be 93.11%. This paper also provided a comparison between HOS feature extraction and Power spectrum feature extraction. All this work is done with help of the Gaussian Mixture Model (GMM) as a classifier. Hence GMM was able to classify the signal into three classes namely normal, ictal, interictal.

3   Methodology

EEG datasets are available online. One of the standard datasets found on the Internet is Bonn Dataset. It consists of 100 text files for each set and there are such 5 sets. Each file has 4096 samples. Input EEG waves are prone to noises because EEG is easily varied by blink of eye, movement or due to thinking process. Hence there is a need for filtering the signal (Fig. 1).

As we know, EEG signals are low frequency signals, hence a low pass filter is required. Based on the sampling frequency and cut off frequency, the best order of filter that can eliminate the noise is found to be 6. Hence, a 6th order Butterworth filter is designed in MATLAB. Equation (1) expresses the butterworth filter equation.

$$[b, a]butter(n, f_{normalized}) \qquad (1)$$

Where a, b = Butterworth Coefficients

$$n = \text{Order of the filter}$$

$f_{normalized}$ = Normalized Frequency = cutoff frequency/((sampling frequency)/2)

Following Eq. (2) builds a butterworth filter using its coefficients in Matlab.

$$data\, Out = filter(b, a, input\, Signal); \qquad (2)$$

Input EEG is filtered and following images shows the input and filtered signal, processed in Matlab (Figs. 2 and 3).

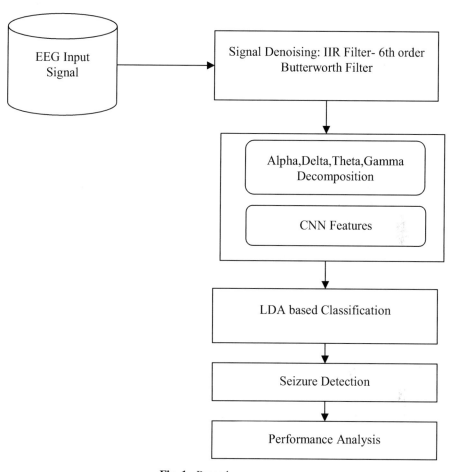

Fig. 1. Procedure sequence

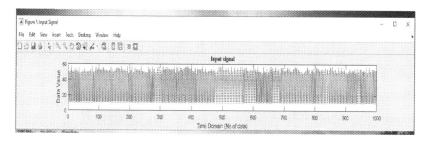

Fig. 2. Input signal

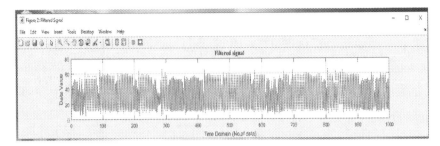

Fig. 3. Filtered signal

4 Convolutional Neural Networks

CNNs are best used to represent a block of data by a single quantity. This single quantity is obtained based on the relationship between the data. Data keeps minimizing when it is passed through several layers of CNN.

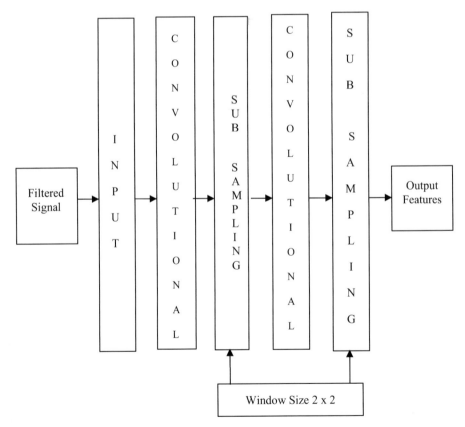

Fig. 4. CNN layers

In this paper, the layers are kept minimum to 5. Proposed work consists of an input layer, which allows input samples to enter further layers. After the input layer, there is a convolutional layer, which is defined with feature map size and kernel size. It derives the relationship between data available in the neighborhood.

Immediately next to the convolutional layer, there exists a pooling or subsampling layer, which minimizes the data samples/parameters that are needed to be evaluated. It minimizes the parameters according to the window size that is specified (Fig. 4).

CNN structure is defined along with types of layers and their specifications such as number of layers, type of it, kernel size, map size and window size. In this work, a 2×2 window in pooling layers is used. CNN Features are extracted as output. A single feature is obtained as output. This single feature represents the entire input data (Fig. 5).

Fig. 5. CNN feature – output

4.1 Linear Discriminant Analysis

Linear Discriminant Analysis provides a way to classify the objects into two or three classes of objects. Hence, a single feature obtained from CNN is introduced to LDA. LDA evaluates it and puts it in the region to which the data is belonged. This serves as a classifier and input signal is identified either as a normal or severe condition of epilepsy.

5   Results

In this segment, Bonn university dataset is used for validating the performance of the proposed system. In this research study, epileptic seizure detection is implemented on a digital signal processing platform for classifying two classes: mild and severe. Here, the performance evaluation is validated for 150 random EEG signals with 80% training and 20% testing of data. According to the input introduced, undergoing all the above process, output is popped out either as mild or severe.

5.1 Performance Analysis

The performance measures of the ILDA-CNN methodology are sensitivity, specificity and classification accuracy. These performances are usually used in biomedical research. The sensitivity and specificity performances are used for defining the relationship between the input and output variables. The effectiveness of normality and abnormality of seizure detection rate is described by the classification accuracy.

Sensitivity
Sensitivity (SEN) is defined as the ratio of accurately classified ictal (Seizure activity) EEGs to total number of labeled ictal EEGs. The sensitivity is expressed in Eq. (3).

$$SEN = \frac{TP}{TP + FN} \times 100\% \tag{3}$$

Specificity
Specificity (SPE) is defined as the ratio of accurately classified interictal (Seizure free) EEGs out of the total number of labeled interictal EEGs. The specificity is given in Eq. (4).

$$SPE = \frac{TN}{TN + FP} \times 100\% \tag{4}$$

Classification Accuracy
Classification accuracy (CA) is defined as ratio of the accurately classified EEGs out of the total number of EEGs. The following Eq. (5) represents the classification accuracy.

$$CA = \frac{TP + TN}{TP + FN + TN + FP} \times 100\% \tag{5}$$

Where, TP = True Positive, FN = False Negative, TN = True Negative, FP = False Positive, SEN = Sensitivity, SPE = Specificity, CA = Classification Accuracy.

Accuracy, sensitivity and specificity of the work is calculated. Following the standard definitions for accuracy as ratio of total classified to total applied patterns, it is found to be 96%. Similarly, sensitivity is the ratio of total classified positive to total actual positive patterns, value obtained is 92%. Specificity is total negative classified to total actual negative patterns, and it is observed to be 100% (Tables 1, 2, 3 and Figs. 6, 7, 8).

Table 1. Performance analysis

Parameter	Percentage
Accuracy	96.67%
Sensitivity	92%
Specificity	100%

Table 2. Performance evaluation of proposed system by means of sensitivity and specificity

Classifier	Classes	TP	FP	FN	TN	Sensitivity (%)	Specificity (%)
LDA	Mild	10	2	0	18	91.67	100
	Severe	9	0	1	20	91.37	100

Table 3. Performance valuation of proposed system in terms of PPV, NPV and accuracy

Classifier	Classes	TP	FP	FN	TN	PPV (%)	NPV (%)	Accuracy (%)
LDA	Mild	9	0	1	20	100	95.23	96.67
	Severe	9	0	1	20	100	95.23	96.67

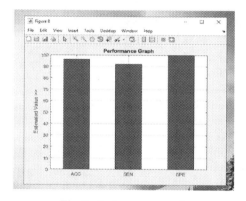

Fig. 6. Performance graph

Fig. 7. Output when data shows mild nature

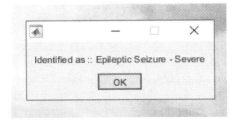

Fig. 8. Output when data shows severe condition

6 Conclusion

Therefore, detection of epileptic seizures using Improved Linear Discriminant Analysis (ILDA) with the support of Convolutional Neural Networks (CNN) based feature extraction is done successfully. It provides whether the data belongs to mild or severe conditions of epilepsy. The epileptic condition detection is purely based on trained modules. Results are obtained based on trained data. Machine learns the details by itself when CNN is used. Later LDA classified the extracted features.

The proposed work gave the result with accuracy of 96%, sensitivity of 92% and specificity of 100%, which when compared with other existing systems of detection, has done a decent job.

References

Epilepsy Fact Sheet (2018). http://www.who.int/mediacentre/factsheets/fs999/en/

Acharya, U.R., Sree, S.V., Swapna, G., Martis, R.J., Suri, J.S.: Automated EEG analysis of epilepsy: a review. Knowl. Based Syst. **45**, 147–165 (2013)

Puce, A., Hämäläinen, M.S.: A review of issues related to data acquisition and analysis in EEG/MEG studies. Brain Sci. **7**(6) (2017)

Joshi, V., Pachori, R.B., Vijesh, A.: Classification of ictal and seizure-free EEG signals using fractional linear prediction. Biomed. Signal Process. Control **9**, 1–5 (2014)

Ghaderyan, P., Abbasi, A., Sedaaghi, M.H.: An efficient seizure prediction method using KNN-based undersampling and linear frequency measures. J. Neurosci. Methods **232**, 134–142 (2014)

Pachori, R.B., Patidar, S.: Epileptic seizure classification in EEG signals using second-order difference plot of intrinsic mode functions. Comput. Methods Progr. Biomed. **113**(2), 494–502 (2014)

Hassan, A.R., Subasi, A.: Automatic identification of epileptic seizures from EEG signals using linear programming boosting. Comput. Methods Progr. Biomed. **136**, 65–77 (2016)

Sharma, M., Dhere, A., Pachori, R.B., Acharya, U.R.: An automatic detection of focal EEG signals using new class of time–frequency localized orthogonal wavelet filter banks. Knowl. Based Syst. **118**, 217–227 (2017)

Faust, O., Acharya, U.R., Adeli, H., Adeli, A.: Wavelet-based EEG processing for computer-aided seizure detection and epilepsy diagnosis. Seizure **26**, 56–64 (2015)

Kumar, Y., Dewal, M.L., Anand, R.S.: Relative wavelet energy and wavelet entropy based epileptic brain signals classification. Biomed. Eng. Lett. **2**(3), 147–157 (2012)

Sharma, R., Pachori, R.B.: Classification of epileptic seizures in EEG signals based on phase space representation of intrinsic mode functions. Expert Syst. Appl. **42**(3), 1106–1117 (2015)

Kumar, A., Mukherjee, S., Luhach, A.K.: Deep learning with perspective modeling for early detection of malignancy in mammograms. J. Discrete Math. Sci. Cryptogr. **22**(4), 627–643 (2019)

Shallu, N.P., Kumar, S., Luhach, A.K.: Detection and analysis of lung cancer using radiomic approach. In: Luhach, A.K., Hawari, K.B.G., Mihai, I.C., Hsiung, P.A., Mishra, R.B. (eds.) Smart Computational Strategies: Theoretical and Practical Aspects, pp. 13–24. Springer, Singapore (2019). https://doi.org/10.1007/978-981-13-6295-8_2

Pradeepa, S., Manjula, K.R., Vimal, S., et al.: DRFS: detecting risk factor of stroke disease from social media using machine learning techniques. Neural Process. Lett. (2020). https://doi.org/10.1007/s11063-020-10279-8

Bajaj, V., Pachori, R.B.: Epileptic seizure detection based on the instantaneous area of analytic intrinsic mode functions of EEG signals. Biomed. Eng. Lett. **3**(1), 17–21 (2013)

Facial Emotional Recognition Using Legion Kernel Convolutional Neural Networks

Sukanya Ledalla$^{(\boxtimes)}$, R. Bhavani, and Avvari Pavitra

Department of IT, Gokaraju Rangaraju Institute of Engineering, JNTU (H), Hyderabad, India

Abstract. Facial expressions can be verbal, and nonverbal, which play an important part of communication. We can convey a message to another person by means of an expression. Automatic recognition of facial expressions through machines can be developed using natural human interfaces. Although, we know that humans can recognize the expression of a person quickly by looking at the person but recognition of expression using a machine is difficult. This paper presents an overview of automatic expression recognition including the expressions of persons who are mentally ill, retarded, etc. It highlights the components of a system and provides research challenges. By definition, the appearance of a face is the facial component in outward appearance acknowledgment. This paper also helps to recognize the emotions of mentally ill people including children.

The primary research works finishes up six substance, face distinguished by photographs, settled by Open Source Computer Vision Library (OpenCV), and facial dataset, settled by Kaggle's Fer2013, the handling preparing and testing the facial dataset, settled by the model Convolutional Neural Network (CNN).

Keywords: Machine learning · Deep learning · Convolutional neural network · Image processing

1 Introduction

With the fast improvement of society, individuals are feeling the squeeze. Nowadays, people, whether children, teenagers, adults or the elderly, are generally in a bad state of mind, usually ignored by themselves or ignored by those around them. According to words from experts, there is a growing group which has been diagnosed and treated for minor or moderate mental health issues. At the same time, with the popularization and application of artificial intelligence, the method, using this technology reasonably, begins popularity to ease the needs for human resources. This project aims at recognizing the emotions of people including patients' mental change, especially at the children's mental change, as a result of it, people can realize the emotional change that they may ignore sometimes. So in this paper, the module of Convolutional Neural Network is built for training, testing and detecting facial emotion changes, then identifying and recognizing the emotional statuses of the people.

Facial emotion recognition is one of the known themes in the fields of PC vision and man-made brainpower. This test can be led utilizing various sensors, however our primary center is to utilize facial pictures, since outward appearances are very significant in relational correspondence. This paper gives the data of the examinations directed by different investigates in the field of FER over the previous decades. Here, we use conventional Neural Networks and their algorithms. We also use Deep Learning techniques to implement this experiment. Taking everything into account, we give a concise data of openly accessible assessment measurements with benchmark results. This examination can help newcomers in the field of FER, giving essential information and a general comprehension of the most recent best in class considers, just as to experienced scientists searching for profitable bearings for future work.

In this venture, this paper utilize profound learning and run the code through pycharm. Profound learning contains various ideas, (for example, CNN, RNN, Backpropagation, and so forth.). Here, we use Convolution Neural Network to build up this task [7]. It helps in perceiving discourse, recognizing pictures or making forecasts. We typically sort out information to go through predefined conditions however profound learning has various layers which help in preparing of information [8].

2 Method

In this venture, this paper utilize profound learning and run the code through pycharm. Profound learning contains various ideas (for example, CNN, RNN, Backpropagation, and so forth). Here, we use Convolution Neural Network to build up this task. It helps in perceiving discourse, recognizing pictures or making forecasts [9]. We typically sort out information to go through predefined conditions however profound learning has various layers which help in preparing of information.

Humans generally express their emotions using different facial expressions. However, facial recognition using machine is difficult to develop to find out the emotions of a person. In this paper, we developed a program which helps in detecting emotions of a person using machine. Initially, we take the image. Later we do image partition and go for processing [10]. Then we obtain the emotion of a person as a result.

Functional Analysis: In this paper, The webcam first locates the persons face and captures his picture and saves the image as ".jpg" type. Then data of the captured image goes into the native computer.

CNN is used to build 4 layers of convolution and 2 full-connected layers, Kaggle's "fer2013.csv" is used as facial emotional dataset and trained through the CNN structure, as a result of this, a file of ".h5" type was created named "model_4layer_2_2_pool" which contains all the special features of the emotional dataset.

After receiving the pictures from a robot, these pictures will be trained and tested through the CNN structure and will be analyzed and recognized via the pre-trained file.

Finally, all the analysis of the results will be summarized and visualized on the display in the values of angry, fear, happy, sad, surprise and neutral.

In this paper, Tensor Flow was used as a backend and Keras was used as the interface to call the functions of Tensor Flow to build the CNN structure.

2.1 Model Architecture

See Fig. 1.

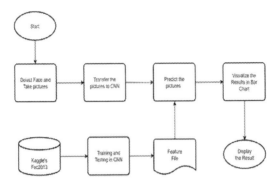

Fig. 1. Architecture of the proposed model

2.2 Dataset Training Flowchart

In this paper, the facial emotional dataset is Kaggle's Fec2013, which is compressed at a size of 92 M and the uncompressed version size is 295 M. The dataset contains 28,000 training photos and 30,000 test photos. Each photo is stored as 48 × 48 pixels.

This dataset contains image pixels (48 × 48 = 2,304 values), facial expressions in each image, and usage types (used as training or tests). The data file is mainly "Fec2013.csv", a total of two columns: emotion, pixels, and usage. There are 7 tags: 0 = Angry, 1 = Fear, 2 = Happy, 3 = Sad, 4 = Surprise, 5 = Neutral. The pixels column is 48 × 48 pixels (Figs. 2 and 3).

Fig. 2. Examples picture of Fer

"Fer.csv" will be transferred into CNN structure for training and testing, and then output a feature file in ".h5" type which contains all the facial emotional characteristics, named "model_4layer_2_2_pool" (Fig. 4).

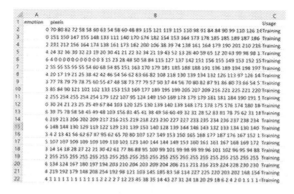

Fig. 3. Fer.csv file

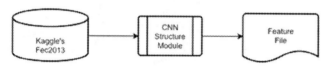

Fig. 4. CNN structure

2.3 Output Data Flowchart

After all the images captured by the webcam have been identified by deep learning, all the results will be aggregated to the average, and finally, the aggregated results will be visualized (Fig. 5).

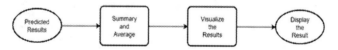

Fig. 5. Output data flowchart

3 Experiment and Results

3.1 Procedure

- Keras is a High-level Neural Networks API for building network models.
- In this paper, keras is a front-end interface which is used for running the model.
- In command prompt, Enter cd filename i.e., cd facial recognition
- After that enter emotiondetection.py which is a coded file written is python.
- This command helps in compiling the code
- Then enter python emotiondetection.py which runs the code.
- Successful completion of code opens a window saying tensorflow running in the background.

- Tensorflow is an open source software library for machine learning applications such as Neural Networks.
- Here, Tensorflow acts as a backend.
- After that we can see the camera started capturing images and showing the expression.

3.2 Results

4 Advantages and Disadvantages

4.1 Advantages

- It helps company managers to identify the employee mood which helps in business growth and increasing productivity.
- It is done by using only software which is used to sense the emotions and no hardware is required which helps in reducing the cost.
- It helps children and old people by providing medical care alerts to their family members.
- It is used in clinical practice.
- It is used to determine the patient mental state.

4.2 Disadvantages

- The dataset may not work well in order to give accurate recognition.
- Results of the paper depend on sensors such as cameras and algorithms which will be more expensive because of costly components.
- It doesn't support voice based recognition.

5   Conclusion

This paper specifies that the understanding of the structure and principle of artificial neural networks in deep learning, as well as the learning of related knowledge of convolutional neural networks are all very core parts. In the process of building a CNN structure, there are many factors that influence the accuracy of the deep learning result and the speed of training, like the quantity of convolution layers and completely associated layers, the activation function, and the dropout and so on. This paper contains very big problems which require a heavy effort to analyze the performance of emotion recognition. Facial emotion sensing are developed gradually at the stage at which once it full-grown, advantages of this sensing technology will help to the society in various aspects of life. The most advantage of this paper is that it will reduce accidents or crimes which happens due to the driver's state of mind, illness and irritation etc. It will help to reduce the limitations or disadvantages of sensing technology before it full-grown.

References

1. Akhtar, N.: Social network analysis tools. In: Fourth International Conference on Communication Systems and Network Technologies, pp. 382–388 (2014)
2. Ekram, T.: Tahmid140/twitter-opinion-mining. https://github.com/tahmid140/twitter-opinion-mining (2015). Accessed 31 July 2015
3. Anwar Hridoy, S.A., Tahmid Ekram, M., Islam, M.S., Ahmed, F., Rahman, R.M.: Localized twitter opinion mining using sentiment analysis. Decis. Anal. **2**, 8 (2015). https://doi.org/10.1186/s40165-015-0016-4
4. Kouloumpis, E., Wilson, T., Moore, J.: Twitter sentiment analysis: the good the bad and the OMG!. In: Proceedings of the Fifth International AAAI Conference on Weblogs and Social Media (2011)
5. Medhat, W., Hassan, A., Korashy, H.: Sentiment analysis algorithms and applications: a survey. Ain Shams Eng. J. **5**(4), 1093–1113 (2014)
6. Becker, L., Erhart, G., Skiba, D., Matula, V.: AVAYA: sentiment analysis on Twitter with self-training and polarity lexicon expansion. In: Second Joint Conference on Lexical and Computational Semantics (*SEM), Volume 2: Seventh International Workshop on Semantic Evaluation (SemEval 2013), pp. 333–340, 14–15 June 2013
7. Gerber, M.S.: Predicting crime using twitter and kernel density estimation. Decis. Support Syst. **61**, 115–125 (2014)
8. Zimbra, D., Ghiassi, M., Lee, S.: Brand-related twitter sentiment analysis using feature engineering and the dynamic architecture for artificial neural networks. In: 2016 49th Hawaii International Conference on System Sciences (HICSS)
9. Ganapathi Raju, N.V., Vijay Kumar, V., Srinivasa Rao, O.: Authorship attribution of Telugu texts based on syntactic features and machine learning techniques. J. Theor. Appl. Inf. Technol. **85**(1), 95–103 (2016)
10. Vijay Kumar, V., Ganapathi Raju, N.V., Srinivasa Rao, O.: Histograms of Term Weight Feature (HTWF) model for authorship attribution. Int. J. Appl. Eng. Res. **10**(16), 36622–36628 (2015)

An Attention Based Automatic Image Description Generation

R. Lakshmi Tulasi[✉]

RVR & JC College of Engineering, Guntur, India

Abstract. With the recent advancements in object detection and machine translation techniques, we proposed an attention based model that automatically performs
the image caption generation. We have used two kinds of attention mechanisms
named hard stochastic attention and soft deterministic attention. We can train
the model using backpropagation techniques and our model concentrates on the
important objects present in the image. By considering these salient objects it
can generate the corresponding captions word by word as the output sequence of
LSTM. We validated our model on the standard MSCOCO dataset.

Keywords: Image captioning · Soft attention · Hard attention · LSTM

1 Introduction

The task of an automatic image description is a challenging one. This involves consider
an image, analyze the visual content, and generate the textual description in a natural
sentence form that describes the most salient aspects of the image. This is one of the
prime objectives of computer vision. Previous research works of computer vision mainly
focused on object detection or image classification in which the main objective is to
detect or recognize a predefined and limited set of objects. Some advancement that deals
with the above-affirmed challenge of generating image description have been developed.
This imposes limits because most of the existing models depend on hard-coded visual
concepts and predefined templates. When compared with traditional approaches, on
datasets having more images, Deep NN based techniques have accomplished very good
results.

Though it is a very challenging task, a lot of research work is done by many
researchers. Recent works used the neural networks based approaches and better quality
of results is achieved.

The Image-captioning task involves two very important areas: the first one is a
computer vision and the second is NLP. The generated sentence should capture object
classes contained in the image and also the relationship present among objects. This
is very helpful for the children to understand the content of images on the web in a
better way. The majority of the image description generation methods are based on the
sequence to sequence in machine translation. The framework takes an input image to
the predefined CNN, then after extracting the features that are passed to RNN decoder

© Springer Nature Singapore Pte Ltd. 2021
A. K. Luhach et al. (Eds.): ICAICR 2020, CCIS 1393, pp. 254–263, 2021.
https://doi.org/10.1007/978-981-16-3660-8_24

to predict every word of the caption based on the visual contents of an image and earlier generated words.

Attention is one of the most important facets which concentrate on the salient features of an image. An important and powerful mechanism is required to drive the model. In this paper, we elaborate on image description generation approaches that use two variants of attention-based mechanisms: stochastic hard attention and deterministic soft attention. The usage of attention increases the ability of the model to visualize the contents. This can pay attention to the salient portion of an image at the time of generating its caption.

The very important contributions of the paper are mentioned here:

- Introduce the two variants of attention mechanisms: a stochastic hard and deterministic soft attention under a single common framework.
- Quantitatively validated the use of attention in caption generation by testing on standard MSCOCO dataset.

The rest of our paper is organized as follows: the literature review is briefed in Sect. 2; the proposed work is discussed in Sect. 3; the training process is explained in Sect. 4; the experimental part of the proposed system is detailed in Sect. 5; the conclusion is given in Sect. 6; the future scope of the problem is mentioned in Sect. 7.

2 Related Work

Despite it is a very challenging task, many researchers worked to address this problem. In this, we provide brief work done by various researchers in the area of image captioning. Till today various methods have been proposed by researchers for image description generation.

Before the usage of neural network approaches for generating image descriptions, two approaches are used commonly. The first approach uses templates to generate captions. For a given input image the existing templates are filled with the appropriate words based on the object detection and attribute finding [1].

Kuznetsova et al., [2] proposed the second approach which is based on the given query. It retrieves the images having similar captions from a large database. These kinds of approaches involve a generalization process to extract the details of the caption which are relevant to the retrieved image. Later neural networks are used for this purpose to achieve better results.

Most of the techniques are RNN based and those are motivated by the sequence to sequence machine translation. Dizmetry et al., [3] proposed the encoder-decoder based machine translation framework which is used for translating an image into an appropriate sentence.

Donahue et al., [4] proposed the LSTM Recurrent Neural Network approach. In these, the image to the RNN is given at the beginning of the process. He tested his approach of LSTMs for videos to generate video descriptions along with the image data. Oriol et al., [5] proposed a deep recurrent based generative model and that is trained to generate the maximum likelihood of the target sentence for the given image. Siming Li et al., [6] proposed a method that considers the web-scale n-grams to generates the captions completely from the scratch. It is a simple but effective approach to automatically generate image captions for computer vision-related inputs.

Ankush Gupta, Prashanth Mannem, et al., [7] considered the annotation of the images and designed an automatic image description generation system. They used computer vision techniques to decide the labels or make use of the existing captions of the trained images to compose a new caption of the image in the testing phase.

Cesc Park et al., [8] Proposed a novel image description model under the name Contextual Sequence Memory. This method generates a caption, by considering the prior knowledge of the user's active vocabularies. Leiquan Wang et al., [9] proposed a dual attention-based model for image description generation on the MS COCO dataset by blending the user's attention and visual attention concurrently.

Gunawardena, P., Amila, O., et al., [10], proposed the novel video highlight generation method. It uses static image processing and data clustering to process the video in static and dynamic feature streams. Multi-scene videos are also processed using this method.

3   Proposed Work

This section describes the three major components of the proposed system which include convolutional feature extraction of an Image, RNN Decoder with attention over the image, Word sequence generation using LSTM.

3.1   Architecture

Input image. Our proposed model of attention-based image caption generation takes an input image 'i' and produces a caption 'x' which is encoded as a sequence of N words.

$$x = \{x_1, x_2, \ldots \ldots, x_c\}, x_i \in R^N$$

where N represents the size of the vocabulary and c represents the number of words present in the generated caption (description).

Convolutional Feature Extraction (Encoder). In this module, L number of D-dimensional features of an image are extracted using a convolutional neural network by considering the scaled 254×254 image as an input. The features are stored in a vector of length k, (v1,v2,v3……vk). Let it call as annotation vector v.

$$v = \{v_1, \ldots \ldots v_L\}, v_i \in R^D$$

To get the correlation among the feature vectors of an image and its portions, we extract features from a bottom layer of the convolutional neural network. This permits the decoder to particularly focus on certain portions of the image by considering the subset of the feature vectors (Fig. 1).

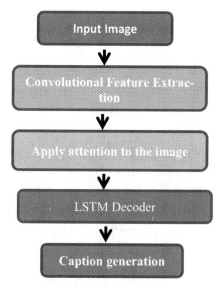

Fig. 1. Architecture for attention-based image description generation

Applying attention to the image. In our model, we have used two attention-based mechanisms, "hard" stochastic attention, and the "soft" variable deterministic attention.

Hard stochastic attention model. In this, we treat the attention locations as intermediate latent variables and $\hat{z}_t$ as the random variable. The novel objective function O_s is defined which is a changing lower bound on the marginal log-likelihood $\log p(x|v)$ where x is the series of words and 'v' is the features of an image. The following function O_s is optimized to derive the learning algorithm of the model.

$$Os = \sum_{s}^{n} p(s|v)\log(x|s, v)$$

$$\leq \log \sum_{s}^{n} p(s|v)p(x|s, v)$$

$$= \log p(x|v) \tag{1}$$

Soft deterministic attention model. In this, first, we calculate the soft attention weighted annotation vector $\emptyset(\{v_i\},\{\alpha_i\}) = \sum_{i=1}^{L} \alpha i \, vi$. We consider the expectation of the context vector $\hat{z}_t$ directly and create a deterministic attention model. This refers to giving in a soft α_i weighted context into the system. The entire model is smooth and differentiable under soft deterministic attention.

Doubly stochastic attention. We introduced a doubly stochastic regularization to train the deterministic version of the model. This can be helpful to give uniform attention to each portion of the image, to improve the BLEU score, and is also helpful to generate more rich and descriptive captions. To summarize the model is trained totally by minimizing the

$$L_d = -\log(P(y|x)) + \lambda \tag{2}$$

Word Sequence Generation using LSTM (Decoder). In our proposed method we have used the LSTM to generate the word sequence of a particular sentence. LSTM is trained to predict and generate the succeeding word of a sentence based on the given word. The diagram which shows the representation of the LSTM cell is given in Fig. 2.

Each LSTM Cell learns the process of weighing it's input components through its input gate. It uses the input modulator to learn the process of modulating and it's contribution towards the memory. Through the forget gate it also learns the weights required to erase the memory cell, and through the output gate, it learns the weights that control how this memory should be emitted. LSTM is represented by

$$h_t = \text{LSTM}\big(Ey_{t-1}, h_{t-1}, z_t\big) \tag{3}$$

$$\begin{pmatrix} i_t \\ f_t \\ o_t \\ g_t \end{pmatrix} = \begin{pmatrix} \sigma \\ \sigma \\ \sigma \\ \tanh \end{pmatrix} W_{\text{LSTM}} \begin{pmatrix} S_{t-1} \\ h_{t-1} \\ z_t \end{pmatrix} \tag{4}$$

$$C_t = f_t \odot c_{t-1} + i_t g_t \tag{5}$$

$$h_t = O_t \odot \tanh c_t \tag{6}$$

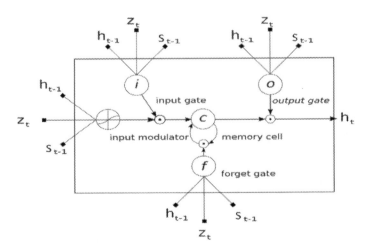

Fig. 2. The structure of LSTM cell.

Here i_t, $\mathbf{o}_t$, $\mathbf{f}_t$, $\mathbf{C}_t$, and $\mathbf{h}_t$ are the input, output, forget, memory, and hidden states of the LSTM respectively. The context vector $\mathbf{z_t}$ represents the visual feature. The S_t represents the embedded vector of the tth word. The σ denotes the logistic sigmoid activation and $\odot$ denotes the element-wise multiplication operation. The $\hat{\mathbf{z}}_t$ (Eqs. (4)–(6)) is the context vector that corresponds to a dynamic characterization of the specific portion of the image at a time 't'. Based on the features extracted at various locations, the mechanism $\hat{\mathbf{z}}_t$ is derived to compute from annotation vectors. The weight generated is interpreted as the probability that the location 'j' is an appropriate location to focus on generating the next word in sequence. The attention model is used to generate weight α_j of every annotation vector. The multilayer perceptron which is trained on the earlier hidden state (h_{t-1}) is used for this purpose.

The weight α_j of every annotation vector v_j is calculated by using the attention model f_{atten}. For that we make use of ae_{tk}

$$e_{ti} = f_{atten}\left(v_j, h_{t-1}\right) \tag{7}$$

$$\alpha_{ti} = expo(e_{ti})/\sum_{k=1}^{L} expo(etk) \tag{8}$$

After the computation of weights, the context vector $\hat{\mathbf{z}}_t$ is computed by using $\hat{\mathbf{z}}_t = \emptyset$ $(\{vj\},\{\alpha j\})$. The initial hidden state, h_0, and the memory state, c_0 of the LSTM are forecasted by averaging the annotation vectors provided with two separate multilayer perceptrons.

$$c_0 = f_{ini,c}(\frac{1}{L}\sum_{i}^{L} v_i) \tag{9}$$

$$h_0 = f_{ini,h}(\frac{1}{L}\sum_{i}^{L} v_i) \tag{10}$$

In this work, we use the output layer of the deep neural network to calculate the probability of the next output word for the given state of LSTM, the context vector, and the previously generated word [10].

$$p\left(y_t|v; \ y_1^{t-1}\right) \alpha \exp(L_o(Ey_{t-1} + L_h h_t + Lz\hat{\mathbf{z}}_t)) \tag{11}$$

Where $L_0 \in R^{Kxm}$, $L_h \in R^{mxn}$, $Lz \in R^{mxD}$, and E are learned parameters initialized randomly.

4 Training Process

The stochastic gradient descent based adaptive learning rate algorithms is used to train both of our variant attention models. To train the MS COCO dataset, we have used the Adam algorithm [11]. We used oxford VGGNet which is pre-trained on ImageNet to create annotations v_i, used by our decoder. Besides, the rest of the model is trained with any encoding function. In our experiments, we used the $14 \times 14 \times 512$ feature map of the fourth convolutional layer prior to applying the max-pooling function. In our model, we used the early stopping of the BLEU score.

5   Experiments Conduction and Result Analysis

In this section, we discuss the experimental methodology used in our model and the results obtained to validate the effectiveness of it.

5.1   Data set

We considered the MS COCO dataset for validation of our method. MSCOCO dataset has 82K images and considered the five of the existing reference sentences though it has more than five. As they need more execution time we considered 5,000 images for our experiments. We performed the basic preprocessing (tokenization) on the dataset (Fig. 3).

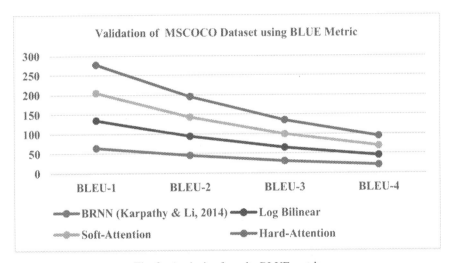

Fig. 3. Analysis of results BLUE metric

5.2   Visualizations from Our Attention Models

The visualization of hard and soft attention models of a sample image is shown in Fig. 4 and Fig. 5.

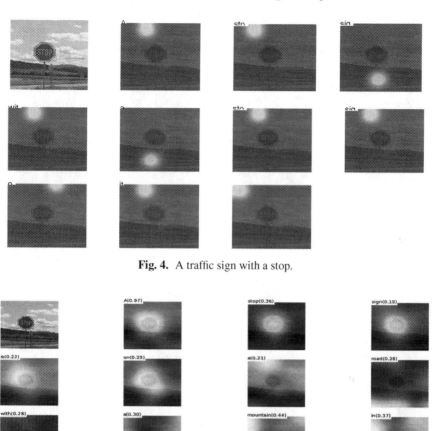

Fig. 4. A traffic sign with a stop.

Fig. 5. A stop sign with a mountain background and the sky

5.3 Results Obtained

Experimental results obtained in our attention-based image description model are recorded in Table 1. We have evaluated the results using the BLEU which is a standard metric in image description generation.

The results are analyzed and compared with BRNN, and Log Bilinear. We obtained better results after applying Soft attention, and hard attention methods. The performance of various methods is represented graphically as in Fig. 3.

Table 1. Results of validation of MSCOCO dataset using BLEU

Dataset used	Model used	BLEU metric			
		BLEU1	BLEU2	BLEU3	BLEU4
MS COCO	Google NIC	66.6	46.1	32.9	24.6
	BRNN [13]	64.2	45.1	30.4	20.3
	Log bilinear	70.8	48.9	34.4	24.3
	Soft-attention	70.1	49.1	34.4	24.5
	Hard-attention	72.2	52.3	35.8	25.0

6   Conclusion

In this paper, we proposed two kinds of attention named hard attention and soft attention approaches for image description generation. We have used the LSTM to generate word by word of our caption using the previously generated word. We have evaluated our model on the standard MSCOCO dataset using the BLEU metric. We have obtained better results than the models without using attention. We also hope that the encoder and decoder model along with the attention is used in various domains. We have demonstrated how the learned alignments correspond very well to human perception.

7   Future Scope

The future scope of our model is discussed in this section. In the proposed work, we have used a single model approach. We will propose the ensembling techniques to enhance the efficiency of our model. In the future, we can also introduce active learning to update the model continuously by asking questions to generate unambiguous captions.

References

1. Kulakarni, G., et al.: Babytalk: understanding and generating simple image descriptions. IEEE Trans. Pattern Anal. Mach. Intell. **35**(2), 2891–2903 (2013)
2. Kuznetsova, P., Ordonez, V., Berg, A., Berg, T., Choi, Y.: Collective generation of natural image descriptions. In: Proceedings of the 50th Annual Meeting of the Association for Computational Linguistics, pp. 359–368. Jenu, Republic of Korea (2012)
3. Bahdanau, D., Kyunghyun, C., Yoshua, B.: Neural machine translation by jointly learning to align and translate. In: ICLR 2015, pp. 1–15. Semantic Scholar (2015)
4. Donahue, J., et al.: Long-term recurrent convolutional networks for visual recognition and description. arXiv:1411.4389v2 (2014)
5. Vinyals, O., Toshev, A., Bengio, S., Erhan, D.: Show and tell: a neural image caption generator. arXiv:1411.4555 (2014)
6. Li, S., Kulakarni, G., Berg, T., Berg, A., Choi, Y.: Composing simple image descriptions using web-scale n-grams. In: Proceedings of the 15th Conference on Computational Natural Language Learning, pp. 220–228. ACM, Portland, USA (2011)

7. Varma, Y., Gupta, A., Mannem, P.: Generating image descriptions using semantic similarities in the output space. In: IEEE Conference on Computer Vision and Pattern Recognition Workshops, pp. 23–28. IEEE (2013)
8. Chunseong, C., Byeongchang, K., Gunhee, K.: Personalized image captioning with context sequence memory networks. arXiv:1704.0648 (2017)
9. Wang, L., Chu, X., Zhang, W., Wei, Y., Sun, W., Chunlei, W.: Social image captioning: exploring visual attention and user attention. Sensors **18**(2), 646 (2018). https://doi.org/10.3390/s18020646
10. Gunawardena, P., et al.: Real-time automated video highlight generation with dual-stream hierarchical growing self-organizing maps. J. Real-Time Image Process. 1–19 (2020)
11. Sutskever, I., Vinyals, O., Le, Q.V.: Sequence to sequence learning with neural networks. In: NIPS, pp. 3104–3112 (2014)
12. Pascanu, R., Gulcehre, C., Cho, K., Bengio, Y.: How to construct deep recurrent neural networks. In: ICLR (2014)
13. Kingma, D., Ba, J.: A method for stochastic optimization. arXiv:1412.6980 (2014)
14. Karpathy, A., Fei-Fei, L.: Deep visual-semantic alignments for generating image descriptions. arXiv:1412.2306 (2014)

Providing Safety for Citizens and Tourists in Cities: A System for Detecting Anomalous Sounds

Balnur Kendzhaeva[1], Bakhytzhan Omarov[2(✉)], Gaziza Abdiyeva[2],
Almas Anarbayev[2], Yergali Dauletbek[3], and Bauyrzhan Omarov[4]

[1] Akhmet Yassawi International Kazakh-Turkish University, Turkistan, Kazakhstan
[2] International University of Tourism and Hospitality, Turkistan, Kazakhstan
[3] International Information Technology University, Almaty, Kazakhstan
[4] Al-Farabi Kazakh National University, Almaty, Kazakhstan

Abstract. Alert the public about emergencies is to bring to public alerts and emergency information on dangers arising from the threat or occurrence of emergency situations of natural and technogenic character, as well as the conduct of hostilities or owing to these actions, the rules of behavior of the population and the need for protection activities. When developing projects in the security and video surveillance industry, the audio characteristics of the systems are often overlooked. At the same time, audio plays a key role in some intercom solutions, but very often it is not taken into account when it comes to security and event management. This applies to many security systems, as audio recorded by surveillance cameras can affect the privacy of individuals caught on camera recordings in different ways. In the current research, we try to apply machine learning techniques to detect dangerous situations. In order to do it, we collected data of audio events of dangerous situations. In the next stage, we applied different machine learning algorithms for dangerous event detection problem.

Keywords: Audioanalytics · Sound · Events · Machine learning · SVM · Audio signal

1 Introduction

In recent years, we have increasingly encountered various audio content that is distributed for both commercial and non-commercial purposes. Due to the growing availability of audio materials and the growth of computing power, automated processing of audio signals based on signals is currently at the center of various studies [1–3]. We understand what is being said, recognize voice, and can guess their emotional state and events. We do this automatically, quickly and effortlessly. However, all this is made possible by a complex process involving a number of brain structures that specialize in auditory (sound) perception and recognition of various sub-components of hearing.

In the past decade, artificial intelligence has experienced a revolution based on machine learning. You no longer have to painstakingly program all intelligence, instead

© Springer Nature Singapore Pte Ltd. 2021
A. K. Luhach et al. (Eds.): ICAICR 2020, CCIS 1393, pp. 264–273, 2021.
https://doi.org/10.1007/978-981-16-3660-8_25

you provide the artificial intelligence with sample data and ask it to study the patterns of this information. This idea is not new, but it has only recently become possible with the advent of affordable GPUs. Originally designed for gaming, these chips have proven to be more versatile than their designers anticipated. Key machine learning algorithms developed around the turn of the century are suddenly productive. Fortunately, these new methods were very flexible. Still image recognition neural network algorithms can also move to video and audio analytics. Audio Analytics Service is a machine learning-based sound and speech recognition technology that detects and analyzes any sounds or a combination of sounds in an audio stream. Audio and video analytics are two types of pattern recognition, branches of artificial intelligence.

Depending on the storage format, user requirements, data volume, and many other parameters, various applications and trends have emerged for solving various audio analysis tasks. The following popular audio analysis tasks can be distinguished [4]: speech recognition, speaker identification, music information search (MIR), event detection, emotion recognition, and film content analysis [5, 6].

This research tries to detect dangerous situations using audioanalytics. For example, at the moment of a shot or other dangerous sound signal, the system recognizes and determines the location of the incident and within a few seconds sends a signal about the event to law enforcement agencies. The camera turns in the direction of the sound source, so that the operator can observe what is happening from a monitor installed in the surveillance center or in the car. The signal is transmitted over a mobile network. City cameras will recognize gunshots, explosions, the rumble of falling, hitting or colliding cars, as well as a scream. A special acoustic monitoring system will allow the camera to instantly focus on the point from which it comes when such a sound occurs, and get the most accurate image of what is happening. "In the event of a loud bang, similar to a shot or explosion, the system will orient the camera to the point of sound to capture what is happening at the moment."

The goal of the project is to teach the computer to listen to the world around it and make decisions based on audio information.

2   Materials and Methods

Building machine learning models for classifying, describing, or generating sound usually concerns modeling tasks where the input data is audio samples (Fig. 1) [7].

These audio samples are usually represented as time series, where the y-axis measurement represents the amplitude of the signal. The amplitude is usually measured as a function of the change in pressure around the microphone or receiver that initially picked up the sound. If your audio samples don't have metadata associated with them, these time series signals will often be your only input for model fitting.

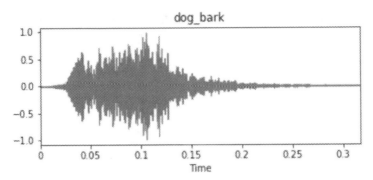

Fig. 1. Audio event detection architecture

2.1 Audio Features in the Time Domain

Energy. Let $xi\,(n)$, $n = 1,\ldots, WL$ – this is a sequence of audio fragments of the ith frame, where $W L$ is the length of the frame. The energy value can be obtained by the formula 1.

$$E(i) = \sum_{n=1}^{W_L} |x_i(n)|^2 \tag{1}$$

Typically, the energy is normalized by dividing it by $W L$ to remove the dependence on the frame length. Then you can get formula 2 from formula 1.

$$E(i) = \frac{1}{W_L} \sum_{n=1}^{W_L} |x_i(n)|^2 \tag{2}$$

This characteristic of the signal often changes, alternating between high and low energy States [5]. Therefore, the standard deviation of energy is often used for classification (Fig. 2).

2.2 Zero-Crossing Rate

The zero crossing frequency is the rate at which the signal sign changes over the course of a frame [8]. The zero crossing frequency can be interpreted as a measure of signal noise (Fig. 3). For example, it usually shows higher values in the case of noisy signals. ZCR is widely applicable, including speech recognition, music recognition, speech detection, and music genre classification. This attribute is determined in accordance with formula 3.

$$Z(i) = \frac{1}{2W_L} \sum_{n=1}^{W_L} |sgn[x_i(n)] - sgn[x_i(n-1)]|, \tag{3}$$

where sgn is a signed function, the logic of which is described by formula 4.

$$sgn[x_i(n)] = f(x) = \begin{cases} -1, x_i(n) < 0 \\ 1, x_i(n) \geq 0 \end{cases} \tag{4}$$

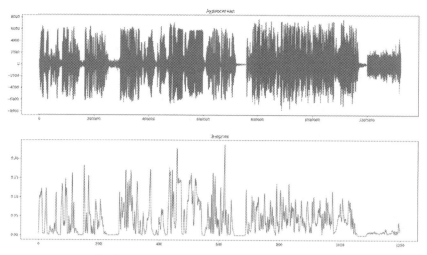

Fig. 2. Visual representation of audio signal energy

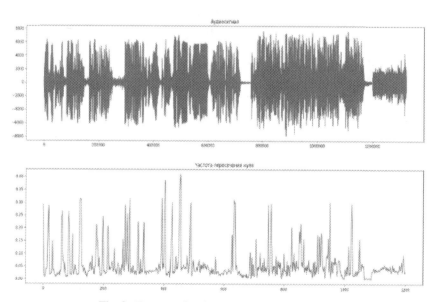

Fig. 3. Zero crossing frequency of the audio signal

When filtering, an FIR filter is used, due to which the signal becomes less sensitive to various background noise that occurs during processing.

Window weighting must be applied because the audio frame is limited in time, therefore when switching to the frequency domain, the effect of seepage of the side lobe spectrum will occur, due to the shape of the spectrum of the rectangular window function (it has the form sin(x)/x). Therefore, to reduce the effect of this effect, the source signal is weighted with different types of Windows with a shape other than rectangular. The

Table 1. Comparative analysis of training models for recognizing audio events

Classifier	A Bayesian classifier	(Gaussian Mixture Model	SVM	Hidden Markov Model	Neural network
Principle	Maximum a posteriori probability	Probability distribution of observations in the General population	Translates the original feature vectors to a space with a higher dimension and finds the maximum separating hyperplane from the recognized classes	A sequence of random variables, where each value xt+1 depends only on the previous th and, under the condition of th, is conditionally independent with the previous th-K)	Built on a multi-layer perceptron, which allows you to classify the input signal in accordance with the pre-configuration of the network
Function	probability density	"Mixture" of several Gaussians	Linear function, polynomial, and RBF	Statistical model simulating a Markov process with unknown parameters	Mathematical model based on the principle of organization of biological neural networks
Dignities	to train and then to interrogate large data sets; the relative ease of interpretation	The recognition model has become more accurate, and the recognition result will improve accordingly	Finds the maximum width of the band, which provides greater accuracy	The model is simple and flexible enough to integrate into many systems	The neural network itself detects uninformative noises and filters them out
Disadvantages	relatively poor classification quality in most real-world tasks	High sensitivity to variations in the training data sample when selecting a large number of Gaussian distributions	Sensitivity to the standardization of data and noise	There is a high probability of an erroneous conclusion when several hidden States are connected to a single observed result	Problems of mathematical nature;

input sequence samples are multiplied by the corresponding window function, which causes the signal values at the sample edges to be reset. The most common weighted functions are Hamming, Blackman, ploskoe, And Kaiser Bessel Windows.

The next step is feature extraction, i.e. reducing signal redundancy, by extracting the necessary information and getting rid of irrelevant information. As a rule, the audio signal is isolated from:

1. Statistics in the time domain
2. Statistics in the frequency domain
3. Mel-frequency cepstral coefficients
4. The coefficients of the linear prediction

After extracting the necessary signal features, the features are normalized. The technique of finding the average value is often used when averaging features over a set of consecutive frames. The interval for averaging is usually from 1 to 10 s.

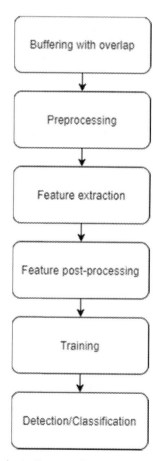

Fig. 4. Audio event detection architecture

The last step in recognizing audio events is to select a training model. Currently, the following model classifiers are used: Bayesian classifier, GM (Gaussian Mixture Model), SVM (SupportVectorMachine), HMM (HiddenMarkov Model), Neural networks [9] (Table 1).

The expected complex structure is demonstrated in Fig. 4. The system consists of the parts as buffering with overlap, preprocessing of audio data, feature extraction, feature post-processing, model training, and in the last step is audio event detection problem.

Audio event detection problem is classified into 2 subtasks as detection and classification [10]:

In our case, we try to detect audio events as glass shattering, burglar alarm, explosion, dog barking, siren (police siren, fire siren, and ambulance car siren), fire alarm, and baby crying.

3   Results

3.1   Dataset

In order to train machine learning models we collected abnormal sounds that contains impulsive sounds like police sirens, gunshots, explosions, alarms, glass screams and etc. The dataset consists of 10 000 thousand sounds of abnormal events. Table 2 shows the samples of the collected sounds.

We applied machine learning for data classification problem. So, in our case we classified impulsive sounds, and in the result our system detects abnormal events. Table 3 demonstrates the abnormal event classification results.

Table 2. Samples of different impulsive sounds

Table Column Head		
Impulsive sounds	*Time (sec)*	*Image*
Glass shattering	3.84	
Burglar alarm	11.13	
Artillery shell explosion	4	
Dog barking	22.15	
Ambulance siren	15.41	
Constant Wail from Police Siren	56.87	
Fire alarm	2.3	
Single gun shot	3.84	
Baby crying	6.66	
Fire alarm beeping	1.41	
Fire alarm bell	1.59	
Explosion	7.78	
Police siren	24.19	
Smoke alarm	0.99	

Table 3. Impulsive audio event detection

Event type	Accuracy	Precision	Recall	F1 score	AUC ROC
Gunshot	0.9215	0.9102	0.9401	0.9002	0.9634
Broken glass	0.9345	0.9648	0.9103	0.9108	0.9572
Fire	0.9102	0.9231	0.9018	0.9311	0.9508
Siren	0.9012	0.9410	0.9029	0.9634	0.9607
Explosion	0.8031	0.8345	0.8279	0.8018	0.9326
Cry	0.9345	0.8134	0.8837	0.8624	0.9445
Dog barking	0.8456	0.8325	0.8537	0.8254	0.9305
Fire alarm bell	0.8654	0.8452	0.8576	0.8457	0.9472

4 Conclusion

In this research, we applied machine learning techniques to abnormal event classification problem. The research consists of several parts. In the first part, we analyzed materials and literature that related to current research. In the next stage of our research, we collected data that consists of different dangerous events. The data were collected mp4 format. In the last stage of the current research, we applied machine learning algorithms to classify audio events. The results shown high comparatively high accuracy. In the next part of our research, we going to increase the accuracy rates by suppression of extraneous noise, increasing the data and applying hybrid algorithms.

Moreover, in further, we are going to apply deep learning techniques to detect dangerous situations also apply parallel computing in GPU to fast recognize audio events.

References

1. Tharwat, A., Mahdi, H., Elhoseny, M., Hassanien, A.E.: Recognizing human activity in mobile crowdsensing environment using optimized k-NN algorithm. Expert Syst. Appl. **107**, 32–44 (2018)
2. Omarov, B.: Applying of audioanalytics for determining contingencies. In: 2017 17th International Conference on Control, Automation and Systems (ICCAS), pp. 744–748. IEEE, October 2017
3. Goldenberg, A., et al.: Use of ShotSpotter detection technology decreases prehospital time for patients sustaining gunshot wounds. J. Trauma]Acute Care Surg. **87**(6), 1253–1259 (2019)
4. Gabriel, D., Kojima, R., Hoshiba, K., Itoyama, K., Nishida, K., Nakadai, K.: 2D sound source position estimation using microphone arrays and its application to a VR-based bird song analysis system. Adv. Robot. **33**(7–8), 403–414 (2019)
5. Wang, K., Yang, L., Yang, B.: Audio event detection and classification using extended R-FCN approach. In: Proceedings of the Detection and Classification of Acoustic Scenes and Events 2017 Workshop (DCASE2017), pp. 128–132, September 2017

6. Romanov, S.A., Kharkovchuk, N.A., Sinelnikov, M.R., Abrash, M.R., Filinkov, V.: Development of an non-speech audio event detection system. In: 2020 IEEE Conference of Russian Young Researchers in Electrical and Electronic Engineering (EIConRus), pp. 1421–1423. IEEE, January 2020

7. Cao, Y., Iqbal, T., Kong, Q., Galindo, M., Wang, W., Plumbley, M.: Two-stage sound event localization and detection using intensity vector and generalized cross-correlation. DCASE 2019 Challenge, Technical report (2019)

8. Cerutti, G., Prasad, R., Brutti, A., Farella, E.: Neural network distillation on IoT platforms for sound event detection. In: Proceedings of Interspeech, vol. 2019, pp. 3609–3613 (2019).

9. McFee, B., Salamon, J., Bello, J.P.: Adaptive pooling operators for weakly labeled sound event detection. IEEE/ACM Trans. Audio Speech Lang. Process. 26(11), 2180–2193 (2018)

10. Sammarco, M., Detyniecki, M.: Car accident detection and reconstruction through sound analysis with Crashzam. In: Smart Cities, Green Technologies and Intelligent Transport Systems, pp. 159–180. Springer, Cham (2018). https://doi.org/10.1007/978-3-030-26633-2_8

Mobilenet V2-FCD: Fake Currency Note Detection

Tejaswi Potluri[✉], Somavarapu Jahnavi, and Ravikanth Motupalli

VNR Vignana Jyothi Institute of Engineering and Technology, Hyderabad, India
{tejaswi_p,jahnavi_s,ravikanth_m}@vnrvjiet.in

Abstract. The technology advancement has made lot of changes to printing and scanning industry. The printing and scanning technologies are affecting economy. There is a big challenge to the entire world in terms of fake currency. These real time problems can be solved easily using Deep Learning techniques. Convolution Neural Networks can be used for detecting Fake Currency note. Our proposed Mobilenetv2-FCD is trained to detect the Indian Fake currency Notes. The proposed network detects fake notes with 85% accuracy. The network can be trained for any nation's currency and can be used accordingly.

Keywords: Fake currency note detection · Deep learning · Feature extraction · MobileNetV2 · Dense layer

1 Introduction

Recent advancement in the technology results in the creation of fake in every field. The banking sector is also facing the same problem with the technology advancement. Reserve Bank of India (RBI) is authorized for printing currency notes. The development in printing and scanning technology lead to increase in fake currency notes which in turn are affecting the economy.

Manual detection of fake currency is a very hectic process. The same technology can be used for detecting the fake currency. Various image processing techniques are used for identification of fake currency. The features like watermarks, optically variable inks and security threads are embedded into currency threads to differentiate from fake. All these features are processed by using image processing. Edge detection techniques, Feature Extraction, Image segmentation etc. are used for detecting fake currency. The detection accuracy is less for these approaches as feature extraction phase is a challenging task. The multilayer networks used in Deep Learning are very effective for different real time applications [8].

Deep learning supports Transfer Learning, which reduces the time and cost required for training [6]. The network will be fine-tuned which in turn can be trained only selected layers with small and customized datasets. The problem of handling huge datasets can also be solved using transfer learning. We have fine-tuned Mobilenet v2 to get Mobilenet v2-FCD which is trained using transfer learning.

The remaining paper includes Literature Study, Proposed System, Implementation details, Experimental Results, Future Scope and Conclusion.

© Springer Nature Singapore Pte Ltd. 2021
A. K. Luhach et al. (Eds.): ICAICR 2020, CCIS 1393, pp. 274–282, 2021.
https://doi.org/10.1007/978-981-16-3660-8_26

2 Literature Study

Recently used popular neural network for image classification problem is Convolutional Neural Networks (CNN). These Convolution Neural Networks analyses images in a better way. The main benefit of CNN is that it the CNN models take less time to learn by having only a fewer parameter and it also reduces the amount of data required for learning. CNN just uses required weights to analyze a small patch of image instead of fully connected network of weights.

Some existing methodologies also used the features of the note image like dominant color, shape, Surf, Harris, Brisk features [2–4] for detecting the fake currency from the complete dataset.

Each convolution layer implements a specific number of filters to the input image [1]. As the window slides across the whole image sum of the pixel values of the image is calculated and that weighted sum is called as convolution. Filter is an array of numbers with same number of rows and columns. The filter is moved over all the pixels. During this process, each pixel value is multiplied with the respective filter value and the sum of product is stored in the output array. The same process can be observed in the following Fig. 2. These filters are used for detecting fake currency (Fig. 1).

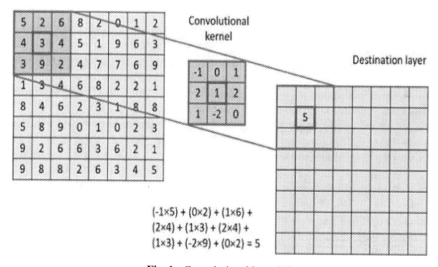

Fig. 1. Convolutional layer [1]

In some papers, the neural networks have been combined with model-based reasoning and data mining techniques. Some existing systems of India implements Edge based detection using Sobel operator. In this, the edges are segmented and classified using different classifiers. Some papers used latent image and watermarks which are embedded in the original currency notes.

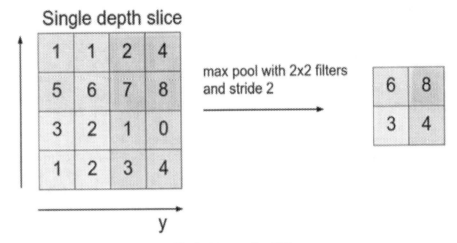

Fig. 2. Max pooling [18]

3 Proposed System

Our model i.e., MobileNet-V2 FCD: Fake Currency Detection is designed in such a way that the most famous convolutional neural network MobileNet-v2 is fine-tuned and it is trained by using customized dataset by using transfer Learning.

MobileNet is a CNN model which consists of layers like convolutions, max pooling, Relu activations, dropout and fully connected layers. We can get the layers from the Fig. 3. MobileNet-v2 consists of 161 layers. We implement transfer learning in which, the last three layers are fine tuned to implement of our proposed work.

To the above architecture of MobileNetV2 model extra dense layers can be added to improve the accuracy of the model. Adding a dense layer with activation function Relu helps to extract more specific and in-depth features of currency note so that distinguishing fake notes which are almost like real notes can be more accurate. After adding dense layer, a dropout layer is added to avoid overfitting of data. Then a dense layer with SoftMax function which acts as an output layer to classify the input image into real or fake is added. By adding these three layers the total number of layers in our model will be 164. The Proposed methodology to build the system includes following steps.

3.1 Data Collection

Data for our model is currency images. The model has been trained for Indian 500-rupee currency notes. So, the dataset includes real and fake 500 note images. The dataset contains a total of 85 images from which 70 are used for training and 15 are used for testing. There are 60 real currency images and 25 fake currency images.

3.2 Data Pre-processing

The size of images collected may vary due to different cameras and devices. The input size for the layers of convolutional neural networks will be fixed. For MobileNetV2

Type / Stride	Filter Shape	Input Size
Conv / s2	$3 \times 3 \times 3 \times 32$	$224 \times 224 \times 3$
Conv dw / s1	$3 \times 3 \times 32$ dw	$112 \times 112 \times 32$
Conv / s1	$1 \times 1 \times 32 \times 64$	$112 \times 112 \times 32$
Conv dw / s2	$3 \times 3 \times 64$ dw	$112 \times 112 \times 64$
Conv / s1	$1 \times 1 \times 64 \times 128$	$56 \times 56 \times 64$
Conv dw / s1	$3 \times 3 \times 128$ dw	$56 \times 56 \times 128$
Conv / s1	$1 \times 1 \times 128 \times 128$	$56 \times 56 \times 128$
Conv dw / s2	$3 \times 3 \times 128$ dw	$56 \times 56 \times 128$
Conv / s1	$1 \times 1 \times 128 \times 256$	$28 \times 28 \times 128$
Conv dw / s1	$3 \times 3 \times 256$ dw	$28 \times 28 \times 256$
Conv / s1	$1 \times 1 \times 256 \times 256$	$28 \times 28 \times 256$
Conv dw / s2	$3 \times 3 \times 256$ dw	$28 \times 28 \times 256$
Conv / s1	$1 \times 1 \times 256 \times 512$	$14 \times 14 \times 256$
$5\times$ Conv dw / s1	$3 \times 3 \times 512$ dw	$14 \times 14 \times 512$
Conv / s1	$1 \times 1 \times 512 \times 512$	$14 \times 14 \times 512$
Conv dw / s2	$3 \times 3 \times 512$ dw	$14 \times 14 \times 512$
Conv / s1	$1 \times 1 \times 512 \times 1024$	$7 \times 7 \times 512$
Conv dw / s1	$3 \times 3 \times 1024$ dw	$7 \times 7 \times 1024$
Conv / s1	$1 \times 1 \times 1024 \times 1024$	$7 \times 7 \times 1024$
Avg Pool / s1	Pool 7×7	$7 \times 7 \times 1024$
FC / s1	1024×1000	$1 \times 1 \times 1024$
Softmax / s1	Classifier	$1 \times 1 \times 1000$

Fig. 3. MobileNetV2 Architecture [19]

model the images should be of size 224×224. The images collected from various sources need to be pre-processed to get of same size without any loss of information.

3.3 Data Augmentation

Wide range of image capturing resources results in different qualities of images. Images captured can vary in terms of lighting, brightness, resolution etc. All these changes can affect in the quality of images. For processing various types of images using a single model, all these images to be pre-processed to unique format so that it can be given as an input to a model. Data Augmentation is used for this step.

Data augmentation is used to increase the diversity to get the training data without using any new data. So, it is a technique used to virtually expand the size of a training dataset by recreating modified versions of images in the dataset. Transformation of images are done by applying various operations like Image flip, Image rotate, image shift, Image brightness and Image Zoom.

3.4 Training Model

The images for training set are obtained from the data augmentation step. These images are given annotations and training dataset is made available.

There are only 70 images which are not enough for a neural network to learn and provide results with high accuracy. Instead of building a new CNN and training it, we have implemented transfer learning. In transfer learning, a set of layers only will be trained based on the requirement. The initial layers can only be trained, or only the final layers can also be trained. Usually, we fix the initial layers which extracts the features, and the final layers are modified which involves the steps like edge detection segmentation, classification etc. Only the final layers are trained with our customized dataset. The proposed model is to learn more features. So to increase the accuracy of the model and to extract high level features three more layers are added – Dense layer with Relu activation, dropout layer and SoftMax layer as shown in Fig. 4. We can notice a decent increase in the accuracy of the model after adding these layers.

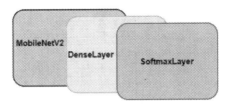

Fig. 4. MobileNetV2_fakecurrency

4   Implementation Details

The model is trained for 100 epochs with a batch size of 8 and uses categorical loss function and SGD optimizer to optimize the loss. The extra layers added are again trained for 100 epochs with batch size 8 and uses binary cross entropy loss function and Adam optimizer. The configuration used for our model is Intel Core i7–9700 processor with 16-GB DDR4 RAM. The model is implemented in Windows 10 operating system.

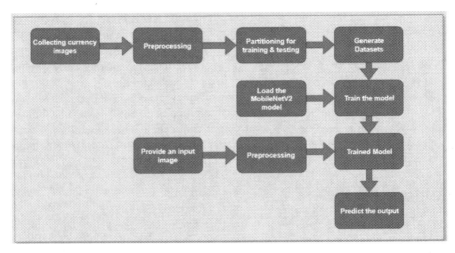

Fig. 5. Workflow of the proposed system

The method is tested in real time using camera of smart phone. When the user captures the image of a currency note the model reads the input from the camera and extracts features. These features are compared with the learned features during training to differentiate fake note from original note. The step-by-step process is displayed in Fig. 5.

5 Experimental Results

The Proposed model is tested on data that it has never seen before. The Testing data has 25 500-rupee images. The database image of real and fake 500-rupee currency is shown below.

Fig. 6. Real 500 rupee note image

Fig. 7. Fake 500 rupee note image [20]

The model has been tested and accuracy is evaluated. We can observe from the Table 1 that our proposed model MobileNet V2 - FCD is far better than the existing MobileNetV2 [5] in terms of accuracy. We have tested our model with old and new

Table 1. Accuracy comparison for existing and proposed models

	MobileNetV2	MobileNet V2-FCD
500 New Note (Front side)	0.85	0.98
500 New Note (Back side)	0.90	0.96
500 Old Note (Front side)	0.83	0.93
500 Old Note (Back side)	0.88	0.92

500 currency notes. We have observed that accuracy is more with new currency notes compared with old currency notes for both the models as training is done with new currency notes. We also tested our model by taking snaps of the notes from both the directions. Again, we can see that accuracy is better for the front side snaps compared to back side snaps.

The proposed MobileNet V2-FCD is compared with existing methodology MobileNet V2 by constructing Receiver Operating Characteristic (ROC) curve as shown in Fig. 8. From this figure we can observe that both the systems are performing same at the low false positive rates and low true positive rates. For the false positive rate 0.4, both models are performing equally from then, both are deviating, and we can observe that our model is performing well compared to existing model.

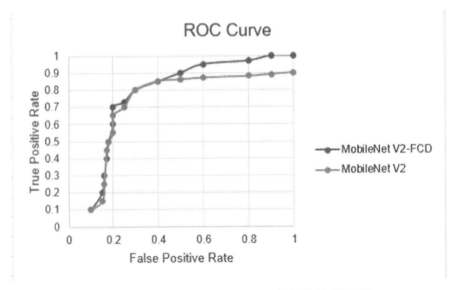

Fig. 8. ROC Curve for MobileNet V2 and MobileNetV2-FCD

6 Future Scope

The main limitation of this system is the small datasets available. Provided with large datasets the model can be trained efficiently to give more accurate results. The model can also be trained for different currency notes like 10, 20, 50, 100, 200 etc. To increase the accuracy of model, it can be trained from scratch which requires high computational power.

7 Conclusion

The use of counterfeit currency is one of the major problems the world is facing nowadays. Due to advancement in technology real notes are printed almost like fake notes and identifying a fake currency note by just seeing it is a very difficult task. An average individual may not be aware of all its security features and is vulnerable to fraud. So, our proposed system can be a better solution in this direction. The CNN model has been trained on a real time dataset and then deployed into a mobile application. This mobile application can be used in fake currency note detection through smart phones.

References

1. Laavanya, M., Vijayaraghavan, V.: Real time fake currency note detection using deep learning. Int. J. Eng. Adv. Technol. (IJEAT) (2019)
2. Potluri, T., Nitta, G.: Content based video retrieval using dominant color of the truncated blocks of frame. J. Theor. Appl. Inf. Technol. **85**(2), 165 (2016)
3. Potluri, T., Sravani, T., Ramakrishna, B., Nitta, G.R.: Content-based video retrieval using dominant color and shape feature. In: Satapathy, S.C., Prasad, V.K., Rani, B.P., Udgata, S.K., Raju, K.S. (eds.) Proceedings of the First International Conference on Computational Intelligence and Informatics. AISC, vol. 507, pp. 373–380. Springer, Singapore (2017). https://doi.org/10.1007/978-981-10-2471-9_36
4. Potluri, T., Gnaneswara Rao, N.: Content Based Video Retrieval Using SURF, BRISK and HARRIS Features for Query-by-image. In: Santosh, K.C., Hegadi, R.S. (eds.) RTIP2R 2018. CCIS, vol. 1035, pp. 265–276. Springer, Singapore (2019). https://doi.org/10.1007/978-981-13-9181-1_24
5. Zhang, Q., Yan, W.Q., Kankanhalli, M.: Overview of currency recognition using deep learning. J. Bank. Financ. Technol. **3**(1), 59–69 (2019). https://doi.org/10.1007/s42786-018-00007-1
6. Sutskever, I., Martens, J., Dahl, G., Hinton, G.: On the importance of initialization and momentum in deep learning. In: International Conference on Machine Learning, pp. 1139–1147 (2013)
7. Vijayaraghavan, V., Karthikeyan, M.: Denoising of images using principal component analysis and undecimated dual tree complex wavelet transform. Int. J. Biomed. Eng. Technol. **26**(3–4), 304–315 (2018)
8. Jadav, M., Sharma, Y.K.: Forged multi national currency identification and detection system using deep learning. Int. J. Comput. Appl. **177**(44), 36–40 (2020)
9. Thakur, M., Kaur, A.: Various fake currency detection techniques. Int. J. Technol. Res. Eng. **1**(11), 1309–1313 (2014)
10. Rathee, N., Arun K., Sachdeva, R., Dalel, V., Jaie, Y.: Feature fusion for fake Indian currency detection. In: 2016 3rd International Conference on Computing for Sustainable Global Development (INDIACom), pp. 1265–1270. IEEE (2016)
11. Upadhyaya, A., Shokeen, V., Srivastava, G.: Analysis of counterfeit currency detection techniques for classification model. In: 2018 4th International Conference on Computing Communication and Automation (ICCCA), pp. 1–6. IEEE (2018)
12. Raval, V., Shah, A.: iCu□e—an IoT application for Indian currency recognition in vernacular languages for visually challenged people. In: 2017 7th International Conference on Cloud Computing, Data Science and Engineering-Confluence, pp. 577–581. IEEE (2017)
13. Singh, S., Choudhury, S., Vishal, K., Jawahar, C.V.: Currency recognition on mobile phones. In: 2014 22nd International Conference on Pattern Recognition, pp. 2661–2666. IEEE (2014)
14. Mirza, R., Nanda, V.: Design and implementation of Indian paper currency authentication system based on feature extraction by edge based segmentation using Sobel operator. Int. J. Eng. Res. Dev. **3**(2), 41–46 (2012)
15. Mahajan, S., Rane, K.P.: A survey on counterfiet paper currency recognition and detection. In: International Conference on Industrial Automation and Computing (ICIAC)-(12–13 Apr 2014)

16. Kulkarni, A., Kedar, P., Pupala, A., Shingane, P.: Original vs counterfeit Indian currency detection. In: ITM Web of Conferences, vol. 32, p. 03047. EDP Sciences (2020)
17. Srinivasu, L.N., Srinivasa Rao, K.: Cash note with high performance security. Int. J. Appl. Res. Bioinf. (IJARB) **9**(1), 20–35 (2019)
18. http://cs231n.stanford.edu/
19. https://medium.com/@lixinso/mobilenet-c08928f2dba7
20. https://trak.in/tags/business/2019/08/30/currency-alert-fake-rs-500-notes-increase-by-121-rs-100-notes-will-be-polished/

Breast Cancer Classification Using Convolution Neural Network (CNN)

Rohit Yadav, Sagar Pande[✉], and Aditya Khamparia

School of Computer Science, Lovely Professional University, Jalandhar, India

Abstract. Machine learning and AI plays a crucial role in the recent advancements of multiple science disciplines. The medical field has seen new developments and achievements with the boost of technology. Breast cancer is one of the most dominant types of cancer in women. Recent studies indicate that there is an increase in the numbers globally. Many researchers started using the power of deep learning and created a model which helps doctors to diagnose and treat this cancer effectively. In this paper, we have used Kaggle dataset of histopathology images which contains 2,77,524 images. A deep learning CNN model is created and used with 80% training and 20% testing split. Without tuning hyperparameters, 61.01% accuracy is achieved. However, with parameters tuning 81% accuracy is achieved.

Keywords: Breast Cancer · Deep learning · Convolution neural network

1 Introduction

In India, breast cancer is the most common cancer in women. As per official reports, 25%–30% of all female related deaths were resultant of this cancer [1]. A study showed that in 2018, 1.6 million new cases were registered, and 87,090 deaths were reported [2]. A major reason for this is less public awareness along with none or very fewer screenings with high testing prices. Statistics from [3] shows, number of cases when compared to 25 years ago shows an increase in breast cancer in the age group between 20–50. Although the exact reason for the development of breast cancer is still unknown, several lifestyle guidelines are stated which decreases the chances of development of breast cancer. Maintaining balanced BMI with regular physical exercise and breastfeeding are several suggestions [4]. But not all reasons cannot be controlled, menstruation in younger age, menopause in the older age, late marriage, contraceptive drug are namely a few which increases the chances of breast cancer.

Different imaging modalities exist for the diagnosis of breast cancer. Authors of this paper [5], have presented a review off all the imaging modalities extensively. While the usage of these techniques depends on the availability the medical devices, X-ray source imaging and Magnetic field imaging are widely used [6].

Implementation of Machine Learning, Deep Learning and AI algorithms have increased drastically in different application with an increase of computation availability and power. Since the increase in computation power, algorithms which were once not feasible can be used today. Image processing is a major research area with a lot of

© Springer Nature Singapore Pte Ltd. 2021
A. K. Luhach et al. (Eds.): ICAICR 2020, CCIS 1393, pp. 283–292, 2021.
https://doi.org/10.1007/978-981-16-3660-8_27

practical and real-life application uses. With help of computational power, we can create a human brain like architecture which can help us in solving real-life problems. Deep learning helps us in a way that it learns from examples. With this, there exists many advantages and disadvantages of using it. Novel ideas are easy to implement as deep learning does not require specific feature extraction and training [7, 8]. To train a specific model, we can use multiple examples, or we can use a very basic training set and simply order it to learn. However, it is much harder to decide the architecture of the model, on which the accuracy depends. It also takes much computational time and memory for training purposes. Since it learns by examples, learning depends on the dataset and deep learning requires a huge amount of dataset for better performance [9, 10].

By taking the advantage of human brain architecture, deep learning takes advantages by different model architecture. Figure 1 shows the basic structure of a neural network. Multilayer Perceptron Neural Network (MLPNN) [11], Backpropagation [12], Convolutional Neural Network (CNN), Recurrent Neural Network (RNN), Long Short-Term Memory (LSTM) [13], Generative Adversarial Network (GAN) [14], Restricted Boltzmann Machine (RBM) [15], Deep Belief Network (DBN) [16] are few of the deep learning networks available but this paper focus mainly on CNN.

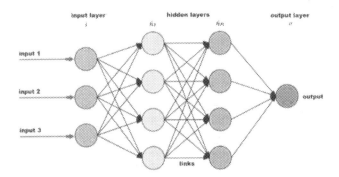

Fig. 1. A simple neural network

CNN is mostly used for images classification and consists of hidden layers which consists of convolution layer, dense layer, flatten layer, dropout layer and more. The input of CNN is an image having height, width, and colour channel. Dropout layer randomly removes some nodes temporarily to check the performance of the network without them which helps to solve to overfitting issues in CNN.

2   Literature Review

This section reviews the existing work in this field with the use of deep learning techniques and the methods they used for the classification of breast cancer. Different researchers have used different imaging modalities for their research purpose.

[17] in their paper, presented a multilayer perceptron neural network (MLP) for classification. MLP is a non-recurrent fully connected neural network. While using

the dataset from the University of Medicine Center, Institute Of Oncology, Ljublijana, Yugoslavia, they had 286 data and 10 attributes. While they were using the small dataset, they pointed out that the output can be improved with an increase in the dataset. In their pre-processing step, they sorted and labelled the dataset they obtained and using 10-fold cross-validation they were able to achieve 96.5% accuracy and 69.93% high evaluation using 10-fold.

[18] presented a computer-aided detection (CAD) for classification of benign and malignant mass tumours in mammograms. They used DDSM and CBIS-DDSM dataset for their experiment. For image enhancement, they used contrast-limited adaptive histogram equalization (CLAHE) technique instead of AHE. For image segmentation, they used two techniques, one based on manual ROI extraction and second on threshold and region based. They used DCNN i.e. AlaxNet for feature extraction and connected the final fully connected layer to support vector machine (SVM) for better accuracy. They tested their methods both with and without SVM and able to achieve the highest accuracy of 87.2%.

While authors of [19] also used mammograms for their research. The model they created was tested on two datasets CBIS-DDSM and full-field digital mammography (FFSM) from INbreast dataset. While using CNN, they were able to achieve 86.1% sensitivity, 80.1% specificity, AUC of 0.91 in CBIS-DDSM and 86.7% sensitivity, 96.1% specificity, AUC of 0.98 in FFSM.

[20] showed their work on MITOS, ICPR 2012 and AMIDA-13 datasets. They created a CNN model with 11 layers (5 convolution, 4 max-pooling, 4 ReLU, 2 fully connected). They used Rely as an activation function and used the dropout layer to solve the overfitting problem. Intensity, textural and morphological features were handcrafted for better results and they were able to achieve 92% precision, 88% recall and 90% F-score.

Authors of paper [21] used the same combination as of [18], but used thermal imaging modality for their research. For thermogram images, they used Research dataBase (DMR) dataset. While the dataset contains a large imaging area of the person, they extracted the region of interest (ROI) and used ImageNet for tumour detection. For a specified output of ImageNet, they used linear SVC, an extension of SVM for further classification and to increase the accuracy. 0.94 is the highest confidence they were able to achieve by their model.

[22] while also working on mammograms used CNN for their experiment. They used mini-MIAS dataset which consists of 322 images. Since the dataset is less for deep learning models, they used augmentation techniques to expand the dataset to get better results. While cropping input images to 48 × 48 and using ReLU activation function, they created their CNN with 5 layers (Convolution-Pooling-Convolution-Pooling-Fully Connected) and were able to achieve 82.71% highest accuracy.

Authors of [23] also presented a CAD system for breast cancer detection using mammograms. In pre-processing, they used an adaptive mean filter to remove the noise and contrast enhancement algorithm for contrast enhancement. Next, they used CNN deep features and Unsupervised Extreme Learning Machine (US-ELM) clustering for mass detection. They created a feature set having multiple features and used ELM with the fused feature for classification. They compared the ELM with SVM and were able to achieve 86.5% accuracy, 85.10% sensitivity, 88.02% specificity and 0.923 AUC.

[24] created and tested two models, shallow DCNN and pre-trained DCNN (AlaxNet). While using DDSM dataset they divided it into 70% training and 30% testing. After resizing the images, they use augmentation to create more images with rotation. Their experiment showed that AlaxNet was able to achieve the highest accuracy of 89%, while shallow DCNN highest accuracy was 80.47%.

[25] experimented by using DDSM dataset which contains 2026 cases. IN their pre-processing step, the removed the text tables in the images and created an automated ROI segmentation framework. Then they used CNN for classification which was able to achieve 93.5% accuracy and AUC of 92.3%.

[26] presented a graphical user interface for doctors to validate the diagnosis. They used INbreast dataset for their experiment and notified that along with the accuracy, recall matrix should also be included for performance measurements. They used Multiview CNN with 4 views and implemented their experiment using Keras [27] with TensorFlow with input images of size 150 × 150. They were able to achieve 80.1% accuracy for 5-fold cross-validation and 0.78 AUC.

3   Materials and Methods

3.1   Datasets

This study was conducted using Kaggle dataset [28] containing histopathology images. The original dataset consisted of 162 whole mount slides from which this dataset is created and consists of 198,738 IDC negative and 78,786 IDC positive images of 50 × 50 size. The output is only 2 classes with labels 0 and 1 for positive and negative. Figure 2 shows the snapshot of the dataset.

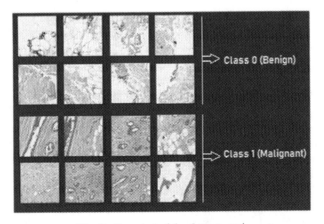

Fig. 2. Snapshot of the dataset used.

3.2 Pre-processing and Data Augmentation

The images in dataset are of PNG format. We have used ImageDataGenerator from tensorflow.keras.preprocessing.image module in python. The dataset was divided into 80% training and 20% testing part. Image augmentation was applied with a horizontal flip, vertical flip, zoom of 0.04 and rotation and images were converted to 48 × 48.

3.3 Architecture of Convolution Neural Network

A sequential model was created having 23 layers. The architecture of the model is shown in Fig. 3. The model was trained with 30 epochs and with a learning rate of 0.001 (Figs. 4 and 5).

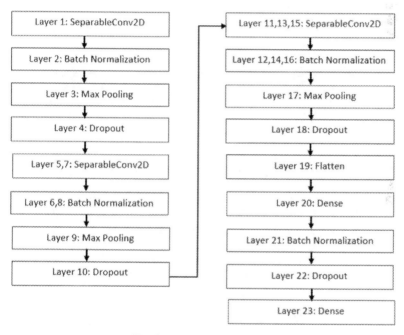

Fig. 3. Layers in CNN model

Layer 1- A SeparableConv2D layer, 3 × 3 filter, activation = ReLU, input shape = 48 × 48 × 3.
Layer 2 - Batch Normalization Layer.
Layer 3 - Max pooling, pool size = (2, 2).
Layer 4 - Dropout layer is used of value 0.25.
Layer 5 - A SeparableConv2D layer, 3 × 3 filter, activation = ReLU.
Layer 6 - Batch Normalization Layer.
Layer 7 - A SeparableConv2D layer, 3 × 3 filter, activation = ReLU.
Layer 8 - Batch Normalization Layer.
Layer 9 - Max pooling, pool size = (2, 2).

Layer 10 - Dropout layer is used of value 0.25.
Layer 11 - A SeparableConv2D layer, 3 × 3 filter, activation = ReLU.
Layer 12 - Batch Normalization Layer.
Layer 13 - A SeparableConv2D layer, 3 × 3 filter, activation = ReLU.
Layer 14 - Batch Normalization Layer.
Layer 15 - A SeparableConv2D layer, 3 × 3 filter, activation = ReLU.
Layer 16 - Batch Normalization Layer.
Layer 17 - Max pooling, pool size = (2, 2).
Layer 18 - Dropout layer is used of value 0.25.
Layer 19 - A flatten layer is used to flatten the image into 1-D array.
Layer 20 - A Dense layer is used with 'ReLU' as activation function.

```
Model: "sequential"

Layer (type)                    Output Shape            Param #
=================================================================
separable_conv2d (SeparableC    (None, 48, 48, 32)      155

batch_normalization (BatchNo    (None, 48, 48, 32)      128

max_pooling2d (MaxPooling2D)    (None, 24, 24, 32)      0

dropout (Dropout)               (None, 24, 24, 32)      0

separable_conv2d_1 (Separabl    (None, 24, 24, 64)      2400

batch_normalization_1 (Batch    (None, 24, 24, 64)      256

separable_conv2d_2 (Separabl    (None, 24, 24, 64)      4736

batch_normalization_2 (Batch    (None, 24, 24, 64)      256

max_pooling2d_1 (MaxPooling2    (None, 12, 12, 64)      0

dropout_1 (Dropout)             (None, 12, 12, 64)      0

separable_conv2d_3 (Separabl    (None, 12, 12, 128)     8896

batch_normalization_3 (Batch    (None, 12, 12, 128)     512

separable_conv2d_4 (Separabl    (None, 12, 12, 128)     17664

batch_normalization_4 (Batch    (None, 12, 12, 128)     512

separable_conv2d_5 (Separabl    (None, 12, 12, 128)     17664

batch_normalization_5 (Batch    (None, 12, 12, 128)     512

max_pooling2d_2 (MaxPooling2    (None, 6, 6, 128)       0

dropout_2 (Dropout)             (None, 6, 6, 128)       0

flatten (Flatten)               (None, 4608)            0

dense (Dense)                   (None, 256)             1179904

batch_normalization_6 (Batch    (None, 256)             1024

dropout_3 (Dropout)             (None, 256)             0

dense_1 (Dense)                 (None, 2)               514
```

Fig. 4. Model summary of CNN architecture

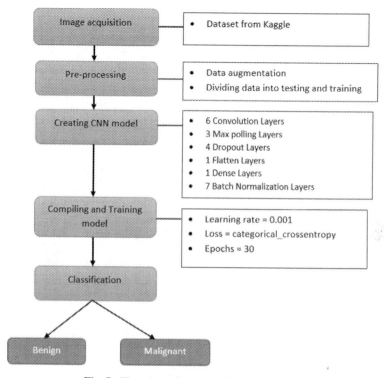

Fig. 5. Flowchart of steps involved in process.

Layer 21 - Batch Normalization Layer.
Layer 22 - Dropout layer is used of value 0.5
Layer 23 - A Dense layer is used with 'softmax' as activation function.

4   Results

We performed this experiment on Kaggle dataset consisting of 2,77,524 images, out of which 80% (2,22,020 images) was used for training purposes and 20% (55,504 images) were used for testing. While using binary cross-entropy for loss and learning rate of 0.001, we were able to achieve 96.03% specificity, 47.05% sensitivity and 80.3% accuracy and Matthew correlation coefficient of 0.40 (Fig. 6).

Fig. 6. Training loss, Validation loss, Training accuracy, Validation accuracy

5   Conclusion

Computer science has played a major role in new insights into the medical area. With the latest development of Machine learning and AI algorithms, simulation can be made to detect and predict new diseases. New medicines chemical compounds can be artificially created with these methods which will reduce the overall development cost. As presented in this paper we have used CNN for classification, but a review of other papers shows us that more can be achieved in breast cancer detection using deep learning methods.

References

1. Trends of Breast Cancer in India. http://www.breastcancerindia.net/statistics/trends.html. Accessed 29 Jan 2020
2. Cancer Statistics - India Against Cancer. http://cancerindia.org.in/cancer-statistics/. Accessed 29 Jan 2020
3. Siegel, R.L., Miller, K.D., Jemal, A.: Cancer statistics, 2019. CA. Cancer J. Clin. **69**(1), 7–34 (2019)
4. Sarosa, S.J.A., Utaminingrum, F., Bachtiar, F.A.: Mammogram breast cancer classification using gray-level co-occurrence matrix and support vector machine. In: 3rd International Conference on Sustainable Information Engineering and Technology (SIET) 2018 - Proceedings, pp. 54–59 (2018)
5. Iranmakani, S., et al.: A review of various modalities in breast imaging : technical aspects and clinical outcomes. Egypt. J. Radiol. Nucl. Med. **51**, 57 (2020). https://doi.org/10.1186/s43055-020-00175-5

6. Kumar, A., Mukherjee, S., Luhach, A.: Deep learning with perspective modeling for early detection of malignancy in mammograms. J. Discret. Math. Sci. Cryptogr. **22**, 627–643 (2019)
7. Pradeepa, S., Manjula, K.R., Vimal, S., Khan, M.S., Chilamkurti, N., Luhach, A.K.: DRFS: detecting risk factor of stroke disease from social media using machine learning techniques. Neural Process. Lett. 119 (2020). https://doi.org/10.1007/s11063-020-10279-8
8. Sharma, S., Nanglia, P., Kumar, S., Luhach, A.: Detection and Analysis of Lung Cancer Using Radiomic Approach, pp. 13–24 (2019). https://doi.org/10.1007/978-981-13-6295-8_2
9. Pak, M., Kim, S.: A review of deep learning in image recognition. In: 2017 4th International Conference on Computer Applications and Information Processing Technology (CAIPT), pp. 1–3 (2017)
10. Yang, X., Wang, L., Zeng, Z., Chandrasekhar, V., Teo, S.G., Hoi, S.: Deep learning for practical image recognition: case study on kaggle competitions. In: Proceedings of the 24th ACM SIGKDD International Conference on Knowledge Discovery & Data Mining, pp. 923–931 (2018)
11. Heidari, A.A., Faris, H., Aljarah, I., Mirjalili, S.: An efficient hybrid multilayer perceptron neural network with grasshopper optimization. Soft. Comput. **23**(17), 7941–7958 (2018). https://doi.org/10.1007/s00500-018-3424-2
12. Lillicrap, T.P., Santoro, A.: Backpropagation through time and the brain. Curr. Opin. Neurobiol. **55**, 82–89 (2019)
13. Zaremba, W., Sutskever, I., Vinyals, O., Brain, G.: Recurrent Neural Network Regularization (2015)
14. Yi, X., Walia, E., Babyn, P.: Generative adversarial network in medical imaging: a review. Med. Image Anal. **58**, 101552 (2019)
15. Liao, L., Jin, W., Pavel, R.: Enhanced restricted Boltzmann machine with prognosability regularization for prognostics and health assessment. IEEE Trans. Ind. Electron. **63**(11), 7076–7083 (2016)
16. Abdel-Zaher, A.M., Eldeib, A.M.: Breast cancer classification using deep belief networks. Expert Syst. Appl. **46**, 139–144 (2016)
17. Jasmir, et al.: Breast cancer classification using deep learning. In: Proceedings of the 2018 International Conference on Electrical Engineering and Computer Science (ICECOS 2018), vol. 17, pp. 237–242 (2019)
18. Ragab, D.A., Sharkas, M., Marshall, S., Ren, J.: Breast cancer detection using deep convolutional neural networks and support vector machines. Peer J. **2019**(1), 1–23 (2019)
19. Shen, L., Margolies, L.R., Rothstein, J.H., Fluder, E., McBride, R., Sieh, W.: Deep learning to improve breast cancer detection on screening mammography. Sci. Rep. **9**(1), 1–12 (2019)
20. Saha, M., Chakraborty, C., Racoceanu, D.: Efficient deep learning model for mitosis detection using breast histopathology images. Comput. Med. Imaging Graph. **64**, 29–40 (2018)
21. Mambou, S.J., Maresova, P., Krejcar, O., Selamat, A., Kuca, K.: Breast cancer detection using infrared thermal imaging and a deep learning model. Sensors (Switz.) **18**(9), 2799 (2018)
22. Tan, Y.J., Sim, K.S., Ting, F.F.: Breast cancer detection using convolutional neural networks for mammogram imaging system. In: Proceeding 2017 International Conference on Robotics, Automation and Sciences. ICORAS 2017, vol. Mar 2018, pp. 1–5 (2018)
23. Wang, Z., et al.: Breast cancer detection using extreme learning machine based on feature fusion with CNN deep features. IEEE Access **7**(c), 105146–105158 (2019)
24. Mechria, H., Gouider, M.S., Hassine, K.: Breast cancer detection using deep convolutional neural network. In: ICAART 2019 – Proceedings of the 11th International Conference on Agents and Artificial Intelligence, vol. 2, no. Icaart, pp. 655–660 (2019)
25. Platania, R., Zhang, J., Shams, S., Lee, K., Yang, S., Park, S.J.: Automated breast cancer diagnosis using deep learning and region of interest detection (BC-DROID). In: ACM-BCB 2017 – Proceedings of the 8th ACM International Conference Bioinformatics, Computatinaol Biology Health Informatics, pp. 536–543 (2017)

26. Ahmed, A.H., Salem, M.A.M.: Mammogram-based cancer detection using deep convolutional neural networks. In: Proceedings - 2018 13th International Conference on Computer Engineering System (ICCES 2018), pp. 694–699 (2019)
27. Ketkar, N.: Introduction to Keras, pp. 95–109 (2017)
28. Breast Histopathology Images | Kaggle. https://www.kaggle.com/paultimothymooney/breast-histopathology-images. Accessed 26 Oct 2020

Deep Bi-linear Convolution Neural Network for Plant Disease Identification and Classification

Ch Ramesh Babu[1], Srinivasa Rao Dammavalam[2]([✉]) [ID], V. Sravan Kiran[2],
N. Rajasekhar[4], B. Lalith Bharadwaj[2] [ID], Rohit Boddeda[3] [ID],
and K. Sai Vardhan[2] [ID]

[1] Department of CSE, GCET, Hyderabad, India
[2] Department of IT, VNR VJIET, Hyderabad 500090, India
srinivasarao_d@vnrvjiet.in
[3] Department of CSE, VNR VJIET, Hyderabad 500090, India
[4] Department of IT, GRIET, Hyderabad, India

Abstract. Plant diseases that occur through various sources is a threat which causes a huge loss in production of farming. Detection of infected plants is necessary to take required preventive measures to protect the plant and preserve it. As manual identification of the disease requires expertise to determine the pathological status of the plant regarding the infection levels. So, automated identification is preferred by driving human-level intelligence to the machine using deep-vision approaches to provide fast, reliable and accurate solutions.

In this research, automated identification and classification of 9 distinct plant-leaves with healthy and infection classes is developed using Bi-Linear Convolution Neural Network (Bi-CNN's). This neural architecture is constructed inspiring from the visual perception of the human brain with two cortical pathways. The hyperparameters are fine-tuned by the scheduling training procedure to attain faster convergence. The model is generalized on a triad of testing splits ranging from 10 to 50%. This model is evaluated on various standard classification metrics and when testing samples are increased by 5x (i.e. from 10 to 50%) the deviation in the accuracy score is very minute (0.27%) which resembles the resilience to unseen samples. The AUC obtained for all the models for variant test samples is at least 99.92%.

Keywords: Bilinear CNN's · Plant automated diagnosis · Computer vision · Fine-tuning CNN's · Neural networks · Plant leaf classification

1 Introduction

Agriculture is a source of livelihood and is the means of crop production. Plant diseases have become a major threat in farming and provision of food. Various plant diseases have affected the natural growth of the plants and the infected

© Springer Nature Singapore Pte Ltd. 2021
A. K. Luhach et al. (Eds.): ICAICR 2020, CCIS 1393, pp. 293–305, 2021.
https://doi.org/10.1007/978-981-16-3660-8_28

plants are the leading cause in loss of crop production. In most of the cases regarding plants, we could recognize the infected one by observing different sections of the leaf as diseases cause some visible symptoms which help us to take necessary precautions and preventive measures to put an end to the further growing infection. Over the past few decades, most followed and practised approach to detect the condition of the plant was through direct observation through naked-eye by experts and agricultural scientists which involves much human effort and a lot of time-consuming processes.

The annually estimated average loss due to pathogens and pests are nearly 13–22% on the world's major crop productions like Rice, Wheat, Maize, Potatoes etc. Pests include animal pests (insects, mites, nematodes, rodents, slugs and snails, birds), plant pathogens (viruses, bacteria, fungi, chromista) and weeds (competitive plants).

In this research, we mainly focus on developing automatic, accurate and less expensive mobile-API to detect and classify 9 different kinds of leafs with infected and healthy images (18 classes) using Bi-Linear Convolution Neural Networks (Bi-CNNs).

2   Previous Research

A. Kaya et al. [4] proposed a CNN model and analyzed how the transfer learning models play an important role in plant classification models. They have considered four transfer learning models and carried out experimentation on four different public datasets. The study had proven that transfer learning can come up with better results when compared to their proposed model. AlexNet and VGG16 are combined with LDA (Linear Discriminant Analysis) and SVM classifiers to extract deep features from the data and are trained with fivefold cross-validation procedure. The proposed model comprehends with fine-tuning and cross-dataset fine-tuning and trained with a split ratio of 70% as training and 30% testing by considering an input size of 100×100. The proposed model got a classification accuracy of 96.93% whereas the transfer learning model (VGG16) got an accuracy of 99.80%.

Karthik. R et al. [5] proposed two different deep architectures for detecting the disease in tomato leaves. The first architecture considers residual learning and the second architecture is based on attention embedded residual CNN. The proposed network consists of a Residual Progressive Feature Extraction (RPFE) block which has 2D Convolutional layer, a MaxPooling layer and a BatchNorm layer to learn the spatial features and for effective learning. The model consumed around 0.6M parameters only. The proposed model archives an accuracy of 98% with 5-fold cross-validation sets. Mohanty et al. [6] implemented transfer learning models (AlexNet & Google Net) on plant village dataset for detecting plant diseases. They used 2 different approaches 1. Transfer learning 2. Training from scratch. The dataset was considered in 3 different types such as color, grayscale and leaf segmented. They have considered five different splits. GoogleNet attained an accuracy score of 99.34%,98% and 99.25% on

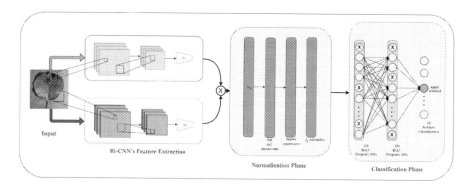

Fig. 1. Architecture of proposed Bi-CNN's for plant leaf identification and classification

color, grayscale and segmented images respectively on 20% test samples when compared to AlexNet. Sandeep Kumar et al. [8] proposed a novel optimization method for identifying diseases in plants. An Exponential Spider Monkey Optimization (ESMO) method is introduced and the feature extraction is done by using SPAM to distinguish between healthy and diseased leaf images. Various machine learning approaches such as KNN, SVM, ZeroR and LDA classifiers are used. It is observed that compared to other models, SVM obtains greater accuracy score of 92.12%. Ahmed et al. [10] proposed a CaffeNet model which is processed into Caffe framework for classification of paddy pests and paddy diseases. The database consists of 9 class paddy pests and 4 class paddy diseases. The CaffeNet model was trained for 30,000 iterations and got an accuracy of 87%. Islam et al. [11] used machine learning and image processing techniques for segmentation and detection of potato diseases. The dataset was collected from plant village database and with the use of SVM the classification accuracy of over 300 images is 95% (Fig. 1).

3   Methodology

3.1   Data Description

The data is collected from an open repository [12] where their motive is to provide publicly available data for plant disease identification via a feasible mobile API. The complete data is not considered where certain classes are collected and a model was created for it. To which apple, pepper, cherry, corn, grape, peach, potato, tomato and strawberry leaf images are considered in which each leaf class contains a single healthy and single or multiple unhealthy contrastive class (es). But, all the multiple unhealthy contrastive classes regarding leaf images are grouped into a unique unhealthy class. Suppose tomato leaf has a different infection/unhealthy classes and where they are grouped into a single, unhealthy class group containing all infection class units. So, at last, 18 unique classes are created for a distinct plant leaf image. In the next step, the data is segregated into train and test positions as, considering gross validation would be computationally expensive. The complete Dataset D is divided into train and test proportions (D_{train}, D_{test}). During the division, the samples are divided randomly by maintaining stratification. The train and test strategy is implemented thrice for understanding the generalization of the proposed model. So, D_{train}, D_{test} are divided into 90–10%, 80–20% and 50–50%. Further, the D_{train} samples are fed into the proposed model to analyse its behaviour and validate using D_{test} to depict performance (Table 1).

3.2   Bi-linear Convolution Neural Network (Bi-CNN's)

The Bi-CNN's are motivated by the visual perception of the human brain through two cortical visual pathways [1,2]. So, a neural network is created by merging the input into two CNN for extracting the features. These features are extracting using Network-A where VGG-16 [13] run in the backend. Similarly, features are extracted using Network-B are from VGG-19 [13]. These bottleneck features of Network-A, B are linearised into feature vectors fv_1 and fv_2 respectively. Now, these features can employ first-order pooling statistics such as maximum and element-wise aggregations which eventually ruins the extracted feature vector quality. This can further diminish the power of capturing fine-grained features such as part-based and also texture-based [14]. In order to overcome this problem, second-order pooling is imparted to retrieve fine-grained features from the given input.

$$fv_1, fv_2 \leftarrow Network - A(D_{train}), Network - B(D_{train}) \tag{1}$$

$$fv_z \leftarrow fv_1 \odot fv_2 \tag{2}$$

$$fv_i : L * I \rightarrow \mathbb{R}^{X*Y} \tag{3}$$

Where i = 1,2 and L is features vector (regarding location) and I is the feature vector (regarding the morphology of the input). X, Y are latent dimensions of feature matrix after feature extraction using a network. Finally, $\odot$ determine the outer-product of the two feature vectors fv_1, fv_2.

It is presumed that bottleneck feature activations from Network-A produce features related to location (e.g. shape, colour etc.). Whereas, Network-B produces features relating location such as scale and position. Now, these feature vectors fv_1, fv_2 are pooled via second-order pooling i.e. an outer-product is

Table 1. Training and testing splits of dataset

Generalization	Train	Test
G-1 (50–50)	20,006 (50%)	20,004 (50%)
G-2 (80–20)	32,007 (80%)	8003 (20%)
G-3 (90–10)	36,008 (90%)	4002 (10%)
	Total Samples	40,010

obtained between them. Next, the matrix is obtained by the outer-product of feature vectors which is linearised to form a vector fv_z. Finally, this linearised feature vector fv_z is passed onto three normalization layers. These three normalization layers are imparted to provide a better understanding of feature representations driven from fv_z. The first normalization layer is either $\log^{(fv_z)}$ or $\sqrt{fv_z}$. Where the statistical significance of using log or square-root is to minimize the redundancy in the feature vector fv_z. Next, signed square-root i.e. $sgn(fv_z).\sqrt{|fv_z|}$ is applied to previous normalization layer. Then, l_2-normalization is applied to the antecedent normalization layer. When activations are not initialized properly maximal probability mass for individual samples is assigned by sigmoid. These assignments could cause fragility in activations i.e. there is a chance for saddle points. So to prevent such scenarios l_2-regularization is imparted as one of the normalization layers. Finally, this triad of normalizations is constructed to improvise both generalization and feature representations captured from fv_z by properly addressing the gradient flow during the course of training via backpropagation.

$$fv_{zk} \leftarrow \log^{(fv_{zk})} \ (or) \ fv_{zk} \leftarrow \sqrt{(fv_{zk})} \tag{4}$$

$$fv_{zk} \leftarrow sgn(fv_{zk}).|fv_{zk}|^{\frac{1}{2}} \tag{5}$$

$$fv_{zk} \leftarrow l_2 - normalize(fv_{zk}) \tag{6}$$

Here, k = 1,2,3,..r and where r is the length of feature vector fv_z. The succeeding step is to classify the captured features Tsung-Yu et al. [15] utilized SVD, LYAP methods for computation of matrices. But, they do not provide GPU computing and only rely on CPU computations. For an efficient computation of matrix functions, fully connected layers are imparted with successive batch normalization, dropout layers. For classification, an architecture (256-128-18) is chosen for discriminating 18 unique classes from the extracted features fv_z. The numerical values provided in the architecture are no of neurons served at each layer. Training a complete neural architecture has an additional advantage of end-to-end training by properly analysing and updating gradients. It is observed that Bi-CNN's provide visual attention to the high informative regions from the provided input, such as infected portions in an unhealthy leaf class. This is provided by the means of second-order pooling.

3.3   Architecture Parameters

In this section, it is aimed to discuss all the hyperparameters tuned during optimization of Bi-CNNs. The complete network architecture consumed 2.13 million parameters when an image of size $128 \times 128 \times 3$ is inserted into it. As the bottleneck features are utilized during feature extraction the cost for the training has eventually reduced. In the classification architecture (256-128-18), the feed is forwarded with ReLU non-linearity. Further, to overcome the problem of covariate shift in the networks batch normalization [16] layers are attached after the 256 and 128 fully connected layers. Additionally, to provide two dropout

(a) Apple infected leaf   (b) CAM of respective infected leaf

Fig. 2. Class activation maps (CAM) of infected apple leaf

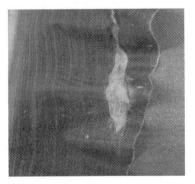
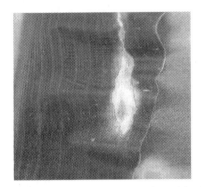

(a) Corn infected leaf   (b) CAM of respective infected leaf

Fig. 3. Class activation maps (CAM) of infected corn leaf

[17] layers are imparted subsequently after batch norm layers with a drop rate of 30%. The network weights are initialized using glorot-normal [18]. The cost function for calculating error is the aggregation of negative log-likelihood of all the class-instances and is formulated as in Eq. 7.

$$Loss = -\sum_i \sum_{c=1}^{18} y_c^{(i)} . \log^{(\hat{y_c}^{(i)})} \tag{7}$$

Where, i is no. of instances (feature samples) and c is no. of class labels. $y_c^{(i)}$ is the ground truth class labels for the class c with i^{th} instance. $\hat{y_c}^{(i)}$ is the predicted class label. Further to optimize the model, adam [19] is chosen as optimizer with an initial learning rate of $0.5*10^{-3}$. Fine-tuning is done cautiously [20,21] analysing the error-rate at each learning schedule. Tensorflow [22] is used in the back-end for constructing the computational graph for proposed model.

4   Results and Discussion

To evaluate the performance of the model, a series of metrics are utilized based on their significance. Accuracy, Area Under the Curve (AUC) [23] and Mean Squared Error (MSE) are imparted to access the models' performance. Accuracy is considered as a standard evaluation metric to access classification performance as it aggregates the correctly classified instances and divides with all the instances which are classified correctly and incorrectly. Next, MSE is formally used as a regression metric to observe the deviation from the actual to that of predicted instances. So, the deviation can also help determine the performance of the model even when ground truth labels are provided. Finally, AUC is calculated to understand the distribution of true positive and false positives for an individual class.

Table 2. Performance evaluation of Bi-CNNs (sqrt and log)

Models	Generalization	Accuracy (%)	AUC (%)	MSE
Bi-CNNs (log)	G-1	96.72	99.92	2.02
	G-2	**97.36**	**99.94**	**1.66**
	G-3	96.95	99.93	2.17
Bi-CNNs (sqrt)	G-1	97.26	99.94	1.91
	G-2	**97.88**	**99.94**	**1.27**
	G-3	97.53	99.95	1.58

As discussed in the previous section, Bi-CNNs are evaluated on two different variants settings. One model is either applying square-root as first normalization layer and other is performing log. Each of the models is assessed on the mentioned classification metrics and it is observed that Bi-CNN model with square-root as first normalization layer (Eq. 4) outperformed the other in all of the generalization circumstances. Additionally, to assess the classification performance class-wise metrics such as precision, f1-score, recall is evaluated for Bi-CNN (sqrt) and clearly illustrated in the Table 3, 4, 5 with various testing splits.

But, to know whether the proposed model is providing visual attention to the required regions or not class activation maps (aka. heat maps) [25] are generated. Heat maps visually describe the final layer activations of the model and impart colour to the highly activated regions (i.e. colouring the region of interest). So, to understand these activations from the bottleneck layer fv_z heat map is plotted for two different plant leaf kinds (apple, corn) with infection classes and visually depicted in the Fig. 2, 3. Further, AUC-ROC curves [23] are generated for an individual class. AUC is used as a metric in Table 2 as they provide detailed characteristics of the classifier. They have the unique property of being insensitive to alterations in the class distributions and can provide good relative

Table 3. Performance of Bi-CNNs (sqrt) class wise for 50% test

Model	Classes	Precision	Recall	F1-score
Bi-CNNs (sqrt 50%)	Apple healthy	0.99	0.93	0.96
	Apple infected	0.96	0.89	0.93
	Pepper healthy	0.97	0.99	0.98
	Pepper infected	0.99	0.94	0.96
	Cherry healthy	0.98	0.99	0.99
	Cherry infected	1.00	0.94	0.97
	Corn healthy	0.99	1.00	0.99
	Corn infected	1.00	0.99	1.00
	Grape healthy	1.00	0.98	0.99
	Grape infected	1.00	0.99	0.99
	Peach healthy	0.96	0.98	0.97
	Peach infected	0.99	0.97	0.98
	Potato healthy	1.00	0.81	0.90
	Potato infected	0.98	0.93	0.95
	Strawberry healthy	1.00	1.00	1.00
	Strawberry infected	0.99	0.96	0.98
	Tomato healthy	1.00	0.89	0.94
	Tomato infected	0.96	1.00	0.98

instance scores. For handling multiple classes, ROC is calculated by considering one class (chosen) as positive and remaining classes are considered to be negative ones. So, 18 different AUC-ROC curves are generated. These AUC-ROC curves are generated for the model Bi-CNN (sqrt), as its performance was optimal, for all the generalization splits and visualized in the Fig. 4(a), 5(a). Further, the goodness of fit curves is generated which contains the information regarding the samples in the class and their distribution pattern of predicted and ground truth class labels. This goodness of fit visualizations are provided by assuming ground truth labels in the x-axis and predicted labels on the y-axis for the Bi-CNN model. The visualizations regarding Bi-CNN's (sqrt) are illustrated in Fig. 4(b), 5(b).

Most of the previous research was held in extracting the features using machine learning methods which do not capture invariances for generic kinds i.e. these models are task-specific and required hand-engineered features. To overcome the problem of extracting features from hand-picked learning mechanisms deep-vision approaches are imparted. Most of the previous work was on developing a convolution neural architecture for extracting features with precise optimization. But, after the evolution of transfer learning [24], many researchers tend to imply these pre-trained weights onto a similar task. As the advantage is they do not require precise hyperparameter tuning and reduce the computa-

Table 4. Bi-CNNs (sqrt) performance class wise for 20% test

Model	Classes	Precision	Recall	F1-score
Bi-CNNs (sqrt 20%)	Apple healthy	0.98	0.94	0.96
	Apple infected	0.95	0.94	0.94
	Pepper healthy	0.97	0.95	0.96
	Pepper infected	0.92	0.93	0.92
	Cherry healthy	1.00	0.97	0.99
	Cherry infected	1.00	0.99	0.97
	Corn healthy	0.99	1.00	0.99
	Corn infected	0.99	0.99	0.99
	Grape healthy	1.00	0.99	0.99
	Grape infected	1.00	1.00	1.00
	Peach healthy	0.99	0.95	0.97
	Peach infected	0.98	0.98	0.98
	Potato healthy	0.96	0.83	0.89
	Potato infected	0.96	0.94	0.95
	Strawberry healthy	1.00	0.99	0.99
	Strawberry infected	0.99	0.99	0.99
	Tomato healthy	0.98	0.94	0.96
	Tomato infected	0.98	0.99	0.98

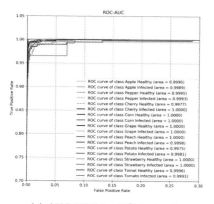
(a) AUC-ROC for 20% test split

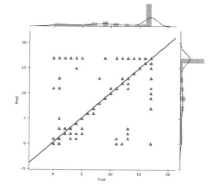
(b) Goodness of fit for 20% test split

Fig. 4. AUC-ROC and goodness of fit plots for individual classes using Bi-CNN (sqrt) on 20% test split

Table 5. Bi-CNNs (sqrt) performance class wise for 10% test

Model	Classes	Precision	Recall	F1-score
Bi-CNNs (sqrt 10%)	Apple healthy	0.98	0.92	0.95
	Apple infected	0.91	0.95	0.93
	Pepper healthy	0.91	0.99	0.95
	Pepper infected	0.99	0.78	0.87
	Cherry healthy	0.97	0.99	0.98
	Cherry infected	0.99	1.00	1.00
	Corn healthy	0.98	1.00	0.99
	Corn infected	0.99	0.99	0.99
	Grape healthy	0.97	1.00	0.99
	Grape infected	1.00	0.99	0.99
	Peach healthy	1.00	0.95	0.97
	Peach infected	0.96	0.98	0.97
	Potato healthy	1.00	0.76	0.87
	Potato infected	0.97	0.93	0.95
	Strawberry healthy	1.00	1.00	1.00
	Strawberry infected	0.96	0.99	0.98
	Tomato healthy	0.98	0.94	0.96
	Tomato infected	0.98	0.99	0.99

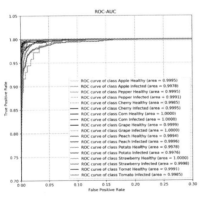

(a) AUC-ROC for 50% test split

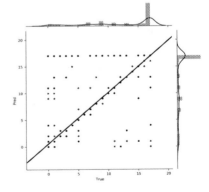

(b) Goodness of fit for 50% test split

Fig. 5. AUC-ROC and goodness of fit plots for individual classes using Bi-CNN (sqrt) on 50% test split

tional budget to a greater extent. Hence, these architectures provide pre-trained weights and many kinds of research apply these transfer learning techniques to extract innate bottleneck feature vectors from the given input to classify either using fully connected neural networks or utilizing machine learning classifiers such as SVM, decision trees etc. But, most of the research lack in providing appropriate visual attention to the models which is the most important property of visual recognition task. Providing visual attention to the models can extract fine-grained features containing detailed and precisive information regarding each entity. Further, training mechanisms should be appropriate for the model to converge fast and generalize well.

These problems are overcome by providing a resilient model for capturing detailed invariances and providing 3 level generalizations sets with faster convergence. The Bi-CNN's model performs outrageously even for large test samples providing minute deviation (0.27% for Bi-CNN (sqrt)) from test samples when increased by 5x. Bi-CNN (sqrt) model obtained the highest accuracy 97.88% for 20% test split and have accuracy (Table 6).

Table 6. Performance comparison with existing literature

Authors	Method proposed	Generalisation test	Classes	Accuracy (%)
Siddharth et al. [3]	BRBFNN	–	6	–
Mohanty et al. [6]	CNN (GoogleNet)	80-20	38	99.35
U.P. Singh et al. [7]	MCNN	80-20	4	97.13
Q. Liang et al. [9]	PD^2-SENet50	–	9,27,45	91,99,98
Cruz et al. [26]	CNN (Abstract-level Fusion)	75-35	3	98.6 ± 1.47
A. Marco et al. [27]	PDNet	70-30	42	93.67
J. Miaomiao et al. [28]	CNN(Inception+ResNet50)	80-20	4	98.57
K. Adithya et al. [29]	CNN+Auto encoders	60-30	6	97.50
E.C. Toor et al. [30]	CNN (DenseNet)	80-20	38	99.75
Dammavalam et al. [31]	CNN(VGGNet)	80-20	2	97.5%
Proposed	**CNN (Bi-CNN's)**	**50-50;80-20;90-10**	**18**	**97.26;97.88;97.53**

5 Conclusion

In this study, a Bi-CNN's is practically implemented, from a neuroscience perspective, on 9 variants of plant leaf with each consisting infection and unhealthy classes by providing a mobile-API. The proposed model attained the highest AUC of 0.9995 for 20% test whereas for 50% split the AUC is 0.9992 which depicts is resilience by attaining fast convergence and powerful generalising ability utilizing appropriate training schedules. The model extracts fine-grained features and provides *visual attention* to the important features. Bi-CNN's can be insightful when two variant extractors capture detailed features with varying morphological and spatial characterises instead of utilizing bottleneck features.

Even with several impressive properties, the model did not use 10-fold cross-validation. Where 10-fold would acquire high computational budget for large samples. Bottleneck features extracted from various state-of-the-art models would provide transferability of weights but, a fine-tuning model from the scratch would give a generic interpretation of features. Second-order pooling methods providing precise self-attention mechanisms are to be developed. Instead of carrying out experimentation on single leaf images, in future, it is aimed to imply aerial imaging techniques to develop a model to extract a bunch of features from multiple plant leaf images for multiple classes.

References

1. Mishkin, M., Ungerleider, L.G., Macko, K.A.: Object vision and spatial vision: two cortical pathways. Trends Neurosci. **6**, 414–417 (1983)
2. Ungerleider, L.G., Haxby, J.V: 'What' and 'where' in the human brain. Curr. Opin. Neurobiol. **4**(2), 157–165 (1994)
3. Chouhan, S.S., Kaul, A., Singh, U.P., Jain, S.: Bacterial foraging optimization based radial basis function neural network (BRBFNN) for identification and classification of plant leaf diseases: an automatic approach towards plant pathology. IEEE Access **6**, 8852–8863 (2018)
4. Kaya, A., Keceli, A.S., Catal, C., Yalic, H.Y., Temucin, H., Tekinerdogan, B.: Analysis of transfer learning for deep neural network based plant classification models. Comput. Electron. Agricu. **158**, 20–29 (2019)
5. Karthik, R., Hariharan, M., Anand, S., Mathikshara, P., Johnson, A., Menaka, R.: Attention embedded residual CNN for disease detection in tomato leaves. Appl. Soft Comput. **86**, 105933 (2020)
6. Mohanty, S.P., Hughes, D.P., Salathé, M.: Using deep learning for image-based plant disease detection. Front. Plant Sci. **7**, 1419 (2016)
7. Singh, U.P., Chouhan, S.S., Jain, S., Jain, S.: Multilayer convolution neural network for the classification of mango leaves infected by anthracnose disease. IEEE Access **7**, 43721–43729 (2019)
8. Kumar, S., Sharma, B., Sharma, V.K., Sharma, H., Bansal, J.C.: Plant leaf disease identification using exponential spider monkey optimization. Sustain. Comput. Inf. Syst. **28**, 100283 (2018)
9. Liang, Q., Xiang, S., Hu, Y., Coppola, G., Zhang, D., Sun, W.: PD2SE-Net: computer-assisted plant disease diagnosis and severity estimation network. Comput. Electron. Agric. **157**, 518–529 (2019)
10. Alfarisy, A.A., Chen, Q., Guo, M.: Deep learning based classification for paddy pests & diseases recognition. In Proceedings of 2018 International Conference on Mathematics and Artificial Intelligence, pp. 21–25 (Apr 2018)
11. Islam, M., Dinh, A., Wahid, K., Bhowmik, P.: Detection of potato diseases using image segmentation and multiclass support vector machine. In: 2017 IEEE 30th Canadian Conference on Electrical and Computer Engineering (CCECE), pp. 1–4. IEEE (2017)
12. Hughes, D., Salathé, M.: An open access repository of images on plant health to enable the development of mobile disease diagnostics. arXiv preprint arXiv:1511.08060 (2015)
13. Simonyan, K., Zisserman, A.: Very deep convolutional networks for large-scale image recognition. arXiv preprint arXiv:1409.1556 (2014)

14. Lin, T.-Y., RoyChowdhury, A., Maji, S.: Bilinear convolutional neural networks for fine-grained visual recognition. IEEE Trans. Pattern Anal. Mach. Intell. **40**(6), 1309–1322 (2017)

15. Lin, T., Maji, S.: Improved bilinear pooling with CNNs. arXiv preprint arXiv:1707.06772 (2017)

16. Ioffe, S., Szegedy, C.: Batch normalization: Accelerating deep network training by reducing internal covariate shift. arXiv preprint arXiv:1502.03167 (2015)

17. Srivastava, N., Hinton, G., Krizhevsky, A., Sutskever, I., Salakhutdinov, R.: Dropout: a simple way to prevent neural networks from overfitting. J. Mach. Learn. Res. **15**(1), 1929–1958 (2014)

18. Glorot, X., Bengio, Y.: Understanding the difficulty of training deep feedforward neural networks. In: Proceedings of the Thirteenth International Conference on Artificial Intelligence and Statistics, pp. 249–256 (2010)

19. Kingma, D.P., Ba, J.: Adam: A method for stochastic optimization. arXiv preprint arXiv:1412.6980 (2014)

20. Smith, S.L., Kindermans, P.J., Ying, C., Le, Q.V.: Don't decay the learning rate, increase the batch size. arXiv preprint arXiv:1711.00489 (2017)

21. Bottou, L.: Stochastic gradient descent tricks. In: Montavon, G., Orr, G.B., Müller, K.-R. (eds.) Neural Networks: Tricks of the Trade. LNCS, vol. 7700, pp. 421–436. Springer, Heidelberg (2012). https://doi.org/10.1007/978-3-642-35289-8_25

22. Abadi, M., et al.: Tensorflow: Large-scale machine learning on heterogeneous distributed systems. arXiv preprint arXiv:1603.04467 (2016)

23. Fawcett, T.: An introduction to ROC analysis. Pattern Recogn. Lett. **27**(8), 861–874 (2006)

24. Pan, S.J., Yang, Q.: A survey on transfer learning. IEEE Trans. Knowl. Data Eng. **22**(10), 1345–1359 (2009)

25. Zhou, B., Khosla, A., Lapedriza, A., Oliva, A., Torralba, A.: Learning deep features for discriminative localization. In: Proceedings of the IEEE Conference on Computer Vision and Pattern Recognition, pp. 2921–2929 (2016)

26. Cruz, A.C., Luvisi, A., De Bellis, L., Ampatzidis, Y.: X-FIDO: an effective application for detecting olive quick decline syndrome with deep learning and data fusion. Front. Plant Sci. **8**, 1741 (2017)

27. Arsenovic, M., Karanovic, M., Sladojevic, S., Anderla, A., Stefanovic, D.: Solving current limitations of deep learning based approaches for plant disease detection. Symmetry **11**(7), 939 (2019)

28. Ji, M., Zhang, L., Wu, Q.: Automatic grape leaf diseases identification via United-Model based on multiple convolutional neural networks. Inf. Process. Agric. **7**(3), 418–426 (2020)

29. Khamparia, A., Saini, G., Gupta, D., Khanna, A., Tiwari, S., de Albuquerque, V.H.C.: Seasonal crops disease prediction and classification using deep convolutional encoder network. Circ. Syst. Signal Process. **39**(2), 818–836 (2020)

30. Too, E.C., Yujian, L., Njuki, S., Yingchun, L.: A comparative study of fine-tuning deep learning models for plant disease identification. Comput. Electron. Agric. **161**, 272–279 (2019)

31. Dammavalam, S.R.: Leaf image classification with the aid of transfer learning: a deep learning approach. Curr. Chin Comput. Sci. **1**, 61–76 (2020)

Comparative Study on Data Embedding Techniques in Image Text-Based Steganography

Venu Madhavan Mangena(⊠) and Rahul Malik

Lovely Professional University, Punjab, India
{madhavan.11601828,rahul.23360}@lpu.in

Abstract. The network usage is increasing day by day not only for common communication among the individuals but also the confidential information between the organizations, and military and secret agencies to secure their national interests. In this scenario, securing confidential information is of higher priority that can be done through steganography. Yet, the major concern is which kind of methodology suitable for which format of the image. So, this article mainly deals with the comparative study of various popular image-text based steganographic methodologies with effective to the various image formats such as JPEG, PNG, and BMP. For such a study, the methodologies are classified based on the image format as well as the corresponding effective domain for the image-text based steganography. The conclusion withdrawn from this comparative study with the aid of PSNR and SSIM is that the image formats JPEG and BMP are effective image formats for image text-based steganography.

Keywords: Steganography · Frequency domain · Spatial domain · Palette · JPEG · BMP · PNG · PSNR · SSIM

1 Introduction

Internet usage has been increasing for the last two decades that includes various aspects related to work, education, entertainment, and social networking, and so on. For all these, the network plays a vital role as a mediator. The basic requirements for the network to be secure are confidentiality, integrity, availability, and non-repudiation. To maintain these requirements various approaches are followed to secure a system such a system referred to as an information securing system. One of the popular approaches that are utilized for securing confidential information is steganography. It is the approach deals with embedding a confidential file format (text, image, audio, and video) within another file format (text, image, audio, and video) for preventing the identification of confidential information from the intruder. The steganographic security system can be visualized as mentioned in Fig. 1.

Steganography has wide applications such as online voting systems, protecting the contents with the generation of captioning, surveillance systems, private image retrieval, protecting the medical archives of the patient, and secured communication between

© Springer Nature Singapore Pte Ltd. 2021
A. K. Luhach et al. (Eds.): ICAICR 2020, CCIS 1393, pp. 306–317, 2021.
https://doi.org/10.1007/978-981-16-3660-8_29

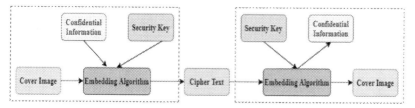

Fig. 1. Steganographic security systems

receiver and sender. Steganography approaches can be broadly classified into two categories based on the kind of embedding the information into the cover image such as Spatial domain approaches and Frequency domain approaches. Spatial domain approaches mainly deal with the modification of the information of the images at pixel level itself to enhance the imperceptibility and the payload of the confidential information. Frequency domain approaches mainly deal with the transformation of data embedding coefficients that are obtained from various Fourier transformations such as the discrete wavelet transformation, discrete Fourier transformation, and discrete cosine transformation. These approaches have strength and hardiness against threats based image processing approaches with limited payload. Yet, these approaches are computationally complex which makes us utilize the computational aspect to attain various new methodologies to improve the payload of the confidential information in the cover image.

The complete document is organized in the following manner: Sect. 2 discusses the steganography related latest work literature. Section 3 discusses the various methods that are used for embedding the information into the cover image. Section 4 discusses the comparative study on the various methodologies based on the image format and their corresponding efficient domains. And, finally, Section 5 deals with the discussion of the possible future work and the conclusion of the related work scenarios.

2   Related Work

The concept of image steganography was adopted by Kadhim, I. J., et al. in 2019 [1] and explained the classification of security systems and their characteristics, the tradeoff among the characteristics of data hiding methodology, evaluation metrics, various types of image-based steganographic methodologies that include various machine learning algorithms based methodologies. The various developments in image-based steganography were discussed in detail along with data hiding algorithms in the aspect of performance of those methodologies by Laishram, D., and Tuithung, T. in 2018 [2] with the aid of various cover images and this article also included the various challenges in these methodologies in the present aspects. Extensive research is going on with various methodologies in the aspect of image-based steganography, for instance, Emad, E. et al. in 2018 [3] implemented a methodology that includes data hiding method was framed by approximating the Integer Wavelet Transformation coefficient attaining the LSB for hiding the confidential information into the cover image. Chikouche, S. L. and Chikouche, N. in 2017 [4] implemented a methodology based on the combination of steganography and cryptography that includes compressing the confidential information utilizing the combination of LZ77 and Huffman methodologies, the information encrypted with the aid of AES-256, and obtained information embedded using LSB methodology. Arya, A. and Soni, S. in 2018 [5] compared the performance of the LSB methodology and the modified LSB methodologies to hide the confidential information in the cover image.

The efficiency of the LSB methodology on image-based steganography was measured by Hashim, M. M. et al. in 2018 [6] based on various types of image formats. Another comparative study was made by Sajid Ansari, A. et al. in 2019 [7] to study the efficiencies of various methodologies of image-based steganography with variation in the format of the cover image and data hiding methodologies. This comparison identified that the JPEG images are more efficient when compared to other formats for steganography. A survey was conducted based on various data hiding methodologies by Narayana, Lakshman, V. et al. in 2018 [8] to identify the pros and cons involved in these methodologies and came up with a new methodology to coverup the cons identified. Muhammad, K. et al. in 2018 [9] proposed a hybrid methodology with a combination of color image-based steganography and encryption. The data hiding methodology considered was adaptive LSB methodology, and the encryption methodology considered was IMMEA. Muhammad, K. et al. in 2017 [10] proposed a new hybrid methodology for image-based steganography along with encryption to enhance the authenticity of the images that are floating on social networking sites. The encryption considered was three-level encryption, data hiding methodology was MS-directed LSB substitution methodology. Security is necessary for the information related to the telemedicine systems and it was identified by Santoso, B. in 2019 [11]. In this aspect, this article implemented a new proposed methodology for securing the confidential information of the patient through image-based steganography. The embedding methodology considered was PVD.

Similar to image steganography, watermarking methodologies also play a vital role in the aspect of authenticity. It was identified by Singh, L., et al. 2020 [12] and surveyed to identify the various aspects of existing methodologies. Sahu, A. K., and Swain, G. in 2019 [13] proposed a methodology for image-based steganography and it was based on the modification of the rightmost bits. The proposed framework was built on certain goals such as to enhance the PSNR ratio, to enhance the embedding capabilities, preventing the fall of boundary issues, and sturdiness against the salt-pepper-noise and RS threat. Swain, G. in 2019 [14] proposed a methodology for enhancing the capacity that can hide in the cover image to obtain the stego-image through image-based steganography. The data hiding methodology with two levels such that lower-level utilizes LSB and QVD utilized for higher-level. This methodology reduced the fall-off boundary issue and enhanced data hiding capabilities. Caviglione, L. in 2018 [15] provided a summary of malware-compatible data hiding methodologies. They explain current and evolving attacks using multiple ways of data hiding methodologies, in a bid to track and suggest successful countermeasures.

3   Methodology

Many methodologies are being used in the research of steganography. These methodologies include most conventional as well as non-conventional methodologies. Yet, in this section, the discussion is based on certain popular methodologies of steganography such as Distortion Methodology, Adaptive Methodology, Least Significant Bit Methodology, Statistical Methodology, Spread Spectrum Methodology, and Discrete Cosine Transformation/Discrete Wavelet Transformation methodologies [25]. In the case of Distortion Methodology, the confidential information is embedded into the image by identifying the regions of distortion in the cover image. During the stage of extraction of confidential information from the stego image, through the evaluation of error between the original and stego images. This methodology is applied for the process of steganography that utilizes the distortion functions as well as error evaluation functions. Distortion methodology is popularly utilized for the JPEG image format.

In the case of Adaptive Methodology, it utilizes to hid the confidential information in the cover images through the spatial and transform domains with the utilization of statistical attributes of the cover image. By depending on the evaluation of the various coefficients or pixels of the cover image determines the changes that can be done on the cover image. In the case of the Least Significant Bit Methodology, it is the most common technique utilized for hiding confidential information in the cover image as part of steganography processing [26]. The confidential information into binary form and each bit of the confidential information will be placed into the least significant bit of the pixel of images. While extraction, the LSBs of each pixel can be collected to get the confidential information. In the case of Statistical Methodology, it utilizes for statistical characteristics of the cover image and then modifies to embed confidential information into the cover image. Firstly, the cover image will be partitioned into various sub-images, and each bit of the confidential information is embedded into each of the sub-images in such a way that modifications in the statistical characteristics of the cover image will not be detectable. In the case of Spread Spectrum Methodology, it is highly popular for the scenario of robust steganography by mixing up this methodology with noise correction function [27]. The methodology mainly deals with the noise that exists in any level of frequency in the signal. This methodology mainly hides confidential information bits in the noise that exists in the cover image and distributes the confidential information entire cover image.

In the case of Discrete Cosine Transformation/Discrete Wavelet Transformation methodologies, DCT methodology is one of the most popular methodologies that is used for hiding confidential information in a cover image. This method works with consideration of data in the form of a summation of the weighted cosine function. Firstly, the cover image will be partitioned into various squares in the form of 8x8 and then, this methodology will be applied to each of the squares separately. For a two dimensional image whose size is represented as MxN, discrete cosine transformation can be represented as mentioned in Eq. 1.

$$I(j, k) = \alpha(j)\alpha(k) \sum_{u=0}^{M-1} \sum_{v=0}^{M-1} f(u, v) cos\left[\frac{(2u + 1)j\pi}{2M}\right] cos\left[\frac{(2v + 1)k\pi}{2M}\right] \quad (1)$$

Where $(j, k) = 0, 1, 2, ..., N1$, $I(j, k)$ represents the pixel of an image, $\alpha(j) = \sqrt{1/N}$, for $j = 0$ and $\alpha(j) = \sqrt{2/N}$, for $j = 1, 2, ..., N - 1$, and $\alpha(k) = \sqrt{1/N}$, for $k = 0$ and $\alpha(k) = \sqrt{2/N}$, for $k = 1, 2, ..., N - 1$. The quantization will be applied finally and then rounded off to obtain the integers for pixel values. DWT methodology was also implemented as similar to that of DCT methodology. Firstly, the cover image will also be partitioned into various sub-images of 4 sub-bands, then image processed with various operations on pixels such as additions and subtractions by scanning the cover image by pixel by pixel from left to right and top to bottom. There are high varied image formats that exist and these will be structured with divergent characteristics with separate header data. These formats are mainly varied among themselves with the nature of compression. For an instance, consider an image of an RGB colored image of 30 bits requires 12 mb to store if the compression is not utilized. If the compression technique is applied then it requires much less storage. There are two different types of compression techniques such as lossy compression and lossless compression. Lossy compression deals with compressing the images and when retrieving the original image from the compressed image certain information will be lost. Lossless compression deals with compressing the images and when retrieving the original image from the compressed image no information will be lost. The popular lossy compression format of the images are JPEG and TIFF, the popular lossless compression format of the images are BMP, PNG, and TIFF. The format of the image TIFF deals with both lossy and lossless compression techniques. The proposed comparative framework considered image formats are JPEG (Joint Photographic Experts Group) format, BMP (Bitmap) format, PNG (Portable Network Graphics) format.

The various methodologies related to steganography categorized based on the various cover image formats such as JPEG, BMP, and PNG and their corresponding domain aspects. These can be classified as mentioned in Fig. 2.

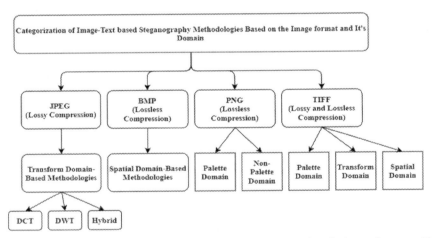

Fig. 2. Classification of various steganography methodologies based on the image format and its domain information

Frequency domain-based transform methodologies majorly worked with JPEG image formats. These methodologies deal with the modification of various pixel information in the spatial domain. Frequency domain-based transform methodologies are further categorized into a high-frequency domain-based transform methodology which dealt with edges and a low-frequency domain-based transform methodology which dealt with smooth and plane zones of the images. The modifications in the lower frequencies in the image are very apparent, yet DCT (Discrete Cosine Transform) and DWT (Discrete Wavelet Transform) methodologies will show a good impact and those are utilized for embedding the confidential information on the cover image. The frequency domain-based methodologies are more vulnerable to various threats than the spatial domain-based methodologies. In the aspect of security, JPEG format performance is better compared to all other formats.

Spatial domain-based transform methodologies majorly worked with BMP(Bitmap) image formats. These methodologies deal with direct modifications in the pixel information of the cover images. BMP methodologies have great ability, however, lesser security because pixels can be changed according to the curves and edges of the images explicitly. Bitmap image format images are more efficient with various embedding methodologies such as Least Significant Bit (LSB) substitution methodology, Most Significant Bit(MSB) substitution methodology, pixel indicator methodology, optimal pixel adjustment methodology, and image realization secure key methodology. Embedding the confidential information into PNG can be implemented in two ways, either the confidential information bits can be inserted into pallets or the confidential information bits into the image pixels. The methodology based on the information bits inserted into the palette possibly simple to enforce but the palette size is very minimal to store the data bits. In this particular scenario, the palette having 256 colors can be confused with just only 210 bytes of the information. Further, no bit can be stored into it as if it is inserted that can be distinguishable with or without the confidential information. When the palette colors are ordered, the encoder somehow encodes the confidential information in a PNG image file. In comparison, the second approach of embedded images has more capacity but security is hard to enforce. At least 1 bit to 7 bit can be embedded per pixel in the image without disrupting the image.

4 Comparative Analysis

This segment shows important comparative findings for different file formats of some of the recorded Steganography methods. The object of comparative analysis is to evaluate the output with consistent experimental settings of different approaches. This methodology will provide instructions for researchers who are prepared to develop current procedures. I evaluated current approaches based on such criteria as perceptibility of stego imaging, functional features, and safety aspects. To compare multiple processes, the PSNR and SSIM evaluation parameters are utilized. High PSNR readings demonstrate the increased quality of stego images: over 40 db PSNR stego images, can be considered as better quality images. High SSIM value indicates that the variation in the stego image when compared to the original image is very less which means that particular methodology has a very good scope to utilize in steganography. For this comparative study, the standard images such as Lena, Pepper, and Baboon are utilized as cover images with different formats such as JPEG, BMP, and PNG. Each image of color with a size of 512-by-512 pixels.

Firstly, the methodology dealt with the JPEG image format. The obtained PSNR values and SSIM values are represented in Table 1 and Table 2. The comparative study of these values is represented graphically as mentioned in Fig. 3 and Fig. 4. From this comparative study, one can identify that the Adaptive PVD methodology working effectively.

Table 1. PSNR values for methodologies applied to JPEG image format

S. no.	Methodology	Lena cover image	Peppers cover image	Baboon cover image
1	Adaptive RDHS methodology [16]	48.26	45.34	32.57
2	Adaptive PVD methodology [17]	51.46	52.18	52.87
3	Transform domain methodology [18]	43.72	43.93	44.05
4	Complementary embedding methodology [19]	35.09	34.93	39.74
5	Integer wavelet transform methodology [20]	43.78	43.96	44.09

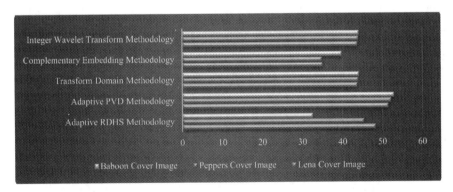

Fig. 3. PSNR comparison for methodologies applied to JPEG image format

Secondly, the methodology dealt with the BMP image format. The obtained PSNR values and SSIM values are represented in Table 3 and Table 4. The comparative study of these values is represented graphically as mentioned in Fig. 5 and Fig. 6. From this comparative study, one can identify that MSB matching and LSB matching methodologies working effectively.

Lastly, the methodology dealt with the PNG image format. The obtained PSNR values and SSIM values are represented in Table 5 and Table 6. The comparative study of these values is represented graphically as mentioned in Fig. 7 and Fig. 8. From this comparative study, one can identify that both are not that effective.

Table 2. SSIM in terms of percentages for methodologies applied to JPEG image format

S. no.	Methodology	Lena cover image	Peppers cover image	Baboon cover image
1	Adaptive RDHS methodology [16]	96.43	97.73	98.73
2	Adaptive PVD methodology [17]	95.83	95.47	95.23
3	Transform domain methodology [18]	97.40	97.83	97.29
4	Complementary embedding methodology [19]	98.58	98.67	99.07
5	Integer wavelet transform methodology [20]	97.42	97.58	97.16

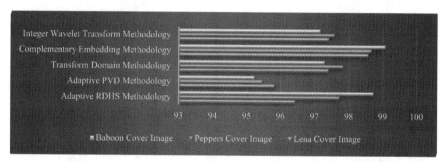

Fig. 4. SSIM in terms of percentages are utilized for comparison of methodologies applied to JPEG image format

Table 3. PSNR values for methodologies applied to BMP image format

S. no.	Methodology	Lena cover image	Peppers cover image	Baboon cover image
1	LSB substitution methodology [21]	43.67	63.24	62.26
2	LSB matching methodology [22]	54.62	54.71	54.23
3	MSB substitution methodology [23]	48.71	55.82	67.19
4	MSB matching methodology [22]	56.73	56.86	56.09

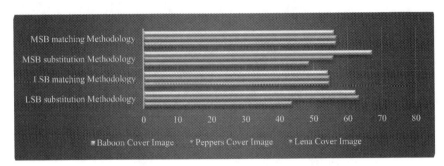

Fig. 5. PSNR comparison for methodologies applied to BMP image format

Table 4. SSIM in terms of percentages for methodologies applied to BMP image format

S. no.	Methodology	Lena cover image	Peppers cover image	Baboon cover image
1	LSB substitution methodology [21]	98.61	96.48	96.83
2	LSB matching methodology [22]	97.21	97.19	97.89
3	MSB substitution methodology [23]	97.86	97.07	94.76
4	MSB matching methodology [22]	96.23	96.17	96.44

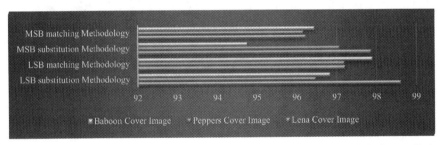

Fig. 6. SSIM in terms of percentages are utilized for comparison of methodologies applied to BMP image format

Table 5. PSNR values for methodologies applied to PNG image format

S. no.	Methodology	Lena cover image	Peppers cover image	Baboon cover image
1	EZ-stego methodology [24]	14.27	19.58	14.64
2	Fridrich scheme [24]	31.72	26.27	20.46

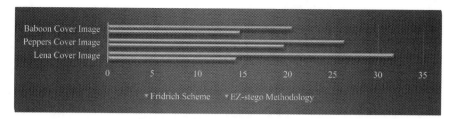

Fig. 7. PSNR comparison for methodologies applied to PNG image format

Table 6. SSIM in terms of percentages for methodologies applied to PNG image format

S. no.	Methodology	Lena cover image	Peppers cover image	Baboon cover image
1	EZ-stego methodology [24]	99.73	98.83	99.54
2	Fridrich scheme [24]	97.43	98.07	98.49

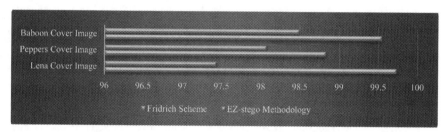

Fig. 8. SSIM in terms of percentages are utilized for comparison of methodologies applied to PNG image format

5   Future Scope and Conclusion

The comparative study frame will provide detailed knowledge about the format of the image that is suitable for the kind of methodology and it will be helpful for the researchers to expand their research based on these methods, the JPEG and BMP image formats are more suitable for steganographic methodologies. For one who is a beginner in steganography, this document will provide the popular methodologies to be applied to which type of image formats. The future works based on steganography are a bit slow but the research on this specific area is very essential to improve the confidentiality, integrity, availability, and non-repudiation of the network. Steganography can also combine with cryptography to form a hybrid system for ensuring security for the confidential data that is in transit through the network between the sender as well as the receiver.

References

1. Kadhim, I.J., Premaratne, P., Vial, P.J., Halloran, B.: Comprehensive survey of image steganography: techniques, evaluations, and trends in future research. Neurocomputing **335**, 299–326 (2019)
2. Laishram, D., Tuithung, T.: A survey on digital image steganography: current trends and challenges. SSRN Electron. J. (2018)
3. Emad, E., Safey, A., Refaat, A., Osama, Z., Sayed, E., Mohamed, E.: A secure image steganography algorithm based on the least significant bit and integer wavelet transform. J. Syst. Eng. Electron. **29**(3), 639–649 (2018)
4. Chikouche, S.L., Chikouche, N.: An improved approach for LSB-based image steganography using AES algorithm. In: 5th International Conference on Electrical Engineering - Boumerdes, ICEE-B 2017, vol. 2017, no. 1, pp. 1–9 (2017)
5. Arya, A., Soni, S.: Performance evaluation of secrete image steganography techniques using the least significant bit (LSB) method. Int. J. Comput. Sci. Trends Technol. (IJCST) **6**(2), 160–165 (2018)
6. Hashim, M.M., Rahim, M.S.M., Johi, F.A., Taha, M.S., Hamad, H.S.: Performance evaluation measurement of image steganography techniques with analysis of LSB based on variation image formats. Int. J. Eng. Technol. **7**(4), 3505–3514 (2018)
7. Ansari, S.A., Mohammadi, S.M., Parvez, T.M.: A Comparative study of recent steganography techniques for multiple image formats. Int. J. Comput. Netw. Inf. Secur. **11**(1), 11–25 (2019)
8. Narayana, L.V., Peda Gopi, A., Ashok Kumar, N.: Different techniques for hiding the text information using text steganography techniques: a survey. Inf. Syst. Eng. **23**(6), 115 (2018)
9. Muhammad, K., Sajjad, M., Mehmood, I., Rho, S., Baik, S.W.: Image steganography using uncorrelated color space and its application for security of visual contents in online social networks. Futur. Gener. Comput. Syst. **86**, 951–960 (2018)
10. Muhammad, K., Ahmad, J., Rho, S., Baik, S.W.: Image steganography for the authenticity of visual contents in social networks. Multimed. Tools Appl. **76**(18), 18985–19004 (2017)
11. Santoso, B.: Color-based microscopic image steganography for telemedicine applications using pixel value differencing algorithm. J. Phys. Conf. Ser. **1175**(1), 012057 (2019)
12. Singh, L., Singh, A.K., Singh, P.K.: Secure data hiding techniques: a survey. Multimed. Tools Appl. **79**(23–24), 15901–15921 (2020)
13. Sahu, A.K., Swain, G.: A novel n-rightmost bit replacement image steganography technique. 3D Research, **10**(1), 118 (2019)
14. Swain, G.: Very high capacity image steganography technique using quotient value differencing and LSB substitution. Arab. J. Sci. Eng. **44**(4), 2995–3004 (2018). https://doi.org/10.1007/s13369-018-3372-2
15. Caviglione, L., Wendzel, S., Woodward, A., Zander, S.: The new threats of information hiding. IT Professional **20**(6), 31–39 (2018)
16. Srinivasan, A., Wu, J., Shi, J.: Android-stego: a novel service provider imperceptible MMS steganography technique robust to message loss. In: Proceedings of the 8th International Conference on Mobile Multimedia Communications, ICST, Institute for Computer Sciences, SocialInformatics, and Telecommunications Engineering, pp. 205–212 (2015)
17. Pradhan, A., Sekhar, K.R., Swain, G.: Adaptive PVD steganography using horizontal, vertical, and diagonal edges in six-pixel blocks. Secur. Commun. Netw. (2017)
18. Huang, F., Huang, J., Shi, Y.Q.: New channel selection rule for JPEG steganography. IEEE Trans. Inf. Forensics Secur. **7**, 1181–1191 (2012)
19. Liu, C.L., Liao, S.R.: High-performance JPEG steganography using a complementary embedding strategy. Pattern Recogn. **41**(9), 2945–2955 (2008)

20. Hemalatha, S., Dinesh Acharya, U., Renuka, A., Kamath, P.R.: A secure and high capacity image steganography technique. Signal Image Process. Int. J. (SIPIJ), **4**, 83 (2013)
21. Rai, P., Gurung, S., Hose, M.K.: Analysis of image steganography techniques. Int. J. Comput. Appl. **114**(1), 11–17 (2015). ISSN 0975-s8887
22. Umbarkar, A.J., Kamble, P.R., Thakre, A.V.: Comparative study of edge-based LSB matching steganography for color images. ICTACT J. Image Video Process. **6**(3), 1185–1191 (2016)
23. Sharma, A., Poriye, M., Kumar, V.: A secure steganography technique using MSB. Int. J. Emerg. Res. Manag. Technol. **6**, 6 (2017)
24. Chen, Y.F., Chien, S.W., Lin, H.H: True color image steganography using the palette and minimum spanning tree. In: Xi, L. (ed.) WSEAS International Conference Proceedings Mathematics and Computers in Science and Engineering. no. 3. World Scientific and Engineering Academy and Society (2009)
25. Kumar, A., Luhach, A.K., Pal, D.: Robust digital image watermarking technique using image normalization and discrete cosine transformation. Int. J. Comput. Appl. **65**, 18 (2013)
26. Singh, C., Luhach, A.K., Kumar, A.: Improving focused crawling with genetic algorithms. Int. J. Comput. Appl. **66**, 4 (2013)
27. Gunawardena, P., et al.: Real-time automated video highlight generation with dual-stream hierarchical growing self-organizing maps. J. Real-Time Image Process. 1–19 (2020)

Mobile Net Convolutional Neural Networks for Video Classification

Sudhakar Putheti[✉], Bhimavarapu Sravya Pranati, and Vishwaksen Bairisetti

Computer Science and Engineering, Vasireddy Venkatadri Institute of Technology, Guntur, AP, India

Abstract. Current data and correspondence advances give the foundation to send bits anyplace, however don't dare to deal with data at the semantic level.s This paper researches the utilization of video content investigation and high- light extraction and bunching strategies for additional video semantic arrangements. This system can be applied to the applications, for example, on-line video order- ing, separating and video synopses, and so forth. Grouping recordings as indicated by content semantics is a significant issue with a wide scope of uses. In this paper, we propose a combination significant learning structure for video request, which can show static spatial information, transient development, similarly as momen- tary snippets of data in the chronicles. Specifically, the spatial and the transient development features are extricated freely by two Convolutional Neural Networks (CNN). The standard commitment of this work is the cream learning framework that can show a couple of huge pieces of the video data. We in like manner show that joining the spatial and the flashing development highlights in the regularized combination arrange is better than direct grouping and combination utilizing the CNN with a delicate max layer, and the sequence-based LSTM is profoundly cor- responding to the conventional characterization technique without considering the transient casing orders. Recordings can be characterized by utilizing MobileNet Classification.

Keywords: Convolutional neural networks · Video classification · MobileNet architecture · Videos

1 Introduction

Video Classification is the best move toward interactive media content comprehension. The video can be characterized at a low level, at a center level, or at an exceptionally elevated level. Large Huge scope datasets, for example, MobileNet [1] have been key empowering influences of late advancement in picture understanding. By supporting the learning procedure of profound systems with a large number of parameters, such datasets have assumed a pivotal job for the quick advancement of picture comprehension to move toward human level precision. Besides, temporary layer institutions of such frameworks have shown to be stunning and interpretable for various tasks past arrangement.

While video course of action at a lower level can consistently be developed using fea- tures from single system, more raised level gathering by and large necessities to accept

© Springer Nature Singapore Pte Ltd. 2021
A. K. Luhach et al. (Eds.): ICAICR 2020, CCIS 1393, pp. 318–328, 2021.
https://doi.org/10.1007/978-981-16-3660-8_30

verification from a couple of modalities to be compelling, since a solitary methodology doesn't give adequate data to precise characterization. For instance, it is hard to dependably recognize activity films from detective [2] motion pictures in the event that we consider just shading information. Joining proof from various modalities for video grouping has been appeared to improve characterization precision in a few investigations, including combining overlay text and faces, shading, movement and sound.

Current methodologies [3] for video examination regularly address ac- counts by features isolated from continuous housings [4], trailed by incorporate conglomeration [12] after some time. Model methods for highlight extraction intertwine huge convolutional neural frameworks (CNNs) pre-organized on static pictures [11]. Other further made models utilize dynamic spatio transient convolutional structures to both concentrate and momentarily outright video fuses simultaneously.

2 Related Work

In previous years, supervised learning [5] based models have been wind up being more serious than the standard techniques on dealing with complex learning issues in various regions. For example, the compelling neural framework [15] (DNN) has been viably used for acoustic showing in the gigantic language talk affirmation issues [2]. Likewise, the supervised learning [13] related methods has been shown to be incredibly weighty [10] in the image space. In the substance space, compelling models have in like manner been adequately used for sentence parsing [4], feeling estimate and language understanding issues [14]. On video data, nevertheless, compelling adjusting regularly showed more deplorable [6] results than the traditional strategies [7, 8].

This is generally a result of the difficulties in exhibiting the extraordinary ascribes of the chronicles. On one hand, the spatial-common nature demands progressively complex framework structures and conceivably similarly pushed learning procedures. On the other hand, up until this point there is obliged proportion of getting ready data with manual clarifications in the video space, which controls the headway of developing new strategies as neural frameworks [9] consistently require expansive planning. As of late two-stream CNN, a fruitful approach that trains two CNNs using static edge and transient development autonomously [18].

The common development stream is changed over to reformist optical stream pictures so the customary CNN. The Knowledge Graph contains an enormous number of focuses. Each subject has at any rate one sorts, that are arranged with high accuracy. For sufficient, there is an comprehensive synopsis of objects with type object and a careful onceover of substances with type sustenance.

3 Proposed System

Deep learning has powered huge advancement in the field of PC vision with neural systems more than once pushing the outskirts of visual acknowledgment innovation. While a significant number of those innovations, for example, object, milestone, logo and text acknowledgment are accommodated web associated gadgets through the Cloud Vision API [16], we accept that the ever-expanding computational intensity of cell phones can empower the conveyance [17] of these advancements un- der the control of our clients, whenever, anyplace, paying little mind to web association. Be that as it may, visual acknowledgment for on gadget and installed application presents numerous difficulties models must run rapidly with high precision in an asset obliged condition utilizing restricted calculation [19], force and space.

YouTube-8M is the dataset that we can proceed our project information in the variation of the data into different formats [22]. We proceed with different accounts since they are a nice wellspring of data for different classes containing Arts and Entertainment, Games, Food and the various activities of the info. To proceed with YouTube, we should follow different procedures in the various process of steps in the data mining. Data Mining process involves the information [21] gain, we perform Data Cleaning and the various information gathering process.

Then we proceed the process of MobileNet application in the various fields of the gain information of the dataset. This is how we are going to proceed with the info gain of the increase in the accuracy of the model and then we proceed with the split of the train and test data [20]. The main key objective is to proceed with the increase in the split of the variation in the key subject and language deprecation and the information ratio on the user dataset keeping knowledge gain ratio for the user. This helps us to improve the maintenance of the project data and paper representation of the data. Data must be cleaned before we train the data. In the next section let us discuss about our proposed system MobileNet Architecture.

3.1 MobileNet Architecture

MobileNet [1] are light weight profound neural organizations most appropriate for portable and inserted vision applications. MobileNet depend on a smoothed-out engineering that utilizes profundity savvy divisible convolutions. MobileNet utilizes two basics worldwide hyperparameters that proficiently compromises among exactness and inactivity. MobileNet could be utilized in item location, fine grain characterization, face acknowledgment, huge scope geo restriction and so forth.

MobileNet configuration proceeded with the normal 3×3 convolution and its based on the follow up of the information of the converting the squares of the info that is to be given to the data of the square constant. This can be done only with the information of the layers that can be propounded into the image formatting of the various formats of the available ones.

In this process, each box contains the different advancement layers in the information given according to the image data. It is followed by the box advancement of the insight of the various proposals that can be proceeded with the information of the various textual format of the data of the info that is given to the architecture.

The information which we give to the convolutional layer, will give up the channels which depend on the factor of the data that gives the insightful network. This helps in the constructing the square in the movement of points in the framework.

Layer in the normalization and the activation function in the network helps us to calculate in the extra points in the framework. Normalization in the framework in the form of getting the information of the extra layer information.

ReLU is the activation function that is used in the getting the projection layer in the middle of the information of the pooling layer in the gain of the variation in the getting of the information of the normal pooling and the dense convolution.

From top to bottom in the particular convolutions in the standard convolutional layers. The common convolutional layer examples are pooling and the dense layer. The main configuration of the variation in the network.

There are many efficient applications that are made based on the network architecture. This helps in the information of the variant points of the framework. It applies to the different convolutions in the getting the information that is present in the various layers that are present in the architecture.

While we consider the convolutional layers the standard information getting from the different layers in the architect of MobileNet. Thus the particular convolutions that can be maintained in the one layer so that process can be made easy for the architecture.

In any case, the yield of the projection layer doesn't have an incitation work. The full MobileNet configuration contains 17 of bottleneck remaining squares straight adhered to by a standard 1 × 1 convolution, an overall typical pooling layer, and a course of action layer Normal pooling.

From top to bottom astute particular layers that can be in trade for the standard layers, the work done almost similar to the convolutions in the welcome of the profundity of the information that can be particularly by the factor of k2. MobileNet uses the different parameters for the information of the different pooling layers. This can be implemented

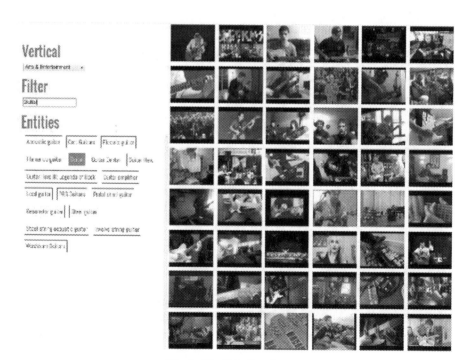

Fig. 1. YouTube 8 m dataset

in the various convolutions in the computational cost of the different parameters that can be change or improvement in the accuracy (Fig. 1).

The size of the 8M dataset is in the terabyte format. It covers the more than 8 million videos in the getting the train data and the test data of the dataset. It is impossible to maintain all the videos in the local system. So we have given only ids of the dataset and we downloaded all the videos into the machine and we converted all those videos of the dataset into the set of images. This images are given to the information of the convolutional layers of the architecture.

One video is converted into the images of the data set and it doesn't take so much time for the conversion of the video into the images. This is how the information is maintained in the dataset. Now the variation in the getting of the image data is kept on

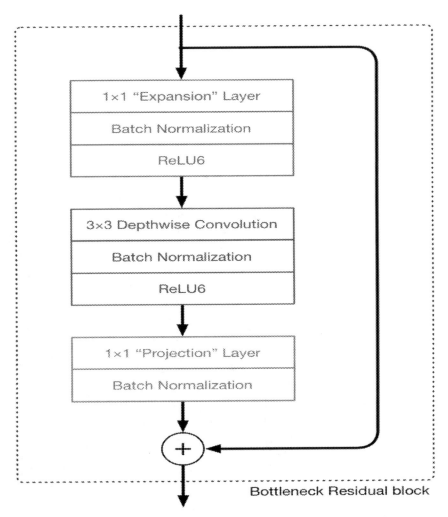

Fig. 2. Architecture of MobileNet

the local machine and the process is continued in the variation in the implementation of the work that is represented in the procedure of the information that is given in the various formats of the image dataset.

Top tier significant model: the uninhibitedly available Inception mastermind arranged on MobileNet. Progressing work shows reliable misfortunes from development incorporates as the size and nice amendment of the video data increases. Positively, we interpret each video reasons (Fig. 2).

MobileNet Architecture contains three layers. One is Expansion layer, Two is Depth wise Convolution and the last one is Projection layer. First we pass the data into the expansion layer the data is processed and then it is sent to the depth wise convolution. In the expansion layer, ReLU is used as the activation function of the neural network. Now the main depth wise convolution is done in the second layer. This is the most important layer in the architecture of the mobilenet architecture.

After that it is sent to the architecture of the projection layer. The meaning of the projection layer that will be mentioned in the different format of the projections. The residual block of the architecture is maintained in the information of the different layers.

Table 1. MobileNet Body Architecture

Type / Stride	Filter Shape	Input Size
Conv / s2	$3 \times 3 \times 3 \times 32$	$224 \times 224 \times 3$
Conv dw / s1	$3 \times 3 \times 32$ dw	$112 \times 112 \times 32$
Conv / s1	$1 \times 1 \times 32 \times 64$	$112 \times 112 \times 32$
Conv dw / s2	$3 \times 3 \times 64$ dw	$112 \times 112 \times 64$
Conv / s1	$1 \times 1 \times 64 \times 128$	$56 \times 56 \times 64$
Conv dw / s1	$3 \times 3 \times 128$ dw	$56 \times 56 \times 128$
Conv / s1	$1 \times 1 \times 128 \times 128$	$56 \times 56 \times 128$
Conv dw / s2	$3 \times 3 \times 128$ dw	$56 \times 56 \times 128$
Conv / s1	$1 \times 1 \times 128 \times 256$	$28 \times 28 \times 128$
Conv dw / s1	$3 \times 3 \times 256$ dw	$28 \times 28 \times 256$
Conv / s1	$1 \times 1 \times 256 \times 256$	$28 \times 28 \times 256$
Conv dw / s2	$3 \times 3 \times 256$ dw	$28 \times 28 \times 256$
Conv / s1	$1 \times 1 \times 256 \times 512$	$14 \times 14 \times 256$
$5\times$ Conv dw / s1	$3 \times 3 \times 512$ dw	$14 \times 14 \times 512$
Conv / s1	$1 \times 1 \times 512 \times 512$	$14 \times 14 \times 512$
Conv dw / s2	$3 \times 3 \times 512$ dw	$14 \times 14 \times 512$
Conv / s1	$1 \times 1 \times 512 \times 1024$	$7 \times 7 \times 512$
Conv dw / s2	$3 \times 3 \times 1024$ dw	$7 \times 7 \times 1024$
Conv / s1	$1 \times 1 \times 1024 \times 1024$	$7 \times 7 \times 1024$
Avg Pool / s1	Pool 7×7	$7 \times 7 \times 1024$
FC / s1	1024×1000	$1 \times 1 \times 1024$
Softmax / s1	Classifier	$1 \times 1 \times 1000$

Fig. 3. MobileNet body architecture

This is the complete description of the MobileNet Architecture. In the below diagram the complete filter shape and the input size of the architecture is mentioned (Fig. 3).

4 Results

We convert the dataset of the videos into the two parts of train and test data. Then we segregated the videos into some of the labels. Then we thought of taking the graph id of the video so that we can pass the video id then we used the different libraries then we can first view the video in the YouTube then we download the video into our local system. Now it's time to train our dataset. We took 70 percent of the data as training data and 30 percent of the data as the test data. After considering the data into the various considered that 70 percent of the training data and started the process using MobileNet Architecture. In the MobileNet architecture, there are three different layers that are to be pooling, dense and other layers. We started the training the data by keeping 10 epochs. If the two epochs make the consideration of accuracy if there is no increase in the accuracy then it doesn't go to the next epoch. This is how we started the training dataset. But fortunately, we have the increase in the accuracy from every epoch to epoch. There is an increase in the accuracy and precision values. We calculated the accuracy and precision values in the standard format. The formula for the accuracy is as follows:

$$\text{Accuracy} = \frac{TP + TN}{TP + TN + FP + FN}$$

Where

TP = TRUE POSITIVES
TN = TRUE NEGATIVES
FP = FALSE POSITIVES
FN = FALSE NEGATIVES

and the formula for the precision is as follows:

$$\text{Precision} = \frac{TP}{TP + FP}$$

Where

TP = TRUE POSITIVES
TN = TRUE NEGATIVES
FP = FALSE POSITIVES
FN = FALSE NEGATIVES

Now we downloaded the training model and started testing on our test data. In the process of the testing of the data, we considered 20 videos of different strategies. We got the result as the 14 as correct result and the remaining 6 are the incorrect result. This is how we started doing our testing on the different videos. After testing the data, we got the accuracy as 75 percent. So, we have defined the trained model as MobileNetClassification.h5 model into 8 million YouTube accounts of train and test data. As of now we have arranged the ages (Fig. 4).

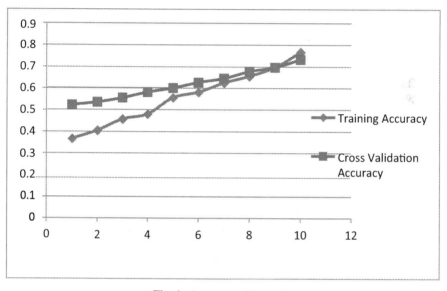

Fig. 4. Accuracy with epochs

Data cleaning includes eliminating the commotion and treatment of missing qualities. The clamor is taken out by applying smoothing methods and the issue of missing qualities is addressed by supplanting a missing an incentive with most generally happening an incentive for that trait. Adaptability alludes to the capacity to develop the classifier or indicator productively; given enormous measure of data Accuracy of classifier alludes to the capacity of classifier. It anticipates the class mark effectively and the exactness of the indicator alludes to how well a given indicator can figure the estimation of anticipated property for another data. Data can likewise be diminished by some different techniques, for example, wavelet change, binning, histogram (Figs. 5 and 6).

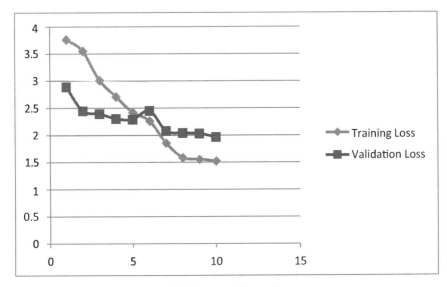

Fig. 5. Loss with epochs

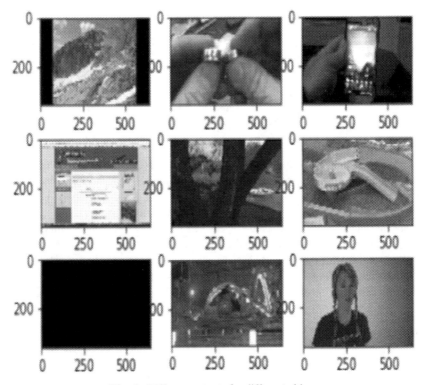

Fig. 6. Different outputs for different videos

5   Conclusion

In this paper, we done a video classification and variation practice. Like creation tremendous extension picture datasets for picture understanding, our goal with YouTube-8M is to get the video insight in advance in the field of any check or information in the video of maintaining the information of the video before watching the video in the wave format of the video. While analyzing the video, we have to concentrate on the information of getting the video id we download the video into our local machine then we process the video in the defined format. This can be done by the way of maintaining the information of the video i.e. the name of the video and the storage of the video in the format of maintaining the information. Then we start the process in the form of defined steps.

These will be maintained the information of which we can maintain the data of the video in the formatting the necessary information in the awaiting component or label it belongs to the way of informing the user to which field it belongs to and the video information is given to the user about the label it belongs to in the process. The image representation of the data is in the format of the image according to the computer knowledge and the it is stored in the correct format of the information that can be implemented in the variety of the awaiting moments of the variation of the video formatting. MobileNet process can be defined in the variation of different pixel images that can be implemented in the different format.

Finally, the information of the variation in the video insight of the information in the library. In the variation in the video then the accuracy increases the challenges of the information of the variant features of the video datasets and using academic process and unreasonable in the variation in the dataset for the feature of the dataset of the variation in the manual creation in the YouTube and we depict the different measures in the various frames in the video datasets and analyze the video on the open-source machine.

The different types of data can be maintained the information of the data. Data format can be done in the maintenance of the data. Visual Clarification vocabularies and the variation in the deep networks and this dataset from the awareness of the video information of the video of the network.

References

1. MobileNets: Efficient Convolutional Neural Networks for Mobile Vision Applications Switzerland, IBM Research - Zürich, 8803 Rüschlikon, Switzerland, Università di Bologna, Italy (2020)
2. He, K., Zhang, X., Ren, S., Sun, J.: Deep Residual Learning for Image Recognition. In: CVPR (2016)
3. Tensorflow: Image recognition. https://www.tensorflow.org/tutorials/image_recognition
4. Krizhevsky, A., Sutskever, I., Hinton, G.E.: Imagenet classification with deep convolutional neural networks. In: NIPS (2012)
5. Simonyan, K., Zisserman, A.: Very deep convolutional networks for large-scale image recognition. In: ICLR (2015)
6. Blank, M., Gorelick, L., Shechtman, E., Irani, M., Basri, R.: Actions as space-time shapes. In: Proceedings of the International Conference on Computer Vision (ICCV), (2005)
7. Szegedy, C., Ioffe, S., Vanhoucke, V.: Inception-v4, inceptionresnet and the impact of residual connections on learning. arXiv:1602.07261v1 (2016)

8. Deng, J., Dong, W., Socher, R., Jia Li, L., Li, K., Fei-fei, L.: Imagenet: a large-scale hierarchical image database. In: Proceedings of the IEEE Conference on Computer Vision and Pattern Recognition (2009)
9. Tran, D., Bourdev, L., Fergus, R., Torresani, L., Paluri, M.: Learning spatiotemporal features with 3d convolutional networks. In: ICCV (2015)
10. Feichtenhofer, C., Pinz, A., Zisserman, A.: Convolutional two-stream network fusion for video action recognition. In: CVPR (2016)
11. Everingham, M., Gool, L.V., Williams, C.K.I., Winn, J., Zisserman, A.: The pascal visual object classes (voc) challenge (2009)
12. Laptev, I., Marszalek, M., Schmid, C., Rozenfeld, B.: Learning realistic human actions from movies. In: CVPR (2008)
13. Fei-fei, L., Fergus, R., Perona, P.: One-shot learning of object categories IEEE Trans. Pattern Anal. Mach. Intell. **28**(4), 594–611 (2006)
14. Girshick, R.: Fast R-CNN. In: Proceedings of the International Conference on Computer Vision (ICCV) (2015)
15. Schuldt, C., Laptev, I., Caputo, B.: Recognizing human actions: a local SVM approach. In: ICPR (2004)
16. Wang, H., Schmid, C.: Action recognition with improved trajectories. In: ICCV (2013)
17. Griffin, G., Holub, A., Perona, P.: Caltech-256 object category dataset Technical Report 7694, California Institute of Technology (2007)
18. He, K., Zhang, X., Ren, S., Sun, J.: Deep residual learning for image recognition. CoRR, abs/1512.03385 (2015)
19. Heilbron, F.C., Escorcia, V., Ghanem, B., Niebles, J.C.: Activitynet: a large-scale video benchmark for human activity understanding. In: IEEE Conference on Computer Vision and Pattern Recognition (CVPR), pp. 961–970 (2015)
20. Baccouche, M., Mamalet, F., Wolf, C., Garcia, C., Baskurt, A.: Sequential deep learning for human action recognition. In: Salah, A.A., epri, B. (eds.) HBU 2011. LNCS, vol. 7065, pp. 29–39. Springer, Heidelberg (2011). https://doi.org/10.1007/978-3-642-25446-8_4
21. Ioffe, S., Szegedy, C.: Batch normalization: accelerating deep network training by reducing internal covariate shift. In: Proceedings of the International Conference on Machine Learning (ICML), pp. 448–456 (2015)
22. Jegou, H., Perronnin, F., Douze, M., Sanchez, J., Perez, P., Schmid, C.: Aggregating local image descriptors into compact codes. IEEE Trans. Pattern Anal. Mach. Intell. **34**(9), 1704–1716 (2012)

A Blockchain Based Online Voting System: An Indian Scenario

Srinivasan Selvaraj[1]([✉]), P. Shobha Rani[1], A. Gnanasekar[1], and Vignaraj Anand[2]

[1] Department of Computer Science and Engineering, R.M.D. Engieering College, Kavaraipettai, India
{ssn.cse,psr.cse,ags.cse}@rmd.ac.in

[2] Department of Computer Science and Engineering, Thiagarajar College of Engineering, Madurai, India
vignaraj@tce.edu

Abstract. The conventional paper based voting system has many limitations including poor security and privacy. Hence, the internet based online voting system has been evolved as an alternate to the paper-based voting system in the recent years. This paper proposes a novel architecture for online voting system which uses block chain to record electoral data. It describes the various steps like block creation and block sealing for creating adjustable block chain for the polling process. It uses private block chain which is accessible to authorized agencies including government bodies (i.e., Election commission). Moreover, it uses AADHAAR information to verify the voter details and uses SHA hashing algorithms to protect the voting data stored in the block. The proposed system is implemented using PHP and JSON. The proposed method has improved the security and manifestation of electronic voting process significantly compared to the existing systems.

Keywords: Blockchain · Online voting · Security · Hashing · SHA algorithm

1 Introduction

Voting plays an important role in all democratic countries as various administrative bodies have used it to choose a leader. Electronic Voting Machines (EVMs) have been adopted in many countries, including India for voting. It has many benefits such as accuracy, convenience, flexibility, privacy, verifiability and mobility compared to the paper based voting systems. However, Manual verification is essential before casting a vote in the existing voting process. Such a verification process increases time to cast a vote. Furthermore, the malfunctioning of EVM leads a many questions about EVM's credibility in many occasions. Hence, it is important to have a more reliable voting system from the voter's perspective.

Block chain technology has been proposed for online voting system to improve the overall voting turnout in recent years. In a block chain based system, a network of computers is used to store the database instead of a single centralized system. It also defines several rules to modify the stored data in the database. To modify the stored

A. K. Luhach et al. (Eds.): ICAICR 2020, CCIS 1393, pp. 329–338, 2021.
https://doi.org/10.1007/978-981-16-3660-8_31

data, all computers in the network should agree to change the database state. As a result, no single computer has the power to falsify the stored data or censor changes. The block chain further requires an audit trail for all sorts of modifications in the database. Each change to the database is called as audit trail or transaction. The details about a group of transactions are stored in a single node or block. Additionally, each block has a reference to its preceding block. This process subsequently forms a chain of blocks called "block chain". And, each block contains a link to its previous block and a list of new transactions. When a new node (computer) is added to the chain, it has an empty database in the block. Subsequently, it downloads all transactional details from other blocks and creates its own database. Hence, it will have the same database state like other nodes in the chain. It enables to verify and rebuilt the database from the scratch.

Most of the existing e-voting systems are vulnerable to hacking. So there is a possibility of changing the outcome of the election. To overcome these problems, this paper proposes a block chain based voting system in the context of India. The proposed system uses digital identity of voters for voter verification. It uses Aadhaar which is a unique and verifiable 12-digit identification number issued by Unique Identification Authority of India (UIDAI) to all the resident of India.

The proposed system uses digital identity for voter verification, unlike the existing e-voting systems. It relies on Aadhaar which is a unique and verifiable 12-digit identification number issued by Unique Identification Authority of India (UIDAI) to every resident of India. The Aadhaar number is used to retrieve all data including the biometric to verify voter credentials during e-voting. It ensures that all authorized voters can cast their vote more confidentially and improves the overall voting turnouts by facilitating the remote voting. A block chain based online voting system hides both identity and political preferences of voters. It improves the trustworthiness of the voting process by assuring that each voter casts exactly one vote and tampering vote is impossible. It enables the online voting system more difficult to hack.

This paper is organized as follows. Section 2 presents the various blockchain based voting systems and Sect. 3 describes the architecture of the proposed system. Section 4 shows how the system is implemented and Sect. 5 concludes the paper.

2   Related Work

Generally, two types of block chains are used in e-voting systems. The first type uses public block chain in which contents of all transactions are visible to the public. However, transactional data are accessible to authorized users alone in the private block chain. Moreover, the public block chain needs encryption algorithms such as Advanced Encryption Standard (AES) to protect transactional data. However, the usage of both encryption and decryption algorithms pulls down the performance of e-voting system. Hence, the private block chain is predominately used in block chain based e-voting systems [2, 3]. In [1], Votem have proposed a token based voting system using block chain to ensure the anonymity and security. However, their system failed to authenticate the voters.

Johnson et al. have used block chain for electronic voting in which voters are recognized based on the addresses. As a result, the system will fail if the user's generates multiple addresses to cast many votes. Hjalmarsson et al. have proposed an e-voting framework which is more secure and reduce the overall cost of conducting elections [4]. Kshetri and Voas have developed a Smartphone based system for internet voting at small scale [5]. Zhang et al. discussed how the private blockchain maintained by an organization such as election commission of the country can be used to keep the details of the votes and transaction and the voting process does not remain visible to the voters. [6–8]. However, it affects the transparency of the voting process.

Zheng et al. presented the various issues of using the blockchain for the e-voting. They emphasized the need for responsive and scalable blockchain to guarantee the successful usage. Moreover, there is a necessity to fix the block size optimally to contain adequate information about a vote [9]. BasitShahzad and Jon Crowcroft have used consortium blockchain to conduct voting by government organizations using efficient hashing techniques [10].

Amrita Dhillon et al. presented the centralized architecture of the online voting system and its vulnerabilities to various electoral frauds [15]. They also described how block chain technology could be used to address the limitations of the existing centralized systems. They have analyzed both merits and demerits of block chain based electoral system. However, they did not implement the proposed system. In [16], proposed a block chain based decentralized voting system which protects voter privacy without the help of third parties. They have demonstrated the system on Hyperledger Fabric is more feasible for real election process.

Shalini Shukla et al. have proposed a block chain based voting system which uses Aadhaar number and encryption technique. They have used Ethereum block chain for the implementation. However, they did not have mechanism to verify the voter identity. Yang et al. has proposed new voting protocol based on block chain and homomorphic encryption to ensure end to end voter verification.

3 The Proposed System

The schematic diagram of the proposed system is shown in Fig. 1. The proposed system operates in two stages. In the first stage, it verifies whether the user is a valid voter or not using the Aadhaar and Biometric authentication system. The biometric system is used to collect the fingerprint of the voter for authentication. The finger print is then compared with the fingerprint of the user retrieved from the Aadhaar Server to determine whether the particular voter is legitimate voter or not. It then allows the verified voters to cast the vote online in the second stage. It continues the polling process until the voting time ends. It subsequently updates the voting details in blockchain database server.

The proposed system is accessible by two types of users: administrator and voter. The administrator has complete control over the system. He has the privilege to accept or reject any voter request even after verifying his credentials. Since Electoral system involves many Electoral Officers, the administrator has the right to create multiple administrators to manage and monitor the voting process. On the other hand, the second type of user, called voter, must register by providing all the relevant information for voting

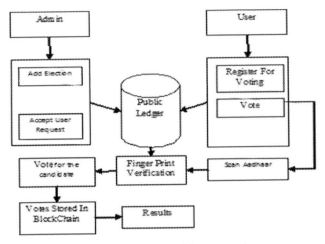

Fig. 1. Schematic diagram of the proposed system

including the Voter ID. Moreover, each user must upload his AADHAAR card during the registration process. The administrator retrieves voter information using AADHAR and checks whether he has provided all information correctly. Then, the user is asked to send his fingerprint which is subsequently compared with the one retrieved using the AADHAAR using the ASIF algorithm. The electoral officer allows the user to cast his vote only if the user details are correct. If there is any mismatch, the electoral officer will not allow the user to participate in the voting process. The proposed system allows the legitimate voter is allowed to cast the vote at point of time in the polling day. At the same time, no voter is allowed to register on the polling day.

As soon as the electoral officer issue an election notification, the information is sent to all eligible voters belongs to the particular constituency. The election process will be started on the specific date and time automatically. All voters can cast his vote on the voting date within voting hours. Once a voter has casted his vote, vote detail is stored in a block of blockchain. Hence, it can be altered or ignored during counting. Moreover, a voter can view his vote detail as it has been hashed using SHA256 algorithm. The electoral officer will publish the result of the election once the election is over.

4 System Implementation

The system is implemented using PHP7.2, MySQL8.0 and JSON on a system with a Core i3 processor with Windows10 Operating System. The following Fig. 2 shows the home page of the proposed system used by both the electoral officers and voters.

Figure 3 shows the various options available to the Electoral officers such as Voters Approval, Posting Election Date, Adding new Electoral Officers and Publishing the election results. To cast a vote on the polling date, each voter must register their details using the ADD User option. Each voter must submit their name, Date of Birth, Aadhaar Number, Constituency, preferred user name and password for their account. The user must provide his provide his fingerprint using the scanner. The Voting officer can view a

Fig. 2. Home page

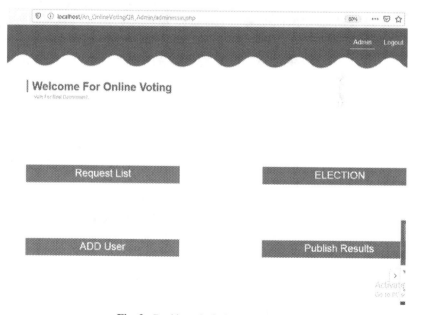

Fig. 3. Dashboard of Electoral Officer

list of all voters using the request list option and check the whether the voter has provided correct information. The voter request will be rejected and the same information is sent to the voter.

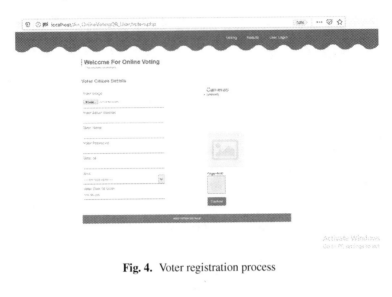

Fig. 4. Voter registration process

Fig. 5. Voter approval process

Figure 4 shows the registration page of voters where the end user should provide all his information and Fig. 5 shows a list of approved online voters to be participating in the election process. On the polling date, the registered voters can login into the system. The voters can cast their voting page where he/she has to choose the candidate of their choice in the list of candidates contested in the election. After the selection, each voter must confirm the selection and cast their vote.

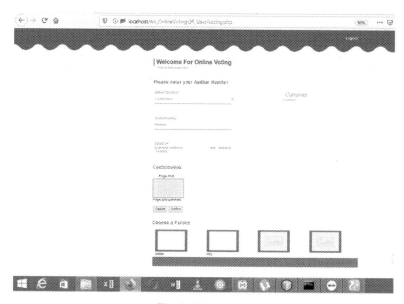

Fig. 6. Voting page

Figure 6 shows the list of candidates who contested in the election. Each voter can cast his vote by clicking on the image of the candidate.

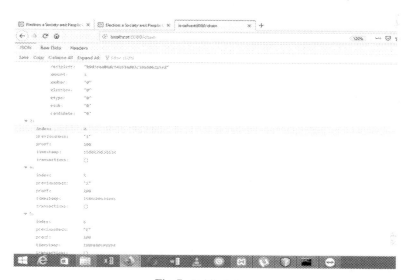

Fig. 7. Public ledger

Figure 7 shows how the voting data is stored in the public ledger. Finally, the votes registered for each candidate are counted to determine the winner of the election. The electoral officer will publish the results with votes registered for each candidate (Fig. 8).

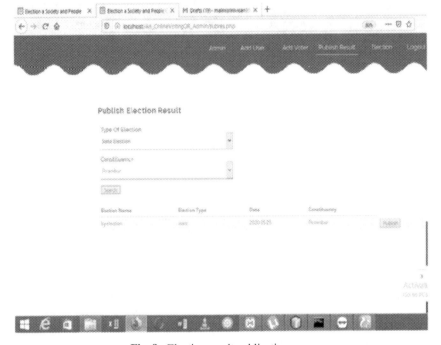

Fig. 8. Election result publication page

The Election officer has the right to publish the result. The election officer must select the appropriate type of election and the constituency for which the election result should be published. Upon submission of the form, the details about the election will be retrieved from the block chain and the same will be presented to the election officer. The results will be available to the public once the election officer presses the publish button on the page.

Figure 9 shows the election result page for the voters. When the voter submits the constituency name to the system, it presents the list of candidates and the number of votes recorded for each candidate to the voters.

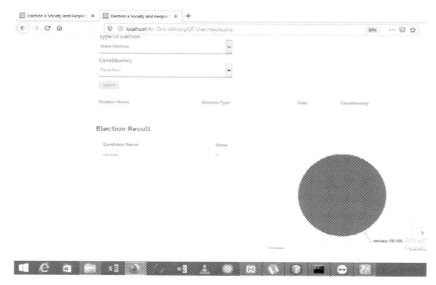

Fig. 9. .

5   Conclusion

Online e-Voting System is essential to enable all voters to participate in the election process irrespective of their location in the world. One of the key issues in the adaptation of online voting is security and authentication. There are a lot of issues raised about the credibility of the current ballot system which uses Electronic Voting Machines (EVMs) by voters. The proposed system preserves voter privacy and allows audit ability. It also provides a transparent system for verification of the election. The proposed system is highly cost efficient as compared to the existing system and can be implemented easily on Internet. This eliminates the need of any central authority to monitor the process. Additionally, the distributed ledger technology ensures that each vote is tamper-proof.

References

1. Stern, J.: Votem—Voting for a Mobile World. https://votem.com/. Accessed 31 July 2018
2. Pilkington, M.: 11 Blockchain technology: principles and applications. In: Research Handbook on Digital Transformations, pp. 225–232 (2016)
3. Gabison, G.: Policy considerations for the blockchain technology public and private applications. SMU Sci. Tech. Rev. **19**, 327–333 (2016)
4. Hjalmarsson, F.P., Hreioarsson, G.K., Hamdaqa, M., Hjalmtysson, G.: Blockchain-based e-voting system. In: Proceedings of the IEEE 11th International Conference on Cloud Computing (CLOUD), San Francisco, CA, USA, pp. 983–986 (2018)
5. Kshetri, N., Voas, J.: Blockchain-enabled e-voting. IEEE Softw. **35**(4), 95–99 (2018)
6. Zhang, Y., Deng, R.H., Shu, J., Yang, K., Zheng, D.: TKSE: trustworthy keyword search over encrypted data with two-side verifiability via blockchain. IEEE Access **6**, 31077–31087 (2018)

7. Zhang, Y., Deng, R.H., Liu, X., Zheng, D.: Blockchain based efficient and robust fair payment for outsourcing services in cloud computing. Inf. Sci. **462**, 262–277 (2018)
8. Shahzad, B.: Quantification of productivity of the brands on social media with respect to their responsiveness. IEEE Access **7**(1), 9531–9539 (2019)
9. Zheng, Z., Xie, S., Dai, H.N., Chen, X., Wang, H.: Blockchain challenges and opportunities: a survey. Int. J. Web Grid Serv. **14**(4), 352–375 (2018)
10. Shahzad, B., Crowcroft, J.: Trustworthy electronic voting using adjusted blockchain technology. IEEE Access **7**, 24477–24488 (2019)
11. Pilkington, M.: 11 Blockchain technology: principles and applications. In: Research Handbook on Digital Transformations, pp. 225–234 (2016)
12. Wolchok, S., et al.: Security analysis of India's electronic voting machines. In: Proceedings of the 17th ACM Conference on Computer and Communications Security, pp. 1–14 (2010)
13. Alonso. L.P., Gasco, M., del Blanco, D.Y.M., Alonso, J.A.H., Barrat, J., Moreton, H.A.: E-voting system evaluation based on the council of Europe recommendations: Helios voting. IEEE Trans. Emerg. Top. Computing. (2018). https://doi.org/10.1109/TETC.2018.2881891
14. Yaser, N., Mahsud, N., Chaudhry, I.A.: Effects of exposure to electronic media political content on voters' voting behavior. Berkeley J. Soc. Sci. **1**(4), 1–22 (2011)
15. Dhillon, A., Kotsialou, G., McBurney, P., Riley, L.: Voting over a distributed ledger: an interdisciplinary perspective. CAGE working paper no. 416 (2020)
16. Zhang, W., et al.: A privacy-preserving voting protocol on blockchain. In: 2018 IEEE 11th International Conference on Cloud Computing (CLOUD), San Francisco, CA, pp. 401–408 (2018)
17. Chaieb, M., Yousfi, S., Lafourcade, P., Robbana, R.: Verify-your-vote: a verifiable blockchain-based online voting protocol. In: Themistocleous, M., Rupino da Cunha, P. (eds.) EMCIS 2018. LNBIP, vol. 341, pp. 16–30. Springer, Cham (2019). https://doi.org/10.1007/978-3-030-11395-7_2
18. Shukla, S., Thasmiya, A.N., Shashank, D.O., Mamatha, H.R.: Online voting application using ethereum blockchain. In: 2018 International Conference on Advances in Computing, Communications and Informatics (ICACCI), pp. 873–880 (2018)
19. Yang, X., Yi, X., Nepal, S., Kelarev, A., Han, F.: Blockchain voting: publicly verifiable online voting protocol without trusted tallying authorities. Future Gener. Comput. Syst. **112**, 859–874 (2020)

Detection of Emphasis Words in Short Texts – A Context Aware Label Distribution Learning Approach

Meghana[✉] and Bhaskarjyoti Das

PES University, Bengaluru, India

Abstract. In multi-label classification problems, the predominant approach is to transform the problem into a single-label classification problem that can result in the affirmative classification of multiple labels of a single sample. However, for data such as image, video, or text segment - a realistic scenario is that of a distribution across multiple labels for any particular sample. This work adopts a label distribution approach to determine the segments of text that need emphasis. Additionally, it focuses on short text samples that make it challenging to understand the context and the author's intent. A context-aware approach is proposed by employing a composite embedding, thereby obtaining contextual information while also focusing on fine-grained details about the text samples. The proposed model outperforms the selected baseline by a significant amount, rendering the amalgamation of the context-aware embeddings and the non-binary nature of the Label Distribution Learning fittest for estimating emphasis.

Keywords: Label Distribution Learning · Emphasis detection · Multi-task learning · Pre-trained embedding

1 Introduction

A generic learning process typically assigns one or more class labels to an instance of an object, and one can either use Single-Label Learning (SLL) or Multi-Label Learning (MLL) for the same. In the former approach, a single label is assigned to an instance whereas, in the latter, each instance may be associated with multiple class labels. Common examples of multi-label learning are emotion classification, scene classification, genre classification for literary works, text topic classification, and personality prediction. In a "Problem Transformation" approach, an MLL problem is treated as an SLL problem effectively ignoring the correlation with other labels while a particular label is being investigated. In the MLL approach that employs a problem transformation to SLL, a single instance can be associated with multiple labels and each such association will be 100%. However, that is not necessarily accurate. There are other approaches of MLL that attempt to extend the binary relevance [1] based approach in SLL with the concept of label correlation. On the contrary, Label Distribution Learning (LDL) [2] is a more generic approach based on the assumption that every instance may belong to more than

© Springer Nature Singapore Pte Ltd. 2021
A. K. Luhach et al. (Eds.): ICAICR 2020, CCIS 1393, pp. 339–347, 2021.
https://doi.org/10.1007/978-981-16-3660-8_32

one label at the same time though the extent of the association can vary for each label. It addresses this issue and answers the question of "To what extent is each label associated with an instance?". In a way, LDL is a general case of both single-label learning and multi-label learning.

Throughout the history of mankind, humans have striven to find effective means of conveying a message, either driven by underlying propagandistic intent or simply to put forward a message for the general good. A multitude of instruments have been employed to convey the message - speeches, plays, advertisements, posters, and billboards to name a few. While the medium of propagation of these instruments varies between speech and text, they all share a common concept of emphasis that plays a pivotal role in putting the message across. For a text sample, being able to estimate the degree of emphasis for each word demands knowing the context of the sentence and the sample as a whole. Emphasis estimation for longer text instances is simpler because determining the context of longer instances is easier. However, the shorter the instance gets, the more challenging it becomes to discern the context, thereby making the determination of emphasis a challenging task.

In a text sample, for the task of identification of emphasis words, it is an oversimplification to identify some words as emphasis words and the rest as non-emphasis words. In reality, the extent of emphasis of a word in a text sample is not necessarily binary. Hence an LDL approach is more suitable to an emphasis detection problem in the text domain. For the specific case of emphasis detection in short text, to overcome the context detection challenge, this paper proposes a context-aware emphasis selection architecture along with an LDL approach, which is seen to give impressive results by outperforming the baseline to a significant extent.

2 Related Work

2.1 Label Distribution Learning

Each instance in LDL terminology is associated with a real-valued vector where each element represents the extent of association of the instance with a particular label. If x_i denotes the ith instance and y_j denotes the jth label, the extent of association of the label y_j to the instance x_i is denoted by the real-valued vector V_i whose elements are denoted by $V_{x_i}^{y_j}$. Each such element of the vector represents the description degree for a particular label and is a real value that lies in the interval [0, 1]. The sum of all such elements of the LDL vector is 1 for any instance x_i. Few extensions of existing machine learning algorithms to incorporate LDL have also been proposed by researchers, Label Distribution Learning Forest [3] for example. There has been some research on using LDL specifically to address scenarios where each instance of the dataset can be associated with multiple labels and such associations need not be binary. Xin Geng et al. [4] used LDL to predict crowd opinion before a movie release. Crowd opinion is different from individual opinion after release as it is better described by a distribution. Bin-Bin Gao et al. [5] used deep label distribution in the visual recognition task using deep CNN. Ke chen et al. [6] used LDL to generate pseudo-age labels from the visual image. Miaogen LING et al. [7] used LDL to describe video segments. Personality consists of multiple traits and DI XUE et al. [8] used LDL along with feature engineering from Chinese blog data to assign personality labels to social media users. Supervised learning problem on social media data is another scenario where binary labels fail to capture the reality and a label distribution approach is more appropriate. Ehsan Mohammady Ardehaly et al. adopted this approach [9] for mining the demographics behind political sentiment in social media.

2.2 Transfer Learning

In recent years, transfer learning [10, 11] has emerged as a key technique in deep learning. The transfer learning framework can be defined in terms of different aspects in the source and target domain i.e. task, features, labels, and the marginal probability of features as well as labels. Inductive Transfer Learning represents the case when different learning tasks are performed in the source as well as target domain and target domain has labeled data. Multi-Task learning is a type of inductive transfer learning. By training a model on different but related tasks, we generalize better by sharing representation across all related tasks. In multitask learning, both the source and target are trained together, while in Sequential Task Learning (a type of inductive transfer learning), first the source is trained and later the target. This is typically referred to as "pre-training". In this work, both sequential task learning and multi-task learning have been experimented.

2.3 Learning Emphasis

Detection of emphasis words in speech has been a popular research problem that can help detect emotion, intention, and attitude. The learning approaches in the existing research so far have used both classical machine learning approaches based on feature engineering and deep learning [14–18]. However, there is very little if not no research on finding emphasis words in text, specifically short text that suffers from lack of context. Amirreza Shirani et al. [19] first investigated this problem of detection of emphasis words in short written text. To the best of our knowledge, this is the only published work available as of now. In this work, two labels are considered with the LDL methodology paired with neural learning techniques using various pre-trained embedding and BiLSTM. Conditional Random Field (CRF) has been attempted but the performance has been poor. The work described in this paper extends their research.

3 Dataset

The dataset [19] utilized in this study is composed of 2,742 short excerpts spanning slogans, quotes, and some conversational sentences. The lengths of the text samples range from 1 to as long as 38 with a mean length of 11.82. Every instance is annotated using votes of nine experts. Each expert has done a token-wise evaluation of every instance using the standard *BIO* tagging notation. Hence, for every token in an instance, one may find a nine-fold annotation enumerating the label that each of the nine experts assigned to it. For example, "Stay Healthy" has two tokens - "Stay" and "Healthy". The votes for "Stay" may be *[O, O, O, O, B, O, B, O, B]*, indicating that three out of the nine experts voted for "Stay" to be the beginning of an emphasized segment. Similarly, those for "Healthy" may be *[B, B, B, B, O, B, I, O, O]* where six (including both *B* and *I* labels) experts voted for healthy to be emphasized, whereas three voted otherwise.

4 Preprocessing

The regular preprocessing task of eliminating the stop-words is not carried out since in many cases, the words that require emphasis are those as trivial as stop-words. For instance, in the sentence "If *you* work, it *will* work", where the italicized words represent emphasized words, both "you" and "will" fall under the common set of stop-words.

4.1 Label Distribution

As mentioned in Sect. 3, the samples in the dataset are annotated with the votes of nine experts using *BIO* tags. This must be translated to a format that the model can understand. In this case, the data must be "label distributed". In other words, the ground truth of each label under every sample must be distributed across the complete set of labels. The set of labels employed in this study is *{IEmph, O}* where *IEmph* signifies "inside emphasized segment" and *O* signifies "outside emphasized segment". To get the label distributions, the proportions of positive and negative votes are calculated. Since *BIO* notation is employed for the votes, both *B* (Beginning of emphasized segment) and *I* (Inside the emphasized segment) votes are considered as *IEmph*.

4.2 Preprocessing Before Training

To be able to pass the text samples into the model, they must all have the same length. Therefore, the text samples are padded with a padding character so that their length fits a predetermined maximum sequence length. In a similar vein, the ground truth is also padded with labels corresponding to "outside emphasized segment", *O*. In this study, a maximum sequence length of 40 is taken.

5 Implementation

The major deterrent in determining the emphasis for shorter instances of text is that there is very little available information to discern the context of the sample. Since context is key to determining the degree of emphasis, we propose a context-aware approach.

5.1 Pre-trained Embeddings

This study utilizes two levels of embedding - ELMo [20] to obtain word-level encoding and Universal Sentence Encoder (USE) [21] to obtain sentence-level encoding. The rationale behind using two levels of embedding is to capture the global information of the sentence (through USE) alongside the word level information (through ELMo). Context-aware nature is achieved by using Universal Sentence Encoder, which encodes the sentence-level information, hence also encoding the context. Furthermore, to obtain fine-grained details about the text sample, we use ELMo, which returns a word-wise embedding. ELMo embeddings used here are 1024 length vectors, whereas USE embeddings are 512 length vectors. For each text sample, the single USE embedding is concatenated to each of the ELMo word embeddings to yield 1536 length composite vectors.

5.2 Label Distribution Learning

This study employs the LDL paradigm of learning as specified in Sect. 2.1. This methodology is especially of the essence in cases where available data is meager. Moreover, the labels are continuous - in problem statements like the one at hand, where there are no definite rules to estimate the degree of emphasis, it only makes more sense to have a continuous probabilistic distribution across all the labels, rather than having discrete binary labels. As mentioned in Sect. 4.1, the set of labels used is {*IEmph, O*}. Furthermore, since the primary task is to model the distribution of the labels presented by the ground truth, we use Kullback-Leibler (KL) Divergence as the loss function.

5.3 Architecture

Figure 1 shows the architecture employed for this study. As mentioned in Sect. 5.1, a composite embedding comprising word-level ELMo embedding and sentence-level USE embedding is used. The composite embedding is fed to the next segment of the network. The remaining network is composed of two Bi-Directional Long Short Term Memory (BiLSTM) layers, each of size 1024. Following this is a time-distributed 40-fold fully connected layer, which finally connects to a time distributed 2-fold fully connected layer, representing the output of the network. Additionally, to prevent overfitting, dropout layers with a value of 0.5 are employed in the BiLSTM layers.

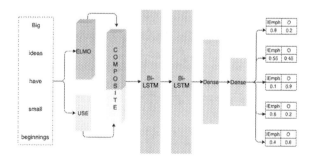

Fig. 1. Proposed LDL architecture with composite embedding

6   Results

The network is trained for 50 epochs on a Tesla K80 GPU. KL Divergence and Adam are utilized as the loss function and optimizer, respectively, while training; and a learning rate of 0.01 is employed. This study considers the highest performing model in [19] (LDL with ELMo and attention) as the baseline. Additionally, MTL models are also evaluated and compared to the proposed model. Two MTL models are employed - one with ELMo embeddings and the other with the proposed composite embeddings.

6.1 Multi-task Learning

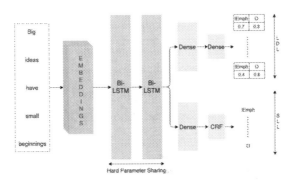

Fig. 2. Multi-task learning architecture

While MTL is mostly used to model two distinct but related tasks with fairly similar architectures, here, it is used for modeling the same task done in two distinct ways. In other words, the main task here would be emphasis detection but the "multi" aspect lies in the method of learning. The two tasks, therefore, are emphasis detection using LDL and Single Label Learning (SLL). The former is the primary task, while the latter is the auxiliary task. Hard parameter sharing is employed, where the two BiLSTM layers specified in Fig. 1 are shared. The parts following these components are branched to serve the respective models. Figure 2 illustrates the MTL architecture employed.

The SLL task is achieved using BiLSTM-CRF, which expects binary labels. The conventional method of setting a hard threshold of 0.5 did not result in acceptable labels, especially in the case of shorter text samples. To better model the labels, a heuristic that is a function of length is devised. The rationale used is that the shorter the text gets, the higher is the consensus about which words to emphasize. Therefore, for a shorter instance, the agreement between the voters is usually higher, and this agreement gradually reduces as the length increases. Consequently, the heuristic dynamically assigns a threshold to an instance based on its length, assigning a higher threshold for shorter texts, and a relatively lower threshold for longer ones. It must be noted that the MTL configuration is a close second in terms of performance and this is a method that can be entirely discounted given the limited dataset used in this work.

6.2 Evaluation

In order to evaluate the models, $Match_m$ [19] metric is used. This metric is employed because it provides a fair way of evaluating models producing continuous, probabilistic

Table 1. matchM scores (in percentage) for m = 1 to m = 8 for various architectures

Model	Model type	m − 1	m = 2	m = 3	m = 4	m = 5	m = 6	m = 7	m = 8
M1	LDL: GloVe+Att	57.5	69.7	76.7	80.7	–	–	–	–
M2	LDL:ELMo	0.6	71.7	78.7	84.1	–	–	–	–
M3	LDL:ELMo +Att	59.6	72.7	77.7	84.6	–	–	–	–
M4	MTL:EMLo	53.2	50.9	57.4	62.4	66.9	70.9	73.8	75.6
M5	MTL:EMLo+USE	70.5	75.7	80.1	83	85.6	87.6	88.9	89.7
M6	LDL:ELMo+USE	72.6	79.3	83.3	85.8	88.0	89.9	91.2	**91.9**

outputs. If L_m^x and $\widehat{L}_m^x$ are sets comprising top m $IEmph$ probabilities in the ground truth and predicted labels respectively, for a datapoint x in dataset D, $Match_m$ is:

$$Match_m = \frac{\sum_{x \in D}\left|L_m^x \cap \widehat{L_m^x}\right|/min(m, |x|)}{|D|} \tag{1}$$

For the evaluation, $Match_m$ with m value ranging from 1 to 8 are taken. An average $Match_m$ over two training datasets obtained with different seed values is used for evaluation to ensure the integrity of the results.

Table 1 displays the performance of various models for comparison. Models M1–M3 depict the $Match_m$ scores of the top three highest-scoring models in [19], whose $Match_m$ scores are available only from m = 1 to m = 4 in [19]. As mentioned previously, we choose the highest performing model in [19], model M3, as our baseline. M4 and M5 represent the models employing multi-task learning. M6 shows the results for the LDL approach trained as part of this study. We begin by comparing the performances of LDL models with models employing multi- task learning. Table 1 shows that LDL models surpass the MTL models across all the combinations of embeddings, with M5 being the only model that closely competes with the proposed model in terms of its performance. Furthermore, when the various models employing LDL are compared, the proposed model, M6, employing ELMo and USE, outperforms all other LDL variants at every value of m. It beats all the models employed for comparison, giving the highest $Match_m$ score of 91.9% at $m = 8$. It can, therefore, be inferred that the composite embeddings comprising ELMo and USE embedding work fabulously in capturing the right information to estimate emphasis.

7   Conclusion

This paper proposes a novel context-aware approach for determining the degree of emphasis in short excerpts of text. Owing to the over-simplification of a binary approach for supervised label learning, Label Distribution Learning is employed to model this task. Additionally, a composite embedding composed of ELMo and USE embeddings is utilized to capture both the context and the fine-grained details of a text sample whose short length offers inadequate context. The model is seen to outperform the baseline in terms of their performance, thereby corroborating the need to efficiently determine context alongside getting word-wise information while proving the suitability of Label Distribution Learning in such problems.

8 Future Work

This study focuses on emphasis detection in short texts and improves upon the approach of Label Distribution Learning by proposing an innovative learning model. The ability to detect emphasis words in a text sample can be an important component in the Natural Language Processing (NLP) pipeline for many downstream NLP tasks such as emotion detection and multi-target stance detection. Furthermore, the feasibility of emphasis detection as an auxiliary task in a multi-task learning setup shall be explored. Finally, this work solely illustrates performance in English text. Future work shall explore utilizing LDL on longer instances of text and exploring ways of determining the degree of emphasis in text samples of other languages.

References

1. Zhang, M.L., Li, Y.K., Liu, X.Y., et al.: Binary relevance for multi-label learning: an overview. Front. Comput. Sci. **12**, 191–202 (2018)
2. Geng, X.: Label distribution learning. IEEE Trans. Knowl. Data Eng. **28**(7), 1734–1748 (2016)
3. Shen W., Zhao, K., Guo, Y., Yuille, A.L.: Label distribution learning forests. In: Advances in Neural Information Processing Systems, pp. 834–843 (2017)
4. Geng, X., Hou, P.: Pre-release prediction of crowd opinion on movies by label distribution learning. In: IJCAI, pp. 3511–3517 (2015)
5. Gao, B., Xing, C., Xie, C., Wu, J., Geng, X.: Deep label distribution learning with label ambiguity. IEEE Trans. Image Process. **26**(6), 2825–2838 (2017)
6. Chen, K., Kämäräinen, J.-K.: Learning with ambiguous label distribution for apparent age estimation. In: Lai, S.-H., Lepetit, V., Nishino, K., Sato, Y. (eds.) ACCV 2016. LNCS, vol. 10113, pp. 330–343. Springer, Cham (2017). https://doi.org/10.1007/978-3-319-54187-7_22
7. Ling, M., Geng, X.: Soft video parsing by label distribution learning. Front. Comput. Sci. **13**(2), 302–317 (2019)
8. Xue, D., et al.: Personality recognition on social media with label distribution learning. IEEE Access **5**, 13478–13488 (2017)
9. Ardehaly, E.M., Culotta, A.: Mining the demographics of political sentiment from Twitter using learning from label proportions. In: 2017 IEEE International Conference on Data Mining (ICDM), pp. 733–738. IEEE (2017)
10. Tan, C., Sun, F., Kong, T., Zhang, W., Yang, C., Liu, C.: A survey on deep transfer learning. In: Kůrková, V., Manolopoulos, Y., Hammer, B., Iliadis, L., Maglogiannis, I. (eds.) ICANN 2018. LNCS, vol. 11141, pp. 270–279. Springer, Cham (2018). https://doi.org/10.1007/978-3-030-01424-7_27
11. Ruder, S., Peters, M.E., Swayamdipta, S., Wolf, T.: Transfer learning in natural language processing. In: Proceedings of the 2019 Conference of the North American Chapter of the Association for Computational Linguistics: Tutorials, pp. 15–18 (2019)
12. Okazaki, N.: CRFsuite: a Fast Implementation of Conditional Random Fields (CRFs) (2007). http://www.chokkan.org/software/crfsuite/

13. Huang, Z., Xu, W., Yu, K.: Bidirectional LSTM-CRF models for sequence tagging. arXiv preprint arXiv:1508.01991 (2015)
14. Zhang, L., et al.: Emphasis detection for voice dialogue applications using multi-channel convolutional bidirectional long short-term memory network. In: 2018 11th International Symposium on Chinese Spoken Language Processing (ISCSLP), pp. 210–214. IEEE (2018)
15. Heba, A., Pellegrini, T., Jorquera, T., André-Obrecht, R., Lorré, J.-P.: Lexical emphasis detection in spoken French using F-Banks and neural networks. In: Camelin, N., Estève, Y., Martín-Vide, C. (eds.) SLSP 2017. LNCS (LNAI), vol. 10583, pp. 241–249. Springer, Cham (2017). https://doi.org/10.1007/978-3-319-68456-7_20
16. Do, Q.T., Sakti, S., Nakamura, S.: Toward expressive speech translation: a unified sequence-to-sequence LSTMs approach for translating words and emphasis. In: INTERSPEECH, pp. 2640–2644 (2017)
17. Mass, Y., et al.: Word emphasis prediction for expressive text to speech. In: INTERSPEECH, pp. 2868–2872 (2018)
18. Ning, Y., et al.: Learning cross-lingual knowledge with multilingual BLSTM for emphasis detection with limited training data. In: 2017 IEEE International Conference on Acoustics, Speech and Signal Processing (ICASSP), pp. 5615–5619. IEEE (2017)
19. Shirani, A., et al.: Learning emphasis selection for written text in visual media from crowd-sourced label distributions. In: Proceedings of the 57th Annual Meeting of the Association for Computational Linguistics, pp. 1167–1172 (2019)
20. Peters, M.E., et al.: Deep contextualized word representations. In: Proceedings of NAACL (2018)
21. Cer, D., et al.: Universal Sentence Encoder. arXiv preprint arXiv:1803.11175 (2018)

The Effective Study of Transfer Learning with VGG-16 on Detection and Classification of Brain Tumor

Kallempudi Sai Sowjanya[✉] and Ishan Kumar

Lovely Professional University, Phagwara, Punjab, India
ishan.23347@lpu.co.in

Abstract. Nowadays transfer learning is a popular area of research and it is giving a very huge impact particularly when dealing detection and classification of various classes of a specific disease with the aid of biomedical images. In this context, the proposed framework is based on brain MRI images for the detection and classification of various classes of brain tumors such as Meningioma, Glioma, and Pituitary tumors. The dataset utilized is openly available and it is popularly known as "Brain tumor dataset-Figshare". It consists of all three classes of MRI images. The proposed framework is considered based on the concept of transfer learning with pre-trained CNN architecture, VGG-16. The proposed framework able to attain an overall accuracy of around 92% for the detection of the tumor, and the accuracy attained for the detected tumors to classify into meningioma, glioma, and pituitary tumors is 98.66%, 98.53%, and 99.54% respectively.

Keywords: Transfer learning · VGG-16 · CNN architecture · Brain tumor

1 Introduction

One of the deadliest and rising diseases are brain tumor cancer. The brain is the core of the human body and the most important organ including the cells and tissues that control the main functions of the body such as respiration, muscle, and senses. The cell has its capacity; some of the cells are flexible, some lose control, reject, and are aberrant [1]. Such unusual mass cell collections are classified as tumors. Uncontrolled and irregular brain cell growth of brain cancer tumors. It is one of life's deadliest diseases. Brain tumor analysis was reported to almost 23,000 individuals in the United States in 2015. Brain tumors have been estimated according to 2017 cancer estimates as one of the nation's leading causes of diseases connected to cancer, morbidity, and mortality in children and adults. Benign and malignant are two types of brain tumors. A benign tumor is known to be a less aggressive and non-cancerous tumor, whereas a malignant tumor is considered an aggressive and cancerous tumor [2]. There are common brain tumors, namely meningioma, glioma, and pituitary tumors. The classification aspect of the implementation presented in this paper is covered in these three categories. The attack on brain cancer has risen over time. In the past two decades, the incidence of brain cancer in all ages has risen. It reflects the need to take care of the brain. In Northern

© Springer Nature Singapore Pte Ltd. 2021
A. K. Luhach et al. (Eds.): ICAICR 2020, CCIS 1393, pp. 348–358, 2021.
https://doi.org/10.1007/978-981-16-3660-8_33

Europe and Africa, national statistics indicate the highest and lowest incidence of brain cancer. Early indications include headache, vision disorder, epilepsy, voice confusion, and paralysis for brain cancer. Both are focused on histopathology and physiological areas. This cancer affects patients in many detrimental ways i.e. both physically and mentally, lead to increased death rates globally. The basic essence of detecting these cancers is therefore very necessary for appropriate care at the right time [3]. Besides, under the direction of humans. To prevent this scenario there is a strong possibility for human complications, a technology that identifies tumors based on the patterns of the brain tumor images must be produced.

Huge progress is ongoing to classify and recognize brain tumors. The machine-learning methodologies have been used in the main study process and the CNN, neural networks, mathematical simulation have been used in the later stages [4]. The research has now entered to the extent where already existing CNN architectures are used for classification purposes and new completely linked layers are introduced. This research has been useful in recognizing and classifying brain tumors. In extracting features from an image dataset, CNN is highly efficient. CNN architecture can also be made of completely connected or dense layers, used for the extraction of features and the further classification of brain tumors. The key purpose of this document is to identify the different brain tumor types based on the image data collected from the MRI (Magnetic Resonance Imaging). The dataset is used for implementation is taken from Kaggle public domain. If the dataset is collected, each image must be pre-processed in the very first step. The next step is an essential aspect of implementation is feature extraction from the images. During the final step of development, the feature was moved over to the fully integrated layers for classification. The model was based on measurement metrics including accuracy, precision, recall, and F1-score.

The complete document organized into various sections such as Sect. 1 discusses the impact of brain tumor and the various steps involved in the process of identification and classification of various tumors through MRI images, Sect. 2 discusses the research and literature related to brain tumor identification and classification, Sect. 3 discusses the dataset and system description, ANN and VGG-16 and the various methodologies for the partitioning of training and testing datasets, Sect. 4 presents the obtained results from the proposed framework, and finally, Sect. 5 discusses the conclusion as well as the future work related to the framework.

2 Related Work

Sneha Khare et al. 2014 [5] proposed a methodology i.e. Genetic algorithm for optimization, SVM algorithm, and curve-fitting algorithm. Optimization is used to execute the suggested methodology. The technique, machine learning, and technique for curve-fitting to detect the tumor and current work was 16.39% accurate and 9.53% precise. K.B. Vaishnavee and K. Amshakala 2015[6] discuss automated brain MRI segmentation and detection. Before the Segmentation, For feature extraction, Histogram Equalization is used to enhance the precision of segmentation. The extraction of features using the Gray Level Co-occurrence Matrix. Although SOM clustering with Histogram Equalization is a simple procedure for segmentation, the PSVM-GLCM-PCA method is a more robust scheme.

Dena Nadir George et al. 2015 [7] proposed methodology i.e. Adaptive Threshold, C4.5 Decision tree, MLP are used for identification of a brain tumor. The two classifiers rely upon using the proposed method; the first classifier was the decision tree algorithm C4.5 and the decision tree algorithm and MLP algorithm for the second classifier. The classifiers are used to assign the case of the brain is divided into one type of benign tumor and five types of a malignant tumor. Maximum accuracy achieved by taking 174 samples of brain MR images and 95% is achieved. Yuehao Pan et al. 2015[8] explain grading brain tumors using Multiphase MRI images. In comparison to other research studies, Involving extra effort to design and select features, the technique used in this paper leverages the learning processes deep learning machine capability. The results suggest a maximum increase in the 18% on CNN grading based on sensitivity and specificity dependent networks as related to Neural Networks.

Eman Abdel-Maksoud et al. 2015 [9] discuss the segmentation of images relates to the process of separating an image into mutually exclusive regions. This paper provides a successful approach to image segmentation using the Fuzzy C-means algorithm-integrated K-means clustering technique. The suggested technique can bring advantages to K-means clustering in terms of minimum processing time for image segmentation. Marco Alfonse and Abdel-Badeeh M. Salem 2016 [10] discuss the identification of the type of brain tumor that is benign or malignant through MRI. The evaluation of the system is based on a series of brain tumor images. Experimental results show the framework proposed has a classification of 98.9% accuracy. Ali Isin et al. 2016 [11] discuss today's healthcare society, brain tumor diagnosis is very normal. Segmentation of the image used for brain treatment of abnormal tumors. In this article, we concentrated on the interest of DWT soft thresholds for enhanced image segmentation and genetic algorithms. SNR value was achieved by the established method from 20 to 44 and the accuracy of segmentation from 82% to 97% of tumor pixels observed based on ground reality. Iván Cabriaa and Iker Gondra 2017 [12] presented a new Potential Field Segmentation algorithm (PFS) that suggests the use of ensemble methods that incorporate PFS. In specific, if the potential area is less than an adaptive potential, each pixel in the MRI is determined and the tumor area is related to the pixel threshold. This segmentation criteria "limited potential" is intuitive, since the tumor pixel has a greater "density" and thus its potential is much higher than or not the "density" in other parts of the immediate field. Javeria Amin et al. 2019 [13] discuss an approach suggesting segmentation and classification of the brain tumor by using MRI. Seven layers are used in the proposed model category of 03 convolutional, 03 ReLU, and a softmax layer. The model proposed increases its accuracy and the proposed CNN model has an estimated processing time of 5.502 set practically this model can be used at an early level for brain damage diagnosis.

Javaria Amin et al. 2019 [14] discuss Weiner filtering is for de-noise and enhancement of input with multiple wavelet bands. The values of the error (MSE) and standardized similarity index (SSIM) are 76.38, 0.037, and 0.98 on T2 and On Flair 76.2, 0.039, and 0.98 respectively. The 0.93 FG and 0.98 BG and 0.010 EA solutions are accomplished on a local dataset. BRATS 2013. 0.97 FG and 0.98 BG precision and 0.015 ER are obtained. The average Q value is 0.88 and 0.017 as far as consistency is concerned. Aditya Khamparia et al. 2020 [15] suggested a new deep learning system powered by the internet of health stuff (IoHT). The feature mining from cervical images is proposed in the framework is performed by using pre-trained CNN models such as InceptionV3, VGG19, SqueezeNet, and ResNet50 for normal and irregular cervical cell classification which are feeding into thick and fattened layers. The approach suggested was validated by precision analysis, recall, F1 ranking, training time, and testing time. Gopal S. Tandel et al. 2020 [16] uses 5 multiclass clinically significant datasets were created. A transfer-learning-based artificial intelligence model using a CNN has been proposed and contributed to better success with magnetic resonance imaging in the classification and ranking of brain tumors. The transference system AlexNet based on CNN provided mean exactness from three types of cross-validation of 100, 95.97, 96.65, 87.14, and 93.74%, respectively. The transfer learning method, AI is effective for multiclass brain tumor grading and has greater outcomes than ML systems performance.

Muhammad Attique Khan et al. 2020 [17] provide a multimodal automated brain tumor recognition system that uses deep learning. The approach suggested is made up of five main steps. The first step is to expand the linear contrast. In the second step, a profound study function extraction. In stage three, A joint research strategy focused on correntropy. In step four, the partial least square (PLS) is in one matrix stable covariant characteristics are fused. ELM was provided with the combined matrix for the final classification. Sakshi Ahuja et al. 2020 [18] explain about brain tumor diagnosis based on transfer learning and segmentation is performed. At the beginning step, brain images are divided into three distinct groups, Low-Grade Glioma (LGG) and High-Grade Glioma (HGG) depends on tumor functionality. On the VGG19 at 6th epoch, training data output 99.82% accuracy, 96.32% accuracy of validation, and test accuracy of 99.30%. The specificity obtained is 100% and 97.81% sensitivity and 0.99% of Area Under-Curve (AUC). In the 2nd step, LGG and HGG segmentation of the tumor images. Segmentation of super-pixels contributes to 0.932 ground data average detection dice index. Anindya Apriliyanti Pravitasari et al. 2020 [19] discuss MRI can be used for brain tumor diagnosis. The U-Net and VGG16 hybrids are a model or architecture with f U-Net architecture for simplification. This method in the learning data collection has a high accuracy of about 96.1%. This UNet-VGG16 could be seen by a CCR value is approximately 95.69% to recognize the region of the brain tumor.

3 Methodologies

This specific section is organized into three categories such as the first category discusses the dataset and system description that are utilized for the implementation of the proposed framework, the second category discusses the methodologies which were utilized as a part of the implementation, and finally mentioned the various methodologies that are utilized for the partitioning of training and testing datasets. These categories of discussion mentioned as follows.

Dataset and System Description: The dataset considered was openly available brain MRI images and popularly known as "Brain Tumor Dataset -Figshare" which consists of 3064 brain MRI contrast-enhanced images. These images can be categorized into three categories such as meningioma, glioma, and pituitary tumors. There are about 708 images of meningioma tumors, 1426 images of glioma tumors, and 930 images of pituitary tumors as mentioned in Table 1. For effortlessly handling these categories, the categories meningioma, glioma, and pituitary tumors are encoded as 1, 2, and 3 respectively. For obtaining training and testing data, stratified- K fold is utilized by considering the number of folds as 8. The proposed framework mentioned was implemented in google Colab on the windows 10 operating system.

Table 1. Details of the brain tumor dataset - Figshare

Type of tumor	Number of MRI images	Percentage (%) of the total
Meningioma tumor	708	23.11%
Glioma tumor	1426	46.54%
Pituitary tumor	930	30.35%
Total	**3064**	**100%**

Deep Learning. Deep learning is the model inspired and mimicked by the human brain and it can be considered as an expansion of the neural network and a sub-section of machine learning. There is various type of deep learning models exists according to their specific usage. Some of the popular deep learning methodologies are classified according to the learning model such as a supervised learning model, and an unsupervised learning model. The supervised learning model includes classic neural networks which can also be considered as multilayer perceptron networks, convolutional neural networks (CNN), and recurrent neural networks (RNN). The Unsupervised learning model includes self-organizing maps (SOM), Boltzmann machines, and Autoencoders.

The classical NN used in the scenario utilizes the structured dataset that is ordered in rows and columns, it will be utilized in the problems related to classification and regression, and this model requires a higher level of flexibility and applicable to various data types.

Convolutional neural networks are used for the image type of datasets. Any CNN network architecture consists of various layers such as Convolutional layers, pooling layers, flattening layers, and fully connected layers. Convolution layers are responsible for feature mapping from the input data supplied and then the vital features will be extracted from filter mappings. Pooling layers are responsible for diminishing the size of the data obtained from convolutional layers. The flattening layer is responsible for converting multi-dimensional data into single-dimensional data. Single-dimension data passed on to fully-connected layers to get the output and then evaluate the loss function of the utilized model. CNN used in scenarios in which the dataset is of images.

A recurrent neural network (RNN) is majorly used for predicting the output of the sequential input. The populist RNN algorithm is Long short-term memory (LSTM). RNN can be utilized in the case of image classification, image captioning, sentiment analysis, and video classification.

Self-organizing maps are majorly used for an aspect of dimensional reduction by using the concept of the best-matching unit. SOM can be utilized in the case of dimensionality reduction and projects that are dealing with music or text or video directing towards artificial intelligence.

Boltzmann machines, unlike other neural network models or SOM, having no direction of implementation and it is defined over hyperspace parameters and so, this kind of model referred to as stochastic models. Boltzmann machines can be utilized for the building of recommendation systems, working with a monitoring system, and implementation of models with a very particular dataset.

Autoencoders are the models utilized to encode the provided input dataset according to the inputs and then passed on to the activation function then the obtained output will be decoded to generate the proper output. Different types of autoencoders exist such as sparse autoencoders, denoising autoencoders, contractive autoencoders, and stacked autoencoders. Autoencoders are mainly used for the detection of features or reducing the dimensionality of the dataset, for the construction of strong influential recommendation systems, and encoding various features from the input dataset. So, one can understand that while dealing with images, the more suitable deep learning model is a convolutional neural network (CNN). There are various CNN architectures are already exist in the research scenario.

VGG-16: A CNN Architecture. The VGG models are CNN architecture type designed to produce outstanding results in the ImageNet challenge, suggested by Karen Simonyan & Andrew Zisserman, of the Visual Geometry Group (VGG), Oxford University. In this article, we are using VGG-16 architecture. VGG16 is the CNN architecture used in 2014 to win ILSVR (Imagenet). It is recognized as one of the best architectural vision models until now. The most unique feature about VGG16 is to concentrate on providing convolution layers with 3×3 filters with phase 1 and using the same padding and max pool layer with 2×2 strands filter, instead of having a huge number of hyper-parameters. It is consistent in the architecture, follows this arrangement of convolution and max layers. In the end, it has 2 FC (fully-connected layers). The 16 in VGG16 corresponds to a weight of 16 layers. The network is quite wide and has about 138 million parameters and it is a very broad network. VGGNet-16 has 16 convolutionary layers, and it is very standardized architecture makes it very appealing. It just has 3×3 convolutions, but many filters, similar to AlexNet. The training will take 2–3 weeks on 4 GPUs. It is also the community's favorite alternative for extracting image functionality. The VGGNet's weight configuration is available and is used as a standard function extractor in many applications and challenges. VGGNet consists of 138 million parameters that can be a little difficult to manage. Transfer Learning allows VGG to be accomplished. The algorithm is pre-trained and modified for greater precision in a data set and you can use the parameter values. VGG-16 architecture can be seen as mentioned in Fig. 1.

Transfer Learning. Transfer learning is a type of machine learning methodology where the existing model is utilized for training aspects and certain additional layers are attached to the existing deep learning model to achieve better accuracy in the identification of certain aspects that are related to the problem. In the proposed framework, VGG-16 was used for the aspect of transfer learning for the detection and classification of various

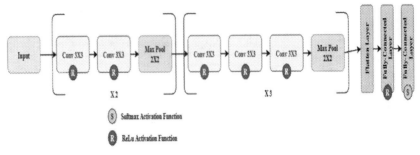

Fig. 1. VGG-16 architecture

brain tumors. The customized input layer was attached to the VGG-16 and three more fully-connected layers for the existing architecture.

Stratified K-Fold: It is the method utilized for the consideration of training and testing datasets to overcome the drawbacks in k-fold or probabilistic methods. Except for the method of partitioning the dataset, the procedure is the same as that of the K-Fold approach. In this approach, the partitioned data in such a way that the entire data can be best represented by each partition such that the bias can be removed and the uniformity of each partition can be combined to represent the entire data.

4   Results and Discussion

The approach was implemented by using conventional and popular CNN architecture called VGG-16 based transfer learning. The number of folds and the number of epochs considered are 8 and 15 respectively. The obtained training and validation accuracy can be mentioned as mentioned in the Table 2.

The key goal of the proposed approach is to obtain reasonable precision in the overall diagnosis and classification of each tumor. The accuracy obtained for the detection of the Meningioma Tumor is 98.66%, the accuracy obtained for the detection of the Glioma Tumor is 98.53%, and the accuracy obtained for the detection of the Pituitary Tumor is 99.54%. For justification of the obtained accuracies, more supporting evaluation metrics were evaluated such as precision, recall as well as F1-score. Higher the values of precision, recall, and F1-score, then those metrics strongly support the accuracies obtained which in return indicates the efficiency of the proposed model. The measurement parameters for each of the tumors derived from the proposed model are referred to in Table 3.

The mentioned evaluation metrics in Table 3 based on a report of the tumor-wise comparison of those metrics, as mentioned in Fig. 2. It shows the evaluation of metrics across various categories of tumors and is represented in graphical form. From this graphical representation, one can understand that the proposed model is highly effective with the pituitary tumors when compared with the other two tumors such as Meningioma and Glioma tumors.

Table 2. Training and validation accuracy details of the model VGG-16

Fold no	Training accuracy (%)	Validation accuracy (%)
1	89.63	82.51
2	92.50	94.26
3	93.88	96.87
4	95.49	97.91
5	96.23	93.47
6	95.74	98.43
7	98.14	93.73
8	97.35	97.65
Overall	**92.99**	**92.89**

Table 3. Evaluation metrics according to the tumor category

Tumor category	Accuracy (%)	Precision (%)	Recall (%)	F1-score
Meningioma tumor	98.66	95.25	99.15	97.16
Glioma tumor	98.53	99.36	97.48	98.41
Pituitary tumor	99.54	99.35	99.14	99.25

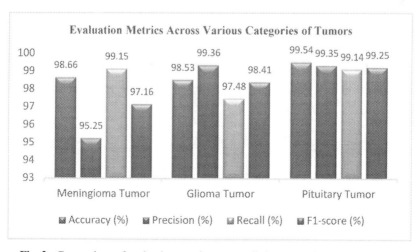

Fig. 2. Comparison of evaluation metrics across all the categories of brain tumors

To understand the effectiveness of the proposed model, the training loss and validation loss pair, as well as training loss and validation loss pair comparison are important.

So, in Fig. 3 and 4, those pairs of comparisons are mentioned. The comparison between training accuracy and validation accuracy is presented in Fig. 3, and the comparison between training loss and validation loss is represented in Fig. 4.

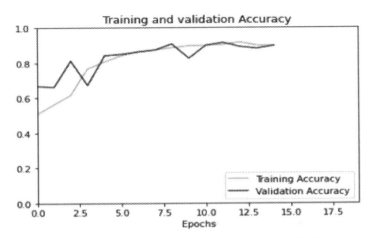

Fig. 3. The comparison between training accuracy and the validation accuracy

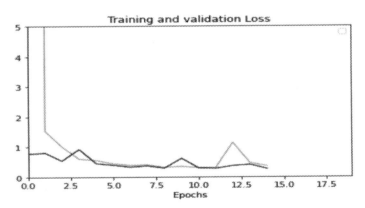

Fig. 4. The comparison between training loss and the validation loss

5   Future Scope and Conclusion

The detection of the classification of various brain tumors is very essential to make it reach common people for cost-effective as well as effective detection. Transfer learning is the extended version of a deep learning scenario. In this context, the additional layers will be attached to the existing model to achieve better accuracy and to reduce the training time. The proposed framework was based on VGG-16 with the concept of transfer learning attained an overall accuracy of about 92%. The accuracy of detection of meningioma tumors is 98.66%, The accuracy of detection of glioma tumors is 98.53%, and

The accuracy of detection of pituitary tumors is 99.54%. Besides, VGG-16 more CNN architectures adopted new concepts such as batch normalization, convolution blocks, and Identity blocks. Due to these, the accuracy of the model can be improved without increasing the depth of the model unnecessarily. This raises the scenarios of implementing the modern CNN architectures such as Inception-v3, ResNet-50, Inception-ResNets, and ResNeXt-50.

References

1. Kumar, A., Mukherjee, S., Luhach, A.K.: Deep learning with perspective modeling for early detection of malignancy in mammograms. J. Discrete Math. Sci. Cryptogr. **22**(4), 627–643 (2019)
2. Singh, C., Luhach, A.Kr., Kumar, A.: Improving focused crawling with genetic algorithms. Int. J. Comput. Appl. **66**(4) (2013)
3. Pradeepa, S., et al.: DRFS: detecting risk factor of stroke disease from social media using machine learning techniques. Neural Process. Lett. (2020). https://doi.org/10.1007/s11063-020-10279-8
4. Shallu, P.N., Kumar, S., Luhach, A.K.: Detection and analysis of lung cancer using radiomic approach. In: Luhach, A.K., Hawari, K.B.G., Mihai, I.C., Hsiung, PA., Mishra, R.B. (eds.) Smart Computational Strategies: Theoretical and Practical Aspects. Springer, Singapore (2019). https://doi.org/10.1007/978-981-13-6295-8_2
5. Khare, S., Gupta, N., Srivastava, V.: Optimization technique, curve fitting, and machine learning are used to detect brain tumors in MRI. In: Proceedings of IEEE International Conference on Computer Communication and Systems ICCCS 2014, pp. 254–259. IEEE, February 2014
6. Vaishnavee, K.B., Amshakala, K.: An automated MRI brain image segmentation and tumor detection using SOM-clustering and proximal support vector machine classifier. In: 2015 IEEE International Conference on Engineering and Technology (ICETECH). IEEE (2015)
7. George, D.N., Jehlol, H.B., Oleiwi, A.S.A.: Brain tumor detection using shape features and machine learning algorithms. Int. J. Adv. Res. Comput. Sci. Softw. Eng. **5**(10), 454–459 (2015)
8. Pan, Y., et al.: Brain tumor grading based on neural networks and convolutional neural networks. In: 2015 37th Annual International Conference of the IEEE Engineering in Medicine and Biology Society (EMBC). IEEE (2015)
9. Abdel-Maksoud, E., Elmogy, M., Al-Awadi, R.: Brain tumor segmentation based on a hybrid clustering technique. Egypt. Inform. J. **16**(1), 71–81 (2015)
10. Alfonse, M., Salem, A.-B.M.: An automatic classification of brain tumors through MRI using support vector machine. Egypt. Comput. Sci. J. **40**(3) (2016)
11. Işın, A., Direkoğlu, C., Şah, M.: Review of MRI-based brain tumor image segmentation using deep learning methods. Procedia Comput. Sci. **102**, 317–324 (2016)
12. Cabria, I., Gondra, I.: MRI segmentation fusion for brain tumor detection. Inf. Fusion **36**, 1–9 (2017)
13. Amin, J., et al.: Big data analysis for brain tumor detection: deep convolutional neural networks. Future Gener. Comput. Syst. **87**, 290–297 (2018)
14. Amin, J., et al.: Brain tumor detection using statistical and machine learning method. Comput. Methods Programs Biomed. **177**, 69–79 (2019)
15. Khampuria, A., Gupta, D., de Albuquerque, V.H.C., Sangaiah, A.K., Jhaveri, R.H.: Internet of health things-driven deep learning system for detection and classification of cervical cells using transfer learning. J. Supercomput. **76**(11), 8590–8608 (2020). https://doi.org/10.1007/s11227-020-03159-4

16. Tandel, G.S., et al.: Multiclass magnetic resonance imaging brain tumor classification using artificial intelligence paradigm. Comput. Biol. Med. **122**, 103804 (2020)
17. Khan, M.A., et al.: Multimodal brain tumor classification using deep learning and robust feature selection: a machine learning application for radiologists. Diagnostics **10**(8), 565 (2020)
18. Ahuja, S., Panigrahi, B.K., Gandhi, T.: Transfer learning based brain tumor detection and segmentation using superpixel technique. In: 2020 International Conference on Contemporary Computing and Applications (IC3A). IEEE (2020)
19. Pravitasari, A.A., et al.: UNet-VGG16 with transfer learning for MRI-based brain tumor segmentation. Telkomnika **18**(3), 1310–1318 (2020)

An Automatic Emotion Analysis of Real Time Corona Tweets

A. Kalaivani[1(✉)] and R. Vijayalakshmi[2]

[1] Department of Computer Science and Engineering, Saveetha School of Engineering,
Saveetha Institute of Medical and Technical Sciences, Chennai, Tamil Nadu, India
[2] IBM, Bangalore, India

Abstract. Emotion Analysis from text is a recent research field originated from Sentiment Analysis. The Sentiment Analysis identify the sentiments and classify them to positive, neutral, or negative sentiments based on the text. Emotion Analysis ocus to detect and recognize emotions through the text expression which are anger, disgust, fear, happiness, sadness and surprise. The real time applications of emotion analysis can be widely applied in software engineering, website customization, education, and gaming domains. Emotion Analysis can be done by gathering social media data such as twitter, reviews, blogs. Emotion Analysis can be done on the public opinion on a particular product or on a particular topic.

In this paper we are focusing to do emotion analysis of the public on real time recent corona tweets. The tweets are collected through twitter application interface. The collected real tweets are applied to pre-processing strategies to remove inconsistent and redundant factors and the pre-processed tweets are visualized through word cloud. The emotions scores are obtained using nrc_sentiment dictionary which contains basic emotions and both sentiments of positive or negative. The emotions score levels of the public are identified from the Corona Tweets and depicted through graphical analysis.

Keywords: Emotion analysis · COVID-19 tweets · Word cloud · nrc_sentiment dictionary

1 Introduction

Sentiment Analysis applies natural language processing to a text documents to understand the sentiments of the text. The outcome of Sentiment classification will classify the text into positive sentiments, negative sentiments or neutral sentiments. Sentiment polarity can be applicable to a whole textual document, sentence and word. The sentiment analysis can be applied to marketing to identify customer trends and then to medical to find the opinion of the patients on a particular disease. Twitter analysis can be used to identify the impact of the education system in the society. Twitter Analysis can be used to track trends and also expanded to disseminate health information during viral epidemics.

Coronavirus disease (COVID-19) is a global infectious disease originated in China during year end of 2019. COVID-19 started spreading across the world and people

© Springer Nature Singapore Pte Ltd. 2021
A. K. Luhach et al. (Eds.): ICAICR 2020, CCIS 1393, pp. 359–370, 2021.
https://doi.org/10.1007/978-981-16-3660-8_34

are still in pandemic situation. The symptoms of COVID-19 virus will have a mild to moderate respiratory illness and can be recovered easily at the initial stage without special treatment. Patients infected by COVID-19 virus are aged people with medical health issue related to heart problems, diabetics patient, respiratory irregularity and cancer patient have a chance of adaptability to this disease easily. Prevention Mechanism can be carried out to slow down COVID transmission by informing public about COVID-19 virus and also conduct awareness program. Simple mechanism is to protect ourself is by wash your hands frequently or using an sanitizer to keep yourself free. The COVID-19 virus spreads through personal contacts of the infected person with cough or cold by means of saliva droplets or nose discharge.

Our human being can interpret the sentiments of writing or speech. Based on the contextual understanding user can classify the sentHumans are gifted with the capability to interpret the tone of a piece of writing. Consider the sentence: "My flight"s been delayed. Brilliant!" Most of them quickly interpret the person as sarcastic, but having a delayed flight is not a good experience. By applying this contextual understanding user can classify the sentence into negative sentiments. Without contextual understanding, a machine look at the sentence "brilliant" and identify sentiment as positive. In this paper we are collecting some real time data on corona and we are going to show what people are thinking about Corona in terms of sentiment analysis.

Sentimental analysis is a resource available for any organization used to analyze and enhance their products and services. Mobile Usage is found with all communities and before purchase of any mobile we can analyze feedback from mobile users through online tweets. Online Mobile tweets from customers of their mobile products can be

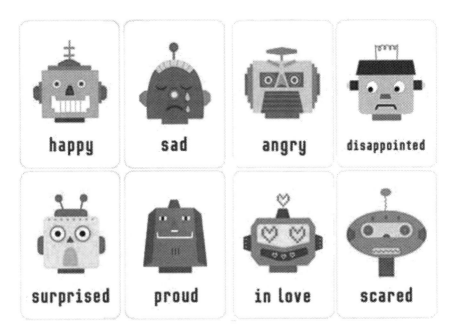

Fig. 1. Basic emotions classification

used for conducting a sentiment analysis. In this paper, the online mobile tweets are collected and processed to identify the emotion scores of mobiles users using R tool. The online mobile tweets are extracted and pre-processed and then classified the tweets into positive and negative sentiments and also their emotion scores are identified for the customers. The basic emotion classification system for online mobile tweets are depicted in Fig. 1.

The organization of the paper flow is as follows: Sect. 2 describes the researchers work on this domain and Sect. 3 describes system methodologies on process of gathering twitter data to emotion classification. The implementation of the proposed work in a stage by stage way is discussed in Sect. 5 and the paper is concluded with the contributions of the proposed work and future enhancement.

2 Literature Review

Many researchers contributed for their research work on pre-processing online tweets and twitter classification and further work also expanded on emotion score. Researchers concentrated much on stop phrase removal to achieving higher accuracy, formation of word cloud to identify frequent words, frequency count of accuracy for number of words present in the word cloud and finally sentiment emotions of overall tweets. Vijayalakshmi R, and A.Kalaivani, [1] proposed a brief information about word cloud formation and also pre processing techniques for apple mobile tweets finally accuracy of sentiment emotion score are depicted through bar graph.

Naramula Venkatesh and A.Kalaivani [2], proposed a preprocessing techniques for mobile tweets and formed word cloud visualization on apple mobile data sets and finding the frequency of the words. Bhattacharajee [3] et al. proposed a preprocessing algorithm for noise reduction based on lexicon. The Cosine Similarity Algorithm is proposed to classify the sentiment comment into a five point scale of -2 (highly negative) to $+2$ (highly positive). Ghag and shah [4] produced a research work by using movie document datasets to analyze the effect of stopwords removal on sentiment classification models. The proposed improved algorithm to produced better accuracy than traditional classifier. The survey is carried out with the classifier based on term weighting technique.

S. Rill et al. in [5], invented a system *PoliTwi* to detect emerging political topics in Twitter rather than other standard information channels. The identified *Top Topics* are shared via different channels towards wider publicity. The topics are compared with Google Trends and observed topics emerged in Twitter than in Google Trends. Finally, these topics can be used as a knowledge bases for concept-level sentiment analysis.

F. H. khan [6] et al. proposed an hybrid algorithm for twitter feeds classification. The proposed method applies contributed on multiple pre-processing steps before sent to the classifier. Proposed techniques overcomes the previous limitations and achieves higher accuracy when compared to the state-of-art techniques.

Rehab Duwairi, Mahmoud El-Orfali [7] anayzed the role of text pre-processing, feature selection and representation and classification using support vector machines. The level of accuracy achieved is improved when compared to the existing literature work. Duwairi and El-orfali [8] discussed sentiment analysis related to Arabic text. The sentiment analysis was investigated for Arabic text datasets with multiple classifiers of SVM, Naive Bayes and K-Nearest Neighbour. The experimental results shows that selection of preprocessing strategies on the input tweets increases the performance of the classifiers.

E. Haddi, X. Liu, and Y. Shi [9] demonstrated the role of text pre-processing in sentiment analysis. The experimental results focussed on appropriate feature selection and representation, sentiment analysis accuracies using support vector machines (SVM) achieved improved performance. Alexander Pak, Patrick Paroubek [10] performed Sentiment Analysis using microblogging. It is a popular communication tool among Internet users. The proposed work automatically collect a corpus for both sentiment analysis and opinion mining purposes. A textual analysis is performed on the collected corpus and a sentiment classifier is built to determine different types of sentiments. Proposed techniques are efficient and performed better than state of art techniquues. The research currently focussed on English language and in future can be expanded for any other languages. The primary issues discussed in literature review are classification accuracy such as most of the tweets with a very high percentage as neutral. The other issues to be considered by the researchers in future work are data sparsity and sarcasm.

3   System Methodology

Datas are gathered from users through web analytics tools which are independent, semi based and unreadable manner. From twitter API we are collecting some real time data on corona what people tweet about the virus and how they are protecting themselves from covid-19 and then the collected data is converted in the form of.csv files. The twitter data collected from the users is unstructured, incomplete, noisy and inconsistent. The data processing strategies are applied to discover knowledge records.

The general data pre-processing steps are removal of lowercase, punctuation, number, URL, special characters and expression. In the raw text stop words removal elimates noise from text by removing words such as "the," "and" and "a". Tokenization and Visualization are effective method to discover abstract thoughts and express information in the raw text. The outcomes of Sentiment analysis are represent in the form of Graphs, Histogrrams and Matrices. The most famous representation are Interactive Maps and Word Cloud. Visualization presentation are used in multimedia, medicine, education, engineering and technological applications. The words with biggest size is most frequently used and with much less length are least used.

In our proposed system, the dataset chosen for sentiment analysis is real time corona dataset. The datasets is applied to pre-processing strategies to remove inconsistent and redundant factors. Our proposed pre-processing techniques involves elimination of punctuations, special characters, digits, escaping HTML characters. Further the dataset is fine-tuned by applying removal of stop words, removal of URLs and removal of expressions. The pre-processed data visualization is represented as word cloud with the frequency of the key words. Finally the tweets are classified into emotions based on nrc-sentiment dictionary and descriptive analysis for the emotions in the form of graph. In Real-world the data may contain unreadable formats which lack in trends, unpolished, disorder and noisy data with errors. Data processing is the best pre-processing techniques to resolve and the proposed block diagram is shown in Fig. 2.

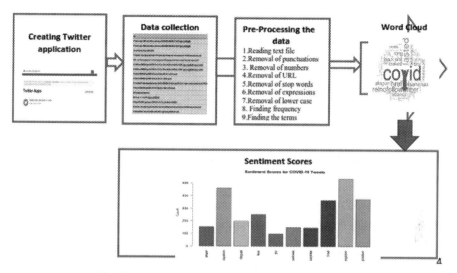

Fig. 2. Proposed system for automatic emotion analysis

a. *Data Collection*

Customers are free to express their comments on public forums like blogs, discussion boards and reviews. Public opinions are collected on private or public social network sites like Facebook and Twitter. Opinions and feelings are expressed in terms of vocabulary, context writing, short forms and slang. The data collected through pubic forums or social network are unstructured and huge disorganized data. The manual analysis of sentiment data is virtually impossible, so in our proposed work we used "R" tool for the efficient data analysis.

b. *Text Preparation*

The data collected through public forums should be filtered to extract the data for data analysis. Text preparation is done by eliminating non-textual content in the data collection. After the text preparation process the relevant data alone exist which can be used for further data analysis.

c. *Sentence Classification*

Preprocessed sentence are examined for subjectivity and objectivity expressions. Each sentence of the tweets are examined for subjectivity and objectivie expressions. Sentences with subjective expressions are retained and that which conveys objective expressions are discarded. The various computational techniques used for identifying subjective sentences are unigrams, lemmas, negation.

d. *Sentiment Scores*

The subjective sentence identified are further classified into two groups as positive and negative. Sentiment Anaysis plays a vital role to analyze and categorize the sentence into positive and negative tweets and the emotion scores are also calculated.

4 System Implementation

The steps to connect R and twitter API to extract Tweets on COVID-19 are

1. Make a Twitter account with the mobile number.
2. Create first Twitter app from this link -http://apps.twitter.com
3. Snap on Create New App. Pick a name for your app and give a concise depiction to your application and give your profile link.
4. Snap on "Create your Twitter application". On the off chance that your application is made and it should look like this as shown in the Fig. 3.

Fig. 3. Creation of Twitter APP

5. Open your application and go to "Keys and Access Tokens" to learn your Consumer Key (Programming Interface Key) and Consumer Secret (API Secret) key as shown in Fig. 4.

Fig. 4. Twitter data extraction -"Keys and Access Tokens"

6. If you're doing this for the primary time then you've got to scroll down on an equivalent keys and access tokens page and generate your Access tokens as shown in Fig. 5.

   R Studio is installed using the following steps:
1. Install necessary packages and load the libraries as shown in Fig. 6. These packages are important to install as they permit R interface to associate with twitter and offers validation to outsider applications.

Your Access Token

This access token can be used to make API requests on your own account's behalf. Do not share your access token secret with anyone.

Access Token	▬▬▬▬▬▬▬▬▬▬▬▬▬▬▬▬▬▬▬▬▬▬▬▬▬▬
Access Token Secret	▬▬▬▬▬▬▬▬▬▬▬▬▬▬▬▬▬▬▬▬▬▬▬▬▬▬
Access Level	Read and write
Owner	
Owner ID	

Fig. 5. Twitter data extraction

```
install.packages(c("twitteR","ROAuth","base64enc",
                   "httpuv","tm","SnowballC","wordcloud",
                   "RCplprBrewer"))
setwd("/users/parumohan/Desktop/project 4")
library(twitteR)
library(ROAuth)
library(base64enc)
library(httpuv)
library(tm)
library(SnowballC)
library(wordcloud)
library(RColorBrewer)
```

Fig. 6. Installing packages in R- studio

```
cred <- OAuthFactory$new(consumerKey=
                         consumerSecret=
                         requestURL='https://api.twitter.com/oauth/request_token',
                         acccesURL='https://api.twitter.com/oauth/access_token',
                         authURL='https://api.twitter.com/oauth/authorize')
##Usage of the following function
##Setup_twitter_oauth(consumer_key,consumer_secret, access_token, access_secret)
setup_twitter_oauth(
```

Fig. 7. Setting the connections between keys

2. Now set up the following commands to establish connections between keys as shown in Fig. 7.
3. The environment and connection for R to speak with Twitter has been found out and tweets are extracted. There are a few orders to remove tweets of a client or by utilizing a particular word. The R code to extract tweets on a particular word are specified in Fig. 8.

```
#To extract tweets based on a particular word
tweets <- searchTwitter("corona", n=1000, lang = "en", resultType = "recent")
class(tweets)
str(s_tweets)
tweets[1:10]
tweets <- twListToDF(tweets)
```

Fig. 8. Tweets extraction for a particular word

4. Finally the tweets are downloaded as shown below in Fig. 9.
5. Nearly 1500 recent tweets are downloaded. After downloading the tweets are easily converted into an.csv file for comfortable view. The tweets are downloaded using following queries Fig. 10.

[1] RT @sardesairajdeep: Good PM stayed away from expected China bashing: leave that to generals! Good he reiterated need to be corona consciou...

[2] RT @abbygov: bro I looked up how long the Black Plague lasted in an attempt to reassure myself about corona and that shit lasted 800 years...

[3] RT @surnell: #Coronil Ok Ok Not a cure for #Corona It is immunity booster that serves the same purpose. Let us buy it in big numbers now

[4] RT @abbygov: bro I looked up how long the Black Plague lasted in an attempt to reassure myself about corona and that shit lasted 800 years...

[5] @elonmusk @RationalEtienne @TimothyBuffett @WhatsupFranks @kimbal There is so little solid information about this -.. https://t.co/2eSBeYSEQx

[6] RT @nitinsehra10: On National Doctors Day today.. \nI salute all the doctors of this nation.. \n\nYou are taking so much pain to save us.. \n\nA...

[7] @lagosfather Boss the Corona virus is real actually. This hard saying this but I just recovered. So please stay safe

Fig. 9. Tweets after downloading

```
write.table(s_tweets,"/Users/parumohan/Desktop/COVID-19.csv",
            append = T, row.names = F, col.names = T, sep = "," )
```

Fig. 10. Tweets conversion into .CSV

From that csv file around 5–10 tweets are taken for data pre processing of tweets. The tweets are applied to tokenization in different structure, single tokenizers can include number of words present in sentences and shown in Fig. 11. The tweets upper case characters are converted into lowercase which are shown in Fig. 12.

[1] rt @sardesairajdeep: good pm stayed away from expected china bashing: leave that to generals! good he reiterated need to be corona consciou...

[2] rt @abbygov: bro i looked up how long the black plague lasted in an attempt to reassure myself about corona and that shit lasted 800 years...

[3] rt @surnell: #coronil ok ok not a cure for #corona it is immunity booster that serves the same purpose. let us buy it in big numbers now

[4] rt @abbygov: bro i looked up how long the black plague lasted in an attempt to reassure myself about corona and that shit lasted 800 years...

[5] @elonmusk @rationaletienne @timothybuffett @whatsupfranks @kimbal there is so little solid information about this -.. https://t.co/2esbeyseox

[6] rt @nitinsehra10: on national doctors day today.. \ni salute all the doctors of this nation.. \n\nyou are taking so much pain to save us.. \n
\na...
[7] @lagosfather boss the corona virus is real actually. it's hard saying this but i just recovered. so please stay safe

Fig. 11. Tweets after tokenization

[1] rt @sardesairajdeep: good pm stayed away from expected china bashing: leave that to generals! good he reiterated need to be corona consciou...

[2] rt @abbygov: bro i looked up how long the black plague lasted in an attempt to reassure myself about corona and that shit lasted 800 years...

[3] rt @surnell: #coronil ok ok not a cure for #corona it is immunity booster that serves the same purpose. let us buy it in big numbers now

[4] rt @abbygov: bro i looked up how long the black plague lasted in an attempt to reassure myself about corona and that shit lasted 800 years...

[5] @elonmusk @rationaletienne @timothybuffett @whatsupfranks @kimbal there is so little solid information about this -.. https://t.co/2esbeyseox

[6] rt @nitinsehra10: on national doctors day today.. \ni salute all the doctors of this nation.. \n\nyou are taking so much pain to save us.. \n
\na...
[7] @lagosfather boss the corona virus is real actually. it's hard saying this but i just recovered. so please stay safe

Fig. 12. Tweets converted to lower case

The tweets are further applied with the pre-processing and the tweets upper case characters are converted into lowercase which are shown in Fig. 12. Pre-processed tweets after the removal of punctuation mark are shown in Fig. 13 and removal of numbers are shown in Fig. 14. The pre-processed tweets after the removal of stop words are shown in Fig. 15 and removal of URL are shown in Fig. 16. Further, they are processed to remove whitespaces and the output of the tweets after removal of white space are shown in Fig. 17.

[1] rt sardesairajdeep good pm stayed away from expected china bashing leave that to generals good he reiterated need to be corona consciou..

[2] rt abbygov bro i looked up how long the black plague lasted in an attempt to reassure myself about corona and that shit lasted 800 year s..

[3] rt surnell coronil ok ok not a cure for corona it is immunity booster that serves the same purpose let us buy it in big numbers now

[4] rt abbygov bro i looked up how long the black plague lasted in an attempt to reassure myself about corona and that shit lasted 800 year s..

[5] elonmusk rationaletienne timothybuffett whatsupfranks kimbal there is so little solid information about this .. httpstco2esbeyseox

[6] rt nitinsehra10 on national doctors day today \ni salute all the doctors of this nation \n\nyou are taking so much pain to save us \n\n a..

[7] lagosfather boss the corona virus is real actually its hard saying this but i just recovered so please stay safe

Fig. 13. Tweets after removal of punctuations

[1] rt sardesairajdeep good pm stayed away from expected china bashing leave that to generals good he reiterated need to be corona consc iou..

[2] rt abbygov bro i looked up how long the black plague lasted in an attempt to reassure myself about corona and that shit lasted year s..

[3] rt surnell coronil ok ok not a cure for corona it is immunity booster that serves the same purpose let us buy it in big numbers now

[4] rt abbygov bro i looked up how long the black plague lasted in an attempt to reassure myself about corona and that shit lasted year s..

[5] elonmusk rationaletienne timothybuffett whatsupfranks kimbal there is so little solid information about this .. httpstcoesbeyseox

[6] rt nitinsehra on national doctors day today \ni salute all the doctors of this nation \n\nyou are taking so much pain to save us \n \nna..

[7] lagosfather boss the corona virus is real actually its hard saying this but i just recovered so please stay safe

Fig. 14. Tweets after removal of numbers

[1] rt sardesairajdeep good pm stayed away expected china bashing leave generals good reiterated need corona conscio u..

[2] rt abbygov bro looked long black plague lasted attempt reassure corona shit lasted years..

[3] rt surnell coronil ok ok cure corona immunity booster serves purpose let us buy big numbers now

[4] rt abbygov bro looked long black plague lasted attempt reassure corona shit lasted years..

[5] elonmusk rationaletienne timothybuffett whatsupfranks kimbal little solid information .. httpstcoesbeyseox

[6] rt nitinsehra national doctors day today \n salute doctors nation \n\n taking much pain save us \n\n..

[7] lagosfather boss corona virus real actually hard saying just recovered please stay safe

Fig. 15. Tweets after removal of stop words

The preprocessed tweets are applied to tokenization, where the tokens are extracted from the input tweets. The frequency of the words extracted are computed and depicted using bar graph as shown in Fig. 18. Word cloud is the visual representation of the tokenized words which are depicted in Fig. 19.

The final preprocessed tweets are applied to src_dictionary to identify the emotion scores and also to classify the tweets as positive or negative. The various emotions showed by the tweets are anger, disgust, fear joy, surprise and so on. The sentiment emotion score for COVID-19 Tweets are shown in Fig. 20.

[1] rt sardesairajdeep good pm stayed away expected china bashing leave   generals good reiterated need   corona conscio u...

[2] rt abbygov bro looked   long black plague lasted   attempt reassure   corona   shit lasted years...

[3] rt surnell coronil ok ok   cure corona   immunity booster serves   purpose let us buy   big numbers now

[4] rt abbygov bro looked   long black plague lasted   attempt reassure   corona   shit lasted years...

[5] elonmusk rationaletienne timothybuffett whatsupfranks kimbal   little solid information   .. httpstcoesbeyseox

[6] rt nitinsehra national doctors day today \n salute   doctors   nation \n\n taking much pain save us \n\n...

[7] lagosfather boss corona virus real actually hard saying   just recovered please stay safe

Fig. 16. Tweets after removal of URL

[1] rt sardesairajdeep good pm stayed away expected china bashing leave generals good reiterated need covid conscio u...

[2] rt abbygov bro looked long black plague lasted attempt reassure covid shit lasted years...

[3] rt surnell coronil ok ok cure covid immunity booster serves purpose let us buy big numbers now

[4] rt abbygov bro looked long black plague lasted attempt reassure covid shit lasted years...

[5] elonmusk rationaletienne timothybuffett whatsupfranks kimbal little solid information ...

[6] rt nitinsehra national doctors day today salute doctors nation taking much pain save us ...

[7] lagosfather boss covid virus real actually hard saying just recovered please stay safe

Fig. 17. Tweets after removal of whitespace

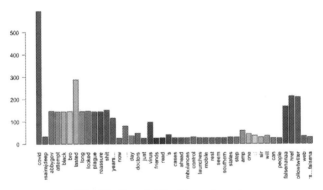

Fig. 18. Bar plot for frequent words

Fig. 19. Word cloud formation

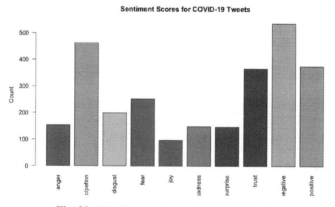

Fig. 20. Emotion scoring on COVID-19 tweets

5   Conclusion

Sentiment Emotion Scoring for COVID-19 tweets shows the negativity as high because all people think that is very dangerous and no medicine was found still. People are afraid of that diseases so the emotion scoring for negativity is high. People who are recovered from covid have tweeted on how to take self-care and their experience on covid. Future scope of the proposed work can be related to any other pandemic diseases or on products to give direction for the customers. Emotion scoring identified for the whole tweets based on words and in future we can classify sentiments for individual tweets based on the emotion score of individual tweets and can further analyse the data at an extreme point of view.

References

1. Vijayalakshmi, R., Kalaivani, A.: Sentiment emotion scoring for Apple mobile tweets. Test Eng. Manag. **82**, 6756–6763 (2020)

2. Kalaivani, A., Venkatesh, N.: Word cloud for online mobile phone tweets towards sentiment analysis. Int. J. Eng. Adv. Technol. **8**(6), 2249–8958 (2019)
3. Bhattacharjee, S., Das, A., Bhattacharya, U., Parui, S.K., Roy, S.: Sentiment analysis using cosine similarity measure. In: IEEE 2nd International Conference Recent Trends in Information Systems (ReTIS), pp. 27–32 (2015)
4. Ghag, K., Shah, K.: Comparing analysis of effect of stop words removal on sentiment classification. In: IEEE International Conference on Computer Communication and Control, pp. 2–7 (2015)
5. Rill, S., Reinel, D., Scheidt, J., Zicari, R.: Early detection of emerging Politics topic on twitter and the impact on concept-level sentiment analysis. Knowl.-Based Syst. **69**, 24–33 (2014)
6. Khan, F.H., Bashir, S., Qamar, U.: TOM: Twitter opinion mining Frame work using hybrid classification scheme. Decis. Support Syst. **57**(1), 245–257 (2014)
7. Duwairi, R., El-Orfali, M.: A study of the effects of preprocessing strategies on sentiment analysis for Arabic text. J. Inf. Sci. 215–221 (2014)
8. Duwairi, R., Elorfali, M.: A study of the effects of preprocessing strategies on sentiment analysis for Arabic text. J. Inf. Sci. 1–13 (2013)
9. Haddi, E., Liu, X., Shi, Y.: The role of text pre-processing in sentiment analysis. Procedia Comput. Sci. **17**, 26–32 (2013)
10. Pak, A., Paroubek, P.: Twitter as a corpus for sentiment analysis and opinion mining. In: Proceedings of the International Conference on Language Resources and Evaluation, pp. 17–23 (2010)

Human Activity Classification Using Machine Learning Techniques with Feature Selection

P. Maneesha$^{(\boxtimes)}$ and Nagadeepa Choppakatla

Department of Electronics and Communication Engineering, VNR Vignana Jyothi Institute of Engineering and Technology, Hyderabad, India
nagadeepa_ch@vnrvjiet.in

Abstract. Recognition of human activities is a field of rising interest in the present transformation. Recognizing the activities allows the applications in constructing the activity profiles for every subject that could be used efficiently for the health and safety applications. Nowadays smartphones are upgraded with remarkable motion sensors to revitalize the entryways in machine learning. According to human activity recognition, datasets for the corresponding work have been increased that paves the way for certainties in different research areas. The human activity recognition dataset includes accelerometer sensor data with respect to six different human activities for example sitting, standing, lying, walk, upstairs walk, downstairs walk. The paper presents the human activity recognition process by analyzing the filter-based feature selection methods in the machine learning model. For activity classification, various classifiers are used as Support Vector Machine (SVM), K Nearest Neighbor (KNN), Random Forest and Decision Tree classifiers. The performance of the model is validated using Train/test split approach. Therefore, for activity recognition, we proposed a model giving better results with a random forest classifier and correlation-based feature selection with best-first search.

Keywords: Accelerometer · Correlation-based feature selection · Human activity recognition · KNN · SVM · Random forest

1 Introduction

Tracking the activities of the human has become the trendy topic with the fusion of machine learning with the vision based and sensor-based technologies. Recognition of human behaviour is one of the open challenges that draws further attention in many fields. It is needed by a number of other applications such as health monitoring, defence, military and many more [12]. Recognition activities can allow the computing system to assist individuals with his or her needs. Sensor-based and vision-based methods can be used for the monitoring the required activities. Any of the above mentioned approaches are not so impressive and cannot impact human activities in any way. It is found that the usage of the sensor-based methodology of information gathering from humans is superior to the other method besides. The sensor-based method might corrupt the collected information and is more concious to noise [20].

© Springer Nature Singapore Pte Ltd. 2021
A. K. Luhach et al. (Eds.): ICAICR 2020, CCIS 1393, pp. 371–380, 2021.
https://doi.org/10.1007/978-981-16-3660-8_35

The smart mobiles are used to constitutive for successful day-to-day apprehend of human activities just for standing, sitting, walking upstairs, walking downstairs, and walking. Having the smart mobiles equipped with sensors paves the way for tracking human activities. The information or data collected through the accelerometer sensors will aid in tracking the elderly and help in assisting them with medical treatment if needed. The purpose of human activity recognition is used to establish a model that removes the distinction intervening the planned activity and real activity that has been carried out. Extraction of the required features is the key for recognizing human activities. To recognize the activities, feature selection and classifiers are used for predicting activities, WEKA is used as a machine learning tool for implementing machine learning strategies.

The paper presents, how different supervised machine learning approaches are used to classify human activities. The rest of the paper is structured as: Sect. 2 includes the summary of related literature. Section 3 evolves the methodology suggested for this analysis. Section 4 addresses the findings obtained and their success assessment and the paper concludes in Sect. 5.

2   Literature Review

The human activity recognition system faces several challenges in the current world. The related studies are discussed in this section. Pierluigi Casale et al. [1] made an activity recognition system that can be portable enough to carry them. Recognition is done by a random forest classifier with twenty computational features. In this experiment, nearly 94% accuracy is obtained in classifying human activities. Dean M. Karantonis et al. [2] projected the real-time classification system for implementing the human movements which are obtained from a waist mounted tri-axial accelerometer device. Various movements with normal day-to-day activities with a total of twelve tasks with 238 tests involving 6 subjects were considered. The accuracy obtained was 90.8%. A. M. Khan et al. [3] presented a global approach to address the problems related to triaxial accelerometer activity recognition. Validation has been done by using six day-to-day physical activities. The accuracy obtained is nearly 95%. The activity information was obtained from the most apparent body positions of the triaxial accelerometer. Martin Berchtold et al. [4] proposed a Recurrent Fuzzy Inference System with modular classification methodology. An explicit study showing the system reaction when adding a new classifier set is presented with the existing system. This methodology is presented by using the bit masking which is recognized using a genetic algorithm.The Dynamic queue can be used to improve the old and new approaches. The accuracy of 95% is obtained by using the filtering approach to it. Mark A. Hall [6] analysed the usage of correlation based feature selection for recognizing the human activities.

3   Methodology

All the previous papers proposed mostly does not necessarily make uses feature selection method. The proposed work describes the process of classifying the activities by using machine learning techniques such as KNN, SVM, Random forest and Decision tree algorithms with selected features. The model focuses on classification preceeded by feature selection and normalization. The proposed model is shown in Fig. 1.

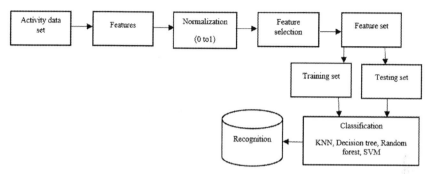

Fig. 1. Frame work for Activity recognition

3.1 Activity Dataset

In this research, we consider the smartphone accelerometer sensor fratures in the HAR dataset. This data is an imbalanced dataset and is associated from UCI machine learning archive and comprise six different activities [18] with a total of 7352 training feature instances and 2947 testing feature instances as given in Table 1.

Table 1. Human activity recognition dataset

Class	Activity	Test instances	Train instances
1	Standing	532	1374
2	Sitting	491	1286
3	Lying	537	1407
4	Walking	496	1226
5	Walking upstairs	471	1073

The data gathered from 30 volunteers and the movements including Upstairs walk, Downstairs walk, Sitting, Standing, and Lying are to be sensed. The sensors that are used are gyro and accelerometer embedded for detecting the angular velocity and linear acceleration of the three-axis at a 50 Hz frequency constant rate. By adding noise and later using a tight width sliding window of 2.5 s for 50% overlap, pre-processing and sampling were enforced to the captured sensor data. Butterworth low-pass filter has been accustomed to separate the sensor's longitudinal and body motion components from data about gravity and body acceleration. The cutoff frequency of 0.3 Hz filter is to provide the gravitation force that only has components of lower frequencies. Time and frequency-domain variables endure building the feature vector against each window. Dataset descriptions are given in Table 1 [12]. Figure 2 portrays six activities performed by 30 different volunteers with different instances.

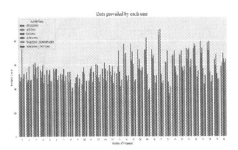

Fig. 2. Activity instances collected from 30 volunteers.

3.2 Features

Every sampled window produces a feature vector. In conventional methods correlation, mean, signal magnitude area and autoregression coefficients were used as the extracted features. In this work angle between vectors, frequency skewness and frequency bands are the new features are included in feature extraction. The total number of accelerometer features taken from the sensor feature vector are listed in Table 2. In this, Time-domain signals and Fast fouriar transforms are applyed for raw accelerometer data. (note t indicates time and f indicate frequency).

Table 2. Total Accelerometer data measure for computing feature vector

Feature vector	Signals
tBodyAcc-XYZ, tBodyAccJerk-XYZ, tBodyAccMag, tGravityAccMag, tBodyAccJerkMag, fBodyAccJerk-XYZ, fBodyAccMag, fBodyAccJerkMag	mean, std, mad, max, min, sma, energy, iqr, entropy, arCoeff, correlation, maxInds, meanFreq, skewness, kurtosis, bands Energy, angle.

3.3 Normalization

A normalization is an approach that is intermittently constituted in machine learning data processing. The purpose of normalization is to accommodate a standard scale from binary column values in the dataset, without altering the value ranges is using Eq. (1).

$$M_{normalized} = \frac{M - M_{min}}{M_{max} - M_{min}} \tag{1}$$

Where M_{max} is maximum value in the dataset and M_{min} is the minimum value in the data set.

3.4   Feature Selection

The proposed approach is a filter-based feature selection. The Model has divided into two categories; they are the Best first search and the Greedy search. The workflow of the human activities is classified as shown in Fig. 3.

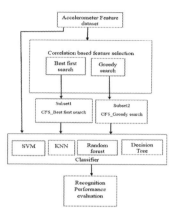

Fig. 3.   Activity classification with filter-based feature selection.

There are six activities are collected from the accelerometer feature dataset and it consists of 348 features per each activity and a total of 10299 instances. Figure 4 depicts the accelerometer sensor based feature dataset which is an imbalanced dataset. The horizontal axis depicts different activities and the vertical axis is the count of a number of instances. The data set is further processed with correlation based feature selection.

Fig. 4.   Accelerometer feature dataset

3.4.1   Feature Reduction Using Correlation Based Feature Selection

Using the standardization method, we changed the values 0 to 1 after applying the selection technique to use the set of correlation-based functions. Correlation based Feature Selection (CFS) is filter based feature selection algorithm that ranks the feature subsets allows the heuristic evaluation function based on correlation. The evaluation function's bias is towards subset1 and subset2. Here subset1 is extracted from best first search and subset2 is extracted from greedy search and these subsets contain the features which are highly correlated among the class and uncorrelated to one another. Unimportant features would be overlooked, in that they would get the poor class correlation. Irrelevant features would be filtered out because one or more of the remaining features can strongly overlap with them. Accepting a function may lean on the degree to which it anticipates classes in areas not already predicted by other features in the instance space. The subset evaluation function [6] of the CFS feature is given in Eq. 2.

$$Z_s = \frac{N\left(\overline{r_{ij}}\right)}{\sqrt{N + N(N-1)\left(\overline{r_{ij}}\right)}} \tag{2}$$

Where Z_s is the heuristic merit for feature subset S, the number of features is N, the mean correlation of feature to class is $\overline{r_{ij}}$, the average correlation feature to feature is $\overline{r_{jj}}$.

First, we apply the best first search method in correlation-based feature selection and then we apply the Greedy search method. These methods are used for feature dimensionality reduction.

3.5   Classification

The activities are classified based on the features set and feature subset1, feature subset2. The proposed work uses four classifiers. They are:

3.5.1   KNN

The algorithm k-nearest to neighbours (KNN) supports both classification and regression [5]. It works by maintaining and quantifying the entire training dataset to find similar training patterns of different tasks in k while making a prediction. As it stands, there is no model other than training the raw dataset, and where the prediction is made, the only computation performed is to query the training data set. KNN will take the mode (most common class) of the most related instances of time domain and frequency domain activities in the training dataset when making predictions on classification problems. Different values of K-nearest neighbours the accuracy is determined shown in Table 3.

3.5.2   SVM

Support Vector Machine (SVM) is designed for problems of binary classification, while extensions to the technique were developed to support problems of multi-class classification and regression [5]. SVM works by finding a line that properly classifies the dissimilar activities. Certain instances considered from a training set are called support vectors.

3.5.3   Random Forest

Random forests or random decision forests are an ensemble learning method for classification, regression, and other tasks that by work by building a number of decision trees at training period and this data which is also known as bootstrapped data is useful for estimating the status of individual trees [9].

3.5.4 Decision Tree

A decision tree is a hierarchical node mapping technique that helps in predicting the response of the dataset [5]. The branch roots depicts the classification outputs such as standing, sitting and other activities considered.

3.6 Train/Test Split Approach for Validating the Proposed Model

Assessing the models with the resampling procedure helps in estimating the precision of the classification process as shown in Fig. 5.

Fig. 5. Train/test split approach

The splitting uses few data instances for training and the remaining data for testing instances. This validation process helps in evaluating the model accuracy. The accelerometer data is split into 70% training data and 30% testing data. And 80% traing data and 20% testing data.

4   Results and Discussion

In this research, we analysed the feature extraction and selection effects on classification accuracy and are discussed in Table 3. Here total extracted features are of 348 features are used for activity recognition. Among these features, two feature subsets are generated with the application of correlation based feature selection. By applying CFS_best first search method 44 selected attributes are obtained and are called subset1. By applying CFS_ greedy search method 44 selected attributes are obtained and are called as subset2. For subset1 selected feature plot is shown in Fig. 6. It shows six activities with 44 features per each activity and total of 10299 instances.

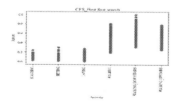

Fig. 6. Selected feature plot using CFS_Best first search

By using the best first search in correlation based feature selection method 44 features are obtained and its labels are described in Fig. 7. These features that make most of the contribution in prediction value are selected. The selected features are used in the classification process with different algorithms.

tBodyAcc-max()-X	tBodyAcc-max()-X	fBodyAcc-max()-X	tBodyAcc-max()-X	fBodyAcc-max()-X
tBodyAcc-entropy()-X	tBodyAcc-entropy()-X	fBodyAcc-entropy()-X	tBodyAcc-entropy()-X	fBodyAcc-entropy()-X
tBodyAcc-correlation()-X,Y	fBodyAcc-correlation()-X,Y	tBodyAcc-correlation()-X,Y	fBodyAcc-correlation()-X,Y	tBodyAcc-correlation()-X,Y
tGravityAcc-mean()-X	tGravityAcc-mean()-X	tGravityAcc-mean()-X	tGravityAcc-mean()-X	tGravityAcc-mean()-X
tGravityAcc-mean()-Y	tGravityAcc-mean()-Y	tGravityAcc-mean()-Y	tGravityAcc-mean()-Y	tGravityAcc-mean()-Y
tGravityAcc-std()-X	tGravityAcc-std()-X	tGravityAcc-std()-X	tGravityAcc-std()-X	tGravityAcc-std()-X
tGravityAcc-max()-X	tGravityAcc-max()-X	tGravityAcc-max()-X	tGravityAcc-max()-X	tGravityAcc-max()-X
tGravityAcc-max()-Y	tGravityAcc-max()-Y	tGravityAcc-max()-Y	tGravityAcc-max()-Y	tGravityAcc-max()-Y
tGravityAcc-max()-Z	tGravityAcc-max()-Z	tGravityAcc-max()-Z	tGravityAcc-max()-Z	tGravityAcc-max()-Z

Fig. 7. Selected features- Subset1 labels with CFS_Best first search

Here activity classification is done with three different feature sets are Accelerometer feature data with 348 features, Subset1 (CFS-Best first search) with 44 features, and Subset2 (CFS-Greedy search) with 44 features which are shown in Table 3. Evolution of test results involved accelerometer data analyzing the extracted feature data and selected feature data.

Table 3. Performance of activity recognition with various classifiers

Feature set	Number of features	Decision Tree	Random forest	KNN K=1	KNN K=3	KNN K=5	SVM
Accelerometer feature data	348	93.8693%	96.0287%	94.3264%	93.7378%	93.6593%	95.1942%
Subset 2 (CFS-Greedy search)	44	95.0971%	97.1162%	91.9903%	92.6699%	93.0097%	93.5437%
Subset 1 (CFS-Best first search)	44	95.0485%	97.2813%	91.8932%	92.6698%	92.9612%	95.4931%

On applying different algorithms to 10299 instances, different performance characteristics are observed. In KNN, for k = 1 with greedy search feature selection method, the performance of the model is 91.9903% accurate, for k = 3 the model is 92.6699% accurate and for k = 5 the model is 93.5437% accurate. In the Decision Tree greedy search feature selection method, the performance of the model is 95.0971% accurate. The model performs its best when the SVM algorithm is applied without any feature selection technique. Random forest CFS_Best first search method performance of the model is 97.2813% accurate. Among all classifiers, the Random forest classifier yields the best performance for activity recognition with CFS-Best first search method.

For validating the proposed machine learning model using Randomforest classifier with CFS-Best first search for activity recognition. Analysed the model with Train/Test Split approach and without split approach. In this Train/Test Split approch 70:30 and 80:20 are used for analysis.The performance of the model is shown in Fig. 8. The complete accelerometer data is used without splitting the instances with 10299 intsances.

The activities are classified using random forest classifier without split and with split approach on three feature datasets are of featre data, selected feature subsets are subset1 and subset2. By analysing the results the proposed model gives the better accuracy with 80:20 split approach for subset1- selected feature dataset.

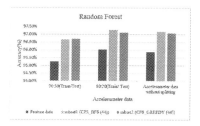

Fig. 8. Train /Test split approach for model evolution for random forest

5 Conclusion

In this paper, feature selection is applied to the human activity recognition UCI dataset (accelerometer dataset). This dataset contains the 6 activity classes, 348 features and 10299 instances.The data set is split into 70% training, 30% testing and 80% training, 20% testing. The approach uses the correlation based feature selection with best first search and greedy search methods and the classifiers such as KNN, SVM, Decision tree and Random forest are used for activity recognition with three feature sets. By analysing the filter based feature selection methods and by analysing the validation approaches we are concluding that for activity recognition, random forest classifier with CFS-Best first search yields the best results.

References

1. Casale, P., Pujol, O., Radeva, P.: Human activity recognition from accelerometer data using a wearable device. In: Vitrià, J., Sanches, J.M., Hernández, M. (eds.) Pattern Recognition and Image Analysis, pp. 289–296. Springer, Heidelberg (2011). https://doi.org/10.1007/978-3-642-21257-4_36
2. Karantonis, D.M., Narayanan, M.R., Mathie, M., Lovell, N.H., Celler, B.G.: Implementation of a real-time human movement classifier using a triaxial accelerometer for ambulatory monitoring. IEEE Trans. Inf. Technol. Biomed. **10**(1), 156–167 (2006). https://doi.org/10.1109/TITB.2005.856864
3. Khan, M., Lee, Y.K., Lee, S.Y.: Accelerometers position free human activity recognition using a hierarchical recognition model. In: The 12th IEEE International Conference on e-Health Networking, Applications and Services, Lyon, pp. 296–301 (2010). https://doi.org/10.1109/HEALTH.2010.5556553
4. Berchtold, M., Budde, M., Schmidtke, H.R., Beigl, M.: An extensible modular recognition concept that makes activity recognition practical. In: Dillmann, R., Beyerer, J., Hanebeck, U.D., Schultz, T. (eds.) KI 2010. LNCS (LNAI), vol. 6359, pp. 400–409. Springer, Heidelberg (2010). https://doi.org/10.1007/978-3-642-16111-7_46
5. Bullbul, E., Cetin, A., Dogru, I.A.: Human activity recognition using smartphone. In: 2018 2nd International Symposium on Multidisciplinary Studies and Innovative Technology (ISMSIT), p. 16 (2018)
6. Hall, M.A., Smith, L.A.: Feature subset selection: a correlation based filter approach. Department of Computer Science, University of Waikato, Hamilton, New Zealand (1999)
7. Gopika, N., Kowshalaya, A.M.: Correlation based feature selection algorithm for machine learning. In: 3rd International Conference on Communication and Electronics Systems (ICCES), Coimbatore, India, pp. 692–695 (2018)

8. Blessie, E.C., Karthikeyan, E.: Sigmis: a feature selection algorithm using correlation based method. J. Algorithms Comput. Technol. **2012**, 385–394 (2012)

9. Subasi, A., Radhwan, M., Kurdi, R., Khateeb, K.: IOT based mobile healthcare system for human activity recognition. In: 2018 15th Learning and Technology Conference (L&T), Jeddah, pp. 9929–9934 (2018)

10. Cheng, L., Guan, Y., Zhu, K., Li, Y.: Recognition of human activity recognition using machine learning methods with wearable sensors. In: IEEE 7th Annual Computing and Communication Workshop and Conference (CCWC), Las Vegas, NV, pp. 1–7 (2017)

11. Bayat, A., Pomplun, M., Tran, D.A.: A study on human activity recognition using accelerometer data from smartphones. Procedia Comput. Sci. **34**, 450–457 (2014). https://doi.org/10.1016/j.procs.2014.07.009

12. Bharathi, B., Bhuvana, J.: Human activity recognition using deep and machine learning algorithms. Int. J. Innov. Technol. Exp. Eng. (IJITEE) **9**(4), 1–7 (2020). ISSN 2278-3075

13. Hall, M.A.: Correlation-based feature selection, for machine learning. This thesis is submitted in partial fulfilment of the requirement for the degree of Doctor of Philosophy at the University of Waikato (1999)

14. Yang, J.-Y., Wang, J.-S., Chen, Y.-P.: Using acceleration measurements for activity recognition: an effective learning algorithm for constructing neural classifiers. Pattern Recogn. Lett. **29**(16), 2213–2220 (2008)

15. Khan, M., Lee, Y., Lee, S.Y., Kim, T.: Human activity recognition via an accelerometer-enable-smartphone using kernel discriminant analysis. In: 5th International Conference on Feature Information Technology, Busan, pp. 1–6 (2010)

16. Chen, Y., Xue, Y.: A deep learning approach to human activity recognition based on single accelerometer. In: IEEE International Conference on Systems, Man, and Cybernetics, Kowloon, pp. 1488–1492 (2015)

17. Chattya, G., Whiteb, M., Akthera, F.: Smart phone based data mining for human activity recognition. In: International Conference on Information and Communication Technologies, ICICT (2014)

18. Anguita, D., Ghio, A., Reyes Ortiz, J.L., et al.: A public domain dataset for human activity recognition using smartphone. In: 21st European Symposium on Artificial Neural Networks, Computational Intelligence and Machine Learning ESANN, Bruges, Belgium (April 2013)

19. Anguita, D., Ghio, A., Oneto, L.: Energy efficient smartphone based activity recognition using fixed point arithmetic. J. Univ. Comput. Sci. **19**(9), 1295–1314 (2013)

20. Bhattacharyya, S., Mukul, M.K., Luhach, A.K., Rodrigues, J.J.P.C.: Motor imagery-based neuro-feedback system using neuronal excitation of the active synapses. Ann. Telecommun., 1–16 (2019). https://doi.org/10.1007/s12243-019-00740-8

21. Dinh Le, T., van Nguyen, C.: Human activity recognition by smartphone. In: 2nd National Foundation for Science and Technology Development Conference on Information and Computer Science (NICS), Ho Chi Minh City, pp. 219–224 (2015). https://doi.org/10.1109/NICS.2015.7302194

Analysis and Prediction of Covid-19

Abrar Athar Hashmi$^{(\boxtimes)}$ and Abdul Wahed

Department of Computer Science and Engineering, CBIT, Hyderabad, India

Abstract. Coronaviruses are a family of related viruses that cause diseases in mammals. Middle East Respiratory Syndrome (MERS-CoV) and Severe Acute Respiratory Syndrome (SARS-CoV) are pandemics the world has already faced. It's a contagious virus that originating in Wuhan, spreading across the World, and was later declared a Pandemic by WHO. It has led to a total of 75 million+ cases and 1.4 million+ deaths across the globe. It has become necessary to understand its spread. There is no doubt that this epidemic has become a disaster for all mankind. This paper is an effort to analyze the cumulative number of deaths, active cases, and recovered cases since its inception. Intuitive visualizations and inferences are made. Time series forecasting models are developed to predict the number of active cases in India.

Keywords: Covid-19 · ARIMA · K-means clustering

1 Introduction

The pandemic has led to adverse effects on human lives and loss of livelihood. A huge number of companies are going out of business and the 200 countries span a variety of social, economic, health, and climatic conditions. It's imperative to develop data processing tools that will facilitate scientists in finding valuable insights. The COVID-19 dataset is a real-time comprehensive collection of data available for transformation into meaningful patterns. This will enable data scientists across the world to share their insights with doctors helping them develop preventive measures and medications.

Every Pandemic has three stages [1]:

Stage 1: Beginning of Local Transmission
Stage 2: Countries impacted with local transmission
Stage 3: Significant Transmission across the World.

2 Related Work

This paper is an effort to analyze the cumulative number of deaths, active cases, and recovered cases. The primary goal is to obtain valuable insights related to the spread of this virus all over the World.

The Dataset consists of time-series data from 22 JAN 2020 to Till date (Updated on daily Basis) [2] (Table 1).

It consists of the following data (Table 2)

© Springer Nature Singapore Pte Ltd. 2021
A. K. Luhach et al. (Eds.): ICAICR 2020, CCIS 1393, pp. 381–393, 2021.
https://doi.org/10.1007/978-981-16-3660-8_36

Table 1. List of parameters analyzed from the world Covid-19 data

| Province/State |
| Country/Region |
| Date |
| Confirmed |
| Deaths |
| Recovered |
| Active |

Table 2. Sample data

	Province/State	Country/Region	Date	Confirmed	Deaths	Recovered	Active
0		Afghanistan	2020-01-22	0	0	0	0
1		Albania	2020-01-22	0	0	0	0
2		Algeria	2020-01-22	0	0	0	0
3		Andorra	2020-01-22	0	0	0	0
4		Angola	2020-01-22	0	0	0	0
...	...	...	...	...	...	...	...
87205		Vietnam	2020-12-28	1451	35	1303	113
87206		West Bank and Gaza	2020-12-28	134310	1332	110927	22051
87207		Yemen	2020-12-28	2096	607	1384	105
87208		Zambia	2020-12-28	19943	384	18296	1263
87209		Zimbabwe	2020-12-28	13148	354	10705	2089

87210 rows × 7 columns

3   Proposed System

There are three steps:

1. Preprocessing of Data
2. Visualization of Data
3. Training and Testing

3.1   Preprocessing of Data

3.1.1   Data Cleaning

Noisy, irrelevant data is identified and removed. We also understand through visualization which factors are more important an highly correlated.

3.1.2 Identifying Missing Values

There can be missing values. We will investigate each column with total missing values. We will not be replacing it with the mean or median value since the dataset is big enough to perform analysis.

3.2 Visualization Data

Various technologies are used to obtain inferences from the data through intuitive patterns.

3.2.1 Pandas

It is a high-level package for doing practical, real-world data analysis in Python [3].
    Pandas is well suited for different kinds of data:

- Ordered and unordered time series data.
- Tabular and Random matrix data (homogeneously or heterogeneous) with row and column labels.

3.2.2 Matplotlib and Plotly

Matplotlib is a plotting package that provides MATLAB-like plotting functionality. Matplotlib utilities lie under the pyplot submodule. Matplotlib is designed to be as usable as MATLAB, with the ability to use Python.
    Plotly is another high-level Python visualization library which is capable of handling geographical, scientific and statistical data.

3.2.3 K-Means Clustering

K-Means Clustering: It is an unsupervised algorithm used to classify data into a specific number of clusters (k). Elbow method is a popular method to determine the optimal value of k by running k-means clustering for a range of values e.g.: 1 to 10 by using Within Cluster Sum of Squares [4] (Fig. 1).

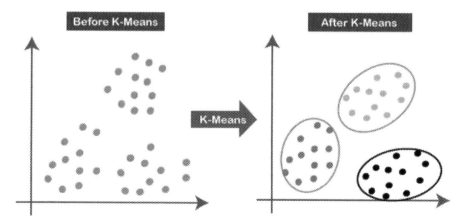

Fig. 1. K-means clustering explained

3.3 Training and Testing

3.3.1 Validation

Machine learning, particularly supervised learning techniques need data to train, test, and validate the model. A big quantity of the training data is to be used to train the model and a small quantity is utilized for verifying the predictions. This validation process gives us information that helps in adjusting our hyperparameters to improve accuracy. After training the model, testing data is used to test it. This testing data is different from the training and validation data used earlier.

The dataset is split into a ratio like 60:40, 80:20 based on the use case, with the greater proportion making up the training data. To achieve the appropriate splitting ratio, Cross-validation techniques are popularly applied.

3.3.2 ARIMA Model

ARIMA stands for AutoRegressive Integrated Moving Average. It creates a time series model based on its past values. It is a class of statistical models for analyzing and forecasting time series data [5].

An Auto-Regressive (AR only) model is one where the Predicted lag (Yt) depends only on its own lags. A non-seasonal ARIMA model is classified as an "ARIMA (p, d, q)" model, where [6]:

- p: order of Auto Regressive term.
- d: order of Moving Average term.
- q: the no. of differences required to make the time series stationary.

$$\text{If } d = 0 : \quad y_t = Y_t \tag{1}$$

$$\text{If } d = 1 : \quad y_t = Y_t - Y_{t-1} \tag{2}$$

$$\text{If } d = 2 : \quad y_t = (Y_t - Y_{t-1}) - (Y_{t-1} - Y_{t-2}) = Y_t - 2Y_{t-1} + Y_{t-2} \tag{3}$$

A pure **Auto Regressive (AR only)** model is one where Yt depends only on its own lags. That is, Yt is a function of the 'lags of Yt'.

$$Y_t = \alpha + \beta_1 Y_{t-1} + \beta_2 Y_{t-2} + \dots + \beta_p Y_{t-p} + \in_1 \tag{4}$$

Moving Average (MA only) model is one where Yt depends only on the lagged forecast errors.

$$Y_t = \alpha + \in_t + \phi_1 \in_{t-1} + \phi_2 \in_{t-2} + \dots + \phi_q \in_{t-q} \tag{5}$$

In ARIMA, the time series is differenced at least once to make it stationary and you combine the AR and the MA terms. So the equation becomes:

$$Y_t = \alpha + \beta_1 Y_{t-1} + \beta_2 Y_{t-2} + \dots + \beta_p Y_{t-p} \in_t + \phi_1 \in_{t-1} + \phi_2 \in_{t-2} + \dots + \phi_q \in_{t-q} \tag{6}$$

3.3.3 SARIMA Model

SARIMA stands for Seasonal AutoRegressive Integrated Moving Average. It is an ARIMA model with a seasonal component. It creates a time series model based on its past values. It is a class of statistical models for analyzing and forecasting time series data [5].

- p and seasonal P: order of Auto Regressive term
- d and seasonal D: order of Moving Average term
- q and seasonal Q: no. of differences required to make the time series stationary
- s: seasonal length in the data

$$SARIMA \underbrace{(p,d,q)}_{non-seasonal} \underbrace{(P,D,Q)_m}_{seasonal} \tag{7}$$

3.3.4 Root Mean Squared Error

RMSE is a measure of how spread out the prediction errors are [10].

$$RSME = \sqrt{\frac{1}{n}\sum_{j=1}^{n}(y_j - \hat{y}_j)^2} \tag{8}$$

3.3.5 Mean Absolute Error

It is the absolute difference between the actual values and the values that are predicted [10].

$$MAE = \frac{1}{n}\sqrt{\sum_{j=1}^{n}(y_j - \hat{y}_j)} \tag{9}$$

4 Results and Discussions

4.1 Data Visualization

4.1.1 Visualizing Core Trends in the World

The no. of Active Cases has been drastically increasing across the Globe since April with 16 million cases as of December which has been greater than the no. of recoveries except for a brief period in May. December has shown a positive impact on the no. of Active cases on the decline and Recoveries showing a drastic improvement (Figs. 2 and 3).

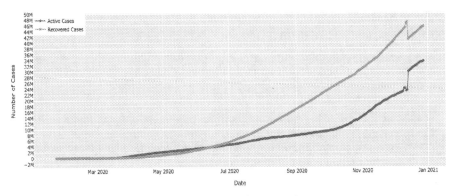

Fig. 2. No. of active and recovered cases

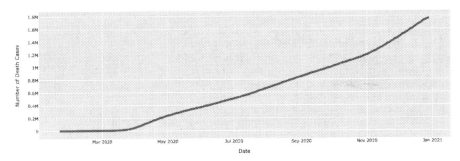

Fig. 3. Number of deaths

There is a uniform increase in the no. of deaths because of COVID-19.

Recovery Rate
See Fig. 4

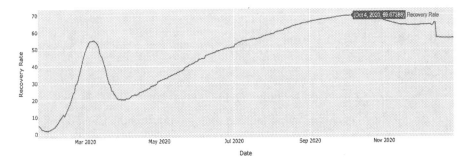

Fig. 4. Recovery rate

Recovery Rate% = (No. of Recovered Cases/No. of Confirmed Cases) × 100

(10)

Where No. of Confirmed Cases = No. of Active Cases + No. of Recoveries + No. of Deaths.

Average Recovery Rate 48.34832333732928

Recovery Rate fell in April and has started to rise again to a high point of 69.67 which is a positive sign and implies that the number of recoveries is increasing.

Mortality Rate

See Fig. 5

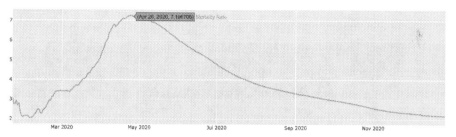

Fig. 5. Mortality rate

Mortality rate = (No. of Death Cases/No. of Confirmed Cases) × 100   (11)

Average Mortality Rate is 3.9654806396761617

The mortality rate, which climbed up to a record high of 7 in May has shown a significant decline, which is a positive sign.

4.1.2 Growth Factor for the No. of Deaths, Active and Recovered Cases

Growth factor is the rate of increase over a very short period example 1 day.

The formula used is:

Formula: (Active/Recovered/Death Cases)/(Active/Recovered/Death Cases on the previous day).

(i)   G.F > 1: Increase in the no. of respective cases.
(ii) A constant G.F = 1: No change in the number of respective cases.
(iii) G.F < 1; Decrease in the no. of respective cases.

The growth factor above 1 indicates a huge increase in all forms of cases. There has been a sudden spike in the growth rate of Active Cases in December which is very concerning (Fig. 6).

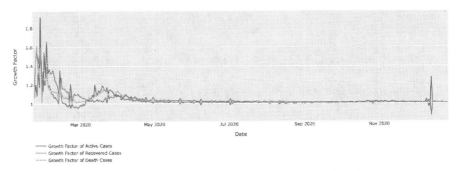

Fig. 6. Date wise growth factor of active, recovered, and death cases

4.1.3 Country Wise Analysis

The US has the highest number of Confirmed Cases followed by India (Fig. 7).

Now let's look at countries without any recoveries having a high mortality rate (Fig. 8).

The highest number of Confirmed Cases, without any recovered patient, is in Sweden. MS Zaandam has a higher mortality rate than the overall mortality rate of the World (3.9).

Let's look at ideal Countries with less than 1000 Confirmed Cases, zero Deaths, and a substantially higher Recovery Rate than the average rate of the World (48.3) (Fig. 9).

Here we find an excellent scenario where these countries such as Cambodia, Bhutan, etc., have the highest Recovery rates without any deaths which could be used as models to study preventive approaches.

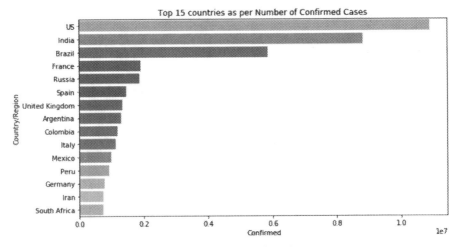

Fig. 7. Country-wise confirmed cases

Country/Region	Confirmed	Deaths	Recovered	Mortality Rate
MS Zaandam	9	2	0	22.2222
Sweden	177355	6164	0	3.47552
Belgium	531280	14303	0	2.69218
Serbia	81086	989	0	1.21969

Fig. 8. Countries with zero recoveries

Country/Region	Confirmed	Recovered	Deaths	Recovery
Seychelles	160	157	0	98.125
Cambodia	302	289	0	95.6954
Bhutan	375	353	0	94.1333
Eritrea	493	444	0	90.0609
Mongolia	428	328	0	76.6355

Fig. 9. Countries with zero deaths

4.1.4 Clustering

We will be clustering countries based on their Mortality rate (M.R) and Recovery rates (R.R). This is because M.R and R.R differ for every country based on different social and economic factors. Another reason for considering these two factors is that they cover all types of cases i.e., Active, Recovered, and Deaths.

K-Means clustering with the Elbow method is applied. We obtain K = 3 to be the optimal number of clusters (Fig. 10).

```
Avergae Mortality Rate of Cluster 0:  25.59107294317218
Avergae Recovery Rate of Cluster 0:  71.9041560644614
Avergae Mortality Rate of Cluster 1:  1.830590245731186
Avergae Recovery Rate of Cluster 1:  84.64982646961421
Avergae Mortality Rate of Cluster 2:  2.0869620557582733
Avergae Recovery Rate of Cluster 2:  23.07397219116931
```

Cluster 0 consists of countries that have an extremely High M.R and moderate R.R. These countries have suffered the most but are now recovering with a High R.R. e.g., Yemen and MS Zaandam.

Country/Region	Confirmed	Recovered	Deaths	Mortality	Recovery	Clusters
India	10224303.00	9807569.00	148153.00	1.45	95.92	1.00
Brazil	7504833.00	6712757.00	191570.00	2.55	89.45	1.00
Russia	3047335.00	2446412.00	54559.00	1.79	80.28	1.00
Turkey	2162775.00	2037433.00	20135.00	0.93	94.20	1.00
Italy	2056277.00	1408686.00	72370.00	3.52	68.51	1.00
US	19301543.00	0.00	334836.00	1.73	0.00	2.00
France	2619616.00	196642.00	63235.00	2.41	7.51	2.00
United Kingdom	2336688.00	5102.00	71217.00	3.05	0.22	2.00
Spain	1879413.00	150376.00	50122.00	2.67	8.00	2.00
Netherlands	781467.00	9150.00	11135.00	1.42	1.17	2.00
Yemen	2096.00	1384.00	607.00	28.96	66.03	0.00
MS Zaandam	9.00	7.00	2.00	22.22	77.78	0.00

Fig. 10. Clustering of countries for K = 3

Cluster 1 consists of countries having a very low M.R and a High R.R. Such countries have seen a lot of cases due to their enormous population but have been able to recover from the adverse impact of the pandemic, e,g., India, Brazil, Russia, and Argentina.

Cluster 2 consists of countries having a low M.R and low R.R. Although they have seen less number of deaths, the recovery rates are too low causing a negative impact on the number of deaths. These countries recorded a significantly high number of active cases but low M.R which is a positive sign, e.g., US, France, Spain, and the UK.

4.1.5 Training and Testing the Model

Here Time Series Forecasting is applied for the number of active cases in India. The model is trained with the number of active cases since the epidemic began until mid-December and tested with data until the last week of December. The value of the p, d, q and s parameters are chosen by analyzing the ACF and PACF plot. The 'best' fitted ARIMA and SARIMA model is selected using AIC and BIC values for each training dataset [9] (Fig. 11).

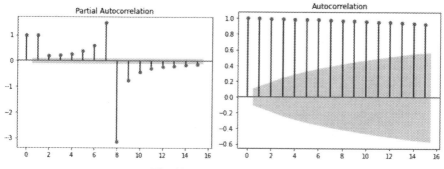

Fig. 11. ACF and PACF plots

4.1.5.1 ARIMA Model

The fitted ARIMA model is ARIMA(5,2,5).

Dep. Variable:	D2.y	**No. Observations:**	322
Model:	ARIMA(5, 2, 5)	**Log Likelihood**	-3105.423
Method:	css-mle	**S.D. of innovations**	3711.944
Date:	Wed, 30 Dec 2020	**AIC**	6234.845
Time:	06:37:35	**BIC**	6280.140
Sample:	2	**HQIC**	6252.928

Here the ARIMA model is fitted with training data and validated (Fig. 12).

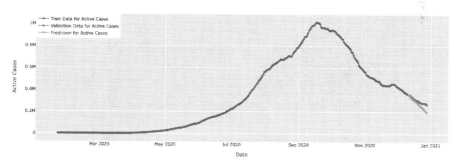

Fig. 12. Active cases ARIMA model prediction

The model can predict the number of active cases with low accuracy.

SARIMA Model

The fitted SARIMA Model is SARIMA(4,2,3)(1,0,2)9.

Dep. Variable:	y	**No. Observations:**	324
Model:	SARIMAX(4, 2, 3)x(1, 0, 2, 9)	**Log Likelihood**	-3125.893
Date:	Wed, 30 Dec 2020	**AIC**	6275.786
Time:	06:36:14	**BIC**	6321.081
Sample:	0	**HQIC**	6293.869

Here the SARIMA model is fit with training data and validated (Fig. 13).

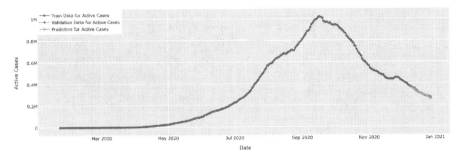

Fig. 13. Active cases SARIMA model prediction

The model can predict the number of active cases with high accuracy (Table 3).

Table 3. Error analyzed for the ARIMA and SARIMA model

Performance metrics	ARIMA	SARIMA
Root mean square error (RMSE)	35700.92673014	6159.371902318
Mean absolute error (MAE)	29705.53742292	4864.176662640

To evaluate the predictive performance of the models, RMSE and MAE have been used in the paper. The SARIMA model greatly improves performance of the model with a very low mean absolute error of 4864 (Table 4).

Table 4. SARIMA model forecast data for future dates

	Deaths	ARIMA model forecast	SARIMA model forecast
1	2020-12-29	190129.40	253715.23
2	2020-12-30	182942.83	248354.15
3	2020-12-31	174155.22	240880.66
4	2021-01-01	165519.71	234684.73

5   Conclusions

COVID-19 doesn't have a very high mortality rate which is continuously dropping. The recovery rate is constantly rising which is a very positive take away. There is a significant increase in the growth factor of the infection due to which the number of Active cases is rapidly increasing.

Countries like the USA, India, Spain, Brazil, and the United Kingdom are facing serious troubles in containing the disease. It's necessary to perform COVID-19 testing on a large scale and Contact Tracing to carry out Quarantining efficiently. The growth factor of the number of deaths and Active Cases has slowed down in the first 2 weeks of December, which is a positive takeaway. The USA, India, and Brazil seem to be the three hotspots of Covid cases and hopefully, there shouldn't emerge any other.

The SARIMA model can predict cases with high accuracy and can be utilized by Scientists for different regions and parameters. Both the time forecasting models indicate a decrease in the no. of active cases in India.

References

1. The Weather Channel. COVID-19 Explainer: Four Stages of Virus Transmission, and What Stage India Currently Finds Itself In (2020). https://weather.com/en-IN/india/coronavirus/news/2020-04-09-four-stages-of-virus-transmission-stage-india-currently-finds
2. GitHub: COVID-19 Data Repository by The Center for Systems Science and Engineering (CSSE) at Johns Hopkins University (2020). https://github.com/CSSEGISandData/COVID-19
3. Pandas.pydata.org: Package Overview—Pandas 1.2.0 Documentation (2020). https://pandas.pydata.org/docs/getting_started/overview.html
4. GeeksforGeeks. Elbow Method for Optimal Value of K in Kmeans (2019). https://www.geeksforgeeks.org/elbow-method-for-optimal-value-of-k-in-kmeans/
5. Towards Data Science – Medium: Time Series Forecasting — ARIMA Models (2018). https://towardsdatascience.com/time-series-forecasting-arima-models-7f221e9eee06
6. Prabhakaran, S.: ARIMA Model - Complete Guide to Time Series Forecasting in Python | ML+. [online] ML+ (2020). https://www.machinelearningplus.com/time-series/arima-model-time-series-forecasting-python/
7. Gunasegaran, T., Cheah, Y.: Evolutionary cross validation. In: 2017 8th International Conference on Information Technology (ICIT) (2017)
8. Gondauri, D., Mikautadze, E., Batiashvili, M.: Research on COVID-19 virus spreading statistics based on the examples of the cases from different countries. Electron. J. Gen. Med. 17(4), em209 (2020). https://doi.org/10.29333/ejgm/7869
9. Chakraborty, T., Ghosh, I.: Real-time forecasts and risk assessment of novel coronavirus (COVID-19) cases: a data-driven analysis. Chaos Solitons Fractals 135, 109850 (2020)
10. Performance measures: RMSE and MAE - The Data Scientist: https://thedatascientist.com/performance-measures-rmse-mae/

On the Comparison of Static and Dynamic Metrics Toward Fault-Proneness Prediction

Navneet Kaur[(✉)] and Hardeep Singh

Department of Computer Science, Guru Nanak Dev University, Amritsar, Punjab, India
navneetsandhu02@gmail.com, hardeep.dcse@gndu.ac.in

Abstract. The notion of predicting fault-proneness by utilizing software metric data has acquired the attention of many researchers in the past three decades. The fault-proneness prediction can assist in the systematic distribution of the software development resources, as testers need to put efforts and time on only those software classes where the chances of faults are very high. This study investigates the dichotomization capability of thresholds identified through Receiver Operating Characteristic (ROC) curve and F-measure. These methods were utilized to compute the cut-off values of the software measures extracted from the jEdit software system. Besides Chidamber and Kemerer metric suite, we also assessed the prediction capability of a dynamic measure - Dynamic Coupling between Object classes (DCBO). The dynamic metrics are capable of revealing true execution behaviour of the software system as here the values can only be extracted at the run-time, therefore can handle the object oriented features, such as, polymorphism, inheritance, and dynamic binding, better than the static metrics. The experimental results highlighted the good performance of the DCBO measure, indicating this particular metric as a promising candidate for the purpose of fault proneness prediction.

Keywords: Fault-proneness · Software metrics · Static and dynamic measure · Threshold techniques

1 Introduction

The unavoidable occurrence of faults during software development has led to an increased interest of researchers in the utilization of statistical and machine learning based models for the anticipation of faulty classes. The fault prediction models can identify the faulty classes by utilizing the software metrics quantifying the structural properties of the software system. These metric based models can identify the high fault-prone classes, therefore, can be helpful in cutting down the cost related to the testing process. However, the idea of execution of these models does not seem practical in the software industries [1]. On the other hand, the idea of threshold values is easy to implement, where the software developers and testers needs some threshold values based on which they can separate the faulty from non-faulty classes.

A threshold technique is a mathematical equation producing an optimal cut-off value of a variable and the yielded threshold helps to map an instance into one of the multiple

© Springer Nature Singapore Pte Ltd. 2021
A. K. Luhach et al. (Eds.): ICAICR 2020, CCIS 1393, pp. 394–403, 2021.
https://doi.org/10.1007/978-981-16-3660-8_37

predefined groups, i.e. yes or no. In the domain of Software Engineering, the threshold values of software metrics can assist in the process of decision making. The testers can observe the peculiarity in the class based on the recognized thresholds of the different metrics. This notion can reduce the overall testing cost by helping the testers to concentrate on high risk-prone classes whose metric values exceed the identified threshold. In this study, we have utilized ROC curve and F-measure methods to compute the threshold value of the selected software measures.

In this study, besides very well known Chidamber and Kemerer (CK) metric suite, we also computed the threshold value of DCBO metric and utilized these metrics for predicting the class fault-proneness. The static and dynamic metrics are different, as in the former case, there is no need to execute the source code of the software systems, the metric values can be obtained on the compilation of the source code, whereas, the values of dynamic metrics can only be obtained on the execution of the code. As the true behaviour of some features, such as inheritance, dynamic binding, and polymorphism can only be revealed at run-time, therefore, dynamic metrics are more efficient in capturing the stated features. The experimental results of the current study revealed the better capability of the selected dynamic metric in predicting faults as compared to the static metrics.

The main contribution of this paper are as follow:

- To compare the predictive capability of the static and dynamic metrics.
- To compare the capability of ROC curve and F-measure in identifying the efficient thresholds.

The remained of the paper is organized as follows. The Sect. 2 contains the related studies. The Sect. 3 presents the set-up of the current study. The Sect. 4 contains the results obtained during the experiment. In Sect. 5, we discuss various threats to the current study. And in the last section, we present the conclusions and scope for the future work.

2 Related Work

Many studies are available in the literature investigating the discrimination strength of the threshold techniques in separating the software classes based on the fault outcome. Some of these studies performed the discrimination process by utilizing the thresholds based on the expert opinion [2, 3]. There are also other studies present in the literature that employed the data-driven techniques capable of selecting the threshold value by utilizing the past fault information [4].

The Value of an Acceptable Risk Level (VARL) is another very commonly utilized technique for the threshold identification which basically utilizes the existing fault information to identify the optimal cut-off value [5–9]. Shatnawi et al. [1] employed ROC curve for the threshold identification process where authors selected the point producing maximized summation of sensitivity and specificity as an optimal cut-off value. On the contrary, Catal et al. [10] adopted different criterion to select the optimal point on the ROC curve, here the authors selected the point producing the maximized area under curve as the optimal cut-off point. The current study has also selected the ROC method, but opted different method for choosing the appropriate cut-off point as from the previous studies.

Shatnawi, in another study [11], tested the effectiveness of standard deviation plus mean method in yielding an optimal cut-off value. Boucher and Badri [12] compared the prediction performance of the ROC curve, Alves Ranking, and VARL methods on the dataset available publicly, among which the ROC curve performed the best and VARL trailed significantly as compared to other two techniques. The authors also compared the threshold based models with the models constructed using machine learning algorithms and found the former one better for the purpose of fault proneness prediction.

All of the above studies tested the prediction proficiency of the threshold techniques by applying them on the static metrics. Despite the existence of many dynamic metrics [13–17], the work done in the field of associating the Object Oriented dynamic metrics with fault-proneness is considerably small. We found single study conducted by Lavazza *et al.* [18] in which the authors correlated the dynamic measures with fault-proneness. The authors compared the static and dynamic metrics for their fault prediction ability. The dynamic measures considered in the study were Distinct method invocation, Dynamic messages, and Distinct classes. The selected measures were tested for their ability to predict the number of faults in four open source software systems.

In the current study, the authors have employed the ROC curve and F-measure to acquire the optimal threshold values of the static and dynamic measures and utilized them to discriminate the faulty and non-faulty classes of the jEdit software system.

3   Methodology

This section contains the details about the methods and techniques which were used to execute the objective of the current study.

3.1   Data Collection

The authors of the current study utilized the metric values of an open source software system - jEdit. The selected software system is written in the Java programming language. The source code and fault information of the jEdit system was collected from GitHub. The jEdit is a text editor and consists of 585 Classes. To track the classes containing bugs, the GitHub entries were examined and the entries containing 'fix' or 'bug' word were further analyzed and the classes which were modified to correct the faults were recorded.

3.2   Dependent and Independent Variables

In this study, the fault outcome is considered as a dependent variable. And, the software metrics quantifying the design properties of the jEdit software system are considered as the independent variables. The static metrics considered in the current study were proposed by Chidamber and Kemerer [19] and the selected metrics are *Weighted Methods per Class (WMC)*, *Coupling Between Object classes (CBO)*, *Lack of Cohesion in Methods (LCOM)*, *Depth of Inheritance Tree (DIT)*, *Response For a Class (RFC)*, and

Number of Children (NOC). The dynamic measure considered in this study is *DCBO*. Basically, "CBO is a count of the number of other classes to which a class is coupled" [13]. The DCBO metric measures the same information, but at the run-time.

3.3   Software Metrics Extraction Tool

In recent years, the use of publicly available dataset, i.e. NASA and PROMISE repositories has been increased in the fault prediction domain. Various studies have utilized the metric and fault information available in these repositories to predict the fault-proneness of a class. However, the current study has also considered the DCBO measure, the information about which has not been provided in any of the above mentioned public repositories. Also, no tool is available to extract the values of the dynamic measures, therefore, a program was implemented by the authors of the current study to extract the value of the DCBO measure. Different approaches have been followed by the existing studies to extract the values of the dynamic measures. In [14], profiler based tracing was adopted, in studies [15, 20] Aspect Oriented Programming (AOP) was utilized, and in [21] dynamic modelling diagrams were opted to execute the dynamic analysis process. In the current study, we employed AOP approach for capturing the value of DCBO measure. Basically, AOP is a programming paradigm that assists in enhancing the modularity by separating the concerns in software implementation. For the purpose, we have used AspectJ which utilizes constructs, such as, pointcuts, joinpoints, advices, and aspects, capable of incorporating additional behaviour in the software system without actually changing the source code of the system. The following is the code of the most pertinent portion of the defined aspect.

```
Public aspect counter
{
    Before(): call (* *.* (..));
    {
        System.out.println(thisEnclosingJointPointStaticPart.getSignature().
        getDeclaringType()

        - - - -

        System.out.println(thisJointPointStaticPart.getSignature().
        getDeclaringType());
        ------
    }
}
```

On the other hand, sci tool[1] has been employed to extract the values of the considered static metrics.

The dynamic metric extraction procedure is completely different from the static one. The former requires more resources in term of efforts and time. The static metrics tool can produce the result for all of the classes at ones. Whereas, in a dynamic environment, the result of a particular metric depends on the input given to the software system in a particular scenario. A scenario represents a sequence of interactions took place among

---

[1] https://scitools.com/.

objects on the execution of code on a particular input [21]. The result of the same metric might be different in different scenarios when distinct values are given as input to the software. For e.g., if module *A* is being used in three different scenarios, there may be a probability of getting dissimilar metric value in each of the scenarios. In this case, a decision needs to be taken regarding which scenario's outcome should be taken. This situation has been handled differently by the different authors in the existing literature. Arisholm [17] gave different values to the software with intent to cover the maximum amount of code and the input value covering the maximum code was further selected as a final metric value. Whereas, Geetika and Singh [22] have executed the software on different inputs, and for each metric the minimum, maximum and average values over all scenarios were recorded. Our study has followed the execution approach adopted by Arisholm [17] for choosing the metric value. In our study different inputs were given to the system with the intent of maximum code coverage.

3.4   Threshold Techniques

The strong association between the software metrics and fault outcome do not necessarily imply that any threshold technique can separate the two groups efficiently. Therefore, it is imperative to validate the threshold techniques before to apply them in the real industrial environment. In the experiment, we tested the following two techniques for the dichotomous purpose.

The Point Closest to (0, 1) Criteria
The ROC analysis has been frequently utilized in the fault prediction domain to quantify how accurately the developed model can identify the faulty and non-faulty classes. Another most common use of this curve is to recognize the optimal cut-off point that can be used by software developers and testers to discriminate the faulty and non-faulty classes. The ROC curve shows sensitivity against 1 minus specificity for each cut-off value. The formula of the sensitivity and specificity is given in the Eq. (1) and Eq. (2).

$$\text{Specificty} = 1 - \text{False Positive}/(\text{False Positive} + \text{True Negative}) \qquad (1)$$

$$\text{Sensitivity} = \text{True Positive}/(\text{True Positive} + \text{False Negative}) \qquad (2)$$

Table 1. Confusion matrix

	Actual classification	
	Faulty	Non-faulty
Faulty	True Positive (TP)	False Positive (FP)
Non-faulty	False Negative (FN)	True Negative (TN)

The threshold identification process requires the identification of the indices given in the Table 1 for each of the values present in the metric range, which further helps to identify the sensitivity and specificity statistics. On the mapping of the computed values of sensitivity and 1-specificity onto the ROC plot (where x-axis and y-axis represents 1-specificity and sensitivity respectively), a curve will be formed coincided with the upper left corner. Any of the points on the formed curve can be selected to separate the faulty from the non-faulty classes, but in order to retrieve the effective results the same should be chosen very carefully. Herein, we selected the point closest to the (0, 1) coordinate of the ROC plot as the optimal cut-off point. The Euclidean Distance (ED) is calculated for all of the thresholds available in the metric range.

$$ED(t) = \sqrt{(1 - sensitivity(t))^2 + (1 + specificity(t))^2}$$

The threshold value t minimizing the $ED(t)$ function was selected as the optimal cut-off value during the experiment.

F-measure

The F-measure is the harmonic mean of precision and recall or sensitivity. The precision measures the number of actual faulty classes from the classes predicted as faulty (the formula given in the Eq. (3)). This is widely used measure to evaluate the success of the developed fault prediction model in case of imbalanced dataset (formula given in the Eq. (4)).

$$Precision = TruePositive/(TruePositive + FalseNegative) \qquad (3)$$

$$F - measure = \left(\frac{(1 + \beta^2) * precision * recall}{\beta^2 * (precision + recall)} \right) \qquad (4)$$

In order to identify the optimal cut-off point through this method, the F-measure was calculated for all of the values in the threshold range and the threshold producing the maximum value of the F-measure was selected as the optimal cut-off value.

4 Results

This section contains the detailed results recorded during the experiment.

Only the appropriate software measures showing a significant association with the fault outcome were selected for the experiment. To execute the metric selection process, Univariate Logistic Regression (ULR) was utilized which can quantify the existing level of association between the dependent and independent variable. Table 2 contains the results based on Univariate Logistic regression. We have calculated the values of p-value, R^2, and Wald Chi-square to identify whether the corresponding metric is significant for predicting the fault-proneness. The CBO, DCBO, RFC, and WMC metrics were found statistically significant for predicting fault-proneness as their p-value was below .05. The results showed higher values of R^2 and Wald Chi-square of the previously mentioned software metrics.

Table 2. Results based on Univariate Logistic regression.

	Wald Chi square	R^2	p-value
CBO	88.03	.358	<.000
DCBO	96.823	.456	<.000
DIT	3.368	.009	0.066
NOC	1.714	.009	0.190
WMC	15.489	.125	<.000
RFC	34.801	.192	<.000
LCOM	7.090	.086	0.063

The cut-off values acquired on the application of ROC curve and F-measure is shown in Table 3. The different threshold values were acquired for the static CBO and dynamic CBO.

For the evaluation of the discrimination ability of the threshold values derived through the selected techniques, the authors of the current study have applied sensitivity, specificity, False Negative Rate (FNR), False Positive Rate (FPR), and G-mean measures. The FPR and FNR indices should be low, whereas G-mean should be high. The formula of FPR, FNR, and G-mean is given in the Eq. (5), Eq. (6), and Eq. (7). Furthermore, in order to make the whole experiment more rigorous, the threshold values were derived and tested by following the K-cross validation procedure. The steps followed to obtain the threshold value through cross-validation are summarized in the Algorithm 1.

Table 3. Cut-off values on the application of ROC curve and F-measure

	CBO	DCBO	WMC	*RFC*
ROC curve	12	10	6	36
F-measure	16	11	5	36

$$G-mean = \sqrt{sensitivity * specificity} \tag{5}$$

$$FPR = False\ Positive/(False\ Positive + True\ Negative) \tag{6}$$

$$FNR = False\ Negative/(False\ Negative + True\ Positive) \tag{7}$$

Algorithm 1: Threshold Based fault detection

1: Given a list of software metrics ($M=\{M_1, M_2, M_3.\_\_\_\_ M_n\}$), Where N is the total number of software metrics for which the threshold values is to be calculated.

2: Divide data into K-folds with approximately equal distribution of cases.

3: For fold k_i in K folds: do

    a.   Set fold k_i as the test set

    b.   Train the methods on the remaining K-1 folds

         • Compute basic measures:

           TP, TN, FP, FN, sensitivity or recall, specificity, precision.

         • Compute final threshold measures:

CP	$\max(sensitivity * specificity)$
F1 measure	$\max\left(\frac{(1+\beta^2)*precision*recall}{\beta^2*(precision+recall)}\right) \; where \; \beta=1$

    c.   Evaluation of method's performance on fold k_i.

4: Calculation of average performance over K folds.

The performance results obtained on the application of the derived thresholds on the testing dataset are shown in the Table 4 and Table 5. The results of ROC curve were slightly better than the F-measure in case of CBO and DCBO metrics. Furthermore, in the context of software metrics, the dynamic measure performed significantly better than the static CBO and other static measures. The number of false predictions was low in case of dynamic measure. The performance results of the RFC and WMC measures were trailed significantly.

Table 4. The prediction results achieved through the ROC curve.

	Specificity	Sensitivity	G-mean	FPR	FNR
CBO	.738	.780	.759	.262	.219
DCBO	.801	.896	.848	.198	.104
WMC	.564	.768	.658	.436	.232
RFC	.748	.548	.64	.252	.452

Although the experimental results manifest the superiority of DCBO in terms of prediction accuracy as compared to other static metrics, but the dynamic metrics have their associated drawbacks. The dynamic metric extraction process is very time consuming, the program has to execute repeatedly on the different inputs, whereas in case of static metrics, the values of all incorporated classes can be retrieved on the compilation of the source code. Also, the values of static metrics can be obtained at early design phase,

Table 5. The prediction results acheived through F-measure.

	Specificity	Sensitivity	G-mean	FPR	FNR
CBO	.849	.645	.740	.15	.354
DCBO	.825	.822	.824	.174	.177
WMC	.564	.768	.658	.436	.232
RFC	.748	.548	.64	.252	.452

whereas dynamic values can only be retrieved at later stages of software development process, i.e., after the implementation phase.

5 Threat to Validity

The current study has tested the effectiveness of only one dynamic metric, therefore, cannot generalize the findings to other dynamic measures. This threat can be reduced by investigating the similar study on other dynamic metrics.

In this study, the F-measure has also been proved effective for discriminating the faulty and non-faulty classes. But, its validity should be tested on other software systems possessing different data distribution.

6 Conclusions and Future Work

In this study, the authors have calculated the threshold values of the software metrics by using ROC curve and F-measure techniques and assessed the effectiveness of the derived thresholds in separating the faulty and non-faulty classes. In addition to the CK metric suite, the DCBO measure was also tested for their anticipation capability and then compared with the outcome of the CK metrics. The results showed the better anticipation capability of dynamic measure as compared to the static metrics.

In future work, we will replicate the study to assess the fault prediction capability of other dynamic metrics.

References

1. Shatnawi, R., Li, W., Swain, J., Tim, N.: Finding software metrics threshold values using ROC. J. Softw. Maint. Evol. Pract. **22**, 1–16 (2010)
2. Mccabe, J.: A Complexity Measure, vol. SE-2, no. 4, pp. 308–320 (1994).
3. Nejmeh, B.A.: Npath: a measure of execution path complexity and its applications. Commun. ACM **31**(2), 188–200 (1988)
4. Erni, K., Lewerentz, C.: Applying design-metrics to object-oriented frameworks. In: Proceedings of the 3rd International Software Metrics Symposium, pp. 64–74 (1996)
5. Shatnawi, R.: A quantitative investigation of the acceptable risk levels of object-oriented metrics in open-source systems. IEEE Trans. Softw. Eng. **36**(2), 216–225 (2010)

6. Malhotra, R., Bansal, A.J.: Fault prediction considering threshold effects of object-oriented metrics. Exp. Syst. **32**(2), 203–219 (2015)
7. Singh, S., Kahlon, K.S.: Object oriented software metrics threshold values at quantitative acceptable risk level. CSI Trans. ICT **2**(3), 191–205 (2014). https://doi.org/10.1007/s40012-014-0057-1
8. Arar, K., Ayan, O.F.: Deriving thresholds of software metrics to predict faults on open source software. Exp. Syst. Appl. **61**, 106–121 (2016)
9. Hussain, S., Keung, J., Khan, A.A., Bennin, K.E.: Detection of fault-prone classes using logistic regression based object-oriented metrics thresholds. In: Proceedings - 2016 IEEE International Conference on Software Quality, Reliability and Security QRS-C 2016, pp. 93–100 (2016)
10. Catal, C., Alan, O., Balkan, K.: Class noise detection based on software metrics and ROC curves. Inf. Sci. (NY) **181**(21), 4867–4877 (2011)
11. Shatnawi, R.: Deriving metrics thresholds using log transformation: deriving metrics thresholds. J. Softw. Evol. Process **27**(2), 95–113 (2015). https://doi.org/10.1002/smr.1702
12. Boucher, A., Badri, M.: Software metrics thresholds calculation techniques to predict fault-proneness: an empirical comparison. Inf. Softw. Technol. **96**, 38–67 (2017)
13. Mitchell, J.F., Power, A.: Run-time coupling metrics for the analysis of Java programs-preliminary results from the SPEC and grande suites (2003)
14. Mitchell, J.F., Power, A.: An empirical investigation into the dimensions of run-time coupling in Java programs, pp. 9–14 (2004)
15. Hassoun, Y., Johnson, R., Counsell, S.: A dynamic runtime coupling metric for meta-level architectures. In: Proceedings of the European Conference on Software Maintenance and Reengineering, CSMR, pp. 339–346 (2004)
16. Zaidman, A., Demeyer, S.: Analyzing large event traces with the help of coupling metrics. In: Proceedings of the 5th International Workshop on Object-Oriented Reengineering, Technical Report of the Department of Mathematics and Computer Science of the University of Antwerp (2004)
17. Arisholm, E., Briand, L.C., Foyen, A.: Dynamic coupling measurement for object-oriented software. IEEE Trans. Softw. Eng. **30**(8), 491–506 (2004)
18. Lavazza, L., Morasca, S., Taibi, D., Tosi, D., Mazzini, V.: On the definition of dynamic software measures, pp. 39–48 (2012)
19. Chidamber, S.R., Kemerer, C.F.: A metrics suite for object oriented design. IEEE Trans. Softw. Eng. **20**(6), 476–493 (1994)
20. Gupta, V., Chhabra, J.K.: Dynamic cohesion measures for object-oriented software. J. Syst. Archit. **57**(4), 452–462 (2011)
21. Yacoub, S.M., Ammar, H.H., Robinson, T.: Dynamic metrics for object oriented designs. In: Proceedings of the 6th International Software Metrics Symposium, pp. 50–61 (1999)
22. Geetika, R., Singh, P.: Empirical investigation into static and dynamic coupling metrics. ACM SIGSOFT Softw. Eng. Notes **39**(1), 1–8 (2014)

Development of an Automatic Road Damage Detection System to Ensure the Safety of Tourists

Batyrkhan Omarov[1,2(✉)], Moldir Kizdarbekova[2], Bauyrzhan Omarov[1], and Nurzhan Omarov[3]

[1] Al-Farabi Kazakh National University, Almaty, Kazakhstan
[2] Akhmet Yassawi International Kazakh-Turkish University, Turkistan, Kazakhstan
[3] Kazakh University of Ways of Communications, Almaty, Kazakhstan

Abstract. Transportation, particularly the automobile, has become an integral part of our daily lives. Like any other device, mechanism or invention, the car carries both positive and negative qualities, and also strongly depends on the state of the surrounding conditions. There is a problem of poor-quality maintenance of highways, namely the possible dangerous consequences of the interaction of the road – road system. Damaged roads are considered one of the main factors contributing to car accidents. This is especially true for roads in the regions, since they are used for most of the transportation of goods and not only from city to city. Many factors (such as rain, snow, high temperatures, and traffic congestion) because various road damage that affect road performance, safety, and vehicle costs. Countries allocate a large budget for road repair. Therefore, it is very important to know in advance about the damage on the roads, so as to start repairing them as soon as possible. In our research, we propose an automatic road damage detection system using smartphone camera and neural network techniques. To detect road damages we use CNN model. Our system demonstrated practical efficiency and high detection rate with more than 80% accuracy.

Keywords: Road damage detection · Neural networks · Deep learning · CNN · Safety

1 Introduction

As it says, there is a major problem all over the world—these are roads. Investing in a large number of disparate repairs is about fighting the symptoms, not treating the disease. The system approach assumes that at the beginning we should understand the problem: what is the condition of our roads, which roads need to be repaired first? Let's give an example: let's say there are two roads that need to be repaired. A detailed diagnosis is carried out, and as a result, it is concluded that the cost of repair of both sites is approximately the same at the moment [1]. Another conclusion based on the results of the diagnosis may be that in a year the repair of the first road will require ten times more funds than the repair of the second. This development can be predicted as a result

© Springer Nature Singapore Pte Ltd. 2021
A. K. Luhach et al. (Eds.): ICAICR 2020, CCIS 1393, pp. 404–413, 2021.
https://doi.org/10.1007/978-981-16-3660-8_38

of a detailed analysis of the structure and nature of roadway damage [2]. Thus, in a resource-constrained environment, diagnostics is a cornerstone.

Highways are associated with the space and landscape of an area that can be mountainous, flat, hilly, swampy, or with other features. The aesthetics of the road gives an idea of the visual qualities of the road, which is harmoniously integrated into the surrounding landscape with the provision of safety, convenience and comfort of movement. The basis of road aesthetics is the high-quality condition of the road and all its elements, the correct solution of road landscaping. The ecology of space, aesthetic perception and traffic safety are interrelated. The main features of the road that distinguish it from other engineering structures are the large length, the variety of information received by a person during speed. Diverse impressions of the road is tiring, and monotonous-dulls attention.

Road maintenance is expensive. Weather conditions and vibrations from the movement of cars naturally destroy the road surface. Salt, fuel and water penetrate cracks in the asphalt and over time lead to more serious damage, which is harder, longer and more expensive to repair [3, 4]. A multiple increase in the load on the roadbed leads to its intensive wear and loss growth, which in turn causes an increase in accidents and vehicle repair costs. Reducing the load of the existing road network is possible by building a new road infrastructure [5]. However, this measure is highly expensive and difficult to implement given the dense urban development. Thus, there is a contradiction between the requirement to reduce the load of roads and increase cargo traffic. This makes it relevant to use the hardware and software complex for monitoring, modeling and forecasting the condition and wear of the road surface, to solve the problem of maintaining the required quality of the road surface, in the context of an annual increase in traffic flow, while reducing repair costs by making standard management decisions [6]. One example of such solutions to this problem is the adoption of operational and preventive measures that prevent intensive wear and tear of emergency areas.

The goal of this project is to automate the detection of various types of damage on roads in real time using images taken using a conventional smartphone.

2 Literature Review

Violation of the stability of the exploited roadbed is most often predetermined by the entire history of its life cycle. Such deformations almost never appear immediately after construction. They are usually preceded by long internal processes that ultimately reduce the strength properties of soils and contribute to the formation of weakened zones in the body of the roadbed. Sometimes, at first glance, minor violations and damages develop into defects that create emergency situations and entail significant economic damage.

In the areas of the road surface directly adjacent to the expansion joints, deep cracks, abrasion of the surface up to 3 cm and depressions were found, from which large pieces of asphalt concrete were knocked out by vehicles. This condition of the expansion joints and adjacent sections of the road surface is dangerous for vehicles and can cause serious accidents.

As a rule, the provision of emergency medical assistance to victims of accidents, emergencies and emergencies on highways is preceded by work on localization of the consequences of these accidents and emergencies, as well as emergency rescue operations. Therefore, there is an important task to organize joint actions of the traffic police, fire and rescue and medical services [7].

To respond effectively to accidents and emergencies, the relevant services need to have the following information:

- data on the location of an accident or emergency;
- approximate number of people affected;
- number of vehicles involved in an accident;
- the presence of additional aggravating factors affecting (Pajaro explosive, chemically and radiation hazardous substances, fires, collapse of buildings, landslides, etc.) [8–13].

The obvious first measure to mitigate the consequences of accidents is their rapid detection and restoration of normal work of roads, which in turn requires fast and accurate detection of the accident. There is a question of creating a modern and effective system for detecting road accidents [14].

Accident detection systems combine tools for data collection and processing. The effectiveness of road accident detection systems is determined by the ability to track and detect accidents using processing algorithms and notify you of the need to take appropriate measures as soon as possible [15]. In some cases, even seconds are crucial. Lives may depend on the rapid and effective coordination of rescue services. Immediate response allows you to avoid danger and reduce damage to road infrastructure to a minimum. And here time is crucial – it is extremely important to react immediately at the very first signs that something has gone wrong, whether it is a collision, the first puff of smoke indicating a car fire, a box with a load that flew out of the back of a truck and got under the wheels of cars behind, or the sudden appearance of a pedestrian where it should not be [16].

Automatic detection of accidents today is possible through the use of intelligent transport systems, using a wide range of sensors: sensors embedded in the road surface, motion sensors and video monitoring, sensors installed on vehicles [17].

Technological means of ensuring security should first of all be equipped with infrastructure objects of particular importance, such as tunnels, bridges, open road sections, intersections and other objects. this will save human lives and protect the infrastructure from threats and dangers of the road situation. In addition, it will allow road authorities to control traffic more effectively. The speed of incident detection depends on the degree to which road facilities are equipped with the necessary technologies [18].

3   Problem Statement

An important feature of the road is continuous traffic with space deformation, with an independent arrangement of oncoming traffic lanes, which eliminates the collision of cars. Landscape design and landscaping includes smooth tracing and combining the road itself with the landscape, organizing the space of the future road with green spaces and natural landforms.

The quality of highways determines their architectural appearance. The road cannot be considered beautiful when quality indicators are broken, when there are defects. Damaged roads are considered one of the main factors contributing to car accidents. This is especially true for roads in the regions, since they are used for most of the transportation of goods and not only from city to city. However, their maintenance is given the least attention, and due to this, the condition of these roads leaves much to be desired. In our case, it is necessary to determine the characteristics of road damage using mobile video measurements. In this case, the characteristics of the object are its area and volume. There are 2 main factors that have a greater impact on the condition of roads: the factor of excessive load and weather conditions.

1) Excessive load or congestion has a significant impact on the road's service life. Overloading leads to premature damage to roads, which leads to high costs for repairing them. Deviation of the traffic load occur when heavy vehicles are carrying goods in excess of permissible carrying capacity. The more vehicles with excessive loads pass, the faster the service life of the road surface will be reduced.
2) From studies conducted in developing countries, heavy rains and rainy weather also play an important role in road destruction. Precipitation intensity determine the level of road damage in this location. Floodwaters and prolonged torrential rains threaten the road surface and affect delamination, cracks and potholes. Stagnant water will reduce the strength of the bond between the road surfaces.

Consequently, it is difficult for employees to apply the results of these studies directly to practical purposes. In this research we do the following tasks:

1) We put together a lot of images of damaged roads. The dataset contains open hatches, tire tracks, construction joints, partial asphalt pavement, potholes and cracks, blurring of road crossings, and blurring of dividing lanes.
2) Built and trained a neural network, as well as evaluated the modern method of object detection based on deep learning.
3) Using a set of data, we evaluated the efficiency and accuracy of the model.
4) Developed an Android mobile app and showed that the type of road damage can be identified with high accuracy.

4   Materials and Methods

A computerized road damage detection system should consist of a number of components, including.

1) A comprehensive data collection process that allows you to obtain the necessary information;
2) A database that can store information in the format
3) Necessary processing and clearing of data before using it in model training

4) Training a neural network on training data, as well as evaluating its effectiveness and accuracy on test data.

The system consists of four stages:

1. Training the model on servers with daily accumulated data of citizens.
2. Determine the state of the road using only the smartphone camera.
3. Upload images of roads to the servers.

In order to detect road damage, we use CNN model that is a deep learning technique. Structure of the model were given in Fig. 1.

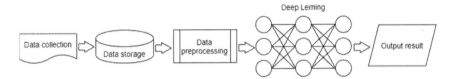

Fig. 1. The proposed structure

4.1 Data Collection

We created our own data set that includes six types of road damage. All images were annotated manually. Table 1 shows the injury types and their classes. Our data contains 1800 images that includes by 300 images of each category. During the data collection process, to identify damage class identifications and types we considered some literatures as [19–23]. Taking into account the features of the image of roadway defects (lack of clear borders, presence of foreign objects, insignificance of some defects), it is necessary to provide for the possibility of "manual" intervention. The roadmaster should be provided with an interface that allows you to select the characteristic points by moving the graphical cursor.

4.2 Neural Network Architecture

Convolutional neural network (also CNN or ConvNet) is one of the most popular algorithms in deep learning, it is a type of machine learning in which the model learns to perform classification tasks directly on an image, video, text or sound. Convolutional neural networks are particularly useful for finding patterns in images to recognize objects, faces, and scenes. They learn directly from images, using templates to classify images and eliminating the need for manual feature extraction. Convolutional neural network (CNN) is the main tool for classifying and recognizing objects, faces in photos, and speech recognition. There are many applications of CNN, such as Deep Convolutional Neural Network (DCN), Region-CN (R-CN), Fully Convolutional Neural Networks (FCNN), Mask R-CNN, and others.

Table 1. Road damage photos for model training

Photos of road damage for model training	Damage class	Type of injury
	D00	Open hatches
	D01, D11	Construction of the connecting part
	D20	Partial asphalt pavement
	D40	Potholes, broken concrete, road cracks
	D43	Blurring a road crossing
	D44	Blurring the dividing lines

All elements of the convolutional filter core are trained on the basis of data under observation by studying a marked set of examples. At each convolutional level, CNN performs subsampling operations to sum the responses of characteristics by neighboring pixels. Figure 2 illustrates our model of CNN for detecting road damages.

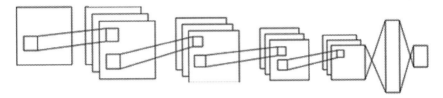

Fig. 2. Structure of a convolutional neural network

5   Experiment Results

To process a test image, CNN can provide each point centered within the image with a probability that it will crack or not. This gives a probability map. The probability of a point can be calculated by averaging the probability $\{P_1, ..., P_N\}$ each patch generated by randomly rotating around its Central pixel c, i.e., $p(c|\{P_1(c), ..., P_N(c)\}) = \frac{1}{N}\sum_{i=1}^{N} P_i(c)$, where $P_i(c)$ i - this is the CNN classification probability calculated for the I-th individual patch, and the number of probabilities is 5 for the calculation efficiency [20]. This fact makes CNN probably overestimate the probability of determining a crack. Therefore, you must use the appropriate threshold. Define precision and recall:

$$P = \frac{true\_positive}{true\_positive + false\_positive} \tag{1}$$

$$R = \frac{true\_positive}{true\_positive + false\_negative} \tag{2}$$

Then the F-measure will look like:

$$F_1 = \frac{2PR}{P + R} \tag{3}$$

The threshold used for revaluation of the final probability is defined so that it gives the highest score in the verification dataset [25]. In this study, the threshold value of t is set to 0.64, at which the indicator is maximal.

After successful training of the neural network, it is necessary to check its performance.

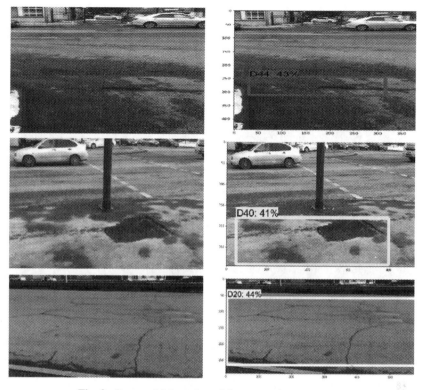

Fig. 3. Successful detection of damage at the new photos

6 Conclusion

Road surfaces during their entire service life operate under cyclic loading of the transport load under a given climatic influence. In order to decrease car accidents due to road damages, we proposed real time road damage using deep learning techniques. We have proposed an automated road damage detection method using CNN that characteristics are automatically extracted from manually annotated patches of images obtained by a smartphone. In this project, we used a data set to detect and classify road damage. These images were then visually classified into six classes. Of these, most of the images were annotated and used as a set for training data. Based on the results, we achieved results and accuracy of more than 80%. We believe that a simple method of road inspection using only a smartphone will be useful in regions where there are not enough experts and financial resources. In further we try to get high accuracy in detection by increasing our dataset, improve the deep learning model, and using GPU performance. Moreover, the proposed approach can be install to smartphones and help to detect road damages in real time. The proposed approach will allow for an objective assessment of road surface damage with minimal costs for its implementation.

References

1. Yu, B.X., Yu, X.: Vibration-based system for pavement condition evaluation. In: AATT 2006, pp. 183–189 (2006)
2. Li, Q., Yao, M., Yao, X., Xu, B.: A real-time 3d scanning system for pavement distortion inspection. MST **21**(1), 015702 (2009)
3. Zhang, A., et al.: Automated pixel-level pavement crack detection on 3d asphalt surfaces using a deep-learning network. CACAIE **32**(10), 805–819 (2017)
4. Zhang, L., Yang, F., Zhang, Y.D., Zhu, Y.J.: Road crack detection using deep convolutional neural network. In: ICIP 2016, pp. 3708–3712. IEEE (2016)
5. Akarsu, B., Karaköse, M., Parlak, K., Akin, E., Sarimaden, A.: A fast and adaptive road defect detection approach using computer vision with real time implementation. Int. J. Appl. Math. Electron. Comput. **4**, 290–290 (2016)
6. Omarov, B.: Exploring uncertainty of delays of the cloud-based web services. In 2017 17th International Conference on Control, Automation and Systems (ICCAS), pp. 336–340. IEEE (October 2017)
7. Omarov, B., et al.: Indoor microclimate comfort level control in residential buildings. Far East J. Electron. Commun. **17**(6), 1345–1352 (2017)
8. Altayeva, A.B., Omarov, B.S., Aitmagambetov, A.Z., Kendzhaeva, B.B., Burkitbayeva, M.A.: Modeling and exploring base station characteristics of LTE mobile networks. Life Sci. J. **11**(6), 227–233 (2014)
9. Omarov, B., et al.: Ensuring comfort microclimate for sportsmen in sport halls: comfort temperature case study. In: Hernes, M., Wojtkiewicz, K., Szczerbicki, E. (eds.) Advances in Computational Collective Intelligence: 12th International Conference, ICCCI 2020, Da Nang, Vietnam, November 30 – December 3, 2020, Proceedings, pp. 626–637. Springer, Cham (2020). https://doi.org/10.1007/978-3-030-63119-2_51
10. Alfarrarjeh, A., Shahabi, C., Kim, S.H.: Hybrid indexes for spatial visual search. In: ACM MM Thematic Workshops, pp. 75–83. ACM (2017)
11. Chun, P., Hashimoto, K., Kataoka, N., Kuramoto, N., Ohga, M.: Asphalt pavement crack detection using image processing and naïve Bayes based machine learning approach. J. Jpn. Soc. Civ. Eng. Ser. E1 (Pavement Eng.) **70**(3), I_1–I_8 (2015)
12. Wang, W., Wu, B., Yang, S., Wang, Z.: Road damage detection and classification with faster R-CNN. In: 2018 IEEE International Conference on Big Data (Big Data), pp. 5220–5223. IEEE (December 2018)
13. Alfarrarjeh, A., Trivedi, D., Kim, S.H., Shahabi, C.: A deep learning approach for road damage detection from smartphone images. In: 2018 IEEE International Conference on Big Data (Big Data), pp. 5201–5204. IEEE (December 2018)
14. Chun, C., Ryu, S.K.: Road surface damage detection using fully convolutional neural networks and semi-supervised learning. Sensors **19**(24), 5501 (2019)
15. Cao, M.T., Tran, Q.V., Nguyen, N.M., Chang, K.T.: Survey on performance of deep learning models for detecting road damages using multiple dashcam image resources. Adv. Eng. Inf. **46**, 101182 (2020)
16. Manikandan, R., Kumar, S., Mohan, S.: Varying adaptive ensemble of deep detectors for road damage detection. In: 2018 IEEE International Conference on Big Data (Big Data), pp. 5216–5219. IEEE (December 2018)
17. Pereira, V., Tamura, S., Hayamizu, S., Fukai, H.: A deep learning-based approach for road pothole detection in timor leste. In: 2018 IEEE International Conference on Service Operations and Logistics, and Informatics (SOLI), pp. 279–284. IEEE (July 2018)

18. Shohel Arman, M., Mahbub Hasan, M., Sadia, F., Shakir, A.K., Sarker, K., Himu, F.A.: Detection and classification of road damage using R-CNN and faster R-CNN: a deep learning approach. In: Touhid Bhuiyan, M., Mostafijur Rahman, M., Ali, A. (eds.) Cyber Security and Computer Science: Second EAI International Conference, ICONCS 2020, Dhaka, Bangladesh, February 15-16, 2020, Proceedings, pp. 730–741. Springer, Cham (2020). https://doi.org/10.1007/978-3-030-52856-0_58

19. Jo, Y., Ryu, S.: Pothole detection system using a black-box camera. Sensors **15**(11), 29316–29331 (2015)

20. Zalama, E., Gómez-García-Bermejo, J., Medina, R., Llamas, J.: Road crack detection using visual features extracted by Gabor filters: road crack detection. Comput. Aided Civil Infrast. Eng. **29**(5), 342–358 (2014). https://doi.org/10.1111/mice.12042

21. Kokusai Kogyo Co., Ltd.: Mms (mobile measurement system) (2016)

22. Yu, X., Salari, E.: Pavement pothole detection and severity measurement using laser imaging. In: 2011 IEEE International Conference on Electro/Information Technology (EIT), pp. 1–5. IEEE (2011)

23. He, K., Zhang, X., Ren, S., Sun, J.: Deep residual learning for image recognition. In Proceedings of the IEEE Conference on Computer Vision and Pattern Recognition, pp. 770–778 (2016)

24. Maeda, H., Sekimoto, Y., Seto, T.: Lightweight road manager: smartphone-based automatic determination of road damage status by deep neural network. In: Proceedings of the 5th ACM SIGSPATIAL International Workshop on Mobile Geographic Information Systems, pp. 37–45. ACM (2016)

25. Zhang, A., et al.: Automated pixel-level pavement crack detection on 3d asphalt surfaces using a deep-learning network. Comput. Aided Civ. Infrastrut. Eng. **32**(10), 805–819 (2017)

Performance Analysis of Machine Learning Algorithms for Text Classification

Manda Thejaswee[(✉)], V. Srilakshmi, K. Anuradha, and G. Karuna

Computer Science and Engineering GRIET, Hyderabad, India

Abstract. In the current century, the number of complex documents and messages requiring a top-to-bottom understanding of ML strategies that precisely identify texts in different applications is increasing. In natural language processing, several ML techniques have produced impressive results. The achievement of these learning calculations relies on their ability to comprehend complex models and non-linear data relationships. In any case, identifying right text classification structures and procedures is still a test for researchers. A brief overview of text classification algorithms is presented in this paper. This review includes numerous methods of selecting text elements, current algorithms and techniques and methods of evaluation. In this analysis different TF-IDF Vectorizer features are compared to find the set that works best under different classification models. The objective of phishing website URLs is to purloin the personal information like user name, passwords and online banking transactions. Phishers use the websites which are visually and semantically similar to those real websites. As technology continues to grow, phishing techniques started to progress rapidly and this needs to be prevented by using anti-phishing mechanisms to detect phishing. Machine learning is a powerful tool used to strive against phishing attacks. This paper surveys the features used for detection and detection techniques using machine learning.

Keywords: Text mining · Text classification · Text categorization · Document classification

1 Introduction

In the last few decades, text classification issues have been discussed in many real-world applications [1, 2]. Classification Many researchers are interested in developing applications that relate to text classification methods, particularly with the latest developments in natural language processing (NLP) with text mining. Artificial Neural Networks were new emerging technologies that help solve problems with the classification of machine learning [20, 22]. Most text categorization systems can be divided into the following phases: pre-processing of text, selection of functions, selection of classifiers and evaluation.

© Springer Nature Singapore Pte Ltd. 2021
A. K. Luhach et al. (Eds.): ICAICR 2020, CCIS 1393, pp. 414–424, 2021.
https://doi.org/10.1007/978-981-16-3660-8_39

Text Classification
A. Document Collection
The records to be classified are of different kinds, such as text, music, images, etc.

B. Pre-processing
The information found in the records is conflicting, unreliable and are prone to have errors and should therefore be pre-processed. Tokenization, stop-word elimination and stemming are incorporated into the pre-processing phase (Fig. 1).

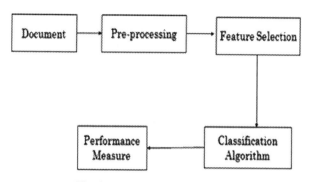

Fig. 1. Text classification process

C. Feature Selection
After pre-processing, the significant stage in text classification was Feature collection. Objective of the Feature collection theory was to pick a subset without affecting the output of the classifier [4].

D. Classificational Algorithms
In recent years, dynamic research on text classification has been carried out. Much of the text classification research work has concentrated on using ML methods to arrange text based on words from a training collection. Naïve Bayes (NB) classifiers, SVM, K-Nearest Neighbor (KNN), Decision Tree [5] are integrated into these methodologies.

E. Evaluation Metrics
The assessment metric assumes a simple task during classification training to achieve the ideal classifier. As a consequence, the selection of an acceptable assessment metric is an important key to segregating and obtaining the ideal classifier.

Text Pre-processing
Several text and documents have some words in the natural language process (NLP) that are unimportant for text classification, as like stop words, mis-spellings, slangs, etc. We tend to briefly clarify few methods and ways for text cleaning and pre-processing of text documents. Numerous algorithms are used, such as statistical and probabilistic methods of learning, because noise and unnecessary features can have a negative effect on results.

2 Feature Selection

- The classifier's precision is not entirely based on the classification algorithm, but also on the collection of features. The choice of irrelevant and inappropriate characteristics can lead to misunderstanding of the classifier and improper performance. The solution to this problem is to select characteristics i.e., to improve classifier competence and accuracy, it is important to select characteristics. The features function selected by eliminating the unapplicable and obsolete features from the initial data set a subset of features from the original feature. The list of attributes is also known.
- Feature selection decreases the spatiality of the dataset, improving the precision of the training. The methods of feature selection are known as evaluation algorithms for attributes and evaluation algorithms for subsets. Features are graded on an individual basis in the 1st technique, then each} feature is assigned a weight per all feature's range of importance to mark feature.
- In comparison, second method picks feature subsets, then ranks them on basis of exact criteria for analysis. Methods for attribute assessment do not calculate the association between attributes, so it is possible to yield subsets of redundant features. In removing redundant features, subset evaluation methods are efficient. Different types of algorithms for the selection of features are expected. The techniques for the selection of features are typically divided into three types of methods for filtering, wrapping, and embedding [7, 8]. Each feature selection algorithm employs one of the three feature selection techniques (Fig. 2).

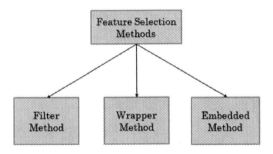

Fig. 2. Types of feature selection

Filter Method

Scoring technology is used as theory criterion in the Filter technique. The variables are provided with a score based on an acceptable ranking criterion and the variables below a certain threshold value are therefore removed. Calculation filtering methods are cheaper, but these techniques neglect dependencies between the functions, preventing over fitting. The chosen subset could therefore not be the best, and a redundant subset is obtained. The algorithms for the critical filter function selection are as follows:

Chi-Square Test

The technique of the chi-squared filter tests the independence of two events. When both the event X, Y are specified as independent, $P(XY) = P(X)(Y)$ or equivalent $P(X/Y) = P(X)$ and $P(Y/X) = P(Y)$. In particular, it is used in the selection of features to verify If a word selected is occurring and a class selected is occurring separately. High $\beta 2$ values indicate the dismissal of the null independence hypothesis (H0) and therefore the term and class occurrence depend. When based, the text classification feature is normally selected.

Document Frequency Technique (DF)

A term's document frequency is classified like total amount of documents containing term within the document set. DF's basic principle is that unusual items should be omitted from the collection of features [11, 12]. In particular, a ranking process is performed in the document collection vocabulary to determine the goodness or value of the word; and the frequency of the document is considered the measure of goodness for words here. The most relevant terms k are chosen as classification functions, followed by filtering the rest. DF is easy and efficient, because within the number of training documents, its time complexity is just about linear. However, the drawback of DF is that some of the terms sometimes used in certain documents might not be racist.

Wrapper Methods

Instead of merely relevant features, wrapper approaches are better at identifying optimal features [6]. Using the learning algorithm heuristics and even the training set, they do this. By the wrapper process, backward exclusion is used to eliminate the irrelevant characteristics from the subset. To spot the relevant function, some pre-defined learning algorithm is required for the wrapper process. It interacts with the algorithm for classification. While wrapper techniques are costly in computation and take longer than the filter process, they give more accurate results than the filter model.

Sequential Selection Algorithms

The SFS-Algorithm begins with an empty set and adds a feature, which in the first step provides the highest value for the objective function. The remaining features are added to the current subset individually after the first stage and the new subset is tested. The individual characteristics which offer the highest classifying accuracy are permanently incorporated into the subset. The process is continued until we have the requisite number of features. This algorithm is called a native SFS algorithm as it does not take into account the dependency between the features.

The SFS algorithm is correctly reversed by a Sequential Backward Selection (SBS) algorithm. Initially, the algorithm begins with the entire set of variables and eliminates an unnecessary function at a time when removal leads to the smallest decrease. The SFFS algorithm is more robust than the naïve SFS, as it introduces an additional backtracking step. The algorithm begins with the SFS algorithm and, depending on the objective function, adds one feature at a time.

The SFFS algorithm then uses the SBS algorithm to delete from the first phase subset a single function and to evaluate the new subsets [13, 14].

Embedded Methods

Unlike the above two methods, before learning tasks begin, the integrated methodology does not conduct the selection process directly. Instead the role selection action is integrated in the learning process [15]. For feature selection, many optimization techniques such as bio-inspired and meta-heuristic algorithms are often used to boost the efficiency of the classification [21, 22].

3 Classification Algorithms

Active research on text classification has taken place over the past few years. Much of the text classification research work has concentrated on the application of machine-learning techniques to classify text based on terms from a training collection. These approaches include SVM, K-Nearest Neighbor (KNN), Tree Decision, Neural Networks, and also by a mixture of approaches [24].

K-Nearest Neighbor

K Nearest Neighbor is an algorithm for supervised machine learning and is a calculation oriented. For instance, it gains from a named preparing set by taking up the preparing data X close by is names y and figures out how to design the data X to is ideal yield the k-NN algorithm is apparently the least difficult or the easiest of algorithms in machine learning. The model just comprises of the preparation data, i.e., the model essentially learns the whole preparing set and for expectation gives the output as the class with the lion's share in the *k' closest neighbours discover concurring to some separation metric. The working in somewhat more derail is as per the following: After the model has put away the preparation set for expectation, it steps through an examination picture to be anticipated, as certain the separation to each picture in the preparation set and gets the 'k' preparing pictures nearest to the test picture. It at that point yields the class as per some democratic methodology from the names of these 'k' neighbours, by and large a greater part vote [18, 19].

Linear SVC

The aim of a Linear SVC (Support Vector Classifier) is to adapt to the information we provide, restoring our data to a "best fit" hyperplane that separates or classifies. From that point on, you will then be able to take those features to your classifier after receiving the hyperplane to envision what the "predicted class is. This makes this particular algorithmic rule less suitable for our needs, but for some cases you will be able to use it [19].

SGD Classifier

Stochastic Gradient Descent (SGD) was a fundamental but efficient optimization algorithm used toward evaluate the parameter/capacity coefficient values that limit a cost function. Often used for the discriminatory learning of linear classifiers, as well as SVM and logistical regression, in convex loss functions. It was used in large-scale datasets effectively because, rather than at the end of instances, the update to the coefficients is performed for each training instance [18, 19].

Naïve Bayes Classifier

It would be troublesome and for all intents and purposes difficult to group a website page, an archive, an email or some other protracted content notes physically. This is the place Naïve Bayes Classifier AI calculation acts the hero. A classifier is a capacity that allots a populace's component esteem from one of the accessible classifications. For example, Spam Filtering is a well-known utilization of Naïve Bayes calculation. Spam channel here, is a classifier that allocates a name "Spam" or "Not Spam" to all the messages. Innocent Bayes Classifier is among the most mainstream learning strategy gathered by likenesses that takes a shot at the well-known Bayes Theorem of Probability-to fabricate AI models especially for sickness expectation and archive grouping. It is a straightforward arrangement of words dependent on Bayes Probability Theorem for emotional investigation of substance. The classifier's value depends on the Bayes theorem.

$$P(AB) = \frac{P(B/A)P(A)}{P(B)}$$

Evaluation Metrics

Performance tests usually assess various aspects of the performance of the classification mission, but similar knowledge is not necessarily available. For example, recall, precision, f-measurement, micro average and macro average are examples of these metrics. Depending on the classification application, the importance of these four parts can differ. Accuracy [18] is called the fraction of accurate predictions for all predictions. The fraction of correctly predicted well-known positives is referred to as sensitivity, i.e. true positive rate or recall [19]. Specificity [20] is called the ratio of negatives correctly predicted. The correctly foresaw proportion of positive elements is called accuracy, i.e. positive predictive value, for any or all positive aspects.

4   Experiment

In this analysis, we compare various features of TF-IDF Vectorizer to find the set which works the best under various classification models. By first considering no stemming and lemmatization in the vectorizer, we begin with the procedure. Then we will simply apply stemming, and we will only apply lemmatization to the vectorizer at the end. We initially use only unigrams as the resulting features of the TF-IDF Vectorizer in each of the three settings and compare it with the effects of considering both unigrams and bigrams in the features range. Therefore, four distinct classification models are considered for all these combinations to verify how they work on the test results. These include Naive Bayes, Logistic Regression, K Nearest Neighbors, and Stochastic Gradient Descent Classifier. The research is done in Python using the Sklearn library. We are using a data collection of 20 newsgroups for this experiment.

Not performing TF-IDF Vectorizer Stemming and Lemmatization: With TF-IDF Vectorizer we can extract "bag of phrases" from the text and apply weights of TF-IDF (term frequency - inverse document frequency). We find through preliminaries that the use of sublinear tf scaling $(1 + \log(tf))$ improves overall performance. The TF-IDF

Vectorizer generated a Matrix document term with ~11000 documents and ~68,000 words (without stemming/lemmatization) within the training set.

We first extract the best unigrams to form the vectorizer from the text data. We are testing four classifiers at that point: Multinomial Naive Bayes, Logistic Regression, Classifier of Stochastic Gradient Descent, and k Nearest Neighbors. We used grid search to change their parameters for Logistic Regression and K Nearest Neighbors.

The 'penalty' parameter was calibrated to the {'L1' and 'L2'} norm values for Logistic Regression. When the 'L2' norm is used in penalization, the best logistic regression efficiency is obtained. The parameter 'n neighbors' was tuned with values {5, 10, 100 and 200} for k nearest neighbours, and the parameter 'weights' was tuned with values{'uniform 'and' distance'} for k nearest neighbours. The best was provided by using 'n neighbours' as 5 and 'weights' as 'width' (Table 1).

Table 1. Performance of classifiers on test data

Ngrams	Classifier			
	Multinomial NB	Logistic regression	SGD classifier	K neighbors classifier
Unigram	66.49	69	70.18	8.42
Unigram + Bigram	65.59	68.34	70.66	I.5

Applying only Stemming in the TF-IDF Vectorizer: Presently we use stemming approach, i.e., slicing the words to their root form. We use Snowball English Stemmer algorithm from the NLTK package in Python and we defined a class to symbolize the Snowball Stemmer. We again implemented the four classifiers, first with least difficult unigrams after which with each unigrams and bigrams in the vectorizer.

Once again, performing grid search on Logistic Regression provided the best results when using the 'L2' standard in the penalization. Similarly, when 'n neighbours' was tuned to 5 and 'weights' to 'distance', k Nearest performed best. The average performance of the test data is presented in Table 2.

Table 2. Performance of classifiers on test data

Ngrams	Classifier			
	Multinomial NB	Logistic regression	SGD classifier	K neighbors classifier
Unigram	66.49	69	70.18	8.42
Unigram + Bigram	65.59	68.34	70.66	8.5

Applying Just Lemmatization in the TF-IDF Vectorizer: Finally, with the use of morphology, we apply lemmatization, for example having the word's grammatically correct normal form. We use the NLTK package's Word Net Lemmatizer and part of-speech word labelling and define a class to represent the Lemma Tokenizer. The four classifiers are again evaluated, first with only unigrams and then with both unigrams and bigrams in the vectorizer.

Once again when the 'L2' standard was used in the penalization, performing grid search on Logistic Regression provided the best results. Similarly, when 'n neighbours' was tuned to 5 and 'weights' to 'width', k Nearest Neighbors got the best results. Table 3 displays the results of the test data gathered.

Table 3. Performance of classifiers on test data

n-grams	Classifier			
	Multi nominal NB	Logistic Regression	SGD Classifier	K-Neighbors Classifier
Unigram	66.87	69.01	69.92	8.71
Unigram +Bigram	65.72	68.36	70.58	8.03

5   Results and Discussions

For every classifier, the best results obtained are shown in the graph. We see that the Stochastic Gradient Descent Classifier, followed by Linear SVC and Multinominal Naïve

Graph 1. Comparison of training time with various classifiers

Bayes, achieves the greatest precision of 90.3%. The bar plot displays every classifier's testing time, training time and accuracy.

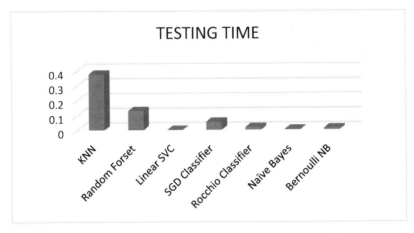

Graph 2. Comparison of testing time with various classifiers

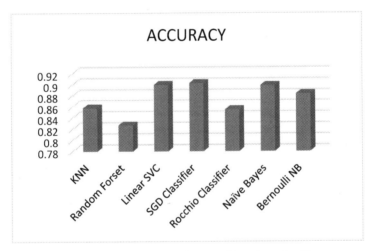

Graph 3. Comparison of accuracy with various classifiers

6 Conclusion

The state-of-the-art feature selection and texting methods in this paper have been extensively analyzed. We have also seen that the use of TF-IDF Vectorizer has provided preferred results over Count Vectorizer. By using Stemming along with both unigrams and bigrams derived from TFIDF Vectorizer, the best accuracy for Stochastic Gradient

Descent was achieved. In addition, unigrams have helped us achieve high accuracy much of the time, so we don't normally need to expand the features and increase the time the classifiers take. Given that training time for different classifiers is more in the random forest algorithm, testing time is more in the KNN algorithm and accuracy is more in the classifier for Stochastic Gradient Descent. We will expand our work in the future to improve the efficiency of the classifier by using algorithms inspired by nature.

References

1. Kwak, N., Choi, C.H.: Input feature selection for classification problems. IEEE Trans. Neural Netw. **13**, 143–159 (2002)
2. Wang, S., Zhu, J.: Variable selection for model-based high dimensional clustering and its application on microarray data. Biometrics **64**, 440–448 (2008)
3. Cateni, S., Colla, V., Vannucci, M.: A genetic algorithm-based approach for selecting input variables and setting relevant network parameters of a SOM-based classifier. Int. J. Simul. Syst. Sci. Technol. **12**, 30–37 (2011)
4. Tang, B., Kay, S., He, H.: Toward optimal feature selection in Naive Bayes for text categorization. IEEE Trans. Knowl. Data Eng. **28**(9), 2508–2521 (2016)
5. Guan, S., Liu, J., Qi, Y.: An incremental approach to contribution- based feature selection. J. Intell. Syst. **13**(1) (2004)
6. Kabir, M.M., Islam, M.M., Murase, K.: A new wrapper feature selection approach using neural network. In: Proceedings of the Joint Fourth International Conference on Soft Computing and Intelligent Systems and Ninth International Symposium on Advanced Intelligent Systems (SCIS&ISIS2008), Japan, pp. 1953–1958 (2008)
7. Gasca, E., Sanchez, J., Alonso, R.: Eliminating redundancy and irrelevance using a new MLP-based feature selection method. Pattern Recogn. **39**, 313–315 (2006)
8. Hsu, C., Huang, H., Schuschel, D.: The ANNIGMA-wrapper approach to fast feature selection for neural nets. IEEE Trans. Syst. Man Cybern.—Part B Cybern. **32**(2), 207–212 (2002)
9. Chou, C.H., Sinha, A.P., Zhao, H.: A hybrid attribute selection for text classification. J. Assoc. Inf. Syst. **11**(9), 491 (2010)
10. Gunal, S.: Hybrid feature selection for text classification. Turk. J. Electr. Eng. Comput. Sci. **20**(sup. 2), 1296–1311 (2012)
11. Molina, L.C., Belanche, L., Nebot, A.: Feature selection algorithms: a survey and experimental evaluation. In: Proceedings of 2002 IEEE International Conference on Data Mining 2002. ICDM 2003, pp. 306–313. IEEE (2002)
12. Oh, I.S., Lee, J.S., Moon, B.R.: Hybrid genetic algorithms for featureselection. IEEE Trans. Pattern Anal. Mach. Intell. **26**(11), 1424–1437 (2004)
13. Xing, E.P., Jordan, M.I., Karp, R.M., et al.: Feature selection for high-dimensional genomic microarray data. In: ICML, vol. 1, pp. 601–608 (2001)
14. Padmavathi, K., Krishna, K.S.R.: Myocardial infarction detection using magnitude squared coherence and support vector machine. In: International Conference on Medical Imaging, m-Health and Emerging Communication Systems. MedCom 2014, pp. 382–385 (2014). Article no. 7006037
15. Cortes, C., Vapnik, V.: Support vector machine. Mach. Learn. **20**(3), 273–297 (1995)
16. Cestnik, B.: Estimating probabilities: a crucial task in machine learning. In: ECAI, vol. 90, pp. 147–149 (1990)
17. Song, Q., Ni, J., Wang, G.: A fast clustering-based feature subset selection algorithm for high dimensional data. IEEE Trans. Knowl. Data Eng. **99**, 1 (2011). https://doi.org/10.1109/TKDE.2011.181

18. Kumari, A., Behera, R.K., Sahoo, K.S., Nayyar, A., Luhach, A.K., Sahoo, S.P.: Supervised link prediction using structured-based feature extraction in social network. Concurrency Comput. Pract. Exp. e5839 (2020)
19. Singh, K., Singh, S.S., Luhach, A.K., Kumar, A., Biswas, B.: Mining of closed high utility itemsets: a survey. Recent Adv. Comput. Sci. Commun. **14**, 6–12 (2020)

Prediction of Sales Figure Using Machine Learning Techniques

Shaleen Kumar Srivastava[1]([✉]), Amit Misra[2]([✉]), and Pratapsinh Chauhan[3]

[1] Saurashtra University, Rajkot, India
[2] Central Bank of India, Mumbai, Maharashtra, India
[3] Shri Govind Guru University, Godhara, Gujrat, India

Abstract. Growth of the business depends on the number of sales. Sales of products are an important part and parcel of any business. In the uncertain world like today, business leaders need to know the sales predictions to allocate resources efficiently and manage cash flow. Sales predictions also helps businesses to estimate their expenditure and revenues which in turn enable businesses to evaluate their short term and long-term performance. This paper is focused on solving the sales problem faced by many organisations by predicting the sales figures and analysing trends and seasonality using exponential moving averages. The algorithm written in this paper can be applied to any database with minor modification.

Keywords: Sales · Exponential moving average · Trends · Seasonality · Linear regression · Random forest regression · Lasso · Ridge and Elastic regression

1 Introduction

Every business entity has objectives to improve the sales and for that, they address questions like - how to grow business, how to select which region is suitable for the growth of business and what are the parameters that can be considered to increase profit margins. In earlier days, it required a lot of manual efforts and mental exercise to solve such problems, but machine learning and data analysis techniques have revolutionized the way business works and elevated the accuracy of predictions to make critical business decisions.

The algorithm proposed in this paper has been drawn using various Machine learning techniques to predict sales figures and analyse trends and seasoning.

2 Proposed Solution

To solve the sales problem, we have come up with the following methodology:

1. Analyse the Dataset by using Exploratory Data Analysis.
2. Use of Exponential Moving Averages (EMA) to analyse Trends and Seasonality
3. Perform Regression analysis using following prediction analysis methods:

© Springer Nature Singapore Pte Ltd. 2021
A. K. Luhach et al. (Eds.): ICAICR 2020, CCIS 1393, pp. 425–434, 2021.
https://doi.org/10.1007/978-981-16-3660-8_40

1. Linear Regression Analysis
2. Elastic Regression (Lasso and Ridge Regression).
3. Random Forest Regression.

We applied this methodology on the Roseman data set available on the Kaggle and we are presenting the results of methodology on the Roseman data set.

In this methodology we are using traditional simple model like EMA analysis which analyse past data and gives simple visual representation of trend and seasonality along with well-advanced Machine Learning Techniques gives future prediction. Consolidation of all the techniques gives dual approach of understanding visual analysis using past EMA analysis and future predictions using various Machine Learning Algorithms. Overall, this methodology gives complete analysis of problem with utmost Simplicity and Accuracy.

2.1 Roseman Sales Dataset

This dataset is a live dataset of Roseman Stores on Kaggle. On analysing the problem of Roseman data stores we observed that the Roseman problem is a problem of how to improve sales and grow business. Our methodology which we proposed is the best to solve this problem by predicting the sales figures, analysing trends and seasoning.

2.1.1 Let's Understand Roseman Dataset

Roseman Dataset Consists of Two Tables Below

A.   store.csv – store.csv table consists of master data of different types of stores.

#	Column	Non-Null Count	Dtype
0	Store	1115 non-null	int64
1	StoreType	1115 non-null	object
2	Assortment	1115 non-null	object
3	CompetitionDistance	1112 non-null	float64
4	CompetitionOpenSinceMonth	761 non-null	float64
5	CompetitionOpenSinceYear	761 non-null	float64
6	Promo2	1115 non-null	int64
7	Promo2SinceWeek	571 non-null	float64
8	Promo2SinceYear	571 non-null	float64
9	PromoInterval	571 non-null	object

B. train.csv- Details of train dataset consists of more than a million records of sales figures of each and every table.

#	Column	Non-Null	Count	Dtype
0	Store	1017209	non-null	int64
1	DayOfWeek	1017209	non-null	int64
2	Date	1017209	non-null	object
3	Sales	1017209	non-null	int64
4	Customers	1017209	non-null	int64
5	Open	1017209	non-null	int64
6	Promo	1017209	non-null	int64
7	StateHoliday	1017209	non-null	object
8	SchoolHoliday	1017209	non-null	int64

Here is our analysis for this dataset:

1. Both the dataset consists of Object type columns, which needs to be converted to integer type in order to predict future sales using Machine Learning, a mandatory requirement for sklearn ML technique.
2. Import the dataset in Python in following tables,

   1. Roseman – train.csv
   2. Store - store.csv

3. Roseman Dataset consists of four store types. Our primary goal is to analyse trends and seasonality in all the stores for achieving this goal we first join both the tables.
4. Since the dataset is very huge and consists of more than a million records to improve performance, we changed the datatype of each column as int32 from int64.
5. **Feeling of Roseman Problem Using Exponential Moving** - Since Roseman problem is a problem of continuous sales data. Exponential Moving Averages are (EMA) is a best indicator to analyse this problem. In layman terms Moving Average is an average past data example 20 days moving average means average data of the last 20 days and the same is moving. Moving Average gives best information about trend and seasonality higher the moving average higher the stability means 200 days moving average is more stable than 10 days. In case sales data supports lower moving averages (example supports 20 days moving average) means data is in strong trend if sales data supports 200 days moving average means data is in week uptrend. Exponential Moving Average is a type of Moving Average having weightage of current data also. Now using EMA we analyse following,
A. **Trend in Data** - This means that sales data is in an uptrend or downtrend.
B. **Seasonality in a data**- This means where sales figure increases in some specific timeframes.
6. For analysing regression problems ExpmyParaonential Moving Average (EMA) figures give a complete picture of data. By analysing this data, we can understand whether doing business is feasible and what are the important opportunities when we are able to get optimum benefits.

```
#Exponential Moving Average chart of Sales figure
rosemanall_weekly = rosemanall.groupby(['year','week'],as_index = False)
rosemanall_weekly.groups
rosemanall_weekly = rosemanall_weekly.agg({'Sales':np.mean})
rosemanll_weckly = rosemanall_weekly.sort_values(by =
['year','week'])rosemanall_weekly['weekrow']= rosema-
nall_weekly.reset_index().index
rosemanall_weekly['10weeks_ema']
=rosemaall_weekly.Sales.ewm(span=10).mean()
rosemanall_weekly['50weeks_ema'] = rosema-
nall_weekly.Sales.ewm(span=50).mean()
rosemanall_weekly['200weeks_ema'] = rosema-
nall_weekly.Sales.ewm(span=200).mean()
rosemanall_weekly.plot('weekrow',
['10weeks_ema','50weeks_ema','200weeks_ema'])
plt.show()
```

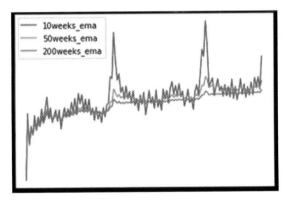

Fig. 1. Exponential moving average chart of sales figure

Conclusion and Observations: While Analysing Exponential Moving Average chart Roseman sales we analyse following observations,

1. Trend - EMA chart analyse that Roseman data is in uptrend and it always above the 200 Exponential Moving Average figures but 200 EMA line is not a steep slope informs that Roseman sales figure is in slow uptrend.
2. Seasonality - 10 days EMA chart figures show that sales has upward seasonality and for some weeks sales figures improve drastically.

Store Type Wise Exponential Moving Average Analysis - While analysing database we observe that Roseman have four different types of stores. After analysing complete dataset, we now analyse Exponential Moving Average Analysis of Sales figures Store-type wise means how the behaviour of different store types in order to go deeper and understand how to improve sales.

```
#Moving Average Chart of Store Wise Sales Figure
rosemanall_a = rosemanall.loc[rosemanall['StoreType'] == 1]
rosemanall_b = rosemanall.loc[rosemanall['StoreType'] == 2]
rosemanall_c = rosemanall.loc[rosemanall['StoreType'] == 3]
rosemanall_d = rosemanall.loc[rosemanall['StoreType'] == 4]
#EMA Analysis Store wise
rosemanall_a_weekly = rosemanall_a.groupby(['year','week'],as_index = False)
rosemanall_a_weekly.groups
rosemanall_a_weekly = rosemanall_a_weekly.agg({'Sales':np.mean})
rosemanll_weekly = rosemanall_a_weekly.sort_values(by = ['year','week'])
rosemanall_a_weekly['weekrow']= rosemanall_a_weekly.reset_index().index
rosemanall_a_weekly['20days_ema'] =
rosemanall_a_weekly.Sales.ewm(span=20).mean()
rosemanall_a_weekly['50days_ema'] =
rosemanall_a_weekly.Sales.ewm(span=50).mean()
rosemanall_a_weekly['200days_ema'] =
rosemanall_a_weekly.Sales.ewm(span=200).mean()
rosemnall_a_weekly.plot('weekrow',['20days_ema','50days_ema','200days_ema'])
plt.show()
```

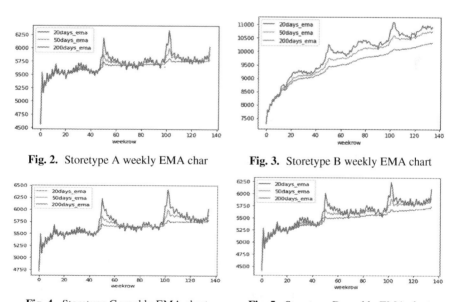

Fig. 2. Storetype A weekly EMA char   **Fig. 3.** Storetype B weekly EMA chart

Fig. 4. Storetype C weekly EMA chart   **Fig. 5.** Storetype D weekly EMA chart

Observations and Conclusions. After analysis of Roseman Storetype wise Exponential Moving Average Charts. After analysing consolidated data we now analyse Roseman Data Storewise. Following observations found

1. STORETYPE A - While analysing Exponential Moving Average Chart of Store Type A, we observe that -Store type A sales figure in slight uptrend 20 days EMA never crosses 200 days EMA. -We observe seasonality in the EMA chart and found sales of Store type A sharply increased at Week 50 and Week 105.

2. STORETYPE B - While analysing Exponential Moving Average Chart of Store Type B, we observe that

    o Storetype B Sales figures are in strong uptrend and 20 days EMA never crosses 50 days EMA sales chart of Storetype B is very strong.
    o Although this chart is very strong, we observe seasonality in upward seasonality at week 50 and week 105.

3. STORETYPE C - While analysing Exponential Moving Average Chart of Store Type C, we observe that -Store type A sales figure in slight uptrend 20 days EMA never crosses 200 days EMA. -We observe seasonality in the EMA chart and found sales of Store type A sharply increased at Week 50 and Week 105.

4. STORETYPE D - While analysing Exponential Moving Average Chart of Store Type D, we observe that

    o Storetype D sales chart is in uptrend and better chart than Storetype A and C. In this EMA chart we observe that support of 20 days EMA at 50 days EMA and most of time 20 days EMA line not cuts downward 20 days EMA line.

After analysing all the EMA charts store wise we observe following out of all the store type Roseman has to focus aggressively on opening new Store type B and D and focus on closure of Store type A and Exponential Moving Average Analysis is a part of Time Series Analysis and Roseman problem is a time series analysis problem our conclusion is that EMA chart analysis gives us very in depth understanding of Roseman sales.

1. **Predicting Sales of Roseman Dataset Using Machine Learning Techniques –** We now do prediction of RoseMan sales using Machine Learning techniques. We observe that the Roseman Sales problem is a regression problem means the predicted variable is in trend.

2. **Prediction of Roseman Sales using Linear Regression Model-** We start with a very simple model i.e. Linear Regression model and we are using Pipeline to pre-process the data and apply Linear Regression Model.

```
# Since Roseman Store is a regression problem we first build Linear
Regression Model
from sklearn, linear_model import LinearRegression
from sklearn.metrics import mean_squared_error
from sklearn.preprocessing import OneHotEncoder
from sklearn.compose import make_column_transformer
from sklearn.metrics import r2_score
from sklearn.preprocessing import OrdinalEncoder
SS = StandardScaler()
OHE = OneHotEncoder()
OE  = OrdinalEncoder()
LR = LinearRegression()
preprocess = make_column_transformer(
(SS,num_cols),
(OHE,obj_cols))
pipeline_linreg = make_pipeline(preprocess,LR)
#8.2 Fit the Pipeline in Training data
pipeline_linreg.fit(X_train,y_train)
#Predict the Pipeline in test data
y_predict_linreg = pipeline_linreg.predict(X_test)
```

```
#Score of Linear Regression pipeline
score_linreg =r2_score(y_predict_linreg,y_test)
score linreg
Out[21]:1.0
rmse = np.sqrt(mean_squared_error(y_test,y_predict_linreg)) rmse
Out[22]: 5.894694597725905e-12
```

Conclusion of Linear Regression Model - We observe that Root Mean Square Error figures are fine, in this model we are getting an excellent score of 1. Our personal opinion on this model is that getting score 1 means some over fitting issues in this model.

Regularization of Linear Regression Model Using Elastic Net. Elastic Net uses both Lasso and Ridge regression - Since Linear Regression model gives very high scores we now do some regularisation using Elastic Net regularisation which uses both Lasso and Ridge regressions. Theory of Lasso and Ridge regression is given below.

Courtesy- Towards Data Science **Linear regression (in scikit-learn)** is the most basic form, where the model is not penalized for its choice of weights, at all. That means, during the training stage, if the model feels like one feature is particularly important, the model may place a large weight on the feature. This sometimes leads to overfitting in small datasets. Hence, following methods are invented. **Lasso** is a modification of linear regression, where the model is penalized for the sum of absolute values of the weights. During training, the objective function becomes: Image for post as you see, Lasso introduced a new hyperparameter, alpha, the coefficient to penalize weights. **Ridge** takes a step further and penalizes the model for the sum of squared value of the weights. Thus, the weights not only tend to have smaller absolute values and more evenly distributed, but also tend to be close to zeros. The objective function becomes: Image for post **Elastic Net** is a hybrid of Lasso and Ridge, where both the absolute value penalization and squared penalization are included, being regulated with another coefficient l1_ratio:

```
# Regression Analysis using Elastic Net uses both Lasso and Ridge regressions
# Regularisation of Linear Regression Model using L1 and L2 regularization.
from sklearn.linear_model import ElasticNet
EN = Elastic Net()
pipeline_elasticnet = make_pipeline(preprocess,EN)
parameters = {'elasticnet__l1_ratio':np.linspace(0,1,30)}
# Calling Grid Search CV
Grid_Search_EN = GridSearchCV(pipeline_elasticnet,parameters)
Grid_Search_EN.fit(X_train,y_train)
# Compute and print the scores
r2 = Grid_Search_EN.score(X_test,y_test)
print("Tuned ElasticNet Alpha: {}".format(Grid_Search_EN.best_params_))
print("Tuned ElasticNet R squared: {}".format(r2))
OUT:
Tuned ElasticNet Alpha: {'elasticnet__l1_ratio': 1.0}
Tuned ElasticNet R squared: 0.9999999325274912
```

3   Prediction of Roseman Sales Using Random Forest Regression Analysis

Courtesy- Wikipedia Evaluation using Random Forest Regressor Model- Random forests or random decision forests are an ensemble learning method for classification, regression and other tasks that operate by constructing a multitude of decision trees at training time and outputting the class that is the mode of the classes (classification) or mean/average prediction (regression) of the individual trees [1, 2]. Random decision forests correct for decision trees' habit of overfitting to their training set. [3]:587–588 Random forests generally outperform decision trees, but their accuracy is lower than gradient boosted trees.

```
# Roseman Store problem using Random Forest Regressor
from sklearn.ensemble import RandomForestRegressor
RF = RandomForestRegressor(max_depth =5)
pipeline_rf = make_pipeline(preprocess,RF)
pipeline_rf.fit(X_train,y_train)
y_predict_rf = pipeline_rf.predict(X_test)
score_rf = r2_score(y_predict_rf,y_test)
score_rf
Out[26]:
0.9978271803344585
```

Our Observations and Conclusion for Random Forest Model.   We observe that Random Forest model gives nice results but at the same time Linear Regression which is a simple model also gives best results.

Final Conclusion - Roseman problem is an interesting problem to analyse future sales. In this presentation we analyse both past sales using Exponential Moving Averages, analyse the trend and seasonality in Roseman Sales figures. We observe that overall sales figures of Roseman stores are stuck from the last three years. It is in a very weak uptrend.

We observe that Roseman has four different types of stores, in this sheet we also analyse the performance of different store types using Exponential Moving Average. We observe that performance of store B is outstanding as compared to performance of all other stores. Our recommendation is that the Roseman team has to focus more on Store Type B and D and focus for closure of Store A and C.

We observe that performance of models is also nice to predict future Roseman Sales.

Future Works

1. In **the Corporate world** Sales is the most important aspect for any organisation. Sales is an engine for any organisation. By just changing the dataset we can analyse sales using Exponential Moving Average Analysis and predict future sales using Linear Regression and Random Forest Regression analysis.
2. **Banking** – Being Bankers we envisage that this project is helpful in Banking in following ways

    1. **Loan Analysis** – By using minor changes in our EMA model we can analyse which customer types have higher EMA figures means strong charts and which have lower EMA figures means weak charts. Banking Industry gets benefit from this analysis to encourage customers having uptrending EMA and discourage those customers having downtrend EMA figures. We also predict future Loan Portfolio using our prediction models.
    2. **Foreign Exchange Analysis and Treasury Business** – Foreign Exchange is one of best Milk Cow for any Banking organisation by using our EMA analysis we encourage those customers having better EMA in Packing Credits, Export Negotiations, Imports under LC/Non-LC.
    3. For treasury business using EMA analysis which currency is in uptrend and which currency in down trend, which treasury instrument is in uptrend and which instrument is in down trend. We also predict the future value of foreign exchange instruments.

3. **Medical Sector** – EMA analysis can be used in the Medical sector like in the present scenario we analyse whether EMA figures of COVID 19 are in uptrend or downtrend. By our Machine Learning models we can predict future figures.
4. **Stock Market, Commodity Markets and Currency Markets** – By using our EMA model we can analyse various stock market indices of the world like Dow Jones, Nasdaq of USA, Nikkei of Japan, Bovespa of Brazil, Nifty of India. Since we are analysing the world chart also, we observe that Stock markets of world are in very high EMA uptrend

Emerging Business Markets – Using EMA analysis we observe that world markets are shifting from US to Emerging Countries like performance of NIKKAI of Japan, Nifty 50 of India in very high uptrend whereas due to very high infusion of liquidity in US markets showing somewhat consolidation. By minor changes in our model we can do EMA analysis of Stock markets as well as prediction using Machine Learning Models.

References

1. Rosemann store dataset for our case study analysis. www.kaggle.com
2. Beheshti-Kashi, S., Karimi, H.R., Lütjen, M., Thoben, K.-D., Teucke, M.: A survey on retail sales forecasting and prediction in fashion markets. Syst. Sci. Control Eng. Open Access J. **3**(1), 154–161 https://doi.org/10.1080/21642583.2014.999389
3. Anaconda and Python for Machine Learning Models i.e. Linear Regression, Elastic Net and Random Forest Regression model. https://machinelearningmastery.com/
4. Lasso, Redge and Elastic Net model. https://towardsdatascience.com/
5. Wikipedia for describing Random Forest Model

Particle Swarm Based Optimal Key Generation: Block Chain Assisted Secure Information Sharing in Supply Chain Management

D. Kalyani[1]($\boxtimes$) and P. Vijay Kumar[2]($\boxtimes$)

[1] VNR Vignana Jyothi Institute of Engineering &Technology, Bachupally, Hyderabad, India
kalyani_d@vnrvjiet.in
[2] DRK Institute of Science and Technology, Hyderabad, India

Abstract. The supply chain is essentially a network of businesses and people, who are involved in manufacturing or delivering products and services. As businesses have enlarged, the supply chains have become more complex, making them difficult to manage and optimize. In this scenario, "Blockchain" has emerged as a technology that helps in the efficient management of these complicated supply chains. In this research work, the block chain assisted "Supply Chain Management (SCM)" is introduced. With the intention of enhancing the security of the proposed SCM, a new privacy preservation approach is adopted, where the "Data Sanitization and Data Restoration" takes place with the optimally selected key. More importantly, in both the processes, the optimal key is generated via a standard "Particle Swarm Optimization Algorithm (PSO)". The proposed secures blockchain based PSCM model is validated by comparing it over the traditional models in terms of attack analysis.

Keywords: PSCM · Block chain technology · Optimal key generation · PSO

1 Introduction

The SCM is the mechanism of managing the flow of commodities as the raw materials from the manufacturer to the finished goods to the supplier. The entire process of the SCM is determined by taking the "right quality at the right time to the right place". The SCM is being highly revolutionized by a key technology termed as the block chain [5–8]. The block chain technology is a peer-to-peer infrastructure that is based on the smart contracts and the distributed database of the business. Block chain is the approach towards implementing the aspects of the supply-chain for improved data protection [4, 9–11]. In the supply chain system of international trade, millions of transactions take place between hundreds and thousands of actors. More particularly, in SCM, when a product change from hand to hand, each and every transactions taking place are documented and as whole a complete history of the product will be recorded yet from the manufacturer level to the sales level. This reduces the time delay, shipping cost and human-errors in transactions as well.

© Springer Nature Singapore Pte Ltd. 2021
A. K. Luhach et al. (Eds.): ICAICR 2020, CCIS 1393, pp. 435–445, 2021.
https://doi.org/10.1007/978-981-16-3660-8_41

It is an effort challenge to manage this all reliably and securely. Therefore, the privacy preservation techniques can be implied for enhancing the security of the network. After the introduction of the privacy preservation techniques with optimization tactics [15–19] based key generation, the SCM with block chain becomes:

- Easy to authenticate/validate data
- Share data easily (using digital keys and selective record sharing)
- Automate processing or audits for online financial transactions.

The most important contribution of this research work is:

- Introduces a PSCM model with block chain technology, where the transactions are secured via the proposed privacy preservation model.
- In the "proposed privacy preservation model", the optimal key for data sanitization and restoration is generated via the renowned meta-heuristic algorithm, PSO.

The leftovers section of this paper is organized as: Sect. 2 addresses the recent works done in SCM with block chain based security management. Section 3 depicts about the proposed SCM with blockchain technology: an overview. Section 4 discusses the acquired results and Sect. 5 concludes this research work.

2   Literature Review

2.1   Related Works

In 2019, Xiong, *et al.* [1] have constructed a private-key distribution protocol in blockchains with key recovery for securing the privacy of the private keys. This model was good in recovering the lost keys. In addition, the author's have introduced the network protocols to ensure the secret key transmission. But, here the convergence of the proposed work was lower.

In 2020, Jangirala *et al.* [2] have developed LBRAPS to make sure the "security of the data" in the supply chains. The proposed LBRAPS was based on "bitwise exclusive-or (XOR), OW-CH and BRO". The proposed work was found to be good in solving the security issues. Apart from this, it suffers from privacy disclosure.

In 2020, Cha *et al.* [3] have projected a framework for enhancing the traceability of the supply chains. This works has utilized the KEES and blockchain for optimizing the security of the supply chains. This approach was found to be more complex in computations.

In 2017, Toyoda *et al.* [4] have proposed a new POM in the post supply chain of RFID-attached products. The authors have merged the blockchian technology with SCM, such that the purchase of counterfeits can be avoided with genuine RFID tag information. But, here the delivery deadline is not reached.

3 Proposed SCM with Blockchain Technology: An Overview

3.1 Traditional SCM

The architecture of the traditional SCM is shown in Fig. 1. It includes 4 major phases: 1st phase $\rightarrow$ Manufacturer, 2nd phase $\rightarrow$ manager, 3rd phase $\rightarrow$ Delivery and 4th phase $\rightarrow$ Vendor. Initially, the raw data from different suppliers are collected and it is send to the manufacturers located in diverse geographical locations. In the next phase, the raw materials are sent to mangers of diverse departments and finally they are transformed into a final product. This product is delivered to the vendors based on the needs and demands. At the end, the vendors directly sell the products to the end-users.

Shortcoming:

- Lack of Transparency and Product Traceability
- Lack of Trust
- Shipping of Expired products
- Deliver of Counterfeit Products

To overcome these drawbacks, a new PSCM is introduced in this research work.

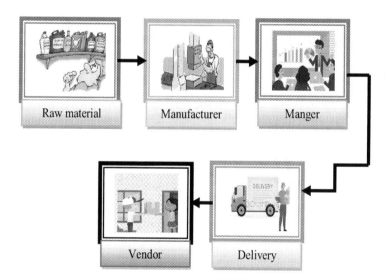

Fig. 1. Traditional SCM

3.2 P-SCM (Proposed Supply Chain Management) Construction

In the PSCM, each and every phases of the SCM are recorded into a block chain network. The PSCM includes 4 major phases: 1st phase $\rightarrow$ Manufacturer, 2nd phase $\rightarrow$ manager, 3rd phase $\rightarrow$ Delivery and 4th phase $\rightarrow$ Vendor. In the end-to-end chain, the immutable block holds every transaction, and product in the PSCM can be tracked. Moreover, the

PSCM permits any of the entity to enter the network, but do not permit them to access the sensitive data in the network. In case of authorized users, the key based authentication verifies the authenticity and then permits them to access the data allocated to them alone. Figure 2 illustrates the constructed PSCM with block chain.

In the initial phase, the raw materials are supplied to manufacturer and the transactions like the "raw material name, quantity, and quality of material, location of the supplier, etc." are loaded into the block chain. Once, the "manufacturer" gets the raw material" they are transferred to the mangers of diverse departments, and the corresponding data is stored in the block chain. From the manger end, the finished products are delivered to the vendors by recoding the truncations data like the name of the manufactured goods, manufacturing cost, and expiry of the product as well. Based on the needs, the vendors can access the block chain and get the appropriate products. However, the security is being the key challenge in the block chain based PSCM; therefore a new Privacy Preserving Security Model is introduced.

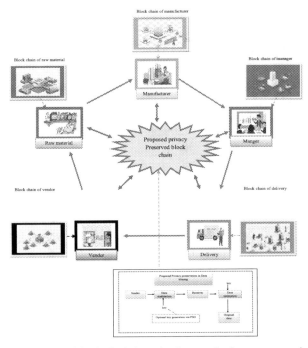

Fig. 2. Proposed SCM with Block chain technology and privacy preservation approach

3.3 Proposed Privacy Preserving Security Model

"The privacy preserving security model commenced in this research work encapsulates three major phases: data sanitization, optimal key generation and data restoration". The original data is sanitized before it is placed in the blocks of the block chain. The transferred sanitized data is restored at the receiver end. More importantly, in both the processes, OKG plays a major role, where the key is optimally selected via the renowned PSO algorithm. The major objective fixed for generating the optimal key for P-PDM is exhibited in Eq. (1).

$$\min\ Fn = \max(Fn_1, Fn_2, Fn_3, Fn_4) \tag{1}$$

In which,

$$Fn_1 = \frac{fun_1}{\max(fun_1)\forall iterations} \tag{2}$$

$$Fn_2 = \frac{fun_2}{\max(fun_2)\forall iterations} \tag{3}$$

$$Fn_3 = \frac{fun_3}{\max(fun_3)\forall iterations} \tag{4}$$

$$Fn_4 = \frac{fun_4}{\max(fun_4)\forall iterations} \tag{5}$$

HFR: In Eq. (2), Fn_1 is the normalized Hiding failure rate and fun_1 is the HFR is the function of the sensitive rules. The sensitive rules count (SRs) in block chain BC is given as $f_1 = |BC \cap SRs|$. The "association rule" A is generated in prior to the "sanitization process" and hence fun_1 is modelled as per Eq. (6). In addition, $\max(fun_1)$ is the worst fun_1 of all the iterations and A' indicates the association rules attained from sanitized block chain BC^{san}.

$$fun_1 = \frac{|A' \cap SRs|}{|SRs|} \tag{6}$$

Data preservation rate Fn_2: The rate of non- sensitive rules in the sanitized block chain is (BC^{san}) and it is also said to be the "reciprocal of information loss". The mathematical formula for rate of N-SR fun_2 is given in Eq. (7)

$$fun_2 = 1 - \frac{|A - A'|}{|A|} \tag{7}$$

FDG Fn_3: The block chain produces the artificial rules fun_3 generated in the sanitized block chain BC^{san} and it is expressed as per Eq. (8).

$$fun_3 = \frac{|A - A'|}{|A'|} \tag{8}$$

MD Fn_4: The count of modifications fun_4 produced in BC^{san} is defined as per Eq. (9). Here, $dist$ is the Euclidean distance between BC and BC^{san}

$$f_4 = dist(BC, BC^{san}) \tag{9}$$

By considering these objectives, a secure data sharing model is introduced.

Data Sanitization Model: In the proposed data sanitization model, BC having the sensitive fields are sanitized. The pruned key matrix K_2 is binarized and the sanitization of BC is done here. The result is fed as input to the RHP, where XOR function is carried out with binarized BC with the dimensions of identical matrix and summed up with one to generate BC^{san}. Then, BC^{san} achieved from the sanitization process generates A' and sensitive rules (SRs). Mathematically, the adopted santization model is given in Eq. (10).

$$BC^{san} = (BC \oplus K_2) + 1 \tag{10}$$

Proposed Key Generation: It has the solution transformation and here K is transformed using the "khatri-rao product". Initially, K_1 is remodelled from K in the dimension $\left[\sqrt{Count_{BC^{san}}^{(n)}} \times BC_{\max} \right]$, where $BC_{\max}$ is the maximal transaction length and the count of transaction is $C_{BC}^{(n)}$ and its adjacent maximal perfect square is $Count_{BC}^{(n)}$.

$$A_1 = \begin{bmatrix} 1 & 1 & 1 \\ 2 & 2 & 2 \\ 1 & 1 & 1 \end{bmatrix}_{\left[\sqrt{Count_{BC^{san}}^{(n)}} \times BC_{\max} \right]} \tag{11}$$

With this $Count_{BC^{san}}^{(n)}$, the sanitized database is achieved with the rule hiding process and sensitive rules. Then, the sanitized sanitized database $Count_{BC^{san}}^{(n)}$ is send to the receiver.

Data Restoration Process: At the receiver end, $Count_{BC^{san}}^{(n)}$ and K_2 are binarized. Then, the binarized SRs is reduced from unit step. Meanwhile, "XOR operation" is carried out for the database and the binarized key matrix, and thereby extracts the restored database. The solution fed as input to PSO is chromosome (keys) $K = K^1, \ldots K^N$, which is equivalent to the "count of the sensitive fields". The solutions are shown in Fig. 3 and here n denotes the count of keys.

Generated Keys

Fig. 3. Solution encoding

At the receiver end, BC^{san} is restored $\left(BC^{rest} \right)$ using Eq. (12).

$$BC^{rest} = \left(BC^{san} - 1 \right) \oplus K_2 \tag{12}$$

3.4   Particle Swarm Optimizarttion

The PSO [13, 14] was developed based on the inspirations acquired from the swarm intelligence behaviour of the particles (search agents). This algorithm has faster convergence and acquires the global optimal solutions without getting trapped into the local optimal. Therefore, PSO is chosen in this research work for generating the optimal keys. The steps followed in the PSO model is depicted below:

Step 1: Initialize the position of the search agents as $X = X_1, X_2, \ldots, X_M$, where M is the count of search agents. In addition, the velocity of the search agents are initialized as $V = V_1, V_2, \ldots, V_M$. The current iteration is denoted as $iter$ and the maximal iterations is denoted as $\max^{iter}$.

Step 2: while $iter < \max^{iter}$, move to step 3 else terminate.

Step 3: Compute the fitness of the search agent using Eq. (1).

Step 4: Update the position and the velocity of the particles, respectively. The mathematical formula for veloicty upadte of jth particle is $V_j(iter+1)$ is given in Eq. (13).

$$V_j(iter + 1) = \varpi.V_j(iter) + ac_1.ra_1\big(G_{bj}(iter) - X_j(iter)\big)$$
$$+ac_2.ra_2\big(G_{bj}(iter) - X_j(iter)\big) \tag{13}$$

Where, ra_1 and ra_2 are the randomly distributed variables and acceleration coefficient are ac_1 and ac_2, respectively. The interia weight is denoted as ϖ, the local best and the

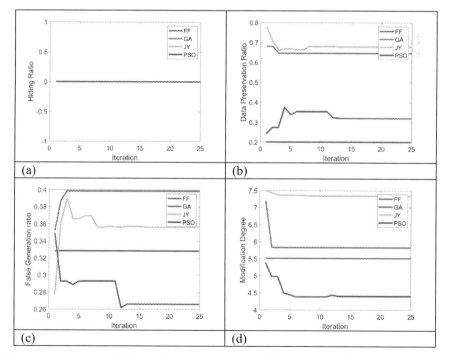

Fig. 4. Achievement of defined objectives in terms of (a) HFR, (b) Data Preservation, (c) FDG and (d) MD.

global best particles are denoted as $G_{pj}(iter)$ and $G_{bj}(iter)$, respectively. The position f the search agent is updated using Eq. (14)

$$X_j(iter + 1) = X_j(iter) + V_j(iter) \; ; j = 1, 2, .., J \tag{14}$$

Step 5: Enforce search space boundaries based on the position of the particle.
Step 6: Terminate.

4   Results and Discussion

4.1   Simulation Procedure

The PSCM based on block chain technology for secure information sharing was implemented in MATLAB and the outcomes were noted. The data for evaluation was collected from: "https://www.kaggle.com/divyeshardeshana/supply-chain-shipment-price-data-analysis" [Access date: 2020–11-07]. "Dataset Description: This data set provides supply chain health commodity shipment and pricing data". The evaluation of the proposed work with PSO and existing models is evaluated in terms of cost function, CCA, CPA, KCA and KPA, respectively. The purpose of CPA & KPA is not to decrypt the message in hand, rather to reconstruct the secret key that was used. This evaluation is done by varying the count of iterations.

4.2   Analysis on Attacks: CCA, CPA, KCA and KPA

CCA of planned secures blockchain based PSCM model with PSO is lower, when contrasted to the proposed work with existing models like FF, GA and JA, respectively, and this is clearly verified from Fig. 5 (a). The CCA of the proposed work with PSO is 9.5%, 8.6% and 11.45 better than the proposed work with existing models like FF, GA and JA, respectively at 30th iteration. The result of CPA of the presented work with PSO and existing models is shown in Fig. 5 (b). Here, the CPA of the presented work is lower with PSO and hence proved to be more secured. The KPA and KCA of the presented work with PSO is lower. Then, for 8000 records, the KPA of the presented work with PSO has the lowest value and it is 20%, 28.5%, and 55.5% improved than extant approaches like FF, GA and JA, respectively. Thus from the overall evaluation, a clear conclusion can be derived that the proposed SCM with block chain based privacy model is highly robust against the attacks, and hence said to be more secure for information transmission.

4.3   Convergence Analysis

The convergence analysis tells about the achievement of the defined objective function given in Eq. (1). In this research work, the objective being the minimization function is achieved more significantly by the proposed model and this is evident from Fig. 6. In the initial iterations, the presented work with PSO has higher convergence, however, not as much higher than the existing works. As the count of iterations increases, the cost function has decreased to its lowest range.

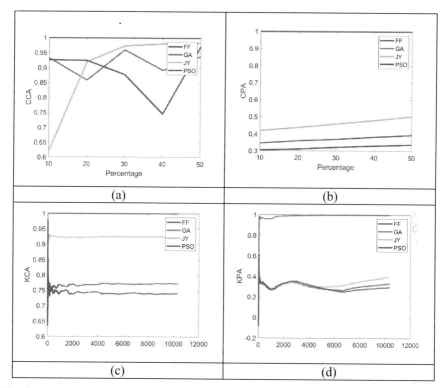

Fig. 5. Analysis of proposed work with PSO and existing works for diverse attacks: (a) CCA, (b) CPA, (c) KCA and (d) KPA

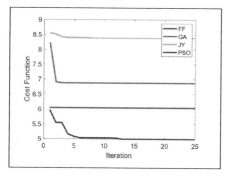

Fig. 6. Analysis on convergence of the Proposed and extant PSCM with blockchain based security model

4.4 Analysis on Key Sensitivity

The key sensitivity of secures blockchain based PSCM model with PSO and extant works is tabulated in Table 1. This valuation is undergone by varying the "percentage level of key to 10%, 30%, 40%, 50% and 70%", respectively. At every variation in the percentage level of key, the secures blockchain based PSCM model has achieved the least possible value, which indicates that the proposed model is stronger and less sensitive to attacks.

Table 1. Key sensitivity evaluation

Key %	FF	GA	JA	PSO
10	0.982194	0.96947	0.998695	0.435675
20	0.9739	0.932933	0.998723	0.425655
30	0.957112	0.99286	0.998707	0.77467
40	0.93495	0.985562	0.998715	0.77024

5   Conclusion

In this paper, a block chain assisted PSCM was introduced. Particularly, to enhance the security of the proposed SCM, a new privacy preservation approach was introduced. In the privacy preservation approach, the "optimal key for data sanitization and data restoration" was generated via a standard PSO. Finally, an attack evaluation is undergone with the projected and the extant works. The CCA of planned work with PSO is 9.5%, 8.6% and 11.45 better than the proposed work with existing models like FF, GA and JA, respectively at 30th iteration.

References

1. Xiong, F., Xiao, R., Ren, W., Zheng, R., Jiang, J.: A key protection scheme based on secret sharing for blockchain-based construction supply chain system. IEEE Access **7**, 126773–126786 (2019)
2. Jangirala, S., Das, A.K., Vasilakos, A.V.: Designing secure lightweight blockchain-enabled RFID-based authentication protocol for supply chains in 5G mobile edge computing environment. IEEE Trans. Industr. Inf. **16**(11), 7081–7093 (2020)
3. Cha, S., Baek, S., Kim, S.: Blockchain Based Sensitive Data Management by Using Key Escrow Encryption System From the Perspective of Supply Chain. IEEE Access **8**, 154269–154280 (2020)
4. Toyoda, K., Mathiopoulos, P.T., Sasase, I., Ohtsuki, T.: A novel blockchain-based product ownership management system (POMS) for anti-counterfeits in the post supply chain. IEEE Access **5**, 17465–17477 (2017)
5. Hadway, S.D., Carnovale, S., Hazen, B.: Understanding risk management for intentional supply chain disruptions: risk detection, risk mitigation, and risk recovery. Ann. Oper. Res. **283**, 179–198 (2017)
6. Karamchandani, A., Srivastava, S.K., Srivastavam, R.K.: Perception-based model for analyzing the impact of enterprise blockchain adoption on SCM in the Indian service industry. Int. J. Inf. Manage. **52**, 102019 (2019)
7. Vaioa, A.D., Varriale, L.: Blockchain technology in supply chain management for sustainable performance: evidence from the airport industry. International Journal of Information Management (2019)

8. Xiong, F., Xiao, R., Ren, W., Zheng, R., Jiang, J.: A Key Protection Scheme Based on Secretm Sharing for Blockchain-Based Construction Supply Chain System. Digital Object Identifier 7 (2019)
9. Yang, A., Li, Y., Liu, C., Li, J., Wang, J.: Research on logistics supply chain of iron and steel enterprises based on block chain technology. Futur. Gener. Comput. Syst. **101**, 635–645 (2019)
10. Chen, T., Wang, D.: Combined application of blockchain technology in fractional calculus model of supply chain financial system. Chaos, Solitons & Fractals, in communication (2019)
11. Behnke, K., Janssen, M.F.W.H.A.: Boundary conditions for traceability in food supply chains using blockchain technology. Int. J. Inf. Manag. Commun. **52**, 101969 (2019)
12. Tönnissen, S., Teuteberg, F.: Analysing the impact of blockchain-technology for operations and supply chain management: An explanatory model drawn from multiple case studies. International Journal of Information Management, in communication (2019)
13. Tanweer, M.R., Suresh, S., Sundararajan, N.: Self regulating particle swarm optimization algorithm &quot. Inf. Sci. **294**, 182–202 (2015)
14. kulkarni, Y.R., Murugan, T.S.: Hybrid weed-particle swarm optimization algorithm and C-mixture for data publishing. Multimed. Res. **2**(3), 33–42 (2019)
15. Boothalingam, R.: Optimization using lion algorithm: a biological inspiration from lion's social behavior. Evol. Intel. **11**(1–2), 31–52 (2018). https://doi.org/10.1007/s12065-018-0168-y
16. Kalyani, D., Sriidevi, R.: Robust Distributed key Issuing protocol for Identity based cryptography. In: International Conference on Advances in Computing, Communications and Informatics, ICACCI, September 21–24, 2016, Jaipur, pp. 821–825. https://doi.org/10.1109/ICACCI.2016.7732147.
17. Kalyani, D., Sriidevi, R.: Survey on Identity based and hierarchical identity based encryption schemes. Int. J. Comput. Appl. **134**(14), 32–37 (2016)
18. Kalyani, D., Sriidevi, R.: Private Communication based on hierarchical Identity based cryptography. In: International Conference on Emerging Technologies in Data Mining and Information Security,(IEMIS-2018). AISC. Springer (2018)
19. Kalyani, D., Sriidevi, R.: New hierarchical Identity based encryption with maximum hierarchy. Int. J. Network Secur. IJNS **21**(1), 40–46 (2019)

Big Five Personality Traits Prediction Using Deep Convolutional Neural Networks

Manisha Nilugonda[✉], Karanam Madhavi, and Krishna Chythanya Nagaraju

Gokaraju Rangaraju Institute of Engineering and Technology, Hyderabad, India
kcn_be@rediffmail.com

Abstract. The automated review of video interviews to identify specific applicant personality traits has grown an intense interview section. It has applicability
in human-computer interaction (HCI), personality computing, and psychological (PE) evaluation. Various Approaches in computer concepts based on deep
learning approaches pointed to the corporation of the CNN (convolutional neural network) approach, which can identify human personality cues and associate
their character features using a webcam. This paper proposed a deep learning-
based Deep Convolutional Neural Network (DCNN) to identify personality traits.
It is a semi-supervised deep learning method, suggested AVI (asynchronous video
interview)-AI that can partially replace human raters' work in the beginning step
of vocation and to guess an applicant personality trait strongly. The proposed
method experimental results show recognizing the applicant's Conscientiousness,
openness, extraversion, and neuroticism is observed by trained HR experts. The
results show that an AVI-AI-based interview tool can strongly identify an interviewee's "big five" traits at an accuracy between 96.9% and 99.5%. Also, the
proposed method compared with traditional classifiers of RF and SVM, and it
shows a better recognition rate compared to previous methods.

Keywords: Big five personality traits · Asynchronous video interview ·
Automatic personality recognition

1 Introduction

Personality is defined as a set of traits that make an individual special, and observation of character is a primary goal of psychology [1]. One of the most influential and
classic personality theories is the idea of the Great Five, which includes five simple
developments: extraversion, kindness, Conscientiousness, frankness, and neuroticism
in the formation of the human personality [2]. With the ubiquity of social networking
sites today, Facebook has become one of the most popular social networking services
globally. More than 1.3 billion customers have an average daily capacity as of June 2017.
As a result, Facebook plays a vital role in the everyday life of humans. Therefore, the
platform provides an ideal online platform for personal and comparative benefit studies.

The information disclosed through personal assessment can be used in various applications. These include, but are not limited to, add alignment, fine-tuning advertising and

© Springer Nature Singapore Pte Ltd. 2021
A. K. Luhach et al. (Eds.): ICAICR 2020, CCIS 1393, pp. 446–455, 2021.
https://doi.org/10.1007/978-981-16-3660-8_42

marketing campaigns, and helping bloggers narrow their target audience primarily based on personality traits previously discovered on the web [3]. Many different packages can take advantage of the personality recognition systems. For example, an organization promoting weapons might display a selective commercial ad describing its wares as a sign of electricity and power to departing humans while also showing robbery statistics and highlighting visible protection improvements for nerves and individuals.

1.1 Industrial Psychology

Industrial and organizational analysts have perceived that character is a universal indicator applied in job reservation [4]. Various employers use self-suggested questionnaires to estimate employment candidates' personalities, but applicants can also lie while reporting personal inclinations to take advantage of additional task capabilities [5]. Some employers rate applicants' personalities based on their facial expressions and various non-verbal cues in the context of job interviews because applicants have great difficulty simulating non-verbal cues.

But it is not practical for each job candidate to visit a face-to-face activity interview or participate in telephone or internet conference interviews because of time limits and cost. The AVI format tool can apply to conduct a computerized conversation with job applicants in a time factor. This method allows employers to verify audiovisual information at a later time [6]. Human evaluators have cognitive difficulty in properly checking a candidate's character attitudes based entirely on video pictures. Barrick et al. [7] discovered that the human evaluators could not correctly identify the candidate to view the videotaped interviews. All applicants with a background in I/O psychology and computer technology recommended that AI outperform humans to identify or divine an applicant's character in selecting a job candidate. The use of AI strategies for data sets is visible in Voice can acquire greater predictive and reliable power than human evaluators. The AI is a department specialized knowledge division that seeks to provide exceptional devices that can react in a comparable way to human intelligence and increase human potential. Acquiring knowledge of ML is a fundamental technique for achieving AI, which "gives computer systems the possibility to be examined without doing listed." Deep learning (DL) is a method of applying machine learning and can 'simulate the human mind's machinery to interpret information, including images, sounds, and text." In conventional ML evaluation, DL feature extraction is computerized rather than guided.

This introduction section describes the big five personality traits in social networking sites and various machine learning algorithms are essential to retrieve psychological information through the public.

2 Background Work

The interview process is challenging in current conditions since it deals with characters with various mentalities and mindsets. Organizations spend a lot of funds and efforts to hire. It grows very demanding when it comes to video interviews. Still, in some situations, they can't understand what type of employee he is and whether he is capably suitable for the jobs the company is trying. Sometimes it is difficult for a company representative (HR's) to judge the applicant's personality. Hence, technical support is required to fill this gap, so artificial intelligence (AI) represents an essential to provide clarifications through the deep learning method described asynchronous video interview through webcam.

2.1 Individuality Taxonomy

Personality commits to a person's 'variations in the specific models of questioning, awareness, and performing' [8]. Typically, this combination predicts whether an organization candidate will perform well in a particular role in the system and participate adequately in a cultural environment of capacity [9]. However, various fashions can evaluate the character of the 'Big Five' features. The Five Aspects Model (FAM) or The Ocean Model provides researchers and practitioners with a well- defined class. For selecting applicants for activities, the five essential factors are categorized and implemented in impressive cultural connections. These determinants are openness, conscience, extroversion, compatibility, and neuroticism. There are various measures to measure a specific five major attitudes, with self-evaluation and interviewer score. Self-evaluation reveals the self-photos, while the guide score indicates personal opinions, and others recognize the person's personality.

2.2 Individuality Computing

Based on preparing social records [10], humans study and understand others' ideas and conclude their characters through interviews. The Brunswik's lens model, tested in Fig. 1, shows how the interviewer accepts arguments to identify the person being interviewed and exposes the connection between the self-rated interviewer and the interviewer's perceptual observations [11]. Respondents define their applicant personality through

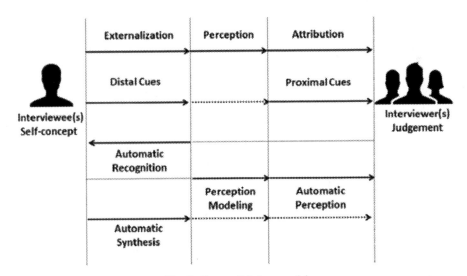

Fig. 1. Brunswik's lens model

different cues (i.e., any visible behavior that the interlocutor may also perceive, including facial features, body movement, speech, and presentations). Instead, the observer needs a "camera" to describe the person's unobserved personal traits being interviewed through close cues (that is, the interviewee's behavior may also understand it, along with significant indirect nudges); However, the interviewer can translate these signals into thoughts.

Figure 1 shows the online interview process as per Brunswik's lens model [11]. It has various stages of Externalization, perception, and attribution with every section declaration.

3 Proposed System

The interview process is one of the challenging tasks for many companies, and they invest heavily in the process. Especially when it comes to video interviews, it becomes much more challenging. In the existing system, we have got a personality prediction system, but there need to be some changes to be done to take to the next level. In the proposed method, there are many features used to implement the big five personality traits prediction. This system can be implemented in the interview process to assess the personality based on facial expressions. It is a perfect tool that will be useful for companies to predict the candidate's personalities. In the proposed system, we have a facial recognition and validation system that not only detects the user's character and validates whether the candidate attended the interview before or is he attending for the first time. The system developed using deep learning techniques like Convolutional Neural Network (CNN) techniques. The method will be done through a webcam. The CNN has been approved as better-performed livestock can stock method photos and understands first impacts from digital images. This experiment performed semi-supervised Deep Learning approaches, including CNN, to growing a corresponding agent mainly dependent on AI. That can routinely identify an applicant's personality using the smallest private data sets of applicants' facial expressions.

People interpret the displayed signs using others and conclude their characters at some point in the interactions, including interviews. The Brunswick lens copy explains how the interviewer uses the signals to choose the interviewed person's personality and shows the relationship between the interviewer's character and the perceptive notes of the interviewee's personality. The big five personality traits can useful in society by applied various behavior analyses like Clinical, Counselling, Community Consumer, and Critical, educational. These connections recommend five general dimensions used in everyday language to explain the human personality and character.

3.1 Data Collecting

In the data collection process, to prepare the dataset in the context of a real activity interview, we developed a cloud-based AVI program, just like existing panels. The AVI tool needs massive storage with Google's cloud and can get registered video ads, make transcripts for interviews, stream video claims for the conference, and get video replies. Content materials for video responses can be used for computational analyzes, including audio analysis and observed video replies records. During AVI, responders' solutions can be recorded as a factor over time but are then reviewed with the help of a set of rules, human evaluators, or both at any other time.

3.2 Data Labeling

To get real rankings of the Five Big traits, we used an international personality item pool (IPIP) stock of 50-items developed in [Goldberg et al. 1992] to measure trends in the top five self-evaluated by applicants. Before collaborating on AVI, all candidates had to perform. The IPIP studied online and declared that the study outcomes could be presented to the most active investigators and those not relevant to the employment reference. This measure was implemented to minimize the impacts of human preference, which could also deteriorate the characteristics of self-personality features along the way to take advantage of a business opportunity.

3.3 Feature Extraction and Modeling

To expand the AVI-AI tool that can use to anticipate interpersonal communication skills and person developments as viewed by human evaluators, we have created a 3- level version described in Featured Video data processing, training classifier, and classifier verification. At the video data processing level, we have to develop AVI to extract facial expressions with people interviewed from each body using our data set in Fmpeg. The facial potential was revealed with OpenCV and Dlib by observing 86 body-consistent reference factors. Each frame's face feature is extracted in 5 s interval of AVI information for each interviewed person. Pre-processing has become essential to reduce unwanted noise inside feature extraction, including hair and cosmetic interference. This paper discovers and crop facial images, as shown in

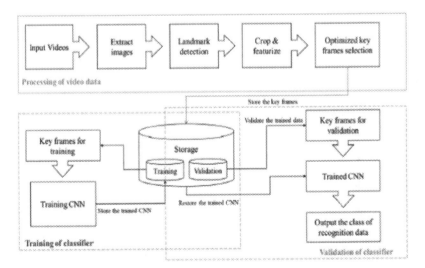

Fig. 2. Processing video data, training of classifier, and validation of classifier

Figure 2 shows; it shows how, obtained the first facial image, expose facial features, and harvest the face image to learn the classifier. Then we switched the captured shot to grey to reduce the lighting effect and accentuate facial features and movement features. Then we identified 86 validated reference points for the face in Fig. 4 without experience. Any unrecovered box was removed.

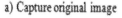

a) Capture original image   b) detect the facial expression as happy

Fig. 3. a) Capture original image b) detect the facial expression as happy.

a) Capture original image   b) Detect the facial expression as Neutral

Fig. 4. a) Capture original image b) Detect the facial expression as neutral

As shown in Fig. 3 and Fig. 4, the proposed method detected a given input image's facial expression and provided a seen expressional image as output.

This paper combines labeled data for 57 people interviewed with their selected characteristics to practice a prediction rule for the big five personality features and candidates communication skills. The proposed TensorFlow-based deep convolutional neural network (DCNN) model shows in Fig. 5.

Does a neural community include four convolutional layers, three grouped layers, ten grouped layers, one fully connected layer, and a SoftMax layer as output? The length of the inserted images was converted to 640 pixels (beautiful width), which was

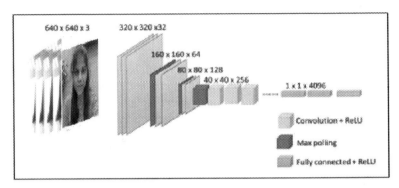

Fig. 5. Proposed DCNN model architecture

normalized through face image processing because the cropped images can also fluctuate in rotation, shift, and reliable and fast pixel ratio (VGA: 640 * 480), which may distort the single-sided image. We used facial expressions drawn from interviewees due to input and assessments of verbal exchange skills. The five colossal abilities seen across three human subjects were used due to an exit from the nervous community. In addition to the input, each layer contains training parameters (conduction weights). Also, we used the rectified nonlinear Unit (ReLU) to withstand the gradient pain leakage that can withstand the characteristic of candidate personality. The last layer of the release was an easy one with a maximum of 60 applicable effects. In the classifier verification score, the educational organization (50%) and the verification organization (50%) receive random sampling. Each person had six unique skills: the ability to communicate and five unusual tendencies. We conducted 4,000 academic repetitions, with lesson fees becoming 0, repeating scores of 10, and school repetition rate 256.

To learn about the apparent factors in pre-treated tires' personality traits, we first use CNN. Deep convolutional neural networks (DCNNs) achieve advanced reputation results on a wide range of severe and imaginary computing problems and may be best suited for this task. We do various deep neural networks and provide comparisons. We used a "warm start" from the pre-trained ResNet-v2-cent, educated in the ILSVRC-2012-CLS photography data set, with a good fit to get a healthy image of the problem. ResNet is part of a larger model, where it corresponds to the downgrade layers, and the additional layers are placed on top of the ResNet.

4   Results and Discussion

This paper implemented a semi-supervised DCNN approach based on TensorFlow to guess for the applicant personality traits automatically. The consequences help human signaling theory and webcam model. They designate that personal evaluators can determine candidates' communication skills and different personality features that correspond to non-verbal conversation signs, along with exceptional human evaluators as well. They may have a similar evaluation webcam to understand non-verbal cues and target characteristics. Consequently, we follow the AVI to obtain the person's facial features being interviewed and combine the AVI with the AI tool to identify the traits used to expect the talents of verbal exchange and develop the person's personality.

All big five trait dimensions have successfully been received and prophesied by the AVI-AI TensorFlow tool. The APR can predict all valid self-ratings for the 'big five' personality traits. The Pearson connected with any aspect between 0.972 and 0.987. R^2 for every dimension was between 0.945 and 0.970. All bindings were determined to be significant (pp < 0:01), while the MSE for every measurement was within 0.045 and 0.031. The higher the R^2 volume (100% perfect). On the contrary, the more under the MSE (0 ideally), the smaller the estimated error. Also, the Classification Accuracy results showed that the Average Accuracy of Classifiers (ACC) was 98.12% (Table 1).

Table 1. Experimental results.

Output Factors	R	R^2	MSE	ACC (%)
Openness	0.972	0.945	0.045	99.5
Conscientiousness	0.987	0.970	0.031	98.8
Extraversion	0.974	0.949	0.120	97.0
Agreeableness	0.978	0.957	0.038	96.9
Neuroticism	0.982	0.964	0.037	98.4

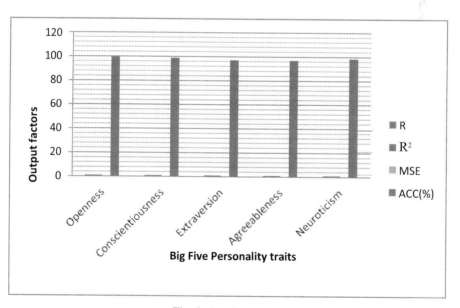

Fig. 6. Resultant graph

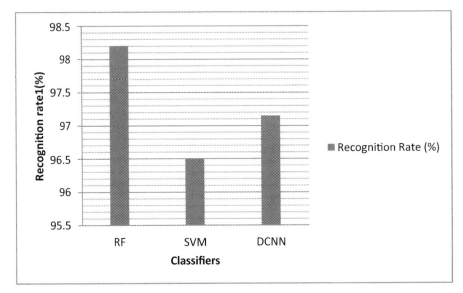

Fig. 7. Recognition rate vs. classifiers

Figure 5 indicates that the proposed deep convolutional neural network-based classifier to recognize the big five traits is compared with the previous classifiers of Random forest (RF), the support vector machine (SVM). The achievement result shows that the proposed method recognition rate is higher than the existing methods (Fig. 6 and 7).

5   Conclusion

This paper proposed an integrated AVI-AI with a semi-supervised deep learning method based on TensorFlow to explicitly identify an interviewee's personality traits based on 120 actual samples from job applicants. A deep learning-based deep convolutional neural network (DCNN) can also be performed in the interview method to judge the personality traits based on his facial expressions. Also, we designed a facial recognition and validation process to identify the user's personality and test whether the candidate attended the interview before or if he attended for the first time. The experimental results show that the proposed Deep Convolutional neural network (DCNN) compared with previous classifiers of RF and SVM. The proposed method provided a higher recognition rate compared to existing methods.

References

1. Lamdan, Y., Madiel, N.: Personality characteristics of Wikipedia members. CyberPsychology & Behavior, pp. 679–681 (2008)
2. Stopfer, D., Gosling, S.: Facebook profiles reflect actual personality, not self-idealization psychological science, pp. 372–374 (2010)

3. Bin, T., Meinel, C.: Identifying Audience Attributes: Predicting Age, Gender and Personality for Enhanced Article Writing, pp. 79–88 (2017)
4. Ryan, M.A., et al.: Culture and testing practices: Is the world _at?, pp. 434–467 (2017)
5. Schneider, T.J., McLarnon, M.: Faking it! Individual differences in types and degrees of faking behavior, pp. 88–95 (2019)
6. Ortner, T.M., Brenner, F.S.: Asynchronous video interviewing as a new technology in personnel selection: The applicant's point of view, p. 863 (2016)
7. Patton, G.K., Barrick, M.R.: Accuracy of interviewer judgments of job applicant personality traits, pp. 925–951 (2000)
8. Mikulincer, M., Shaver, R.: APA Handbook of Personality and Social Psychology. Personality Processes and Individual Differences (2015)
9. Dilchert, S., Hough, L.M.: Personality: Its measurement and validity of employee selection, pp. 298–325 (2017)
10. Walther, J.B.: Theories of computer-mediated communication and interpersonal relations, pp. 443–479 (2011)
11. Mohammadi, G., Vinciarelli, A.: A survey of personality computing, pp. 273–291 (2014)
12. Goldberg, L.R.: The development of markers for the big-five factor structure. Psychological Assessment, pp. 26–42 (1992)
13. Ramesh, G., Madhavi, K.: Summarizing Product Reviews using NLP based Text Summarization. International Journal of Scientific & Technology Research, September 2019. (Scopus)
14. Ramesh, G., Madhavi, K.: Best keyword set recommendations for building service-based systems" International Journal of Scientific and Technology Research, October 2019
15. Madhavi, K., Rajesh, G., Sowmya Priya, K.: A secure and robust digital image watermarking techniques. Int. J. Innov. Technol. Exploring Eng. (IJITEE) ISSN: 2278–3075, Volume-8 Issue- 12, October 2019 2758. https://doi.org/10.35940/ijitee.L2563.1081219
16. Nallella, T., Madhavi, K., Ramesh, G., Sowmya Priya, K.: Data Storage in Cloud Using Key-Policy Attribute-Based Temporary Keyword Search Scheme (KP- ABTKS), pp 630–636
17. Nilugonda, M., Madhavi, Dr.: A Survey on Big Five Personality Traits Prediction Using Tensorflow. E3S Web of Conferences. 184. 01053 (2020). https://doi.org/10.1051/e3sconf/202018401053.
18. Khamparia, A., Singh, S.K., Luhach, A.K., Gao, X.Z.: Classification and analysis of users review using different classification techniques in an intelligent e-learning system. Int. J. Intell. Inf. Database Syst. **13**(2–4), 139–149 (2020)
19. Kumari, A., Behera, R.K., Sahoo, K.S., Nayyar, A., Kumar Luhach, A., Prakash Sahoo, S.: Supervised link prediction using structured-based feature extraction in the social network. Concurrency and Computation: Practice and Experience, e5839 (2020)
20. Singh, K., Singh, S.S., Luhach, A.K., Kumar, A., Biswas, B.: Mining of closed high utility itemsets: a survey. Recent Adv. Comput. Sci. Commun. **13**, 1 (2020) https://doi.org/10.2174/2213275912666190204134822.

Crowdsourced Mobile Service for Preventing Child Trafficking Using Image Analytics

K. Dhinakaran[1], S. Udhayakumar[2(✉)], R. Nedunchelian[3], V. J. Varshini[1], and D. Swathi[1]

[1] Rajalakshmi Institute of Technology, Chennai, India
{varrshini.vj.2018.cse,swathi.d.2018.cse}@ritchennai.edu.in
[2] Saveetha School of Engineering, Saveetha Institute of Medical and Technical Sciences, Chennai, India
[3] Karpaga Vinayaga College of Engineering and Technology, Chennai, India

Abstract. Child trafficking are increasing in urban locations and the count is only increasing. Mostly the children are abused and exploited for begging, involuntary domestic servitude, forced child labor, commercial sex, and other illegal activities. In India, trafficking has grown over 14 times over the last decade according to National Crimes Records Bureau (NCRB) and the country has become a transit point for traffickers. The necessity to prevent child trafficking and engaging them in self-development, is the responsibility of every citizen towards nation building. Technological advancements have taken a huge leap in the domain of mobile analytics and social networking and therefore it should be used as a tool to mitigate this burning issue. Empowering every individual to report child trafficking using mobile devices and let the technology do the rest of analytics to identify vulnerable spots, missing child, type of trafficking and reporting to authorities can make a difference. Therefore, our proposed work is to develop an mobile application environment with the general public as the frontline workers, who can capture an image or video of the scene of trafficking along with the location information. The crowd sourced data is pulled from the cloud and segregated based on location. Further the date is pre-processed using image processing algorithms specifically Convolutional Neural Network (CNN) is used. As a case study, the work identifies a missing child, by applying the crowdsourced data to the CNN based training algorithm to match with the available sources. The algorithm also classifies the gender and age using cascade classifier and physical impairments using MAX pooling filter.

Keywords: Crowdsourced image analytics · Child trafficking · Deep learning algorithms · Convolutional Neural Networks

1 Introduction

Child trafficking is an issue that needs to be addressed immediately with iron hand, it is one of the national problems which is trivial to solve with traffickers sometimes are in coordination with parents of the child. As technology progresses the crime also

© Springer Nature Singapore Pte Ltd. 2021
A. K. Luhach et al. (Eds.): ICAICR 2020, CCIS 1393, pp. 456–465, 2021.
https://doi.org/10.1007/978-981-16-3660-8_43

increases, the present networking through sophisticated technology like social media platforms and mobile technology are being used predominantly by the organized crimes rather than those who prevent it.

Disheartening statistics about child labor is that there are more than 168 million children are engaged around the world and around half of them are into some hazardous works. Such a kind or forced labor through trafficking by criminals or due to poverty by parents can inevitably affect the livelihood of the child from school, their physical, emotional and social well-being. Despite increased efforts to combat trafficking by governments, everyday you find children being exploited for begging in traffic signals and places of interest like tourist spots, multiplexes, and commercial hotspots. The worst is that many parents from villages are duped by conman for city life and attractive packages and their children's, especially the girls are dumped into flesh trade. Without much support from either the government or from the general public they strive hard to go back, and inescapably end up on the streets of city.

Of these various problems faced by our children of the future, the most burning issue that every citizen of India faces daily is child begging. An estimated 300,000 children are drugged, beaten and forced to beg. Over 40,000 children are abducted every year in India, according to National Human Rights Commission. Man's inherent nature of sympathy towards beggers and giving more alms makes this into an organized begging cartel. Empowering a citizen to prevent this child begging voluntarily with the use of advanced technology is the scope and motivation of our research work.

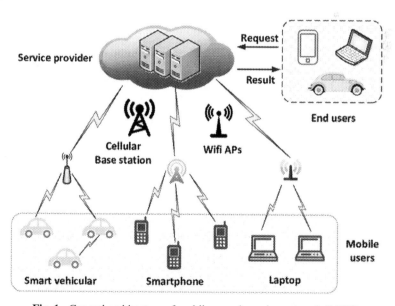

Fig. 1. General architecture of mobile crowdsourcing network (MCN)

Proliferation of advanced processing mobile devices and collaboration with mobile cloud for processing whatever data that comes from the mobile is an emerging paradigm for Mobile Crowdsourcing Network (MCN) as shown in Fig. 1. Technology enabled services like crowd sourcing can gather intelligent information's about child begging using location data with which it is possible to identify the hotspots of begging.

2 Literature Survey

Modern slavery in the form of forced child begging is critical issue that must be eliminated and the challenge of ending the child labour remains a formidable task. Sustainable developmental efforts undertaken by many world non-government organizations like International Labour Organization (ILO) [1], United Nations Children's Fund (UNICEF), International Program on Elimination of Child Labour (IPEC) have failed to effectively stop the children begging on the streets. Though these organization plan and execute it at the highest level with full autonomy they are ill equipped to deal this organized crime, which mostly revolves with the support of anti-social elements and even some times the parents of the child. In-order to prevent it, the technology like mobile crowdsourcing helps to power every individual to fight against organized crime [2]. Mobile based crowdsourcing is helpful for traffic analysis as presented in the project Signalguru [3]. Various challenges and issues have been discussed to understand the benefits and applications of mobile crowdsourcing [4].

The use of crowdsourcing technology by common man, especially among Indian population is explored by Microsoft Research India have demonstrated the economic viability of building a crowdsourced platform [5]. Haifeng Niu et al. has briefly explained about the crowd sourced extracting for urban activities, data sources reviews, applications, and methods. Data is gathered form social media, point of interest (POI) and collaborative websites that are generated by the crowd have become finely grained proxy data of urban activities and universally used in research on application [6]. According this paper, bibliometric analysis conducted first that recognizes underpinning domains, pivot scholar, and papers around this topic. This review blends preceding results into three parts: dominant applications with different data sources and fuses; mobility pattern, functional areas, and event detection are analyzed with spatial analysis; and application of sociodemographic and perception analysis in city attractiveness, demographic characteristics and sentiment analysis. The challenges about the kind of data are talked at the conclusion of the paper. This paper gives a organized and current review for both researchers and practitioners those who are interested in the applications of crowd sourced data mining for urban activity.

Ji Hwan Park et al. has explained briefly about the crowd analytics. From crowd sourcing, the annotations of medical data image were obtained, and they were explored. This was done to perform crowd analytics for clinical imaging data. Based on various measures like annotation clustering, observation rate, logging occasions, the crowd sourced medical data were contemplated, categorized, and refined with the help of CMed. For a specific video and the corresponding workers, analysis of the results of crowd annotation is carried out by the dependent visualization components that are provided by the CMed [7]. For detecting the pattern and for accumulating insight on crowd sourced clinical data, they permit an analyst and thereby help them to design a system for getting proficient results. Two clinical crowd sourcing studies were used for explaining the effectiveness of their architecture. One is, detection of lung nodule using projection videos of CT which has a slab that is thin with maximal intensity. Another one is, detection of polyp in videos of virtual colonoscopy. They also yield professionals' opinion to display the efficacy of their architecture. Finally, for performing the integration of their architecture into a clinical enterprise, they will provide recommendations based on their learnings from their architecture.

Zijing Lin et al. has discussed about the designing bicycle volume using crowd sourced data from strava application in smartphone [8]. Crowdsourced data that are utilized for modeling the bicycle volume in the City of Chatlotte, North Carolina. By using the strava's metro the data is collected from the user's smartphone applications. The essential information for processing the data are manual count of bicycle volume, data of crowd sourced bicycle, road characteristics, sociodemographic, zoning, temporal, and bicycle facility are integrated using the ArcGIS and SAS. The succeeding of processing is two linear regression models that are developed to quantify the relationship between bicycle manual count data and Starva Metro bicycle data as well as another relevant variable. Modeling results in the estimation of bicycle volume on most of the road segments in the city of charlotte.

3   Crowd Sourced Analytics Environment

We propose a model to find the impaired facial feature that was desecrate by someone, "Desecrate Net" that uses image input to find the age and gender of the child and check the facial features of the child with huge number of images are used for training to find the required output from the input image data. The image of the children is captured by any sort of camera like traffic camera, digital camera, mobile camera, etc. By using the camera Exif data camera model and settings, GPS information, and date and time the photo was taken input the location of the children is pinned by the geotagging technique. The information is gathered using integration of crowdsourcing with data analytics and convolutional neural network. The detailed architecture of the proposed crowdsourced analytic environment is presented in Fig. 2.

The input image is converted to Grayscale, to find the age and gender from the data, Grayscale images may be a assortment of shades with no obvious shading. On a screen, each component of a grayscale comes alive of sunshine, starting from the delicate live of sunshine, or black to the powerful live of sunshine, or white. Grayscale simply has brightness info from a picture not the opposite color info. Grayscale is sample representing of import of every component is just live of lights in image that's, it comes solely intensity of the brightness of the image.

A face recognition system is the innovative technologies used to detect and verify a person from the digital image or video frames. Detection of face is an PC innovation that are utilized in the recognition of face of the human in digital framework. Face recognition likewise alludes to the mental procedure by which humans find and go to look in a visual scene.

Cascading is a specific instance of outfit learning dependent on the link of a few classifiers, utilizing all data gathered from the yield from a given classifier in the course. Falling classifiers are prepared with a few hundred "positive" example perspectives on a specific article and self-assertive "negative" pictures of a similar size. After the classifier

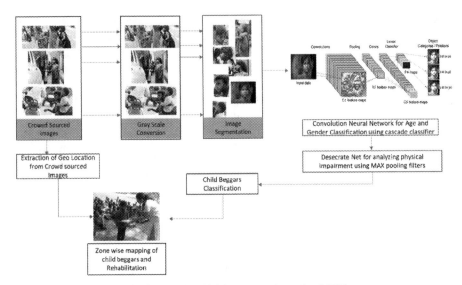

Fig. 2. Child trafficking prevention using MCN

is prepared it tends to be applied to a district of a picture and distinguish the article being referred to. To scan for the item in the whole edge, the hunt window can be moved over the picture and check each area for the classifier. This procedure is most usually utilized in picture preparing for object identification and following, basically facial location and acknowledgment.

3.1 Age and Gender Classification

There are two important facial attributes that play a vital role are age ang gender. The estimation age and gender estimation from a single face image an tedious task in intelligent applications, such as access control, human computer interaction, law enforcement, marketing and visual surveillance, etc. From the camera input the age and gender of the child is estimated by convolutional neural network for the children below age 18 who are treated as labour are found and helped [9].

Where acquiring the age and gender data from social image repositories is a tedious process and often requires access to private data. Informational indexes for age and sex estimation from genuine social pictures are along these lines generally constrained in size and by and by no match in size with a bigger picture arrangement informational collection [10]. Overfitting is a regular issue when AI put together techniques are utilized with respect to such little picture assortments. This issue is exacerbated while considering profound convolutional neural systems because of their immense quantities of model parameters. Care should in this way be taken so as to abstain from overfitting under such conditions.

To generate Age and gender featured outcomes various essentials of various sizes are to be applied on the input data using CNN. These featured outcomes are mapped as input for upcoming processes which is described as substitute sampling where the activations are taken from their neighbourhood [11]. These operations are important in minimizing the dimension of featured operation and getting translation non-variation up to decent degree. The next important layer of CNN is the tube connected layer, where the top most level abstractions are modelled from the input model and it should be compared with CNN implementations used for face recognition, that are trained with huge number of images to find the required output from the input image data.

3.2 DesecrateNet

This system uses the Input pictures to find the physical impairment of the child. The desecrateNet Networks on 54 Layers of Convolutional layers which has Pooling, Normalization, image Flattening, Fully Connected layers and finally the building block layer is convolutional layer. The children's in India are exploited to work and beg by some illegal guardians [12, 13]. Our solution is to identify the children working and begging in the streets of India, and those who are exploited by illegal means can be easily recovered by the officials. They children are sometimes made physically desecrate by local goons can be found using our proposed algorithm, which has 3 separate steps.

I). It checks for handicapped
II). It checks for visible Scars on face
III). It checks for any facial damage and facial muscle impairment.

Algorithm to find age gender and physical attributes

      {IMG-xyz} to GRAYSCALE.
      {IMG-xyz-GRAY} to object{Scale factor
=1.2,step_ratio=1,min_size(60,60),max_size(123,123)};
      {object}(CCF 24x24)
      // (note: CCF =Cascaded face size 24x24)
      {object} MAX pooling (gender,age) :
            {object} MAX (gender)
            {object} (Gender features ,F-0XY,M-0XX);
            {object} MAX (age)
            {object} (FACIAL MUSCLE DATASET ,F-0XY,M-0XX);

   As {object N }at (--Gender--,--age--);

   For 1 to n
      If {object N} at (age=<18)
      Upload IMG-xyz to get {GPS coords in exif(IMG-xyz) };
   //To find the physical impaired,scars and facial muscle and eyes damage
      {IMG-xyz} to Classifier 1- Dimentional CNN of Human Child
      Body of SAME {age}
      Return
      Confusion Matrix {Physcial attributes},
   upload(detail Analysis).

Pseudocode-Damaged Facial Detection

//Aim to determine the age, gender and to do detailed analysis of physical //attributes of the person using input image

//Input : image in the following format .jpg and .png.

//Output : Age , Gender and Damage Analysis.

i ← IMG-xyz (grayscale)
j ← Scale(i) to MAX(123,123) or MIN(60,60)
k← Cascade(j) in SIZE(24,24)
G←gender features
A←Facial muscle features
Repeat
MAX POOLING <- G //To find Gender
Until Match [G]
g ← Match[G]
Repeat
MAX POOLING <- A //To find Age
Until Match [A]
 a ← Match[A]
If a >=18 then
GC←exif(IMG-xyz)
S←system
S←Upload IMG-xyz ,a,g,GC;   //To find the physical impaired, scars and facial

//muscle and eyes damage

DA← i[1-Dimentional CNN of Human child body]   // DA-stands for Detailed //Analysis
Repeat
Apply ← Classifier 1-Dimentional CNN
Until Match[a]
DA ← Confusion matrix[Physical attributes]
Upload S← DA

4   Analysing the Data Set

Here to build a Convolutional Neural Network we used Intel i5–7200 @clock speed of 2.7 Ghz with 1 TB of Hard disk and Nvidia GeForce 970 for Facial damage prediction system. This system can also be used to perform mobile cloud analytics, whereby the collected images are processed within the location itself by offloading concept instead of the images sent to distance cloud [14] (Table 1).

The dataset here has different sets of children's faces, adults' faces children's faces with scars, with walking sticks and eyes. The validation loss and validation accuracy are shown in Fig. 3 and training loss and training accuracy are shown in Fig. 4.

Table 1. Analysis of the training dataset for validating the children face

Epoch	Train loss	Train accuracy	Validation loss	Validation accuracy
1	1.534	0.4115	0.812	0.698
2	1.245	0.455	0.763	0.75
3	1.021	0.492	0.712	0.724
4	0.943	0.523	0.54	0.682
5	0.82	0.545	0.43	0.621
6	0.745	0.572	0.402	0.593
7	0.655	0.582	0.389	0.537
8	0.523	0.63	0.352	0.498
9	0.43	0.674	0.312	0.431

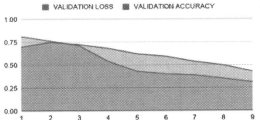

Fig. 3. Validation loss vs Validation accuracy

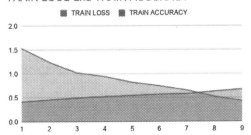

Fig. 4. Training loss vs Training accuracy

The system increases the accuracy over number of times where the loss is extremely low over 'n' number of trains. The system has Pre-trained datasets which helps in increasing accuracy over other existing networks. Datasets used here are featured with Data Augmentation, which is a main feature that helps as a major advantage over Inception V3 and MobileNet Model.

5 Conclusion

Mobile crowdsourcing network has the potential to harness vast amount of data from general public. Utilizing this data for preventing child trafficking is one of the novel attempts of this research. The DesecrateNet model and the Convolutional Neural Network approach helps to analyse the image and train it for classifying the child among multiple images based on age, gender and disability factor is the primary object. The DesecrateNet Model added an extra layer of convolution to increase the accuracy from 92.4% to 96.5%. This performance is higher in comparison to the existing models namely Inception V3 and MobileNet Model. Our model used less training data and identified the required objective in time because of the added advantage of using Max Pooling algorithm. Thus it is an effort to support the cause of deprived children who need a desperate escape from the clutches of the trafficker.

References

1. Global Estimates of Child Labour, Results and trends, 2012–2016, International Labour Organization (2017)
2. Ren, J., Zhang, Y., Zhang, K., Shen, X.: Exploiting Mobile Crowdsourcing for Pervasive Cloud Services: Challenges and Solutions. IEEE Commun. Mag. **53**(3), 98–105 (2015)
3. Koukoumidis, E., Peh, S., Martonosi, M.R.: Signalguru: leveraging mobile phones for collaborative traffic signal schedule advisory. In: Proceedings of ACM MobiSys, pp. 127–40 (2011)
4. Yang, K., Kuan Zhang, J., Ren, X.S.: Security and privacy in mobile crowdsourcing networks: challenges and opportunities. IEEE Commun. Mag. **53**(8), 75–81 (2015)
5. Chopra, M., et al.: Exploring crowdsourced work in low-resource settings. CHI 2019, 4–9 May 2019, Glasgow, Scotland Uk © 2019 Association for Computing Machinery (2019)
6. Haifeng, N., Elisabete, A.S.: Crowdsourced data mining for urban activity: review of data sources, applications, and methods. J. Urban Plann. Dev. **146**(2), 04020007 (2020)
7. Park, J.H., Nadeem, S., Boorboor, S., Marino, J., Kaufman, A.: CMed: crowd analytics for medical imaging data. IEEE Trans. Vis. Comput. Graph. **27**(6), 2869–2880 (2021). https://doi.org/10.1109/TVCG.2019.2953026
8. Zijing, L., Wei (David), F.: Modeling bicycle volume using crowdsourced data from Strava smartphone application. Int. J. Transp. Sci. Technol. **9**(4), 334–343 (2020)
9. Dhinakaran, K.: Distributed data analytics for improving Indian economical growth using recommendation system. J. Adv. Res. Dyn. Control Syst. **12**(SP4), 134–140 (2020)
10. Lea, S.G., D'Silva, E., Asok, A.: Women's strategies addressing sexual harassment and assault on public buses: an analysis of crowdsourced data. Crime Prev. Community Saf. **19**(3–4), 227–239 (2017)
11. Casana, J.: Global-scale archaeological prospection using CORONA satellite imagery: automated, crowd-sourced, and expert-led approaches. J. Field Archaeol. **45**(S1), S89–S100 (2020)
12. Kaushik, A.: Rights of children: a case study of child beggars at public places in India. J. Soc. Welfare Hum. Rights **2**(1), 01–16 (2014)
13. Srivastava, R.N.: Children at work, child labor and modern slavery in India: an overview. Indian Pediatr. **56**(8), 633–638 (2019)
14. Nandhini, U., Tamilselvan, L.: Computational analytics of client awareness for mobile application offloading with cloud migration. KSII Trans. Internet Inf. Syst. **8**(11), 3916–3936 (November 2014)

Human Fall Detection Using Motion History Image and SVM

K. Lakshmi[(⊠)] and T. Devendran

Periyar Maniammai Institute of Science and Technology, Thanjavur, India
lakshmi@pmu.edu

Abstract. Fall detection system is a most challenging system in artificial intelligence research, especially in healthcare. It is very vital for elderly people who are frequent victims of age-related factors. In this paper, we propose a vision-based fall detection system. This paper compares the performance of HOG (Histogram of Oriented Gradients) features and Motion History Images. The feature extracted is given to SVM (Support Vector Machine) classifier for classifying fall or non-fall movements in the image. UMA fall dataset is used for the experiment. Experiment result shows Motion History Image features gives better performance than the hog features. Further, the performance of Motion History Image based SVM classifier is tested on many other data sets, including the author's own dataset.

Keywords: Human fall detection · Vision based · HOG features · Motion history image

1 Introduction

Elder people sometime cannot balance themselves due to age related factors and illness. They tend to fall easily. This may cause severe injury or even death sometime. According to the World health organization, falls are major public health problem. In each year 6, 46,000 fatal falls are occurring, and it is the second leading cause of unintentional injury death after the road traffic accidents [1]. There are many methods and techniques available to address this issue. Researchers propose automatic Human Fall Detection system. This fall detection system is mainly classified into two categories namely vision-based system and sensor-based system. In sensor-based system the fall events are detected through the sensors fixed in wearable devices and/or floors. Sensors fixed in the floor are used to sense the vibration and detect the heavy weight movements on the floor. These movements of the person are analyzed to identify the fall movements [11]. Wearable gadgets sense the linear motion and angular motion through sensors and detect the fall movements. When there is a fall identified, it is informed to the caretaker by message/ alert system. But the main drawback of this sensor-based system is that the person should always wear the gadgets or always keep a gadget with them. This may be a burden for elder people mentally as well as physically. Comparatively the vision-based system is easy to use for the elder people.

© Springer Nature Singapore Pte Ltd. 2021
A. K. Luhach et al. (Eds.): ICAICR 2020, CCIS 1393, pp. 466–476, 2021.
https://doi.org/10.1007/978-981-16-3660-8_44

1.1 Computer Vision Based Fall Detection System

Computer Vision based fall detection system acquires the input video or images. First the image is pre-processed, like re-shaping, converting the image into grayscale, *etc.* Moving object is identified in the image. In this system, moving object is the human. Features are extracted from the moving object. These extracted features are given to a classifier to train it. Once the classifier is trained it can be used to classify the video or image to identify the fall or non-fall movement. The system is given as block diagram in Fig. 1.

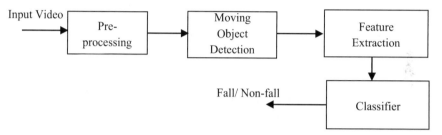

Fig. 1. Human fall detection system

In this paper we propose a vision-based fall detection system using Motion History Images. In this work we test the performance of using HOG (Histogram of Oriented Gradients)features with SVM and Motion History Image with SVM. Further the system is tested with other types of datasets.

This paper is organized as follows; the Sect. 2 discusses the related works. Section 3 elaborates the proposed system. Section 4 discusses the datasets and experimental results and Sect. 5 gives the conclusion.

2 Related Work

Basic methodology of the vision-based system is to get input video from the camera and divide the videos into number of frames. These video frames processed, and the fall movements are detected. The fall detection may be based on rules or classifier based. Many researchers use different kinds of datasets and algorithms to detect the fall movements. Many datasets are available publicly like SDU dataset [12], UR fall dataset [14], MobiFall [13], Multi model Multiview fall dataset [15], EDF and OCCU Fall dataset [16].

The author of [2] used a multivariate exponentially weighted moving average chart to detect the fall movements. MEWMA chart takes the correlations between variables and at the same time monitors a set of cross correlated variables. This chart statistics is a time weighted average of all previous observations. The chart can detect even small shifts. It is used to detect the fall movements.

Author of [3] combines two techniques namely ellipse approximation and motion history image. In ellipse approximation two important characteristics are there orientation and eccentricity. The standard deviation of orientation and eccentricity will consider as sudden change of human position. This motion history of images is used to find how fast the motion has occurred. From that they identify the fall movements.

Gaussian mixture model to detect the moving person in the frame is proposed by [4]. Rules are framed to identify fall detection. Since there are lot of chances for falls positive in fall detection two rules were proposed by the authors. One rule identifies the fall based on the features, orientation angle and distance of contour pixels. Second rule reconfirms fall using change of centre of mass width, change of Hu moments invariants.

Next, author of [5] combines three techniques to detect the fall movements, human shape analysis, head tracking and centre of mass detection. Moving person is identified by background subtraction technique and the head information is tracked by particle filter. While analysing head position any variation in human shape and centre of mass are analysed. If there is any large variation that indicates fall movement.

The author of [6] uses the shape analysis method. Here, the entire body is covered with three points and two lines. Any changes in the distance and the orientation of the lines can indicate a change in the shape of the person in the image. Fall is identified when changes in these two lines differences and orientations.

The author of [7] uses the back propagation neural network learning algorithm. They use Gaussian mixture model for foreground extraction. For feature extraction they use, aspect ratio of bounding box, orientation of ellipse and vertical velocity of centre point. All the three features are used for training the BPNN and detect the fall events.

Next author of [8] use three machine learning algorithms. For feature extraction, Openpose software was used to detect 24 key points on human body. Data of eight subjects were used as training data and data of 4 subjects were used as test data. The SVM, Logistic regression, and linear discrimination analysis are used to identify the fall movements.

Author [10] proposed an Activity Recognition system for Fall Detection using Convolution Neural Network. The authors used their own data sets. Focus is to distinguish between actual fall and near fall possess (fall alarms). They suggest that combining RGB background subtracted and Depth with CNN gives good result.

3   Proposed System

As shown in Fig. 1, the proposed system uses a hardware setup for capturing the video as given in Fig. 2.

The hardware setup has Raspberry pi board [9] with pi camera for recording the activities. The board has SD card to store the video captured. The video is transmitted to the laptop for further processing. In the Laptop/PC Fall detection method using SVM training and testing takes place. Once the SVM is trained, when there is a fall identified the system sends a message to the caretaker.

This section elaborates the method used for fall detection. Implementation of method is done using the Python 3 program [10, 11, 16]. Here we use two methods; first one uses the HOG features and second one uses MHI.

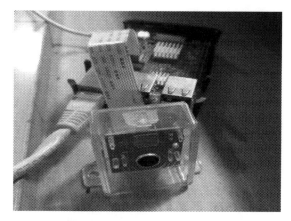

Fig. 2. Raspberry pi camera setup

3.1 HOG Feature with SVM

Video captured is taken as input and it is split into frames. Frame is converted into grey scale image. In-built function in OpenCV based on Guassian Mixture is used to extraction the foreground image. A sample frame from our own data set and a sample foreground image is given in Fig. 3, (a) and (b) respectively.

From the foreground image HOG [9, 12] features are extracted. HOG features are commonly used in the object detection applications. The technique is based on the gradient orientation in localized portions of an image. The HOG descriptor gives the shape of an object [11, 12]. Reason behind selecting HOG is that the descriptor would help us to differentiate the shape of fall and non-fall body.

This HOG features are given as input to the SVM classifier. Since, SVM classifier's performance is good, it is proposed to use this classifier (Fig. 4). The main objective of this SVM is to best fit hyper plane that categorize the data [15]. The trained SVM is given with the test images/video. The accuracy measure is used to evaluate the performance of the classifier.

3.2 Motion History Image with SVM

The Motion History Image (MHI) is an image template that has temporal images compacted into a single image. The MHI pixel intensity is a function of the motion history at that location, where brighter values correspond to the most recent action. The main advantage of using MHI is that it represents motion sequence in one single frame (Fig. 5).

Video captured is taken as input; the frames are read one by one. The moving object (human) is identified using frame differencing. First frame is taken as the reference frame and the consecutive frames are subtracted from the reference frame. Noise in difference image is handled by the dilation technique. Noise removed image is given as input to the MHI function to create the MHI image. This image matrix is flattened and used to train the SVM.

(a) Man standing

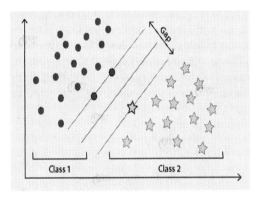

b) Foreground image of man falling frame

Fig. 3. Sample real image and foreground image

Fig. 4. Support Vector Machine Classification

4 Experimental Results

Dataset we used to test the performance of HOG and MHI features is UMA Fall dataset. This dataset is created by [17] for sensor-based fall detection system. In this experiment, the video of the UMA Fall dataset is used to train and test the systems. To evaluate the

(a)   Man standing

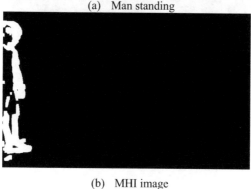

(b)   MHI image

Fig. 5. Sample MHI image

system, we used the accuracy [16] measure.

$$Accuracy = (TP + TN)N \tag{1}$$

TP-True Positive
TN-True Negative
N-Total no.of frames

We have used four fold cross-validations for confirming the performance of the classifier. 65% of data are used as training set and 35% are used as test data.

4.1 Comparison Between the HOG Feature and MHI

As given in section III, HOG features of the image are taken, and dataset is prepared with suitable class label. Class label 0 is given to indicate "non-fall" and 1 is to indicate "fall". Likewise, MHI are created and dataset is prepared. The SVM used is a linear SVM. The accuracy is measured as given in the Eq. 1. We have taken the "fall_backwards" video of UMA fall dataset to compare the performance of the HOG and MHI.

Fig. 6. Sample fall frames from UMA "fallback" data set

When the video is read frame by frame, more than 400 frames obtained, ranging from standing, slightly bending, semi-falling to falling as shown in the sample images given in Fig. 6. The classification results are given in the Table 1.

Table 1. Classifier performance on HOG and MHI

Features	Accuracy	Cross val score
HOG	98	87
MHI	99	95

Next, we used other datasets to check the performance of MHI. Performance of MHI is consistent on other datasets too. The results are given in Table 2.

4.2 Performance of MHI on Other Datasets

We have used other fall videos, "fall-forward" and "fall-backward" videos in the collection UMA dataset. We have also used a multiple camera fall dataset [17] for this experiment (Fig. 7).

Performance of MHI features with SVM classifier is shown in Table 2.

In "fall-forward" many frames actions are ambiguous hence the performance is low when we do cross-validation.

Next, we have taken the random videos from Youtube. These are not dataset recorded for fall detection experimental purpose, these are real videos recorded. Elderly people activities were recorded in care-centre, these videos were used to check the performance of the system. Sample frames of the video are shown in Fig. 8.

Performances of the other fall videos are given in Table 3. We can observe in the table that the Classifier performance is not good when video have more than one person in the screen.

(a)   UMA Fall dataset – Fall-forward images

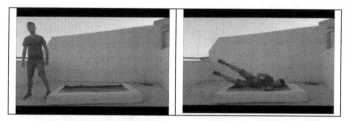

(b)   UMA Fall dataset – Fall-lateral images

(c)   Multiple Camera Fall dataset

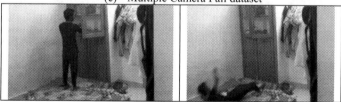

d) Own video data set

Fig. 7. Sample images of various datasets

Table 2. Classifier performance on another UMA dataset

Features	Accuracy	Cross val score
UMA fall forward	99	74.7
UMA fall lateral	99.3	95.5
Multi cam dataset	99.7	90.1
Own data set	98.7	97.5

a) Old man Playing with Balloon

b) Old people walking with a dog

c) Old lady walking with walker

Fig. 8. Random video samples

Table 3. Classifier performance on other videos

Features	Accuracy	Cross val score
Video1(Old man Playing with Balloon)	1	95
Video2(Old people walking with a dog)	1	64.4
Video3(Old lady walking with walker)	1	88

5 Conclusion

In this paper we implemented the vision-based fall detection system using raspberry pi tool kits and raspberry pi v2 cameras, and SVM classifier. We have observed that more the training frame better the performance (results are not shown here). Using frame-based HOG features gives lower performance. Drawback in using single frame feature is that it may not distinguish between falling movement and near falling position like slant standing position, sitting position etc. This drawback is eliminated in MHI. MHI records the history of frame, hence it is can distinguish between falling movement and near falling normal movements. However, the performance of the system is not good with the video input of old people walking with a dog. In another video there is only one person in the video, in this video more than one person are there in the frame. For this type of videos, other features may need to be added to improve the performance of the fall detection system.

Another limitation in this system is that it used the full matrix of MHI. It takes lot of memory to train the SVM. MHI matrix needs to be reduced to reduce the consumption of memory.

References

1. World Health Organization. https://www.who.int/en/news-room/fact-sheets/detail/falls Accessed 27 Aug 19
2. Harrou, F., Zerrouki, N., Sun, Y.: Houacine: A Vision-based fall detection system for improving safety of elderly people. IEEE Instrum. Meas. Mag. **20**, 49–55 (2017)
3. Basavaraj, G., Ashok, K.: Vision based surveillance system for detection of human fall. In: 2nd IEEE International Conference on Recent Trends in Electronics Information & Communication Technology (RTEICT) (2017)
4. Rajabi, H., Nahvi, M.: An intelligent video surveillance system for fall and anesthesia detection for elderly and patients. In: 2nd International Conference on Pattern Recognition and Image Analysis (IPRIA), Rasht, pp. 1–6 (2015)
5. Fairouz M., Nadia, B.: Depth camera based fall detection using human shape and movement. In: IEEE International Conference on signal and Image Processing (ICSIP), pp. 586–590 (2016)
6. Chua, J.-L., Chang, Y.C., Lim, W.K.: A simple vision-based fall detection technique for indoor video surveillance. SIViP **9**(3), 623–633 (2013)
7. Hsu, Y.W., Perngl, J.W., Liu, H.L.: Development of a vision based pedestrian fall detection system with back propagation neural network. In: 2015 IEEE/SICE International Symposium on System Integration (SII) (2015)

8. Hiroaki, K., Takeshi, K., Shuji, A.: Video-based fall risk detection system for the elderly. In: IEEE 1st Global Conference on Life Sciences and Technologies (LifeTech), pp.147–149 (2019)

9. Dalal, N., Triggs, B.: Histograms of oriented gradients for human detection. In: IEEE Computer Society Conference on Computer Vision and Pattern Recognition (CVPR 2005), vol. 1, pp. 886–893 (2005)

10. Adhikari, K., Hamid, B., Nait-Charif, H.: Activity recognition for indoor fall detection using convolutional neural network. In: IEEE Fifteenth IAPR International Conference on Machine Vision Applications (MVA), pp. 68–71 (2017)

11. Eduardo, C., Santoyo-Ramón, J.A., Cano-García, J.M.: UMA fall: a multisensor dataset for the research on automatic fall detection. In: Procedia Computer Science, vol. 110, pp. 32–39 (2017)

12. Yilmaz, M.: SDU dataset (2018)

13. Vavoulas, G., Pediaditis, M., Spanakis, E.G., Tsiknakis, M.: The MobiFall dataset: an initial evaluation of fall detection algorithms using smartphones. In: 13th IEEE International Conference on BioInformatics and Bioengineering, pp. 1–4 (2013)

14. URFall Detection dataset: http://fenix.univ.rzeszow.pl/~mkepski/ds/uf.html

15. Tran, T.: A multi-modal multi-view dataset for human fall analysis and preliminary investigation on modality. In: 2018 24th International Conference on Pattern Recognition (ICPR), Beijing, pp. 1947–1952 (2018)

16. Zhang, Z., Conly, C., Athitsos, V.: Evaluating depth-based computer vision methods for fall detection under occlusions. In: Bebis, G. et al. (eds.) Advances in Visual Computing. ISVC 2014. Lecture Notes in Computer Science, vol. 8888, pp. 196–207. Springer, Cham (2014) https://doi.org/10.1007/978-3-319-14364-4_19

17. Auvinet, E., Rougier, C., Meunier, J., St-Arnaud, A., Rousseau, J.: Multiple cameras fall dataset, Technical report 1350, DIRO - Université de Montréal (2010)

Robust Indian Currency Recognition Using Deep Learning

Swathi Gowroju[1(✉)], K. Sravani[1], N. Santhosh Ramchandar[1], D. Sai Kamesh[2], and J. Nasrasimha Murthy[2]

[1] Sreyas Institute of Engineering and Technology, Telangana, Hyderabad, Telangana, India
{swathigowroju1,sravani2,nsramchander3}@sreyas.ac.in
[2] Sreyas Institute of Engineering and Technology, Hyderabad, Telangana, India

Abstract. The applications of currency counting are vast in real-time. From the ATM to small entrepreneur business applications includes currency recognition. In contrary, currency recognition is one of the HCI applications that can be taken for any human-computer application. This technology limits the manpower and human supervision. The emerging technologies such as AI and Machine Learning were now part of every application. In this regard, the proposed methodology is a robust methodology built on deep learning technique using relatives less number of images in the database with high noise, including rotated notes, tilted notes, held by hand note images. The proposed methodology extracts denomination in 90 s. It uses a Convolution Neural Network (Inception using transfer learning) to extract currency denomination. We acquired the accuracy of 83% in predicting the denomination.

Keywords: Image processing · Feature extraction · Denomination · Convolution neural networks

1 Introduction

India is one among economically growing counties. Ongoing businesses, investments, transactions need money as the source. Developing countries like India needs such kind of activities in a much better way than in the current scenario. The need for counting money and recognizing the denomination is a specific target in most of the banks and transaction areas. Currently, the Indian currency system has the denomination of Rs. 10, 20, 50, 100, 200, 500 and 1000. Every currency note will have value on it. We generated a neural network application which accurately predicts the denomination (value) of the note. The emerging technology such as CNN is the best-chosen option for the proposed methodology as the rate of prediction is high for the network rather than blindly analysing the pattern using analysis tools. By choosing so, we not even predicted the value accurately but also minimized the time of prediction successfully.

© Springer Nature Singapore Pte Ltd. 2021
A. K. Luhach et al. (Eds.): ICAICR 2020, CCIS 1393, pp. 477–486, 2021.
https://doi.org/10.1007/978-981-16-3660-8_45

2 Literature Survey

The need for counting and predicting the denomination on the note recognition is encouraging research area which combines the features of image processing, pattern recognition, security check and digital image processing tools to work with. It's a hybrid computing aspect where a researcher can use any of the traditional application or the evolving deep learning technique to implement. An economic system in India is consistent over the decades. The Government of India introduced 1, 2, 5, 10, 100 and 1000 rupees notes from its evolution. Currently, the Indian currency system has the denomination of Rs. 10, 20, 50, 100, 200, 500 and 2000. Every note has its value on it.

There were several authors [1–19] who worked on the proposed system using different techniques. In our literature survey, we studied traditional systems for the recognition such as, using Hue, Saturation and Value (HSV), that uses Saturation and Intensity values of an image pixel values to predict the denomination [1]. [2] Used region of interest (ROI) analysis with a pattern recognition technique to predict the denomination. The estimated time for the proposed system for 100, 500 and 1000 notes is 0.21135, 0.22134, and 0.2231 respectively.

[3] Used CNN with 2 Convolution operations, 2 max-pooling operations, 2 ReLU activation layers and 2Fully Connected Layers in their architecture to process the input image of 227*227*1 size. They used 20epochs and a batch size of 64 for classification. [4] used size, colour and text extraction feature to identify various notes collected from 20 different countries. The centre region is extracted and checked their value by using the ratio of the number of black pixels to the number of pixels as a predicted ration to compare with different country r values. Using a template matching technique they determined the denomination value. The Indian currency was detected in 45.4 s during the process.

Faster RCNN using inception model in [5] predicted the currency with the accuracy of 87% and loss of 0.201. Feature map is constructed on pre-trained Image-Net CNN. The denomination value is displayed by the bounding box to all the predicted denominations. [7] used template matching technique on an extracted feature from the localized image. He used Edge detection to perform image localization. There is a need for a system that processes the information without human intervention. However, this becomes difficult because of the various features and the security aspects regarded with the banknotes. Numerous methods were proposed [8–10] using various features. There have been various systems with image processing techniques were proposed in [12–14]. However, we can learn that considering the parameters mentioned in these papers are useful but there is a need for more than one parameter. In the papers [15, 16] the classification model is created using an artificial neural network. Various properties such as the direction of note, face-value were recognised using neural network-based bill recognition and verification method, the learning vector quantization (LVQ) and SURF Features (Table 1).

First, we input the image to the proposed system, and then the image is reshaped to (299 × 299) and fed to the inception network. The complexity constraints such as simplicity, high speed, efficiency and security were pioneer parameters to develop the algorithm.

Table 1. Literature survey on denomination methods

Author	Year	Methodology used	Accuracy (%)	Dataset used	Denominations used	Time taken for prediction	Comments
[3]	2020	CNN	93.4	Own dataset with 5322 images	6	255 min	Pics collected from a smartphone of core i5 7th generation processor
[4]	2015	Aspect Ratio & HSV	93.3	-	20	53 s	Note sfrom20 different countries
[5]	2019	Edge detection and pixel intensity values	76.6	30 input Images	15	-	Feature extracted based on image segmentation methods
[6]	2020	Faster RCNN	87	Own dataset	10		Used Regions Proposal Network (RPN) to predict the regions of CNN
[7]	2018	Edge Detection	-	Own dataset	5	60s	Did not explain the template matching
[2]	2012	Sobel Filter		Own dataset	3	23s	Edge-based segmentation by Sobel operator
[9]	2007	Markov chain concept	95	Own dataset	100		Process the texture of currency
[12]	2013	ROI and pattern matching	—	Own dataset	10		Only denomination numerals are matched using filters
[16]	2020	ORB Algorithm	—	Own dataset	4	-	Cost of computation is high and additional hardware 2required
[19]	2016	SIFT Algorithm	60.5	Own dataset	5	72s	The visibility of the objects using different annotated points

Segmentation algorithms [17] are time consuming as the ROI needs to be accurately predicted and these algorithms are quite useful when the object identity needs to be detected. Instead the classification algorithms [18] are much easier comparatively as generalization is predominant factor in such algorithms. Invariant Gaussian distribution [19, 20] is used to detect the currency that includes size, colour and texture to identify the currency. Table: 1 brief the methods used by various authors. Segmentation algorithms Classification algorithm.

3 Proposed Method

According to the literature survey, the currency recognition is performed using various techniques such as surface, blueprint and colour. We use digital image processing techniques to acquire the image, after that the deep learning model and the ImageNet model Inception is used to predict the output. The Inception network is trained with the 1729 train set images and then tested validated with the 210 validation set images. Proposed algorithms are discussed in Fig. 1.

Step 1: Input an Image.

Step 2: Resize the image into (299 x 299).

Step 3: Image Conversion process: Image into numpy array.

Step 4: Feed the array into the inception model.

Step 5: Use the optimal learning rate of 0.001 and batch size 10.

Step 6: The network goes through several convolution layers and pooling process that reduces the trainable parameters using batch normalization.

Step 7: Add an extra layer at the end of output layer of model using the softmax activation function to classify the value.

Step 8: Compile the model with "adam" optimizer and set loss to "categorical cross entropy"

Step 9: Now use "fit generator()" to train the model with 50 epochs

---

Fig. 1. Algorithm of proposed method

Image acquisition is the process of creation of a digital image, typically from the database. The acquired image is then converted into an array which can be used for processing. The image is reshaped to (229 × 229) and fed to the model for prediction. The image then goes through a network of dense layers or convolution layers where different filters are applied for the processing of the image. The array is then normalized so that the trainable parameters are reduced. Max Pooling is applied to the network. The softmax layer is used to predict the class of the image.

3.1 Proposed Architecture

The Inception network is greatly structured that invades the proposed system both in terms of speed and accuracy. The proposed system uses convolution, pooling to extract the feature map. The proposed system used resized input image of 299 × 299 with 3 filters. A 1 × 1 convolution is used to map an input pixel with all its respective channels to an output pixel. 1 × 1 convolution is used as a dimensionality reduction module to reduce computation to an extent. The proposed architecture has 22 layers (27 including the pooling layers). To make the computation to minimize we limited the convolution to 1 × 1 before 3 × 3 and 5 × 5 convolutions. To avoid the middle part of the network from dying out, two auxiliary classifiers are introduced in the model. The concatenation used 2048 channels altogether to build a model. The Inception model replaces the FCNs used at the end that averages the pooling channel values with 2D feature map reduces the total number of parameters used. The proposed flowchart is described in Fig. 2.

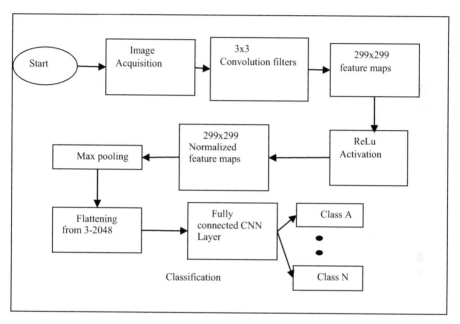

Fig. 2. Flowchart of the proposed system

3.2 Implementation

As described in Fig. 2, the proposed system uses a convolution neural network of 3 × 3 filters. These are convolved with the image to detect the presence of features dictated by them. Each 3 × 3 generates a feature map of 32 × 32 sizes with 0 paddings. The generated feature map is an array containing convolved output at each pixel. ReLu is an activation function which generates the output of the maximum feature element. Max pooling operation s performed to diminish the size of the input image to half. As we are using 2 × 2 max-pooling operation, it outputs 4 values under its dimension. The final fully connected layer flattens the concatenated output into a single feature map. This layer is classified into either of the classes in the output.

4 Experiment and Results

The proposed system uses 1749 images belonging to 10 classes to train and 210 images belonging to 10 classes to test. Hence 10 denominations get predicted. The sample dataset is collected from imagenet database and contains 1749 images in the training set and 210 images in the test set under 10 classes.

4.1 Training

In the implementation, we considered 4 parameters under training the model. They are accuracy, value loss, value accuracy and loss. Loss is calculated using Log-loss function.

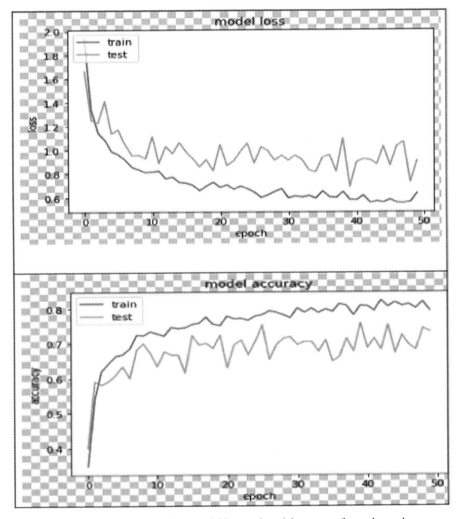

Fig. 3. Plot is drawn against model loss and model accuracy for each epoch

The training parameters are shown in Table 2. The parameter values are considered at every 5th epoch and tabularized. The model is trained with a batch size of 10 and 50 epochs. The plots are drawn against each parameter and shown in Fig. 3. The model exhibited the best accuracy at 50th epoch. Figure 3 show plots of accuracy over each epoch.

Table 2. Training parameter values of the proposed at every 5 consecutive epochs

EPOCHS	TIME	LOSS	ACC	VAL_LOSS	VAL_ACC
1	286s 819 ms	1.9388	0.3469	1.6624	0.4000
5	286s 819 ms	0.9865	0.6634	1.1392	0.6095
10	285s 817 ms	0.8110	0.7339	0.9267	0.6414
15	288s 824 ms	0.7268	0.7448	1.0599	0.6743
20	285s 815 ms	0.7275	0.7506	0.8244	0.7238
25	286s 819 ms	0.6710	0.7781	1.0535	0.7348
30	286s 820 ms	0.6694	0.7795	0.9528	0.7590
35	288s 824 ms	0.5903	0.7976	0.8111	0.7795
40	290s 830 ms	0.5798	0.8073	0.6875	0.8071
45	286s 818 ms	0.5563	0.8177	1.0279	0.8314
50	289s 827 ms	0.6318	0.8336	0.9062	0.8333

4.2 Results

During experimentation, Total parameters found were 21,823,274. The trainable parameters are 20,490 and Non-trainable parameters 21,802,784. The average time taken to run the trained model under each epoch is 390 s. To predict the output class, the proposed system took 78Secs with an accuracy of 87%. The results of the proposed system are shown in Table 3.

Table 3. Results of proposed method

Input Image	Output of Prediction
	Class: 10 New
	Class: 20
	Class: 200
	Class: 500

5 Conclusion

In this proposed work, we used a robust approach for denomination detection in the currency of India. The proposed system experiments on various denominations and physical conditions including new notes folded notes reversed notes and tilted notes in different illuminations and background. The proposed system used the database of 1729 train set images and then tested validated with the 210 validation set images. The database is trained using the neural network and the denomination is extracted using edge detection on the extracted feature. The result obtained is with 84% accuracy using deep CNN. We would like to increase the accuracy of over 90% in future.

References

1. Amirsab, S.A., Mudassir, M., Ismail, M.: An automated recognition of fake or destroyed Indian currency notes. Int. J. Adv. Sci. Res. Eng. Trends **2**(7), (2017)
2. Mirza, R., Nanda, V.: Design and implementation of Indian paper currency authentication system based on feature extraction by edge-based segmentation using Sobel operator. Int. J. Eng. Res. Dev. **3**(2), 41–46 (2012)
3. Chowdhury, U.R., Jana, S., Parekh, R.: Automated system for Indian banknote recognition using image processing and deep learning. In: 2020 International Conference on Computer Science, Engineering and Applications (ICCSEA), pp. 1–5 (March 2020)
4. Abburu, V., Gupta, S., Rimitha, S.R., Mulimani, M., Koolagudi, S.G.: Currency recognition system using image processing. In: Tenth International Conference on Contemporary Computing (IC3), pp. 1–6 (August 2017)
5. Sharan, V., Kaur, A. (2019). Detection of counterfeit Indian currency note using image processing. In: International Journal of Engineering and Advanced Technology (IJEAT), vol. 9, no. 1, (October 2019) ISSN: 2249 – 8958
6. Bhavsar, K., Jani, K., Vanzara, R.: Indian currency recognition from live video using deep learning. In: Chaubey, N., Parikh, S., Amin, K. (eds.) COMS2 2020. CCIS, vol. 1235, pp. 70–81. Springer, Singapore (2020). https://doi.org/10.1007/978-981-15-6648-6_6
7. Venugopal, V., Thomas, D., Prasad, A.: Indian currency recognizer and counter system. Int. J. Innov. Technol. Exploring Eng. (IJITEE) **4**(5), 34–37 (2014)
8. Pujar, M.R.: Indian currency recognition and verification using image processing. Int. J. Adv. Res. Dev. **3**(2), 175–180 (2018)
9. Hassanpour, H., Yaseri, A., Ardeshiri, G.: Feature extraction for paper currency recognition. In: 2007 9th International Symposium on Signal Processing and Its Applications, pp. 1–4 (February 2007)
10. Vishnu, R., Omman, B.: Principal features for Indian currency recognition. In: 2014 Annual IEEE India Conference (INDICON), pp. 1–8 (December 2014)
11. Yi, C., Tian, Y., Arditi, A.: Portable camera-based assistive text and product label reading from hand-held objects for blind persons. IEEE/ASME Trans. Mechatron. **19**(3), 808–817 (2013)
12. Jain, V.K., Vijay, R.: Indian currency denomination identification using image processing technique (2013)
13. Reel, P.S., Krishan, G., Kotwal, S.: Image processing based heuristic analysis for enhanced currency recognition. Int. J. Adv. Technol. **2**(1), 82–89 (2011)
14. Sarfraz, M.: An intelligent paper currency recognition system. Procedia Comput. Sci. **65**, 538–545 (2015)
15. Gogoi, M., Ali, S.E., Mukherjee, S.: Automatic Indian currency denomination recognition system based on artificial neural network. In: 2015 2nd International Conference on Signal Processing and Integrated Networks (SPIN), pp. 553–558 (February 2015)
16. Swathi, A., Rani, S.: Intelligent fatigue detection by using ACS and by avoiding false alarms of fatigue detection. In: Saini, H.S., Sayal, R., Govardhan, A., Buyya, R. (eds.) Innovations in Computer Science and Engineering: Proceedings of the Sixth ICICSE 2018, pp. 225–233. Springer, Singapore (2019). https://doi.org/10.1007/978-981-13-7082-3_27
17. Swathi, A., Saneep, K.: A smart application to detect pupil for small dataset with low illumination. Innov. Syst. Softw. Eng. **17**, 29–43 (2020) https://doi.org/10.1007/s11334-020-003 82-3
18. Khamparia, A., Singh, S.K., Luhach, A.K., Gao, X.Z.: Classification and analysis of users review using different classification techniques in intelligent e-learning system. Int. J. Intell. Inf. Database Syst. **13**(2–4), 139–149 (2020)

19. Mirza, R., Nanda, V.: Paper currency verification system based on characteristic extraction using image processing. Int. J. Eng. Adv. Technol. (IJEAT) **1**(3), 68–71 (2012)
20. Behera, H.S., Swain, B.K., Parida, A.K., Sahu, G.: A new proposed round robin with highest response ratio next (rrhrrn) scheduling algorithm for soft real-time systems. Int. J. Eng. Adv. Technol. **37**, 200–206 (2012)

A Review on Various Deep Learning Techniques for Identification of Plant Diseases

Akash Sirohi[1(✉)], Arun Malik[2], Isha[2], and Ashish Kr. Luhach[3]

[1] Lovely Professional University, Punjab, India
[2] Department of Computer Science, Lovely Professional University, Punjab, India
{arun.17442,isha.17451}@lpu.co.in
[3] The PNG University of Technology, Lae, Papua New Guinea

Abstract. Plants are the most important for the living of human beings as well as for our environment. Agriculture plays an important role in the economy of our country, so it becomes important to save the plants from diseases. It is necessary to detect the diseases in an earlier stage to save the plants, which is one of the most difficult things so, In order to detect or identify the diseases in the plants there are some traditional methods which are done by manually becomes very difficult and they require lots amount of time, expertise in plant diseases and has excessive processing time. Nowadays machine learning and deep learning is used widely for this purpose with the help of images. So this paper, perform a survey on the various deep learning techniques or models for the identification of plants diseases.

Keywords: Diseases · Deep learning · Technique · Image processing · Machine learning

1 Introduction

Infection in plants becomes one of the biggest problems in agriculture farming, to overcome this detection of infection in plants or crops should be identified in earlier stages. The detection or identification can be done manually but it raised some error because data is in image form and it is a challenging task too [3]. So to overcome this situation automatic identification techniques are used which makes the process reliable and easy. The main problem in the identification of infections is, getting the symptoms disease or extraction of patterns that contain information about the diseases. But with the help of present computer vision techniques, the information or portion that contains disease symptoms can be acquired by segmentation [3]. So to spare our time and increment the precision of expectation we use PC vision: Machine learning [5].

Previously, Machine learning techniques were used to identify the infection on the plant using image data [1]. There are many machine learning algorithms that can be used for this purpose, depend upon the requirements. Machine learning is the technique that learns with the data and to classify the data use the training as an experience [3] and gives the result. Nowadays machine learning are used in various ways like virtual assistance,

© Springer Nature Singapore Pte Ltd. 2021
A. K. Luhach et al. (Eds.): ICAICR 2020, CCIS 1393, pp. 487–498, 2021.
https://doi.org/10.1007/978-981-16-3660-8_46

predictions, video surveillance, and many more. Machine learning techniques can be used as an image classifier but they don't provide a satisfactory result then deep learning comes into existence.

Deep learning is the subset of machine learning; it is the technique that resembles the human brain. Deep learning based on the neural networks which are basically the basic unit of the human brain that's why they provide better results as an image classifier. The convolutional Neural Network, a deep learning technique acquires the best position as an image classifier among all the techniques [1, 15]. Deep learning has various working fields like recognition, image classifier, NLP, Vision, and many more. Generally deep learning model have at least 3-layers and each and every layer is link with data feature with neurons [3]. To understand the problem, a lot of agriculture data and a good understanding of deep learning are required. So this paper reviewed some existing deep learning techniques of identification of plant infection through images after analysis of several articles.

2 Literature Review

Junde Chen et al. in [1] used the pre-owned transfer mastering method of serious convolutional neural community, to determine the condition of growing foliage. They utilized a pre-trained design on Inception module, VGGNet, and ImageNet, these models were used by them to delegate the weights somewhat compared to beginning coming from zero then qualified types with the own dataset of theirs and they also determine which the proposed techniques of theirs accomplished the 91.83% precision on a public dataset, as well as 92% on grain, grow. They altered the pre-trained model in such a manner that they put in a convolutional level by changing the final level for batch normalization.

Minu Eliz Pothen et al. in [2] proposed a method for better classification of rice leaf diseases i.e. Bacterial leaf blight, Leaf smut, and Brown spot disease. They used Otsu's method for segmentation, after segmentation they used Local Binary Patterns (LBP) and Histogram of Oriented Gradients (HOG) for classification features, and SVM was used to train the system which gave 94.6% accuracy with the polynomial kernel.

M.Nagaraju and Priyanka Chawla in [3], reviewed the existing deep learning techniques used to identification or detection of plant diseases, systematically. They also analyse the results of different techniques and gives the future scope for data analysis.

Manpreet Kaur and Dr. Rekha Bhatia in [4] proposed a method for tomato disease detection, implemented on MATLAB, and collected the dataset from PlantVillage which contains 6 diseases and one healthy leaf set. They used the pre-trained models of ResNet to extract the feature, with an ECOC linear learner for classification. In the end, they concluded that their method gave accuracy of 98.8%.

A.S.M. Farhan AI Haque et al. in [5] proposed a disease detection technique using the deep learning CNN model for guava, they considered some diseases which were anthracnose, fruit rot, and fruit canker. They collected their dataset from different districts of Bangladesh. In the end, they concluded that their proposed technique gave 95.61% accuracy rate.

Radhamadhab Dalai and Kishore Kumar Senapati in [6] used the deep learning models to identify the pest disease, they used the RCNN model for detection and according to them its give better result.

Malik Hashmat Shadab et al. in [7] identified whether the deep learning models can work fine in uncontrolled conditions. For that, they used a dataset that consists of 5 diseases of sugarcane acquired from 5 different regions of Karnataka. They concluded that they achieved 93.20% accuracy on their dataset and 76.40% on images from different sources of the internet. Also, they used two models YOLO and Faster-RCNN for object detection and achieved 58.13% on average.

Mehmet Metin Ozguven and Kemal Adem in [8] proposed a technique to detect and classify the diseases in sugar beet leaves automatically using deep learning. They used a faster R-CNN which was formed by changing the parameters of the CNN model. They trained their model with 155 images and predicted the accuracy which was 95.48%. According to them by changing the parameters of the CNN model their proposed model not only gives better accuracy but it can becomes fast also.

Hu Gensheng et al. in [9] determined the condition of tea leaf's by using a very low photo mastering technique, they applied SVM for segmented the picture following removal of color as well as consistency element in addition to C-DCGAN for augmented the condition area test. So that they utilized the segmented picture as feedback plus they additionally utilized DCNN for creating a brand new education established, essentially, a mix of rich mastering style, as well as classical mastering model, were used by them and they also determined that they attained 90% reliability.

Md. Helal Sheikh et al. in [10] proposed a method to determine the condition of Peach and Maize leaf utilizing AI. They utilized picture processing methods along with a full mastering version CNN to instruct, on the foundation of the dataset of theirs, and also additionally they also concluded that their model attained 99.28% accuracy.

Ramar Ahila Priyadharshini et al. in [11], proposed the full CNN method to determine the maize leaf diseases, he utilized the plant-Village dataset for the maize actually leaves image. This model was used by him to identify the three illnesses as well as nourishing leaves; he concluded that this method accomplished the 97.89% reliability.

Jayme Garcia Arnal barbedo in [12] attempted to determine the grow diseases utilizing heavy learning with specific spots and lesions rather than utilizing total leave. He concluded that utilizing lesions and spot, accomplished reliability was 12% much more than the accuracies attained using whole foliage.

Aditya Khamparia et al. in [13] proposed a method for the identification of diseases in several crops in the early stage by using deep learning techniques for which they used 200 images of individual crop dataset and also they compare their method with several other methods like SVM, KNN, genetic algorithm, and ANN. In the end, they concluded that their method gave the accuracy of 92% and 93.7% with 32 * 32 * 3 and 64 * 64 * 3 filter size respectively.

Konstantinos P. Feretinos in [14] created a unit to determine the disease using leaves photos as well as identify the healthy leaves. He utilized a convolutional neural network to develop a unit also he applied the receptive data source to teach as well as evaluate the networking plus attained 99.53%.

Jayme GA Barbedo in [15] attempted to discover the variables which engage in a crucial job inside the layout and also the usefulness of serious neural networks utilized to identify the condition of vegetation. Also, he formed the database of his pictures employed within the research as well as tests. He concluded that every last method has several limits no matter if we apply to plant life elements quite compared to foliage or even make use of CNN.

Budiarianto Suryo Kusumo et al. in [16] utilized picture processing methods to draw out the functions on the picture of corn grow actually leaves to determine the sicknesses. They used attributes including RGB, scale-invariant element transform (SIFT), speeded upwards strong features (SURF) plus Oriented Fast and also turned Histogram and bref (ORB) of focused gradients (HOG), next they utilized a few printer mastering methods for the category as SVM, choice tree, Naive Bayes and Random Forest. They determined the RGB attribute may be the important and best element amongst them for a category that has the greatest precision.

K.R.Aravind et al. in [17] attempted to determine the maize leaf's diseases for they accumulated 2000 pictures coming from receptive data source i.e. PlantVillage. And then, the characteristics at the picture were extracted by them as well as histogram influenced by textural characteristics. They utilized a piece of equipment mastering method i.e. multiclass SVM for the category, Within the conclusion, they determined that having a popcorn bag of attributes they obtained 83.7% while employing mixed statistical attributes they obtained 81.3% reliability.

Juanhua Zhu et al. in [18] proposed a strategy to determine the grape grow leaf's illness instantly that was dependant on picture evaluation along with a back-propagation neural network (BPNN). They denoised the pictures together with the Wiener Filtering technique that was influenced by wavelet transform additionally they made use of the Otsu segmentation way of segmenting the picture as well as morphological way of improving the lesion design. The 5 illnesses i.e. leaf area, Sphaceloma ampelinum de Bary, round spot, anthracnose, along downy mildew was identified by them. They determined which the proposed method of theirs attained 91% reliability.

Aravind Krishnaswamy Rangaranjan et al. in [19] used the pre-trained model of deep learning to detect the diseases of tomato crops. They used the PlantVillage dataset for training and testing, they used two models i.e. AlexNet and VGG16net. They also conclude that they achieved 97.29% in VGG16net and 97.49% in AlexNet.

Andreas Kamilaris et al. in [20] survey the deep learning techniques used in the field of agriculture, also they examined they result, data pre-processing, models, and their frameworks. They examined these qualities from 40 research, which used deep learning for the production or detection of disease. In the end, they concluded that deep learning gave a better result than image processing techniques.

Zahid Iqbal et al. in [21] performed a survey on different image processing techniques to detect the disease on citrus plants. They studied different methods of segmentation, image pre-processing, features selection & extraction, and one important method i.e. classification.

Edna Chebet Too et al. in [22] performed certain experiments over different deep learning models to find out the best technique. They used VGG 16, Inception V4, ResNet with 50, 101, and 152 layers, and DenseNets with 121 layers and they used data from plant village of 14 different plants having healthy leaf and 38 different classes. In the end, they found that DenseNet perform well among them and gave 99.75% accuracy with less number of parameters and less chance of overfitting.

Hyeon Park et al. in [23] developed a mechanism which analyses the images dynamically with the help of deep learning. They mainly used strawberry fruits and leaves. After analyses images were sent to the farmer to collect feedback from farmer and to diagnose it rapidly. They used CNN architecture to develop their model which also works well in smartphone.

Bharat Mishra et al. in [24] performed a survey on the techniques of image processing which were used to detect the leaf diseases. They compared several types of techniques/approaches and highlight the challenges in leaf disease detection and they also concluded that there was a scope of hybrid algorithms like genetic algorithms for detection.

Usama Mokhtar et al. in [25] used the Gabor wavelet transform method to extract the features from images with using support vector machines (SVMs) with different kernel methods to detect the diseases on tomato leaves. They used datasets of 100/type of diseases in tomato images and they conclude that their technique achieved 99.5% accuracy.

Halil Durmus et al. in [26] used deep learning techniques for detecting the tomato diseases and also they tested the two deep learning models like AlexNet and SqueezeNet. They used Nvidia Jetson TX1 for training and testing the models and they used the PlantVillage dataset for tomato leaf images. They concluded that AlexNet gave 95.65% accuracy and SqueezeNet gave 94.3% accuracy (Table 1).

Table 1. Literature Review

Reference no.	Author	Crop name	Model used	Accuracy
1	Junde Chen et al.	Multiple	VGGNet & ImageNet	91.83% & 92%
2	Minu Eliz Pothen & Dr. Maya L Pai	Rice	SVM	94.6%
4	Manpreet Kaur & Dr. Rekha Bhatia	Tomato	ResNet	98.8%
5	A.S.M Farhan Al Haque et al.	Guava	CNN	95.61%
7	Malik Hashmat Shadab et al.	Sugarcane	FR-CNN	93.2% (on their dataset) & 76.4% (on internet pics)
8	Mehmet Metin Ozguven et al.	SugarBeet	FR-CNN	95.48%
9	Hu Gensheng et al.	Tea	SVM&VGG16	90%

(continued)

Table 1. (*continued*)

Reference no.	Author	Crop name	Model used	Accuracy
10	Md. Helal Sheikh et al.	Maize	F-CNN	99.28%
11	Ramar Ahila Priyadharshini et al.	Maize	D-CNN	97.89%
14	Konstantinos P.Ferentinos	Multiple	AlexNet, AlexNetOWTBn, GoogLeNet, Overfeat, VGG	99.06%, 99.44%, 97.27%, 98.96% and 99.48%
17	K.R.Aravind et al.	Maize	SVM	83.7%
18	Juanhua Zhu et al.	Grape	BPNN & Weiner	91%
19	Aravind Krishnaswamy Rangarajan et al.	Tomato	VGG16 & AlexNet	97.29% & 97.49%
25	Usama Mokhtar et al.	Tomato	SVM	99.5%
26	Halil Durmus et al.	Tomato	AlexNet & SqueezeNet	95.65% & 94.3%

3 Deep Learning Techniques

CNN (Convolutional Neural Network): A unique kind of neural system is utilized for grouping and acknowledgment of pictures. It is the fundamental model for characterization which gives preferred outcomes over the customary techniques [1]. The fundamental CNN contains primarily 3 layers for example convolutional layers, pooling layers, and full association layers [1].

Convolutional Layers: This layer is utilized to removes the particular highlights of the picture rely on its convolution portion size. We can separate a lot of highlights by simply applying the convolutional layer a few times.

$H_i = \phi(H_{i-1} W_i + B_i)$.

Where, H_i = feature map, $H_i\text{-}1$ = convolution feature of previous layer, W_i = weight of ith layer.

B_i = offset vector of ith layer, ϕ = ReLU function.

Pooling layers: It is utilized to lessen the spatial measurement to decrease computational multifaceted nature and furthermore diminish the danger of over-fitting [1].

$$x_j^l = down\left(x_j^{l-1}, s\right)$$

Where, $l = l^{th}$ pooling layer, j = o/p properties local receptive, down() = down-sampling function.

x_j^{l-1} = feature vector in previous layer, s = pooling size.

Fully-Connected Layers: It is utilized after the two layers recorded above to separate the highlights for the arrangement of pictures. Softmax Function used to foresee the class by utilizing the aftereffect of past layers [1] (Fig. 1).

$$\text{Softmax}(z)_i = e^{z_j} / \sum_1^k e^{z_k} \, (for j = 1, 2..k)$$

Where k = dimension of z vector.

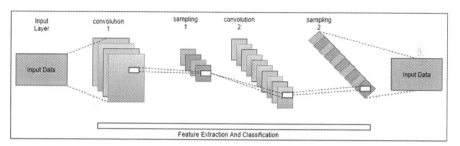

Fig. 1. Convolutional neural network [27]

AlexNet: Fundamentally AlexNet comprises 5 convolutional layers and 3 completely associated layers. Every convolution layer is trailed by the ReLU work then a layer is utilized for speculation called the Normalization layer which is trailed by the pooling layer and full-associated layer. The completely associated layer used to foresee the class and furthermore used to decrease the over-fitting. The last completely associated layer contains the class probabilities of the information picture which are ordered further by softmax work or softmax classifier [26] (Fig. 2).

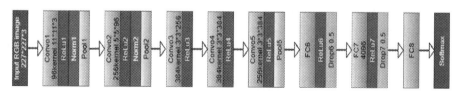

Fig. 2. AlexNet structure [26]

SqueezeNet: It is one of the packed models of profound realizing which gives better outcomes and it a presentation of system design building. It depends on three structure methodologies to diminish its size. Lessening channel size, diminishing info channels, and down sampling late in the system are the 3 techniques. It has five modules that comprise of a crushed layer with 1 * 1 channels and extends layer with 1 * 1 and 3 * 3 channels which are trailed by ReLU work [26] (Fig. 3).

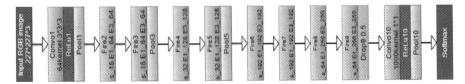

Fig. 3. SqueezeNet structure [26]

RESnet 101: ResNet has numerous variations like ResNet 50, ResNet 18, and so forth yet ResNet 101 gives better exactness among them and generally appropriate for enormous datasets. It is a pre-prepared model of CNN which depends on two areas: Feature Learning and Classification. Fundamentally it utilized DAG (Direct Acyclic Graph) strategy [4]. It has one info layer and one yield layer however it can take different contributions from various layers. It has:

Input layer: Take input according to channel.

Convolution layer: generate feature map, equal to the convolution filters.

Batch Normalized layer: used to reduce covariance shift before activation layer.

ReLU function: Also called as Activation function.

Pool layer: reduce the dimensions of images.

Fully-connected layer: Contains the class labels.

LeNet: It is the principal design for CNN which was made acknowledgment of transcribed and machine-printed character. It is 5 layers organize for example 2 convolution layers and 3 completely associated layer [11]. It likewise has learnable loads and predispositions. It takes a few contributions with weighted entirety at that point apply initiation capacity and gives the yield [5] (Fig. 4).

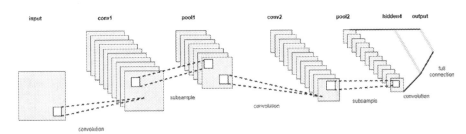

Fig. 4. LeNet architecture [11]

VGG-19: It has 16 convolution layers that are trailed by 3 completely associated layers lastly followed by a SoftMax layer. It just uses 3 × 3 convolution with both steps and cushioning of 1. The arrangement of stacked convolution layers additionally contains MaxPool layers which utilize a 2 × 2 channel and a step of 2. It contains around 143.6 million boundaries [9, 19].

4   Strategy

In analysing the deep learning model lot of challenge occurs during the process. This section contains the strategy that tells how and which points are to be focus to analyse the deep learning model.

4.1   Groundwork

To review the deep learning techniques, 25 articles studied. These articles collected from standard journals like IEEE, Springer, Research Gate and etc. A keyword-search is performed to collect articles like Deep Learning, CNN, and Artificial intelligence, Machine learning, Diseases identification.

4.2   Conduction

This, shows what points to be focus to analyse the deep learning technique and the dataset: Source of Dataset, Feature Extraction Techniques, Quality of Images, and Overfitting.

4.2.1   Dataset

Dataset is one of the most crucial element to analyse the techniques. Without the dataset, there is no meaning of analysing the technique, because the dataset is required to train and test the deep learning systems. So to obtain the dataset researchers use PlantVillage, Google Sites, and other open-source databases. The dataset should contain high-quality images. The more accurate the dataset more will be the accuracy.

4.2.2   Feature Extraction Technique

Feature Extraction is one of the most challenging tasks in CNN models. Ancient methods deal with predefined features. Feature extraction means to find out the patterns which contain the information of the plant infection. The more accurate the feature extraction more will be the accuracy. Pre-processing techniques of images are used to improve the feature extraction [3]. The most worthy pre-preparing activity is picture resize or design all pictures into similar size and types [3]. And, feature extraction can also be improved by segmentation by finding the regions that contain information about diseases or by increase the dataset. There are many other method also for feature extraction like ORB (Oriented quick and pivoted brief), Color-slope histogram and so on.

4.2.3   Image Quality

As image data is used to train the model, so if low-quality images are used then the model cannot be able to identify correctly that's why the quality of image has the effective role in the identification or training of the model. Quality means Noise, high quality images mean low noise. To train the model high-quality images should be used [6], so to enhance the quality of images some pre-processing techniques are used like Noise filtering, augmentation, and segmentation [3].

4.2.4 Overfitting

Due to the overfitting the error percent chance can be increased, so to avoid this chance activation functions are used in deep learning models like ReLU (Rectifier linear unit), PReLU (Parametric Rectifier Linear Unit), sigmoidal function and more., but ReLU and PReLU are faster and better than others [3] (Figs. 5, 6).

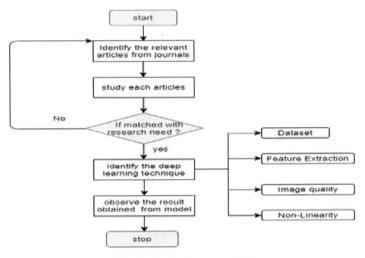

Fig. 5. Analysis structure [3]

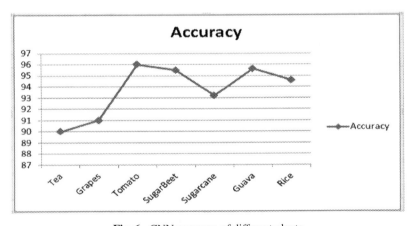

Fig. 6. CNN accuracy of different plants

5 Conclusion

This paper performed a survey of some existing deep learning techniques of identification and classification of plant leaves diseases. So after reviewing some articles, some models of deep learning are comes into the picture i.e. CNN, VGGNet, LeNet, ResNet, and many more, and after analysis, we can say that CNN is the best model for this purpose and there are some points, which consider as important for the analysis of any model and its accuracy i.e. dataset, Feature extraction, image quality, and overfitting. In the future, there should be some technique that can work well with unstructured data because present techniques work well with structured data only.

References

1. Chen, J., et al.: Using deep transfer learning for image-based plant disease identification. Comput. Electron. Agric. **173**, 105393 (2020)
2. Pothen, M. E., Pai, M.L.: Detection of rice leaf diseases using image processing. In: 2020 Fourth International Conference on Computing Methodologies and Communication (ICCMC). IEEE (2020)
3. Nagaraju, M., Chawla, P.: Systematic review of deep learning techniques in plant disease detection. Int. J. Syst. Assur. Eng. Manage. **11**, 1–14 (2020). https://doi.org/10.1007/s13198-020-00972-1
4. Kaur, M., Bhatia, R.: Development of an improved tomato leaf disease detection and classification method. In: 2019 IEEE Conference on Information and Communication Technology. IEEE (2019)
5. Farhan Al Haque, A.S.M.: A computer vision system for guava disease detection and recommend curative solution using deep learning approach. In: 2019 22nd International Conference on Computer and Information Technology (ICCIT). IEEE (2019)
6. Dalai, R., Senapati, K.K.: An intelligent vision based pest detection system using RCNN based deep learning mechanism. In: 2019 International Conference on Recent Advances in Energy-efficient Computing and Communication (ICRAECC). IEEE (2019)
7. Malik, H.S., et al.: Disease recognition in sugarcane crop using deep learning. In: Chiplunkar, N.N., Fukao, T. (eds.) Advances in Artificial Intelligence and Data Engineering. AISC, vol. 1133, pp. 189–206. Springer, Singapore (2021). https://doi.org/10.1007/978-981-15-3514-7_17
8. Ozguven, M.M., Adem, K.: Automatic detection and classification of leaf spot disease in sugar beet using deep learning algorithms. Phys. A **535**, 122537 (2019)
9. Hu, G., et al.: A low shot learning method for tea leaf's disease identification. Comput. Electron. Agric. **163**, 104852 (2019)
10. Sheikh, M.H., et al.: Detection of maize and peach leaf diseases using image processing. In: 2019 10th International Conference on Computing, Communication and Networking Technologies (ICCCNT). IEEE (2019)
11. Priyadharshini, R.A., Arivazhagan, S., Arun, M., Mirnalini, A.: Maize leaf disease classification using deep convolutional neural networks. Neural Comput. Appl. **31**(12), 8887–8895 (2019). https://doi.org/10.1007/s00521-019-04228-3
12. Barbedo, J.G.A.: Plant disease identification from individual lesions and spots using deep learning. Biosys. Eng. **180**, 96–107 (2019)
13. Khamparia, A., Singh, A., Luhach, A.K., Pandey, B., Pandey, D.K.: Classification and identification of primitive Kharif crops using supervised deep convolutional networks. Sustain. Comput. Inform. Syst. **28**, 100340 (2020)
14. Ferentinos, K.P.: Deep learning models for plant disease detection and diagnosis. Comput. Electron. Agric. **145**, 311–318 (2018)
15. Barbedo, J.G.A.: Factors influencing the use of deep learning for plant disease recognition. Biosyst. Eng. **172**, 84–91 (2018)

16. Kusumo, B.S., et al.: Machine learning-based for automatic detection of corn-plant diseases using image processing. In: 2018 International Conference on Computer, Control, Informatics and its Applications (IC3INA). IEEE (2018)

17. Aravind, K.R., et al.: Disease classification in maize crop using bag of features and multiclass support vector machine. In: 2018 2nd International Conference on Inventive Systems and Control (ICISC). IEEE (2018)

18. Zhu, J., Wu, A., Wang, X., Zhang, H.: Identification of grape diseases using image analysis and BP neural networks. Multimedia Tools Appl. **79**(21–22), 14539–14551 (2019). https://doi.org/10.1007/s11042-018-7092-0

19. Rangarajan, A.K., Purushothaman, R., Ramesh, A.: Tomato crop disease classification using pre-trained deep learning algorithm. Procedia Comput. Sci. **133**, 1040–1047 (2018)

20. Kamilaris, A., Prenafeta-Boldú, F.X.: Deep learning in agriculture: a survey. Comput. Electron. Agric. **147**, 70–90 (2018)

21. Iqbal, Z., et al.: An automated detection and classification of citrus plant diseases using image processing techniques: a review. Comput. Electron. Agric. **153**, 12–32 (2018)

22. Too, E.C., et al.: A comparative study of fine-tuning deep learning models for plant disease identification. Comput. Electron. Agric. **161**, 272–279 (2019)

23. Park, H., JeeSook, E., Kim, S.-H.: Crops disease diagnosing using image-based deep learning mechanism. In: 2018 International Conference on Computing and Network Communications (CoCoNet). IEEE (2018)

24. Mishra, B., et al.: Recent technologies of leaf disease detection using image processing approach—a review. In: 2017 International Conference on Innovations in Information, Embedded and Communication Systems (ICIIECS). IEEE (2017)

25. Mokhtar, U., et al.: Tomato leaves diseases detection approach based on support vector machines. In: 2015 11th International Computer Engineering Conference (ICENCO). IEEE (2015)

26. Durmuş, H., Güneş, E.O., Kırcım M.: Disease detection on the leaves of the tomato plants by using deep learning. In: 2017 6th International Conference on Agro-Geoinformatics. IEEE (2017)

27. pyimagesearch: LeNet Convolutional neural network. https://www.pyimagesearch.com/2016/08/01/lenet-convolutional-neural-network-in-python/

28. ResearchGate: CNN. https://www.researchgate.net/figure/CNN-general-architecture_fig3_321787151

Silence Elimination for Robust Speaker Detection in Large Database

S. Venkata Achuta Rao[1]($\boxtimes$) and Pamarthi Rama Koteswara Rao[2]

[1] Department of CSE, SREYAS Institute of Engineering and Technology, Hyderabad, India
dr.achyuth@sreyas.ac.in

[2] Department of ECE, NRI Institute of Technology, Agiripalli, Krishna District, Vijayawada, Andhra Pradesh, India

Abstract. The goal is to build an efficient speaker identification framework for broad sets of data in noisy conditions. The key phases of traditional recognition procedures are feature extraction, network training, and checking features. In this experimental work, Silence removal methodologies are proposed to improve accurate recognition. Pitch & Pitch strength factors are extracted from the original speech digital signals as unique characteristics. Multilinear Principle Factor Analysis (MPCA) is used to minimize the dimension of the feature matrix. During the extraction process, silence elimination using Zero Cross Rate and End State Detection methods are incorporated to source utterance. These properties are considered in later testing phase, where SVM based classification is employed. Forward Loking Schostic (FOLOS) is perhaps the most appropriate algorithm used to classify speakers effectively. The experimental findings demonstrated that the suggested approaches rationally increase performance for massive data in noisy conditions.

Keywords: Support vectors · Pinciple components · Stochastic · End detection · Forward looking

1 Introduction

Increasing structured data measurements are a problem for real-world speech processing, such as high preparation period, low reaction time, and huge memory [1]. In practical speaker identification schemes, robustness and responsiveness seem to be the major elements. From the early research, it is noted that under matching conditions, good performance was obtained for clear high pitched voice. The efficiency of the classification procedure, however, reduces drastically in noisy situations and incongruent circumstances. This enables us throughout the speaker identification process to explore novel approaches at various levels.

A standard method of identification of speakers consists primarily of two stages: registration and recognition [2]. At the registration stage voice details are collected in linear mode from its speaker archive. A set of such models helps to build the data base of the speaker. A representation of an input speaker is correlated to the templates in the dataset and the findings are extended at the differentiation point. Moreover, characteristics are

A. K. Luhach et al. (Eds.): ICAICR 2020, CCIS 1393, pp. 499–509, 2021.
https://doi.org/10.1007/978-981-16-3660-8_47

derived from the input voice and translated into a comparatively quite discriminatory and reliable compact image than the initial signal [3].

This research implies experimental examinations for the different phases; extraction of characteristics, noise removal, reduction in dimension and categorization.

2   Approach Adopted

In this study, silence elimination algorithms are used to remove background noise for good speaker identification from the original utterance (Fig. 1).

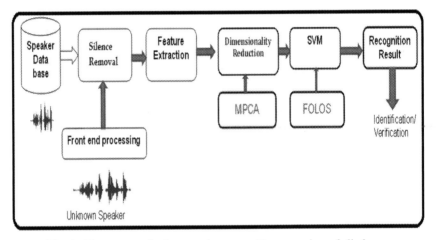

Fig. 1. The process of robust speaker recognition comprises of all phases.

2.1   Extraction of Features

The extraction subsystem identifies a set of parameters that display explicit speaker information from the previous signal. These results are the effects of dynamic data analysis in multiple phases of speaker data acquisition.

The features of voice signal are primarily characterized by listening patterns, vocal tract and speech enthusiasm. The anatomical characteristics of the vocal tract are more stable and less mimicable [4]. Thus, non-conventional characteristics correlated with vocal tract produce strong results in clean and replicated conditions [5]. These approaches are developed with residual linear predictive (LP) signals. But these devices significantly degrade their efficiency in mismatched and distracting environments [6]. Therefore a variety of new characteristics from the source of excitation that are less vulnerable to ambient noise must be extracted. The cognitive and biochemical facets of a speaker demonstrate interesting sources such as pitch power. This work focuses primarily on the extraction of features by collecting features of pitch intensity parameters.

2.2 Removal of Noise

Speech behavior detector algorithms are used for the recognition of a reliability speaker to remove ambient noise from its message articulation. The noise reduction involves two key methods: zero cross rate and voice utterance detector dependent on capacity. For distinguishing the pitched portion of the voice signal, the context is more statistically important.

For robustness, silent component removal is essential in the speaker recognition phase. The preprocessing phase therefore includes the isolation of repetitive details. The speech section consists primarily of incidents such as Unvoiced (U), Voiced (V), Silence (S) [7]. Hardly any speech is possible in silent regions, where sound waves do not expand and contract as that in the unvoice zone. This analysis incorporates the very well techniques of silence reduction.

2.3 Reduction in Dimensionality

This technique minimizes the attribute matrix measurements when retaining the discriminative details of the presenter for the recognition procedure. As the fundamental characteristics increasingly shift, the amount of data obtained from the source utterances is very high. In addition, to determine the attributes of expression, the identification method needs moderately limited details.

A significant amount of extracted features requires large memory and fast processing time in the speaker recognition phase. The dimensions of the function matrix, in which a high-dimensional area is transferred into such a space of smaller dimensions, must then be diminished. In addition to the advantages of computing, precision gains can be made in noisy circumstances [8]. The most effective and well structured projection, being used for dimension reduction for this experimental work, is the Multi-linear Factor Analysis (MFA) [9]. In terms of population density, we performed many surveys and carried out a comparative study. Although these approaches are effective for high recognition activities, original outcomes are influenced with regard to massive recognition of speakers for this work.

2.4 Discrimination

Signal categorization is a complex method in a speech recognition phase to authorize a certain unknown speaker. The discrimination is generally achieved by analogy with the current database. The method is normally split into two categories: training and testing [10]. The convolution neural network is programmed with person speaking knowledge during processing. Validation is a co-ordinate scoring estimation method, which reflects a proportion of similarity between added and current feature values.

The search is checked by contrasting the approximate functionality with the speaker versions. The Vector Support Machine (SVM) is an effective and highly efficient discriminant tool in classification systems [11]. Especially, SVM is used in mathematical learning to allocate the role of mitigating danger. However the SVM's key limitations are machine complexity and low efficiency on broad data environments. Therefore the optimization of broad SVM algorithms was studied. A powerful FOLOS Vector Machine algorithm was implemented and tested [12].

3   Removal of Silence

Two key methods are commonly adopted in voice-based systems for the reduction of silence: zero crossing and energy-based speech utterance detectors. The empirical nature of its context is more critical to distinguish the pitched portion of the voice signals. The following segment explains the essential protocols for silence elimination.

3.1   Short Energy Time (SET) Algorithm

The Short Energy Time algorithm involves 3 measures for extracting and detecting silence and sound from the reported utterance.

Pre-processing. Hanning frame technique separates extracted audio signal into 17 ms-size frame blocks.

Boundary Expression Calculation. The below equations estimate the energies,

$$F(j) = \sum_{m}^{M} y_j(m)^2 \tag{1}$$

Where, from every frame of the original signal, $j = 0$ to L and L is the frame numbers. The intensity of the mth section in j^{th} frame is defined by $y_j(m)$. The Q_1 and Q_2 energy levels are extracted from the signal frames. The following standard parameters measure these quantities.

$$Erg\_Mx = Mx\,(F(j)) \tag{2}$$

$$Erg\_Mn = Mn\,(F(j)) \tag{3}$$

$$Q_1 = Erg\_Mn\left[2 + 3\,Log_{10}(Erg\_Mx\,/\,Erg\_Mn)\right] \tag{4}$$

$$AV = \frac{\sum_l F(k)}{\sum_l 2} \tag{5}$$

Where k is the iterator for frames with $F > Q_1$.

$$Q_2 = Q_1 + 0.45\,(AV - Q_1) \tag{6}$$

By the above calculations, the primary speech signal maximal energy Erg Mx, Erg Mn is the least possible value, and AV is the mean above Q1.

The limits of the utterances are evaluated in terms of the following energy criteria:

1. When Q1 and Q2 go beyond energy, Q1 is referred to as the preliminary start (PL).
2. As energy declines past Q2 and then sinks below Q1, that closing mark of Q1 is regarded as the tentative end point (PT).
3. A little unidentified "word" is recognised as a "noise spike," which is removed while processing.

Elimination of Silence. The frames that were not recognised as "voices" by the measures above are identified as "silence" but will be eliminated by the signals.

3.2 Zero Cross Rate for the Reduction of Silence

Perfect cleaner speech is quite difficult to capture. It is also apparent that any noise level interferes with speech signal. As a consequence, the quiet speech trends have a greater zero cross. For the removal of silence by zero cross segments, the three major steps are included.

Pre-processing. The voice signal is split into 13 ms blocks by the Hann window thnique.

Estimate of Zero Switch Rate. The Zero switch estimate is described as,

$$G_{in} = \sum_{p=1}^{P-1} |sgn[y_q(p+1) - sgn[y_q(p))| \tag{7}$$

There, m is the sector number, and $y_q(p)$ is the pth frame of the qth segment, with sign $(y_q(p))$ being formed,

$$sgn(y_q(p)) = \begin{cases} 1 & if \ y_q(p) \geq 0 \\ 0 & otherwise \end{cases} \tag{8}$$

Elimination of Silence. Unvoiced sections are omitted by making high zero cross rates than a threshold.

3.3 Peak Detection Point Silence Removal

Peak identification point Reduction of silence, the "mean" δ estimate as well as "standard deviation" γ reflecting the ambient noise for a 1250 fragments.

$$\delta = \frac{1}{2450 \sum_{k=1}^{230} y(k)} \tag{9}$$

$$\gamma = \sqrt{\frac{1}{2150} \sum_{k=1}^{2300} (y(k) - \delta)^2} \tag{10}$$

The variance is defined with in recorded signal but graded as a spoken sample if $\frac{|y-\delta|}{\gamma} \leq 4$.

The speech parts were described as voiced or voiceless with "1" and "0". The total segmentation techniques are further separated into 13 ms long Hann window technique.

4 Dimension Reduction: Multilinear Factor Analysis

The MFA technique for dimensional reduction will minimise by considering all vector-ized modes. These predicted tensors explicitly catch the variance in the defined function range. More explicitly, a selected series of characteristics varying [13] was defined. You get Rsel components in each section of the function matrix while Rsel is a squared number. R_T column variables are then chosen from size R_{sel}. Each vector in columns is expressed as $S_i^{(j)}$ in which is defined as $0 \leq i \leq R_{sel} - 1$ and the matrix Z is identified as,

$$Z_{xy}^j = S_x^j : 0 \leq x \leq \sqrt{R_{sel}} - 1, 0 \leq y \leq \sqrt{R_{sel}} - 1 \tag{11}$$

From the above updated matrix, any vector of the jth column is proposed with MFA to minimise dimensionality, where y is indeed an independent factor.

Above in this method the distance-based C for each jth matrix is extracted as,

$$C^J = Z^b - \delta \tag{12}$$

In (12), δ stands for a median matrix, extracted for the word $Z^{(b)}$, and used for distance - based calculation. Tensor vectors $U_1^{(b)}$ and $U_2^{(b)}$ are added to the remote matrix of C to achieve matrix projection β:

$$\beta = \sum_{b=0}^{R-1} U^b (U^b)^T \tag{13}$$

The basic measurement method is defined in (13) and the tensors $U_1^{(b)}$ and $U_2^{(b)}$ must be calculated [14]. This calculation matrix becomes prone to the widespread issue of the eigenvector.

5   Experimental Results and Anaysis

5.1   Setup of Experimentation

Speech Database. In digital signal analysis platform, MATLAB, the suggested speaker identification strategies are applied. These methods are checked using the Neuroscience Foundation speech library [15]. Both 1250 speakers (720 males and 530 females) have been used for preparation and research in an experiment setup [15]. In the second level, 840 speakers were randomly chosen from the built data base including 525 female versus 315 male speakers. Each speaker who talks cleanly is educated at the stage of learning while checking speaker data first from NST dataset with "channel noise" and "white noise" separately. The tests are carried out by planning a database of environmental sound in the initial sterile database voice of various SNRs. This is created dynamically by the MATLAB "toolbox".

Extraction of Features. Forty-five voice samples are taken from each individual in the extraction process to prepare voice functions. Thirty two expression tests are being used for test phase and the remaining samples can be used for identification checking. The voice signals are usually measured at 32 kHz and are set to 30 ms [16]. Every frame consists of 512 FFT-based vectors for creating functional vectors. Next phase, these functional vectors are used to minimize dimensionality to construct an optimized feature set.

5.2 Outcomes and Results

The effects of the proposed technology were assessed on the phrases extracted from the NIST index. The power is calculated by the usage of a noisy database, purposely adding white "Gaussian noise" in the initial database on many SNRs, such as 42 dB, 32 dB and 22 dB. The blue areas in the speaker output signal reflect spoken parts, while the green parts display the unacceptable silence sections as seen by Figs. 2, 3 and 4.

Accuracy vs. SNR. The experimental findings indicate that the SNR greatly enhances efficiency. From the research observations, our approaches are much like the sentences in a sterile noise-free dataset. However, higher SNRs increase performance. At the 22 dB SNR, typical procedures suppress most speech signals in a quiet way, but only quasi sections are excluded.

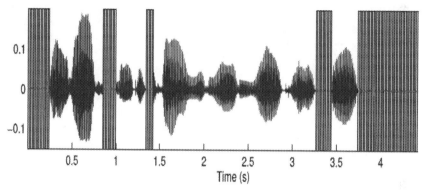

Fig. 2. Silence elimination with 42 dB SNR SET algorithm for "white noise" (Color figure online)

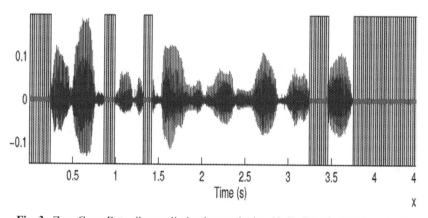

Fig. 3. Zero Cross Rate silence elimination method at 42 dB SNR for "white noise".

The results of the experiments carried out following the silence elimination phase indicate that the new function vectors give a fair improvement against the actual values in Tables 1 and 2. With the addition of ambient noise of 42 dB SNR in particular, the accuracy of the MFA transform is increased by 3.78% compared here to silence exclusion stage. Similarly, channel noise at 42 dB has increased slightly to 2.43%. The enhanced findings demonstrate that the inclusion of more noise is more successful in the output of MFA transformation.

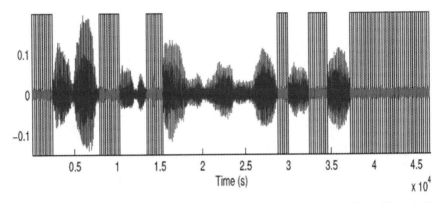

Fig. 4. Peak detection point algorithm silence elimination at 42 dB SNR for "white noise".

The analysis for silence descrimination is summarised by the tables.

Table 1. Additive "Gaussian Noise" speaker identification score

Algorithm	Segments at SNR 42 dB	Segments at SNR 32 dB	Segments at SNR 22 dB
Short energy time	97.34%	95.29%	94.16%
Zero cross rate	98.38%	97.06%	94.87%
Peak detection point	98.03%	96.73%	94.44%

Table 2. Speaker identification performance deteriorated by "Additive channel Noise".

Algorithm	Segments at SNR 42 dB	Segments at SNR 32 dB	Segments at SNR 22 dB
Short energy time	97.86%	94.45%	94.62%
Zero cross rate	97.67%	95.73%	93.78%
Peak detection point	98.32%	96.65%	94.86%

Person Count vs. Accuracy. The validity of the study uses multiple population scales (180, 330, 480, 630, 780, 930, 1080, and 1230). The precision of a given sample size is calculated by the random collection of speaker identification tests for participants from 1650 speakers in the dataset. The impact of user size under turbulent conditions is expressed in Figs. 5 and 6. The exactness of the operation of MFA extraction is enhanced.

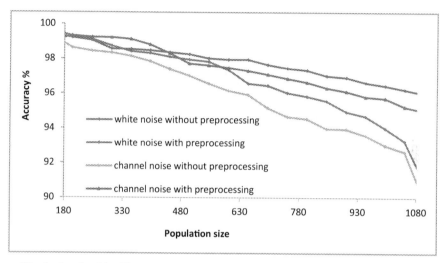

Fig. 5. Speaker identification rate with count for "Channal and White noises" at 22 dB.

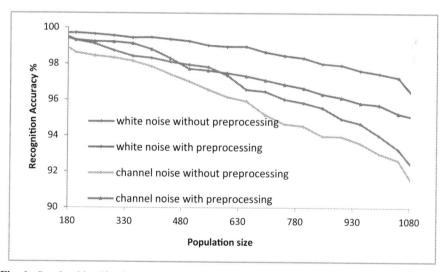

Fig. 6. Speaker identification rate as a result of the amount of speakers for "Channal and White noises" at 32 dB.

The outcome of studies in the "Gaussian noise" at 42 dB increases the detection rate by 2.45% (without noise removal) as well as 3.17% (with noise removal) after MFA transformation and the SVM (Forward Loking Schostic) algorithm. In comparison, the increase for applying noise only to system at 42 dB is 1.79% and 1.84%, accordingly. The findings above demonstrate that the involvement of the output device with destructive process is more dominant.

6   Conclusion and Summery

The experimental findings demonstrate that the Multilinear Factor Analysis (MFA) transition increases precision relative to traditional features. Although computer sophistication is decreased by 28%, MFA- SVM (Forward Loking Schostic) does surpass state-of-the-art speaker recognition technology. The method suggested is often superior than other methods in all cases. However the various voice clarity in the device is greatly increased. As described in the above parts, the preparation and testing processes are a little complicated and do not lead to a substantial grouth. When the overall result of the recognition method is taken, the process for selecting the candidate specified by Forward Loking Schostic (FOLOS) is the optimum set of functional vectors. The methodology suggested is experimentally established and has also been validated to enhance efficiency over technological innovations. It is also remembered that SVM's sophistication is greatly decreased with the vast amount of users during the collection of datasets.

References

1. Wang, S., Wu, Z., Qian, Y.: Data augmentation using deep generative models for embedding based speaker recognition. In: IEEE/ACM Transaction on Audio, Speech, and Language Processing, vol. 2, pp. 2598–2609 (2020)
2. Lee, J.Y., Choi, B.J., Kim, N.S.: Robust alignment using gating mechanism for end-to-end speech synthesis. IEEE Sign. Process. Lett. 27, 2004–2008 (2020)
3. Boulianne, G.: A study of inductive biases for unsupervised speech representation learning. In: IEEE/ACM Transaction on Audio, Speech, and Language Processing, vol. 28, pp. 2781–2795 (2020)
4. He, X., Chen, M., Yang, J.: 3-D Convolutional recurrent neural networks with attention model for speech emotion recognition. IEEE Sig. Proc. Letters 25(10), 1440–1444 (2018)
5. Hanifa, R.M., Isa, K., Mohamad, S.: Comparative analysis on different cepstral features for speaker identification recognition. In: 2020 IEEE Student Conference on Research and Development, IEEE Publisher (2020)
6. Ridha, D., Suyanto, S.: Removing unvoiced segment to improve text independent speaker recognition. In: 2019 International Seminar on Research of Information Technology and Intelligent Systems. IEEE Publisher (2019)
7. Furui, S.: 40 Years of Progress in Automatic Speaker Recognition. Lecture Notes in Computer Science book series. In: Advances in Biometrics, pp. 1050–105 (2011)
8. Imam, S.A., Bansal, P., Singh, V.: Review: speaker recognition using automated systems. AGU Int. J. Eng. Tech. 5, 31–38 (2015)
9. Khamparia, A., Singh, A., Luhach, A.K.: Performance comparison of Apache Hadoop and Apache Spark. In: Proceedings of the Third International Conference on Advanced Information for Computing Research, pp. 1–5 (2019)
10. Rao, P.R.K.: Random forest algorithm with a half-voting and weighted decision trees for interior pedestrian tracking. Int. J. Recent Tech. Eng. 8(3), 6971–6976 (2019)

11. Rao, P.R.K., Rao, Y.S.: Dimensionality reduction techniques and SVM algorithms for large population speaker identification. Int. J. Sig. Proc. Syst. **4**(2), 86–95 (2016)
12. Deshpande, M.S., Holambe, R.S.: Robust speaker identification in the presence of car noise. Int. J. Bio. **3**(3), 234–245 (2017)
13. Zhao, X., Wang, Y., Wang, D.: Robust speaker identification in noisy and reverberant conditions In: IEEE/ACM Transaction on Audio, Speech and Language Processing, vol. 22(4) (2014)
14. Ming, J., Hazen, T.J., Glass, J.R.: Robust speaker recognition in noisy conditions. In: IEEE Transaction on Audio, Speech, and Language Processing, vol. 15(5) (2005)
15. Li, X., Tan, T., Chen, X.: Pattern Recognition Book. Springer (2017). https://doi.org/10.1007/978-1-4613-4154-3
16. Delcroix, M., Watanabe, S., Metze, F.: New Era for Robust Speech Recognition. Springer book (2017). https://doi.org/10.1007/978-3-319-64680-0
17. Chakroun, R., Frikha, M.: Robust features for text-independent speaker recognition with short utterances. Neural Comput. Appl. **32**(17), 13863–13883 (2020). https://doi.org/10.1007/s00521-020-04793-y

Image Classification Using Convolutional Neural Networks

Nishit Handa, Yash Kaushik[✉], Nikhil Sharma, Muskaan Dixit, and Monika Garg

Manav Rachna International Institute of Research and Studies, Faridabad, India
monikagarg.fet@mriu.edu.in

Abstract. The term Deep Learning can be termed as the subset of artificial intelligence with multiple network layers forming neural patterns. People's interest in having the knowledge of deep hidden layers have recently boosted and have begun to takeover various classical strategical performances in numerous fields; especially in pattern recognition and image recognition. One of the most talked-about and important part in deep learning and neural networks is about the Convolutional Neural Network (CNN). We have briefly described about how CNNs plays an integral role in the field of image recognition. Starting from the concepts of Deep Learning and Neural Networks we make our way for CNNs. We have given the idea of how CNN works along with convolutional layers and convolutional filters in a lay-man language and the simplest way possible. Further, how a convolutional filter classifies objects and shapes is also explained in the paper. Later in the paper we have also discussed the advantages of CNN over any other neural network technique.

Keywords: Image recognition · Deep learning · Image classification · Neural networks · Convolutional neural networks · Artificial intelligence

1 Introduction

Deep learning is a small set of machine learning itself that is the foundation of artificial intelligence. Artificial Intelligence is a method that helps a machine to mimic human behavior. AI through Machine learning can be achieved by using algorithms (that are trained) and deep learning. Now, deep learning itself is considered as a type of machine learning that has a structure deeply influenced by the structure of the human brain. In-depth study of this structure can be described as an artificial neural network. In the case of machine learning one will have to place the features by hand which will act as a detector but in deep learning on the other hand the features are taken into account by neural networks and without human intervention. Deep Learning requires a lot of data to train our machine for our machine to give the best optimal results. Deep learning can be used for a variety of purposes such as - Customer support, Medical care, self-driving cars. It is considered to be the most effective way to handle or work with random data and the neural network needs a large amount of data to train which can take hours or months and time increases with the amount of data and layers in the network.

A. K. Luhach et al. (Eds.): ICAICR 2020, CCIS 1393, pp. 510–517, 2021.
https://doi.org/10.1007/978-981-16-3660-8_48

Nowadays, whenever we mention any image recognition or object recognition task, machine learning tools come in handy. In order to get precise results or experience a better performance, one can organize large datasets and learn or acquire much more powerful learning models to prevent over fitting. Until recently, data sets for label photos were very small - by ordering tens of thousands of photos. Easy recognition tasks can be better solved with data sets of such a large size, especially if they are expanded with labelled storage conversions. But the things in the actual settings show a big difference, so in order to learn to see them it is necessary to use very large training sets. And of course, small data databases have become widely known, but more recently it has become possible to collect labelled data sets containing millions of images.

In order to learn about thousands of objects from millions of pictures, we need a model with a great readability. However, the great complexity of the object recognition feature means that even a huge database such as ImageNet cannot solve this issue, so our model should therefore provide more details before paying for all the data we have. Their power is regulated by its depth and width vary, and their assumptions are also strong and accurate, particularly in the nature of the pictures. Therefore, compared to standard feed forward neural networks with layers of the same size, CNNs have very few connections to the boundaries and are therefore easy to train, and their excellent mathematical performance may be much worse.

2 Neural Networks

The concept of artificial neural networks first came in when a paper was written on how the nerves work in 1943 by McCulloch, a neurophysiologist, and junior mathematician, Walter Pitts. They were encouraged with electrical circuits and used them to simulate a uncomplicated neural network. Studies were conducted and people began to see the use of neural networks in various fields but the fear began when the authors began to think that the "thinking machines" could have few consequences on a person. Asimov's series of robots reveals the effects on human behavior and the ways in which machines can do all human work. In 1982 a number of events sparked renewed interest. And today, conversations with neural networks as we all know are omnipresent. Neural Networks have a lot of potential and they seem to have very bright future as mother nature itself is an evidence that this kind of notion functions. Although, the chances of success, which is precisely the key to all technology, lies in the development of the hardware. Currently the evolution of a neural network simply justifies that the principal is functioning. However, the study develops neural networks that, due to processing limitations, take weeks to learn.

Artificial neural networks, usually simply called neural networks, is the foundation of deep learning and a subset of machine learning where the algorithms are influenced by the arrangement of a human brain.

The Neural network trains itself from the input data to recognize data patterns and estimates the results of a new set of the same data. It allows machines to solve complex problems even when using a very different, unstructured and interconnected data set. Neural networks have several applications and image or face recognition is one of them. Not only neural networks but convolution neural networks play a very important role in image recognition and we will describe about convolutional neural networks in detail in our paper further.

2.1   How Does Neural Network Work?

Neural networks are made up of layers of neurons or also known as nodes. These neurons are the main processing component of a network. Each processing node has its own information base, including what you have seen and any rules that were originally designed or created for themselves. The tiers are tremendously interconnected through channels, which means each node in tier n will be connected to many nodes in tier n−1 - input - and in tier n + 1, which supplies input information for those nodes. There can be one or more nodes in the output layer, where the resulted feedback can be read.

Beside all, this artificial neural networks are quite adjustable, which means that they can improve themselves as they learn from training before and next runs provide more details about the world (Fig. 1).

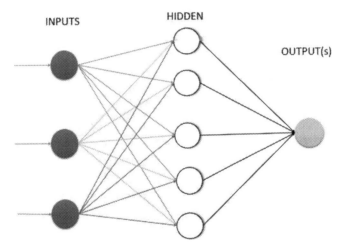

Fig. 1. Neural network layers

3   Convolutional Neural Network

In the beginning we explained how deep learning is now an important area in machine learning. One fine technology which can be implemented using the concepts of deep learning is image recognition. Whenever a machine has to recognize an image, it does so by reading the matrix representation of the pixel values for every part of the image. Now for relatively small binary images like digits or alphabets we can use the Multilayer perceptron model where we utilize more than a single filter to reach out to our conclusion i.e. the binary probability for the classification of data (using logistic regression). But for analyzing more complex visual imagery we switch to regularized versions of multilayer perceptron i.e. CNNs.

The Convolutional Neural Network can be defined as an artificial neural network that plays a major role in the analysis of images. It is also referred to as a comp net or CNN. Although CNNs have most of their use in image analysis but they can also be used in other problems like editing or analyzing several data. A CNN functions in a way that it is able to find out or select meaningful patterns in an image. It is this pattern detection that makes CNN so useful in image analysis. One of the key differences between a multilayer perceptron and a CNN is that the latter has unique hidden layers called as convolutional layers. These hidden convolutional layers like any other layer get the input, then change the input in some way to output this transformed input into the following layer.

The number of filters must be specified for a particular convolutional layer.

3.1 In-Depth Image Classification

If you look closely at the picture you will find numerous things that are going on such as multiple edges, shapes, textures and so on. So, for example, a type of pattern the filter can find can be the edges and images, so this filter will be called the edge detector (Fig. 2).

Fig. 2. Object detector and pattern detector for a particular image

Now some filters will detect corners, squares or circles, which is what we will see in our network's beginning. However, as the network deepens, these filters become more complex. Therefore, our filters will find such items such as eyes, ears, feather and scales in later layers instead of edges and basic shapes. More sophisticated artifacts such as human beings, plants, insects etc. can be contained in even deeper layers.

Technically, a filter can only be seen as a relatively small matrix for which the number of rows and columns is calculated, and random numbers are used in the values within the matrix. When a convolutional layer receives the input the filter will slide over each

MxN (M rows and N columns) set of pixels from the input itself until it has covered every MxN block of pixels from the entire image. This sliding of the filter over an entire image is called as convolving (Fig. 3).

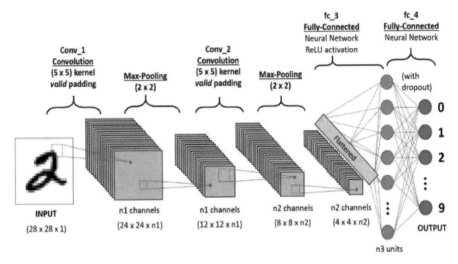

Fig. 3. Layers of CNN

3.2   Advantages of CNN Over Common Neural Networks

There are some advantages of convolutional neural networks over neural networks. Over the years, research on convolutional neural networks (CNNs) has evolved rapidly, but real-world deployments of these types are often limited by computer resources and memory issues. Another reason why CNN is so popular is because of their design – the best thing is there is no need for a feature release. The program learns to perform feature extraction and CNN's main idea is, it uses image rotation and filters to create dynamic features that are transferred to the next layer. CNNs are used for image classification and recognition due to their high accuracy. … CNN follows a sequence model that works to build a network, like a skin, and ultimately provides a fully connected layer where all the sensors are connected to each other and the effect is processed.

4   Literature Survey

[1]   Deep learning finds a complex structure in big data sets using a back propagation algorithm. In-depth study finds advanced structures in massive information sets employing a back-up show algorithmic program to point out however the machine ought to amend the inner parameters to calculate the illustration in every layer from the illustration within the previous layer. Deep learning and neural networks bring enhancements in image process, video, speech and audio.

[2] In-depth readings permit pc models containing multiple layers of process to review information illustration at multiple output levels. These ways have dramatically improved the state of the art in speech recognition, visual recognition, object acquisition and lots of different domains. The report was an improvement that used discussion nets to almost reduce the number of object recognition errors, and disrupted the rapid acceptance of in-depth learning by the computer – watching community.

[3] According to this literature, Deep learning is a multilayered neural network learning algorithm that has come out in recent years. It has given various new ideas to machine learning, and the ingenuity of artificial intelligence and computer to human communication in advance on highways. We applied in-depth reading to handwriting recognition, and explored two common algorithms for in-depth reading: Convolutional Neural Network (CNN) and Deep Belief NetWork (DBN). We performed CNN and DBN performance tests on the MNIST database as well as the actual manuscript database. The degree of accuracy of CNN and DBN in the MNIST database is 99.28% and 98.12% respectively, and in the actual database of manuscripts it is 92.91% and 91.66% respectively. Test results show that in-depth reading has excellent reading ability. You do not need to remove the features manually. In-depth reading can learn many natural aspects of data.

[4] When faced with the challenging task of classifying images, we often define our imagination by distributing the image, and identify the reflective features of one category or another. The growing evidence of each class helps us make our final decision. Deep network design - a unique network component (ProtoPNet), which makes excuses in the same way: the network disseminates the image by obtaining reflective components, and incorporates evidence from prototypes to make the final separation. The model therefore thinks in terms of quality in the way that ornithologists, physicians and others explain to people how they can solve the complex tasks of image classification. When several ProtoPNets are integrated into a large network, it can achieve the accuracy associated with other deep models performing very well. In addition, ProtoPNet offers a rendering that is not available in other translators.

[5] It could be a very intriguing job for the beginner to differentiate among the tasks related to computer vision. For e.g. When we classify an image then there is a difference between localizing an object and detecting it, but they are all considered under recognition of an object. While classifying an image we designate a label to an image and when we are localizing it then we draw a box around the objects that are there in the image, but while detecting we union these tasks. Region-Based-CNNs are the combination of these techniques which are used to address localization of these tasks as well as recognition which are basically configured for the performance of the model.

[6] In recent years, advanced automation networks (including duplicates) have won numerous competitions in pattern recognition and machine learning. This historical study aptly summarizes the relevant work, most of which dates back thousands of years. In-depth students are divided by the depth of their credit-oriented approaches, which are options for learning that may be learning, which is the cause between actions and outcomes. In-depth supervised reading, unchecked reading,

intensified reading and natural enumeration, and indirect searches of short code programs on deep and neural networks.

[7]   Data classification which is performed in the presence of noise will cause profusely worse results than expected for pure patterns. While working on this paper we have a tendency to investigate this downside within the case of deep convolutional neural networks so as to propose a solutions that may try to influence the noise. The most contributions bestowed during this paper area unit experimental examination of influence of various sorts of noise on the convolutional neural network, proposition of a deep neural network operative as a noise reducer, investigation of a deep network coaching with noise polluted patterns, and at last AN analysis of noise addition throughout the coaching method of a deep network as a kind of regularization. Our main findings area in unit construction of the deep network primarily based on noise reducing filter that outperforms progressive solutions, further as proposition of a sensible methodology of deep neural network coaching with clamant patterns for improvement against the clamant take a look at patterns. All results area unit underpinned by experiments that show high effectuality and presumably broad applications of the planned solutions.

[8]   Traditional neural networks although have achieved considerable performance at image classification, they need been characterized by feature engineering, a tedious method that leads to poor generalization to check information. During this report, we prefer convolutional neural network (CNN) approach for classifying CIFAR-10 datasets. This approach has been shown in previous works to realize improved performances while not feature engineering. Learnable filters and pooling layers were accustomed extract underlying image options. Dropout, regularization beside variation in convolution ways were applied to scale back over fitting whereas making certain inflated accuracies in validation and testing. Higher take a look at accuracy with reduced over fitting was achieved with a deeper network.

[9]   Convolutional Neural Network (CNN) is the progressive method for image classification task. In this paper, the authors have mentioned completely different parts and architectures of CNN in brief. They have shown that how CNN advanced from LeNET-5 to the latest SENet model. Model descriptions as well as coaching details of every model is also explained. Additionally, they have also compared the mentioned models.

[10]   Deep convolutional neural networks accomplished a thriving performance in many alternative analysis areas. Deciding the unreal neural network structure and size of the filters is problematic. Rather than coaching a man-made neural network from scratch for image classification tasks, the thought of adapting a pre-trained network has emerged. During this paper, the performance of a man-made neural network trained from scratch with the fine-tuned pre-trained neural network was compared for various datasets. Obtained results showed that mistreatment pre-trained neural network structure provided a performance accelerate to fifty. 65% for exactitude, 42.14% for recall and fifty. 19% for F1-score.

5 Conclusion

For image recognition, multilayer perceptron (MLP) models have been used in the past. Nevertheless, they suffered from the curse of dimensionality due to the complete connectivity between nodes, and did nit scale well with higher resolution images. Through the text of our paper we conclude that convolution neural networks which is a subset of deep learning as a technology will go far in context of image recognition and it has numerous advantages which can't be ignored. We have seen that be it any scientific paper discussing image recognition convolution neural network are used by everyone. Convolution neural network can also be considered as pillars on which image recognition works. In spite of the attractive features of CNN, and in spite of the high efficiency of local architecture, it is still very expensive to use on a large scale in images having very good resolution. Fortunately, the GPUs used in the present, combined with the highly optimized use of 2D convolution, are strong enough to simplify the training of large convolutional neural networks, with the latest data sets contain examples with sufficient labels to train such models without overcrowding. From the literature survey done above, we also conclude that convolution neural network comparatively performs better than DBN (Deep Belief Network) and also much work is not being done using convolution neural network yet and there is a lot to explore and learn.

References

1. LeCun, Y., Bengio, Y., Hinton, G.: Deep learning Published: 27 May 2015
2. Krizhevsky, A., Sutskever, I., Hinton, G.: ImageNet classification with deep convolutional neural networks. In: Proceedings of the Advances in Neural Information Processing Systems, vol. 25, pp. 1090–1098 (2012)
3. Published in: 2015 Chinese Automation Congress (CAC), 27–29 November 2015
4. Chen, C., Li, O., Tao, D., Barnett, A., Su, J.K.: This Looks Like That: Deep Learning for Interpretable Image Recognition (2019)
5. Brownlee, J.: May 22 2019 in Deep Learning for Computer Vision- A Gentle Introduction to Object Recognition With Deep Learning (2019)
6. Schmidhuber, J.: Deep learning in neural networks: an overview. Neural Netw. **61**, 85–117 (2015)
7. Koziarski, M., Cyganek, B.: Image recognition with deep neural networks in presence of noise – dealing with and taking advantage of distortions. Integr. Comput. Aided Eng. **24**(4), 1–13 (2017)
8. Akwaboah, A.D.: Norfolk State University-Convolutional Neural Network for CIFAR-10 Dataset Image Classification, November 2019
9. Sultana, F., Sufian, A.: Paramartha Dutta-Advancements in Image Classification using Convolutional Neural Network, May 2019
10. Sarigul, M.: Mutlu Avci-Effect of pre-trained deep neural network usage on performance of image classification, November 2017

Coding and Detection Techniques Used in SAC-OCDMA System: A Detailed Review

Bhanuja Ahuja and Suresh Kumar[✉]

Department of ECE, UIET, Maharshi Dayanand University, Rohtak, India
skvashist_16@yahoo.com

Abstract. Optical communication has become need of the day being capable of offering high bandwidth and data processing at high speed to meet the requirement of seamless communications. In order to ensure security of data and bandwidth efficiency, coding techniques are mandatory. This paper presents detailed review of the technological developments in the field of Optical Code Division Multiple Access (OCDMA) specifically focusing on one of its implementation i.e. Spectral Amplitude Coded OCDMA (SAC-OCDMA) system. SAC-OCDMA has an inherent advantage in form of complete elimination of the Multiple Access Interference (MAI) that is why it has drawn the attention of researchers. Here various possible coding schemes, which can be implemented like Double Weight (DW), Modified DW (MDH), Enhanced DW (EDW), Multi Diagonal (MD) and Walsh Hadamard (WH) codes along with various detection techniques such as Complementary Subtraction Detection (CSD), Single Photodiode Detection (SPD), Direct Detection (DD), AND detection and modified-AND detection. The latest work on this topic has been thoroughly reviewed and will motivate, to peruse research in the field to develop new and modified technique, in order to improve the parameters such as bit rate, SNR, higher data rate etc.

Keywords: OCDMA · MAI · Sa-coding · EDW code · MDW code · Direct detection

1 Introduction

Optical communication has been tremendously adopted in today's telecommunication due to various advantages. Some of the advantages include its high fidelity rate, high data rates, immunity to atmospheric conditions and chemicals and many more [1]. Optical fiber permits many users to access the channel simultaneously by using various multiple access techniques such as DMA or WDMA or CDMA [2]. Huge number of subscribers with high data rate demand have pushed towards OCDMA implementation. However, OCDMA is gaining more focus and attention due to various pros which are: it's ability to support several users simultaneously without contention, better performance against eavesdropping, less sensitivity for frequency fluctuations, better capacity in bursty networks etc. [3]. On the other hand OCDMA systems suffer from various problems such as MAI, thermal, Phase Induced Intensity Noise (PIIN) and shot noise which deteriorate

© Springer Nature Singapore Pte Ltd. 2021
A. K. Luhach et al. (Eds.): ICAICR 2020, CCIS 1393, pp. 518–528, 2021.
https://doi.org/10.1007/978-981-16-3660-8_49

its performance. Basic block diagram for implementation of SAC-OCDMA is shown in Fig. 1. OCDMA can be implemented by different coding: phase-spectral encoding, time encoding, spectral amplitude coding, spectral temporal coding etc. In SAC-OCDMA or spectral amplitude coding method, selective blocking is used to encrypt frequency content of a signal [4]. This scheme is reported to have removed MAI and suppress PIIN to a large extent and is also a reliable as well as cost effective approach. It can be implemented by using 1D, 2D, ZCC codes. Example of few more codes are namely MDW, Random Diagonal (RD) code, EDW, Multi Diagonal (MD) code, Modified Quadratic Congruence (MQC) code, DW and many more. In this paper Sect. 2 is devoted to explanation of MD, MDW, EDW, WH codes followed by detection techniques in Sect. 3. Further, Sect. 4 presents the tabular comparison of previous works based on their work, coding, detection performance, data rates and in Sect. 5 the paper gets concluded.

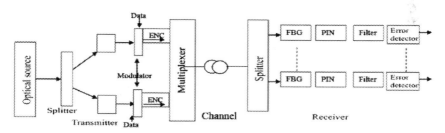

Fig. 1. Basic block diagram - SAC-OCDMA

2 SAC-OCDMA Code Structure

2.1 MD Code

The MD code uses the elements as (N, W, λ) where N represents code length. The symbol W denotes code weight (chips with value 1), and λ depicts in phase cross correlation. When $\lambda = 0$, it concludes that code is having zero cross correlation property. The following steps are followed during construction of MD code [5].

Step 1: Firstly, consider value of weight (W) and then choose K denoting number of subscribers, thereafter develop a sequence having diagonal matrices. Accordingly for these values, i and j_w will be set. $(i = 1, \ldots\ldots K)$ expressed by rows of the matrix, and $(j_w = 1, \ldots\ldots W)$ will shows the number for the diagonal matrices. Here K and W both are chosen as $+$ integer.

Step 2: For the above parameters MD sequences are required to be computed for every diagonal matrix. The function represented by the equation:

$$S_{i,jw} = \begin{cases} (i_n + 1 - i), & \text{For } j_w = \text{even number} \\ i, & \text{For } j_w = \text{odd number} \end{cases} \tag{1}$$

Step 3: Form the position matrix and given by:

$$S_{i,1} = \begin{bmatrix} 1 \\ 2 \\ 3 \\ \vdots \\ K \end{bmatrix} \quad S_{i,2} = \begin{bmatrix} K \\ \vdots \\ 3 \\ 2 \\ 1 \end{bmatrix} \quad S_{i,3} = \begin{bmatrix} 1 \\ 2 \\ 3 \\ \vdots \\ K \end{bmatrix} \quad S_{i,W} = \begin{bmatrix} K \\ \vdots \\ 3 \\ 2 \\ 1 \end{bmatrix} \tag{2}$$

Step 4: Every element in $S_{i,j}$ signifies the value of 1 in the given matrices of dimensions $1 \times K$, then $Q's$ [4]:

$$Q_{i,1} = \begin{bmatrix} 1 \cdots 0 \\ \vdots \ddots \vdots \\ 0 \cdots 1 \end{bmatrix}_{K \times K} \quad Q_{i,2} = \begin{bmatrix} 0 \cdots 1 \\ \vdots \ddots \vdots \\ 1 \cdots 0 \end{bmatrix}_{K \times K} \quad Q_{i,w} = \begin{bmatrix} 1 \cdots 0 \\ \vdots \ddots \vdots \\ 0 \cdots 1 \end{bmatrix}_{K \times K} \tag{3}$$

Step 5: The whole group in the diagonal matrices represents MD code of order given by which is $K \times N$ matrix

$$\begin{bmatrix} Q_{i,1} \; Q_{i,2} \cdots Q_{i,w} \end{bmatrix}_{K \times N} \tag{4}$$

$$\text{i.e.} \quad MD = \begin{bmatrix} a_{1,1} & \cdots & a_{1,N} \\ \vdots & \ddots & \vdots \\ a_{i_n,1} & \cdots & a_{i_n,N} \end{bmatrix} \tag{5}$$

Here the codes have zero cross correlation, therefore, orthogonality is achieved. Also it is observed that in a given diagonal, change in any element of the matrices will not change the constant property of having zero cross correlation. This correlation property ensures cancellation of MAI. The performance of MD code during transmission has been found to be superior to MQC or RD codes. MD codes perform better with large code lengths and more number of users are required.

2.2 MDW Codes

MDW codes have been developed by modifying the DW codes. In DW codes the base matrix is solely dependent upon total users at that instance. Then the base matrix is repeated diagonally and the continuous repetition process called as mapping technique results in the generation of the code. The weight of MDW is always an even number greater than 2. They are $K \times N$ matrix having code length N and numbers of users K given by equations [6]:

$$N = 3 \sum_{j=1}^{w/2} j \tag{6}$$

$$K = \frac{w}{2} + 1 \tag{7}$$

The cross correlation of this code is 1 but in some combinations, codes can have a zero cross correlation as well. Therefore the maximum cross correlation is 1 for MDW codes.

2.3 EDW Codes

EDW codes maintain cross correlation of almost one among the users. They are implemented using same mapping techniques mentioned for MDW codes. A general algorithm for EDW without mapping is also reported, which is presented in this work. The length of code remains constant for each additional user.

Steps involved:

- Select W, N and find L
- Construct M basic matrix
- Repeat M in U^*
- Add rows of M to U^*
- Fill empty spaces of U^{**} with zeros

Construction of code starts with selecting value of weight W and desired users given by N. Length of code is expressed by Eq. (8) as under:

$$L = N * (W - 1) \quad for\ W\ and\ N \tag{8}$$

Basic matrix M is constructed as [6]:

$$M = \begin{bmatrix} R_1 \\ R_2 \end{bmatrix} \quad Where \quad \begin{bmatrix} R_1 \\ R_2 \end{bmatrix} = \begin{bmatrix} \lfloor \frac{w-2}{2} \rfloor 0s & \lfloor \frac{w+1}{2} \rfloor 1s \\ \lfloor \frac{w}{2} \rfloor 1s & \lfloor \frac{w-2}{2} \rfloor 0s \end{bmatrix} \tag{9}$$

After this user code matrix U of size $N \times L$ is constructed which is given as follows: Liaisons matrix U^* is formed by repeating M matrix, $N - 1$ times

$$U^* = \begin{bmatrix} R_1 \cdots\cdots\cdots\cdots \\ R_2\ R_1 \cdots\cdots\cdots \vdots \\ \vdots\ \ R_2\ R_1 \cdots\cdots \vdots \\ \vdots\ \ \vdots\ \ \vdots\ \ \ddots\ \ddots\ \vdots \\ \vdots\ \ \vdots\ \ \vdots\ \ \ddots\ R_1\ \vdots \\ \cdots\cdots\cdots\cdots R_2 \cdots \end{bmatrix} \tag{10}$$

Next add R_1 and R_2 to last row and first column respectively of liaison matrix:

$$U^{**} = \begin{bmatrix} R_1 \cdots\cdots\cdots\cdots R_2 \\ R_2\ R_1 \cdots\cdots\cdots \vdots \\ \vdots\ \ R_2\ R_1 \cdots\cdots \vdots \\ \vdots\ \ \vdots\ \ \ddots\ \ddots\ \ddots\ \vdots \\ \vdots\ \ \vdots\ \ \ddots\ \ddots\ R_1\ \vdots \\ \cdots\cdots\cdots\cdots R_2 \cdots \end{bmatrix} \tag{11}$$

To complete EDW code matrix of $N \times L$ fill up the empty spaces by zeros as follows:

$$U = \begin{bmatrix} R_1 & 0 & 0 & \cdots\cdots & R2 \\ R_2 & R_1 & 0 & \cdots\cdots & 0 \\ 0 & R_2 & 0 & \cdots\cdots & \vdots \\ \vdots & \vdots & \ddots & \ddots & \vdots \\ \vdots & \vdots & \ddots & R_1 & 0 \\ 0 & 0 & 0 & \cdots & R_2 & R_2 \end{bmatrix} \tag{12}$$

2.4 Walsh-Hadamard Codes

This code decompose incoming signal into groups having shape of square pulse having the level as '+1' or '−1'. The code involves in the formation of WH matrix (H_M) which is a $Z \times Z$ matrix having values of 0 s and 1 s. M is to be taken as greater than 2. Also the code length is represented as $N = 2^M$. For H_M code matrix number of users can be calculates by $2^M - 1$.

$$H_m = \begin{bmatrix} H_{m-1} & H_{m-1} \\ H_{m-1} & \overline{H}_{m-1} \end{bmatrix} \tag{13}$$

$$\text{For } M = 1; H_1: \quad H_1 = \begin{bmatrix} 1 & 1 \\ 1 & 0 \end{bmatrix} \tag{14}$$

$$\text{For } M = 2; H_2: \quad H_2 = \begin{bmatrix} H_1 & H_1 \\ H_1 & \overline{H}_1 \end{bmatrix} = \begin{bmatrix} 1 & 1 & 1 & 1 \\ 1 & 0 & 1 & 0 \\ 1 & 1 & 0 & 0 \\ 1 & 0 & 0 & 1 \end{bmatrix} \tag{15}$$

Here every row in H_M contains $\frac{Z}{2} 0's$ and $\frac{Z}{2} 1's$ [8].

3 Detection Techniques

3.1 DD Technique

It is one of the simplest technique for detection of implemented code. It helps in reduction of number of filters required since only single pair of decoder and detector is required per user [9]. Here no subtraction process is involved because recovery of information can be done from any chip which has the property of non-overlapping with any other chip of different channel [10]. Code which can be used in direct detection you should have at least one of the chip as clean signal for every channel for example Modified Quadratic Codes (MQC), EDW, DW and MDW. Basic block diagram showing the DD technique is given in figure Fig. 2.

3.2 Single Photo Detector Detection Technique

Here before sending the data to subtractor, decoding takes place using two sets of decoder. First set exhibits similar spectral response with respect to the encoder which is intended to be used for received data. For weight w and in phase correlation λ. It gives the output data with either λ P.U for interferers or w P.U for active users [11]. Then to cancel out the mismatched signatures the remaining signal is sent to the s-decoder which is the subtractive decoder. The s- decoder outputs either λ P.U for interferers or zero P.U for active users. On implementation of subtraction the output finally results in either zero P.U for interferers or w P.U for active user, where zero P.U signifies that interfering signals are cancelled out. This technique helps in eliminating PIIN as well as MAI both when processed in optical domain itself which gives an advantage of deploying only single photodiode instead of two or more and it also allows more users to access the system simultaneously. Block diagram for SPD is shown in the figure Fig. 3.

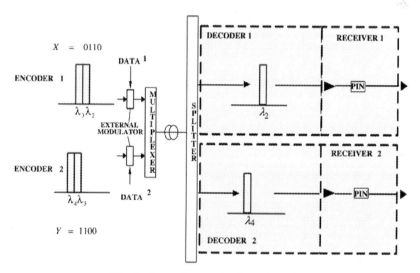

Fig. 2. Basic diagram for direct detection

3.3 CSD Technique

Here the data sequences modulated with the selected data is multiplexed in transmitter and at the receiver end after de-multiplexing the signal splits into two branches of spectral chip which are complementary to each other. The signal is then detected and sent to subtractor. Here overlapping data gets subtracted from expected code and then calculates the correlation difference [12].

The basic block diagram of CSD technique has been drawn in figure Fig. 4. In Fig. 4 different code sequences, in which X = (0110) and the second sequence Y = (1100) are further modulated with data and thereafter given to multiplexer. Mathematically, the cross-correlation is:

$$\theta_{XY}(k) = \sum_{i=0}^{N-1} x_i y_{i+k} \tag{16}$$

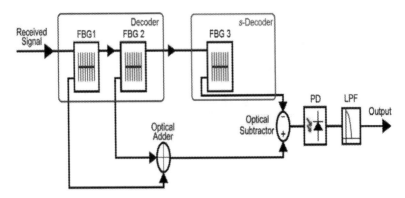

Fig. 3. Basic diagram for SPD

Then correlation of complemented sequence (X) and Y is given as:

$$\theta_{\overline{X}Y}(k) = \sum_{i=0}^{N-1} \overline{x}y_{i+k} \tag{17}$$

We look for the sequence for which

$$\theta_{XY}(k) = \theta_{\overline{X}Y}(k) \tag{18}$$

The cross-correlated output of from the subtractor is:

$$Z_{\text{complementary}} = \theta_{XY}(k) - \theta_{\overline{X}Y}(k) \tag{19}$$

If the output from the sub tractor is 0, indicates absence of signal from other user in the channel under consideration (Fig. 5).

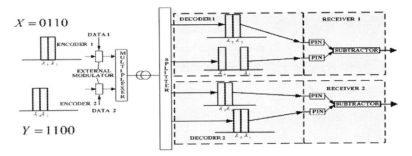

Fig. 4. Block diagram for CSD

3.4 Modified AND Subtraction Detection Technique

The SAC-OCDMA receiver for modified AND subtraction detection is given in the Fig. 6 [13]. Here received signal passes through the splitter-1 which generates two outputs. One

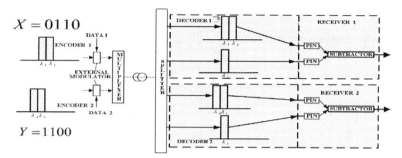

Fig. 5. Block diagram for AND Subtraction detection

of the output is sent to splitter-2 and other is sent to the 3-dB attenuator. The outputs of splitter-2 are sent to the parallel combination of the decoder-1 and decoder-2. This technique is implemented to divide code weight thereby helps in reducing the optical power level in the process of decoding. The 3-dB attenuator sends the signals to the c-decoder where attenuator ensures that, in the event of an inactive user, the photo detector should receive the interfering signals having equal power levels. The upper decoder exhibits spectral response that matches with that of active user. However, the c-decoder is having overlapped bits received from various interferers. This technique can be implemented using FBGs as decoders since they have low insertion losses, compact size and also provide better spectral resolution. After that output goes to Photo detectors. The Photo detectors at each branch is supposed to give electrical output signals.

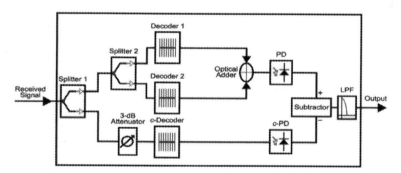

Fig. 6. Block diagram showing Modified AND Subtraction Detection Technique

4 Comparative Study

This section covers a tabular comparison of mentioned coding schemes with different detection techniques. The work considers schemes implemented at sdifferent data rates and different number of users as given in Table 1 below.

Table 1. Comparison of pervious work

Reference	Study	Coding Scheme	Detection Scheme	Data Rate	No Of Users	Bit Rate and Other Findings
Moteal leh, Morteza et al. [4]	Simulation based on high data rate transfer using new design and on a 30km long SMF. Compared it with KS, MFH, MQC, EDW codes	MD	DD	622Mbps 15 Gbps	10	MD at 622Mbps performed better as it allowed 92 users as compared to 43, 59, 27, 39 for MQC, RD, MFH, EDW respectively.
Majeed, M H et al. [8]	Broadband SAC-OCDMA with aim to reduce BER beyond floor value	MD	DD	3 Gbps	3-15	MD codes outstand WH codes and most users shared bandwidth while having BER less than 10^{-9}
		WH	DD			
Kaur, Amanpreet, al. [9]	Simulation of different codes with different schemes while implementing FBGs as encoders and decoders	DW	DD,CSA, AND, modifiedAND,SPD	200Mbps	3 (2 active 1 inactive)	SPD shows best performance for both codes with BER of 1.3011 x 10^{-56}(MDW), 8.4 x 10^{-41} (DW).also MDW showed better results than DW for all .
		MDW				
El-Mottaleb, Abd, et al.[14]	Comparison of performance of codes while observing effect of different photodiode (APD, PIN) and DCF	MDW	SPD	622Mbps 1Gbps 2Gbps	3	MDW outperformed EDW at all bit rates. At 2Gbps and transmission distance of 120km BER: 5.51×10^{-10} (MDW) and 2.5×10^{-9}(EDW)
		EDW				
Sharma Teena et al. [15]	Work on security enhancement	MD	with X-OR GATES	1Gbps	2	BER of 2.50×10^{-25} and Q factor of 10.29 for 1st user and BER of 7.11×10^{-16} and Q factor of 7.95
Yen, C. et al. [16]	Work on unipolar/bipolar spectral codes	WH	using FBGs	200Mbps	-	BER of 10^{-45} for bipolar and 10^{-12} for unipolar scheme.

(continued)

Table 1. (*continued*)

Majeed Majida h H et al. [17]	Performance enhancement coding and three schemes of DCF	MD	DD		15	Multi Diagonal is superior than Walsh hadamard because WH freq bits were too close resulting in possibility of MAI
		WH		200M bps		
Norazi mah, Mat Zain, et al. [18]	Channel spacing effects on performance of codes	MDW	AND	622M bps	-	Modified AND out performed. BER decreases with increasing channel spacing.
			Modified AND			
Negi, C. M., et al. [19]	Focus on performance of codes using parameters of BER, number of filters and received power	DW	DD,AND subtractio n, CSD,	622M bps-1Gbps - 2.5Gb ps	-	For economic feasibility : prefer DW with DD. For accuracy : prefer DW with CSD. Common to prefer AND subtraction
		MDW				

5   Conclusion

This article examined the basic structuring of SAC optical systems. Algorithms for code construction were presented. Further, each mentioned code performed differently with all detection techniques. While comparing previous work as shown in the table, it is seen that high data rates result in some BER decrement. Also quality factor decreases with number of users. Out of the codes which are presented, in maximum cases, MD and MDW performed better than other codes like WH, EDW etc. If considering accuracy, one should prefer SD or CSD detection. Channel spacing too played important role for BER optimization.

References

1. Navpreet, K., Goyal, R., Rani, M.: A review on spectral amplitude coding optical code division multiple access. J. Opt. Commun. **38**(1), 77–85 (2017)
2. Suresh, K., Rai, H.M.: Layout Design of CDMA Cellular Communication System to Control Spill Over of Transmitting Power in Border Areas (2011)

3. El-Mottaleb, S.A.A., Fayed, H.A., Aly, M.H., Rizk, M.R.M., Ismail, N.E.: An efficient SAC-OCDMA system using three different codes with two different detection techniques for maximum allowable users. Opt. Quant. Electron. **51**(11), 1–18 (2019). https://doi.org/10.1007/s11082-019-2065-8

4. Morteza, M., Maesoumi, M.: Simulation of a SAC-OCDMA 10 User× 15 Gb/s system using MD code. Int. J. Opt. Appl. **4**, 20–26 (2014)

5. Kaur, S., Singh, S.: Review on developments in all-optical spectral amplitude coding techniques: Opt. Eng. **57**(11), 116102 (2018)

6. Norazimah, M.Z., et al.: Analytical comparison of various SAC-OCDMA detection techniques. In: 2011 2nd International Conference on Photonics. IEEE, (2011)

7. Kumawat, S., Kumar, M.R.: Generalized optical code construction for enhanced and modified double weight like codes without mapping for SAC–OCDMA systems. Opt. Fiber Technol. **30**, 72–80 (2016)

8. Majeed, M.H., Ahmed, R.K., AbdlJabbar, I.L.: Gb/s broadband spectral amplitude coding-optical code division multiple access (SAC-OCDMA) based on multidiagonal and Walsh Hadamard codes. J. Commun. **14**, 802–812 (2019)

9. Kaur, A., Singh, G.: Performance comparison of various detection techniques for SAC-OCDMA system using DW and MDW code. In: 2015 International Conference and Workshop on Computing and Communication (IEMCON). IEEE (2015)

10. Abdullah, M.K., et al.: Performance of OCDMA systems with new spectral direct detection (SDD) technique using enhanced double weight (EDW) code. Opt. Commun. **281**(18), 4658–4662 (2008)

11. Al-Khafaji, H.M.R., et al.: Reducing BER of spectral-amplitude coding optical code-division multiple-access systems by single photodiode detection technique. J. Eur. Opt. Soc. Rapid Publ. **8**, 13022-1–13022-5 (2013)

12. Sahbudin, R., et al.: Comparative performance of hybrid SCM SACOCDMA system using complementary and AND subtraction detection techniques. Int. Arab J. Inf. Technol. (IAJIT) **5**(1) (2008)

13. Al-Khafaji, H.M.R., Aljunid, S.A., Fadhil, H.A.: Improved BER based on intensity noise alleviation using developed detection technique for incoherent SAC-OCDMA systems. J. Mod. Opt. **59**(10), 878–886 (2012)

14. El-Mottaleb, A., et al.: Enhanced spectral amplitude coding OCDMA system utilizing a single photodiode detection. Appl. Sci. **8**(10), 1861 (2018)

15. Sharma, T., Kumar, M.R.: Novel security enhancement technique for OCDMA and SAC OCDMA against eavesdropping using multi-diagonal code and gating scheme. Opt. Wirel. Technol. 477–486 Springer, Singapore (2020). https://doi.org/10.1007/978-981-13-6159-3_50

16. Yen, C.T., et al: Performance analysis of dual unipolar/bipolar spectral code in optical CDMA systems. J. Appl. Res. Technol. **11**(2), 235–241 (2013)

17. Majeed, M.H., Ahmed, R.K.: Performance enhancement of encoding–decoding multi-diagonal and walsh hadamard codes for spectral amplitude coding-optical code division multiple access (SAC-OCDMA) utilizing dispersion compensated fiber. J. Opt. Commun. 1.ahead-of-print (2020)

18. Norazimah, M.Z., et al: Channel spacing effect on SAC-OCDMA system based modified-AND subtraction detection scheme : Key Engineering Materials, vol. 594. Trans Tech Publications Ltd (2014)

19. Negi, C.M., et al: Optical CDMA networks using different detection techniques and coding schemes. Int. J. Future Gener. Commun. Netw. **4**(3), 25–34 (2011)

Breast Cancer Detection Based on Decision Fusion of Machine Learning Algorithms

Rohit Yadav$^{(\boxtimes)}$ and Richa Sharma

School of Computer Science, Lovely Professional University, Jalandhar, India
richa.18364@lpu.co.in

Abstract. A lot of new methods have been invented in Machine Learning since 1959 when Arthur Samuel first coined the term. The ability to learn and pattern checking in data persuaded many researchers in this field. With so many algorithms and their hybrid combinations, the task to solve a problem includes which combination of methods can produce better and efficient results. In this paper, we have used MIAS dataset for our experiment. First, we have improved the contrast of the mammograms using Contrast Limited Adaptive Histogram Equalization (CLAHE) technique. Second, Region of Interest (ROI) is selected from the images and cropped, then a CNN model used for the extraction of features. Finally, SVM and Decision tree classifier are used for the classification and voting classifier is used for the final decision. After using decision fusion based on a voting classifier, we were able to achieve 93.4% accuracy.

Keywords: Breast Cancer · Deep learning · Machine learning · Image fusion

1 Introduction

Breast Cancer is one of the most common cancers in women. As per official reports, in India, 25%–30% of all female related deaths were resultant of this cancer [1]. A study showed that in 2018, 1.6 million new cases were registered, and 87,090 deaths were reported [2]. A major reason for this is less public awareness along with none or very fewer screenings with high testing prices. Figure 1. shows, number of cases when compared to 25 years ago shows an increase in breast cancer in the age group between 20–50 [3]. Although the exact reason for the development of breast cancer is still unknown, several lifestyle guidelines are stated, which decreases the chances of development of breast cancer. Maintaining balanced BMI with regular physical exercise and breastfeeding are several suggestions [4]. But not all reasons cannot be controlled, menstruation in younger age, menopause in the older age, late marriage, contraceptive drug are namely a few, which increases the chances of breast cancer.

With the advancement of technology in both medicine and computer science, the detection, diagnosis, and treatment of diseases have improved drastically. New methods and techniques are being discovered which aids in the medical process. For breast cancer detection, many imaging modalities exist. In hospitals, various breast imaging methods are used in early breast cancer detection and screening, including MRI [5], computed

© Springer Nature Singapore Pte Ltd. 2021
A. K. Luhach et al. (Eds.): ICAICR 2020, CCIS 1393, pp. 529–538, 2021.
https://doi.org/10.1007/978-981-16-3660-8_50

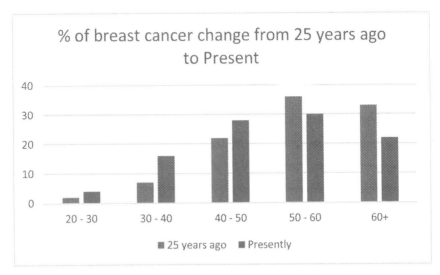

Fig. 1. Brest cancer % change in India of different age group

tomography (CT) [6], magnetic resonance imaging (MRI) [7, 8]. But a mammogram is gaining popularity for its low complexity and better availability. Figure 2 [9] shows all the imaging techniques which are used for breast cancer detection.

However, this paper focuses mainly on Mammograms and used MIAS dataset for experiments. Mammography is achieved through an X-ray exposure of the breast. The breast tissue can absorb X-ray radiation as it is exposed to X-ray. There are various signal levels of the breast tissue and cancer cells. But the question of classifying lumps in mammogram lands on the radiologist, whose prediction is based on experience [10] and, quality of mammogram [11]. Adding to this, breast anomalies are also hidden by the breast tissue structure which makes it more difficult to detect [12]. A major problem in mammogram images is its low contrast [13], which makes it difficult to detect lumps, and have shown a high rate of false-positive cases (regular change as cancerous) and false negative (actual abnormality not detected) [14–16].

Image fusion is a process which applies different methods and techniques for combining several images information either from the same platform or from different spectroscopic platforms to create a single output image. The resultant image (known as fused image) has more detailed and useful or predictable information for machine perception or human understanding [17]. Each input image might have a different focus area, and the complete information might not be presented in a single image. Image fusion process combines these images, which is more detailed than a single image. To combine multiple images, all images should be of the same area, and different angled photos result in difficulty in the fusion process.

Different medical conditions require a separate process to be followed for its treatment, image fusion can combine MRI, CT, PET, SPECT data together for better results. Better achievements have been achieved in improving clinical accuracy by using Multi-modal medical image fusion algorithms [18].

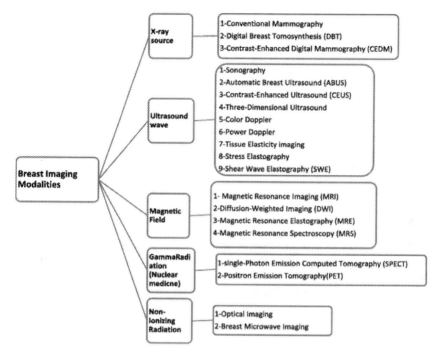

Fig. 2. Different imaging modalities for the diagnosis of breast cancer

Pixel level [19], feature level and decision level fusion [20] are types of fusion techniques and is explained with help of diagram in Fig. 3(a). In this paper, we used decision level fusion for our experiment. In this method, we use the fusion process after the classification step is completed. This process is generally a combination of multiple

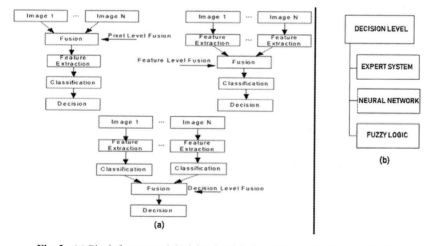

Fig. 3. (a) Pixel, feature and decision level fusion. (b) decision level methods

algorithms to obtain the resultant image. When confidences are used instead of decision, it is known as soft fusion. Otherwise, it is called hard fusion. Methods of decision fusion are shown in Fig. 3(b).

With advancements in algorithms and better computational power, Machine learning has helped to solve many real-life problems. These algorithms help in managing huge amount of data along with finding correlation among data which is not possible to find manually. Deep learning is also a subfield of AI which is gaining a lot of popularity. In this paper, we have used deep learning for feature extraction and used these features for classification using SVM and Decision tree. Finally, we have used voting classifier for decision level fusion to combine the results from these two classifiers and predicted our output.

2 Literature Review

This section reviews the related work done by researchers using fusion techniques. Pixel level, feature level and decision level fusion techniques are used by researchers for different modalities like MRI, CT and mammogram [21] as well as other modalities are also used and reviewed. Multiple authors have also purposed CADx solution [22, 23], pipeline structures and frameworks for fusion and classification of breast cancer.

While using MIAS dataset for their experiment, authors implemented pixel level fusion in their experiment. They conducted their experiment on three different mammograms from dataset of Normal, Benign and Microcalcification X-rays. They tested simple average and weighted average method and documented the results based on Signal to Noise Ratio (SNR), Peak Signal to Noise Ratio (PSNR), Root Mean Square Error (RMSE), Mutual Information (MI), etc. They concluded that, using image fusion provides better results than original image [24].

While using the same MIAS dataset, authors presented their image fusion method using Particle swarm optimization (PSO). The PSO used to calculate the optimum weighted weights for fusion and compared the results with conventional DWT and genetic algorithms. They compared the results on same fusion parameters as of author [24] and concluded that genetic method based DWT provides better results than Weighted average and traditional DWT [25].

Authors of paper [26], presented local entropy maximization based image fusion technique to improve the contrast of mammograms. They used MIAS and TMCH dataset for their experiment. Using Haar wavelet they decomposed the original and CLAHE image into 3 levels. Using sliding window of 5×5 window size, they fused the coefficients while choosing the maximum entropy. Finally, the fused image is reconstructed using these coefficients and validated their outcomes based of edge contents (EC), edge-based contrast measure (EBCM), feature similarity index measure (FSIM) and absolute mean brightness error (AMBE). They achieved 1.87 EC, 120.1 EBCM, 0.97 FSIM and 2.01 AMBE. They compared their results with HE, BBHE and CLAHE and their method showed better results.

Using 400 mammogram images from hospitals, authors [27], have purposed a CAD system using feature fusion techniques. First, they suggested a method of mass detection based on CNN deep features and clustering with Unsupervised Extreme Learning Machine (US-ELM). Second, they establish a collection of features that incorporate deep features, morphological features, texture and density features. Third, using the merged function collection to distinguish benign and malignant breast masses, an ELM classifier is established.

Authors of paper [28], purposed a wavelet fusion along with CLAHE enhancement for their experiment. They used multi-modalities images. In first step, they enhanced the contrast of image using CLAHE and second, they used 2D wavelet transformation fusion to generate the fused image. They compared their results on parameters like SNR and found their method performs better for different medical images with low contrast.

[29] presented a CAD system in which they used DDSM dataset for their experiment. Their experiment includes merging features of MIO and CC views of mammograms for better results. While using five features namely GLRLM, GLCM and others. While using SVM as classifier and using RBF kernel as performance booster they were able to achieve 97.5% accuracy, 100% sensitivity, 97.2% specificity, 97.1% precision, 96.23% F1 score, 0.952% Mathews Correlation Coefficient and 98.74% Balanced Classification Rate.

While using DDSM dataset for their experiment, authors of paper [30], used ensemble of CNN for classification of mammograms. The implemented data cleaning by contrast fading and removed white strips in input images of dataset and in pre-processing padding, dilation and cropping is applied. Since they used CNN for their experiment, they used data augmentation to solve overfitting issues in their model. Finally, they used GoogleNet for their classification step. Their decision fusion is based on max ensemble technique. After training their model for 50000 iterations they were able to achieve 91.3% recall value in stand-alone setup and were able to increase this to 97.3% with ensemble. 94.5% F1 score and 95% precision value is achieved.

[31] while also using decision level fusion used 65 thermography images gathered from [32, 33] and [34]. They purposed a novel texture feature extraction based on Markov Random Field (MRF) model and another texture based on LBP are extracted from images. While implementing decision fusion based on HMM, they were able to achieve 8.3% false negative and 5% false positive rate.

Whereas authors of paper [35] implemented a deep feature fusion of 3 different imaging modalities together. They used mammogram dataset FFDM containing 245 unique images, Ultrasound dataset containing 1125 images and DCE-MRI dataset containing 690 images. While using publicly available VGG19 model they implemented CNN model and were able to achieve AUC = 0.89 for DCE-MRI, AUC = 0.86 for FFDM and AUC = 0.9 for ultrasound (Table 1).

Table 1. Fusion techineques overview.

Author	Year	Fusion Technique	Dataset	Notes
[24]	2015	Pixel Level Fusion	MIAS	• Better results both in simple average and weighted average techniques.
[26]	2018	Pixel Level Fusion	MIAS, TMCH	• Used image fusion for contrast enhancement. • Values achieved(1.87 EC, 120.1 EBCM, 0.97 FSIM and 2.01 AMBE) • Better results than HE, BBHE and CLAHE.
[27]	2019	Feature Level Fusion	400 mammograms images from the hospital.	• Used CNN for mass detection. • Deep features, Morphological, texture and density feature set are created • Used EML classifier for classification.
[29]	2019	Feature level Fusion	DDSM	• Multi view feature fusion • SVM as classifier • 97.5% accuracy, 100% sensitivity, 97.2% specificity, 97.1% precision, 96.23% F1 score, 0.952% Mathews Correlation Coefficient and 98.74% Balanced Classification Rate.
[30]	2017	Decision Level Fusion	DDSM	• Used CNN for their experiment. • Used Google Net and trained for 50000 iterations. • Ensemble fusion achieved 97.3% recall value, 94.5% F1 Score, 95% precision.
[31]	2016	Decision Level Fusion	Self-gathered	• 65 thermography images used. • Texture features extracted based on MRF and LBP model. • Decision fusion based on HMM.

3   Materials and Methods

3.1   Datasets

In this experiment, we have used MIAS dataset. MIAS dataset consists of 161 pair of films of abnormalities and normal cases. It consists of 322 mammograms which are selected from United Kingdom National Breast Screening Program. A major factor for selection MIAS dataset is, it consists of mammograms which are cheap, low complexity and easily available in countries. MIAS dataset is available in two sizes (50 μ and 200 μ). There are other mammography datasets publicly like DDSM, TMCH,B-SCREEN [36] etc.

3.2   Pre-processing

A major problem in mammogram images is its low contrast, which makes it difficult to detect lumps, and have shown a high rate of false-positive cases (regular change as cancerous) and false negative (actual abnormality not detected). To solve this problem, we have implemented the CLAHE enhancement technique. CLAHE is a version of AHE in which we define a threshold level at which the intensities are clipped. Clip limit of 0.2 was used for this experiment and was coded in python.

3.3   Segmentation

Another issue with mammograms is the non-important area in the film. For our algorithms to achieve better results and to reduce the processing time we must trim the images to select the Region of Interest (ROI). Generally, according to the view of the breast (left or right), a majority of the portion is pixels with 0 value which should be removed. In this experiment, we have implemented a sliding vertical line from left or right depending on the image to trim it until pixels with non-zero pixel value is encountered.

3.4   Feature Extraction and Selection

This is one of the main important steps in our workflow. The output of the process heavily depends on the pre-processing techniques to enhance the images and features used for classification. Features more associated to the output class contribute better than non-associated features. In this step, we have used the power of deep learning algorithms for patterns in our input image. A CNN model is created which extracts the features and these features are used by classification algorithm (SVN and Decision Tree). A model of CNN architecture is shown in Fig. 4. A total of 1754 high-level features and 288 low-level features were used by the classification algorithm.

3.5   Classification and Decision Fusion

In this step, we have implemented SVM and Decision classifier. SVM is a machine learning algorithm which can be used for both classification and regression. Decision tree is also implemented for the classification of breast cancer. Finally, a voting classifier

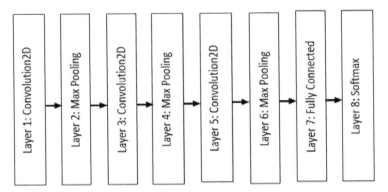

Fig. 4. CNN model architecture for feature extraction

is used for making a decision based on these two input classifiers and final output is generated. Figure 5, shows the workflow of the process which we have used for our experiment.

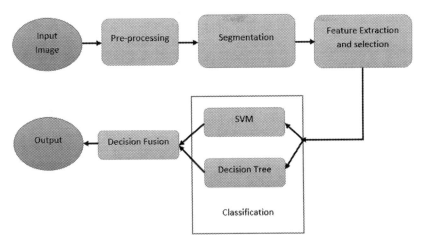

Fig. 5. Workflow of the process for breast cancer detection

4 Results

In this experiment, we have used MIAS dataset consisting of 161 pair of mammograms (322 total). CLAHE enhancement technique is used for improving the contrast of the images and the CNN model is used for the extraction of features. A total of 288 low-level and 1754 high-level features were extracted and were used for classification. Standalone SVM was able to achieve 90.3% accuracy, 87.8% sensitivity and 93% sensitivity while Decision tree was able to achieve 92.03% accuracy. After combining both the classification techniques using a voting classifier, we were able to achieve 93.4% accuracy.

5   Conclusion

Breast cancer is major affected diseases in women. After reviewing many techniques and methods in this paper we found out that a CAD system seems to be a good solution for real-life use by radiologist. With radiologist own expertise and second and helping opinion from CAD system will help to address the accuracy of diagnosis by improving the image, selecting the ROI. Further, a feature fusion along with decision fusion can be implemented to improve the results.

References

1. Trends of Breast Cancer in India. http://www.breastcancerindia.net/statistics/trends.html. Accessed 29 Jan 2020
2. Cancer Statistics - India Against Cancer. http://cancerindia.org.in/cancer-statistics/. Accessed 29 Jan 2020
3. Siegel, R.L., Miller, K.D., Jemal, A.: Cancer statistics, 2019. CA. Cancer J. Clin. **69**(1), 7–34 (2019)
4. Sarosa, S.J.A., Utaminingrum, F., Bachtiar, F.A.: Mammogram breast cancer classification using gray-level co-occurrence matrix and support vector machine. In: 3rd International Conference on Sustainable Information Engineering Technology SIET 2018 - Proceedings, pp. 54–59 (2018)
5. Jalalian, A., Mashohor, S.B.T., Mahmud, H.R., Saripan, M.I.B., Ramli, A.R.B., Karasfi, B.: Computer-aided detection/diagnosis of breast cancer in mammography and ultrasound: a review. Clin. Imaging **37**(3), 420–426 (2013)
6. Chen, B., Ning, R.: Cone-beam volume CT breast imaging: feasibility study. Med. Phys. **29**(5), 755–770 (2002)
7. Mann, R.M., Kuhl, C.K., Kinkel, K., Boetes, C.: Breast MRI: guidelines from the European society of breast imaging. Eur. Radiol. **18**(7), 1307–1318 (2008)
8. Sree, S.V.: Breast imaging: a survey. World J. Clin. Oncol. **2**(4), 171 (2011)
9. Iranmakani, S., et al.: A review of various modalities in breast imaging : technical aspects and clinical outcomes (2020)
10. Michaelson, J., et al.: The pattern of breast cancer screening utilization and its consequences. Cancer **94**(1), 37–43 (2002)
11. Elmore, J.G., et al.: Variability in interpretive performance at screening mammography and radiologists' characteristics associated with accuracy. Radiology **253**(3), 641–651 (2009)
12. Verma, B., McLeod, P., Klevansky, A.: Classification of benign and malignant patterns in digital mammograms for the diagnosis of breast cancer. Expert Syst. Appl. **37**(4), 3344–3351 (2010)
13. Ball, J.E., Bruce, L.M.: Digital mammographic computer aided diagnosis (CAD) using adaptive level set segmentation. In: Annual International Conference on IEEE Engineering in Medicine and Biology - Proceedings, pp. 4973–4978 (2007)
14. Zhang, G., Wang, W., Moon, J., Pack, J.K., Jeon, S.I.: A review of breast tissue classification in mammograms. In: Procedings of the 2011 ACM Research in Applied Computation Symposium RACS 2011, pp. 232–237 (2011)
15. Bird, R.E., Wallace, T.W., Yankaskas, B.C.: Analysis of cancers missed at screening mammography. Radiology **184**(3), 613–617 (1992)
16. Kerlikowske, K., et al.: Performance of screening mammography among women with and without a first-degree relative with breast cancer. Ann. Intern. Med. **133**(11), 855–863 (2000)

17. Suthakar, J.: International journal of computer science and mobile computing study of image fusion-techniques, method and applications. Int. J. Comput. Sci. Mob. Comput. **3**(11), 469–476 (2014)

18. James, A.P., Dasarathy, B.V.: Medical image fusion: a survey of the state of the art. Inf. Fusion **19**(1), 4–19 (2014)

19. Mitchell, H.B.: Image Fusion Theories, Techniques andApplications (2010)

20. Nazar, E., et al.: A comprehensive overview of decision fusion technique in healthcare: a systematic scoping review. Iran. Red Crescent Med. J. **22**(10) SE-Systematic reviews (2020)

21. Kerlikowske, K., et al.: Comparative effectiveness of digital versus film-screen mammography in community practice in the United States: a cohort study. Ann. Intern. Med. **155**(8), 493–502 (2011)

22. Dheeba, J., Singh, N.A., Selvi, S.T.: Computer-aided detection of breast cancer on mammograms: a swarm intelligence optimized wavelet neural network approach. J. Biomed. Inform. **49**, 45–52 (2014)

23. Singh, S.P., Urooj, S.: An Improved CAD system for breast cancer diagnosis based on generalized pseudo-zernike moment and ada-DEWNN classifier. J. Med. Syst. **40**(4), 1–13 (2016). https://doi.org/10.1007/s10916-016-0454-0

24. Kumar, M.P., Svecw, A., Pradesh, A.: Pixel Level Weighted Averaging Technique for Enhanced Image Fusion in Mammography, vol. 3, pp. 10–15 (2015)

25. Kumar, M.P., Kumar, P.R.R.: Image fusion of mammogaphy images using meta heuristic method particle swarm optimization (PSO). Int. J. Appl. Eng. Res. **11**(9), 6254–6258 (2016)

26. Pawar, M.M., Talbar, S.N.: Local entropy maximization based image fusion for contrast enhancement of mammogram. J. King Saud Univ. - Comput. Inf. Sci. **33**, 150–160 (2018)

27. Wang, Z., et al.: Breast cancer detection using extreme learning machine based on feature fusion with CNN deep features. IEEE Access. **7**(c), 105146–105158 (2019)

28. Bhan, B., Patel, S.: Efficient medical image enhancement using CLAHE enhancement and wavelet fusion. Int. J. Comput. Appl. **167**(5), 1–5 (2017)

29. Shanmugam, S., Shanmugam, A.K., Muthusamy, E.: Analyses of statistical feature fusion techniques in breast cancer detection, vol. 17, no. iCAST, pp. 311–316 (2019)

30. Sert, E., Ertekin, S., Halici, U.: Ensemble of convolutional neural networks for classification of breast microcalcification from mammograms. In: Proceedings of the Annual International Conference on IEEE Engineering in Medicine and Biology Society EMBS, pp. 689–692 (2017)

31. Rastghalam, R., Pourghassem, H.: Breast cancer detection using MRF-based probable texture feature and decision-level fusion-based classification using HMM on thermography images. Pattern Recognit. **51**, 176–186 (2016)

32. EtehadTavakol, M., Lucas, C., Sadri, S., Ng, E.: Analysis of breast thermography using fractal dimension to establish possible difference between malignant and benign patterns. J. Healthc. Eng. **1**, 27–44 (2010)

33. EtehadTavakol, M., Ng, E., Lucas, C., Sadri, S., Gheissari, N.: Estimating the mutual information between bilateral breast in thermograms using nonparametric windows. J. Med. Syst. **35**, 959–967 (2011)

34. Rastghalam, R., Pourghassem, H.: Breast cancer detection using spectral probable feature on thermography images. In: 2013 8th Iranian Conference on Machine Vision and Image Processing (MVIP), 2013, pp. 116–120 (2013)

35. Antropova, N., Huynh, B.Q., Giger, M.L.: A deep feature fusion methodology for breast cancer diagnosis demonstrated on three imaging modality datasets. Med. Phys. **44**(10), 5162–5171 (2017)

36. "Mammographic Image Analysis Homepage - Databases. https://www.mammoimage.org/databases/. Accessed 23 Sep 2020

A Modern Paradigm for Diagnosing Novel Coronavirus Disease (COVID-19) Using Multilayer Customized CNN via X-ray Images

Birjit Gope[✉] and Aditya Khamparia

School of Computer Science, Lovely Professional University, Phagwara, Punjab, India
Aditya.17862@lpu.co.in

Abstract. The novel disease that has already been declared a global pandemic that is COVID-19, initially had an epidemic in a major Chinese city called Wuhan, China. This novel virus has now infected more than two hundred countries across the world as it propagates through human activity. In comparison, novel coronavirus signs are very close to general seasonal influenza such as common cold, fever, cough and shortness in breathing. Infected patient monitoring is viewed as a crucial phase in the battle against COVID-19. Detection tools for Positive cases of COVID-19 do not offers distinctive results, so that it has increased the need to support diagnostic tools. Therefore, to prevent further dissemination of this disease, it is extremely important as early as possible to identify positive cases. However, there will be some approaches for identifying positive patients of COVID-19 that are usually conducted on the basis of respiratory samples and amongst them, X-Ray or radiology images are an essential treatment course. Latest data from the techniques of X-Ray imaging show that these samples contain significant SARS-CoV-2 viruses. information. In order to reliably diagnose this virus, the use of deep learning techniques that is DNN which is also offers advanced imaging instruments and techniques will prove to be useful, as can the issue of the absence of trained rural physicians. In this report, we presented a multilayer customized convolution neural network (MC-CNN) system analyzing chest X-Ray images of individuals suffering from covid-19 using an open-source database available in kaggle. In order to propose DNN approach provides 97.36% of classification accuracy, 97.65% of sensitivity, and 99.28% of precision. Therefore, we conclude that this proposed approach will allow health professionals to confirm their initial evaluation of patients with COVID-19.

Keywords: Deep learning · Multilayer customized-CNN · COVID-19 · X-Rays

1 Introduction

The latest coronavirus pandemic, identified as COVID-19, has developed a troubling condition around the globe. Coronaviruses are positive sense RNA viruses that are non-segmented enveloped by the Coronaviridae family and order of the Nidovirales and generally spread to humans and other mammals [1]. However, the coronavirus family also

© Springer Nature Singapore Pte Ltd. 2021
A. K. Luhach et al. (Eds.): ICAICR 2020, CCIS 1393, pp. 539–551, 2021.
https://doi.org/10.1007/978-981-16-3660-8_51

includes Middle East Respiratory Syndrome (MERS) and also Severe Acute Respiratory Syndrome (SARS) viruses that are also responsible [2, 3]. The epidemic of COVID-19 began in December 2019 in Wuhan, a town in Eastern China. With signs such as headache, dry cough, and exhaustion, this infection triggers Pneumonia. In serious situations, the patient has problems breathing. Headaches, fatigue, or vomiting are often found in certain patients. It spreads from individual to individual by droplets of the infected human cough or sneeze [4]. Even if a disinfected individual contacts goutlets without washing or sanitation of his hands and contacts his or her face especially his or her eyes, nose or mouth, will infect him. As of 8 May 2020, 210 countries have been infected by the novel coronavirus, according to the World Health Organization (WHO) Status Survey. On April 25, 2020, the World Health Organization (WHO) announced it a pandemic. One of the main methods of coronavirus research is Reverse Transcription Polymerase Chain Reaction (RT-PCR). This test is carried out with respiratory tests, and The results are given in a few hours or two days. The most popular studies are blood tests to recognize COVID-19. Care specialists will occasionally utilize chest x-ray tests to assess the condition of the lung. In China an infection prevalence of 98% was detected by CT imaging and another testing methods is far behind. The Chinese researchers had insufficient stocks of pharmaceuticals in the early stages of the pandemic flu. The doctors will only detect disease based on a digital chest CT scan. There are several countries utilizing CT imaging also and so does Turkey. Some findings suggest that for early identification of COVID-19 [8–11], laboratory results and clinical picture features are much stronger.

COVID-19 has been distributed across the world and threatened mankind. Because of its high infectivity and transmissibility, some of the largest economies are under competition for capital. To order to forecast the number of cases to future, other strategies would be required due to the increased size of cases and their resulting burden on the health and administration professionals. In this document, in order to predict the number of COVID-19 cases in India ahead of thirty days for ahead and impact of precautionary action such as social isolation and COVID-19 expanded, we used to data-drive estimation methods like deep neural network in transfer learning method VGG16. Prediction of varying factors (number of positive cases, number of failed cases, etc.) achieved using the proposed approach is reliable and will help health officials and administrators.

In 2019 we saw the latest pandemic but it is since 1917. Government, Researchers and Scientist all over the world are working to fight this pandemic (COVID-19) still they can't find its solution to fight. Now it's time novel coronavirus is been detected in humans and the first case were found into a person of Wuhan, China in the fall of December, 2019. In this paper, we reviewed history and taxonomy of coronavirus and findings of authors regards COVID-19 prediction and detection. In this paper we have reviewed the deep learning techniques to detect and predict COVID-19. Since at the time of writing this paper not much research has been published. The focus area of this paper work with X-rays images of lungs, while other medical modality images might also provide better detection and prediction results. This article calls for a public dataset which can help researchers to work on their models in this field. Deep learning is the trend in the today's modern world of technology it gives accurate results as compared to other methods so, we prefer deep learning model that is convolution neural network (CNN) classifier it will work on image to classify the images and obtain better results.

COVID-19 was identified in China in December 2019 and a WHO global pandemic was reported on 11 March 2020, due to SARS-CoV-2 virus. AI is a potentially important weapon in the battle against the pandemic COVID-19. Machine Learning (ML), the natural language for which AI may be defined at present Computer Vision (NLP) and processing applications to teach computers to use big data models to detect, explain and predict patterns. These features can be useful for recognizing (diagnosing), predicting and describing (treating) COVID-19 infections, Support with socio-economic impact management. In these reasons, AI and other data analysis methods have been scrammed for use and discovery since the outbreak of the pandemic.

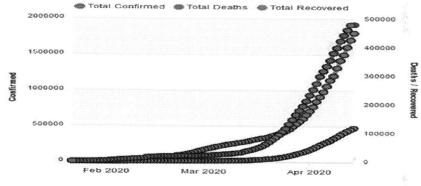

Fig. 1. Outbreak of COVID-19

We will include an early analysis of the AI contribution to combating COVID-19, which was real and feasible, as well as the present limitations on these contributions, in this paper. It is aimed, in order to provide feedback for rapid responses to science, policy and medical study, at quickly taking advantage of an increasingly expanded discussion and function. The human and economic damage caused by the pandemic would be appalling; as it is published, there was considerable confusion in predicting how bad and how effective non-pharmaceutical and pharmaceutical responses could be the development of AI is a worthy endeavour and one of the most promising research methods to minimize this uncertainty has been built over the last ten or so years. Data scientists have taken up the challenge encouragingly (which means that this document's shelf-life may be short). In addition, improvements in X-ray scans were already reported by health professionals before the signs were apparent [12]. In recent years, Deep Neural Network method approaches have been effectively extended to several issues, such as the classification of skin cancer [13, 14], the diagnosis of breast cancer [15, 16], the classification of brain disease [17], the diagnosis of X-ray pneumonia [18], and lung segmentation [19–21]. Therefore, in the rapid increase of this COVID-19 epidemic, accurate, precise, and faster intelligence detection models can help to overcome this issue. We suggest a new framework in this report to detect COVID-19 infection from X-Ray images utilising a broad approach to the Multilayers Customized Convolutional Neural Network

(MC-CNN). We reviewed at the COVID-19 reported X-ray scans and medical histories of other disorders and regular individuals on the basis of an available benchmark dataset of COVID. Also, we have used the VGG-16 network to develop our model for features extraction.

2 Literature Review

In this section can find some analysis on demand forecasts here. There are many approaches to apply the market forecasting techniques. The application fields for automatic demand prediction are various, such as engineering, shipping, leisure, stock exchange, and retail. Time series methods use past data to predict future demand. Techniques for time series include the naive approach, the mean method, and the basic exponential method.

An method was suggested to detect confounder-19 utilising x-ray images [1]. The authors used the YOLO model for classifying the pictures. The model used 17 layers of convolution that were accompanied by filters for each of the layers. In their trial, the authors concluded that the built model could be directly employed across the cloud for screening of patients of coVid-19 in X-ray pictures. Our device is fully integrated without the need for any human feedback. Our sophisticated computer is efficient to process binary and multi class problems. Abbas et al. [4] advocated the usage of deep learning related methods in identifying circulating type 1 diabetes by utilising chest x-ray pictures. The ET can accommodate small anomalies in the x-ray signal.

This helps to boost model production. Das et al. used deep learning to recognise and classify x-ray signatures using medical evidence. The training data was obtained using pre-trained CNN. They also assumed that many such definitions are obsolete. Asif et al. recommended that deep convolutional neural network or a deep CNN should be implemented in speech recognition tasks. Transfer learning method is very helpful in estimating covariate. A convolutional deep CNN for x-ray picture detection was proposed by Majeed and her colleagues in 2011. To investigate their results, they employed a neighbourhood activation map strategy. The CNN article becomes more respectable with out the clinicians' recommendation. Ioannis D. Apostolopoulos and Tzani A. Mpesiana used computer techniques to evaluate lens forms from x-ray image. Results from sample data were promising. Furthermore, these researches do need further confirmation. Heidari et al. presented a scheme to link source of lung injury with X-rays. This was pre-processed to produce a pseudocolor image. This proposed approach improves the precision and usefulness of the model. One solution to medical image acquisition is to use a radiography or a CT-CT scan. The latest one is a lot smoother than the old one. Prabira Kumar Sethy and Santi Kumari Behera created a model for classification using transfer learning and help vector machine. This model worked the most in simulation tasks. Narin, et al. [10] examined five learning strategies. The writers argued that ResNet-50 had the best precision.

"There should be no harm or injury to each other" (2020). This research offers detailed comparison of artificial intelligence and soft computing theories on predicting the outbreak of COVID-19. Two distinct machine learning algorithms (multilayer perceptron and fuzzy adaptive networks) have currently yielded promising performance.

Based on the results described in the review report, I think machine learning can be an effective tool for outbreak modelling. Punn et al. (2020). The aim of this study is to establish the accuracy of COVID across different nations. [14] Farahat et al. (2020). In this post, I will present a time series forecasting model focused on data structure LSTM. COVID19 cases must be dealt by the government so that policies can be properly carried out. Organisational variables are analysed even more thoroughly than HCI variables (2019). The proposal under analysis is stronger than today's techniques. Employing forecasting method, inclusion of neural networks and modern pattern models in the project will guarantee a highly accurate predictor. Finally, due to staffs of this magazine (2020). These psychologists employed a portion of Artificial Intelligence into their review. This was used as the source of influenza, X-ray images and coronavirus. MobileNet V2 and SqueezeNet models and Help Vector Machine has been used to distinguish pictures. An precision of 99.27% is achieved in this direction. Zhang et al. (2020). This work uses deep learning to determine which current drugs are safe for people with zoonotic novel coronavirus. The authors used a modified Dense Net to model protein-ligand binding on a protein. Scientists can find which drugs may cure the virus and which are useless. While more research must be undertaken, compounds like adenosine and vidabrine could be helpful for care [49] Qian Goyue et al. (2020). According to their results using deep learning algorithms implemented Viral Host Prediction. So they figured out that a host which is most potential and it is also found out that the host would get MERS coronavirus and Ebola. The most similar signs came from the bat coronavirus. Researchers were able to learn more about how coronavirus could be spread by observing mink and bats in science. "Chen et al." (2020). In this paper, authors used UNet++ to classify facial features from CT scans.

The authors conducted computerised shape simulation of these scans. The model was quite reliable and had excellent material recall. The model hit a sensitivity rate of 100%, precision of 93.55%, consistency of 95.25%, positive predictive value of 84.62%, negative predictive value of 99.61%, and positive predictive value of 99.16%. The model was estimated for 98.8% and 100% trust rate. The doctor was as correct as an accomplished radiologist on 27 people. The radiologists also removed 65% of radiology reading cycle with the aid of the machine model. The model was especially good at speeding up the work of specialists in imaging. This is a strong indication of AI positively affecting the culture. This is because radiologists may have more CT scan patients in a shorter amount of time. While there was a substantial impact on a small cohort of subjects, the results tended to be suspicious. This shows that all of these patients have the same psychiatric condition. This data also has certain drawbacks. Deep learning is a priority area for artificial intelligence. This approach includes end-to-end simulations that generate desired results with interesting input details. Artificial intelligence systems are becoming more integral in medical diagnostics and care. First process includes utilising reverse transcription quantitative real-time PCR to classify a novel coronavirus. Therefore, this would ensure the world has greater understanding and awareness of COBID. Radiological films are increasingly used to characterise COVID-19 cases. [23] endorsed a profound model, COVID-Net, a deeply-connected, extensible neural network which is highly optimised for COVID 19 only, giving an 87% efficiency across all. Aid Vector

Machine (SVM) algorithms are used to represent X-Ray images for various Convolutional Neural Networks (CNN) models in the series. In this way, this project plays a very important function in personal wellbeing. ResNet 50 demonstrated over 98% sensitivity for COVID-19. He collected approximately 500 pictures of COVID-19 patients from GitHub.

The findings by using ResNet 50 and Inception-V3, 97 and 87%, were obtained using fivefold cross-validation. Compared to other form, COVID-19 offers a result of 98.75% and 93.48% Investigators took many X-ray pictures of COVID-19 illness. Experiments have showed that the X-ray Deep Learning system is capable of extracting important COVID-19-related biomarkers from the urine. COVID-Net proposes an economical model to describe the socio-political dynamics that influence COVID-19. A chest X-ray showed 25 person with recorded COVID-19 In this innovation seven versions of convolutional neural network such as VGG-19 and the second version of the Google Mobile Net were included. In order to categorise a clinical scenario, every classification process is built into neural networks in order to incorporate all of it. A sophisticated and specialised image-based learning simulation approach for medical diagnosis and care is suggested. Retinopathy with diabetes and macular degeneration can be listed since they do not look the same on normal X-ray films. It is most crucial to use a multi-class and hierarchical classification scheme. to assemble the RYDLS-20 Database of chest X-ray photographs of pneumonia severity scores, the writers collected a database called RYDLS-20 of chest X-ray photographs of pneumonia severity scores. In F1 and MLC this ranked beyond 0.7. Artificial intelligence appears to be an effective method for COVID-19 classification. The overall number of the planes which were used in COVID-19 was 108. There were 86 planes with atypical pneumonia among them (COVID-19 group).

Experiments. Special numbers of VGG-16, VGG-19, Squeeze Net, Google Net, MobileNet-V2, ResNet-18, ResNet-50, ResNet-101 and Xception images are part of data of VGG-16, VGG-19, Squeeze Net, Google Net, MobileNet-V2, ResNet-18, ResNet-50, ResNet-101 and Xception. In a broad sample of over 160 suspected of pneumonia, ResNet-101 demonstrated a strong detection rate of 93%. The goal of this report was to look at whether Chest X-rays could be used to analyse the occurrence of COVID-19 injuries. The trial included Pre-qualified Resnet50 and VGG-16 among other CNNs focused on chest x-rays.

3   Proposed Work

3.1   Outline of Methodology

The proposed architecture is a customized convolution neural network (CNN). It consists of a combination of convolution layers, pooling layers, dropout layers, flatten, and dense layers. The type of layers used and corresponding trainable parameters are shown in Table 2. Figure 3 outlines our methodology.

3.2   Data Pre-processing and Augmentation

All the images contained in the dataset were rescaled between 1 and 0. This rescaling of images was done to treat each image in the same manner. In data augmentation, we

Table 1. Comparison of techniques that are used to detect COVID-19.

Authors	Approach	Types of Data	Source of Data	Results
[23]	Deep Transfer Learning for predicting COVID-19 automatically	X-Ray images	GitHub & Kaggle repository	Accuracy = 98%
[24]	Detecting and Classifying Automated Technique for Pneumonia-based using Deep Learning	CT scan samples and X-Ray images	X-Ray, CT scan Dataset publicly source- Internet	Accuracy = 96%
[25]	Screening COVID-19 & pneumonia using Deep Learning	CT scans samples	Hospital of Zhejiang, China	Accuracy = 86.7%
[26]	CNN with pretrained weighted models	X-Ray images	X-ray images of a public dataset	VGG19, DenseNet models: f1-scores = 0.89 normal & Coronavirus = 0.91
[18]	Automated Customized Convolutional Neural Network	X-Ray images	50 Coronavirus patients (GitHub) 50 normal X-ray (Kaggle)	98%
[27]	Support Vector Machine (ML model)	CT scan samples	Total = 150 CT scan images Coronavirus = 53	Classification accuracy GLSZM is 99.68%
[28]	Hybrid method i.e. Support Vector Machine based on deep learning approach (Deep Features)	X-Ray images	Coronavirus cases = 25 Normal cases = 25 (GitHub, Kaggle)	SVM + ResNet50 (FPR value = 95.52%, F1-score = 95.52%, MCC value= 91.41% and Kappa value = 90.76%)

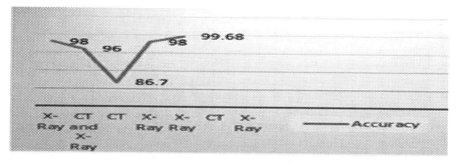

Fig. 2. Table of comparison Graphical Representation

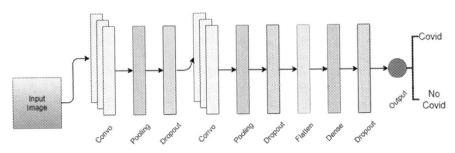

Fig. 3. Proposed methodology architecture

Table 2. Type of layers and corresponding trainable parameters.

Layer Type	Output Shape	Trainable Parameters
Conv2D	(None, 150, 150, 32)	2432
MaxPooling2D	(None, 75, 75, 32)	0
Dropout	(None, 75, 75, 32)	0
Conv2D	(None, 75, 75, 64)	51264
MaxPooling2D	(None, 37, 37, 64)	0
Dropout	(None, 37, 37, 64)	0
Flatten	(None, 87616)	0
Dense	(None, 256)	22429952
Dropout	(None, 256)	0
Dense	(None, 1)	257
Total Parameters: 22,483,905		
Trainable Parameters: 22,483,905		
Non-Trainable Parameters: 0		

applied horizontal flips. Horizontal flip helped in dealing with the presence of covid-19 on both the sides of the x-ray image. Moreover, we also applied a zoom range of 0.2 during the data augmentation process.

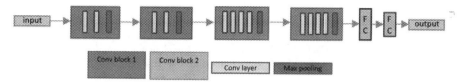

Fig. 4. Multilayers Customized CNN

3.3 Dataset

To train our model we used the dataset obtained from kaggle repository. The total number of x-ray images contained in the dataset is 2295, of which 712 are x-ray images of covid-19 patients and 1583 are normal x-ray images. Figure 5 represents sample x-ray images of both the classes, i.e., covid-19 as well as x-ray images. Table 3 presents a summary of the train and test dataset.

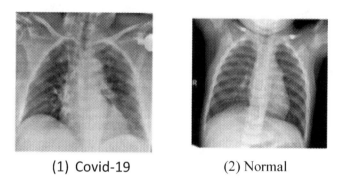

(1) Covid-19   (2) Normal

Fig. 5. (1) Covid-19 x-ray (2) Normal x-ray.

Table 3. Summary of train and test dataset.

Image type	Train size	Test size
Covid-19	545	167
Normal	1266	317
Total	**1811**	**484**

3.4 Extraction and Summarizing of Data

The included articles were examined to extract and summarize the data with respect to our research objectives. Thus, to meet our objectives, we classified the research questions according to some criteria. The criteria included: year of publication, medical discipline, disease type, the objective of research, inputs, and outputs, problem and research gap, and findings, and results.

4 Results

In this report, followed by model validation results, we discuss the loss observations. We performed experiments utilizing X-Ray images to identify and differentiate recorded cases of COVID-19 and to train models of non COVID-19 and COVID-19 in two classes. This latest paradigm was evaluated using the ten-fold cross-validation methodology. To plan, 90% of the X-Rays would be used for testing or confirmation and the remaining 10% were used. In order to understand the excellence of the forecast, the loss function is strongly important. Out of Figs. 5 and 6. We find that, after every 100 epochs, the absence of training and legitimacy is steadily reduced.

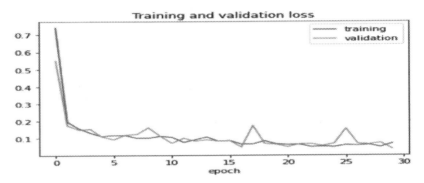

Fig. 6. Training and validation loss

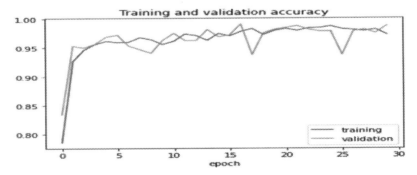

Fig. 7. Training and validation accuracy

It's noteworthy that training efficiency increased in the primary epoch due to the inclusion of a critical group's results (Fig. 6). Measurement, confirmation and determining the outcome through direct image tests ensure that the model is accurate. To affirm the efficacy of it the model is evaluated through cross-validation.

By calculating the time model sufficient to detect and distinguish, the time comparison is accomplished. Our architecture proposed a multitude of examples of chest x-ray pictures (see the four-part Matrix Confusion: True Positive, True Negative, False

Positive and False Negative) (Fig. 7). However, the model created incorrect predictions mostly in bad shots, always projecting the Pneumonia patient as COVID-19 because the picture attributes were parallel.

The success metrics in the proposed model are subjected to 10-fold cross-validation to verify the effectiveness and benchmark of each model. The predicated models showed average accuracy of about 98% and mean sensitivity, precision, and F1 score of 97.65%, 95.48% and 98.46%. It also has a ranking of more than 99%.

5 Conclusion and Future Scope

Covid-19 has disrupted the whole globe. CoVid-19 identification also remains a challenging challenge. There is not a procedure presently accessible that is able to detect 100% precision. This is an aim of this research is to use deep learning methods on chest X-rays in identifying lung spots for covid patients. Detecting covid-19 using deep learning techniques could be used by the clinical personnel as a second opinion. We suggest utilizing a customized convolution neural network to detect X-rays that include the covid-19 from plain X-rays. A high training precision of 98.17% is reached in the model.

In this paper, we presented a profound learning paradigm for the identification of cases of COVID-19 in Chest x-ray images. With an accuracy of 97.36%, without manual feature extraction, this automated system may perform binary classification. Furthermore, this model is also able to evaluate and work for real-time applications that use a larger dataset. Furthermore, it may be useful in cases where the test kit is not appropriate. Until now, the positive case recognition of COVID-19 from radiology images utilizing the deep learning method has not been accepted by the professional community of medical experts. In emergency medical care systems, in the screening of COVID19 patients using an RT-PCR, this proposed system should be considered as a complementary instrument. Under the guidance of radiologists and physicians, this instrument will also serve as an important diagnostic medium for initial evaluation of COVID-19 patients. At this stage, with more COVID-19 images of contaminated cases, we are building a wider custom dataset and to develop our existing method to stabilize our model to distinguish both CT and X-Ray scan images.

References

1. Ozturk, T., Talo, M., Yildirim, E.A., Baloglu, U.B., Yildirim, O., et al.: Automated detection of COVID-19 cases using deep neural networks with X-ray images. Comput. Biol. Med **121** (2020)
2. Narayan Das, N., Kumar, N., Kaur, M., Kumar, V., Singh, D.: Automated deep transfer learning-based approach for detection of COVID-19 infection in chest X-rays Ingenierie et recherche biomedicale (IRBM: Biomedical engineering and research) (2020)
3. Abbas, A., Abdelsamea, M.M., Gaber, M.M.: Classification of COVID-19 in chest X-ray images using DeTraC deep convolutional neural network. Applied Intelligence (2020)
4. Asif, S., Wenhui, Y., Jin, H., Tao, Y., Jinhai, S.: Classification of COVID-19 from Chest Radiography Images Using Deep Convolutional Neural Network. J. Xidian Univ., vol. 14, no. 8 (2020)

5. Majeed, T., Rashid, R., Ali, D., Asaad, A.: Covid-19 Detection using CNN Transfer Learning from X-ray Images. *medRxiv*, p. 2020.05.12.20098954 (2020)

6. Apostolopoulos, I.D., Mpesiana, T.A.: Covid-19: automatic detection from X-ray images utilizing transfer learning with convolutional neural networks. Phys. Eng. Sci. Med. **43**(2), 635 640 (2020). https://doi.org/10.1007/s13246-020-00865-4

7. Heidari, M., Mirniaharikandehei, S., Khuzani, A.Z., Danala, G., Qiu, Y., Zheng, B.: "Improving the performance of CNN to predict the likelihood of COVID-19 using chest X-ray images with preprocessing algorithms. Int. J. Med. Inf. **144**,(2020)

8. Perumal, V., Narayanan, V., Rajasekar, S.J.S.: Detection of COVID-19 using CXR and CT images using transfer learning and Haralick features. Appl. Intell. **51**(1), 341–358 (2020). https://doi.org/10.1007/s10489-020-01831-z

9. Sethy, P.K., Behera, S.K.: Detection of coronavirus disease (covid-19) based on deep features (2020)

10. Narin, A., Kaya, C., Pamuk, Z.: Department of Biomedical Engineering, Zonguldak Bulent Ecevit University, 67100, Zonguldak, Turkey. arXiv Prepr (2020)

11. Pan, S.J., Yang, Q.: A survey on transfer learning. IEEE Trans. Knowl. Data Eng. **22**(10), 1345–1359 (2010)

12. Wilson, D.J., Falush, D., McVean, G.: Germs, genomes and genealogies. Trends Ecol. Evol. **20**(1), 39–45 (2005)

13. Tumpey, T.M., et al.: Pathogenicity of influenza viruses with genes from the 1918 pandemic virus: functional roles of alveolar macrophages and neutrophils in limiting virus replication and mortality in mice. J. Virol. **79**(23), 14933–14944 (2005)

14. Erkoreka, A.: The Spanish influenza pandemic in occidental Europe (1918–1920) and victim age. Influenza Other Respi. Viruses **4**(2), 81–89 (2010)

15. Rothan, H.A., Byrareddy, S.N.: The epidemiology and pathogenesis of coronavirus disease (COVID-19) outbreak. J. Autoimmun. **109**, 102433 (2020)

16. Lai, C.C., Shih, T.P., Ko, W.C., Tang, H.J., Hsueh, P.R.: Severe acute respiratory syndrome coronavirus 2 (SARS-CoV-2) and coronavirus disease-2019 (COVID-19): the epidemic and the challenges. Int. J. Antimicrob. Agents **55**(3) (2020)

17. Wang, Z., Tang, K.: Combating COVID-19: health equity matters, Nat. Med. 26 (April) (2020) 2019–2021. Department of Biomedical Engineering, Zonguldak Bulent Ecevit University, 67100, Zonguldak, Turkey

18. Sun, J., et al.: COVID-19: epidemiology, evolution, and cross-disciplinary perspectives. Trends Mol. Med. **26**(5), 483–495 (2020). https://doi.org/10.1016/j.molmed.2020.02.008

19. COVID-19 related analytics, graphs, and charts Corona Tracker

20. Clinical characteristics of 113 deceased patients with coronavirus disease 2019: retrospective study. Bmj, 1295(March), p. m1295 (2020)

21. Nagendran, M., et al.: Artificial intelligence versus clinicians: systematic review of design, reporting standards, and claims of deep learning studies in medical imaging. BMJ **368**, 1–12 (2020)

22. El Asnaoui, K., Chawki, Y., Idri, A.: Automated Methods for Detection and Classification Pneumonia based on X-Ray Images Using Deep Learning (2020)

23. Xu, X., et al.: Deep Learning System to Screen Coronavirus Disease 2019 Pneumonia, pp. 1–29 (2020)

24. Hemdan, E.E.-D., Shouman, M.A., Karar, M.E.: COVIDX-Net: a framework of deep learning classifiers to diagnose COVID-19 in X-Ray images (2020)

25. M. Barstugan, U. Ozkaya, and S. Ozturk, "Coronavirus (COVID-19) Classification using CT Images by Machine Learning Methods," 5, pp. 1–10, 2020.

26. Kumar, P., Kumari, S.: Detection of coronavirus Disease (COVID-19) based on Deep Features. https://www.Preprints.Org/Manuscript/202003.0300/V1, March, p. 9 (2020)

27. Salehi, A.W., Baglat, P., Gupta, G.: Alzheimer's disease diagnosis using deep learning techniques. Int. J. Eng. Adv. Technol. **9**(3), 874–880 (2020)
28. Gupta, G., Gupta, A., Jaiswal, V., Dilshad, M.: Ansari, a review and analysis of mobile health applications for Alzheimer patients and caregivers. In: 2018 Fifth International Conference on Parallel, Distributed and Grid Computing (PDGC), IEEE, pp. 171–175 (2018)
29. Sharma, L., Gupta, G., Jaiswal, V.: Classification and development of tool for heart diseases (MRI images) using machine learning. In: 2016 Fourth International Conference on Parallel, Distributed and Grid Computing (PDGC), IEEE, 2016, pp. 219–224 (2016)
30. Review on machine and deep learning models for the detection and prediction of Coronavirus Ahmad Waleed Salehi, Preety Baglat, Gaurav Gupta Faculty of Engineering and Technology, Shoolini University, Solan, Himachal Pradesh 173229, India

Automated Identification and Classification of Blur Images, Duplicate Images Using Open CV

Gajula Ramesh, Anusha Anugu$^{(\boxtimes)}$, Karanam Madhavi, and P. Surekha

CSE Department, Gokaraju Rangaraju Institute of Engineering and Technology, Hyderabad, Telangana 500090, India

Abstract. The number of digital images increasing rapidly with the popularization of digital cameras and mobile phones, as they are now available at affordable prices in the market. There is various image quality degradants out of which the blur plays a vital role in the nature. To get the quality and quantified images users will move on with the clicking of same image repeatedly. With the rapid increment of images, the occupation of space in the storage devices also increases. Previously researchers are worked on these problems individually, so the model will provide them combinedly in a single methodology. As the identification of blur images, duplicate images manually by the users has become a critical task, we come up with a new idea of sequential model to identify blur, duplicate images sequentially and storing those images in their respective folders automatically which are created by this model such that the user can review if they want, else they can delete the folder. It also provides the video of original good images (without duplicates) to review the images quickly and easily by the user.

Keywords: Blur images · Duplicate images · Laplacian operator · MD5 hashing · Windows media player · KNN classifier

1 Introduction

Machine Learning is a district of computer science which imparts the systems capability to be told and enhance itself from the previous experience with none human intervention and without being programmed explicitly by humans. Learning stage involves various observations on sample data to make a mathematical model called "training data". Machine Learning has various applications like computer vision and email filtering etc.

Computer Vision. CV is a multidisciplinary logical field that manages how computer can increase significant level comprehension from computerized images or videos. It looks to know and automate tasks that the human sensory system can do.

Image Processing. The method of performing some operations on a picture to induce its effective information or to urge a magnified image is thought as Image Processing. Input for image processing may be a sequence of images, an image or video and output is either a picture or attributes related therewith image.

© Springer Nature Singapore Pte Ltd. 2021
A. K. Luhach et al. (Eds.): ICAICR 2020, CCIS 1393, pp. 552–562, 2021.
https://doi.org/10.1007/978-981-16-3660-8_52

Blur Detection. Images are accustomed store or display information. Images are utilised to point out data which are helpful and important. Now-a-days, with the provision of varied good digital cameras, mobile phones increase day by day at the affordable costs; it has benefited the humans to snap many images. It has become a trend to humans to capture the pictures regardless of the situation is also. Either good or bad humans must store the data pictographically or visually as their lifetime memories. It will be helpful if a scientific technique is presented profoundly with automatic identification of blurred images [1], duplicate images and its deletion which can reduce the glancing time of all images and deleting those one by one. As its equivalent time it'll provide space for the storage of more images. There are mainly three kinds of blur, they are Gaussian blur, Motion Blur, out of focus blur.Gaussian blur is due to the environmental factors like air, water, wind, rain, fire, smoke, fog etc. Motion blur is because of the instant between the thing and camera. Out of focus blur is because of the space between the camera and therefore the object (Fig. 1).

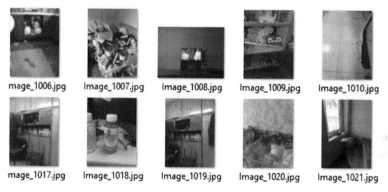

image_1006.jpg   Image_1007.jpg   Image_1008.jpg   Image_1009.jpg   Image_1010.jpg

image_1017.jpg   Image_1018.jpg   Image_1019.jpg   Image_1020.jpg   Image_1021.jpg

Fig. 1. Good and blur images in dataset

In this paper, the process considers only the out-of-focus (De-focused)blur images from the dataset considering interior and exterior parts of an house along with the objects available in the house.

While capturing the pictures, humans will capture the same object repeatedly so and on to get the right and qualified image of that object. Capturing of these many clicks of the same object ends up in the formation of duplicate images. Duplicate Images are the images that are exact to other images [5]. The position of objects within the images is same and there's no difference in the angle of rotation also. Duplicate images accumulate quickly; clutter your photo albums and takes up plenty of space. As we capture the object number of times, the number of images increases the occupation of space within the storage disk which ends up with the wastage of memory. Not only the memory wastage it also wastes the time of humans,as it takes much time for them to spot those duplicate images in the plenty of images (Fig. 2).

From past decades the researchers are researching about the foundation of automatic identification of blur images from a large number of image datasets. Even though there are numerous methods and models individually to identify the blur images and duplicate

Image_1184.JPG   Image_1185.jpg   Image_1186.jpg   Image_1187.jpg

Image_1188.jpg   Image_1189.jpg   Image_1191.jpg   Image_1192.jpg

Image_1193.jpg   Image_1194.jpg   Image_1195.jpeg   Image_1196.jpg

Fig. 2. Duplicate images in dataset

images, there is no recognised method which identifies both the duplicate and blurs images. The proposed model will then makes use of KNN algorithm along with Laplacian operator and image hashing function to get automatically the blur, duplicate images respectively in their folders.

2 Blur Identification Techniques

To decide whether a picture is blurry or nor and the scope to which it is blurry, [6, 9] there are numerous procedures [12, 13], [14]. Among them some of them are:

Haar Wavelet Transform (HWT). The procedure undergoes the splitting of images into NxN by repeating on every individual tile of the 2D HWT, and gathering obliquely, perpendicularly and parallely associated tiles into group of provokes with articulated changes. Little clumps carrying images are then announced as blurred.

Fast Fourier Transform (FFT). The frequencies at various random points of an image are calculated by the algorithm in this procedure. It completely depends on the frequency level of an image to announce that the image is blur or not blur. If there is a low measure of high frequency then the procedure announces that the image is blurry and the software engineers are left with their choice to decide to what will be the abundance of high frequency or few of high frequency.

Laplacian Operator. Laplacian operator, besides a derivative operator but the basic contrast between different operators like Sobel, Kirsch and Laplacian operator is that all other derivatives are first order derivative yet the Laplacian operator is a second order derivative mask. Out of the different procedures that identify the blurriness of images available in the machine learning, to achieve the aim, have opted Laplacian operator and Open CV library on the foundation of python. Picking up the ideal identification strategy shifts concurring to the circumstance and generally relies upon the results produced.

3 Implementation Steps

In the implementation process, initially the input dataset is taken and is trained to the model. In the training process, filtering of images such as images in the formats of JPG, jpg, PNG, png, JPEG are taken by the process. In the image processing by using Laplacian operator we calculate two features or parameters i.e., Laplacian value and maximum Laplacian value of an image. Then with the help of Knn Classifier, images are classified as blur and Good images. Considering good images as input data,MD5 hashing technique identifies the duplicate images followed by converting filtered good images into video using Windows Media Player.

Dataset. We have collected the dataset by gathering the interior and exterior images of a house. We have totally1250 images in which 676 are taken as training dataset and 574 as real data set for testing the methodology. The dataset includes normal good images along with blur and duplicate images.

Input. We have taken a folder of images which consists of good blur and duplicate images in a storage device or a memory space.

Output. We will get separate folder of images for blur, good, duplicate and original good images along with a video of good images folder.

The implementation process of the proposed model is diagrammatically represented as shown in the below figure (Fig. 3).

Data Processing. Data Processing is defined as the process of administrating the information by using a computer. It includes the conversion of unprocessed information to the machine decipherable structure, passing of information into andout of the CPU, memory to output device and arrangement or modification of output. Data Processing includes the performance of characterized operations on the information by any utilization of computers.Once the information or data is successfully loaded, we perform data processing to filter images in the png, jpg, JPG, PNG, jpeg formats and if the image is in other formats then those come under unknown array of images.

Image Processing. In the processing of image we extract two features by using Laplacian operator which is openly available in OpenCV.Then followed by statistical analysis on those features by using describe function to get count, mean, standard deviation, maximum value, Minimum value etc.. By using different models we got to found out the baseline model and standardization is done to get the more accurate model and found KNN classifier gives the best accuracy for the proposed model.

Laplacian Operator. Laplacian function is a high pass filter or gradient filter provided by the Open CV.

$$\Delta \text{src} = \delta^2 \text{src}/\delta x^2 + \delta^2 \text{src}/\delta y^2$$

Where each deprival is found using sobel derivate which a combined Gaussian smoothing plus differentiation operator. It is more unaffected by noise. We can define the direction of derivates to be got gold of horizontal (x order) and vertical (y order)

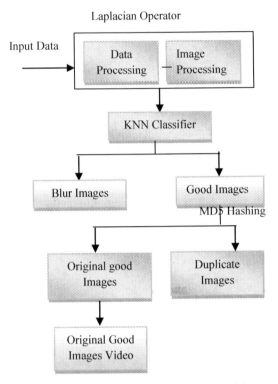

Fig. 3. Implementation Diagram of the methodology

gradually. Unlike first order filters it detects the edges at zero crossings that is where the value changes from negative to positive and vice versa (Fig. 4).

$$\text{Kernel of the Laplacian is } \begin{bmatrix} 0 & 1 & 0 \\ 1 & -4 & 1 \\ 0 & 1 & 0 \end{bmatrix}.$$

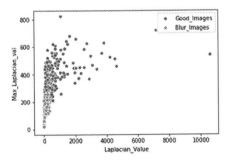

Fig. 4. Scattered plot of laplacian value of good and blur images

By using Laplacian function we have extracted two features of an image i.e., laplacian value and max laplacian value and the above scattered graph shows the features of both good and blur images of the training data set taking laplacian values on x-axis and max-laplacian values on y-axis.The blue coloured dots in the graph represents good images and the orange dots represents the blur images.

Image Hashing. The way towards inspecting the constituents of an image assembling, a value of hash that specially recognizes an input image drew on the constituents of an image.

Hash Algorithm MD5. A few duplicates can also be in any series of digital images, and consequently the time and vitality spent on labelling the similar records (or the dangers identified with part record-keeping) focuses on this for any computerized resource director.

Duplicate records not just possess stockpiling, they additionally cause discontinuity in advanced resource the executives frameworks and on record workers. This discontinuity causes a breakdown of record-keeping, and results in metadata records for the indistinguishable substance being entered over and again. As metadata passage is an upscale activity, and reliable record-keeping is one among the centre advantages of computerized resource the executives programming, copy documents must be kept away from. On the off chance that two indistinguishable records are spared with various file-names, they'll actually be tried as copies by viewing the unmistakable document mark, or hash. This can be acquired effectively utilizing MD5 [8, 11] (a check summing tool) or other proportional devices like SHA1 or CRC.

A hash might be a "message digest" of a huge record, prompting a short string which is clear to look over in contrast with the hash of other record. Following is an example of hash how it looks like:

4b62753267da6995182dec1b7ff523a0

It's profoundly impossible that two non-indistinguishable records will have the similar hash despite of the fact that the hash is shorter and littler than the whole record. At that point it gives a simple gratitude to check for the duplication of information. On the off chance that two records have the similar hash, then they're identified as duplicate copies.

In the proposed model, the hash value of an image is calculated using md5 hashing.Then the process checks whether the hash value of an image is coinciding with the other image hash value using a key value. If the hash values are coinciding then those images are said to be duplicate images. Out of them the process keeps only one image in the original good images and remaining copies are in the duplicate images folder.

KNN Algorithm. K Nearest Neighbour is a supervised machine learning algorithm and is a directed AI calculation. For instance it gains from a named preparing set by taking up the preparing data X close by its names y and figures out how to design the data X to its ideal yield y.

The k-NN algorithm is apparently the least difficult or the easiest of the algorithms in machine learning. The model just comprises of the preparation data, i.e., the model essentially learns the whole preparing set and for expectation gives the output as the class with the lion's share in the *k' closest neighbours discover concurring to some separation metric. The working in somewhat more detail is as per the following: After the model has put away the preparation set for expectation, it steps through an examination picture to be anticipated, ascertains the separation to each picture in the preparation set and gets the 'k' preparing pictures nearest to the test picture. It at that point yields the class as per some democratic methodology from the names of these 'k' neighbours, by and large a greater part vote (Fig. 5).

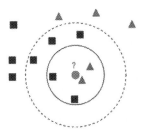

Fig. 5. KNN classification algorithm (source:Google)

The model has two sets of images as good and blur images and are labeled as "1" and "0" respectively. In the above figure let's consider triangles as blur images and squares as good images. Now a new image (circle) comes into where there needs a decision whether it belongs to blur and good. By simply examining the figure the new image can be added to the blur set as those are very near to it this is called simple classification. But according to KNN classification one needs to give weights to all those images in the sets, the images which are near to the new image gets more weight than the image which are at far distance.Then it adds the weights of all those images in the two sets such that the image goes into the set with higher weight.

4   Results and Discussion

The proposed method works effectively with 94% accuracy. Initially, the process results with the threshold value of laplacian's variance, if the laplacian's variance of an image is more than the threshold value of laplacian then those images are considered as good images and else if less than the threshold value of laplacian then those images are considered as blur images.

The following screenshots from the results of the method is the proof towards the effectiveness of the process (Figs. 6 and 7).

As noted earlier, this process uses KNN algorithm for the classification of blur and good images after checking with the other algorithms like SVM algorithm, Decision trees, Logistic Regression LR etc. The following tables show the training and the testing score of images using different algorithms, other metric values of blur and good images respectively (Tables 1 and 2).

Fig. 6. Blur images from the classification model

Fig. 7. Good images from the classification model.

Table 1. Train and test score of images using different algorithms

Algorithm	Train score	Test score	Accuracy
KNN algorithm	0.9454	0.9421	94%
Decision Trees	1	9.0	80%
SVM algorithm	0.9354	0.9364	92.5%
Logistic regression	0.9330	0.9360	92%

Table 2. Metric scores of blur and good images using different algorithms

Algorithm	Blur & good images	Precision	Recall	F1-score	Support
KNN algorithm	0	0.94	0.91	0.93	70
	1	0.94	0.96	0.95	103
Decision Trees	0	0.88	0.87	0.88	70
	1	0.91	0.92	0.92	103
SVM algorithm	0	0.95	0.89	0.92	70
	1	0.93	0.97	0.95	103
Logistic regression	0	0.95	0.89	0.92	70
	1	0.93	0.97	0.95	103

With the assistance of real time dataset the method is tested to test whether it performs correctly or not and located out that the method is functioning accurately as per the knowledge. The method initially creates four folders automatically such as: blur photos, good photos, duplicate photos, original good photos as the subfolders of its parent folder. Then the blur photos are extracted into its respective folder and remaining photos are stored in good photos. Secondly the duplicate photos are identified using hashing function and are stored into duplicate photo folder, and then the left-over images are now original good photos with none duplicate, blur photos. Finally the original good images are automatically converted into video using windows media player (Figs. 8 and 9).

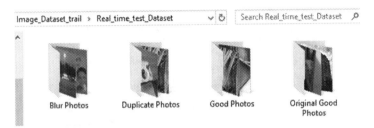

Fig. 8. Automatically created folders with respective images

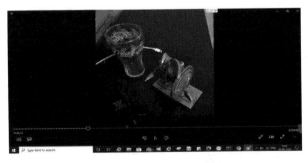

Fig. 9. Video of original good images

The above two figures will show the proof of the results such as screenshot of automatically created folders with classified images and a video playing of original good images.

5   Conclusion and Future Work

The proposed model in this paper is a replacement methodology for the identification of de-focused blur images and duplicate images using Laplacian transform, KNN algorithm and hashing function respectively in Machine Learning. It also classifies the images into good, blur and duplicate images from a folder a folder of images in any storage device. The newly proposed methodology automatically creates separate folders for those classified images and stores them respectively. This methodology is a sequential process as initially it identifies the blur images and classifies them into blur, good images. Then followed by the identification of duplicate images from those good images and classify them into duplicate, original good images.Now,original images are the images with none duplicate and blur images. Finally there carries four folders like good images, blur images, duplicate images and original good images. The methodology also creates a video of those classified original good images automatically using MX windows players which is additionally highlighted automatically once the strategy is finished completely. The purpose of the proposed work can be applied in many real time applications like an album of wedding ceremony, any photo shoot album and also the images captured in a mobile to get only quality images with non repeated one. This process saves time for the users as both duplicate and blur are identified and moved to their folders automatically. And in some cases even if they need blur copies they can recheck their blur photos folder to get it back else if they don't need any blurred ones or duplicate ones then they can delete the complete folder to save space in their devices.

In future this model can be extended by the usage of two or more algorithms which then called as Hybrid Method to identify differing kinds of blur images along with labelling the type of blur. By using still larger datasets one can extend it by using Deep Learning techniques also.

References

1. Sharma, A., Shukla, D.: A novel approach for the detection of blur using SVM and KNN classification techniques in image processing. Int. J. Adv. Technol. Eng. Sci. **4** (2016)
2. Hsu, P., Chen, B.-Y.: Blurred image detection and classification. National Taiwan University. vivace@cmlab.csie.ntu.edu.tw
3. Kim, S., Wang, X.-J., Zhang, L., Choi, S.: Near duplicate image discovery on one billion images (2015)
4. Zhang, S., Shen, X., Lin, Z., Mech, R.: Learning to understand image blur. In: IEEE/CVF Conference on Computer Vision and Pattern Recognition (2018)
5. Hsieh, S.-L., Chen, C.-R.: A duplicate image detection scheme using hash functions for database retrieval. In: IEEE International Conference on Systems, Man and Cybernetics (2010)
6. Landge, R.Y., Sharma, R.: Blur detection methods for digital images-a survey. Int. J. Comput. Appl. Technol. Res. 2(4), 495–498 (2013). https://doi.org/10.7753/IJCATR0204.1019
7. Bansal, R., Raj, G., Choudhury, T.: Blur image detection using laplacian operator and open-CV. In: Proceedings of the SMART - 2016, 5th International Conference on System Modeling & Advancement in Research Trends, 25th–27th November (2016)
8. Legendre, F., Dequen, G., Krajecki, M.: From a logical approach to internal states of hash functions - how sat problem can help to understand SHA-* and MD*. In: Proceedings of the 10th International Conference on Security and Cryptography (SECRYPT), vol. 1, pp. 435–443 (2013)
9. Tong, H., Li, M., Zhang, H.: Blur detection for digital images using wavelet transform. In: IEEE International Conference on Multimedia and Expo (ICME), vol. 1 (2004)
10. Kumar, S.K., Reddy, P.D.K., Ramesh, G., Maddumala, V.R.: Image transformation technique using steganography methods using LWT technique. Traitement du Signal **36**(3), 233–237 (2019)

11. Ragab, A.H.M., Ismail, N.A., Allah, O.S.F.: An efficient message digest algorithm (MD) for data security. In: Proceedings of IEEE Region 10th International Conference on Electrical and Electronic Technology, TENCON (2001)
12. Ramesh, G., et al.: Detection of plant diseases by analyzing the texture of leaf using ANN classifier. Int. J. Adv. Sci. Technol. **29**(8s), 1656–1664 (2020)
13. Madhavi, K., Ramesh, G., Lavanya, G.: Load effectiveness on coverage-technique for test case prioritization in regression testing. Int. J. Innov. Technol. Exp. Eng. (IJITEE) **8**(7) (2019). ISSN 2278-3075

Transfer Learning to Improve Breast Cancer Detection on Unannotated Screening Mammography

Anand[1], Arun Solanki[1], and Anand Nayyar[2(✉)]

[1] Gautam Buddha University, Greater Noida, India
asolanki@gbu.ac.in
[2] Duy Tan University, Da Nang, Vietnam
anandnayyar@duytan.edu.vn

Abstract. Breast cancer ranks in the top half of the division of cancers that prove to be fatal. The early detection of the disease is pivotal for the survival of patients. Recently, advances in deep learning have been used for the detection of breast cancer. These systems are often trained with sizeable medical imaging datasets of screening mammography prepared and annotated by expert radiologists. When developing such models, researchers face difficulty in obtaining the datasets required for training. The study presents a transfer-learning based approach that attempts to address the problems faced by existing breast cancer detection models trained with large annotated screening mammography datasets. Further, these models do not perform well on datasets without such annotations. The study attempts to solve these problems by using a multi-stage approach to train a breast cancer detection model. The initial stage involves training a Convolutional Neural Network (CNN) based model on a large publicly available dataset of annotated breast cancer mammography. The study then uses Transfer Learning to exploit the hierarchical learning properties of CNNs to fine-tune the model on a dataset of unannotated mammograms. An evaluation of the model at detecting breast cancer in unannotated screening mammography resulted in an accuracy of 75% and a reduced false-negative rate, marking an improvement over the benchmarked existing approach. The findings of the study show that transfer learning-based approaches improve the performance of an unannotated screening mammography breast cancer detector. The study also suggests the use of such systems as potential computer-aided diagnosis (CAD) tools.

Keywords: Transfer learning · Deep learning · Convolutional Neural Network · Resnet · Breast cancer screening · Unannotated mammography

1 Introduction

The survival rate for women diagnosed with breast cancer in India is worse than the global average, with 33.9% of women diagnosed with the disease between 2010 and 2014 not surviving [1]. According to the Union Health Ministry, with an incidence rate

© Springer Nature Singapore Pte Ltd. 2021
A. K. Luhach et al. (Eds.): ICAICR 2020, CCIS 1393, pp. 563–576, 2021.
https://doi.org/10.1007/978-981-16-3660-8_53

as high as 258 per million women and a mortality rate of 127 per million women, breast cancer ranks as the most widespread cancer among women in the country. A majority of fatal cases would have been preventable with early detection of the disease. In addition to a lack of awareness of early signs of breast cancer, the unavailability of diagnostic centres and proper screening methods along with a lack of qualified radiologists in tier two and tier three cities are significant reasons for the late diagnosis in most cases. With the increased prevalence of machine learning [2–6] and deep learning [7–11] in the past decade, there has been widespread application of the techniques to medical imaging problems. Application of novel deep learning techniques to medical imaging can increase the accuracy of cancer detection in screening methods, and the development of computer-aided diagnosis systems that combine machine learning methods and medical imaging problems is a very active field of research. Most existing deep learning literature with application to breast cancer detection involves training a CNN to detect cancerous masses in screening mammography by classifying labelled masses in them as malignant or benign. Since training a CNN requires a lot of examples of labelled images, most existing systems are trained with large datasets containing annotated Regions of Interest (ROI). AlexNet, a CNN that spurred deep learning research by performing at near-human levels at the ImageNet classification challenge in 2012, was trained using 1.2 million images [12]. Medical imaging datasets are often short of such requirements as mammograms are difficult to obtain, anonymise, and there is a scarcity of true positives in the datasets. Expert labelling of regions of interest (ROI) is expensive. Additionally, such systems have low performance when used with unannotated mammography, which is common in everyday diagnostic settings. The study aims to create an improved CNN based classifier model for breast cancer classification on unannotated screening mammography, i.e. datasets without ROI information using the technique of transfer learning. The problems identified by the study are:

- A lack of annotated breast cancer screening mammography datasets.
- A lack of deep learning-based breast cancer detection systems for use with unannotated screening mammography.

The concept of Transfer Learning is a technique that can help train neural networks in a computationally efficient manner. Transfer learning or fine-tuning exploits the phenomenon where the first few layers of a CNN are general, i.e. they learn features that are general to a task and this knowledge is extended to specific use cases by training the last few layers on another dataset. Transfer learning or fine-tuning is a machine learning method where models developed for a specific task are used as a point of initialisation for training another model that performs a second task. In practice, transfer learning yields results only if the original task and target task are somewhat related. For example, models pre-trained on the ImageNet dataset are often used as an inception point for models that perform similar classification tasks in computer vision. Transfer learning enables the low-level feature knowledge learnt by a model trained for solving one problem to be reused to solve other related problems. The study leverages this technique, and its main contribution is:

- The development of an unannotated mammography breast cancer detector. The study has achieved this by using transfer learning to utilise the information learned from an annotated screening mammography dataset.

2 Research Paper Organisation

The study is organised into multiple parts, and part I is the introduction which gives a brief overview of the motivation of the study, computer-aided diagnostic systems utilising deep learning and the current state of affairs of medical imaging research. Part II contains the details of the organisation of the study, whereas part III is a thorough discussion of the related work carried out by other researches and authors. Part IV is an explanation of the choice of datasets and the pre-processing steps required before using the data with the proposed model. Part V is a discussion of the CNN used in the system along with the associated characteristics of the chosen model. Part VI lays out the training strategy used for the model, and part VII is a thorough discussion of the obtained results and their significance. Part VIII concludes the findings of the study and part IX discussed some of the limitations and the future scope of the study.

3 Literature Review

This study deals with the application of transfer learning-based deep learning for breast cancer detection in unannotated screening mammography; some researchers have applied similar techniques to detect breast cancer in histology images [13–17]. Acquiring and preparing histology images is difficult due to the specialised sample preparation procedure [18, 19], and as such, the study has focused only on breast cancer detection on screening mammography. Traditionally multi-stage breast cancer detection for screening mammograms using deep learning is done in three stages: detection, analysis, and final assessment/management. The first stage focuses on segmenting the foreground from the background, whereas the second stage focuses on extracting ROIs. The final stage examines these ROIs in detail for a final determination of the presence of malignancy in them. Most of the advances discussed here have focussed on applying deep learning to mass detection where a DNN is used to verify whether a small patch or ROI has a mass in it [20–22]. Most approaches deal with directly classifying masses as benign or malignant. These studies expect that an annotated source of screening mammograms exist [23–26]. Some researchers have tried to combine both the stages [27] and have proposed methods where the mass detection and classification are performed in sequence, forming an end-to-end approach. However, all these state-of-the-art systems are dependent on the performance of the segmentation network and do not provide satisfactory performance on unannotated screening mammography. The reconstruction of such images using generative models [28–31] have been researched but have not resulted in satisfactory performance or are computationally expensive. Another limitation of these studies has been the fact that they have used relatively small datasets for the training of the models. An analysis of the existing studies show that most researchers have focused on training deep learning systems with ROIs or patches from annotated datasets, i.e. assumed that the detected masses are available as input. The various studies have used a combination of pre-processing techniques along with different deep learning architectural advances to incrementally improve the performance of the models at breast cancer detection. However, very few studies have focused on the performance of the models on unannotated screening mammography.

4 Data

A common technique used for timely detection of breast cancer is Screening Mammography. The method involves examining the human breast by taking low energy X-ray images (see Fig. 1) and finding masses or abnormal regions in them. The technique requires trained radiologists to find and label such abnormalities, and the interpretation of the results is often challenging [32].

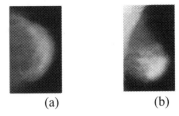

(a)   (b)

Fig. 1. A screening Mammogram in (a) craniocaudal (CC) and (b) mediolateral oblique (MLO) view.

In existing CAD systems, mammography images have been used to extract features and train deep CNN models to perform breast cancer classification. A region of interest (ROI) in medical imaging is any region that is of interest to a pathologist when looking for evidence of disease. The ROIs, in the case of screening mammography, are labelled by radiologists and denote the presence of abnormal tissues. A mammogram with annotated ROI (see Fig. 2) may identify the boundary of a tumour, measure its size, and examine the spread of cancer.

Fig. 2. A Mammogram with ROI labelled showing cancerous tissues.

Since the study uses a two-stage approach to train the model, it is necessary to use two different datasets, an annotated dataset, and an unannotated dataset.

4.1 CBIS –DDSM – Annotated Dataset

The DDSM (Digital Database for Screening Mammography) [33], is a dataset of 2,620 mammograms; digitised using industrial scanners. The images included in the dataset are digitised lossless JPEG images. The study uses the DDSM dataset as it is a large, high quality, publicly available dataset that contains pixel-level annotations or ROI information as verified by pathologists. The study has an accompanying pathological report that labels each mammogram as normal or in the presence of masses, as benign or malignant.

To be specific, the study uses a modernised subset of the DDSM dataset called CBIS-DDSM (Curated Breast Imaging Subset of the Digital Database for Screening Mammography) [34] that is carefully curated by a mammographer to improve the data imbalance of positive and negative cases. The lossless JPEG format that the images are in the original dataset caused problems with newer systems and as such the curated version of the dataset uses the DICOM format. The number of mammography images is slightly lower in comparison. The data has been downloaded from the Cancer Imaging Archive using the NBIA Data Retriever. The pre-processing tasks performed on the mammograms in the dataset included:

Conversion to PNG Format. The Mammograms have been converted into the PNG format from DICOM for model compatibility.

Cropping and Resizing of Mammograms. The Mammograms were cropped around the ROI information as specified in the dataset (see Fig. 3). The cropping highlights the regions with the masses and helps to train the model to be able to identify and classify cancerous tissues accurately. The study resized the mammograms to a resolution of 224 × 224.

Labelling of Images. The mammograms with ROI were labelled as 0 - benign (non-cancerous) or 1 - malignant (cancerous) as shown in Fig. 3, as per the accompanying pathological report.

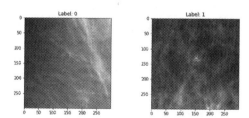

Fig. 3. Mammograms from CBIS-DDSM cropped around ROI with label information used for training.

Data Balance and Train – Test Splitting. In the CBIS-DDSM only a small proportion of the mammograms are cancerous or abnormal. The final divisions were 80:20 for the train and test set. The split of images in the train and test sets is 2068 and 516 images respectively.

4.2 INbreast – Unannotated Dataset

INbreast [35] is a dataset containing 410 mammogram images from 115 cases of women affected with breast cancer. The small full-field digital mammography (FFDM) dataset was created with the intent of being used in (CAD) systems. Although the dataset contains annotations for the mammograms, the study has chosen to ignore them to check the performance of the model after transfer learning on unannotated datasets. The dataset contains the results of the cancer biopsies in accordance to the Breast Imaging Reporting and Data System (BI-RADS). The results need to be mapped before being used to train the model. The mammograms in the dataset are entirely digital and stored in the medical standard DICOM format. Since INbreast is a modern FFDM dataset created with the intent of being used with CAD systems, it is relatively easy to pre-process the mammograms:

Conversion to PNG Format. Systems compatibility dictates the conversion of the mammograms into the PNG format.

Resizing of Mammograms. The mammograms have been resized to a resolution of 224*224 for compatibility with the input layer of the pre-trained model.

Labelling of Images. The images are labelled as 0 - benign or 1 - malignant according to the accompanying BIRADS pathological report, as discussed in Table 1.

Train – Test Split. The 410 images in INbreast were divided into 80:20 for the train and test set. The final split was 326 and 82 images in the train and test set respectively.

Table 1. BIRADS classification of mammogram screenings and mapped model labels.

BIRADS category	Description	Model label
0	Incomplete	0
1	Negative	0
2	Benign findings	0
3	Probably benign	0
4	Suspicious abnormality	1
5	Highly suspicious of malignancy	1
6	Known biopsy with proven malignancy	1

5 Model Design

The model proposed by the study first utilises a fully annotated dataset to train a CNN based deep learning model to recognise annotated ROIs. After that, the model is converted into a general-purpose mammogram classifier, i.e. unannotated screening mammography classifier. This is achieved by further training the model on datasets without

ROI annotations (or unannotated datasets) using Transfer Learning. The overall architecture of the model is divided between the annotated dataset and unannotated dataset modules (see Fig. 4).

The study has opted to use a CNN as the base network of the model. The excellent performance of CNNs on computer vision tasks justifies this choice. CNN is a deep learning network that adds Convolutional layers or filters on top of artificial neural networks to identify the spatial patterns contained in the data. CNNs also reduce the dimensions of the feature maps at each successive stage or layer, which leads to an overall reduction in the number of parameters in the system. There are multiple popular CNN architectures. A thorough analysis of some of these networks has been carried out in [36].

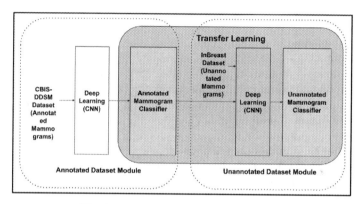

Fig. 4. The architecture of proposed work.

5.1 Residual Network–50

The Residual 50 network (ResNet-50) is the base network in this study. Resnet has been found to have higher accuracy when compared to similar deep learning architectures in computer vision tasks and can help overcome problems faced by very deep neural networks [37]. The details of the network (see Fig. 6) and the various blocks follow.

ResNet Blocks. The design of ResNet consists of stacking multiple 'building blocks' of consecutive layers that lead to a size-reduction of the feature map between them. The used block has a design which uses three Convolutional layers (see Fig. 5). Such blocks are repeated K number of times in a ResNet based network design. A convolution function stride of two is often used in the first Convolutional layer in a block to reduce the feature map size.

To be more specific, the "bottleneck design" of Resnet, shown in Fig. 5, has been used in this study. GPU resources are preserved by performing the expensive 3 × 3 operations less frequently in the block. The 4-Resnet blocks are repeated multiple times and make up the complete Resnet 50 network shown in Fig. 6.

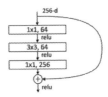

Fig. 5. Residual Network Bottleneck building block featuring 'shortcut' design.

ResNet Shortcut Design. Another essential characteristic of the ResNet block is the 'shortcut' design [38], shown using the long skip-connection between the ends of the block in Fig. 5. This 'skip-connection' helps carry over the weights of the network between the blocks skipping over some intermediate blocks.

The connection helps each unit to focus on identifying the information contained in the feature maps without common problems associated with deep neural networks such as the vanishing and exploding gradients. The shortcut design of the Resnet block overcomes the vanishing gradient problem of deep neural networks during the backprop-agation stage where the weights of the deeper layers of deep neural networks saturate and performance degrades at a point due to the gradients becoming too small to update the weights of the initial layers.

Flatten ResNet 50 Output. The final Resnet block produces an output in the form of a feature map of 256-dimension. The last block is connected to the dense or fully connected layers, and care is taken to flatten the output of the last block before being passed forward to these dense layers.

Fully Connected Layers and Output Classification. Classification of entire mam-mograms using the network involves flattening the output of the preceding layers and passing it through a SoftMax activation function. The SoftMax function outputs the probabilities for the two labels, benign or malignant (see Fig. 6).

6   Training the Model

Training the model proposed in this study has two parts. The first part is to train the discussed network on the CBIS-DDSM dataset with ROI. The second part of training utilises transfer learning to fine-tune the same model with a customised training routine on the unannotated INbreast dataset. The Training strategies and parameters used in both cases follow.

6.1   Training on CBIS-DDSM Annotated Dataset

The CBIS-DDSM has been split into train and test sets in the proportion 80:20. Adam [39] or adaptive motion optimiser is used as it provides a relative speed-up compared to simple stochastic gradient descent-based methods, while the learning rate has been left at the default value of 1e–3 along with a suitable loss function for binary classification;

the Binary cross-entropy loss function. Keeping in mind the GPU memory limitations when training a complex network with high-resolution images, the maximum batch size is set to 32, and the network is trained for 50 epochs.

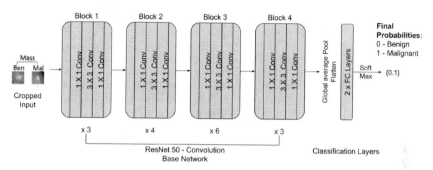

Fig. 6. Complete Resnet 50 based network architecture of the model.

6.2 Transfer Learning on Unannotated INbreast

The second part of training in this study fine-tunes the model using transfer learning on the unannotated INbreast dataset. The strategy used for transfer learning involves splitting the training into parts and only training particular layers at a time. The INbreast dataset was split 80:20 between training and testing sets. Binary cross-entropy is used as the loss function again as the objective of the optimisation is the same, however with an increased batch size of 64. The same optimiser, Adam is used due to the merits discussed above and also to keep variation in the two stages of training to a minimum. The learning schedule is set according to the following strategy:

The model was initialised with the weights of the model trained in section A. This weight-initialisation technique helps prevent the loss of the information contained in them, and a 2-stage [40] training approach was used:

- All layers except the top 4 were 'Frozen', i.e. their weights were not updated. The network was trained initially for 10 epochs with a substantially lowered learning rate of 10^{-4}; this is done in the interest of updating the weights of the model gradually and not to cause large perturbations.
- With all the layers unfrozen, training was continued for a further 40 epochs with a further reduced learning rate of 10^{-5}.

7 Results

The training–validation accuracy graphs (see Graph 1) and training summary table (see Table 2) for both the stages of training are presented in this section.

The model trained without transfer learning is referred to as the existing work or base model in this section, and the proposed model or fine-tuned model is the model

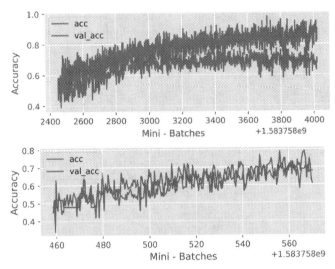

Graph 1. Accuracy of the model, on top – Annotated CBIS-DDSM and bottom – Unannotated INbreast.

Table 2. The validation-set accuracy of the models for the training stages.

MODEL	TRANSFER LEARNING	DATASET	ACCURACY	#OF EPOCHS
ResNet50	N	CBIS-DDSM	90%	50
ResNet50	N	INbreast	55%	50
ResNet50	Y	INbreast	75%	50

trained with transfer learning. Figure 7 shows the predicted probabilities of the presence of benign and malignant masses in unannotated screening mammography made by the two models on a small validation set of mammograms from the INbreast dataset (see Graph 2).

Analysing the results the predictions can be grouped into the following. For most benign samples, the new model is more confident at correctly predicting benign masses, and the probability of a false positive is also low. For samples where both the models make incorrect predictions and miss the cancerous masses, the new model is now less confident of the wrong prediction, i.e. the probability of a false negative is lower, which is a crucial metric for a breast cancer detection system. The prediction for sample 7, 12 is of great interest as the new model can predict malignancy with reasonable confidence even when the previous model missed it completely. This result shows that the proposed model is even able to correct false negatives for some of the samples, which is vital as the model should not miss actual cases of malignancy or cancer in the screening mammography. At no point is the model observed to be making worse predictions than the existing model.

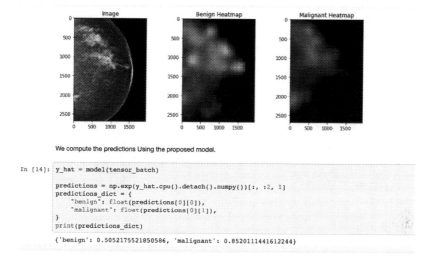

We compute the predictions Using the proposed model.

```
In [14]:  y_hat = model(tensor_batch)

          predictions = np.exp(y_hat.cpu().detach().numpy())[:, :2, 1]
          predictions_dict = {
              "benign": float(predictions[0][0]),
              "malignant": float(predictions[0][1]),
          }
          print(predictions_dict)

          {'benign': 0.5052175521850586, 'malignant': 0.8520111441612244}
```

Fig. 7. Output predictions (probabilities) for the presence of benign and malignant calcifications or masses in mammograms made by the proposed model.

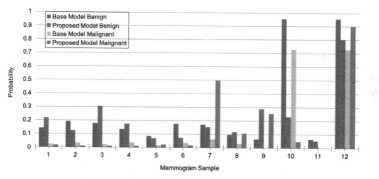

Graph 2. Output predictions (probabilities) for the presence of benign and malignant calcifications or masses in mammograms made by the two models.

8 Discussion and Conclusion

The study shows that transfer learning is a viable approach for training or fine-tuning models on smaller unannotated datasets to create new models that perform significantly better on unannotated datasets. The study has shown that a model trained on an annotated mammography dataset is not able to perform well on other datasets without such annotations. This lack of performance on unannotated mammography is a practical problem as well-annotated mammography datasets do not exist in many hospitals or regions of the world.

An analysis of the predictions shows that the model trained with transfer learning is generally able to make predictions with higher confidence. The model corrects the incorrect predictions made by the existing model for a few samples indicating greater accuracy at identifying and prediction of breast cancer in unannotated mammography and lower probability of false negatives. This result is significant as it validates the claims of the study that transfer learning improves breast cancer detection in unannotated screening mammography. These models can be trained for shorter periods, and reduce the reliance of CAD systems on annotated datasets.

9   Future Work

The results of the training on CBIS-DDSM (see Fig. 7, top) show that the model begins to overfit on the dataset while training. It could be possible to reduce this overfitting by using regularisation techniques. The training on INbreast (see Fig. 7, bottom) show that the training and validation loss are still close for the model, this may indicate that with more complex models it could be possible to refine further the system leading to greater accuracy on unannotated mammography breast cancer detection.

References

1. Agarwal, G., Ramakant, P.: Breast cancer care in India: the current scenario and the challenges for the future. Breast care **3**(1), 21–27 (2008)
2. Pandey, S., Solanki, A.: Music instrument recognition using deep convolutional neural networks. Int. J. Inf. Technol. **13**(3), 129–149 (2019)
3. Agarwal, A., Solanki, A.: An improved data clustering algorithm for outlier detection. Self-organology **3**(4), 121–139 (2016)
4. Rajput, R., Solanki, A.: Review of sentimental analysis methods using lexicon based approach. Int. J. Comput. Sci. Mob. Comput. **5**(2), 159–166 (2016)
5. Kaur, N., Solanki, A.: Sentiment knowledge discovery in twitter using CoreNLP library. In: 8th International Conference on Cloud Computing, Data Science and Engineering (Confluence), vol. 345, no. 32, pp. 2342–2358 (2018)
6. Rajput, R., Solanki, A.: Real-time analysis of tweets using machine learning and semantic analysis. In: International Conference on Communication and Computing Systems (ICCCS-2016), Taylor and Francis, at Dronacharya College of Engineering, Gurgaon, 9–11 September, vol. 138, no. 25, pp. 687–692 (2016)
7. Ahuja, R., Solanki, A.: Movie recommender system using K-means clustering and K-nearest neighbor. In: Accepted for Publication in Confluence-2019: 9th International Conference on Cloud Computing, Data Science and Engineering, Amity University, Noida, vol. 1231, no. 21, pp. 25–38 (2019)
8. Priyadarshni, V., Nayyar, A., Solanki, A., Anuragi, A.: Human age classification system using K-NN classifier. In: Luhach, A.K., Jat, D.S., Hawari, K.B.G., Gao, X.-Z., Lingras, P. (eds.) Advanced Informatics for Computing Research. CCIS, vol. 1075, pp. 294–311. Springer, Singapore (2019). https://doi.org/10.1007/978-981-15-0108-1_28
9. Singh, T., Nayyar, A., Solanki, A.: Multilingual opinion mining movie recommendation system using RNN. In: Singh, P.K., Pawłowski, W., Tanwar, S., Kumar, N., Rodrigues, J.J.P.C., Obaidat, M.S. (eds.) Proceedings of First International Conference on Computing, Communications, and Cyber-Security (IC4S 2019). LNNS, vol. 121, pp. 589–605. Springer, Singapore (2020). https://doi.org/10.1007/978-981-15-3369-3_44
10. Singh, G., Solanki, A.: An algorithm to transform natural language into SQL queries for relational databases. Selforganizology **3**(3), 100–116 (2016)

11. Tayal, A., Köse, U., Solanki, A., Nayyar, A., ve Marmolejo Saucedo, J.A.: Efficiency analysis for stochastic dynamic facility layout problem using meta-heuristic, data envelopment analysis and machine learning. Comput. Intell. **36**(1), 172–202 (2019)

12. Krizhevsky, A., Sutskever, I., Hinton, G.: ImageNet classification with deep convolutional neural networks. Neural Inf. Process. Syst. **25**, 1097–1105 (2012)

13. Jiang, Y., Chen, L., Zhang, H., Xiao, X.: Breast cancer histopathological image classification using convolutional neural networks with small SE-ResNet module. PLoS ONE **14**(3), e0214587 (2019)

14. Cireşan, D.C., Giusti, A., Gambardella, L.M., Schmidhuber, J.: Mitosis detection in breast cancer histology images with deep neural networks. In: Mori, K., Sakuma, I., Sato, Y., Barillot, C., Navab, N. (eds.) Medical Image Computing and Computer-Assisted Intervention – MICCAI 2013. LNCS, vol. 8150, pp. 411–418. Springer, Heidelberg (2013). https://doi.org/10.1007/978-3-642-40763-5_51

15. Cruz-Roa, A., et al.: Automatic detection of invasive ductal carcinoma in whole slide images with convolutional neural networks. In: Medical Imaging, 2014: Digital Pathology, p. 904103 (2014)

16. Araújo, T., et al.: Classification of breast cancer histology images using convolutional neural networks. PLoS ONE **12**(6), e0177544 (2017)

17. Rakhlin, A., Shvets, A., Iglovikov, V., Kalinin, A.A.: Deep convolutional neural networks for breast cancer histology image analysis. In: Campilho, A., Karray, F., ter Haar Romeny, B. (eds.) Image Analysis and Recognition. LNCS, vol. 10882, pp. 737–744. Springer, Cham (2018). https://doi.org/10.1007/978-3-319-93000-8_83

18. Sarmiento, A., Fondón, I.: Automatic breast cancer grading of histological images based on colour and texture descriptors. In: Campilho, A., Karray, F., ter Haar Romeny, B. (eds.) Image Analysis and Recognition. LNCS, vol. 10882, pp. 887–894. Springer, Cham (2018). https://doi.org/10.1007/978-3-319-93000-8_101

19. Vahadane, A., et al.: Structure-preserved color normalization for histological images. In: 2015 IEEE 12th International Symposium on Biomedical Imaging (ISBI), pp. 1012–1015 (2015)

20. Domingues, I., Cardoso, J.S.: Mass detection on mammogram images: a first assessment of deep learning techniques (2013)

21. Dhungel, N., Carneiro, G., Bradley, A.P.: Automated mass detection in mammograms using cascaded deep learning and random forests. In: 2015 International Conference on Digital Image Computing: Techniques and Applications (DICTA), pp. 1–8 (2015)

22. Ertosun, M.G., Rubin, D.L.: Probabilistic visual search for masses within mammography images using deep learning. In: 2015 IEEE International Conference on Bioinformatics and Biomedicine (BIBM), pp. 1310–1315 (2015)

23. Huynh, B.Q., Li, H., Giger, M.L.: Digital mammographic tumor classification using transfer learning from deep convolutional neural networks. J. Med. Imaging. **3**(3), 034501 (2016)

24. Levy, D., Jain, A.: Breast mass classification from mammograms using deep convolutional neural networks (2016)

25. Arevalo, J., González, F.A., Ramos-Pollán, R., Oliveira, J.L., Lopez, M.A.G.: Representation learning for mammography mass lesion classification with convolutional neural networks. Comput. Methods Programs Biomed. **127**, 248–257 (2016)

26. Mordang, J.-J., Janssen, T., Bria, A., Kooi, T., Gubern-Mérida, A., Karssemeijer, N.: Automatic microcalcification detection in multi-vendor mammography using convolutional neural networks. In: Tingberg, A., Lång, K., Timberg, P. (eds.) Breast Imaging. LNCS, vol. 9699, pp. 35–42. Springer, Cham (2016). https://doi.org/10.1007/978-3-319-41546-8_5

27. Akselrod-Ballin, A., et al.: Predicting breast cancer by applying deep learning to linked health records and mammograms. Radiology **292**(2), 331–342 (2019)

28. Eo, T., Jun, Y., Kim, T., Jang, J., Lee, H.-J., Hwang, D.: KIKI-net: cross-domain convolutional neural networks for reconstructing undersampled magnetic resonance images. Magn. Reson. Med. **80**, 2188–2201 (2018)

29. Han, Y., Yoo, J., Kim, H.H., Shin, H.J., Sung, K., Ye, J.C.: Deep learning with domain adaptation for accelerated projection-reconstruction MR. Magn. Reson. Med. **80**, 1189–1205 (2018)

30. Shi, J., Liu, Q., Wang, C., Zhang, Q., Ying, S., Xu, H.: Super-resolution reconstruction of MR image with a novel residual learning network algorithm. Phys. Med. Biol. **63**, 085011 (2018)

31. Yang, G., Yu, S., Dong, H., Slabaugh, G., Dragotti, P.L., Ye, X.: DAGAN: deep de-aliasing generative adversarial networks for fast compressed sensing MRI reconstruction. IEEE Trans. Med. Imaging **37**, 1310–1321 (2018)

32. Barlow, W.E., et al.: Accuracy of screening Mammography interpretation by characteristics of radiologists. J. Natl. Cancer Inst. **96**(24), 1840–1850 (2004)

33. Heath, M., Bowyer, K., Kopans, D., Moore, R., Philip Kegelmeyer, W.: The digital database for screening Mammography. In: Yaffe, M.J. (ed.) Proceedings of the Fifth International Workshop on Digital Mammography, pp.212–218. Medical Physics Publishing (2001)

34. Lee, R.S., Gimenez, F., Hoogi, A., Miyake, K.K., Gorovoy, M., Rubin, D.L.: A curated Mammography data set for use in computer-aided detection and diagnosis research. Sci. Data. **4**(1), 1–9 (2017)

35. Moreira, I.C., Amaral, I., Domingues, I., Cardoso, A., Cardoso, M.J., Cardoso, J.S.: INbreast. Acad. Radiol. **19**(2), 236–248 (2012)

36. Alom, M.Z., et al.: A state-of-the-art survey on deep learning theory and architectures. Electronics **8**(3), 292 (2019)

37. He, K., Zhang, X., Ren, S., Sun, J.: Deep residual learning for image recognition. In: 2016 IEEE Conference on Computer Vision and Pattern Recognition (CVPR), pp. 770–778 (2016)

38. He, K., Zhang, X., Ren, S., Sun, J.: Identity mappings in deep residual networks. In: Leibe, B., Matas, J., Sebe, N., Welling, M. (eds.) Computer Vision – ECCV 2016. LNCS, vol. 9908, pp. 630–645. Springer, Cham (2016). https://doi.org/10.1007/978-3-319-46493-0_38

39. S. Ruder.: An overview of gradient descent optimisation algorithms (2016)

40. Li, J., Wu, W., Xue, D., Gao, P.: Multi-source deep transfer neural network algorithm. Sensors **19**(18), 3992 (2019)

Fatty Liver Disease Prediction Using Supervised Learning

Vala Harshitha Rao[✉], Dheeraj Sundaragiri, and Prasanta Kumar Sahoo

CSE Department, Sreenidhi Institute of Science and Technology, Hyderabad, Telangana, India
{dheerajs,prasantakumars}@sreenidhi.edu.in

Abstract. Fatty liver disease is one of the most common types of liver disease in the modern period. It is one of the most important human diseases and has a very serious impact on human life. Hepatic disease is also known as liver disease. It damages the liver. Some symptoms of liver disease may include jaundice and weight loss, and there are some different forms of liver disease. There are two different kind of liver diseases. They are alcoholic fatty liver disease it develops who consume lot of alcohol, it damages our liver. It leads to cirrhosis. Non alcohol fatty liver is common causes of liver disease in the world. They accumulate fat within liver. So, early prediction of liver disease can save human life. Data mining became an easy for liver disease prediction. The research may be done to predict the liver disease has very challenging task, it calculated from of medical data bases. To overcome this research data mining techniques are used such as classification, regression problems. The patient risk level is classified used data mining techniques. It predicts the liver disease accurately and efficiently.

Keywords: Liver disease · Data mining · Prediction · Classification regression algorithms

1 Introduction

The very first stage of damaged liver is an inflamation. Excessive fat in the liver is known as fatty liver. If we uncheck inflammation it leads to scarring. If scar tissue over time in the liver it lead to liver fibrosis. Gradually increasing of fat in hard scar tissue in the liver continuosly cause cirhosis. The final stage of liver disease is cirrhosis. The liver is an important organ in the body and a second organ. For our body, it has several essential vital organs. The livers main job is filters the blood before passing it to whole body. The blood which comes from digestive track. The role of the liver is it ensure detoxification and metabolizes drugs in our body. Liver secrets bile. It extract nutrients from carbohydrates, lipids, proteins. It stores vitamins and glycogen. It hoards energy in the form of sugar and provides for organism. Liver performs indispensable functions, in our body. Liver keep pure from toxins and other harmful substances. Some important functions of liver are (i) Liver providing energy to our body by the help of storing vitamins iron and sugar. (ii) It removes cholesterol from the body and control the production. (iii) Removing all waste products, such as drugs and other poisonous substances and clears the blood in the body.

© Springer Nature Singapore Pte Ltd. 2021
A. K. Luhach et al. (Eds.): ICAICR 2020, CCIS 1393, pp. 577–587, 2021.
https://doi.org/10.1007/978-981-16-3660-8_54

(iv) After cuts or injuries, it makes clotting factors to stop bleeding. (v) Removes bacteria from bloodstream to combat infection and produce immune factors in body. (vi) Liver secret "bile" it helps in digestive food and absorbing nutrients. Removing all waste products, drugs from removing and filtering harmful substance from the body. Liver doesn't function well it affects whole body. Once degradation begins, it damaged liver in predictable manner. But in today's world liver disease has became the leading cause of death in the world. The main cause of 577 Patients among 377 patients has fatty liver disease [1]. It implemented a feature models for better accuracy for disease prediction. Proposed system concludes PSO feature selection for liver dataset. It predict accuracy in four different phases: patients among 377 patients has fatty liver (i) The liver patient datasets is collected from UCI Repository by applied min max normalization algorithm. (ii) In second phases, from normalized liver patient datasets comprises only significant attributes by the use of PSO feature selection. (iii) In third phases, classification algorithm is applied. (iv) In fourth phase accuracy is calculated [2]. By using machine learning approaches use classification algorithm to identify liver patient based on performance factors.

By using python GUI (graphical user interface) will be developed [3]. Using data mining techniques algorithm is used to increase the accuracy and time. By using genetic algorithm accuracy increased to 93% in work [4]. To develop classification techniques to predict disease 11 algorithms were put it to datasets and compared with the terms of accuracy, precision and recall [5]. Research may be done in various decision tree techniques liver is predicted. The various decision tree techniques such as RF, J48, LMT, RT, decision stump, REPTree and Hoeffiding tree. By analysis of this decision tree techniques decision stump has highest accuracy 70.67%. They want to increase more accuracy furtherly by using decision tree such as CART [6]. Liver disease have became leading cause of death. By using various algorithm such as decision tree, J48, ANN, Navies bayies algorithms to classify the liver disease predictive or descriptive accuracy [7]. By using machine learning it gives improved exactness on discovery of liver disease. Two different algorithms are used for exactness. They are SVM, K_Nearest neighbor [8]. Ultrasound are used for liver applications, the techniques soon it become part in the future armamentarium ultrasound specialist for liver disease [9]. Using medical data mining model has huge amount of data can convert into valuable information. Data mining techniques such as RF, neural network, SVM, Bayesian network and particle PSO_SVM, and PSO_SVM best performance specificity, accuracy, sensitivity, precision, Area under curve, false positive rate and F_measure. PSO_SVM algorithm has highest accuracy [10]. Early prediction of liver disease will save human life. The data mining techniques such as CART and CBR to raise accuracy of liver diagnosis. The CART rate accuracy 92.94%, CBR accuracy rate 90.00% [11]. To evaluate the performance machine learning to reduce high cost of diagnosis by prediction. Using different classification algorithm LR, decision tree, RF, KNN, SVM and navies bayes. Logistic regression achieve high accuracy [12].

STAGES OF LIVER DISEASE:

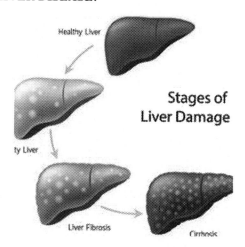

2 Implementation Steps

ALGORITHM

To minimize bias (for example by overfitting), we randomly divided the dataset into training and testing 70% of training and 30% of testing.70% (n = 735) for feature selection and 30% (n = 314) for the model generation (see below).

$$\sum\nolimits_{i=1}^{n} (y_i - \hat{y}_i)^2 + \lambda \times \sum\nolimits_{j=1}^{m} |\beta_j|$$

We used LASSO algorithm. It is one of the regression problem available to analyze the data. LASSO Regression is used for linear regression. Data point shrunk toward central point like mean. The model provide fewer parameters. LASSO encourage sparse model. LASSO Regression can reduce the slope to be exactly equal to zero. It predictors that minimizes prediction error. It gives best accuracy. The cost function is given for LASSO is:

Cost(W) = RSS(W) + α (Sum of squares of weight)

We used python for this project. Python is high level programming language, general purpose, iterative, interpreted and oops. It reduce fewer lines of codes. We used powerful Lasso regression technique. It works magnitude of coefficients of feature with magnitude the error between predicted and actual observations. It is L1 regularization technique. It has minimize cost function is given as Cost(W) = RSS(W) + α(Sum of squares of weight). There are three different cases for values of is α.

1. α = 0; it is a simple linear regression with same coefficient
2. α = ∞ All co-efficient zero
3. 0 < α < ∞ co-efficient between 0

The following code is used for training and prediction through Lasso regression

ALGORITHM STEPS:

1. Lasso regression instantiates the value with alpha of 0.01.
2. The model fits for training the data.
3. Lasso regression predicts the training data.
4. To print MSE, MAE, RMSE, & RSquared on training dataset.
5. Repeat the steps on test dataset (Fig. 1).

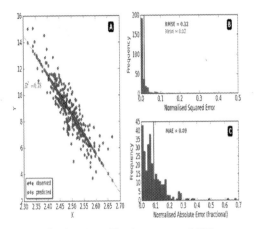

Fig. 1. Mean Absolute error or MSE

DATA SET

In this study, the liver patient dataset is chosen from UCI Repository based on the given liver attributes it predicts the disease. The dataset has 11 attributes it predicts the liver disease and identify the patient result. The dataset is built on real number, categorical, integer types. The dataset consists of 11 characteristics, including age, gender, TB, DB, Alkphos, Sgpt, Sgot, TP, ALB, A/G ratio and class. The attributes age is real number age is one of the essential characteristics for growing the liver disease. Gender is greater risk factor for male 76% patients are affected for liver disease. It denoted by '1'and female 24% patients are affected for liver disease. It denoted by '0'.The class attribute denotes "yes" with Boolean value "1" having liver disease. Class attribute denotes "no" with Boolean value "0" not having liver disease.

DATA PREPROCESSING:

1. Start is initial step to start the project.
2. Data base is collect the data from external source like (kaggle) before providing it to the model.
3. Data preprocessing which is used to transform data into information and efficient format with less effort.
4. Training is used to train an algorithm it minimize the effects of data and later it send to testing it test the model by making predictions.
5. We used Lasso algorithm to predict the liver disease it achieve with more effective and high accuracy.
6. Final step is predicting the disease. If the disease is predict the output will be numerical "1" = yes, disease not predict value is "0" = no.

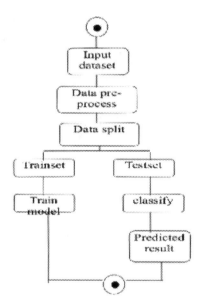

TOOLS AND LANGUAGE:
We use the Jupiter notebook as a tool and python 3.8 as a programming language. Some ML techniques are used for prediction of disease to get the result. Comparing various techniques such as decision tree, hybrid, lasso regression, NN, SVM, and RF finding the best technique to predict the disease.

ANACONDA: Anaconda installed new packages and tools. Install necessary libraries like matplotlib, pandas, numpy, scikit-learn, seaborn, pillow. Python main.py is used to execute the program (Fig. 2, 3, 4, 5, 6, 7, 8).

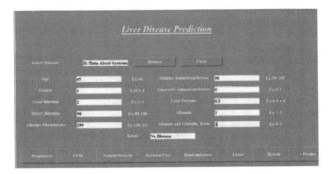

Fig. 2. Implementation

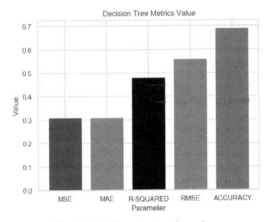

Fig. 3. Decision tree metrics values

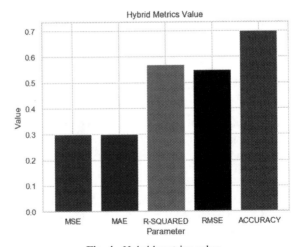

Fig. 4. Hybrid metrics value

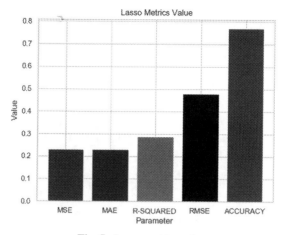

Fig. 5. Lasso metrics value

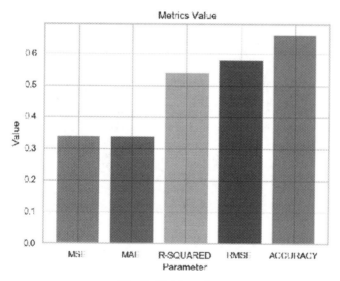

Fig. 6. Metrics value

MSE:

The mean squared error (MSE) compares the original image's "real" pixel values to the degraded image. The MSE is the sum of the squares between the real and the noisy image of the "errors." The error is the sum by which the original image values vary from those of the degraded image. It is portrayed as follows.

$$MSE = \frac{1}{mn} \sum_{0}^{m-1} \sum_{0}^{n-1} \|f(i,j) - g(i,j)\|^2 \tag{1}$$

$$MSE = (1/(m * n)) * \text{sum}(\text{sum}((f - g).^2)) \tag{2}$$

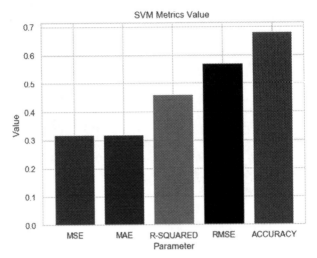

Fig. 7. SVM metrics value

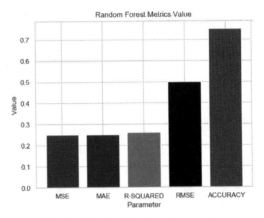

Fig. 8. Random forests metrics value

MAE:

It is the Difference between original and enhanced image is given as

$$MAE = |E(xN) - E(y)| \tag{3}$$

Where E(x)= average intensity of input image E(y)= average intensity of enhanced image. The mean absolute error, where the estimation and the true value are is an average of the absolute errors. Note that alternative formulations can be weight variables that include relative frequencies. The mean absolute error was used on the same scale as the calculated data. This is regarded as a measure of scale-dependent accuracy and can therefore not be used to use various scales to make comparisons between sequences.

R-Squared Parameter:

It takes two measurements that exist in the population of detections, all classes or one as a subset of those detections, and then calculates a best fit line and R-squared value for the resulting data point pairs.

RMSE:

The Root Mean Square Error (RMSE) is given as the MSE square root. This demonstrates that greater image quality is given by a higher PSNR and greater MSE & RMSE value

$$RMSE = \sqrt{MSE} \tag{4}$$

ACCURACY:

Accuracy can be defined as the percentage (TP + TN)/(TP + TN + FP + FN) of correctly classified instances. Where, respectively denote the sum of true positives, false negatives, false positives and true negatives (Fig. 9, 10, 11).

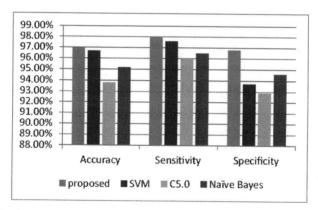

Fig. 9. The overall comparison between SVM, C5.0, and Naïve Bayes.

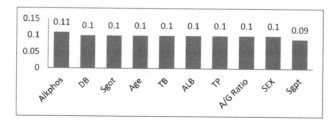

Fig. 10. Prediction of liver disease.

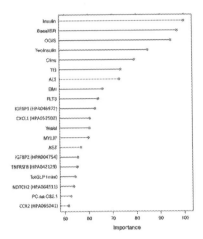

Fig. 11. Variable importance for the advanced model.

3 Results

Image Segmentation Data Set

Data Set Characteristics:	Multivariate	Number of Instances:	2310	Area:	N/A
Attribute Characteristics:	Real	Number of Attributes:	19	Date Donated	1990-11-01
Associated Tasks:	Classification	Missing Values?	No	Number of Web Hits:	206228

4 Conclusion

The proposed system concludes that classification and Regression algorithms are applied for liver disease data set. Researchers have focused to save a human life and predict the liver disease in earlier stage. They used classification and regression algorithms such as decision tree, hybrid, lasso regression, neural network, svm and random forest 69%, 70%, 77%, 66%, 68%, 75% to predict the liver disease. This algorithm gives better results comparing with another algorithms. However in the future, we collect recent data for liver disease with advanced classification and regression techniques to predict the disease.

References

1. Wu, C.C., Yeh, W.C.: Prediction of fatty liver disease using machine learning algorithms. Comput. Methods Programs Biomed. **170**, 23–29 (2019)

2. Banu Priya, M., Laura Juliet, P.: Performance analysis of liver disease prediction using machine learning algorithms. IRJET. **5**(1) (2018)
3. Jacob, J., Chakkalakal Mathew, J.: Diagnosis of liver disease using machine learning techniques. IRJET. **5**(4) (2018)
4. Hassoon, M.: Rule optimization of boosted C5.0 classification using genetic algorithm for liver disease prediction. IEEE (2017)
5. Bahramirad, S., Mustapha, A.: Classification of liver disease diagnosis: a comparative study. IEEE (2013)
6. Nahar, N., Ara, F.: Liver disease prediction by using different decision tree techniques. Int. J. Data Min. Knowl. Manage. Process. **8**(2), 1-9 (2018)
7. Baitharu, T.R., Pani, S.K.: Analysis of data mining techniques for healthcare decision support system using liver disorder dataset. Procedia Comput. Sci. **85**, 862–870 (2016). https://doi.org/10.1016/j.procs.2016.05.276
8. Mehtaj Banu, H.: Liver disease prediction using machine-learning algorithms. Int. J. Eng. Adv. Technol. **8**(6), 1–3 (2019). https://doi.org/10.35940/ijeat.F8365.088619
9. Berzigotti, A., Ferraioli, G.: Novel ultrasound-based methods to assess liver disease: the game has just begun. Dig. Liver Dis. **50**(2), 107–112 (2018). https://doi.org/10.1016/j.dld.2017.11.019
10. Joloudari, J.H.: Computer-aided decision-making for predicting liver disease using PSO-based optimized SVM with feature selection. Inform. Med. Unlocked **17**, 100255 (2019)
11. Lin, R.H.: An intelligent model for liver disease diagnosis. Artif. Intell. Med. **47**(1), 53–62 (2009)
12. Rahman, A.K.M.S.: A comparative study on liver disease prediction using supervised machine learning algorithms. Int. J. Sci. Technol. Res. **8**(11), 419–422 (2019)

LSSA: A Protective Shared Data Communication Mechanism in Cloud Environment

Syed Umar[1](✉), Nilesh Gole[2], Pravin G. Kulurkar[2], Tariku Birhanu Yadesa[1],
and Parmanand Prabhat[2]

[1] Department of Computer Science, Wollega University, Nekemte, Ethiopia
[2] Department of Computer Science and Engineering, Himalayan University, Itanagar,
Arunachal Pradesh, India

Abstract. Users can access shared data warehouses using a cloud infrastructure. It is important to verify the data successfully to ensure mutual data integrity. The accuracy checking of the shared data is carried out by an examination system that encourages Group members to alter data, but this method leads to complicated estimates as per the Group members. The monitoring method of the assigned agent estimates the group members lightly, but lacks the safety threats among the group members and their agents. With the implementation of Hash graph technology and the development of a management Third Party Medium (TPM) approach, a Lightweight Safe Cloud Storage Audition System (LSSA) is suggested, achieving group security protection and a lightweight group measurement. In the meantime, the TCP Sliding Fan Technology incorporates a simulated TPM pool with interconnected features to enhance support for the handler. We test our method in numerical analysis and tests, which prove that our system provides the groups with lightweight computing and ensures the safety data evaluation process.

Keywords: TPM pool · Shared data · Agent security · Lightweight calculation

1 Introduction

Increment of customers' access to a shared pool of networks, software and infrastructures without even needing to demand them from distributed computing is the newest utility-oriented decentralised computing paradigm which has envisaged a massive IT transformation. Cloud computing is divided into three frameworks in the sense of deployment: i) public, ii) private, iii) hybrid, iv) community clouds that are described below:

Public Cloud: Through public cloud computing providers move different applications as a service and enable consumers via access to infrastructure, such as Amazon Web Services, Google App Engine, by concentrating distributed servers over the Internet.

Private Cloud: A success organization requires and manages programmes and structures en.

© Springer Nature Singapore Pte Ltd. 2021
A. K. Luhach et al. (Eds.): ICAICR 2020, CCIS 1393, pp. 588–596, 2021.
https://doi.org/10.1007/978-981-16-3660-8_55

Community Cloud: A collection of organizations that are either supervised personally or by a trustworthy external entity distribute the resources and structure.

Hybrid Cloud: The Hybrid cloud pursues a combination of on-site, proprietary cloud and public cloud third-party providers, in a two-platform structure.

As for the guide and taxonomy design of three service models, i.e. PaaS, SaaS, IaaS, Liu and his colleagues [1] addressed the obstacles to select and improve distributed computing and classes of utility computing and explore their opportunities [2] for selecting and developing them. Buyya and his colleagues [3] suggested a market-oriented cloud asset management system. It offers cluster, grid and cloud features and knowledge of processes for market-driven asset management.

The PaaS system provides designers with runtime requirements, as their individual needs suggest. The PaaS offers the development, delivery and monitoring of the applications through programming framework, libraries and toolboxes. For trading clients, such as S3 (Simple Storage Service) and EC2 (Elastic Cloud Computing), the IaaS provides tracking, repositioning and systems management in a kind of scalable Virtual Machine (VM). Distributed storage offers a cloud storage as a service for the monitoring, monitoring, and remote backup of information that is available via a network to users (usually the Internet). The customer is concerned that the information contained inside the cloud is integral so unauthorized actors can target or change customer information. Therefore, in Cloud Computing a new principle called data auditing for the safe storage of information is implemented. The audit is a consumer information authentication procedure that may either be performed by the consumer itself (informational proprietor) or by a TPA (third party auditor). It helps hold the data stored in the cloud integrity.

The two sections of the role of the verifier are: firstly, private auditing, where the honesty of the data is only reviewed by the recipient or the information holders. No other party has the power to ask the server about the results. However, the average consumer check continues to improve. Secondly, public auditability encourages everyone to question the server, not just the client, and provides a review of the records by TPA. The TPA is a business that is used to work by the consumer. This provides all the required skills, intellect and experience required for the job of certifying honesty which thus reduces customers' overhead. The distributed database information without requiring a local copy of information must be effectively checked by TPA. The details contained on the distributed server should be known zero.

2 Existing Works

Ateniese et al. first suggested a Provable Custody of Data (PDP) in 2007 that would be able to validate cloud data ownership without all data being retrieved [5]. Then Juels et al. suggested to use the retrievability evidence framework to provide evidence that data can be recovered by the verifier [6] by a back-up or archive facilities [6].

The PDP framework that supports complex operations [7] was introduced by Ateniese et al. in a follow-up report. This ensures that a data up loader has complete control of any operation carried out in a cloud application, including block deletions, modifications and insertions. The authenticated table [8] was then introduced by Waters et al. to introduce a fully-dynamic PDP framework. In comparison to these works, [9, 14] is used to analyze the credibility of common data in the following structures. Users may alter and exchange cloud data providers as a collective in this case, where any member of the group can view and alter the shared data, and also share the variant they have updated with the others [11], [21]. In the same way, user can modify and share information.

A BLS based signature scheme to support agile group management was introduced in 2016 by Mr Yang et al. [9] attacks of the Cloud service provider and community participant, Jiang et al. have suggested data confidentiality based on the vector committing methodology [10], [22]. Through integrating proxy encryption with encryption.

Luo et al. introduced a secure consumer revocation system in 2017 [11]. Since then, Huang et al. has introduced an effective, logical hierarchy-bound key distribution among groups, thus maintaining the group's identity privacy [12]. Huang et al. subsequently suggested the removal of the main scrow to provide certificateless audits would further enhance the privacy of the user [13]. The groundbreaking studies preceded by Huang et al. Fu et al. proposed to carry out an audit method to restore accurate common blocks of data by modifying the group's binary tree tracking data [14].

Li et al. introduced a new data cloud audit scheme with cloud audit server [15]. The cloud monitoring service creates customer identification marks before it is submitted to the cloud management system. While this scheme can minimize user overhead computation, it will expose to the cloud audit system entirely the private keys and user details. Malicious cloud service providers will then go through the authentication process without storing customer data.

Guan et al. was using an analogous contradictory approach to creating a cloud storage audit scheme [16], [24], which minimized the time taken for verification labels but expanded the time needed to validate cloud data integrity. Wang et al. incorporated agents to help community members in creating labels of authentication and auditing data integrity [17], thus reducing the strain on group members of computing.

Nevertheless, the community member must encrypt the data before submitting to the server, which ultimately raises the device workload, in order to guarantee data protection. Shen et al. suggested a minor audit scheme to replace members of the community with authentication labels by adding the Third party mechanism (called the agent) [18].

Security is among the most open issues in cloud computing. Various organizations watch cloud infrastructure closely for security risks. Online protection and privacy vulnerabilities can be smaller than cloud storage than those that must be housed in a single server, instead of in the cloud (a network of machines used for remote authentication and conservation) [19], [25, 26].

Smart technology growth will be made possible by cloud infrastructure that is a cornerstone of urban planning, better decision-making and utilities distribution, with an increased standard of life under a cleaner climate, strengthened physical, economic progress, public safety and effective administration. The smart innovations should be well prepared and assisted by an assessment, review and synthesization to handle the vast influx of data from a wide variety of regions [20, 23].

2.1 Problem Definition

A malicious cloud server is capable of discarding all data exchanged by reserving any intermediate outcomes or previous legitimate facts that we call a substitution attack or a re-playing attack, which may provide clear proof of data ownership. A malevolent group member may alter data of other members without being detected in that group. A malicious agent may work with unauthorized members of the community to harvest data from users and identities. The three above things we know continue to be open problems for the creation of a stable integrity audit scheme on customer side for common data with lightweight computing.

2.2 Implementation Procedure

A lightweight, reliable cloud storage data auditing system (LSSA) was introduced here. Similar to the audit system in the cloud computing system [18], a third party medium (TPM) is used in the verification mark measurement instead of group members and the effects of audit data accuracy are easy for group members to measure. We separated the group members as well as the TPM into a group manager in relation to this system, to isolate and control the group and the TPM and to suppress their cooperation. With respect to the participants of the party our contributions to science can be summarized as follows:

(1) This paper offers the data protection and anonymity of the community participants by the use of an effective blind process. This paper removes the secret protection threats of community members by implementing a hash graph and at the same time makes user identification traceable.

(2) The concept for the TPM management was created and the Project Manager designed the interactive TPM pool. The technique guarantees agent protection (TPM) and contributes to light estimates for the agent. The usage of the TPM to measure the mark of authentication and to audit the data integrity ensures that community members are able to determine lightweight

(3) The scheme's security review suggests that the scheme is secure and can survive threats and replay attacks.

(4) The Scheme's experimental analysis reveals that lightweight interventions can be achieved for members of the society and the TPM.

2.3 Implementation Procedure

The Organization Model involves four individual entities: Group (M), Server, Group Manager (GM) and TPM members. The group consists of many sections, as seen in Fig. 1. Any member of the group can access and alter the data file after the data owner (the company or individual that owns the original data) creates and uploads it in the cloud. Note that the original data owner plays GM's position and there is only one GM in each division. The model has two main roles: i) blind data and ii) blind data collected and distributed via a Hashgraph within the community. The cloud offers data store services for group members (iCloud, OneDrive and Baidu Cloud) and offers group members with a forum to exchange data. The GM is playing three critical role models: 1) creating public-private TPM key pairs, 2) multi-purpose the TPM management approach and 3) generating a hidden seed for blinding community members' data and retrieving real cloud information. The TPM has two significant roles: 1) the development of a data 2) authentication symbol for the members of the Community, on behalf of the participants, the checking of cloud data's credibility.

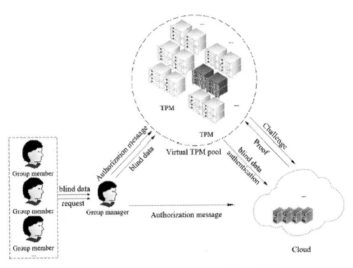

Fig. 1. Architecture model for implementation

The method of implementation is broken down into the data transfer and the audit phase. The data would then be blinded by the hidden seed and saved to the project manager before the group member asks to download the updated data to the server. Under TPM administration, the group management manager picked a TPM for authorization from the simulated TPM pool, and for those blinded data during the time of authorization the approved TPM accumulates the respective authentication labels. While the cloud will also obtain the blind data and authentication mark. The cloud will verify if the TPM permission is active at the present time before obtaining these messages. If it is, the verification mark verifies that it is right or not. If right, he will retrieve the actual data and determine their labels of authentication. Finally, these actual labels and verification data are stored in the cloud. The community manager picks a TPM and establishes the authorisation under the TPM compliance plan before conducting the auditing process. The approved TPM then sends challenge communications to the cloud. The cloud will verify if TPM permissions are correct before these messages are received. If so, the cloud may provide confirmation that the shared data was in custody. Finally, by checking the authenticity of popular data in the cloud, the TPM can verify the accuracy of the evidence.

3   Design of the Implementation

Lightweight Computing: This strategy means that community participants don't have to carry out time-consuming assessments during authentication labels or during mutual data assessments. In the estimation, multiple TPMs take part, which means only one TPM is measured gently.

Identity Traceability: Moving data from unauthorized users may lead to conflicts between members of the community using the same shared data. This aim means that all unauthorized members of the company can be identified and expelled by GM and thus achieves company security management.

TPM Management Security: Each of the TPM operates independently to ensure the TPM's legal presence. This aim means that the cloud embraces and preserves only data from GM-licensed TPMs and addresses the problems of the GM-authorized TPMs only.

Data Privacy and Identity Privacy: The precise data block information cannot be identified if the TPM creates authentication markers instead of the group members. The TPM cannot access the identity information of community members at the moment of downloading data and auditing data.

Audit Correctness and Security: Through the use of the audit process the TPM will check the quality of the data shared. The audit cannot be done by replacing or replaying attacks by malicious cloud service providers.

4   HashGraph Approach

As seen in Fig. 2 below, every circle of the figure represents a hah-value case. In the historical records the earlier vertices represent early occurrences and Mi specifies the user i. In Gossip mode, the message could be distributed over the Hashgraph network. When B happens, user M2 who created B will add its own signature, Sign M2, to this event and randomly transfer it to user M1. This message is received by User M1 and a new event A is generated. Event A comprises two event hashes (a historical event C and a coordinated event B user M2), and user M1 adds event A to his/her sign, Sign M1.

The concept theory of community member management can be suggested using Hash graph technologies. The definition of the TPM management approach is indicated by comparison to the TCP window sliding and the interconnection feature.

Group Member Management Design

The group manager creates an account arbitrarily as the identity mark of the member M of the group, whenever the account is used to determine the real identity of the group member. The project manager deletes the account if the group member is dropped. We specified the following notes for notational convenience.

M: les data are divided into n blocks (m1, m2, ..., mn), where mi is divided into slices (mi;1, mi;2, ..., mi;s) each is repeated as mi and each slice is recorded as mij.

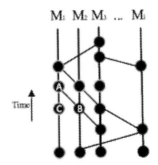

Fig. 2. Hashgraph design of LSSA

mij: The mij-corresponding blind data block.

idi;j: the blind data block public identification information mij.

MOwner: Data owner's account (ID).

Block: Block, e.g., SHA-1, and SHA-256. Hash function.

Sign: The name of the participants is marked.

The MOwner Data Owner transfers the mij blind data block to the team member, which calculates the idi;j value of the hah (idi;j), and then applies a signed signature of the SignMOwner. The Community Member or Group Manager is randomly selected, sending the event to the network nodes, to synchronise it with the initial case. The Group members have access to the original shared data and may change it, but the Mi Group members who have subsequently updated and modified mij must update their blind block identifier. The members then measure the idij hash value for a new case as a modify/access record, and append the SignMi signature to distribute within that community.

The creative director produces the public-private key pair for TPM during the data upload process. He also produces a hidden seed and transfers it to members of the party and the server. Since the port of the project manager is the connection between group members and TPM, the group manager has the power to choose the sending and contact roles, to establish a TPM management plan authorization and then to give the authorization to TPM. Whenever the user wishes to load data into the cloud, the blindness factor is measured to blind this with the occult seed. The blind data are then decided by transmitting them inside the project to the project manager as a transaction record for another event. The community manager may validate before getting the messages whether the member's hash value is true or not. If so, the approval will be submitted to the TPM.

The TPM then generates the necessary authentication markers for the information misguided and stores them in the cloud together. The cloud tests if the TPM permission is current at the present time before retrieving those messages. If so, he can verify whether these marks are right or not. If right, the actual data is retrieved by using the element blindness and their authentication labels are computed. The cloud eventually holds the individual data and codes for authentication.

4.1 Experiment Evaluation

The main theme of this paper is to eliminate future safety risks using a better route. When using data in the audit scheme for common data, team members are often concerned for efficiency problems. This section first calculates and then checks the overhead unit of the LSSA scheme in the actual operating environment. The final results show that the scheme will have limited weight for the members of the party and that LSSA is secure from related audit schemes.

5 Conclusions

The proposal suggested an established pooled data ownership in cloud storage for a lightweight and secure audit process. By implementing a Hash graph the group membership will track, and Hash graph technology will avoid the illicit actions of the group members. Every community member and TPM, defining several TPMs for the measurement and management under the management approach, is different, which means that the mechanism of cloud data testing is safe and that the TPM is measured lightweight.

References

1. Armbrust, M., et al.: Above the clouds: a Berkeley view of cloud computing. Department of Electrical Engineering and Computer Science, University of California, Berkeley, Berkeley, CA, USA, Technical Report UCB/EECS-2009-28 (2009)
2. Mell, P., Grance, T.: The National Institute of Standards and Technology (NIST) definition of cloud computing. NIST, Washington, DC, USA, NIST Special Publication 800-145 (2011)
3. Julisch, K., Hall, M.: Security and control in the cloud. Inf. Secur. J. A Glob. Perspect. 19(6), 299–309 (2010)
4. Feng, D.G., Zhang, M., Zhang, Y., Xu, Z.: Study on cloud computing security. J. Softw. 22(1), 71–83 (2011)
5. Ateniese, G., et al.: Provable data possession at untrusted stores. In: Proceedings of the 14th ACM Conference on Computer and Communication Security (CCS), pp. 598–609 (2007)
6. Juels, A., Kaliski, B.S.: Pors: proofs of retrievability for large files. In: Proceedings of the 14th ACM Conference on Computer and Communication Security (CCS), pp. 584–597 (2007)
7. Ateniese, G., Di Pietro, R., Mancini, L.V., Tsudik, G.: Scalable and efficient provable data possession. In: Proceedings of the 4th International Conference on Security and Privacy in Communication Networks, Istanbul, Turkey, pp. 22–25 (2008)
8. Shacham, H., Waters, B.: Compact proofs of retrievability. In: Pieprzyk, J. (ed.) Advances in Cryptology - ASIACRYPT 2008, pp. 90–107. Springer, Heidelberg (2008). https://doi.org/10.1007/978-3-540-89255-7_7
9. Yang, G., Yu, J., Shen, W., Su, Q., Fu, Z., Hao, R.: Enabling public auditing for shared data in cloud storage supporting identity privacy and traceability. J. Syst. Softw. 113, 130–139 (2016)
10. Jiang, T., Chen, X., Ma, J.: Public integrity auditing for shared dynamic cloud data with group user revocation. IEEE Trans. Comput. 65(8), 2363–2373 (2016)
11. Luo, Y., Xu, M., Huang, K., Wang, D., Fu, S.: Efficient auditing for shared data in the cloud with secure user revocation and computations outsourcing. Comput. Secur. 73, 492–506 (2018)

12. Huang, L., Zhang, G., Fu, A.: Privacy-preserving public auditing for dynamic group based on hierarchical tree. J. Comput. Res. Develop. **53**(10), 2334–2342 (2016)

13. Huang, L.X., Zhang, G.M., Fu, A.M.: Certificateless public verification scheme with privacy-preserving and message recovery for dynamic group. In: Proceedings of the Australasian Computer Science Week Multiconference, Melbourne, VIC, Australia, p. 76 (2017)

14. Fu, A., Yu, S., Zhang, Y., Wang, H., Huang, C.: NPP: a new privacy-aware public auditing scheme for cloud data sharing with group users. IEEE Trans. Big Data (to be published)

15. Li, J., Tan, X., Chen, X., Wong, D.S., Xhafa, F.: OPoR: enabling proof of retrievability in cloud computing with resource-constrained devices. IEEE Trans. Cloud Comput. **3**(2), 195–205 (2015)

16. Guan, C., Ren, K., Zhang, F., Kerschbaum, F., Yu, J.: Symmetric-key based proofs of retrievability supporting public verification. In: Pernul, G., Ryan, P.Y.A., Weippl, E. (eds.) Computer Security -- ESORICS 2015: 20th European Symposium on Research in Computer Security, Vienna, Austria, September 21–25, 2015, Proceedings, Part I, pp. 203–223. Springer, Cham (2015). https://doi.org/10.1007/978-3-319-24174-6_11

17. Wang, H., He, D., Tang, S.: Identity-based proxy-oriented data uploading and remote data integrity checking in public cloud. IEEE Trans. Inf. Forensics Secur. **11**(6), 1165–1176 (2016)

18. Shen, W., Yu, J., Xia, H., Zhang, H., Lu, X., Hao, R.: Light-weight and privacy-preserving secure cloud auditing scheme for group users via the third party medium. J. Netw. Comput. Appl. **82**, 56–64 (2017)

19. Gayatri, P., Venunath, M., Subhashini, V., Umar, S.: Securities and threats of cloud computing and solutions. In: 2018 2nd International Conference on Inventive Systems and Control (ICISC), pp 1162–1166. IEEE Explorer (2018)

Applying Deep Learning for Extremism Detection

Shynar Mussiraliyeva, Batyrkhan Omarov, Milana Bolatbek, Ruslan Ospanov,
Gulshat Baispay$^{(\boxtimes)}$, Zhanar Medetbek, and Zhastay Yeltay

Al-Farabi Kazakh National University, Almaty, Kazakhstan

Abstract. According to recent research, the use of social media to track the spread of radical ideas and extremist threats has attracted the attention of researchers for more than 10 years. In the last 3 years, there has been a surge in research interest in identifying and predicting based on the analysis of the text content of messages in open social networks as extremists actively use social networks and the number of calls to extremism and the number of recruitment through social networks is growing.

In this paper, we consider an important applied problem of using deep learning methods to identify potential extremist and terrorist information on the Internet. It provides an overview of existing solutions and approaches and offers its own method for detecting online extremism. The applicability and effectiveness of the proposed method is demonstrated experimentally on a reference set of real data potentially containing extremist information. The results of the experiment show high accuracy in detecting extremist messages.

Keywords: Extremism · Machine learning · Deep learning · NLP · Classification

1 Introduction

Countering the spread of aggressive information in the global network is an urgent problem of society and government agencies, which is solved in particular by filtering unwanted Internet resources [1–3]. A necessary condition for such filtering is the classification of the content of sites and documents of the information flow. Therefore, the actual problem of information technologies is the classification and categorization of texts in natural languages according to the thematic, psycholinguistic orientation. In particular, discusses the current problems of forensic linguistics related to the study of the "discourse of enmity" as a manifestation of the extremist orientation of texts and speech aggression; characterizes various types of speech hostility [4, 5]. The information and psychological weapons used by extremist and terrorist organizations are aimed primarily at the younger generation, i.e. the object of these weapons is the consciousness of a young person [6]. In this case, it is necessary to keep in mind the empirical fact that it is wrong to consider a person in the modern information society as a kind of autonomous biosocial being, since he is now included in the extensive information computer networks [7].

To solve the problems of countering terrorism and extremism using information from the Internet, it is important to develop software systems that allow:

© Springer Nature Singapore Pte Ltd. 2021
A. K. Luhach et al. (Eds.): ICAICR 2020, CCIS 1393, pp. 597–605, 2021.
https://doi.org/10.1007/978-981-16-3660-8_56

1. Identify user groups, communities and resources on the Internet where information of terrorist or extremist content circulates [8].
2. Monitor, receive and predict the characteristics of message flows and documents distributed in such groups [9].
3. Assess the danger and predict the risks that members of such communities bear [10, 11].

In our research, we try to identify texts that contains extremism related messages or calls to extremism. Structure of current research as following: Second chapter gives information about deep learning methods for text classification and data preparation process. In the third chapter we develop CNN and LSTM model for extremism related text classification. In the fourth chapter, we demonstrated experiment results, and in the end conclude the paper.

2 Development of Deep Learning Methods for Text Classification

Deep learning is ideal for natural language processing (NLP) tasks such as sentiment analysis, classification, and machine translation. For text classification, we use the following deep learning methods: convolutional neural network (CNN) and recurrent neural network (LSTM).

2.1 Preparing Data for Training

Before we start, let's see what data we have. This data set includes marked texts. Each text is assigned a label: 0 for neutral text or 1 for extremist text. Since in our case the data is text, filtering and vectorization can be considered for data preparation. Text filtering is performed to reduce noise and emissions.

Let's start by filtering the text using the following algorithm:

1) Bring all characters to the same case and remove the extra characters "not words".
2) Exclude common words (stop words).
3) perform stemming and lemmatization.
4) Specify the tokenization template (splitting the text into token words) and the n-gram word model (the number of possible words in the token).

Neural networks can only learn to find patterns in numerical data, and so before we enter text into the neural network as input, we must convert each word to a numeric value. This process is often referred to as word encoding or tokenization [12].

For tokenization, we use word attachments. After tokenization we need to tokenize the data. To do this, we need to install Keras using the following command: pip install keras [13].

```
from keras.preprocessing.text import Tokenizer
from keras.preprocessing.sequence import pad_sequences
from keras.preprocessing import text, sequence

tokenizer = Tokenizer(num_words=20000)
tokenizer.fit_on_texts(list(X_train))

X_train = tokenizer.texts_to_sequences(X_train)
X_test  = tokenizer.texts_to_sequences(X_test)

X_train = sequence.pad_sequences(X_train, maxlen=200)
X_test  = sequence.pad_sequences(X_test,  maxlen=200)

print('X_train shape:', X_train.shape)
print('X_test shape: ', X_test.shape)
```

2.2 Deep Learning Model

In a neural network, we know several terms, such as input layer, hidden layer, and output layer. Therefore, the difference between a deep learning architecture and a neural network is the specified number of hidden layers. A simple neural network has only 1 hidden layer, whereas Deep Learning has more than 1 hidden layer.

We start with the input neuron layer, where we enter our feature vectors, and then the values are passed to the hidden layer. Each time we connect, we pass the value forward, while the value is multiplied by the weight, and the offset is added to the value. This happens at each connection, and at the end we get the value of the output layer. The output layer consists of one or more output nodes. In our case, one node, since we have a binary classification problem.

CNN. Convolutional neural networks have revolutionized image classification and computer vision by being able to extract elements from images and use them in neural networks [13]. In the case of text classification, the convolutional core slides through word attachments, only its task is to look at attachments for several words at once. The size of the convolutional core should also change in accordance with this task. To view word embedding sequences, we want the window to look at several (usually 3 or 5) word embeddings in the sequence. The cores will be a wide rectangle with dimensions like 3×300 or 5×300 (with an embedding length of 300). In our case, 4×200, because we set the sequence length to 200 when tokenizing. Each core cell has a corresponding weight. As the kernel slides over the word embedding, the kernel weights are multiplied by the value of the word embedding, then all the multiplied values are added together to get the output value.

A convolutional neural network will include many of these cores, and as the network is trained, these core weights are learned. Each core is designed to view the word and surrounding words in a sequential window. Thus, the convolution operation can be considered as feature selection based on a window. There is another nice feature of this convolutional operation [14]. Recall that similar words will have similar embeddings, and the convolution operation is just a linear operation on these vectors. So, when a convolutional core is applied to different sets of similar words, it will produce the same output value.

To process the entire sequence of words, these kernels will move the list of word attachments sequentially. This is called 1D Convolution (one-dimensional convolution), because the core moves in only one dimension: time. One core will move one by one through the list of input attachments, looking at the embedding of the first word, then the embedding of the next word, the next, and so on. The resulting output will be a feature vector. In the following image, you can see how this convolution works [15] (Fig. 1).

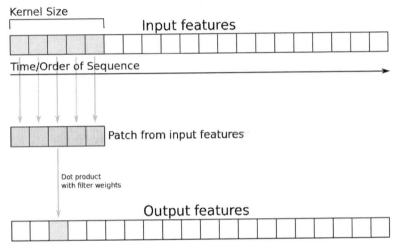

Fig. 1. Convolution

The maximum values obtained when processing each of our convolutional feature vectors will be combined and passed to the last layer. This is called MaxPooling.

And this is what our convolutional neural network looks like (Fig. 2).

Let's move from theory to practice. First, we need to add an embedding layer with the parameters input_dim – the size of the dictionary, the number of unique words that we want to use; input_length – the length of the sequence; output_dim – the dimension of the embedded variable. Then we set an exception layer to exclude 50% of the nodes. Now we add a convolutional layer that has 100 filters with a core size of 4, so that each convolution takes into account a window of 4 word attachments and the relu activation function. Before adding the Max Pooling layer, we add a normalization layer. After the merge layer, we add a dense layer to get the output size of 8 and use the real activation function. At the end, we configure the output layer. Since we are performing binary classification, we use the sigmoid activation function and get 1 result in the output layer.

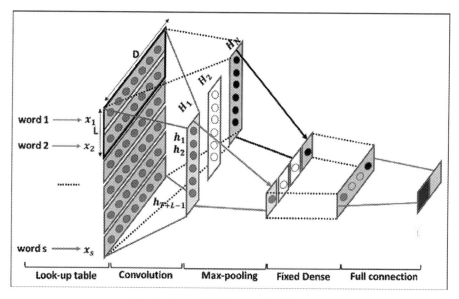

Fig. 2. Deep CNN for text classification

```
cnn_model = Sequential()
cnn_model.add(Embedding(input_dim=20000, input_length=200, output_dim=128))
cnn_model.add(SpatialDropout1D(0.5))
cnn_model.add(Conv1D(filters=100, kernel_size=4, activation='relu'))
cnn_model.add(BatchNormalization())
cnn_model.add(GlobalMaxPool1D())
cnn_model.add(Dropout(0.5))
cnn_model.add(Dense(8, activation='relu'))
cnn_model.add(Dense(1, activation='sigmoid'))

cnn_model.compile(loss='binary_crossentropy', optimizer=Adam(0.01),
                  metrics=['accuracy'])
cnn_hist = cnn_model.fit(X_train, Y_train, batch_size=256,
                  epochs=4, validation_split=0.2)
```

Here we use the "Adam" optimizer and the "cross entropy" loss function. And we got the following result in 4 epochs (Fig. 3).

3 Applying Recurrent Neural Network

LSTM. LSTMS (Long short-term memory) are designed to solve the vanishing gradient problem and allow them to store information for longer periods of time compared to traditional RNNS. Therefore, we use LSTM rather than a traditional recurrent neural network. The lstm architecture is shown below [17] (Fig. 4).

We will classify text data using a deep learning network with long-term short-term memory (LSTM). Text data is naturally consistent. To study and use long-term dependencies to classify sequence data, we use the lstm neural network. An LSTM network is a

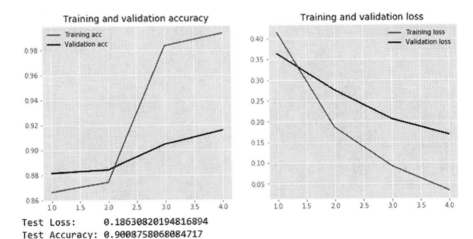

Test Loss: 0.18630820194816894
Test Accuracy: 0.9008758068084717

Fig. 3. Text classification result for 4 epochs

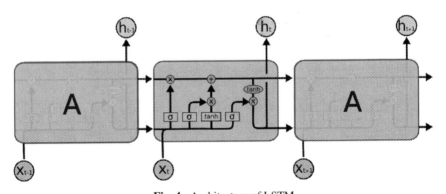

Fig. 4. Architecture of LSTM

type of recurrent neural network (RNN) that can study long-term dependencies between time steps, as shown above, of sequence data [18].

To enter text into the LSTM network, you must first convert the text data to numeric sequences. We have already converted the text to a numeric value when building a model of the convolutional neural network. We will continue to work with those numeric values.

We created exactly the same model for this neural network as for the convolutional neural network. Only instead of the convolutional layer, we added a bidirectional lstm layer.

Bidirectional LSTM is extensions of traditional LSTMS that can improve model performance in sequence classification tasks. In tasks where all time intervals of the input sequence are available, bidirectional LSTMS train two LSTMS instead of one in the input sequence. The first refers to the input sequence as is, and the second refers to an inverted copy of the input sequence. This can provide the network with additional context and lead to faster and even more complete investigation of the problem. Thanks to this form of generative deep learning, the output layer can simultaneously receive information from the reverse and forward States (Fig. 5).

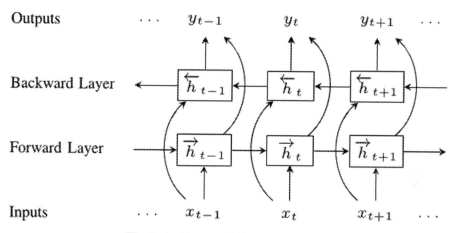

Fig. 5. Architecture of bidirectional LSTM

After 5 years of training our recurrent network model LSTM we obtained the following result (Fig. 6):

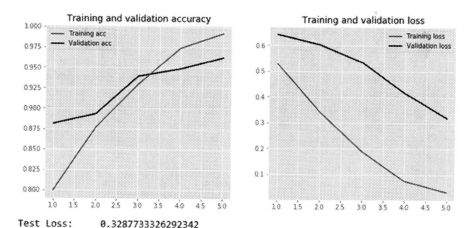

Test Loss: 0.3287733326292342
Test Accuracy: 0.9570063948631287

Fig. 6. Text classification result for 5 epochs

A convolutional neural network (CNN) is limited by the size of the local window and can only extract local text features. For long texts, such as news, CNN cannot study the long-term dependence of long text. Another model of recurrent neural networks with deep learning, based on long-term short-term memory (LSTM), can study the long-term dependence of text. Let's summarize the results of our research on the result of classification of test data (Fig. 7).

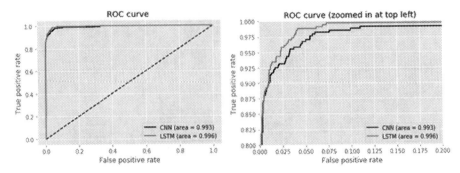

Fig. 7. Result for 5 epochs

4 Conclusion

In this paper, our attempt in extremist message detection on social networks using deep learning techniques is presented. In the first step, we collected data that contains extremist ideation and extremism related keywords. After, applied LSTM and CNN to for text classification problem in the Kazakh language. In our case, we applied binary classification to classify data as extremism related and non-extremism related messages. The results shows that deep learning can successfully be applied in similar problems. In the course of a literary survey, we noticed that the use of natural language processing for extremist texts in the Kazakh language is rare. Thus, the collected corpora and the given research will be useful study in text classification and in detection of radicalism and destructive information in the Kazakh language.

In the next step of this research, we are going to supply the corpus with new texts, make balanced corpus, tonality of posts in social media, and increase the accuracy of extremist text classification.

References

1. Pande, N., Karyakarte, M.: A review for semantic analysis and text document annotation using natural language processing techniques (2019). Available at SSRN 3418747
2. Alshemali, B., Kalita, J.: Improving the reliability of deep neural networks in NLP: a review. Knowl.-based Syst. **191**, 105210 (2019)
3. Yankah, S., Adams, K.S., Grimes, L., Price, A.: Age and online social media behavior in prediction of social activism orientation. J. Soc. Media Soc. **6**(2), 56–89 (2017)
4. Costello, M., Hawdon, J.: Who are the online extremists among us? Sociodemographic characteristics, social networking, and online experiences of those who produce online hate materials. Violence Gend. **5**(1), 55–60 (2018)
5. Ferrara, E.: Contagion dynamics of extremist propaganda in social networks. Inf. Sci. **418**, 1–12 (2017)
6. Awan, I.: Cyber-extremism: ISIS and the power of social media. Society **54**(2), 138–149 (2017)
7. Chetty, N., Alathur, S.: Hate speech review in the context of online social networks. Aggress. Violent. Beh. **40**, 108–118 (2018)

8. Kruglanski, A., Jasko, K., Webber, D., Chernikova, M., Molinario, E.: The making of violent extremists. Rev. Gen. Psychol. **22**(1), 107–120 (2018)
9. Chen, H.: Exploring extremism and terrorism on the web: the dark web project. In: Yang, C.C., et al. (eds.) Intelligence and Security Informatics. LNCS, vol. 4430, pp. 1–20. Springer, Heidelberg (2007). https://doi.org/10.1007/978-3-540-71549-8_1
10. Finlayson, M.A., Halverson, J.R., Corman, S.R.: The N2 corpus: a semantically annotated collection of Islamist extremist stories. In: LREC. – 2014, pp. 896–902 (2014)
11. Chepovskiy, A., Devyatkin, D., Smirnov, I., Ananyeva, M., Kobozeva, M., Solovyev, F.: Exploring linguistic features for extremist texts detection (on the material of Russian-speaking illegal texts). In: 2017 IEEE International Conference on Intelligence and Security Informatics: Security and Big Data, ISI 2017 Institute of Electrical and Electronics Engineers Inc., pp. 188–190 (2017)
12. Tereikovskyi, I., Tereikovska, L., Korystin, O., Mussiraliyeva, S., Sambetbayeva, A.: User keystroke authentication and recognition of emotions based on convolutional neural network. In: Hu, Z., Petoukhov, S., He, M. (eds.) Advances in Artificial Systems for Medicine and Education III. AISC, vol. 1126, pp. 283–292. Springer, Cham (2020). https://doi.org/10.1007/978-3-030-39162-1_26
13. Anthony, L.: Visualisation in corpus-based discourse studies. Corpus approaches to discourse: a critical review, 197–224 (2018)
14. Wolfe, C.R., Dandignac, M., Reyna, V.F.: A theoretically motivated method for automatically evaluating texts for gist inferences. Behav. Res. Methods **51**(6), 2419–2437 (2019). https://doi.org/10.3758/s13428-019-01284-4
15. Danekenova, A., Zhussupova, G., Nurmagambetov, R., Shunayeva, S., Popov, V.: The most used forms and methods of citizens involvement in terrorist and extremist activity. J. Pol. L. **12**, 1 (2019)
16. Nicholls, T., Bright, J.: Understanding news story chains using information retrieval and network clustering techniques. Commun. Methods Meas. **13**(1), 43–59 (2019)
17. Tulkens, S., Hilte, L., Lodewyckx, E., Verhoeven, B., Daelemans, W.: The automated detection of racist discourse in Dutch social media. Comput. Linguist. Neth. J. **6**, 3–20 (2016)
18. Fortuna, P., Nunes, S.: A survey on automatic detection of hate speech in text. ACM Comput. Surv. (CSUR) **51**(4), 1–30 (2018)

An Imperative Diagnostic Framework for PPG Signal Classification Using GRU

Nimmala Mangathayaru[1]([✉])[ID], B. Padmaja Rani[2], V. Janaki[3],
Shilhora Akshay Patel[1][ID], G. Sai Mohan[1][ID], and B. Lalith Bharadwaj[1][ID]

[1] Department of IT, VNR VJIET, Hyderabad 500 090, T.S, India
mangathayaru_n@vnrvjiet.in
[2] Department of CSC, JNTUH, Hyderabad 500 085, T.S, India
Padmaja_jntuh@jntuh.ac.in
[3] Department of CSC, Vaagdevi Engineering College, Warangal 506 006, T.S,
India

Abstract. Cardiovascular disease are one of the leading causes of an increase in the mortality rate due to irregular heart beats. Photoplethysmogram (PPG) technique is one of the noninvasive evaluation of blood pressure (BP) offers a reliable, feasible, and cost-efficient solution than other conventional techniques. PPG technique is highly induced by motion artifacts and its characteristics depend on the physiological condition of the person. While the collection of data, the PGG must be calibrated. In this research, a novel approach using a dual-tree complex wavelet transform (DT-CWT) based feature extraction technique with GRU network for the classification of hypertension is proposed. DT-CWT gives shift invariance compared to Continuous wavelet transforms and dual tree structure helps to extract the real and imaginary coefficients of the features. DT-CWT helps to integrate the signal patterns even disintegrating them during testing procedure. Further, these extracted features are fed into a variant neural architecture consisting of sequential GRU layers stacked over fully connected dense layers. It is observed, utilizing GRU layers led to extract precise features for sequential signal data by out-performing existing models. The proposed model attained an state-of-the-art accuracy score of 98.82% on BIDMC-PGG dataset by overhauling existing loops in research.

Keywords: PPG signal · Dual tree complex wave transform · Deep learning · Coronary heart diseases · Hypertension · Diagnostic model · PPG classification

1 Introduction

Neglect of health amongst young individuals has effectuated in a decrease in mortality rate because of deaths due to hypertension which in turn might be a factor leading to cardiovascular diseases. These diseases are increasing year by year worldwide. In recent years, the mortality of cardiovascular diseases (CVDs)

© Springer Nature Singapore Pte Ltd. 2021
A. K. Luhach et al. (Eds.): ICAICR 2020, CCIS 1393, pp. 606–621, 2021.
https://doi.org/10.1007/978-981-16-3660-8_57

and hypertension related diseases has overtaken cancer. Hypertension plays an immense role in many CVDs which have become a significant contributor to human deaths [1]. There are a distinct group of heart and blood vessel diseases such as cerebrovascular disease, Rheumatic heart disease (RHD), Coronary heart disease (CHD), Peripheral arterial disease (PAD), etc. [3]. Long term abnormal blood pressure can cause many complications in the human organ system including mainly in the kidneys, brain and heart causing irreversible injury. 13% of worldwide deaths are attributed to CVD and hypertension [3]. Identification of hypertension in the early stages can be used to take action against CVDs. From previous research, it is concluded that determining Blood Pressure (BP) of an individual would play a key role to know about CVDs. Invasive and Non-invasive are the two distinct methods that are used to estimate BP. The invasive medium for estimating BP requires the insertion of a cannula in blood-vessel for live tracking. But, Invasive methods often tend to be painful and cause many infections. There can also be a clinical circumstance where the invasive method is difficult to perform safely. Hence, non-invasive continuous BP evaluation may be vital clinically. There are many techniques that can be used noninvasively. Arterial blood pressure (ABP) and Photoplethysmogram (PPG) are the two dominant techniques. ABP technique is not adaptable in real-world applications. PPG signals are reliable for the measurement of BP [2,10] and also studied that ppg can be used for assessing and detection of hypertension [11]. PPG requires high quality, high sampling rate, and sampling precision of the signals and is sensitive to noise. Due to non-invasive methods are of low-cost, PPG sensors are promising and well known established diagnostic tool. Many PPG based BP evaluation techniques that were presented previously had arterial wave propagation theory [5,6], PPG morphology theory [7–9] as the core idea of their work.

Seventh report of the joint national committee on prevention, detection, evaluation, and treatment of high blood pressure. Hypertension (JNC7) [4] report states that BP levels can be categorized into four different categories: Normal, prehypertension, stage1 hypertension, stage2 hypertension. For classification of BP level in a single beat or signals, one should have Systolic Blood Pressure (SBP) or Diastolic Blood Pressure (DBP). Table 1 shows the classification of different BP levels using Systolic and Diastolic Pressure. We can calculate SBP and DBP using Pulse Transit Time (PTT) [25]. Soo-young Ye et al. [25] presented a method to evaluate SBP and DBP. This method has a low error rate compared to others. Also, the error rates are content with the organization of ANSI/AAMI (Fig. 1).

Many experiments are conducted in recent years, most of them using machine learning algorithms or deep learning models for classification. Tjahjadi et al. [19] proposed a KNN based method that has skipped the feature extraction method by considering raw PPG signals and achieved 86.7% accuracy. Liang [15] classified hypertension using google net and continuous wavelet transform (CWT) pre-processing and feature extraction and achieved an F-score of 92.55%. Liang [15] used the wavelet transformation method (WT) using which useful information and features from the raw PPG signal can be extracted. These extracted

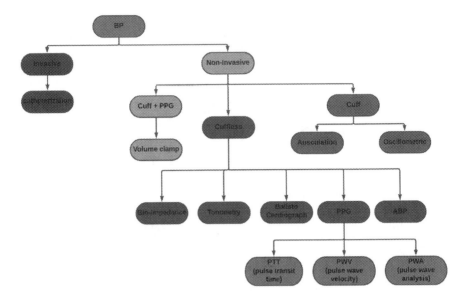

Fig. 1. Shows different cuff and cuff-less techniques for evaluation of blood pressure

features can also be represented in a feature set as important parameters for the classification of hypertension. Cvetkovic et al. [12] had conducted a pilot study on feature selection using WT. The study has been conducted on different signals: ECG, EEG and PPG respectively and have used Discrete wavelet transform (DWT) and stated that DWT features can be used as input for Neural Network for classification of signals. Wavelet transform is useful in pattern recognition in the signal as well as in signal analysis application. There are also many experiments conducted in the classification of hypertension. In this paper, a novel approach is being proposed for the classification of hypertension using the Dual-tree Complex Wavelet Transform (DT-CWT) method for feature extraction. DT-CWT overcomes the limitations of DWT. Due to this reason, DT-CWT has been used for feature extraction. The working of DWT and DT-CWT are explained in Sect. (4). The proposed method was tested on BIDMC PPG and Respiration Dataset [21] respectively. This dataset is taken from PhysioBank [26]. The PPG signals beats are classified according to the JNC7 report [4]. The detailed explanation of the dataset and data collection has been passed into the GRU network for the classification. GRU's has been used because it works best for time series analysis data like signals and forecasted data.

Table 1. Depicts classification of blood pressure to different classes for JNC7 report

SBP mm Hg	DBP mm Hg	BP classification
120	or 80	Normal
120–139	or 80–89	Prehypertension
140–159	or 90–99	Stage 1 hypertension
160 above	or 100 above	Stage 2 hypertension

2   Previous Research

Recently there is a lot of research done in the evaluation of hypertension utilizing machine learning and deep learning. They have used statistical features and some others used morphological features and wavelet transformed features from raw ppg signals to predict hypertension. Nour et al. [16] have proposed automatic hypertension classification. Types based on personal features they compared four different machine learning algorithms C4.5 decision tree classifier (DTC), random forest, linear discriminant analysis (LDA), and linear support vector machine (LSVM) and secured the highest accuracy 99.5%, 99.5%, 96.3%, and 92.7% they did not use any biomedical signal. They have used features that are available in the PPG-BP dataset [20]. Tjahjadi et al. [17] have proposed a novel feature extraction short-time Fourier transform (STFT) method for classifying hypertension using biomedical signals. They have used Bi-LSTM neural network as a classification model and achieved accuracy for 99.33%. The dataset used for this study was the PPG-BP dataset [20]. Liang et al. [15] has made use of Continuous-Wavelet-Transform (CWT) for pre-processing of signals and represented features as images. They applied transfer learning on google-net and achieved a 92.55% F-Score. The dataset used in this study is MIMC. Cvetkovic et al. [12] have conducted a study on feature selection using Wavelet transform (WT). They compared Continuous-Wavelet-Transform (CWT) and Discrete-Wavelet-Transform (DWT) since CWT is not reliable. They have stated that DWT feature extraction may help in the classification task as the patterns are simplified and robustly represented and they also concluded that DWT is a feasible technique for feature extraction. The method was tested on different signals ECG, PPG, and EEG. Liang et al. [14] have used pulse-arrival-time (PAT) as well as photoplethysmogram (PPG) features. Which are extracted from ECG together with PPG signals utilizing Arterial Wave propagation theory as well as PPG morphological theory they used different machine learning algorithm AdaBoost tree, logistic regression, KNN, and bagged tree the PAT features alone achieved F-score of 66.88%, 56.22%, 53%, 66%, and for PPG features alone achieved F-score of 72.76%, 63%, 78%, 78% further they have combined the PAT and PPG features and achieved F-score of 74.67%, 63%, 84%, 83%. KNN and bagged trees performed better when features were combined. The dataset used in this study was to MIMIC.

Yao et al. [18] have used features obtained from the PPG signal along with its derivatives and proposed a feature extraction approach. Although they have obtained morphological features, these features are uniquely associated with hypertension. They have tested on different machine learning models in which SVM performed the best and achieved an accuracy of 88%. The dataset used in this study is an open clinical trial dataset. Sannino et al. [13] have compared different machine learning algorithms in detail. They used cuffless-blood pressure estimation dataset from UCI and MIMIC-II from Physionet in their study and found that random forest works best. They have also inspected the performance of the classifier in terms of risk stratification. The random forest has achieved an accuracy of 80%. Tjahjadi et al. [19] proposed a KNN based method that utilizes unprocessed ppg signal to substitute with ppg feature extraction process and KNN achieved 86.7% accuracy. The dataset used in this study is the PPG-BP dataset. Su et al. [22] have posed a novel deep learning architecture. Which is multilayered LSTM and residual connection permit gradients in RNN to propagate efficaciously. The proposed model was tested as a static continuous bp dataset and achieved RMSE of 3.90 and 2.16 in SBP and DBP. Jindal et al. [23] have used deep belief networks and restricted Boltzmann machines and clustered into individual groups. The model is also robust against motion induced noise; the model has achieved 96.1% accuracy with 10-fold cross-validation. The dataset used in this study is the TROIKA dataset. In this section we have discussed various latest research many researchers have used different techniques for feature extraction and classification methods. There are many drawbacks of using statistical features is that they are not well-generalized features set for prediction; there is no robust features representation when compared to features that are extracted from raw ppg signals using wavelet transform (WT). In this paper, we are going to the DT-CWT wavelet transform method to overcome the limitations of the DWT wavelet transform method. The DWT and DT-CWT are explained briefly in the methodology section and our proposed DT-CWT method was tested on three different datasets.

3   Dataset Description

For this experiment, We have utilized the BIDMC PPG and Respiration Dataset [21]. Which is freely available on PhysioBank [26]. BIDMC PPG dataset contains signals and numeric values extracted from MIMIC-II dataset. BIDMC PPG dataset is manually annotated by two annotators by utilizing impedance respiratory signals. They have annotated every single breath in each recording by utilizing impedance respiratory signals. BIDMC PPG dataset holds 53 recordings instances each one of 8 min time span each instance holds many different physiological signals, in particular PPG, ABP, and ECG. Each one of these physiological signals are sampled 125 Hz. The physiological signal further holds Heart-Rate (HR), Respiratory-Rate (RR), and Blood-Oxygen Saturation-level (SpO2) sampled 1 Hz, as physiological parameters in it. It also contains information about the patient such as age and gender. BIDMC PPG dataset has

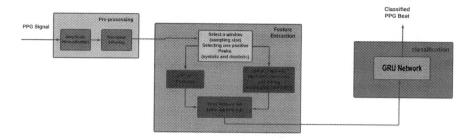

Fig. 2. The above diagram illustrates the proposed diagnostic framework

manually annotations of breaths. PPG signal from this dataset was used to evaluate the BP level and classify it according to the JNC7 report [4]. This dataset is used because it doesn't contain any missing peak or any noisy data. Which is reliable for the experiment. Also, the dataset is manually evaluated for annotations.

4   Methodology

The proposed method consists of three Steps, Step-1: Signal preprocessing, Step-2: Extraction of features, Step-3: Classification. Figure 2 illustration depicts the proposed method.

Signal preprocessing phase involves two parts, one in amplitude normalization and second is filtering. PPG signals are normalized to mean '0' and standard deviation of '1'. To shrink amplitude variance for each signal. The pandemonium in PPG signals are eliminated by utilizing a Chebyshev II with 4th order bandpass filter with a cutoff frequency of 0.5–12 Hz [32]. Preprocessed signals were utilized in Step-2 for extracting predominant attributes. SBP and DBP of PPG signals are calculated using [25]. Attributes which are extracted using DTCWT technique are put in as Input to GRU classifier. The classifier maps Features to their corresponding class labels. Which are extracted from the detail coefficients of D4 and D5. The acquired attributes are attached with five other attributes in particular, SBP, DBP, Skewness, Timing information, and kurtosis. Which are obtained from the PPG Signals.

4.1   Discrete-Wavelet-Transform (DWT)

Wavelet-Transform (WT) allows representing the signals in various scales. WT is the extension of the Fourier transformation. Instead of operating on single scale time or frequency. WT operates on multitudinous scales which provides contemporaneous determination in time and frequency [27]. This is accomplished by Separation through stretching in scale and change in time versions of model wavelet. A given input signal I[.] is fragmented by utilizing two filters (high-pass filter and low-pass filter) which is downsampled by 2 in each stage. Let A[.]

remain high-pass filter and B[.] remain mirror variant and it is low-pass in nature. The downsampling output of High-pass Filters is known as detail coefficients and downsampling output of Low-pass Filters is known as approximation coefficients. A1 (approximation coefficient of First Filter) is further fragmented as depicted in illustration in Fig. 3. The three scale level decomposition is shown in Fig. 3.

The high-pass filter and low-pass filter (two filters) are quadrature mirror filters (QMF) in each phase. QMF constraint is specified by

$$B(f)B(f^{-1}) + B(-f)B(f)^{-1} = 1$$
$$A(f) = fB(-f^{-1})$$

Here A[f] and B[f] is f transform of both filter which are related in the time domain as

$$A[K - 1 - n] = (-1)n.B[n]$$

where K represents the length of the filter. Result of both filters of a given signal I[n] is given by

$$Y_{hpf}(X) = \sum_{n} I[n]A[-n + 2X]$$

$$Y_{lpf}(X) = \sum_{n} I[n]B[-n + 2X]$$

The wavelet utilized for this study is order-2 of Daubechies wavelet (db2), because of morphological similarity towards the PPG Signals. Considering that DWT technique is feasible for analyzing ppg signals. Yet the absence of shift-invariance property in DWT makes it a powerful tool for analyzing 1D signals. But it faces problems like oscillation, aliasing, and shift-invariance. The modelling of signals with distinctiveness turns out to be intricate since wavelet coefficients turn out to be oscillating between negative and positive throughout distinctiveness. As a result of down sampling operation in each phase in DWT gives rise to shift-invariance. Consequently energy of coefficient alters distinctively after a small-time shift in a signal model. Due to this reason, coefficients of DWT fail to discriminate signal shifts.

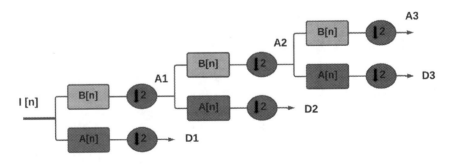

Fig. 3. Three level DWT transformation

4.2 Dual-Tree Complex Wavelet Transform (DTCWT)

The DTCWT is a simple technique which overcomes the limitations of DWT. DTCWT uses complex-valued scaling function and wavelet and they are as follow

$$\Phi_x(t) = \Phi_r(t) + \Phi_i(t)$$
$$\Psi_x(t) = \Psi_r(t) + \Psi_i(t)$$

Here $\Phi_r(t)$ remains an real part in a complex-valued function and $\Phi_i(t)$ remains an imaginary part in a complex wavelet function which Hilbert transforms set to one another. The above-mentioned applies also to the scaling function [28]. DTCWT utilizes two filters made from real wavelet, one is utilized for obtaining imaginary parts and another filter is utilized for obtaining real parts in transform. Amalgamation of both filters is called an analytic filter. This presents us with a new formation identical of two standard DWT filters band structure operations in concurrent. Sub-bands in the lower half of the DWT, Part-B will represent an imaginary part and the sub-band in the upper half of the DWT, Part-A will represent an real part. To fulfil precise reconstruction constraint each half utilizes dissimilar pairs of filters. Let X0 (n) represent the Low-pass filter and X1 (n) represent the High-pass filter belonging to Upper Filter bank and Y0 (n) represent the Low-pass filter and Y1 (n) represent the High-pass filter belonging to Lower Filter bank. Both Low-pass filters (X0 (n), Y0 (n)) are constructed in a way that wavelet function is estimated Hilbert transmute set associated as

$$Y_o(n) = X_o(n - 1/2)$$

1D-Quadratic-shift Dual tree structure given by Kingsburg [29] is illustrated in the Fig. 4. In DT-CWT two filters have been utilized, one pair of filters in level-1 and another pair of filters are utilized at all Higher levels. Filters behind level-1 have equal extent yet not absolutely linear stage and have a batch hold up of 1/4. To accomplish the expected hold up of 1/2 sample. We utilize time contrary of the tree and filter in part-B. Therefore DTCWT applies two DWTs. The complex coefficients only emerge when both the trees are consolidated. This incorporation of both trees helps us in representing distinctive signals (falls, stalks). DTCWT also provides imprecise shift inversion [30] with restriction of 1D signals having the restricted redundancy factor of 21. and that is considerably lesser compared to undecimated DWT. DT-CWT coefficient energy is varied less when compared with DWT coefficient. Therefore it turns out that DTCWT is better than DWT method. Mainly in pattern recognition problems. The length of filters utilized are of 10 at each stage [31].

The summary of using DT-CWT feature extraction is as follows. (i) selecting a positive peak (SBP and DBP) sample size of a single beat cycle. (ii) Perform 1D DTCWT transform until 5 scales for selected signals. (iii) consider 4th, 5th detail coefficients as attributes. The lower tree produces both 4th, 5th scale detail coefficients representing the imaginary part. Whereas the upper tree of

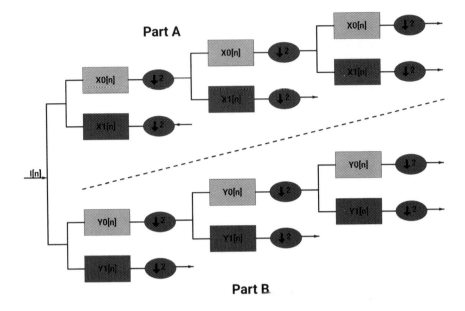

Fig. 4. Three level DTCWT transformation

complex wavelet transform produces both 4th, 5th scale detail coefficients representing the real part. The absolute values of both 4th, 5th scale detail coefficients are determined by making use of real and imaginary coefficients. (iv) Perform 1D Fast Fourier transform (FFT) on the determined features (4th, 5th detail coefficients) after that attach independently along with five attributes which we determined from the PPG signal of every cardiac cycle.

Kurtosis shows the peakedness of the signal and it is calculated using as follow

$$Kur(z) = \frac{E[(z - \nu)^4]}{\sigma^4}$$

Skewness is calculated using as follow

$$Ske(z) = \frac{E[(z - \nu)^3]}{\sigma^3}$$

Timing information is stated as the r–r interval ratio. and it is calculated as follow

$$Ir_i = \frac{t_i - t_{i-1}}{t_{i+1} - t_i}$$

5   Classification

Bi-LSTM and LSTM are widely used for sequential data classification and become start-of-the-art classifiers for sequential data. LSTM and Bi-LSTM are used for continuous SBP and DBP calculation and it has been used for arrhythmia classification [34,35]. LSTM processes the sequential data in one direction (forward) whereas the Bi-LSTM processes the sequential data in two directions (forward and backward) [33]. But, Gated recurrent neural networks (GRUs) [38] did provide an surge in performance while compared to LSTM's. The major advantages of using GRU's over LSTMs that, GRUs have control over the information flow in the absence of memory unit and is computationally cheap to that of LSTM. A detailed study is undergone to understand the use of LSTM and GRUs for sequential data [39]. Thus variant architectures are utilized to extract the features and analyse the performance. Extracted features from the pre-processing step (DT-CWT) with five other features are passed as input to the proposed variant network. The input features are mapped with respect to the output classes. For creating the network we used Keras [36]. Which is a library that is easy to use and to train the model. Four variant architectures are proposed with varying size of input and depth. The first two architectures (1, 2) consists of 3 GRU sequential units, one with 64-32-4 and other with 32-16-4 GRU units. The Next two architectures (3, 4) consists of 2 GRU Sequentail units, one with 64-4 and other with 32-4 GRU units. The layer normalization and dropout layers are adjoined in between these GRU layers for appropriate regularization. To classify these learned sequential data further a series of fully connected layers are attached and consists of dense units similar to that of GRU units utilised in individual architecture. The architectures are visually depicted in Fig. 5, 6. These networks are fully trained from the inception of network by assigning appropriate initialisations.

6   Results

The overview of the GRU network and its parameters are shown in the figure. While training GRU networks we divided the complete data into train and test parts. The overall data is randomly shuffled with considering appropriate stratification. The above-mentioned process is achieved and results are generated with Keras library [36] where backend using Tensor-flow [37]. Results have been evaluated using various classification metrics such as Accuracy, Recall, Precision, and MSE. The proposed architectures are then tested for three different batch size i.e. 16, 32 and 64. This paradigm of increasing is considered to increase the generalisation ability as mentioned [40]. Further, to understand the performance three distinct training and testing procedures are constructed i.e. 10, 25 and 50% of testing samples. So, the performance for individual fully trained architectures is tested on variant batches and variant test samples. Individual model's performance is tested and evaluated with mentioned classification metrics and described in Table 2, 3, 4 and 5.

To our knowledge, there is no previous study which investigated this approach i.e. using DT-CWT feature extraction in PPG signals and utilizing sequential gated recurrent units for classification. The analysis show that the shallow models performs better than deeper networks. This proposed technique is suitable

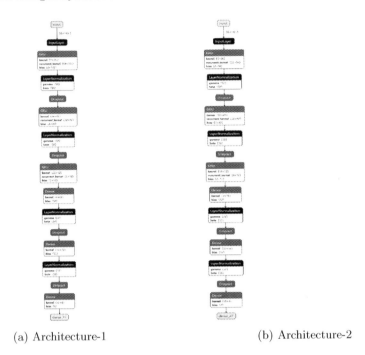

(a) Architecture-1   (b) Architecture-2

Fig. 5. These architectures consists of 3 sequential GRU layers

Table 2. Neural architecture:1 (Net-64-32-4)

Models	Test	Accuracy (%)	MSE (%)	Recall (%)	Precision (%)
Batch-16	0.10	98.31	0.7657	98.13	98.14
	0.25	97.76	0.9402	97.75	97.76
	0.50	96.53	1.3088	96.52	96.54
Batch-32	0.10	98.13	0.7657	98.13	98.14
	0.25	97.76	0.9402	97.75	97.76
	0.50	96.53	1.3088	96.52	96.54
Batch-64	0.10	97.21	1.1544	97.21	97.23
	0.25	96.87	1.1553	96.87	96.87
	0.50	96.29	1.1974	96.88	96.89

and reliable. There is no over-fitting of data in the model i.e. convergence is attained by training and testing samples parallel to each other. The results show that this approach is best when compared to its previous approaches in the classification of hypertension. The Table 6 illustrates the proposed approach and other approach with many standard classification metric (accuracy score). The proposed technique attains an highest accuracy score of 98.8% with 10% testing on minute architecture (architecture 3).

(a) Architecture-3   (b) Architecture-4

Fig. 6. These architectures consists of 2 sequential GRU layers

Table 3. Neural architecture:2 (Net-32-16-4)

Models	Test	Accuracy (%)	MSE (%)	Recall (%)	Precision (%)
Batch-16	0.10	97.00	1.2302	96.99	97.01
	0.25	94.76	2.0390	94.72	94.80
	0.50	92.63	2.8630	92.55	92.69
Batch-32	0.10	96.99	1.2411	96.96	97.01
	0.25	96.67	1.3650	96.66	96.69
	0.50	95.04	1.9093	94.96	95.08
Batch-64	0.10	96.21	1.5339	96.17	96.24
	0.25	95.63	1.7924	95.60	95.66
	0.50	98.10	0.7833	98.08	98.13

Table 4. Neural architecture:3 (Net-64-4)

Models	Test	Accuracy(%)	MSE (%)	Recall (%)	Precision (%)
Batch-16	0.10	98.21	.6939	98.21	98.22
	0.25	98.49	.6271	98.49	98.49
	0.50	97.35	.9905	97.34	97.35
Batch-32	0.10	98.88	.4734	98.88	98.88
	0.25	98.32	.6881	98.32	98.32
	0.50	98.59	.5871	98.59	98.59
Batch-64	0.10	98.83	.4581	98.83	98.83
	0.25	98.45	.6209	98.45	98.46
	0.50	97.30	1.0462	97.29	97.30

Table 5. Neural architecture:4 (Net-32-4)

Models	Test	Accuracy (%)	MSE (%)	Recall (%)	Precision (%)
Batch-16	0.10	97.57	.9497	97.56	97.57
	0.25	98.28	.7182	98.28	98.28
	0.50	97	1.1804	97	97.01
Batch-32	0.10	96.93	1.1836	96.92	96.93
	0.25	97.90	.8572	97.89	97.90
	0.50	96.44	1.3395	96.44	96.44
Batch-64	0.10	98.80	.4789	98.80	98.81
	0.25	98.51	.6239	98.50	98.51
	0.50	97.62	.9368	97.61	97.62

Table 6. Previous novel literature involved in classifying PPG signals

Authors year	Dataset used	Feature extraction	Algorithms	Score
Nour et al. [16] 2020	PPG-BP dataset [20]	No (used existing features)	Random forest,	Accuracy 99.5%,
Tjahjadi et al. [17] 2020	PPG-BP dataset [20]	Short-time Fourier transform (STFT)	BLSTM (100 hidden; 3 Dense layers)	Accuracy 99.33%
Liang et al. [15] 2018	MIMIC	CWT	Pre-trained google net	-
Liang et al. [14] 2018	MIMIC	PAT and PPG features	AdaBoost Tree; LR, KNN, bagged tree	PAT & PPG: F-score: 74.67%, 63%, 84%, 83%
Yao et al. [18] 2020	Open clinical trial dataset	PPG signal	SVM	Accuracy 88%
Sannino et al. [13] 2020	UCI and MIMIC-II	Random-forest	Accuracy 80%	
Tjahjadi et al. [19] 2020	PPG-BP dataset [20]	Raw signals	KNN	Accuracy 86.7%
Jindal et al. [23] 2016	TROIKA dataset	Not specified	DBN & RBM's	Accuracy 96.1%
Proposed	**BIDMIC-PPG dataset**	**DT-CWT**	**GRU+ FC layers**	**Accuracy: 98.82%**

7   Conclusion

An automatic warning system is necessary for the detection of hypertension, therefore is needed for the timely and accurate evaluation of this disease. The users can immediately evaluate blood pressure and check for hypertension easily and accurately using the proposed technique. The proposed technique (combined with DTCWT and GRU's) significantly improves the classification and performance of the system and makes accurate detections. The proposed method is resilient to noise and motion artifacts. It performs better than the traditional machine learning algorithms such as, k-NN, random forest, bagging, and boosting classifiers. By using DT-CWT, feature extraction is simplified by analysing the underlying features using dual tree schema and make it robust. The loss of energy of the signal is low compared to the other feature extraction techniques which uses wavelet transformation. The feature extraction works better than the PPG features, PAT features and PPG morphological features. The proposed technique results have been evaluated using various classification metrics such as Accuracy, MSE, Recall, and Precision. The model performed state-of-the-art by attaining 98.8% accuracy and 98.81% precision for BIDMC PPG dataset [21]. In future, the PGG signal is analysed in variant classes to provide multi-attribute relationship related to CHD.

References

1. Gabb, G.M., Mangoni, A.A., Anderson, C.S., et al.: Guideline for the diagnosis and management of hypertension in adults - 2016. Med. J. Aust. **205**(2), 85–89 (2016). https://doi.org/10.5694/mja16.00526
2. Allen, J.: Photoplethysmography and its application in clinical physiological measurement. Physiol. Measur. **28**(3), R1 (2007)
3. Mendis, S., et al.: Global atlas on cardiovascular disease prevention and control. World Health Organization (2011)
4. Chobanian, A.V., et al.: The seventh report of the joint national committee on prevention, detection, evaluation, and treatment of high blood pressure. Hypertension **42**, 1206–1252 (2003)
5. Mukkamala, R., et al.: Toward ubiquitous blood pressure monitoring via pulse transit time: theory and practice. IEEE Trans. Biomed. Eng. **62**(8), 1879–1901 (2015). https://doi.org/10.1109/TBME.2015.2441951
6. Ding, X., Zhang, Y., Liu, J., Dai, W., Tsang, H.K.: Continuous cuffless blood pressure estimation using pulse transit time and photoplethysmogram intensity ratio. IEEE Trans. Biomed. Eng. **63**(5), 964–972 (2016). https://doi.org/10.1109/TBME.2015.2480679
7. Yoon, Y., et al.: Cuff-less blood pressure estimation using pulse waveform analysis and pulse arrival time. IEEE J. Biomed. Health Inform. **22**(4), 1068–1074 (2018). https://doi.org/10.1109/JBHI.2017.2714674
8. Xing, X., Sun, M.: Optical blood pressure estimation with photoplethysmography and FFT-based neural networks. Biomed. Opt. Express **7**, 3007–3020 (2016)
9. Li, Y., Wang, Z., Zhang, L., Yang, X., Song, J.: Characters available in photoplethysmogram for blood pressure estimation: beyond the pulse transit time. Australas. Phys. Eng. Sci. Med. **37**(2), 367–376 (2014). https://doi.org/10.1007/s13246-014-0269-6
10. Martínez, G., et al.: Can photoplethysmography replace arterial blood pressure in the assessment of blood pressure? J. Clin. Med. **7**(10), 316 (2018)
11. Elgendi, M., et al.: The use of photoplethysmography for assessing hypertension. NPJ Digital Med. **2**(1), 1–11 (2019)
12. Cvetkovic, D., Übeyli, E.D., Cosic, I.: Wavelet transform feature extraction from human PPG, ECG, and EEG signal responses to ELF PEMF exposures: a pilot study. Digital Signal Process. **18**(5), 861–874 (2008)
13. Sannino, G., De Falco, I., De Pietro, G.: Non-invasive risk stratification of hypertension: a systematic comparison of machine learning algorithms. J. Sens. Actuator Netw. **9**(3), 34 (2020)
14. Liang, Y., et al.: Hypertension assessment via ECG and PPG signals: an evaluation using a MIMIC database. Diagnostics **8**(3), 65 (2018)

15. Liang, Y., et al.: Photoplethysmography and deep learning: enhancing hypertension risk stratification. Biosensors **8**(4), 101 (2018)
16. Nour, M., Polat, K.: Automatic classification of hypertension types based on personal features by machine learning algorithms. Math. Probl. Eng. **2020**, 1–13 (2020)
17. Tjahjadi, H., Ramli, K., Murfi, H.: Noninvasive classification of blood pressure based on photoplethysmography signals using bidirectional long short-term memory and time-frequency analysis. IEEE Access **8**, 20735–20748 (2020)
18. Yao, L., Liu, W.: The hypertension assessment based on features extraction using a PPG signal and its derivatives. Physiol. Meas. (2020)
19. Tjahjadi, H., Ramli, K.: Noninvasive blood pressure classification based on photoplethysmography using k-nearest neighbors algorithm: a feasibility study. Information **11**(2), 93 (2020)
20. Liang, Y., et al.: A new, short-recorded photoplethysmogram dataset for blood pressure monitoring in China. Sci. Data **5**, 180020 (2018)
21. Pimentel, M.A.F., et al.: Toward a robust estimation of respiratory rate from pulse oximeters. IEEE Trans. Biomed. Eng. **64**(8), 1914–1923 (2016)
22. Su, P., et al.: Long-term blood pressure prediction with deep recurrent neural networks. In: 2018 IEEE EMBS International Conference on Biomedical and Health Informatics (BHI). IEEE (2018)
23. Jindal, V., et al.: An adaptive deep learning approach for PPG-based identification. In: 2016 38th Annual International Conference of the IEEE Engineering in Medicine and Biology Society (EMBC). IEEE (2016)
24. Sesso, H.D., et al.: Systolic and diastolic blood pressure, pulse pressure, and mean arterial pressure as predictors of cardiovascular disease risk in men. Hypertension **36**(5), 801–807 (2000)
25. Ye, S.Y., et al.: Estimation of systolic and diastolic pressure using the pulse transit time. World Acad. Sci. Eng. Technol. **67**, 726–731 (2010)
26. Goldberger, A.L., et al.: PhysioBank, PhysioToolkit, and PhysioNet: components of a new research resource for complex physiologic signals. Circulation **101**(23), e215–e220 (2000)
27. Faragallah, O.S.: Efficient video watermarking based on singular value decomposition in the discrete wavelet transform domain. AEU-Int. J. Electron. Commun. **67**(3), 189–196 (2013)
28. Chen, G.: Automatic EEG seizure detection using dual-tree complex wavelet-Fourier features. Expert Syst. Appl. **41**(5), 2391–2394 (2014)
29. Kingsbury, N.: Complex wavelets for shift invariant analysis and filtering of signals. Appl. Comput. Harmonic Anal. **10**(3), 234–253 (2001)
30. Selesnick, I.W., Baraniuk, R.G., Kingsbury, N.C.: The dual-tree complex wavelet transform. IEEE Sig. Process. Mag. **22**(6), 123–151 (2005)
31. Manoharan, S.: A Dual tree complex wavelet transform construction and its application to image denoising. Int. J. Image Process. (IJIP) **3**(6), 293 (2010)
32. Liang, Y., et al.: An optimal filter for short photoplethysmogram signals. Sci. Data **5**, 180076 (2018)
33. Cui, Z., et al.: Deep bidirectional and unidirectional LSTM recurrent neural network for network-wide traffic speed prediction. arXiv preprint arXiv:1801.02143 (2018)
34. Lo, F.P.-W., et al.: Continuous systolic and diastolic blood pressure estimation utilizing long short-term memory network. In: 2017 39th Annual International Conference of the IEEE Engineering in Medicine and Biology Society (EMBC). IEEE (2017)

35. Yildirim, O., et al.: A new approach for arrhythmia classification using deep coded features and LSTM networks. Comput. Methods Programs Biomed. **176**, 121–133 (2019)
36. Chollet, F.: Keras: deep learning library for theano and tensorflow. **7**(8), T1 (2015). https://keras.io/k
37. Abadi, M., et al.: Tensorflow: a system for large-scale machine learning. In: 12th USENIX symposium on operating systems design and implementation (OSDI 2016). 2016
38. Chung, J., Gulcehre, C., Cho, K., Bengio, Y.: Empirical evaluation of gated recurrent neural networks on sequence modeling. In: NIPS 2014 Workshop on Deep Learning, December 2014 (2014)
39. Yin, W., Kann, K., Yu, M., Schütze, H.: Comparative study of CNN and RNN for natural language processing. arXiv preprint arXiv:1702.01923 (2017)
40. Smith, S.L., Kindermans, P.-J., Ying, C., Le, Q.V.: Don't decay the learning rate, increase the batch size. In: International Conference on Learning Representations (2018)

Large Scale Efficient Clustering Using DBSCAN and Ensemble Techniques

D. Pradeep Kumar[1(✉)], B. J. Sowmya[1], R. Hanumantharaju[1], Anita Kanavalli[1],
S. Seema[1], and K. N. Shreenath[2]

[1] Department of Computer Science and Engineering, M S Ramaiah Institute of Technology,
Bengaluru, India
{Pradeepkumard,sowmyabj,hmrcs,anithak,seemas}@msrit.edu
[2] Department of Computer Science and Engineering, Siddaganga Institute of Technology,
Tumkur, India
shreenathk_n@sit.ac.in

Abstract. Data clustering techniques are unsupervised machine learning techniques used in the field of data mining. Different clustering technique operate and perform differently based on the characteristics of input dataset. DBSCAN is a popular clustering technique with great ability to cluster datasets of arbitrary shapes and different sizes and densities using the principle of density estimation and noise removal. Density based clustering has proven to be very efficient and has found numerous applications across several domains. But DBSCAN does not perform well with clusters of similar densities and has a worst case run-time complexity of $O(n^2)$ for high dimensional data. In this paper we try to overcome the drawbacks by developing SuperCube based Accelerated Density Based Spatial Clustering algorithm that detects the clusters by performing a dimensionality reduction that is, transforming high dimensional complex data into a lower dimensionality data and uses a unique combination of a virtual grid and employs representative points which reduces the time complexity to $O(n \log n)$. Results from the experiments with Datasets of varying sizes and dimensions are presented which proves that the proposed algorithm performs with greater accuracy and effectiveness.

Keywords: SuperCube · Ensemble techniques · Density based spatial clustering of applications · Superimposing

1 Introduction

Clustering is one of the most widely used methods and one of many effective data analysis techniques for unsupervised learning. It is a helpful approach that attempts to assemble the input data set with respect to any similarities into a list of finite ranges of semantically compatible groups. These algorithms, especially hierarchical algorithms, density-based algorithms, partitioned algorithms, graph-based algorithms, combinational algorithms, model-based algorithms and grid-based algorithms, can be loosely categorized into seven

A. K. Luhach et al. (Eds.): ICAICR 2020, CCIS 1393, pp. 622–636, 2021.
https://doi.org/10.1007/978-981-16-3660-8_58

groups. Density-based algorithms are noted for their concise description and hence the comparatively straightforward implementation of these varieties of algorithms. Another vital feature of this algorithm is that, even in an outlier data set, it is able to discover clusters of varying shapes and different sizes and does not require users to determine the number of clusters. DBSCAN defines denser area clusters and low density regions are classified as noise or outliers, providing high-quality output that depends on two specified parameters, Eps and MinPts. The basic principle behind such a cluster finding algorithm is that the neighbor points of the specified radius Eps would consist of the smallest number of points (MinPts) for each point in the cluster. An item is automatically picked by DBSCAN and evaluated only once. The neighborhood of the object is analyzed in such a manner that a cluster to which objects can be added later is created if it satisfies the minimum requirement for forming a cluster, and if the neighborhood objects do not fulfil the lowest threshold criterion, it is declared a noisy object. Many clustering tools are unable to classify clusters of arbitrary shapes, so DBSCAN has the bonus of being able to recognize a cluster of arbitrary shapes. The drawbacks of DBSCAN include the complexity of the worst case, tending to $O(n^2)$. Additionally, spatial indexing methods do not work efficiently for higher dimensional data, the runtime complexity grows from $O (n \log n)$ to $O (n^2)$ for high dimensions. To overcome these issues, the SuperDBSCAN algorithm which is a combination of the SuperCube based Accelerated DBSCAN algorithm along with PCA (Principal Component Analysis) is proposed. This algorithm runs with a temporal complexity of $O (n \log n)$, even for higher dimensional data and uses a unique combination of a virtual grid, which is imposed on the input data and employs representative points, this significantly reduces the number of comparisons that need to be made, which translates into a significant run time speed up of up to 52.57% when compared to other proposed improvements. The PCA algorithm attempts to derive a low-dimensional set of features from a much larger set while still preserving as much variance as possible and also visualizing higher dimensional data. Another criticism of the DBSCAN algorithm has been that it is sensitive to its input parameters and MINPTS. The Super DBSCAN algorithm eliminates the need for the MINPTS parameter thus making it more accessible to non-expert users. The major contribution of this article is summarized as follows:

1. To reduce High dimensional to low dimensional data.
2. To identify and classify similar density clusters.
3. It maintains 100% accuracy of the original DBSCAN algorithm
4. It achieves a significant speed up in run time when compared to other improvements proposed for the DBSCAN algorithm.
5. It eliminates the need for the MINPTS input parameter, making the algorithm more user-friendly for non-expert users.

2   Literature Survey

DBSCAN was originally introduced by Ester and Kriegel, which was used as an underlying algorithm in many applications. A large amount of work has been done in the area of DBSCAN like parallel computing, dimensionality reductions, cloud computing, etc. to enhance and increase the accuracy and efficiency of DBSCAN clustering method. A research had been carried out to develop an algorithm which could improve the density calculations on the data set and thereby decreasing accuracy loss.

[1] Algorithm makes use of a ranked retrieval technique called WAND in order to improve the results of DBSCAN clustering. It further works by reducing the invoking times of WAND. [2] Another approach introduces in the modification of DBSCAN algorithm that was P- DBSCAN, used for the detection of geo tagged photos using the concept of adaptive density for fast convergence towards high density regions. In this method, the density threshold is also used as one of the factors for efficient working of DBSCAN. [3] Another methodology has been done in Linear DBSCAN calculation dependent on area delicate hashing. The fundamental territories of this paper incorporate including more info boundaries and lacking of over-simplification. Not at all like the first DBSCAN, this procedure utilizes LSH which requires quicker locale inquiry for k neighbors of an information point. This paper incorporates a seed point determination strategy, which depends on impact space and neighborhood closeness, to choose some seed focuses rather than all the area during bunch development is utilized in this work. Therefore, the quantity of district inquiries can be diminished, in this way guaranteeing better calculation precision. [4] An equal DBSCAN bunching calculation was likewise executed in past works for treatment of the huge scope information preparing utilizing the huge information handling stage called Spark. Flash, as another age of quick broadly useful motor for huge scope information handling, gives strong circulated dataset reflection for information stockpiling that dispenses with the requirement for middle outcomes to be shipped off the disseminated document frameworks, and thus it improves continuous information preparing. [5] presents the dimensionality decrease strategies and their appropriateness for different kinds of information and application zones. In this paper they have clarified the Linear Dimension Reduction Technique (LDRTs) and Non-Direct Dimension Reduction Technique (NLRDTs) which thusly have a few administered, solo and semi-managed methods to accomplish low dimensionality. When done a similar report among LDRT and NLRDT can presume that LDRT requires less calculation force and cost. [6] Myat Cho Mon Oo and Thandar Thein have proposed a proficient prescient examination framework for high dimensional enormous information by improving adaptable irregular forest calculation on Apache Spark stage. The viability of the proposed framework is inspected on five-genuine world datasets and results showed that the proposed framework accomplishes profoundly serious execution contrasted and RF calculation actualized by Spark MLib [7]. In this paper, a strategy for coordinating dull information is proposed and Nonnegative grid factorization is applied to the bunching gathering model dependent on dim information. From the start the distinctive base grouping results are acquired by utilizing different bunching designs and NMF is applied to get coordinated outcomes which fills in as appeared in the underneath graph. Test results show that the strategy beats other bunching group procedures [8]. This examination presents an exhaustive

investigation of DBSCAN calculation and the improved adaptation of DBSCAN calculation with its usage utilizing mat lab. In this cycle, the information has been isolated impeccably, at that point new testing strategy will applied so as to decrease the thickness of thick information and get information with just a single thickness circulation (meager information), the consequences of examining were viable. They have utilized three strategies to get the normal yield which resembles the figure underneath. [9] LI Meng'ao and MENG Dongxue, *GU Songyuan, LIU Shufen proposed a paper so as to conquer the time cost of the calculation dependent on lattice cell based calculation. This strategy has been checked tentatively that DBSCAN calculation dependent on matrix cells shows higher exactness and lower time multifaceted nature. [10] In this paper the specialists have proposed a method that decreases the time unpredictability of dbscan calculation contrasted with the first calculation with a period intricacy of O(N). They have proposed a calculation with LSH where It looks for the surmised Nearest Neighbor Points rather than the exact Nearest Neighbor Points and LSH restores a few purposes of the circle whose middle is p and the range is $(1 + \varepsilon)$d. ε is doled out by the clients and $\varepsilon > 0$. [11] This paper which focuses on a new method to solve dimensionality problems where clustering is integrated with correlation measure to produce good feature subset. Evaluated computational time and accuracy of proposed method with Relief and IG methods. Relief (Kira and Rendell, 1992) present a feature selection approach based on instance based attribute ranking scheme called RELIEF algorithm. It deals with incomplete, noisy and multiclass datasets. [12] This paper clarifies about another closeness measure that represents excess of information that are dissipated a similar way from a given point. The run-time assessment shows that both the separation based and common neighbor based thickness gauges have a similar quadratic time unpredictability as for dataset size. Examination of commotion impacts showed that both DBSCAN and CI-DBSCAN have a similar power to the clamor. [13] The archive joins thickness tops grouping and gravitational pursuit strategy to upgrade information bunching which proposes an altered component of choosing the cut-off separation.

[2] The introduced strategy chooses the enhanced starting bunch communities then the age of the underlying populace is executed dependent on the arrangement of applicant groups. They give an improved instrument on boundary choice which will expand the exhibition of grouping. [14] This paper clarifies about building up another DBSCAN calculation for assessing the quantity of groups by advancing a probabilistic cycle, in particular DBSCAN-Martingale, which includes arbitrariness in the choice of thickness boundaries and lessen the quantity of emphases needed to separate all bunches. This work fundamentally centers around logical recipe for the normal number of separated bunches per DBSCAN-acknowledgment by outlining with the time administrator and age in thickness based grouping. [15] The archive clarifies about another upgraded DBSCAN-Martingale probabilistic cycle calculation for assessing the quantity of groups, which includes arbitrariness in the choice of thickness boundaries and lessen the quantity of emphases needed to remove all bunches. The tests acknowledged in this work, in the covering bunch altering issue one can decrease the quantity of between group edges by covering at least two bunches. At that point, it might be smarter to embed vertex in more than one group than to eliminate edges from that vertex.

Grouping calculations are alluring for the assignment of class recognizable proof in spatial information bases. In any case, the notable calculations experience the ill effects of serious downsides when applied to huge spatial information bases, most of which could be the expanding time unpredictability and finding the groups for high dimensional information.

3 Design

The idea aims at finding a better and suitable technique for the clustering purpose in regard with DBSCAN. The propose a method to reduce high dimensional data to low dimensional data and thereby reducing the time complexity. The aim of this work is to design such an algorithm which could be used to increase the efficiency of finding clusters of high dimensional datasets using the DBSCAN approach. Also, it reduces the time complexity for the same. It defines all the necessary modules used for this approach of clustering, for example, with respect to the data analysis for handling high dimensional data is done using PCA technique which projecting the high dimensional data in a space for lower dimensional subspace, data pre-processing techniques involves outlier detection, handling missing values of attributes, redundant data and similar density data. The initial step in our work includes the data pre-processing. Data pre-processing is an integral step in Machine Learning as the quality of data and the useful information that can be derived from it directly affects the ability of our model to learn; therefore, it is extremely important that the pre-process our data before feeding it into our model. Standardize our dataset in such a manner that obtain equal values for the given data, that is convert the strings to integers (Fig. 1).

Unsupervised Learning a Machine Learning technique that has been pre-owned in our idea. This technique has various applications such as segmenting datasets by some shared attributes. Detecting anomalies that do not fit to any group, and simplifying datasets by aggregating variables with similar attributes. The objective of clustering is to find different groups within the elements in the data. To do so, clustering algorithms find the structure in the data so that elements of the same cluster (or group) are more similar to each other than to those from different clusters. Ensuing the data pre-processing takes place the data is split into two sets: the training and the testing data. It is based on a number of points with a specified radius ε and there is a special label assigned to each datapoint. The process of assigning this label is the following:

- It is a specified number (MinPts) of neighbour points. A core point will be assigned if there is this MinPts number of points that fall in the ε radius.
- A border point will fall in the ε radius of a core point, but will have less neighbours than the MinPts number.
- Every other point will be noise points.

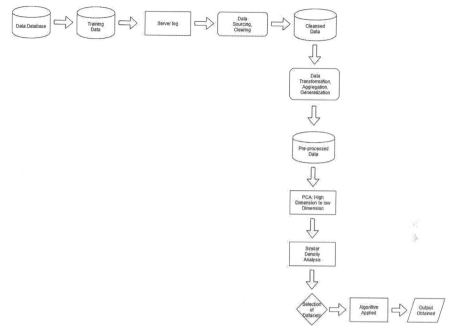

Fig. 1. Proposed framework for the efficient clustering

4 Implementation and Results

Usage of a novel methodology known as SuperCube based Accelerated Density Based Spatial Clustering for Applications, in this algorithm. Here, our algorithm executes with a time complexity of O(nlogn), even for higher dimensional data. It unstratified a virtual cube on the given data set and uses the idea of representative points to reduce the number of comparisons. It provides significant run time speed up when compared to other proposed improvements and eliminates the need for one input parameter MINPTS, thus making it easier to use for naive users.

A series of steps have been followed to obtain accurate results. Commencing the process of data processing, followed by merging conditions and then the superimposing supercube to choosing the representation points.

Pre-processing
Perform a pre-processing step on the input data and sort the data set according to one of the dimensions. For example, a two dimensional data set is first sorted according to the X coordinates and then the result is sorted according to the Y coordinates. Hence this approach of data sorting is extensible for any dimension. This pre-processing speeds up the supercube allocation as explained below.

The Merging Condition

As explained below the algorithm checks if the distance between two points is less than the input parameter. If it is, then the two supercubes that these two points belong to are merged to belong to the same cluster.

Superimposing Super Cubes

One of the key ideas of this proposed algorithm is the formation of the Supercubes. These Supercubes are contributory in providing us an execution speed improvement via the original DBSCAN algorithm. A supercube is an n-dimensional analogue of a square (n = 2) and a cube (n = 3). A Supercube has all the properties that a cube has in three dimensional space, but in n dimensional space, it is a closed, compact, convex figure whose 1-skeleton consists of groups of opposite parallel line segments aligned in each of the space's dimensions, perpendicular to each other and of the same length. So in 1-D a Supercube is a line segment, a square in 2-D, a cube in 3-D, a tesseract in 4-D and so on. Supercubes for the first four dimensions are shown in Fig. 3. Based on the dimensionality of the data, overlay a virtual Supercube on the points such that the length of the space diagonal of the Supercube is.

Deciding the area in space where the 2-D grid needs to be constructed. For this define the boundary by taking the minimum and maximum of X and Y coordinates respectively. Once the scope of the grid is defined, construct the boxes and superimpose this grid on the original data set. The key idea for the construction of this grid is that, construct it in such a way that every point in a particular box is guaranteed to belong to the same cluster. This provides us a significant speed up, as instead of checking each and every point against each point in the data set as in the original DBSCAN algorithm, just need to check if any one point in the box satisfies the merging condition, if it does all the points belonging to that particular box are guaranteed to satisfy the merging condition too. This property is guaranteed by the virtue of creation of the boxes. Choose the diagonal of each box to be equal to the parameter that is input to the algorithm, thus create boxes of length = breadth = $l/\sqrt{2}$. Therefore, the maximum distance between any two points inside the box is never greater than, consequently they belong to the same cluster. This approach scales with dimensions. For two dimensional data set construct a grid consisting of flat boxes, for three dimensional data, create a grid of cubes where the length of the space diagonal is equal to and so on.

Choosing Representative Points

For n dimensional data, need $2(n + 1)$ representative points. For sake of explanation, consider two dimensional data. Hence for each face of the grid, define eight Representative Points. These points are labelled as follows:

- Top
- Top Right
- Right
- Bottom Right
- Bottom
- Bottom Left

- Left
- Top Left

These points are the boundary points of the box.

For example, the Top point is the top-most point inside the box. Use a token ring approach to distribute points to these eight positions which is explained here. To decide which box does the point belong to, divide the point by $l/\sqrt{2}$ in each dimension to obtain the corresponding band in which the point lies. The intersection of these bands gives us the box in which the point lies. In case the grid does not start from the origin, perform a origin shift transformation. If any points are found to lie exactly on the edge of the box round up the division. As the first point is entered into a new box, all of these eight positions are initialized to that point. An ideal position with respect to representative points is defined as a case where representative point lie on the edge of the box as shown in Fig. 2. Now whenever a new point is encountered, each position calculates the Euclidean distance between the ideal position and the current point and the point being examined. If a new point is found to have a smaller distance, the corresponding representative point is updated with the new point. Obviously multiplicity is allowed, that is one point can represent multiple positions. This process is repeated for all the points belonging to a particular box.

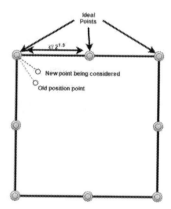

Fig. 2. The distance between the new point and the ideal position is compared with the distance between the representative point and the ideal position, if the former is lesser the new point is updated as the new representative point.

Depth First Search

Now to implement the main clustering; traverse the entire grid in a depth first fashion. Start with the box closest to the shifted origin. At any given point of time, compare the two closest representative points between boxes. For example, in a two-dimensional space, begin by checking if the top representative point of the current box i is within an - distance of the Bottom representative point of the top neighbor box j. Traversal in a clockwise fashion. If the distance between corresponding points is less than, the merging condition is said to be satisfied and all the points in both these boxes are labeled to belong to the same cluster. If the merging condition fails, the next box in the DFS traversal is checked and the cluster IDs are not updated.

Layering

Two points belong to the same cluster if the distance between them is less then, the location of the points inside the boxes are not known. Therefore, it is entirely possible that the distance between points in two consecutive boxes can be less. That is, consider only neighboring boxes in our depth first traversal, the j-layer; bound to miss points that are at a distance which is less than. Consequently, the accuracy of the algorithm suffers. To overcome this problem, introduce a concept of layering. If the traversal for the j-layer box returns a failure, check for the $(j + 1)$ th layer box in the same direction, subject to the condition that the distance between the representative points is less than. Check the $(j + 1)^{th}$ layer box only for non-diagonal neighbors which again reduces the number of iterations. This can be done because the grids are designed in such a way that the diagonal of each box is equal to the value of, therefore two points in the diagonal direction cannot be at a distance less than and not lie in consecutive boxes.

Density based clustering techniques especially DBSCAN have found innumerable applications across domains. The Traditional DBSCAN algorithm has a time complexity of $O(n^2)$ which reduces to $O(n \log n)$ when spatial indexing. However, the complexity again rises to $O(n^2)$ for high dimensional data. Here, proposed a new algorithm, Super DBSCAN, to overcome the drawbacks of DBSCAN. This algorithm runs with a temporal complexity of $O(n \log n)$ which uses a unique combination of a virtual grid, that is imposed on the input data and employs representative points which reduces the number of comparisons that need to be made and in turn reduces the time complexity. Our projected algorithm is an easy but efficient and effective algorithm and it boosts the performance of DBSCAN in adjacent clusters with different densities.

Algorithm 1:
Principle Component Analysis
PCA algorithm(X, k): top k eigenvalues/eigenvectors
X = N × m is a data matrix,
every point in data x_i = column vector, I =1 to m
• X mean x is subtracted from each column vector x_i in the X
• ΣXX^T ... covariance matrix of X
• { λ_i , u_i }i=1..N = eigenvectors/eigenvalues of Σ ... $\lambda_1 \geq \lambda_2 \geq ... \geq \lambda_N$
• Return { λ_i , u_i }i=1..k
% top k principal components

Algorithm 2:
SuperCube creation and initialization
function: GENERATE-SuperCUBE(data set D,)
input: data set D containing all input points and user input parameter
output: SuperCubeDetailsNbPos : coordinates are considered as key and its updated position details as value
foreach dimension i in n **do**
> //n is number of dimension of data set D which is globally defined iBand $\leftarrow$ generate steps of $\sqrt{2}$ by incrementally increasing from shifted origin to boundary of the Supercube container for every axis ;

End
foreach value v in every iBand **do**
SuperCubeList $\leftarrow$ generate all the combination of Supercube for v;
end
foreach SuperCubePoint k in SuperCubeList **do**
> Position $\leftarrow$ IDENTIFY-POSITION-OF-SuperCUBE(k); SuperCubeDetailsNbPos $\leftarrow$ APPEND(k , NEIGHBOURING-POINTS(k), Position);

End
> **return** SuperCubeDetailsNbPos;

Algorithm 3:
Computation of Representative Points
function: COMPUTE-REPRESENTATIVE-POINTS(data set D,)
input: data set D containing all input points and user input parameter
output: SuperCubeDetailsRepPts: coordinates are considered as key and its updated points as value
Foreach data point j in data set D containing data points **do** IdentifiedSuperCube $\leftarrow$ FIND-CORRESPONDING-SuperCUBE-OF-POINT(j);
Status $\leftarrow$ CHECK-VISITED(IdentifiedSuperCube)
if Status is not visited **then** // visiting for the first time
> initialize all the $2^{(n+1)}$ representative points to the current j point; // n is number of dimension for data set D which is globally defined

> end
> else
> foreach representative point l ∈ set$2^{(n+1)}$ representative points) do
>> compare euclidean distance between the ideal point-and-the current point represented by a and ideal point-and-representative point l represented by b ;
>> **if** a < b **then**
>>> updated representative data point l $\leftarrow$ current data point j ;
>> end
>> end
end
> SuperCubeDetailsRepPts $\leftarrow$ insert the current point j in
> IdentifiedSuperCube with its updated $2^{(n+1)}$ representative points ;
> **End**
return SuperCubeDetailsRepPts;

Algorithm 4:
Clustering mechanism for SuperCube
function: CLUSTERING-FUNCTION(SuperCubeDetails, CurrentSuperCube)
input: CurrentSuperCube:Supercube under consideration and SuperCubeDetails:dictionary with Supercube coordinate as key and its updated neighbouring points, representative points, position details as value
output: ClusterList = contains list of complete number of points and cluster in every
cluster **if** CurrentSuperCube is not visited **then**
    if CurrentSuperCube is opened **then**
    foreach NeighbouringSuperCube of CurrentSuperCube **do**
      if distance between corresponding representative points < for NeighbouringSuperCube in jth layer **then**
      ClusterID$_{NeighbourSuperCube}$ ← ClusterID$_{CurrentSuperCube}$; //merging cluster
      Mark CurrentSuperCube as visited;
        CLUSTERING-FUNCTION(NeighbourSuperCube, SuperCubeDetails); // recursive call
      End
      else
      if the NeighbouringSuperCube is not a diagonal Supercube **then**
          if distance metric between respective representative data points < for NeighbouringSuperCube
in (j + 1)th layer of the Supercube **then**
          ClusterIDNeighbourSuperCube ← ClusterIDCurrentSuperCube; // merging cluster
            Mark CurrentSuperCube as visited; CLUSTERING-FUNCTION(NeighbourSuperCube,
SuperCubeDetails); // recursive call
        end
        else
          check for the next NeighbouringSuperCube;
        end
      end
      else
          check for the next NeighbouringSuperCube ; // distance greater than , merging condition
violated
      end
      end
    end
  end
  else
do nothing; // check for the next Supercube in next function call
end
end
else
do nothing; // check for the next Supercube in next function call
end
return ClusterList;

Algorithm 5:
SuperCube based Accelerated DBSCAN
Function: SuperCUBE-BASED-ACCELERATED-DBSCAN(data set D,)
input:data set D containing all input points, user input parameter indicating the density of the clusters needed.
Output: Reduced Data obtained from PCA shifted to LastClusterList.
LastClusterList = aggregation of individual ClusterList for each Supercube initialize
CurrentClusterID=1; SuperCubeDetails1 ← GENERATE-SuperCUBE(data set D,);
SuperCubeDetails2 ← COMPUTE-REPRESENTATIVE-POINTS(data set D,);
SuperCubeDetails ← SuperCubeDetails1 + SuperCubeDetails2
foreach Supercube k in SuperCubeDetails **do**
if k is not visited and k has some points **then**
    mark k as visited;
    ClusterIDk ← CurrentClusterID;
    LastClusterList = LastClusterList + CLUSTERING-FUNCTION(SuperCubeDetails, current Supercube
k,)
    CurrentClusterID = CurrentClusterID+1;
    end
    else
    pass to the next Supercube in SuperCubeDetails
    end
end
return LastClusterList;

To check the time and the efficiency of the proposed SCA-DBSCAN algorithm, conduct multiple experiments. To verify the results, run the DBSCAN algorithm and the FastDBSCAN algorithm on the same data sets with the same input parameters and compare the accuracy of the results as well as the time taken by each algorithm to achieve those results. Run the algorithm on three different data sets that represent three different types of data: sparsely distributed data (synthetic data set 1), tightly coupled data and data with arbitrary shape that classical partition based algorithms fail to identify (synthetic data set 2). After performing the proposed algorithm on the obtained data sets can observe the following results: DATA SET 1.

On comparing both the algorithms, can conclude that the number of clusters formed are 5 with an accuracy of 0.166 for the original DBSCAN while, the proposed algorithm gives us an accuracy of 0.85714 and the time taken is 0.722 s with the number of points obtained individually for each cluster is 50, which results in a tightly coupled data as shown in Fig. 3.

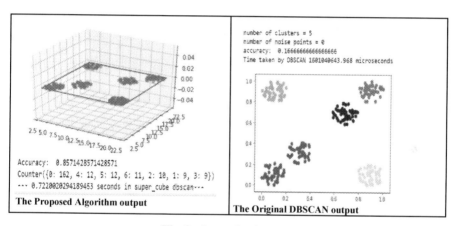

Fig. 3. Output for dataset 1

On comparing both the algorithms the number of clusters formed is 1 with an accuracy of 0.0667 for the original DBSCAN while the proposed algorithm gives us an accuracy of 1.0 and the time taken is 0.3517 s with the number of points obtained is 116, which results in a sparsely distributed data as shown in Fig. 4.

On comparing both the algorithms the number of clusters formed is 0 with an accuracy of 0.0 for the original DBSCAN while the proposed algorithm gives us an accuracy of 0.9714 and the time taken is 1.062 s with the number of points obtained is 1, which results in a sparsely coupled data and as shown in Fig. 5.

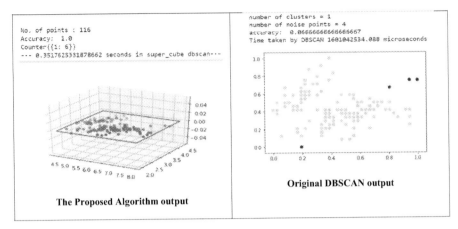

Fig. 4. Output for dataset 2

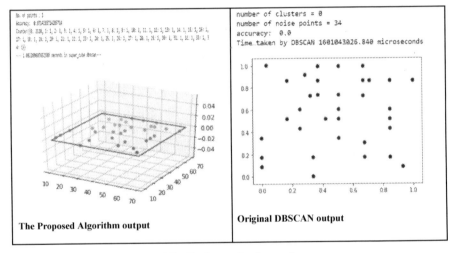

Fig. 5. Output for dataset 3

On comparing both the algorithms the number of clusters formed is 3 with an accuracy of 0.156 for the original DBSCAN while the proposed algorithm gives us an accuracy of 0.8 and the time taken is 0.627 s with the number of points obtained as 50 for cluster 1, 2 and 3 while cluster 4 consists of 42 points, which results in an arbitrary size and shaped data and as shown in Fig. 6.

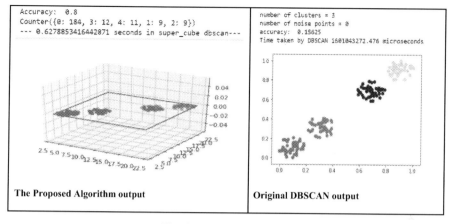

Fig. 6. Output for dataset 4

5 Conclusion

Established an algorithm that centralizes around the drawbacks of a common machine learning technique known as DBSCAN. Through this user a naive user can competently lay hands on understanding the over comings of DBSCAN through a transparent algorithm that have implemented. Conducted a basic comparison with the supercube DBSCAN algorithm and the original DBSCAN where the accuracy and the time complexity are displayed clearly. The main concept of the DBSCAN algorithm is to locate regions of high density that are separated from one another by regions of low density. So it would suggest that while dealing with spatial clusters of different density, size and shape, it could be challenging to detect the cluster of points. The task can be even more complicated if the data contains noise and outliers. DBSCAN tends to be slower when working with large datasets since computation on similar datasets becomes time consuming as the datasets increase. Our research shows how it could be improvised or modified in a way that it identifies outliers easily with anomaly detection and also handles the large datasets thereby reducing the time complexity and also reducing the dimensionality. Aim at incorporating Dimensional reduction so as to increase the cluster performance for our work. Our work proposes a simple yet improvised version of DBSCAN which not only reduces the time complexity but increases the effectiveness and efficiency of the clustering altogether.

References

1. Mehta, J., Mathur, V., Sanjay, S.: HCA-DBSCAN: SuperCube based accelerated density based spatial clustering for applications with noise. IEEE (2019)
2. Zhang, Y., Wang, X., Li, B., Chen, W., Wang, T., Lei, K.: Dboost: a fast algorithm for DBSCAN-based clustering on high dimensional data. In: Bailey, J., Khan, L., Washio, T., Dobbie, G., Huang, J.Z., Wang, R. (eds.) Advances in Knowledge Discovery and Data Mining. LNCS (LNAI), vol. 9652, pp. 245–256. Springer, Cham (2016). https://doi.org/10.1007/978-3-319-31750-2_20

3. Schikuta, E.: Grid clustering: an efficient hierarchical clustering method for very large data sets. In: Proceedings of 13th International Conference on Pattern Recognition, vol. 2, pp. 101–105 (1996)
4. Kisilevich, S., Mansmann, F., Keim, D.: P-DBSCAN: a density based clustering algorithm for exploration and analysis of attractive areas using collections of geo-tagged photos. In: Proceedings of the 1st International Conference and Exhibition on Computing for Geospatial Research and Application (pp. 1–4) (2010)
5. Huang, F., et al.: Research on the parallelization of the DBSCAN clustering algorithm for spatial data mining based on the spark platform. Remote Sens. **9**(12), 1301 (2017)
6. He, Q., Gu, H.X., Wei, Q., Wang, X.: A novel DBSCAN based on binary local sensitive hashing and binary-KNN representation (2017)
7. Ayesha, S., Hanif, M.K., Talib, R.: Overview and comparative study of dimensionality reduction techniques for high dimensional data. Inf. Fusion **59**, 44–58 (2020)
8. Oo, M.C.M., Thein, T.: An efficient predictive analytics system for high dimensional big data. J. King Saud Univ.-Comput. Inf. Sci. (2019)
9. Ye, W., Wang, H., Yan, S., Li, T., Yang, Y.: Nonnegative matrix factorization for clustering ensemble based on dark knowledge. Knowl.-Based Syst. **163**, 624–631 (2019)
10. Kumari, A., Shrivastava, V., Pandey, A.: Reduction of DBSCAN time complexity for data mining using parallel computing techniques (2019)
11. Meng'Ao, L., Dongxue, M., Songyuan, G., Shufen, L.: Research and improvement of DBSCAN cluster algorithm. In: 2015 7th International Conference on Information Technology in Medicine and Education (ITME), pp. 537–540. IEEE (2015)
12. Wu, Y., Guo, J., Zhang, X.: A linear DBSCAN algorithm based on LSH (2007)
13. Chormunge, S., Jena, S.: Correlation based feature selection with clustering for high dimensional data. J. Electr. Syst. Inf. Technol. **5**(3), 542–549 (2018)
14. Ester, M., Kriegel, H.-P., Sander, J., Xu, X.: A density- based algorithm for discovering clusters in large spatial databases with noise. In: Proceedings of 2nd International Conference on Knowledge Discovery and Data Mining, Portland, OR, AAAI Press, 1996, pp. 226–231 (1996)
15. Guha, S., Rastogi, R., Shim, K.: CURE: a~ efficient clustering algorithms for large databases. In: Proceedings of ACM SIGMOD International Conference on Management of Data, Seattle, WA, 1998, pp. 73–84 (1998)
16. https://www.geeksforgeeks.org/dimensionality-reduction/?ref=lbp
17. A fast clustering algorithm to cluster very large categorical data sets in data mining, In: Proceedings of SIG- OD Workshop on Research Issues on Data Mining and Knowledge Discovery, Tech. Report 97–07, UBC, Dept. of CS (1997)
18. https://stackabuse.com/dimensionality-reduction-in-python-withr/

Usability Analysis of E-Governance Applications

Rajul Betala[✉] and Sushopti Gawade

Department of Computer Engineering, Pillai College of Engineering, Mumbai University, Panvel, Maharashtra, India
sgawade@mes.ac.in

Abstract. Ideally, E-Governance application should be simple, usable, and provide all government services online. But many countries are still facing issues in providing this. So, definition of e-governance is studied. 5 Surveys conducted by different organizations such as USA's Digital.gov, United Nations Department of Economic and Social Affairs (UNDESA), Institute for Management Development (IMD), International Academy of Chief Information Officer (IAC) & World Economic Forum are taken into consideration and links of 10 highest performing countries common in all these 5 surveys is used for analysis of usability & related parameters with online tools Qualidator & Site-Analyzer. In Qualidator tool, Australia's application ranks highest with 90.30% usability. In Site-Analyzer tool, Denmark's application ranks highest with 83.30% Overall Percentage. Usability & related parameters like Search Engine Optimization (SEO), Accessibility, Content, Design, and Performance are compared. The issues are studied and to resolve these issues, guiding principles given by Jacob Nielson are studied.

Keywords: E-Governance application · E-Government application · Usability analysis · Performance analysis · E-governance · E-government

1 Introduction

In the early 1990s, two changes swept across the world, which are, the focus on good governance with increasing private sector participation in the delivery of public services & Information Communication Technologies (ICTs) and secondly, the Internet, which contains technologies that potentially could connect anyone in real-time. E-Governance marked a paradigm shift in the philosophy of governance by involving: (i) Citizen Centricity instead of Process Centricity and (ii) Large-scale public participation through ICTs enablement [1]. The main goal of e-governance is to reach the beneficiary and to ensure that the services they need are delivered with high ease-of-use (usability) [5].

Usability is the degree to which a design can be used and achieve the required objectives with maximum effectiveness, efficiency, and satisfaction [8]. According to ISTQB (International Software Testing Qualifications Board) Definition, Usability analysis determines the degree to which an application is simple to understand, learn, and operate. Its main goal is to identify and gather qualitative and quantitative information about usability issues so that its results can help to resolve the issues faced by users. The Usability Analysis report helps to eliminate design problems and end-user frustration.

© Springer Nature Singapore Pte Ltd. 2021
A. K. Luhach et al. (Eds.): ICAICR 2020, CCIS 1393, pp. 637–648, 2021.
https://doi.org/10.1007/978-981-16-3660-8_59

[12] Different parameters are analyzed in Usability Analysis such as the Search Engine Optimization (SEO), Accessibility, Content, Design, and Performance of the application [10].

This paper attempts to bridge the gap present in the literature by analyzing usability and related parameters of the global perspective of e-government applications by taking into consideration a few of the e-government applications of different high performing counties in terms of e-governance. The usability analysis is done using online automated tools and the results of the analysis are compared and discussed.

The remaining paper is structured as follows. In the second section, the Literature Review is given which shows the existing manual or automated analysis done using usability and related paper. The third section shows the Methodology which is used to describe the tools, techniques, and data used for the analysis. Forth section provides the Results and Discussion about it in the context of usability and related parameters. The fifth section gives the Conclusion & Future Scope of the work.

2 Literature Review

Usability analysis of e-governance applications is found to be mostly limited to the study of 1 or 2 countries as depicted in Table 1 and as shown in the following few examples:

- Becker (2005) had written about the importance of usability of e-governance applications for higher aged adults in the US.
- Jaeger (2006) had performed an analysis of e-governance application in which Jaeger measured the accessibility and usability for disabled persons in the US.
- Asiimwe and Lim (2010) performed Usability Analysis of the Ugandan government websites and after analyzing the results they proposed several measures to increase Usability.
- Isa, Suhami, Safie, and Semsuddin (2011) carried out the usability analysis of e-governance applications of 155 Malaysian government with fully automated evaluation tools, then they found many usability issues. So, they provided many suggestions and guidelines for improving the usability of the applications.
- Youngblood and Mackiewicz (2012) tried to compare the usability analysis scores of all the municipal government websites created for the US state of Alabama [13].
- Nissar P. (2014) discussed e-governance in Kerala, in its research, while stating that the use of ICT imperative in any agenda drawn towards achieving good governance [14].
- Sumit Kumar Singh (2018) discussed the overview of e-governance in its research [15].
- There are many sponsored e-government literature series undertaken by the IBM Institute (IBM, 2004).
- Also, UN survey is done in each year or within 2 years (UNDESA, 2001, 2003, 2004, 2005, 2008, 2010, 2012, 2014, 2016, 2018) [16].

Table 1 and above examples of the literature depict that many researchers are studying usability in 1 or 2 governments but there are very few literature usability on an international global perspective. Also, Table 1 depicts that only a few literatures studying Usability with the other parameters such as Search Engine Optimization (SEO), Accessibility, Content, Performance, and Design in a single research. So, this research will act as a bridge that will fill these gaps in the literature.

Table 1. Literature review depicting Usability & related parameter analysis using an online tool or manual survey in 1 or 2 country governments (Abbreviation used are P = Parameter used, U = Usability, AC = Accessibility, S = Security, C = Content, SE = Service)

Year	P	Tools & techniques	Application or system used	Conclusion
2020	U, AC	U – Questionnaire survey (from 4 visually impaired (VI) teachers) AC – AChecker, HTML_CodeSniffer, SortSite, & Total Validator	Saudi electronic government educational systems: Noor, Faris, and iEN	For usability, the main issue reported by all participants is that most systems did not support the screen readers effectively For accessibility, the perceivable principle had 73% errors [2]
2020	U, AC, S	U – GTmetrix AC – WAVE S – Sucuri	25 Hungarian websites of public sector bodies	Results denoted that lot of improvements were needed so the authors came up with proposals to improve the parameters [3]
2020	U, AC	U, AC – Questionnaire survey (With 30 participants belonging to Russia and Bulgaria)	5 Bulgarian and 5 Russian websites of government institutions	Results were analyzed using 8 quantitative metrics given by web user interfaces (WUI) visual analysis service and it was found that overall ratings were significantly higher for Bulgarian websites [4]
2020	U, AC	U – Questionnaire survey AC – WAVE online tool	6 Ethiopian government websites were used. A survey was done with 175 participants for usability	Participants in this research were not satisfied with the services of the website [6]

(continued)

Table 1. (*continued*)

Year	P	Tools & techniques	Application or system used	Conclusion
2019	U, AC, C, S, SE	U – Questionnaire survey. AC – FAE 2.0 (Functional Accessibility Evaluator 2.0)	342 US County websites	An average of 41/100 accessibility score and 14.4/18 usability score was found [7]
2018	U, AC	U – Questionnaire survey (With 5 evaluators) AC – Accessibility Evaluator 2.0	279 e-government websites from 31 Sub-Saharan Africa countries	The average of 36.2% with the highest as 64.8% was found [9]
2017	U, AC	U – Questionnaire survey (conducted by 32 evaluators.) AC – AChecker, TAW	Management & Scholarship website taken by studying 10 Libyan government website	Main features should be at easy to access location as usability was found low in this area. Also, the website failed in many places in accessibility evaluation [11]
2016	U, AC	U,AC – fast link checker, webpage speed analyser, HTML validator, CSS validator, SortSite	51 Turkey Government websites	Serious accessibility problem and negligence in performance and quality is observed [17]

3 Methodology

This paper uses the quantitative research method in which various scores of different usability parameters are taken out using various online automated tools. This study aims to perform descriptive data analysis involving multivariate analysis of different variables such as Usability, Search Engine Optimization (SEO), Accessibility, Content, Performance, and Design. The following subsections describe the tools, techniques, and data used in the usability analysis.

3.1 Tools and Techniques

In this research two different statistical & analytical online automated tools are used to analyze the e-governance applications. These are Qualidator & Site-Analyzer.

Qualidator online automated tool is offered by seven49.net. It analyses & determines the scores of various parameters like Usability, Accessibility & SEO of an application and provides overall quality scores. For analysis, it uses various international standards like ISϴ standards, WCAG of World Wide Web Consortium (W3C). It also utilizes the usability guidelines given by Jacob Nielsen and Google Webmaster Guidelines for usability & other parameter analysis of an application [18].

Site-Analyzer is an online automated tool that provides many services to analyze the website. It provides various features like Page Analysis, Crawl, Rank Tracking, Backlinks, Keyword Research, and SEO Benchmarks. Page Analysis feature is used for the usability analysis of e-governance applications in this paper. Page Analysis instantly provides a complete diagnosis of SEO, Content, Design, Performance, and Accessibility for all the pages of the website. Moreover, it provides an Overall Quality score which is a weighted score calculated by Site-Analyzer based on the score of each criterion [19].

3.2 Data

5 Surveys conducted by different organizations such as USA's Digital.gov [23], UNDESA (United Nations Department of Economic and Social Affairs) [22], Institute for Management Development's World Competitiveness Ranking (WDCR) [20], Waseda-IAC (International Academy of Chief Information Officer) International Digital Government Ranking (IDGR) [21] & World Economic Forum's Global Information Technology Report (GITR) [24] are taken into consideration to find the topmost countries to be used for performing usability analysis.

Among all these 5 surveys, the top 10 ranking countries which are high performing countries according to most of the surveys described above are Singapore, South Korea, Denmark, USA, United Kingdom, Australia, Hong Kong, New Zealand, Norway & Sweden.

The government websites of these 10 countries are randomly taken into considerations for usability analysis and the ranking according to these 5 surveys, links of these

Table 2. List of countries used in this paper with their links and abbreviation used in this paper. (Abbreviation used are D = Ranking according to USA's Digital.gov survey, U = Ranking according to UNDESA survey, W = Ranking according to WDCR, I = Ranking according to IDGR, G = Ranking according to GITR, N = Not taken into consideration in survey)

Country	D	U	W	I	G	Application link	Abbreviation
Singapore	5	7	2	2	1	https://www.mom.gov.sg/	SP
South Korea	7	3	8	6	12	https://www.gov.kr/	SK
Denmark	N	1	3	1	10	https://www.regeringen.dk/	DM
USA	8	11	1	5	8	https://www.usa.gov/	US
United Kingdom	1	4	13	3	7	https://www.gov.uk/	UK
Australia	2	2	15	10	17	https://www.australia.gov.au/	AU
Hong Kong	3	N	5	18	11	https://www.gov.hk/	HK
New Zealand	4	8	22	14	16	https://www.govt.nz/	NZ
Norway	6	14	9	11	4	https://www.norway.no/	NW
Sweden	N	5	4	8	3	https://sweden.se/	SW

websites, and the Abbreviation which will be further used in this paper are denoted in the same Table 2. These links will be fetched to the online automated tools to generate the results.

4 Results and Discussion

The quantitative analysis results from both the online automated tools Qualidator and Site-Analyzer for Usability and related parameters Content, Design, Performance, SEO, and Accessibility are provided in the following subsections.

4.1 Results from Qualidator

Qualidator is an online automated tool for Usability, SEO, Accessibility, and Overall quality of the application based on the scores of Usability, SEO & Accessibility. The URL of 10 countries' websites are provided to this tool and results are noted in following Table 3.

In this analysis, it is found that UK tops in Accessibility scores with 84.22% while the US is at the bottom line with 75.87%. Remaining countries fall in between with NZ 83.59%, HK 83.07%, DM 82.72%, NW 81.58%, AU 80.70%, SP 80.20%, SK 76.90%, and SW 76.49%. This can be seen in Fig. 1(a).

For SEO, it is found that NW ranks highest with 88.90% while SK ranks lowest with 65.40%. Remaining countries rank in between with AU 84.72%, SW 78.86%, US 78.58%, SP 78.00%, HK 77.85%, NZ 75.96%, UK 73.32% & DM 68.10%. This can be represented as in Fig. 1(b).

Table 3. Comparison using Qualidator (Online usability analysis tool available at: https://www.qualidator.com/. Accessed on: 27 March 2020 & 28 November 2020)

Country	Accessibility (%)	SEO (%)	Usability (%)	Total (%)
SP	80.20	78.00	82.20	82.50
SK	76.90	65.40	74.70	74.90
DM	82.72	68.10	76.93	74.35
US	75.87	78.58	75.95	78.80
UK	84.22	73.32	79.21	79.88
AU	80.70	84.72	77.12	80.89
HK	83.07	77.85	76.11	76.95
NZ	83.59	75.96	86.21	79.71
NW	81.58	88.90	75.49	77.14
SW	76.49	78.86	72.99	77.59

In terms of Usability, it is found that NZ is at the top with 86.21% while SW is at last with only 72.99%. Remaining countries fall in between range with SP 82.20%,

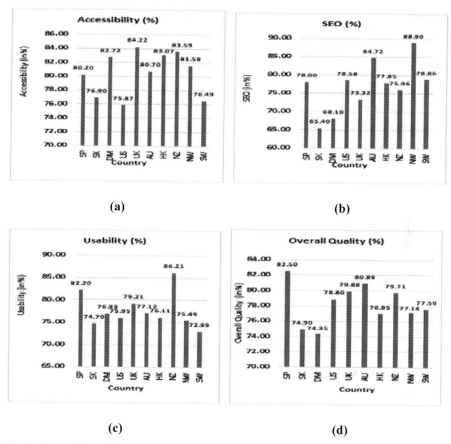

Fig. 1. Comparison of (a) Accessibility, (b) SEO, (c) Usability & (d) Overall Quality scores of 10 countries using Qualidator

UK 79.21%, AU 77.12%, DM 76.93%, HK 76.11%, US 75.95%, NW 75.49% and SK 74.70%. This can be represented as in Fig. 1(c).

In terms of overall quality score, SP ranks highest with 82.50% while DM ranks lowest with 74.35%. Remaining 8 countries fall in between with AU 80.89%, UK 79.88%, NZ 79.71%, US 78.80%, SW 77.59%, NW 77.14%, HK 76.95% and SK 74.90%. This can be found in Fig. 1(d) representation.

4.2 Results from Site-Analyzer

Site-Analyzer is an online automated tool that is used for SEO, Accessibility, Performance, Design, Content, and Overall Usability Analysis. The 10 countries' websites are provided to this tool and results are noted in following Table 4.

While analysis of SEO, it is found that DM ranks highest with 89.20% while NZ ranks lowest with 6.20%. Remaining countries lie in between with US 80.40, SP 80.10%,

Table 4. Comparison using site-analyzer (Online usability analysis tool available at: https://www. site-analyzer.com/. Accessed on: 27 March 2020)

Country	SEO %	Content %	Design %	Performance %	Accessibility %	Overall usability %
SP	80.10	55.20	95.80	61.00	74.80	76.40
SK	63.50	55.40	71.00	73.20	51.30	62.70
DM	89.20	58.30	75.70	61.00	84.50	82.30
US	80.40	72.70	80.10	40.20	87.90	74.30
UK	69.70	55.10	95.80	73.20	66.40	76.30
AU	65.70	51.50	78.30	74.40	63.30	63.40
HK	44.50	56.40	87.30	61.00	74.80	60.50
NZ	06.20	00.00	60.30	87.80	26.60	23.30
NW	68.30	53.60	78.30	61.00	87.90	75.20
SW	62.60	52.80	100.00	61.00	87.90	72.40

UK 69.70%, NW 68.30%, AU 65.70%, SK 63.50%, SW 62.60% and HK 44.50%. This can be represented as in Fig. 2(a).

In the Content analysis, it is found that the US ranks highest with 72.70% while NZ ranks lowest with 0% score. Remaining countries scores were found as DM 58.30%, HK 56.40%, SK 55.40%, SP 55.20%, UK 55.10%, NW 53.60%, SW 52.80% and AU 51.50%. This can be represented as shown in Fig. 2(b).

While design analysis, it is found that SW scores highest with 100% while NZ scores lowest with 60.30%. Remaining countries lie between with UK & SP with 95.80%, HK 87.30%, US 80.10%, NW & AU with 78.30%, DM 75.70% and SK 71.00%. In Fig. 2(c) this is represented.

In this analysis, NZ ranks highest with 87.80% score in Performance analysis while the US ranks lowest with 40.20%. The remaining countries are ranking in between with AU 74.40%, UK & SK with 73.20%, SP, DM, HK, NW & SW with 61% each. This is represented in Fig. 2(d).

In Accessibility analysis, US, NW & SW scored highest with 87.90% while NZ scored lowest with 26.60% and remaining countries are found ranking in between with DM 84.50%, HK & SP with 74.80%, UK 66.40%, AU 63.30%, and SK 51.30%. This is represented in Fig. 2(e).

The overall usability of DM is found to be highest with 82.30% while it is found to be lowest for NZ with 23.30%. Remaining countries score in between with SP 76.40%, UK 76.30%, NW 75.20%, US 74.30%, SW 72.40%, AU 63.40%, SK 62.70% and HK 60.50%. This is represented in Fig. 2(f).

4.3 Usability and Related Parameters

As SEO, Accessibility, Design, Performance, and Content are related to Usability, it is necessary to study & discuss these parameters with respect to the 10 websites used.

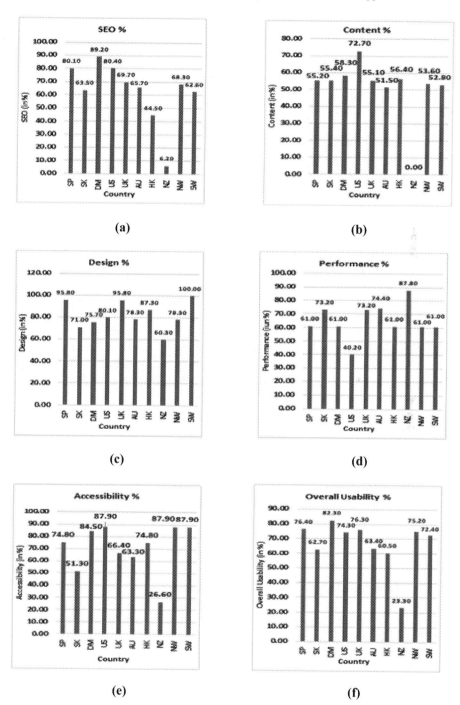

Fig. 2. Comparison of (a) SEO, (b) Content, (c) Design, (d) Performance, (e) Accessibility, (f) Overall usability scores of 10 countries using site-analyzer

In the analysis of SEO, DM has scored highest with 89.20% in results from the Site-Analyzer tool. The tool also shows that it has optimized page title & meta-description, proper indexation & site-map, alternative text are given to multimedia scoring 100% and only 2% are external links when 101 links are studied. But only 91.1% are reliable links. If this is improved, then SEO will be 100% for DM. In the analysis of Qualidator, NW scores the highest with 88.90%. This tool also shows that NW should optimize meta-description and should include keywords to score 100%.

In the analysis of Accessibility, US, NW & SW ranked highest with 87.90% in results from the Site-Analyzer tool. The results depicted that the application of these countries had proper accessibility on different devices even on mobiles as it has Meta-Viewport and proper domain length. The only improvement needed is the Twitter card addition. This will make the accessibility score to 100% of these countries. When tested with Qualidator, UK ranked highest with 84.22%. This tool also depicted that there is still a need of having alternate text for multimedia, reduction or removal of annoying pop-ups, separating adjacent links, optimize printer friendliness, include a sitemap, support access keys, and include resizable fonts to score 100%.

In the Content analysis, the US with 72.70% ranked highest in results from the Site-Analyzer tool. This result depicted that it has 15.53% text/code ratio which is optimum and has enough keywords with 2046 exploitable & 459 single keywords. Only Title coherence and titles should be improved. This will increase the content score.

In the case of Performance analysis, it is found that NZ ranks highest with 87.80% with the Site-Analyzer tool. The result depicts that it has good page weight, optimized execution time of 251 ms, and optimized loading time. But the server should use file compression to make the Performance score of 100% for NZ.

In Design analysis, it is found that SW scores 100% in the result of Site-Analyzer. The results show that the SW has HTML 5 Doctype, UTF-8 charset, SSL enabled, design quality enabled, optimized layout design, ipv6 compatible, DNSSEC enabled and HTTPS enabled. Other countries can check the design of SW and learn from it to get a 100 Design score.

As the usability is related to all the above-discussed parameter, the highest usability score can be achieved by only that application which has highest performance, good and trustworthy content, excellent accessibility, good design, and excellent SEO. Thus, it can be seen that DM scored highest in terms of usability when checked with the Site-Analyzer tool. This can be seen from the result of DM that it had scored 89.20% in SEO (ranking 1st), 58.30% in Content (ranking 2nd), 61% in Performance (ranking 5th), 75.70% in Design (ranking 8th), and 84.50% in Accessibility (ranking 2nd). But still, DM application has much scope of improvement in terms of making reliable links, improving text/code relation, the addition of microdata, improving title coherence, following charset standardization, improving execution time, and performing loading optimization. Also when checked with Qualidator, NZ ranked highest with 86.21% in usability, and from results, it can be seen that it had scored 83.59% in Accessibility (ranking 2nd) and 75.96% in SEO (ranking 7th). But there is still much scope of improvement in terms of use of standard Doctype, removal of annoying pop-ups, improving page ranking, the inclusion of robot.txt, inclusion of sitemap, inclusion of access-key, optimizing the loading time of homepage, and inclusion of keywords to score 100%.

5   Conclusion and Future Scope

The usability and its related parameter analysis on 10 countries using 2 automated online tools Qualidator and Site-Analyzer is carried out. While taking out results from the Qualidator tool, it is found that New Zealand ranks highest with 86.21%, SW ranks lowest with 72.99% and the remaining application ranked in between. While taking out results from the Site-Analyzer tool, it is found that DM ranks highest with 82.30%, NZ ranks lowest with 23.30%, and remaining applications rank in between these ranges.

The analysis report from this tool also depicts that the countries can improve the score by using main keywords, reducing page weight, optimize twitter card, improve security, improving page execution time, optimize Facebook sharing, providing Alternative Text for images, adding more textual content, creating responsive web design and configuring Ipv6 compatibility.

In 1994, Jacob Nielson has identified the following principles to create Usable applications. The same shall be applied to create Usable e-governance applications [25]:

- While designing a usable application, there should be a match between the System and the Real-world.
- Usable application should give full User control and freedom.
- It should maintain Consistency and Standards.
- It should be capable of Error prevention.
- It should give Flexibility and Efficiency of use.
- It should maintain an Aesthetic and minimalist design.
- It should help users recognize, diagnose, and recover from errors.
- It should have proper Help and documentation.
- It should provide Pleasurable and Respectful Interaction with users [25].

This paper research is conducted using 10 countries' e-governance applications. But in the future, this can be conducted using more countries' e-governance applications which will help to analyze more issues coming in the way to provide ideal usability. Further in this research, only 2 automated tools are used. So, in the future, this can be increased to get more insights into results. Also, in this paper, only major parameters having relation with usability are compared for all applications. In the future, this can be extended to all micro parameters related to usability like download time, provision of a transaction form, link to different payment wallets and gateways, proper feedback mechanism, broken links, and browser compatibility issues.

References

1. Maazuddin, K., Vijayashree, L.: Impact of e-governance on employees performance. Int. J. Sci. Res. Publ. **5**, 1 (2015)
2. AlSaeed, D., et al.: Accessibility evaluation of Saudi e-government systems for teachers: a visually impaired user's perspective. Appl. Sci. **10**, 1–32 (2020)
3. Csontos, B., Heckl, I.: Accessibility, usability, and security evaluation of Hungarian government websites. Univ. Access Inf. Soc. **20**(1), 139–156 (2020). https://doi.org/10.1007/s10209-020-00716-9

4. Nacheva, R., Bakaev, M.: Elder users' experience evaluation of Bulgarian and Russian e-government websites. Econ. Sci. Educ. Real Econ. Dev. Interact. Digital Age **1**, 241–256 (2020)

5. Benard, L.: E-governance. Compiled Lecture Notes (2019)

6. Zeleke, Y.: Usability and accessibility model for e-government websites in Ethiopia. In: The 6th Annual ACIST Proceedings, pp. 1–12 (2020)

7. Bai, Y.: The relationship between website accessibility and usability: an examination of U.S county government online portals. Electron. J. e-Gov. **17**, 47–62 (2019)

8. Wikipedia: Usability. https://en.wikipedia.org/wiki/Usability

9. Verkijika, S.F., De. Wet, L.: A usability assessment of e-government websites in Sub-Saharan Africa. Int. J. Inf. Manage. **39**, 20–29 (2018)

10. Cubettech: An overview on usability testing & 6 Tools to automate it. https://cubettech.com/resources/blog/an-overview-on-usability-testing-6-tools-to-automate-it/

11. Karaim, N.A., Inal, Y.: Usability and accessibility evaluation of Libyan government websites. Univ. Access Inf. Soc. **18**(1), 207–216 (2017). https://doi.org/10.1007/s10209-017-0575-3

12. Qatestlab: 3 goals of usability testing. https://blog.qatestlab.com/2011/03/05/3-goals-of-usability-testing/

13. Mete, Y., Nihan, O., Caglar, Y., Kursat, C., Cenay, B.: Usability in local E-Government: analysis of Turkish metropolitan municipality Facebook pages. Int. J. Publ. Adm. Digital Age **3**(1), 53–69 (2016)

14. Nissar, P.: E - governance in Kerala. Abhinav Int. Monthly Refereed J. Res. Manage. Technol. **3**(10), 31–37 (2014)

15. Sumit, K.S.: E-governance: an overview. National J. Multi. Res. Dev. **3**, 223–227 (2018)

16. UNDESA: UN E-government surveys. https://publicadministration.un.org/en/research/un-e-government-surveys

17. Akgül, Y.: Quality evaluation of E-government websites of Turkey. In: 2016 11th Iberian Conference on Information Systems and Technologies (CISTI), pp. 1–7. IEEE (2016)

18. Qualidator. https://www.qualidator.com/de/tools/myrating-overview.htm/

19. Site-Analyzer. https://www.site-analyzer.com/en/analysis

20. IMD World Competitiveness Center. https://www.imd.org/wcc/world-competitiveness-center-rankings/world-digital-competitiveness-rankings-2020/

21. Waseda - IAC International Digital Government Rankings. https://iacio.org/wasada-iac-world-e-government-ranking/

22. United Nations: Gearing e-government to support transformation towards sustainable and resilient societies. In: UNDESA, pp. 90–92 (2018)

23. Digital.gov: The best e-gov websites in the world. /https://digital.gov/2014/12/31/the-best-e-gov-websites-in-the-world/

24. Global Information Technology Report 2015. https://www.weforum.org/reports/global-information-technology-report-2015

25. Nielsen, J.: 10 usability heuristics for user interface design. Nielsen Norman Group (1994). https://www.nngroup.com/articles/ten-usability-heuristics/

Sustainable Smart Society Framework Using ICT

Lakshita Aggarwal[1], Deepak Chahal[2(✉)], and Latika Kharb[2]

[1] Department of Computer Science, SRM University Delhi-NCR, Sonepat, Haryana, India
[2] Department of IT, Jagan Institute of Management Studies, Sector-05, Rohini, New Delhi, India
{deepak.chahal,latika.kharb}@jimsindia.org

Abstract. Smart cities are the urgent need of an hour when there is a need to transform the rural cities to the advanced ones calling them the digitally advanced and smart. We aspire to do it for delivering better quality of life and at a sustainable cost. Smart cities provides a liveable future ahead by providing a digital solutions to the mankind. A smart city is the one which increases efficiency, productivity and sustainability by improving quality of life of increasing population and completing their demands. A data is being collected, stored and analyzed all the time as all the devices around us keeps on collecting all the data from equipment such as vehicles, healthcare, wearable devices, management systems, infrastructural devices etc. Smart cities are made in a manner that they reduce resource consumption, wastage of energy resources and maintaining the overall cost and development in a judicious manner using smart technologies. In this paper, we tried to cover all the areas through which more smart cities can be developed and the quality of life can be enhanced.

Keywords: Smart · Sustainable · Technology · Digital · Roadmap

1 Introduction

Smart means "Connected" and "networked". Smart cities are made in a manner that they reduce resource consumption, wastage of energy resources and maintaining the overall cost and development in a judicious manner using smart technologies. A smart city can be viewed as an integration of a number of solo IoT applications where collaboration of applications from different domains can optimize and simplify many complicated situations [1]. Smart cities expand infinitely over length and breadth to meet the growing demands of people and also involving the need of the community to make smart city a necessity. Smart cities not just includes smart cities but also smart government, smart environment, smart economy, smart people, smart mobility, smart living, smart health and many more via collecting data from various sources and integrating with various advanced technologies producing efficient results.

In this paper, we tried to analyze different frameworks for sustainable smart cities using ICT approach. We also tried to address the roadmap plans for smart cities to be implemented in our society so that the lives of people may revolve to the bigger scales in

© Springer Nature Singapore Pte Ltd. 2021
A. K. Luhach et al. (Eds.): ICAICR 2020, CCIS 1393, pp. 649–657, 2021.
https://doi.org/10.1007/978-981-16-3660-8_60

contributing towards society. The approach followed in this paper to address the problems is we have shown different roadmap plans to address the problem. Different vision strategies are also given that shows the implementation plans followed in traditional approach v/s the new vision zero strategy given (Fig. 1).

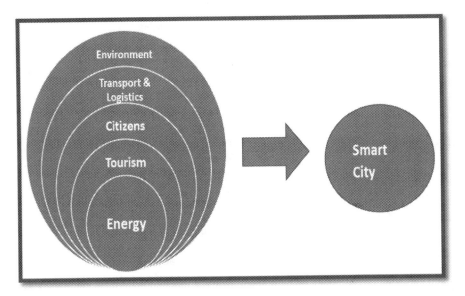

Fig. 1. Components of smart city

The above components of smart city explains that smart means "looking ahead in the future" and "dreaming for a forward living ahead". The smart city revolves around the lives of growing population and urbanization. The growth of cities is not just limited to urban areas but it should also spread its wings even in rural areas and remote regions of the country to make the world transformed and digital.

Smart cities includes:-

- City system
- Infrastructures
- City purpose
- City stake holders

The integration of all these basic components i.e. Energy, Tourism competitively, Transport & Logistics, Citizens including social and human capital participation and the quality of life, environment includes all natural resources comes with the complete solution to smart cities.

2 Literature Review

Liangxiu Han worked on big data driven approach on sustainable smart society showing that the size of the data keeps on accumulating from each and every device like sensors, networks, images, biomedical devices and many more. He also added that as our infrastructure grows with the same pace in digitalization world the data grows along. He focused on new developments and methods based on big data driven approach to address societal challenges or in a way to make our societies smart that becomes ubiquitous for man-kind.

CholaChhetri et al. worked on the privacy framework to be adapted in smart homes according to the usage. He also worked upon the various on-going researches towards the privacy concerns of smart home related devices.

Indrawati et al. tried to analyze the high growth of urbanization that requires smart level of living life to address all the problems. The paper also shows the basic factors or indicators that can be used as a measurement for smart healthcare implementation.

3 ICT Approach

ICT (Information & Communication Technologies) used by smart and sustainable city that helps in improving quality of life and efficiency of urban operation and services.

ITU-T organised keywords and also found different aspects according to their percentage (%). These pie chart and bar graph interprets the study of different parameters according to the definition of ICT (Information & communication technologies) (Fig. 2).

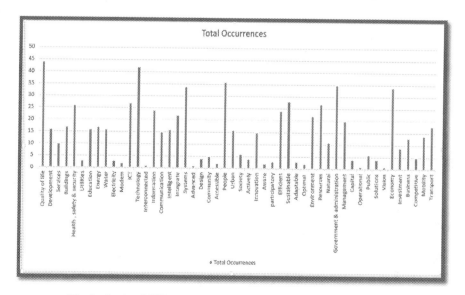

Fig. 2. Study of different parameters according to the definition of ICT

Above graphical representation shows the study of different parameters on the scale according to the definition of ICT. Different parameters that contributes in making of smart society are looked upon to tackle the situation and to grow our cities smart and sustainable (Fig. 3).

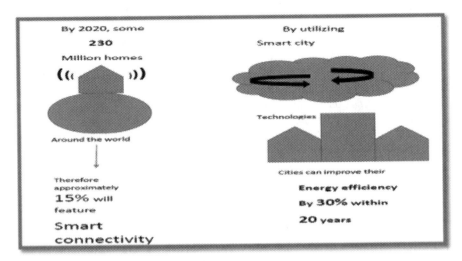

Fig. 3. Smart connectivity

Every day, we consume power but we never give a thought from where it is generated 75% of the city's share of worldwide power consumption. We need solutions that pave the way for innovative and economic growth such as data based mobility infrastructure that can be supplemented by new services like carpooling or logistic services. The more problems smart city solves the more likely people adopt the smart cities.

4   Component of Smart City Framework

These smart cities are beneficiary towards the new method of planning and emphasizing the need of being smart not just by themselves but also creating the surrounding smart which allows the rigorous use of new ideas and technologies to succeed the advancements in the real world (Fig. 4).

The new ideas of real smart world are firmly rooted in data science which allows us to determine the size and location of society parks, playgrounds, sidewalk extensions, community gardens, malls, paths and many other basic necessity of the residential citizens in the smart city. So, where these amenities are needed the most smart cities use data to generate predictive models and they test the accuracy of the models from the past historical records of the data by pre - processing those data sets before moving forward integrating the technologies like IOT(Internet of things), Big data, AI(Artificial Intelligence).

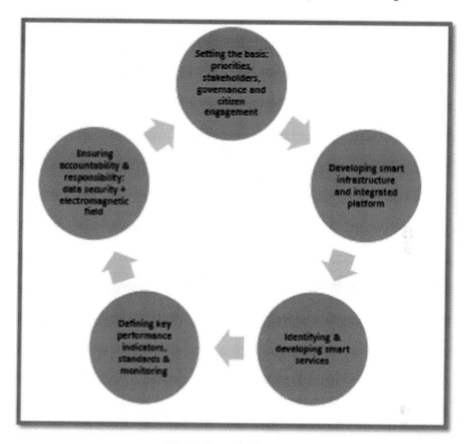

Fig. 4. Smart city framework

5   Roadmap to Smart City

This Digital city practice amendment framework tries to make city smart by integrating web/virtual city, eco environment and making the city ubiquitous for everyone (Fig. 5).

A smart city is the one which involves citizens, infrastructures and all other components digitally providing seek of relief to the residence [2]. Roadmap provides the way in which the cities can be transformed to smart cities by improving the quality of life by using correct and adaptable technological methods for improving the efficiency of services and meeting day to day needs of the people living in (Fig. 6).

Every 8 months, a city's population exceeds the five million in number making it a huge megacity. As the population size grows the number of challenges expands seeking new opportunities and challenges on the way. Because the growing population will demand for more food, resources, sheltering and many more.

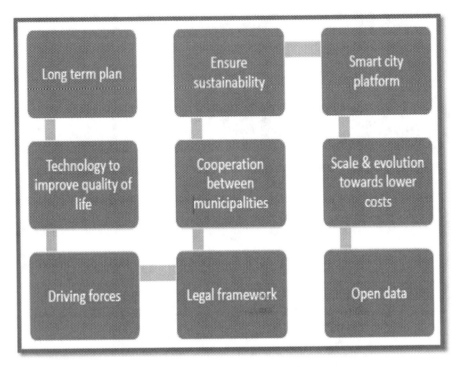

Fig. 5. A roadmap to smart city

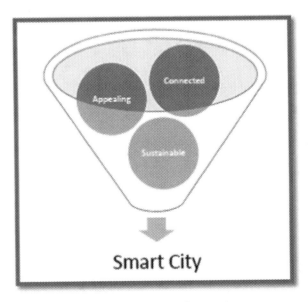

Fig. 6. Components of smart city

6 Pre-processing of Data

As smart things gather enormous amounts of data which even sometimes not computed or processed to convert the data to useful information. Pre-processing of data includes few features such as:

1. Mobility – As the amount of data on the network is so large that we needs cloud storage to store the data.
2. Scalability – Large number of devices increases pressure to the cloud as a result latency also increases.
3. Power limitations – transmission with the data constantly consumes lots of power. Loose powered battery devices might be a constraint to the IOT devices.

To solve all the above problems like mobility, reliable and real time actuation, scalability and power limitations researchers proposed mobile cloud computing (MCC). So, [3] MCC shifted its phase from cloud computing to some compute and storage resources instead of relying on cloud for everything which is known as fog computing. So, fog and cloud works together providing optimal performance to IOT applications A smart gateway can be employed between underlying networks and the cloud to realize fog computing.

7 Connected and Networked Homes

There were the ages when people use to communicate with each other via letters with the ongoing technological developments internet changed the way we communicate. As the technologies advanced time passed by internet raised with internet of things (IOT) which shows how different objects are connected to each other through the internet. For instance, refrigerators are connected to internet and respond about the people with the information of the current fresh food stock available or the food is getting rotten, clothes we wear might able to tell all the useful biomedical information required about the people if any necessary action is required to be taken [4, 5]. The concept behind IOT is "the extensive use of the variety of things or objects that are around us such as sensors and other smart devices that are able to interact and produce intelligent results adjusting with the environment. This is the wide spread in the society as it changes life of one and all with the changing demands of the society. Integration of AI with IOT brings smart and intelligent devices acting logistic and automated help to the human. AI brings not only new challenges but also comes with the developments in the nation with the global labour, economic growth, capital competition and also solves moral, supervisory and legal issues.

8 Architecture

A large amount of data which cannot be stored on the executable machine is stored on the cloud and for any analysis it is accessed from the cloud. The smart gateway is employed in between the cloud and the smart devices. It acts as a gateway from which all the data and APIs have to cross for processing the data. It acts as the middleware layer for all the unstructured data to process those unstructured data sets to transform them into the information. It is the system of numerous elements such as sensors, protocols, actuators, cloud services and other layers (Fig. 7).

Three layers of IOT architecture are:-

1. Client side i.e. IOT Device Layer
2. Operators on the server side i.e. IOT gateway layer
3. A pathway for connecting clients and operators (IOT platform layer)

Making smart cities using IOT does not means:-
☐ Smart! = high speed communication.
☐ Smart! = Big data storage.
Rather
Smart means "Networked"

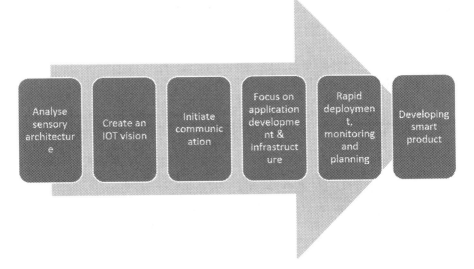

Fig. 7. IOT Architecture

9   Future Work

The process of building applications has been a journey and it varies depending on one's application requirements and purpose [6].

In the near future, we will try to develop some prototype that can be commercially deployed in the society to improve standard of living. The purpose of building the application will be basically to help the humankind in the stressed life to make it comfort living for all. The intervention of smart and connected life will help the society in a better way possible. ICT will improve the efficiency operation of society. Different vision operations will help in developing the society in better way possible.

10 Conclusion

While the world is growing development at every stage whether it be society or people is required. Development is the base foundation of work for developing standard of living. We have included the concept of smart city as the pre – requisite need of an hour. Some workflow plans have also been discussed stating the ways to minimize wastage and developing sustainable standards of living. ICT measures have been included to enhance the quality of life. This paper also discusses the concepts of connected and networked homes also including the different roadmap strategies for making the society ubiquitous for man-kind. Finally, we hope that this article will make some contributions to the world's response to the situation and will also help in providing some references for future research as well.

References

1. Reddy, K.H.K., Luhach, A.K., Pradhan, B., Dash, J.K., Roy, D.S.: A genetic algorithm for energy efficient fog layer resource management in context-aware smart cities. Sustain. Urban Areas **63**, 102428 (2020). https://doi.org/10.1016/j.scs.2020.102428
2. IBM Global Business Services. A Vision of Smarter Cities: How Cities Can Lead the Way into a Prosperous and Sustainable Future, (IBM Institute for Business Value, Somers, NY) (2009). http://public.dhe.ibm.com/common/ssi/ecm/en/gbe03227usen/GBE03227USEN.PDF
3. Wang, D., Pedreschi, D., Song, C., Giannotti, F., Barabasi, A.-L.: Human mobility, social ties, and link prediction. In: Proceedings, International Conference on Knowledge Discovery and Data Mining (2011). http://users.cis.fiu.edu/~lzhen001/activities/KDD2011Program/docs/p1100.pdf
4. Ipeirotis, P.G.: Analyzing the amazon mechanical Turk marketplace. XRDS Crossroads ACM Mag. Students **17**(2), 16–21 (2010)
5. Wisdom, J.P., Chor, K.H.B., Hoagwood, K.E., Horwitz, S.M.: Innovation adoption: a review of theories and constructs. Adm. Policy Ment. Health Ment. Health Serv. Res. **41**(4), 480–502 (2013). https://doi.org/10.1007/s10488-013-0486-4
6. Kharb, L.: A perspective view on commercialization of cognitive computing. In: 2018 8th International Conference on Cloud Computing, Data Science and Engineering (Confluence), pp. 829–832. IEEE (2018)

Statistical Approach for Mining Frequent Item Sets

Deepti Mishra[1]([⊠]) [iD] and Saurabh Sharma[2] [iD]

[1] GL Bajaj Institute of Technology and Management, Greater Noida, India
[2] BITS, Pilani, India

Abstract. Current paper submits an altogether novel method to identify Frequent Itemset which applies approach of statistics further based on association rule mining which otherwise a commonly applied method in transactional database to trace high frequency itemset in data mining arena. The algorithm designs frequency distribution table, Algorithm applies the formulas of class intervals to design frequency distribution table. It calculates the frequency if item sets present in the database. It functions in two phases. Phase 1 is termed as filtering and debulking phase. Phase 2 is termed as application step alongside comparison step among class interval techniques. Threshold values are calculated within the algorithm to find frequent item sets. Threshold numeric is subjected on to the formed table showing frequency distribution and simultaneously products listed are also selected. It generates pairs by applying combination technique. Database is the alone requirement as input. Current paper therefore addresses the worth of identifying and searching frequent item sets in huge transactional database.

Keywords: Association rule · Data mining · Statistical techniques · Transactional database

1 Introduction

Various data mining methods like classification, clustering and association are used to extract out essential information from large data bases. Detection of frequently occurring patterns of item sets in transactional data bases is core function of association rule mining. Every passing day abundant data is generated and accumulated. Organisations dealing in big data and analytics are generating large transactional data sets having diverse and intricate patterns hidden hitherto. Commonly seen transactional databases viz. e commerce databases, data generated from business companies, transactional storages, are a few to be named upon. Frequent itemset mining has a relevance in finding implications and correlations in between products of huge transactional or relational databases [1, 2].

It seems to envisage lucrative correlations and associations in between items in big sized transactional databases. Association rule mining offers helping hand to organizations in stratifying and delineating lucrative patterns and consequent decision making from enormous expanse and big dimension of statistics in giant data. Multiple techniques for association rule mining are in vogue currently. Essential applications include

© Springer Nature Singapore Pte Ltd. 2021
A. K. Luhach et al. (Eds.): ICAICR 2020, CCIS 1393, pp. 658–669, 2021.
https://doi.org/10.1007/978-981-16-3660-8_61

harvesting information, correlations, and relationships among item sets, mining frequent patterns, marketing, intelligent decisions making in business, education and social platforms and the list is not exhaustive [1, 2].

Data mining technique which is known as Association rule mining is almost [3] synonymous as Apriori algorithm. It is two step process, first step to find frequent item sets, while in next step to generate if then rules. It unravels the frequency that is, number of times an item has occurred in the data set.

FPTREE (Frequent Pattern Tree) a distinct approach utilised to search frequent patters from the data set by separating it into conditional datasets [4]. Apriori algorithm is needed in this as a supportive adjunct. It performs to give rise a structure which is like a tree structure having uppermost node with other connected nodes. Furthermore, tree branches being synthesised by scanning the entire data base to search frequent patterns. The authors in their Current endeavour suggest a novel methodology for frequent pattern mining namely Statistical Approach for Mining Frequent Item Sets (FIST). The entire focus is on elucidating the procedure and working of currently proposed algorithm. The algorithm is applied for identifying frequent item sets and interesting patterns from vast transactional database. Unlike Apriori algorithm, it does not need to calculate support count. The technique utilises Association rule mining concept. it goes for finding frequent item sets which highly occurred in the database by implicating statistical formulae and calculations. The notations and topics of statistics that are used in algorithm are frequency distribution table, class interval formulas, median value, and combination formula. It applies Rice and Sturges' rule to create class intervals in the frequency distribution table. Both rules generate different number of classes after retrieving data from database to design frequency distribution table. Database is the only requirement at the time of input.

It is attempted to analyze and review few prior works published previously in different research papers. A comparative approach is discussed and explained between Rice rule and Sturges' rule during implementation process on the proposed algorithm. Paper concurrently has presented the outcomes for frequent item sets generated from the transactional database. It also compared the performance of class interval rules on the database during designing of frequency distribution table.

Current paper endeavours to enrich the fellow researchers by revealing the knowhow of association rule mining in producing frequent patterns from transactional data. The key objective of the paper to offer the knowledge of data mining and its technique i.e., association rule mining. So that, researchers can gain knowledge in the domain of association rule mining to learn to identify frequent patterns from large database. The remaining portions is designated as part 2 having the review of earlier expeditions in frequent mining. Part 3 represents few common annotations and information. Part 4 elaborates about the database utilized for realization of the algorithm. Later Part 5 portion represents a fresh methodology for frequent item mining. Subsequent part exhibits its execution outcomes. Further part 6 debates over the algorithm as well as its expedition and outcomes after the surmise.

2 Literature Review

Multiple research previously performed on mining frequent item generation and varied methodologies advised and applied by prior scholars in big data. Current part of the discourse delivers certain evaluation on procedures applicable for the same job. It seems to envisage lucrative interrelationships and links in between items in big sized transactional databases. Association mining offers helping hand to organizations in stratifying and delineating lucrative patterns and consequent choice making from enormous bulk and big dimension of data in mammoth sized data sets. Multiple techniques for association rule mining are in vogue currently. To begin with let's discuss Apriori algorithm which one of the techniques of association rule mining further applies support and confidence calculations [1]. Upon delivering to Apriori, it is vastly applied in market basket analysis. Apriori algorithm is the calculation of frequent patterns and occurrence of item sets frequently. The representation of association rules A → B, where both A and B are attributes pairs. Calculation of values of Support and Confidence plays vital role in Apriori algorithm. This value implies the association between different attribute pairs.

Authors suggested an algorithm to identify association rules that functions as constraints with confidence measure to build the model. The measure is applied to calculate a constraint value to find frequent patterns which is different from Apriori step [5]. A model-based frequency technique is suggested [6] to find frequent item sets in transactional data set. The technique can also manage and detect outliers i.e., rare items and values which are totally deviated from rest of the data set.

Authors suggested [7] an algorithm to identify frequent item sets by applying some threshold constraints and conditions. Linear time and space are its two ways of functioning. It applies the concept of probability of Poisson approximation and Chen-Stein approximation [8]. The algorithm generates frequent patterns by applying forementioned approximations. Author showing like that the technique that it endeavours to produce frequently occurring patterns by creating a support threshold value. Authors suggested an algorithm namely adaptive miner by reducing time and space complexity by following adaptive strategy [9]. SPARK is used in implementation process. An approach is suggested by authors called PFP (parallel frequent pattern) [10] which follows the idea of MapReduce standard additionally with FP growth algorithm. Authors suggested a new technology namely [11] BPFP (Balance Parallel FP Growth) which is quicker and effectual.

An approach has been proposed that applies both concepts i.e., MapReduce and Apriori algorithm for finding frequent patterns [12]. It offers efficient and quicker outcomes. Authors suggested an approach namely MRFP growth which also applies concept of Map Reduce technique with Hadoop [13, 11]. The functioning of Approach requires two scans where in one scan it identify frequent patterns while in next scan it creates FP tree. Another approach applies sampling and approximation method to detect highly occurred item sets based on their frequency [14]. Authors provides studies and surveys on frequent mining for generating highly occurred patterns [15].

Authors suggested an approach based on Markov Chain [16] which finds similar length transactions additionally with frequencies that create new dataset from original one. A technique is introduced in frequent mining in association rule mining which also consider spurious tuples while processing [17]. It is based on the concept of probability that applies on frequency values of support count to identify frequent patterns. Threshold values are also utilized during calculations. Another approach namely Krimp algorithm is suggested by the authors which follows MDL principle [18] to identify frequent item sets.

3   Prerequisite and Formulas

3.1   Statistics Required

Frequency Distribution Table. Current paper requires statistics techniques in which one of them is frequency distribution table. It is the way of representation of data by generating frequency values of attributes for the class intervals [19]. It displays the frequency values i.e., count of occurrence of column values.

Class Intervals. In algorithm, few class intervals rules are noted applies on transactional database. Those are Sturges' rule and Rice rule.
   Sturges' Rule [20]: Formula for Sturges' rule mentioned in Eq. (1) for logarithm base 2 defined as

$$1 + \log_2 n$$

Hence, logarithm base 10 as

$$1 + 3.3 \log_{10} n \tag{1}$$

here n is samples. Now considering an example, such as for 1000 observations it generates almost 10 classes.
   Rice rule [so called as it was technically introduced by staff in the statistics department at Rice University]: According to this rule, the number of class interval Eq. (2) can be computed as

$$2 * \sqrt[3]{n} \tag{2}$$

here n is samples. Now considering an example, such as for 1000 observations it generates almost 20 classes which slightly greater than Surges' rule.

Combination Techniques. It is an efficient method to generate pairs of combinations of items where order does not matter [21] i.e., pairs by using the formula ^nC_r

$$nCr = \frac{n!}{r!(n-r)!} \tag{3}$$

where n is total elements and r is number of element selection.

Ordered and Unordered Set. An unordered set is a set that has elements but not necessary relation between the elements. for example, in a set if A and B are two elements, then not necessary a relation between them. In ordered pair, if element A is present, then B must be there.

4 Dataset

Information of datasets can be gained from UCI Machine Learning Repository. The database is named as Online Retail. The link for the database Archieve.ics.uci.edu/ml/datasets/online+retail from where it can be easily downloaded. It has the records of transactions between December 2010 to December 2011. Dataset already used in research works [22]. Dataset Information about database.

Columns (Attributes) = 8
Count of rows = 5,41,909.
Distinct rows in Stockcode = 3,958.
Records not found = N/A

5 Aimed Procedure

Here, Notations used in the proposed methodology
F_itemsets = searched interested patterns
TDB = Transactional database
Tsc_R = Records in TDB

5.1 Problem Statement

Now, for defining problem statement equations can be generated as [23, 24]

$$F\_itemsets \in TDB \tag{4}$$

$$F\_itemsets \in Tsc\_R \text{ where } Tsc\_R \in TDB. \tag{5}$$

Equation (4) and Eq. (5) states that F_itemsets belongs to TDB and Tsc_R. Hence, it generates equations in the form of Eqs. 6 and 7

$$F\_itemsets \subset TDB \tag{6}$$

$$F\_itemsets \subset Tsc\_R \tag{7}$$

Formal Problem Statement. Input is TDB with Tsc_R, the problem states identifying F_itemsets in TDB.

5.2 Methodology

The algorithm is slightly different from the standard previous procedures because as input it only requires transactional database. Rest of the calculations and values are done by the algorithm itself. Statistical techniques are used by the algorithm FIST for processing and calculations. Statistical techniques which are applied for calculation are frequency and occurrence calculation of item sets, median value generation, listing frequency distribution table, and finding combinations of pairs. The algorithm functions in two stages.

- Stage 1

  It is the filtering and debulking stage.

  1. Retrieve database
  2. Divide and break the records into classes.
  3. Rice rule and Sturges' rule is used (one by one) to calculate number of classes of frequency distribution table.
  4. Generate frequency distribution table of generated classes including attribute Stockcode.
  5. Choose uppermost 10 data from existing each class
  6. Selected uppermost 10 items are assigned value as threshold t1.

  In stage 1, initially transaction database is retrieved and read. Then records are retrieved from that transactional database. Distinct values are identified to generate exact number of classes to design frequency distribution table. The algorithm checks both the formulas of class intervals which are mentioned in Sect. 3.2. A comparative study is also provided in Sect. 7. The column transaction_id is used to plot class intervals in frequency distribution table. In next step, occurrence of each itemset is checked to calculate their frequency value which refer to column Stockcode of transactional database. In step 3, the item sets having high frequency values and additionally are uppermost 10 records are selected for stage 2.

  Now, the algorithm choses only uppermost 10 records of item set from each class for further calculations because to offer precise outcome. The selection of uppermost item sets having uppermost frequency values may be less than or greater than 10.

- Stage 2

  Stage 2 is the application process of the algorithm which concomitantly presents a comparison step. The outcome provided by the stage 1 i.e., uppermost 10 item sets of attributes Stockcode, from each class are further used to generate combination of pairs. Now, the total number of records processed in stage 2, are very less than those of stage 1. It is because stage 1 applies complete transactional database while in stage 2 only selected records are used for processing. This makes calculation and processing easier.

  1. Combination technique mentioned in Sect. 3.3 is used to design pairs involving item sets.
  2. Number of items sets in the generated pairs = Search the pair having minimum number of items sets from transactional database.
  3. Select only one pair from the pairs having same item sets.
  4. Find out occurrence of each pair from transactional database to calculate frequency value.
  5. Using transaction database calculate median value.
  6. That median value is threshold t2.
  7. If frequency value of generated pairs > t2 then consider those pairs as frequent item sets.

The stage 2 concludes generating pairs from item sets, matching frequency from transaction database and finding highest frequent items. To avoid duplicate pairs, those pairs are deleted which are having the same set of items, designing unordered set mentioned in Sect. 3.4. Next step requires calculation of median value i.e., threshold t2. It is value of the median of the total count of transactions. The generated pairs having frequency value > t2 are counted as frequent pairs.

Now stage 2 processed only on top 10 item sets, it is because first the database is huge which having >5,00,000 records. Now, condition arises, if all the records of attribute Stockcode of transactional database are used to generate pairs then it would be cumbersome data. Total number of distinct records in Stockcode are 3958.

Then, total count of combinations produced is

$$2^{3958} = 2.9972e+11911$$

Now from the above figures of values shows it is more than lacs, which further requires super computers for processing. So, selection of 10 uppermost item sets is considered from each class for further calculation and processing.

5.3 Algorithm

The algorithm functions on designing frequency distribution table using the attribute transaction_id as class interval. Frequency of item sets in Stockcode attribute is calculated in frequency distribution table.

```
Input: TDB
Output: F_itemsets
begin
       retrieve TDB
       for k = 1 to count (Tsc_R)
       display (Tid)
       for k=1 to count (Tid)
       Rules applied for finding class intervals
       Design frequency distribution table
       Assign t1= highest 10 frequency values
       if (frequency of item sets < t1)
       then
       item sets not considered
       l1= top 10 item sets
       for k = 1 to l1
       apply combination technique to make pairs
       find frequency value of each pair in Tsc_R
       Assign t2= median value from Tsc_R
       If (frequency value > t2)
       Then assign F_itemsets
    end
```

6 Implementation and Results

SQL Server 2017 and Power BI tools are referred for verifying the experimental results of the proposed algorithm. Power BI is a data analytics tools which is used for graphical representation of data, building advanced queries, and creating data models. Dataset which is referred for experimental inference in this paper is described in detail in the Sect. 4.

6.1 Outcomes Applying RICE and Sturge's Rule

Now moving ahead on analysis shows that the applied solution for algorithm by implementing Rice Rule for binning the class intervals. From the results of algorithm applying Rice rule, it can be realized that the total number of data rows returned are 57552 which is a large amount of data. Stockcode_freq field shows the frequency of products.

The total number of class interval generated after applying Rice rule are 59, whereas total number of class interval generated after applying Sturges' rule is 28. Class intervals are created by mapping the column transaction_id of the input database. Frequency of occurrence of each item set is calculated on the column Stockcode. It can be defined as; the frequency distribution table includes first column named as class intervals which maps transaction_id column of database. Next column of table is item sets which maps Stockcode column of database. Further next column of table is the frequency of each item set.

Median values are quite conspicuous in the column named Median Row. The uppermost products are taken into consideration so that they can be passed on to next stage because of their maximum occurrence in the created class.

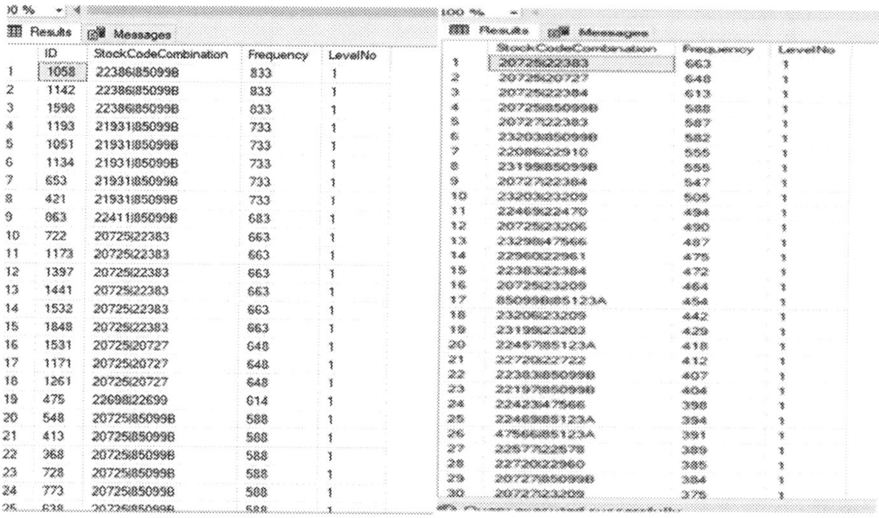

	ID	StockCodeCombination	Frequency	LevelNo
1	1058	22386|85099B	833	1
2	1142	22386|85099B	833	1
3	1596	22386|85099B	833	1
4	1193	21931|85099B	733	1
5	1051	21931|85099B	733	1
6	1134	21931|85099B	733	1
7	653	21931|85099B	733	1
8	421	21931|85099B	733	1
9	863	22411|85099B	683	1
10	722	20725|22383	663	1
11	1173	20725|22383	663	1
12	1397	20725|22383	663	1
13	1441	20725|22383	663	1
14	1532	20725|22383	663	1
15	1848	20725|22383	663	1
16	1531	20725|20727	648	1
17	1171	20725|20727	648	1
18	1261	20725|20727	648	1
19	475	22698|22699	614	1
20	548	20725|85099B	588	1
21	413	20725|85099B	588	1
22	368	20725|85099B	588	1
23	728	20725|85099B	588	1
24	773	20725|85099B	588	1
25	638	20725|85099B	588	1

	StockCodeCombination	Frequency	LevelNo
1	20725|22383	663	1
2	20725|20727	648	1
3	20725|22384	613	1
4	20725|85099B	588	1
5	20727|22383	587	1
6	23203|85099B	582	1
7	22086|22910	555	1
8	23199|85099B	555	1
9	20727|22384	547	1
10	23203|23209	505	1
11	22469|22470	494	1
12	20725|23206	490	1
13	23298|47566	487	1
14	22960|22961	475	1
15	22383|22384	472	1
16	20725|23209	464	1
17	85099B|85123A	454	1
18	23206|23209	442	1
19	23199|23203	429	1
20	22457|85123A	418	1
21	22720|22722	412	1
22	22383|85099B	407	1
23	22197|85099B	404	1
24	22423|47566	398	1
25	22469|85123A	394	1
26	47566|85123A	391	1
27	22577|22578	389	1
28	22720|22960	385	1
29	20727|85099B	384	1
30	20727|23209	375	1

Fig. 1. Representing the results for RICE and Sturge's Rule respectively for rule mining generating frequent item sets.

Figure 1 shows the results of algorithm, by applying both class interval rules, those are Rice rule and Sturge's rule as class interval. Total number of rows returned after executing the query are 50,485 which is lesser than the number of rows returned by Rice rule. Column stockcode combined shows the combination of item sets those occur frequently. The uppermost combination of pairs of item sets are 22386/850998 having highest frequency of occurrence in the database online retail. The generated pairs are the outcome of applying Rice rule for class intervals. Results generated through Sturges' is different from Rice rule.

7   Comparative Results for FIST Approach

In this section, a comparative study is discussed among class intervals formulas which are Rice rule and Sturges' Rule. Power Bi desktop is used for graphical visualization. Both Sturges' rule and Rice rule are used for designing and calculating number of classes in frequency distribution table. A comparison graph is shown in Fig. 2. During processing it is identified that both rules are ideal for calculations. Either of the approaches are adjustable as per functionalities requirement. As both the rules are applied during the processing of the algorithm FIST, it is identified that RICE rule predicts more accurate outcomes in comparison with Sturges' rule because the database is too large.

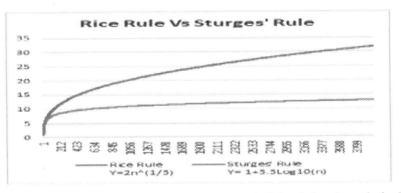

Fig. 2. Showing comparative results of RICE and Sturge's Rule of class intervals for FIST approach

The analysis depicts for Sturges' rule that there is a decrease in the count of classes as the data size increases. Slope in the graph will alter naturally as increase in the data size. Graph in Fig. 2 visualize that count of frequency classes for Sturges' Rule are fewer as related to Rice rule. It is therefore prudent to use Sturges' Rule in for medium or small databases. Whereas in for a medium sized or large sized data set Rice rule is better suited. The current paper therefore has also presented the comparison of outcomes for class interval rules.

The results therefore make it quite conspicuous that uppermost most occurred products are absent in Sturges' results. The difference is summarised in a tabulated form vide infra (Table 1).

Table 1. Comparative outcomes of class interval - Sturges' Rule and Rice Rule

	Sturges' rule	RICE rule
Count of produced classes	28	59
Count of distinct rows	12,428	50,485
Highest frequency value for pairs	663	833
Top 1st item set	Lacking	22386/85099B
Top 2nd item set	Lacking	21931/85099B
Top 3rd item set	Lacking	22411/85099B

It can be visualized that Rice rule for class interval gives better outcomes in compared to Sturges' Rule for large datasets.

8 Discussions

It is noticed that by analysing complete compiled results total number of items within pairs can be >5. The frequency value of itemset is reduced as there is increment in the count and number of itemset in the pair. It can be stated, through Eq. (8)

$$frequency\ value \propto \frac{1}{number\ of\ items\ in\ a\ group} \tag{8}$$

Now, uppermost 10 items which are generated in phase 1, are used for further calculations, because the total records are large in the database. And combination of pairs of all the records will be generated that become enormous in size to handle. So, selecting 10 uppermost items having high frequency of occurrence will make computation easier. Algorithm also removes duplicate values, as it is mentioned that total number of records are >500000. The classes count created by applying RICE rule are 59. During the implementation, in phase 1, rows count generated are $>50,000$.

Now the results show that total number of rows generated in phase 2 are 50,485. As, the algorithm selects uppermost 10 item sets generated in each class, then there should be combinations

$$\left(2^{10}\right) = 1024$$

Further can be $1024 * 59 = 60,416$. It can be concluded total number of rows should returned $>60,000$, which is a greater value from actual obtained rows i.e., 50,845. This is because all the duplicate values are deleted from the combination results.

9 Conclusion

Various DM methods like Association Classification, and Clustering are used to decoct out essential information from large data bases. Detection of frequently occurring patterns of item sets in transactional data bases is core function of association rule mining.

Every passing day abundant data is generated and accumulated. Organisations dealing in big data and analytics are generating large transactional data sets having diverse and intricate patterns hidden hitherto. An algorithm is proposed and implemented which is used to find frequent item sets in large transaction database. It applies the concepts and basics of statistics and its techniques. The topics of statistics those are applied in the algorithm are generating frequency distribution table for item sets, combination technique, median value calculation and finding ordered and unordered sets. The algorithm functions in two phases. Phase 1 is filtering phase and phase 2 is application phase. Later, combination methodology is used on particular sets of items having greater frequency and groups are created and checked for frequent itemset. Current paper therefore addresses the importance of item sets in the foundation mining of frequent itemset and identifying these in big datasets having transactional work. The paper also presents the comparison between two approaches of class intervals. It is attempted to analyze and review few prior works published previously in different research papers. A comparative approach by employing multiple statistical methodologies during application manoeuvre on the proposed algorithm has been attempted. Paper concurrently has presented the outcomes, the comparisons, and evaluation as well by using varied statistical methods for frequent item generation. The future scope of the paper is to compare the algorithm with other renowned algorithms.

References

1. Han, J., Kamber, M., Pei, J.: Data Mining Concepts and Techniques. Elsevier (2011)
2. Goh, D.H., Ang, R.P.: An introduction to association rule mining: an application in counseling and help-seeking behavior of adolescents. Behav. Res. Meth. **39**(2), 259–266 (2007). https://doi.org/10.3758/BF03193156
3. Agrawal, R., Srikant, R.: Fast algorithms for mining association rules. In: 20th International Conference on Very Large Data Bases, VLDB, Santiago, Chile (1994)
4. Han, J., Pei, H., Yin, Y.: Mining frequent patterns without candidate generation. In: Management of Data, SIGMOD 2000, Dallas, TX (2000)
5. Al-Maqaleh, B.M., Shaab, S.K.: An efficient algorithm for mining association rules using confident frequent itemsets. In: 3rd International Conference on Advanced Computing & Communication Technologies. IEEE (2013)
6. Hahsler, M.: A model-based frequency constraint for mining associations from transaction data. Data Mining Knowl. Disc. **13**(2), 137–166 (2006). https://doi.org/10.1007/s10618-005-0026-2
7. Karp, R.M., Shenker, S.: A simple algorithm for finding frequent elements in streams and bags. ACM Trans. Database Syst. **28**(1), 51–55 (2003)
8. Krish, A., et al.: An efficient rigorous approach for identifying statistically significant frequent item sets. ACM Trans. Database Syst. **32**, 333–368 (2009)
9. Rathee, S., Kashyap, A.: Adaptive-miner: an efficient distributed association rule mining algorithm on Spark. J. Big Data **5**(1), 1–17 (2018). https://doi.org/10.1186/s40537-018-0112-0
10. Wang, Y., Li, H., Zhang, D., Zhang, M., Chang, E.: PFP: parallel Fp-growth for query recommendation. In: Proceedings of the 2008 ACM Conference on Recommender Systems, RecSys 2008. ACM, New York (2008)

11. Zhou, L., Zhong, Z., Chang, J., Li, J., Huang, J.Z., Feng, S.: Balanced parallel Fp-growth with Mapreduce. In: IEEE Youth Conference on Information, Computing and Telecommunications, Beijing, China (2010)
12. Li, J., Roy, P., Khan, S.U., Wang, L., Bai, Y.: Data mining using clouds: an experimental implementation of apriori over Mapreduce. In: 12th International Conference on Scalable Computing and Communications (2012)
13. Al-hamodi, A.A.G., Lu, S.: MRFP: discovery frequent patterns using MapReduce frequent pattern growth. In: International Conference on Network and Information Systems for Computers. IEEE (2016)
14. Alon, N., Matias, Y., Szegedy, M.: The space complexity of approximating the frequency moments. In: Proceedings of the ACM Symposium on Theory of Computing, New York (1996)
15. Gibbons, P.B., Matias, Y.: Synopsis data structures for massive data sets. In: Proceedings of the 10th Annual ACM-SIAM Symposium on Discrete Algorithms, Baltimore, Maryland, USA (1999)
16. Gionis, A., Mannila, H., Mielikäinen, T., Tsaparas, P.: Assessing data mining results via swap randomization. ACM Trans. Knowl. Disc. Data 1(3), 14 (2007). https://doi.org/10.1145/129 7332.1297338
17. Bolton, R.J., Hand, D.J., Adams, N.M.: Determining hit rate in pattern search. In: Hand, D.J., Adams, N.M., Bolton, R.J. (eds.) Pattern Detection and Discovery. LNCS (LNAI), vol. 2447, pp. 36–48. Springer, Heidelberg (2002). https://doi.org/10.1007/3-540-45728-3_4
18. Vreeken, J., van Leeuwen, M., Siebes, A.: KRIMP: mining itemsets that compress. Data Mining Knowl. Disc. 23(1), 169–214 (2011). https://doi.org/10.1007/s10618-010-0202-x
19. Spiegel, M.R., Schiller, J., Srinivasan, R.A.: Probability and Statistics. Schaum's Outlines (2012)
20. Sturge, H.A.: The choice of class interval. J. Am. Stat. Assoc. 21(153), 65–67 (1926)
21. Hegland, M., Garcke, J., Challis, V.: The combination technique and some generalisations. Linear Algebra Appl. 420(2), 249–275 (2007)
22. Chen, D., Sain, S.L., Guo, K.: Data mining for the online retail industry: a case study of RFM model-based customer segmentation using data mining. J. Database Mark. Customer Strategy Manage. 19, 197–208 (2012). https://doi.org/10.1057/dbm.2012.17
23. Walpole, R.E., Myes, R.H.P., Myers, S.L., Keying, K.Y.: Probability and Statistics for Engineers and Scientists (2010)
24. Lipschutz, S., Lipson, M.L., Patil, V.H.: Discrete Mathematics. MacGraw Hill Education (2013)

Real-Image Transformation into a Caricature Image Using Neural Network

K. Sonali Swaroop$^{(\boxtimes)}$, Sandeep Kumar, and A. Sowjanya

Sreyas Institute of Engineering and Technology, Hyderabad, India
{sonali.k,drsandeep,sowjanya.a}@sreyas.ac.in

Abstract. Multimedia is an area which is evolving at a greater extent day by day and it forms a great are of interest in machine learning and artificial intelligence. The caricature of a real time image is defined as a cartoon style of the corresponding object. It can be widely used process in the area of computer graphics as performing the same process manually for each picture. And hence this paper proposes a method of converting a real-time image into its caricature. The proposed methodology uses a concept of fully connected network to convert the real time image into its cartoon style. The experiments show improvised results up to 90% when compared to the existing methods. The experiments also prove that our model has strong applicability for translating real time images.

Keywords: Caricature · Fully connected layer · Machine learning

1 Introduction

Cartoon is an area of application which is currently trending in entertainment industry because of increasing the demand of smart phone as well as laptop to make the entire world digitized. It is also a known fact that the making a caricature requires humongous creative skills manually. While the number to convert the images into cartoons in large numbers it happens to be a time consuming process also requires lots of human effort and therefore, it creates a necessity to build a computing system to generate such huge number thereby reducing the time consumption drastically. As per CAGR USA organization report, this industry will generate the revenue of 20.5 Billion USD up to the year of 2020 as shown in Fig. 1.

A few years back, the styling of pictures comprises of a specific area named "non-photorealistic delivering". The traditional calculation was done on the basis of the area for the styling of pictures and they were fruitful in styling any pictures by adding plans, surface, impacts etc. So, forth with the assistance of the calculation, numerous product was created to change over genuine images (snapshot) into animation pictures a portion of the techniques fizzled while a portion of the strategies gave results however didn't fulfill all the prerequisites. Additionally, animation pictures are complicated contrasted with genuine pictures. This issue can be all the more comprehensively portrayed as picture to-picture interpretation, changing over a picture from one portrayal of a given scene, a, to another, b, e.g., grayscale to shading, picture to semantic marks, edge-guide

© Springer Nature Singapore Pte Ltd. 2021
A. K. Luhach et al. (Eds.): ICAICR 2020, CCIS 1393, pp. 670–679, 2021.
https://doi.org/10.1007/978-981-16-3660-8_62

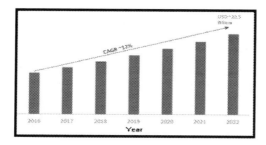

Fig. 1. Growth rate of cartoon based industry up to 2022

to photo. Long periods of exploration in PC vision, picture handling, computational photography, and illustrations have delivered incredible interpretation frameworks in the managed setting. To fulfill all the necessities of changing over genuine pictures for example depiction into animation picture several studies have taken the assistance of Cartoon GAN.

In this paper motivated by [15], we propose a novel model to transform real time image to caricature image. The Proposed model takes the input as an real time image and produces an cartoon image. We introduce a dedicated deep neural network trained for photo translation, which is able to better extract comic style features. Rest of the paper is organized into various sections which describes briefly about the various research work carried on the mentioned application. The next section describes the proposed methodology and then the results and comparison is presented followed by the conclusion of the research work.

2   Related Work

Recent literature focuses mostly on non-photorealistic interpretation methods which aim at generating caricature images using various neural network algorithms. Shuvendu et al. [9] proposed a generative adversarial network (GAN) method for translating real images to caricature images with preserving the details of input image. This model focuses on generating faster and efficient detail animation images and uses custom loss. Kaidi et al. [2] proposed a first deep learning approach for translating unpaired photo to caricature image. This model uses both geometric exaggeration and appearance stylization using two GAN's. Cari-Geo GAN to learn geometry-to-geometry translation. Caristy GAN to learn appearance-to-appearance translation. Zhu et al., [14] developed a cycle-consistent Adversarial network (CycleGAN) model to generate caricature images using unsupervised learning. This method produces natural looking images similar to target domain using a learning approach to translate source image to target image.

Akanksha et al. [1] proposed a neural network-based model (Cartoon GAN) to convert images as well as, video to caricature images. Using loss function, this model generates flexible and clear edge defined images and using computer vision videos are translated into caricature images. Chen et al. [3] proposed a novel method based on deep neural networks (GAN) to translate photos to cartoon images. This method focuses on optimizing target images in gray scale domain, to avoid artifacts of color patches.

Even this method preserves object boundaries better with improved lines and shading. Huang et al. [6] proposed a principled framework for Multimodal Unsupervised Image-to-Image translation (MUNIT). This model produces quality and diversity superior to existing unsupervised methods. Since this method learns the distribution of target domain images using GAN's produces results that are significantly more faithful and realistic. Zhang et al. [8] focuses specially on selfie cartoonization GAN which uses attentive adversarial network (AAN) to improve specific facial features and ignore low-level details. This method design three losses like total variation loss, attentive cycle loss, perceptual loss and outperforms when compared with other state-of-art methods.

Chen et al. [4] proposed Cartoon GAN method which generates caricature image with less details or share corners in images. For removing shape edges, this method focuses on training the edges. Yi et al. [14] proposed Dual GAN model which uses two sets of unlabeled images from two domains for training. The primal GAN learns to translate images from one domain to other, while the dual GAN learns to invert the task. It was observed that Dual GAN produces better results especially for unlabeled data. Also there is a huge research being conducted on video processing by including secure methods to analyze and to convert it into various forms like digital water marking etc. described in [5, 7, and 12] (Table 1).

From the literature survey, it is evident that the research has been done assuming the applications are vivid and wide. Most of the models were created based on the available dataset which is very limited. GAN has provided some results invariably good but the dataset is minimal and it would yield accurate results to the trained data set only.

3   Proposed Methodology

We use FCN model for translating real image into caricature image as it is easy to implement and less computationally complex than CNN.

3.1   Object Classification

A normal order issue means to recognize (or potentially restrict) an item in an information picture. We typically have a solitary focal point in such issues, and subsequently the yield is a vector of probabilities of various classes present in the preparation corpus. The subject is ordered into the class name having the most extreme estimation of likelihood.

3.2   Object Detection

Object detection deals with the process of locating the portions in the image or video input. It generates the bounding area encircling those located portions such that they can be analyzed for its features.

3.3   Semantic Segmentation

Otherwise called thick expectation, the objective of a semantic division task is to mark every pixel of the info picture with the particular class speaking to a particular item/body.

Table 1. Comparison of existing methodology on cartoon GAN

Year	Algorithm/technique used	Advantages	Dataset	Parameters measured
2020 [1]	Generative Adversarial Networks (GAN)	Generates flexible and clear edge defined images	200 Real world images	–
2019 [9]	Generative Adversarial Networks (GAN)	Faster and efficient method	CelebA, Danbooru	(Face Recognition) FR Score-76.24%
2019 [8]	Attentive Adversarial Network (AAN)	Generates satisfactory images	Own Dataset	–
2018 [2]	Two stage framework 1. CariGeoGAN to learn geometry-to-geometry translation 2. CaristyGAN to learn appearance-to-appearance translation	First unpaired translation approach and can be extended to high resolution images	Own dataset	–
2018 [6]	Multi-modal Unsupervised image-to-image Translation (MUNIT)	Achieves superior quality and diversified images	SYNTHIA, Cityscape	(Conditional Inception Score) CIS-1.039 (Inception Score) IS-1.050
2018 [4]	Cartoon Generative Adversarial Network	High quality, high efficiency	Own Dataset	Training time - 1517.69 s
2017 [14]	Cycle-Consistent Adversarial Networks	Generates natural looking images but fails to translate in extreme cases	CMP Façade, UT Zappos50K	FR Score-68.87%, Class IOU-0.56 Per Pixel Accuracy-0.19
2017 [3]	Deep Convolutional Neural Network	Preserves the line structures especially boundaries	Own Dataset	Accuracy-97.25%

(continued)

Division is performed when the spatial data of a subject and how it cooperates with it is significant, as for an autonomous vehicle. Likewise, it is important that this assignment isn't keen on recognizing various articles having a place with a specific class [16, 17].

Table 1. (*continued*)

Year	Algorithm/technique used	Advantages	Dataset	Parameters measured
2017 [13]	Dual Generative Adversarial Network	Proposed Methodology produces better results than GAN	PHOTO-SKETCH, DAY-NIGHT, LABEL-FACADE	Class IOU-0.62 Per Pixel Accuracy - 0.4

For instance, in the event that you have two vehicles of various make and shading, they would in any case be given a typical mark of 'Vehicle' and thought about a solitary element (Fig. 2).

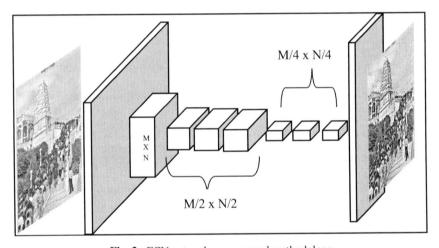

Fig. 2. FCN network on proposed methodology

Fully Convolutional Networks (FCN): The first Fully Convolutional Network (FCN) takes in a planning from pixels to pixels, without extricating the locale recommendations [18, 19]. The FCN network is an expansion of the old style CNN. The primary thought is to make the old style CNN take as information subjective estimated pictures. The limitation of CNNs to acknowledge and create marks just for explicit estimated inputs originates from the completely associated layers which are constant. In opposition to them, FCNs just have convolutional and pooling layers which enable them to make expectations on self-assertive measured sources of info [11]. The major issue or task in this methodology is by traversing through many convolutional and pooling layers, the output characteristics are down sampled. Henceforth, the test results of FCN are generally of lesser quality resulting is poor boundaries. The main advantage of the proposed methodology is that it can work irrespective of the size of the original image. It eliminates the necessity of normalization of the input image size at any later stage given that all connections are local. To obtain a segmentation map (output), segmentation networks usually have 2 parts: The fact that the particularly with FCN is that by spreading through a few exchanged convolutional and pooling layers, the quality of the expected output maps is decimated. Consequently, the immediate forecasts of FCN are ordinarily in low quality, bringing about moderately fluffy article limits. Likewise, the organization can work paying little mind to the first picture size, without requiring any fixed number of units at any stage, given that all associations are nearby [11].To get a division map (output), division networks ordinarily have 2 sections:

- Down sampling path: capture class information in the input image
- Up sampling path: restore the dimensional information

In the figures, convolutional layers are spoken to as vertical lines between pooling layers, which explicitly show the overall size of the element maps. In the organization introduced, it very well may be seen that the info picture of resolution M × N is convoluted to M/2 × N/2 lastly to M/4 × N/4. At this stage we acquire small heat maps of various items, every pixel featured to a power identical to the likelihood of event of the article. As a subsequent stage, these small scale heat maps are up sampled lastly totaled to acquire a High-quality division map, with every pixel arranged into the highest probability class. The following mathematical expression describes the output metric of the model which gives the translated output. The translated output includes all the layers of convolutional networks.

$$q_{ab} = h_{cd}(\{p_{da} + \alpha_a, \ d_b + \alpha_b\} 0 \le \alpha_a, \ \alpha_b \le c)$$

$$h_{cd} \ o \ l_{c'd'} = (h \ o \ l)_{c' + (c-1)_{d'dd'}}$$

Where, c is the size of the window, d is sampling factor involved and h_{cd} determines the type of the layer. The final step of the proposed methodology is explained in the next section.

Transposed Convolution: In contrast to convolution, a transposed convolution layer is utilized to up sample the diminished quality highlight back to its unique goal. A bunch of step and padding is found out to acquire the last output from the lower features highlights. One significant issue with in-network down sampling in a FCN is that it decreases the quality of the contribution by an enormous factor, accordingly during up sampling it turns out to be hard to recreate the better subtleties even in the wake of utilizing complex procedures like Transpose Convolution. Single direction to manage this is by adding skip connections in the Up sampling stage from prior layers and adding the two component maps. These skip associations give enough data to later layers to create exact division boundaries. This blend of fine and coarse layers prompts neighborhood expectations with almost precise worldwide (spatial) structure.

4   Results and Discussion

4.1   Metrics

Per Pixel Accuracy: This measurement is simple, since it yields the class forecast accuracy per pixel.

$$acc(p, GT) = \frac{|pixels\ correctly\ preicted|}{|total\ no\ of\ pixels|}$$

Jaccard: It is a ratio of pixels common between the predicted class and the original class and the division map pixels between the two classes [9].

$$jacc(p(class).GT(class)) = \frac{|p(class) \cap GT(class)|}{|p(class) \cup GT(class)|}$$

Where p is the predicted segmentation map
GT is the ground truth segmentation map
P (class) is then the binary mask indicating if each pixel is predicted as class or not

$$IOU = \frac{Area\ of\ Overlap}{Area\ of\ Union}$$

4.2   Results and Comparison

The proposed methodology was implemented on real-time images which were captured by a smart phone 24MP primary camera, 8MP wide angle sensor and 5MP depth sensor. The dataset consists of 1000 still images of which 80% were used as training samples and 20% were used as testing samples. Few of the output samples are shown in Fig. 3. The proposed methodology was implemented on a PC having 8 GB RAM and NVIDIA graphic card with MATLAB v2015 software. Table 2 summarizes the comparison of results of our model with existing models. While evaluation, proposed work perform better than the other state of art methodologies. The proposed methodology gives the accuracy upto 90.71% and IOU is 0.667.

5   Conclusion and Future Scope

We have developed a neural network model to translate real-time images to caricature images. Experimental results show that CycleGAN [14] performs well but is computationally complex and cannot maintain the content of the input image. Dual GAN [13] gives better results but not produces possible outputs for labeled data. Proposed model outperforms with high accuracy, and quality in converting real-time images to caricature images.

As dataset is limited we can extend our work with new deep learning models which can handle large data. In future we can extend our model to additional areas like video, text, etc. to improve efficiency. Moreover, handling real time videos for supporting interesting applications is another promising research direction.

Fig. 3. Output samples of proposed work

Table 2. Comparison of proposed work with existing state of art methods

Year	Algorithm/technique used	Parameters measured
[9], 2019	Generative Adversarial Networks (GAN)	Accuracy = 76.24% IOU = –
[14], 2017	Cycle-Consistent Adversarial Networks	Accuracy = 68.87% IOU = 0.56
[6], 2018	Multi-modal Unsupervised image-to-image Translation (MUNIT)	Accuracy = 81.20% IOU = 0.59
[13], 2017	Dual Generative Adversarial Network	Accuracy = – IOU = 0.62
2020	**Proposed Methodology**	**Accuracy = 90.71%** **IOU = 0.667**

References:

1. Apte, A., Unnikrishnan, A., Bomble, N., Gavhane, S.: Transformation of realistic images and videos into cartoon images and video using GAN. Int. Res. J. Eng. Technol. (IRJET) **7**, 2118–2121 (2020)
2. Cao, K., Liao, J., Yuan, L.: CariGANs: unpaired photo-to-caricature translation. ACM Trans. Graph. **37**, 1–14 (2018)
3. Chen, Y., Lai, Y.K., Liu, Y.J.: Transforming photos to comics using convolutional neural networks. In: IEEE International Conference on Image Processing (ICIP), pp. 2010–2014 (2017)
4. Chen, Y., Lai, Y.K., Liu, Y.J.: Cartoongan: generative adversarial networks for photo cartoonization. In: IEEE Conference on Computer Vision and Pattern Recognition, pp. 9465–9474 (2018)
5. Gunawardena, P., et al.: Real-time automated video highlight generation with dual-stream hierarchical growing self-organizing maps. J. Real-Time Image Proc. 1–19 (2020). https://doi.org/10.1007/s11554-020-00957-0
6. Huang, X., Liu, M.-Y., Belongie, S., Kautz, J.: Multimodal unsupervised image-to-image translation. In: Ferrari, V., Hebert, M., Sminchisescu, C., Weiss, Y. (eds.) ECCV 2018. LNCS, vol. 11207, pp. 179–196. Springer, Cham (2018). https://doi.org/10.1007/978-3-030-01219-9_11
7. Kumar, A., Luhach, A.K., Pal, D.: Robust digital image watermarking technique using image normalization and discrete cosine transformation. Int. J. Comput. Appl. **65**(18) (2013)
8. Li, X., Zhang, W., Shen, T., Mei, T.: Everyone is a cartoonist: selfie cartoonization with attentive adversarial networks. In: IEEE International Conference on Multimedia and Expo (ICME), pp. 652–657 (2019)
9. Roy, S.: Generating anime from real human image with adversarial training. In: 2019 1st International Conference on Advances in Science, Engineering and Robotics Technology (ICASERT), pp. 1–5 (2019)
10. Shelhamer, E., Long, J., Darrell, T.: Fully convolutional networks for semantic segmentation. IEEE Trans. Pattern Anal. Mach. Intell. **39**(4), 640–651 (2017)
11. Shi, R., Ngan, K.N., Li, S.: Jaccard index compensation for object segmentation evaluation. In: IEEE International Conference on Image Processing (ICIP), pp. 4457–4461 (2014)

12. Singh, C., Luhach, A.K., Kumar, A.: Improving focused crawling with genetic algorithms. Int. J. Comput. Appl. **66**(4), 40–43 (2013)
13. Yi, Z., Zhang, H., Tan, P., Gong, M.: DualGAN: Unsupervised dual learning for image-to-image translation. In: IEEE International Conference on Computer Vision, pp. 2849–2857 (2017)
14. Zhu, J.Y., Park, T., Isola, P., Efros, A.A.: Unpaired image-to-image translation using cycle-consistent adversarial networks. In: IEEE International Conference on Computer Vision, pp. 2223–2232 (2017)
15. Gatys, L.A., Ecker, A.S., Bethge, M.: Image style transfer using convolutional neural networks. In: IEEE Conference on Computer Vision and Pattern Recognition (CVPR), pp. 2414–2423 (2016)
16. Kumar, S., Singh, S., Kumar, J.: Face spoofing detection using improved SegNet architecture with blur estimation technique. Int. J. Biometric **13**, 131–149 (2021)
17. Kumar, S., Singh, S., Kumar, J.: Gender classification using machine learning with multi-feature method. In: IEEE 9th Annual Computing and Communication Workshop and Conference (CCWC), Las Vegas, USA, 7th–9th January 2019, pp. 0648–0653 (2019)
18. Kumar, S., Singh, S., Kumar, J.: Multiple face detection using hybrid features with SVM classifier. In: Jain, L.C., E. Balas, V., Johri, P. (eds.) Data and Communication Networks. AISC, vol. 847, pp. 253–265. Springer, Singapore (2019). https://doi.org/10.1007/978-981-13-2254-9_23
19. Andy, C., Kumar, S.: An appraisal on speech and emotional recognition technologies based on machine learning. Int. J. Recent Technol. Eng. (IJRTE) **8**(5), 2266-2276 (2019). ISSN 2277-3878

Author Index

Printed in the United States
by Baker & Taylor Publisher Services